Voluntary Codes

Private Governance, the Public Interest and Innovation

Kernaghan Webb, *Editor*

cɹᴜise

A publication of the Carleton Research Unit for
Innovation, Science and Environment, Carleton University

The contents of this book are downloadable from the
Carleton Research Unit on Innovation, Science and Environment
Web site (**www.carleton.ca/spa/Research/cruise.htm**).

Library and Archives Canada Cataloguing in Publication

Voluntary codes : private governance, the public interest
and innovation / Kernaghan Webb.

Includes bibliographical references and index.

ISBN 0-7709-0482-3

1. Social responsibility of business. 2. Standardization. 3. Corporate governance.
4. Industrial policy. 5. Commercial policy. I. Webb, Kernaghan R.
II. Carleton Research Unit for Innovation, Science and Environment

HD2741.V65 2004   658.4'08   C2004-905298-5

Contents

Acknowledgments

The chapters in this volume were almost all developed as part of the Voluntary Codes Project of Industry Canada's Office of Consumer Affairs (OCA). Special thanks is owed to Industry Canada, and more particularly OCA, for its consistent support — financial and otherwise — of the Voluntary Codes Project from its inception.

Within OCA, I would especially like to thank Director General Michael Jenkin and Director Maryanne Murphy for agreeing to support the work underlying this volume, which began prior to their tenure. The Voluntary Codes Project would never have gotten off the ground without the original backing of then-Director General Vinita Watson and then-Director Derek Ireland, to whom I remain grateful.

In addition, I would like to thank the Carleton Research Unit on Innovation, Science and Environment (CRUISE) at Carleton University for its assistance in bringing this volume to the publication stage. Dr. Bruce Doern, Director of CRUISE, coordinated the external refereeing process, and helped steer the volume from a collection of somewhat disparate papers to its current, more coherent form. A key objective of undergoing the external academic refereeing process and of publishing the volume through CRUISE was to better engage the broader academic community on issues associated with voluntary codes.

The efforts of a large number of other individuals were key to making this volume possible. David Cohen, Dean of the Faculty of Law at Pace University, New York, played an instrumental role, providing wise guidance to the contributors to this volume, particularly in the Voluntary Codes Project's early stages.

A special and heartfelt debt of gratitude is owed to an impressive contingent of talented, helpful and seemingly inexhaustible University of Victoria Law School co-op students, who did an incredible amount of research and thankless "behind-the-scenes" work — work without which this volume would not have been possible. In chronological order, Lynda Cassels, Gregory Rhone, Andrew Morrison, John Stroud, David Clarke and Kathleen Priestman were all instrumental in this regard. I am fortunate to have had the opportunity to work with them. All of them have now graduated and are gainfully employed in private practice, working for public interest advocacy organizations, or with government. David Clarke has now joined OCA, and deserves particular thanks for his excellent substantive contributions to the volume as well as his superb technical editing. I would also like to thank former OCA staffers Julia von Hahn and Mark Garrett for their assistance.

With tremendous grace under pressure, Nancy Dynes formerly of OCA did a terrific job of formatting and inputting all of the chapters. Cathy Enright of OCA skillfully negotiated the communications angles, working with the very professional crew at Whitehall Associates, led by Amy Heron.

I would like to thank as well the close to 400 members of the online Voluntary Codes Research Forum located around the globe. They have helped to keep me abreast of the latest developments in voluntary codes, and have been highly supportive of our work on voluntary codes from the outset.

Finally, I must thank the authors for their excellent contributions, and the many people who provided comments on drafts of the chapters.

Note that the opinions expressed in this volume are those of the authors, and not necessarily those of any institution to which the authors might be affiliated.

Dr. Kernaghan Webb
July 2004
Ottawa, Canada

Contributors

Colin J. Bennett is Professor of Political Science at the University of Victoria, Victoria, British Columbia.

François Bregha is a Principal at Stratos Inc., Ottawa, Ontario.

David Clarke is a Legal Policy Analyst with the Office of Consumer Affairs, Industry Canada, Ottawa, Ontario.

David Cohen is the Dean of Law at Pace University School of Law, White Plains, New York.

G. Bruce Doern is a Professor of Public Policy at Carleton University in Ottawa and Exeter University in the United Kingdom, and is Director of the Carleton Research Unit on Innovation, Science and Environment, Carleton University, Ottawa, Ontario.

Neil Gunningham is a Professor in the School of Resources, Environment and Society, at Australian National University, Canberra, Australia.

Kathryn Harrison is an Associate Professor of Political Science at the University of British Columbia, Vancouver, British Columbia.

Mary Jane Middelkoop is a Research Associate at Stratos Inc., Ottawa, Ontario.

John Moffet is a Principal at Stratos Inc., Ottawa, Ontario.

Andrew Morrison practices commercial litigation with Shields Harney in Vancouver, British Columbia.

Bryne Purchase was Deputy Minister, Ontario Ministry of Energy, Science and Technology, in Toronto, Ontario, until April 2004.

Gregory T. Rhone is in private practice at Gordon & Velletta, Barristers & Solicitors, in Victoria, British Columbia.

John Stroud is a Legal Policy Analyst with the Canadian Air Transport Security Authority in Ottawa, Ontario.

Kernaghan Webb is an Adjunct Research Professor at Carleton University's Department of Law and School of Public Policy and Administration, Honorary Lecturer with the University of Dundee's Centre for Energy, Petroleum and Mineral Law and Policy, and Sessional Adjunct in the Queen's University School of Policy Studies. He is also Senior Legal Policy Advisor and Chief of Research at the Office of Consumer Affairs, Industry Canada, Ottawa, Ontario.

PART ONE

Introduction

Chapter 1
Understanding the Voluntary Codes Phenomenon

Kernaghan Webb

Introduction

Few would dispute that the command-and-control regulatory model (comprising legislation and regulations) is the pre-eminent instrument used today for developing and implementing norms of acceptable and unacceptable individual and corporate conduct. After all, statutes articulate societal positions on important issues; they are the products of democratically elected legislatures; and they establish the frameworks for command-and-control regulatory approaches, which are enforced by specialized government agencies, backed up by the courts. Regulatory regimes pertaining to consumer, environmental, worker, and health and safety protection, and many other areas, have made considerable progress in improving the lives of millions. But for all of its strengths, the command-and-control regulatory approach is not without limitations, including expensive and protracted development and enforcement processes;[1] jurisdictional constraints on subject matter, approach and scope;[2] vulnerability to inconsistent and inadequate enforcement, due to staff and resource cutbacks and associated downturns in government and public attention; and a tendency toward inflexibility and overformality, which can lead to adversarial and legalistic "going by the book" attitudes to compliance.[3] Some commentators have begun to speak of command-and-control regulation reaching the limits of its capabilities and starting to break down under its own weight.[4]

---

1. See, e.g., itemizations of limitations associated with environmental legislation in C. Coglianese and J. Nash, eds., *Regulating from the Inside: Can Environmental Management Systems Achieve Policy Goals?* (Washington: Resources for the Future, 2001), especially Chapter 1. A Canadian example of cost and time issues associated with regulations is the process of amending the *Metal Mining Liquid Effluent Regulations,* which began in 1990, involved dozens of studies and consultations with hundreds of stakeholders, cost in excess of $1 million, is estimated to necessitate an expenditure of $2 million annually to enforce, and was only completed in June 2002. Information derived from conversations with Department of Environment officials, and from the Regulatory Impact Assessment Statement (RIAS) and revised regulations. The RIAS and revised regulations are published in the *Canada Gazette,* Part II, June 6, 2002, pp. 1412–1462, available at <http://canadagazette.gc.ca/partII/2002/20020619/html/sor222-e.html>.

2. Constitutional division-of-power constraints are particularly a factor in federations where legislative authority is split between federal governments and states/provinces/*landers,* such as is the case in Canada, the United States, Australia and Germany. For example, in Canada, as determined by the *Constitution Act, 1867,* the federal government can only legislate to the extent of its powers; the provinces can only legislate to the extent of their powers; both levels of government are constrained by the *Canadian Charter of Rights and Freedoms,* and the ability of a government to develop legislation having extraterritorial effect is limited. Similar constraints are in place in other jurisdictions. These issues are discussed in greater detail in Kernaghan Webb and Andrew Morrison, "The Law and Voluntary Codes: Examining the 'Tangled Web'," Chapter 5, below.

3. See, e.g., E. Bardach and R. A. Kagan, *Going by the Book: The Problem of Regulatory Unreasonableness* (Philadelphia: Temple University Press, 1982); and Coglianese and Nash (footnote 1).

4. Speaking particularly about environmental law, but noting a similar phenomenon in industrial labour organization law, Professor Eric Orts in "Reflexive Environmental Regulation," *Northwestern University Law Review* 89 (1995), pp. 1227–1340, p. 1241, suggests that "juridification" has set in, in light of the sheer volume

Kernaghan Webb, Editor, *Voluntary Codes: Private Governance, the Public Interest and Innovation.*
This chapter ©2004 Kernaghan Webb, pages 3–32.
Published by the Carleton Research Unit for Innovation, Science and Environment, Carleton University, Ottawa, Canada.

In apparent recognition of these limitations, and of the potential value of other approaches, governments and scholars have begun in recent years to recognize the role of other techniques, including use of non-governmental voluntary code and standards initiatives.[5] Unlike conventional command-and-control regulatory approaches, voluntary codes harness market, peer and community energies to influence behaviour, and draw on the infrastructure of intermediaries such as industry associations, standards organizations and non-governmental organizations for rule development and implementation. In a way, the renewed interest by governments in non-State approaches to governing takes us full circle: voluntary rule systems have been used since earliest times to articulate shared norms and to structure interpersonal relations, and indeed pre-date the modern State.

Religion, culture, tradition and notions of morality and ethics are all examples of cooperative, trust-based non-governmental processes and techniques that have long been employed and continue to play important roles in providing a framework for social and commercial conduct.[6] For thousands of years, merchant behaviour has been controlled through non-governmental techniques.[7] In the Middle Ages in Europe (and much earlier elsewhere), merchant guilds regulated virtually every aspect of a given commercial activity, from market access through means of production, product quality and price, enforcement of contracts, and even an element of welfare protection for guild members and their families.[8] While guilds have faded in importance with the rise of the

---

of environmental legislation that is building up:

> Environmental juridification points to a critical weakness of the command-and-control approach. There are cognitive limits to protecting the environment through detailed orders. As new laws are passed to regulate critical areas and old laws are revised to close or open loopholes, the legal system's capacity actually to process the material becomes impaired. Eventually, traditional command-and-control regulation breaks down under its own weight. (*Footnotes omitted*)

5. See, e.g., discussion in I. Ayres and J. Braithwaite, *Responsive Regulation: Transcending the Deregulation Debate* (New York: Oxford University Press, 1992); N. Gunningham, P. Grabosky and D. Sinclair, *Smart Regulation: Designing Environmental Policy* (Oxford: Clarendon Press, 1998); K. Harrison, "Voluntarism and Environmental Governance," in E. Parson, ed., *Governing the Environment: Challenges and Trends* (Toronto: University of Toronto Press, 2001), Chapter 5; M. Priest, "The Privatization of Regulation: Five Models of Self-Regulation," *Ottawa Law Review* 29 (1998), pp. 233–302, p. 236.

6. For an insightful exploration of the importance of some of these non-State mechanisms and processes in commercial contexts, see F. Fukuyama, *Trust: The Social Virtues and the Creation of Prosperity* (London: Penguin, 1995). Of course, religion, culture, tradition, morality and ethics, like law, are all techniques of control. They can be used to gain and maintain power, they can be manipulated and abused, and they too are rightly the subject of significant critical analysis. See, e.g., the writings of Jurgen Habermas and Michel Foucault on this topic in D. Browning and F. Fiorenza, eds., *Habermas, Modernity and Public Theology* (New York: Crossroads, 1992); J. Carrette, ed., *Religion and Culture by Michel Foucault* (Manchester: Manchester University Press, 1999).

7. J. Braithwaite and P. Drahos, in *Global Business Regulation* (Cambridge: Cambridge University Press, 2000), p. 497, footnote 6, maintain that "strictly speaking, following Durkheim, the Christian church was the first great NGO [non-governmental organization] to supply a set of norms which regulated business practice." Even today, the preparation of food in compliance with religious edicts, such as those associated with halal (Muslim) and kosher (Jewish) foods, provides us with examples of non-governmental food certification systems. See Webb and Morrison, "The Law and Voluntary Codes," Chapter 5, below, for discussion of some of the legal aspects of halal and kosher regimes.

8. Needless to say, these guilds frequently had significant anti-competitive features. For a somewhat more detailed discussion of the history of economic self-regulation, see K. Webb, "Government, Private Regulation and the Role of the Market," in M. MacNeil, N. Sargent and P. Swan, eds., *Law, Regulation and Governance* (Don Mills, Ont.: Oxford University Press, 2002), Chapter 12.

State, private regulatory techniques that use non-governmental intermediaries to ensure compliance have continued to flourish against a backdrop of law. The Better Business Bureau, for example, had its origins in merchant "vigilance committees" first created in the late 1800s.[9] Starting in 1899, various apparel companies agreed to comply with safe labour conditions and be inspected by the National Consumers League (NCL), and thereby were entitled to use the NCL's "White Label" on their apparel.[10] The International Chamber of Commerce first published its *Code of Advertising Practice* in 1937,[11] and many other forms of industry self-regulation were put in place throughout the 20th century.[12]

The recent interest of governments in voluntary codes seems to coincide with considerable activity in this area by private sector and civil society actors — and this is perhaps no accident. A key distinction between earlier use of voluntary instruments and that of today is that modern non-governmental voluntary activity takes place against a backdrop of extensive State regulation, and indeed is often (at least in part) a response to it. Consider the following examples:

> As efforts to negotiate a global forest protection convention sputter, several major international environmental organizations (most notably, WWF, the World Wide Fund for Nature), working with retailers and others, spearhead the development of the Forest Stewardship Council (FSC) and its labelling program for products from sustainably harvested and managed forests. While initially facing much resistance from the forest extraction industry, and despite numerous "start-up" administrative difficulties, there are now more than 24 million hectares of FSC forests worldwide. At the same time, forest producers take leadership roles in developing their own voluntary sustainable forestry programs, in some cases using the services of standards development organizations such as the Canadian Standards Association. In addition to private sector use of the programs, governments in Canada and the United States have begun efforts to have their regulatory forest management regimes certified as being in compliance with the FSC program.[13]

---

9. History of the Better Business Bureau is discussed in David Clarke and Kernaghan Webb, *Market-Driven Consumer Redress Case Studies and Legal Issues* (Ottawa: Office of Consumer Affairs, Industry Canada, 2002), available at <http://strategis.ic.gc.ca/epic/internet/inoca-bc.nsf/en/ca01643e.html>.

10. U.S. Department of Labor, Bureau of International Labor Affairs, *By the Sweat and Toil of Children: Consumer Labels and Child Labor* (Vol. IV) (Washington: U.S. Department of Labor, 1997), especially pp. 5–7.

11. See European Advertising Standards Alliance (EASA), *EASA Guide to Self-Regulation* (Amsterdam: EASA, 1999), p. 8.

12. See discussion in M. Olson, *The Rise and Decline of Nations: Economic Growth, Stagflation, and Social Rigidities* (New Haven: Yale University Press, 1982).

13. E. Meidinger, in "Environmental Certification Programs and U.S. Environmental Law: Closer Than You May Think," *Environmental Law Reporter* 31 (2001), pp. 10162–10179, p. 10169, reports sources indicating that the agencies responsible for managing State-owned lands in Minnesota, New York and Pennsylvania have either achieved Forest Stewardship Council certification or announced they intend to do so. In March 2001, "[the] Honourable John Snobelen, Minister of Natural Resources for the province of Ontario, and Dr. Maharaj Muthoo, Executive Director of the Forest Stewardship Council (FSC), initiated a bilateral process that will result in FSC certification of all Crown-owned forests managed in compliance with Ontario law and the products derived from those forests." Per Ontario Ministry of Natural Resources, *Ontario First in World to Receive Environmental Forest Certification*, press release, March 23, 2001. The FSC and Canadian Standards

In the early 1990s, Gap Inc., a major American apparel retailer, was the subject of negative media attention as a result of alleged non-compliance by its contractor-suppliers with a Gap Inc. voluntary code pertaining to treatment of workers located in developing countries. In theory, supplier factories in these developing countries are subject to a range of statutory protections pertaining to workers, but in practice there is often little enforcement. In the absence of effective State-based programs, codes imposed by retailers as a term of contract take on greater significance (the codes are voluntary in the sense of not being imposed by governments, but are nevertheless contractually binding on those supplier firms that agree to meet their terms). In response to allegations that suppliers were not complying with its code, Gap Inc. worked with its critics to revise and improve the terms of the code, and used local organizations to monitor supplier compliance with the code provisions. As this work progressed, several multistakeholder, industry-wide labour certification regimes were developed (such as the U.S. government-supported Apparel Industry Partnership/Fair Labor Association), with third-party monitoring, in a number of jurisdictions. Monitoring by local, developing country interests has become increasingly common.[14]

In anticipation of new regulations, and in an attempt to reduce the likelihood of another chemical plant disaster like that which occurred in Bhopal, the Canadian Chemical Producers' Association devises and implements "Responsible Care," a 152-point environmental management program pertaining to the research and development, manufacturing, transportation, distribution, waste management and community awareness aspects of the chemical industry. Over time, the program develops compliance verification and public reporting elements. The program is picked up by the chemical producers' associations in more than 40 countries, including the United States. Some claim that the program is being used to stymie needed new legislation and regulations.[15]

In theory, online merchants are subject to the same legislative requirements for consumer protection as those facing conventional "bricks and mortar" merchants, but government enforcement of consumer protection legislation to address Internet problems is hampered by jurisdictional difficulties. Moreover, many consumers have concerns about the reliability and integrity of online merchants. In response, a major United Kingdom consumer organization devises a voluntary code initiative pertaining to consumer protection in

---

Association programs are discussed in greater detail in Gregory T. Rhone, David Clarke and Kernaghan Webb, "Two Voluntary Approaches to Sustainable Forestry Practices," Chapter 9, below. Similar programs in other jurisdictions are discussed in Kernaghan Webb and David Clarke, "Voluntary Codes in the United States, the European Union and Developing Countries: A Preliminary Survey" (hereafter "Other Jurisdictions"), Chapter 13, below. Eco-labelling programs are discussed in Kathryn Harrison, "Promoting Environmental Protection Through Eco-Labelling: An Evaluation of Canada's Environmental Choice Program," Chapter 10, below.

14. Gap Inc.'s program is discussed in greater detail in Gregory T. Rhone, John Stroud and Kernaghan Webb, "Gap Inc.'s Code of Conduct for Treatment of Overseas Workers," Chapter 7, below. The Fair Labor Association and its competitors are discussed in greater detail in Webb and Clarke, "Other Jurisdictions," Chapter 13, below.

15. This program is discussed in greater detail in John Moffet, François Bregha and Mary Jane Middelkoop, "Responsible Care: A Case Study of a Voluntary Environmental Initiative," Chapter 6, below.

electronic commerce, called Web Trader. Under the Web Trader program, online merchants that agree to abide by the terms of the code may display a logo on their Web site that indicates that they are in compliance with the code. Many U.K. businesses apply for and receive approval to use the logo. Following the U.K. lead, consumer organizations in nine other countries offer affiliated programs, in competition with similar, business-led initiatives.[16]

In several cases, Canadian courts require that companies convicted of environmental offences be registered as compliant with ISO 14001, a voluntary environmental management system (EMS) standard developed through the International Organization for Standardization (ISO), a non-governmental organization with a private sector focus. Subsequently, Canadian environmental legislation is amended to require courts, in their determinations of liability, to consider whether companies are complying with EMS standards, and gives the courts express authority to require compliance with EMSs as part of sentencing. Other jurisdictions offer expedited permitting and reduced inspections to companies complying with voluntary EMSs. Through these regulatory reforms, governments are in effect acknowledging the value of voluntary environmental management programs as adjuncts to regulatory regimes and are developing legislative structures that explicitly support use of such approaches.[17]

An Australian supermarket industry association develops and implements a voluntary code pertaining to the accuracy of its bar code scanners. An essential part of the program is the requirement that, if a consumer finds that there is a discrepancy between the price at the cash register and that on the product, he or she gets the product for free. Compliance rates are high, and complaints to government regulators are low, in part because the program creates incentives for both consumers and supermarkets to be vigilant. The program supports regulatory objectives against misleading advertising, but does so through non-regulatory, market mechanisms. Learning from their Australian counterparts, a similar program is developed in Canada, operated by major retail associations, and endorsed by the Canadian Competition Bureau.[18]

Using the services of a reputable Canadian standards development organization, the Canadian federal government, working in conjunction with provincial governments, industry associations and consumer organizations, develops a voluntary code pertaining to the protection of personal information. As the voluntary code is completed, a major industry association that has participated in the development of the code requests that it become the basis for federal and provincial laws. A federal law is developed that draws explicitly on the terms of the voluntary standard.[19]

---

16. This program is discussed in Webb and Clarke, "Other Jurisdictions," Chapter 13, below. It was terminated at the end of 2002.

17. As discussed in Webb and Morrison, "The Law and Voluntary Codes," Chapter 5, below.

18. The Australian code is discussed in Neil Gunningham, "Codes of Practice: The Australian Experience," Chapter 12, below. The terms of the Canadian program are available at <http://cb-bc.gc.ca/epic/internet/incb-bc.nsf/vwapj/ct02381e.pfd/$FILE/ct02381e.pdf>.

19. As discussed in Colin J. Bennett, "Privacy Self-Regulation in a Global Economy: A Race to the Top, the Bottom or Somewhere Else?" Chapter 8, below, and Webb and Morrison, "The Law and Voluntary Codes," Chapter 5, below.

Environmental regulators in a developing country devise a pollution control public rating program, with the objective of creating incentives for compliance through honour and shame. Pursuant to a process involving an advisory panel with environmental organization representatives, individual emitters are rated using data from inspections, and the results are selectively made public through a press conference and Internet site. Research suggests the program galvanizes environmental performance by harnessing community pressure. Six other developing countries devise similar programs.[20]

An industry association is told by a regulatory agency that, if it does not develop and implement customer service standards for its members, the regulatory agency will do it for them. The industry association puts in place standards, monitors compliance and establishes a tribunal to resolve consumer and industry disputes. The tribunal panel includes one consumer representative, one industry representative and a neutral chair (e.g. a retired judge). The decisions (including dissenting opinions) are publicly available. Individuals may still complain to the regulator, but in more than 10 years of operation, the decisions of the private tribunal have never been overturned.[21]

As these examples illustrate, voluntary codes are currently in place or being developed in Canada and around the world to address a wide variety of environmental protection, worker, consumer, community and other issues.[22]

It is perhaps no accident that many of these codes have a significant international dimension. A strong argument can be made that voluntary codes have come into prominence as the result of a confluence of factors associated with globalization. Although difficult to define, globalization can be seen as a complex process of interdependency or convergence resulting from dramatically increasing levels of exchange in goods, information, services and capital.[23] Accompanying the process of globalization has been a growing belief among consumers in Western developed countries that corporations need to meet high standards of care wherever they operate: it is increasingly seen to be no longer acceptable for corporations to behave well "at home" while violating basic norms of consumer, worker, environmental and community

---

20. As discussed in Webb and Clarke, "Other Jurisdictions," Chapter 13, below.

21. As discussed in Webb and Morrison, "The Law and Voluntary Codes," Chapter 5, below.

22. They are also increasingly the subject of scholarly attention. For recent publications, see, e.g., J. Bendell, ed., *Terms for Endearment: Business, NGOs and Sustainable Development* (London: New Academy of Business, 2000); C. Carraro and F. Lévêque, eds., *Voluntary Approaches in Environmental Policy* (Dordrecht: Kluwer, 1999); R. Gibson, ed., *Voluntary Initiatives: The New Politics of Corporate Greening* (Peterborough, Ont.: Broadview Press, 1999); V. Haufler, *A Public Role for the Private Sector: Industry Self-Regulation in a Global Economy* (Washington: Carnegie Endowment for International Peace, 2001); J. Manheim, *Corporate Conduct Unbecoming: Codes of Conduct and Anti-Corporate Strategy* (St. Michaels, Md.: Tred Avon Institute Press, 1999); A. Prakash, *Greening the Firm: The Politics of Corporate Environmentalism* (Cambridge: Cambridge University Press, 2000).

23. See, e.g., Haufler, ibid., p. 20, who states that industry self-regulation is one element of globalization. In H. Holm and G. Sorensen, eds., *Whose World Order? Uneven Globalization and the End of the Cold War* (Boulder, Colo.: Westview Press, 1995), p. 1, the authors define *globalization* as "the intensification of economic, political, social and cultural relations across borders." For a thorough discussion of the concept and its implications, see A. Prakash and J. Hart, eds., *Globalization and Governance* (London: Routledge, 1999).

protection elsewhere.[24] Aided by advances in telecommunications and information technology, and provoked in part by recognition of the weaknesses of international public lawmaking and implementation regimes, non-governmental organizations (NGOs) are playing an increasingly prominent role in devising voluntary codes, stimulating corporations to develop their own codes, and monitoring corporate behaviour.[25] With the widespread use of the Internet, and the proliferation of NGOs in developing countries with access to it, it is now possible for civil society networks to track corporate and governmental misbehaviour wherever it might be, and to communicate monitoring information around the globe virtually instantaneously.[26]

In spite of preliminary evidence suggesting that codes can be effective in generating changes in behaviour,[27] there are many potentially problematic aspects of voluntary codes: those that are poorly designed or implemented can frustrate or mislead intended audiences, attract negative publicity, slow or prevent needed laws, have anti-competitive effects, create barriers to trade, and be difficult to enforce, particularly against those who do not want to participate (free riders).[28] In addition, voluntary codes can have significant legal implications for governments, industry, standards organizations and non-governmental organizations.[29] In short, while voluntary codes appear to show considerable promise as instruments for promoting public policy, there are also many aspects that raise questions about the roles and actions of all parties.

---

24. See, e.g., the results of the 1999 Environics International Millennium poll of 25,000 consumers in 23 countries, which indicated the increasing importance consumers are putting on the social responsibility leadership of companies. According to the survey, 67 percent of consumers in North America and Oceania had "punished" a company seen as not socially responsible in the past year, or considered doing same (*punishment* was defined as avoiding a product or speaking out about the company) or rewarded a company that had behaved in a socially responsible manner. This compared with 53 percent of North European consumers, 40 percent of Mediterranean, 37 percent of African and 31 percent of Latin American and Eastern European consumers. See Environics International, *Consumers Worldwide Expect Business to Achieve Social as Well as Economic Goals,* press release, September 30, 1999.

25. See comments to this effect by A. Florini, ed., in *The Third Force: The Rise of International Civil Society* (Washington: Japan Center for International Exchange and Carnegie Endowment for International Peace, 2000), and G. Gereffi, R. Garcia-Johnson and E. Sasser, "The NGO-Industrial Complex," *Foreign Policy* (July–August 2001).

26. See particularly Florini, ibid., pp. 220–224.

27. For example, as discussed in this volume, the Forest Stewardship Council has, through its affiliates, certified more than 24 million hectares of sustainably harvested forests; Gap Inc.'s program applies to its suppliers in 50 countries; the Fair Labour Association's program applies to more than 5,000 suppliers; there are noted reductions in emissions from Responsible Care members, and companies that are registered to ISO 14001 claim environmental improvements. Of course, as with discussions of the impacts of conventional regulatory programs, it is difficult to attribute improvements to any particular voluntary code; moreover, there may be problems with the reliability of current data, and information concerning compliance with code commitments may not be forthcoming.

28. Per Office of Consumer Affairs and Regulatory Affairs Division, Treasury Board Secretariat (Canada), *Voluntary Codes: A Guide for Their Development and Use* (Ottawa: Industry Canada and Treasury Board Secretariate, 1998), p. 6. The Guide is available at <http://strategis.ic.gc.ca/epic/internet/inoca-bc.nsf/en/ca00880e.html>. See also discussion in Webb and Morrison, "The Law and Voluntary Codes," Chapter 5, below.

29. These points are discussed in detail in Webb and Morrison, "The Law and Voluntary Codes," Chapter 5, below.

It was with these types of issues in mind that the Canadian Office of Consumer Affairs[30] launched the Voluntary Codes Project in 1996. The Project's original aims were to develop a better appreciation of the potential uses of voluntary codes for public policy purposes, and of their strengths and weaknesses, and to identify conditions conducive to success, roles of government, legal and public administration implications, and possible next steps. In the short term, the Project took the form of a research program involving both case studies and more in-depth explorations of the legal, public administration and other implications of voluntary codes, and the experience with voluntary codes in other jurisdictions.[31] Some of those original studies have been modified and updated for this volume. The research program led to a multistakeholder symposium at which the studies and issues were further explored and discussed.[32] At the symposium, support was expressed for the development of a guide to voluntary codes, similar to guides that had been developed in Australia and New Zealand.[33]

Following the symposium, a multistakeholder working group was struck to develop the guide. *Voluntary Codes: A Guide for Their Development and Use*[34] is now in its second printing. The online Voluntary Codes Research Forum is now operated by the Office of Consumer Affairs, with close to 400 government, industry, non-governmental and academic members around the world.[35] An evaluative framework for improving voluntary codes has been published,[36] and the Office of Consumer Affairs continues to participate in the development and monitoring of voluntary approaches — currently, in the areas of electronic commerce, voluntary labelling of genetically modified foods, complaints handling and the electronic transfer of funds (debit cards).

This volume is a logical extension of the Office of Consumer Affairs' work in the area of voluntary codes, an opportunity to bring together in one place some of the thinking and experiences on voluntary codes that may assist all parties in developing a better understanding of the strengths, weaknesses and roles of these codes. Drawing on the scholarly network associated with the Carleton Research Unit on Innovation, Science and Environment at Carleton University (which, among other responsibilities, administered a third-party academic review of this volume in manuscript form), the volume is intended to assist in engaging the broader academic community in explorations of voluntary codes issues. Research in this volume suggests that, when properly developed and implemented, voluntary codes can represent innovative approaches to

---

30. Originally, the Office of Consumer Affairs partnered in this work with Treasury Board Secretariat's Regulatory Affairs Division. The Regulatory Affairs Division has since been disbanded.

31. Summaries of the draft studies are available at <http://strategis.ic.gc.ca/epic/internet/inoca-bc.nsf/en/ca00880e.html>.

32. A summary of the symposium is available at <http://strategis.ic.gc.ca/epic/internet/inoca-bc.nsf/en/ca00819e.html>.

33. The voluntary codes experience in Australia and New Zealand is described in Gunningham, "The Australian Experience," Chapter 12, below.

34. The Guide (footnote 28) is available at <http://strategis.ic.gc.ca/epic/internet/inoca-bc.nsf/en/ca00880e.html>

35. For more information about the Forum, go to <http://strategis.ic.gc.ca/epic/internet/inoca-bc.nsf/en/ca00973e.html>.

36. Available at <http://strategis.ic.gc.ca/epic/internet/inoca-bc.nsf/en/ca00880e.html>.

addressing the concerns and needs of consumers, workers, environmentalists, communities and individual citizens, while at the same time helping companies to be more competitive. They can encourage companies and organizations to conduct themselves in ways that benefit both themselves and the broader community, and can harness market, community and peer pressures. However, in light of the significant problems that can arise from poorly thought out and inadequately implemented codes, it is hoped that it is apparent that the decision to participate in a voluntary code should only be undertaken after a thorough examination of the issues surrounding use of such instruments.

Voluntary Codes Defined

The title of this volume links voluntary codes with three concepts: private governance, the public interest and innovation. Given the centrality of these terms to the volume, a brief exploration of their meaning is in order at the outset. *Voluntary codes*, as used here, are:

- commitments not required by legislation or regulations;
- agreed to by one or more individuals or organizations;
- intended to influence or control behaviour; and
- to be applied in a consistent manner or to reach a consistent outcome.[37]

Several important points about this conception of voluntary codes deserve emphasis or explanation. First, even though a voluntary code is not legislatively required, this is not to suggest that there are no legal aspects to it, or implications flowing from its use; nor is it to intimate that at least part of the impetus for a code's development may not be legal in nature (for example, to forestall the likelihood of new regulations being developed or to decrease legal liability).[38] Second, while industry-wide voluntary codes may attract the most attention, it is entirely possible for an individual firm to develop a voluntary code for application only to itself or to its suppliers.[39] Third, the voluntary codes contemplated in this definition must include both commitments and application: a code without mechanisms to ensure its application is simply a statement of intent.[40] Frequently, voluntary codes are used in conjunction with a labelling or logo program, to signal to audiences that a particular product or member is in compliance with a code. Fourth, this definition of voluntary codes is sufficiently broad to capture the normative

---

37. This is a paraphrase of the definition of voluntary codes found in *Voluntary Codes: A Guide for Their Development and Use* (footnote 28), p. 2.

38. See Webb and Morrison, "The Law and Voluntary Codes," Chapter 5, below.

39. Indeed, a single-firm voluntary code is the subject of one of the case studies in this volume ("Gap Inc.'s Code of Conduct," Chapter 7, below). Moreover, as Kathryn Harrison discusses in her chapter, "Canada's Environmental Choice Program," Chapter 10, below, industry-wide compliance may not be desirable since compliance with a code and use of a label may be intended to show leadership and to gain a competitive advantage.

40. See Colin J. Bennett's contribution to this volume ("Privacy Self-Regulation," Chapter 8, below) for a typology of voluntary instruments, including commitments, codes and standards.

standards of formal, recognized standards bodies[41] such as the International Organization for Standardization (ISO), the Canadian Standards Association (CSA), and its counterparts in other jurisdictions, as well as those normative documents developed by firms, NGOs and other entities outside the formal standards system. Thus, from a functional standpoint, ISO or CSA standards are simply voluntary codes developed through formal standards systems. Both voluntary codes and standards are the subject of examination in this volume, and both terms are used as appropriate throughout this volume.

Voluntary Codes and Private Governance

As used here, *private governance* is intended to encompass the full range of ways that organizations not directly affiliated with the State attempt to organize their affairs.[42] It encompasses activities of both those engaged in the commercial sector as well as those in civil society. The names used by commentators to describe elements or types of private governance are breathtaking in their variety and creativity: some of the terms used include informal regulation, private regulation, communitarian regulation, self-regulation, co-regulation, reflexive law, soft law, self-management, corporate social responsibility, and techniques that go "beyond compliance."[43] Each of these terms is intended to connote or emphasize a distinctive attribute of a particular type of private governance. Taken together, for the purposes of this volume, *private governance* can be seen as a continuing process through which conflicting or diverse interests may be accommodated and cooperative action may be taken by non-State parties.[44] It includes

---

41. According to the World Trade Organization's *Agreement on Technical Barriers to Trade*, a standard is a document "approved by a recognized body, that provides, for common and repeated use, rules, guidelines or characteristics for products or related processes and production methods, *with which compliance is not mandatory*. It may include ... symbols, packaging, marking or labelling requirements as they apply to a product, process or production method," Annex 1, para. 2 (Geneva: WTO, 1994), available at <www.wto.org/english/docs_e/ legal_e/17-tbt.pdf>; emphasis added. An exploration of the significance of this definition to voluntary codes activities of groups such as the Forest Stewardship Council is undertaken in Webb and Morrison, "The Law and Voluntary Codes," Chapter 5, below.

42. The definition of *private governance* provided here draws on the definition of *global governance* in Commission on Global Governance, *Our Global Neighbourhood* (Oxford: Oxford University Press, 1995), p. 2. In the Commission's definition, governance purposefully encompasses public, civil society and commercial actors and activities. While the focus here is on non-State actors and instruments (and, hence, private governance), as the conclusion of this volume discusses, ultimately, a multipartite conception of governance shows considerable promise as a way of bringing to bear the full range of parties and instruments on any public policy problem.

43. In addition to the publications referred to above, see A. King and M. Lenox, "Industry Self-Regulation Without Sanctions: The Chemical Industry's Responsible Care Program," *Academy of Management Journal* 43:4 (2000), available at <www.aom.pace.edu/amj/August2000/king.pdf>, p. 7; S. Pargal and D. Wheeler, "Informal Regulation of Industrial Pollution in Developing Countries: Evidence from Indonesia," *Journal of Political Economy* 104 (1996), pp. 1314–1327; G. Teubner, L. Farmer and D. Murphy, eds., *Environmental Law and Ecological Responsibility: The Concept and Practice of Ecological Self-Organization* (Chichester: John Wiley and Sons, 1994).

44. Using increasingly sophisticated forms of game theory, such as the multiparty stag hunt (as opposed to the two-party prisoner's dilemma) and non-zero-sum games (i.e. games that allow for win-win situations, such as mutually beneficial trades, as opposed to zero-sum games in which one side's gain is another's loss, such as checkers), philosophers have begun to develop interesting explanations for why, over time, actors will tend to choose cooperative as opposed to conflict solutions to problems they face. While the author could find no

formal institutions and regimes empowered to develop rules and enforce compliance (e.g. industry association and NGO-supported rule-making and disciplinary procedures, monitoring and enforcement techniques), as well as informal arrangements that people and institutions either have agreed to or perceive to be in their interest (e.g. peer pressure through quarterly meetings, information disclosure, etc.). Private governance is thus an overarching conceptual framework within which voluntary codes, as non-legislatively required commitments made and applied by a variety of actors, are developed and operate. It should be emphasized that governments can do and are doing much to promote, guide and support private governance techniques that further public policy objectives, and to constrain those that are contrary to public policy. Throughout this volume, examples of such government promotion, guidance, support and constraining efforts are provided.

Voluntary Codes and the Public Interest

As David Cohen makes clear in his chapter, there are a vast number of self-imposed voluntary instruments used by business that, while very important to the development, production, pricing, marketing and distribution of goods and services, have little significance from a public interest standpoint.[45] Many corporate structures, bylaws, policies, operational manuals, standards and contracts fit in this category. The focus of attention in this volume is on those voluntary codes that have a significant public interest component — even though in many cases the motivations of the proponent may very well be largely self-oriented in nature (e.g. increasing or maintaining customers, decreasing risk, increasing productivity and profit, responding to shareholder and investor demands, decreasing insurance premiums, improving worker and community relations, or forestalling development of a new regulation or decreasing the likelihood of a legal violation and liability).[46] It is in recognition of the public policy effects of private voluntary codes that, in a wide number of cases, governments have participated in and supported the development of such codes and indeed have drawn on them for their own purposes.[47]

In a world in which industry, governments and NGOs are increasingly employing market-oriented voluntary codes that address important public policy

---

discussions on point, voluntary codes would appear to be good examples of cooperative multiparty solutions in keeping with stag-hunt and non-zero-sum game theories. The leading proponent of stag hunt theory is Professor Brian Skyrms at the University of Calfornia (Irvine). His paper, *The Stag Hunt*, is available at <http://hypatia.ss. uci.edu/lps/home/fac-staff/faculty/skyrms/Hunt.PDF>. The leading proponent of non-zero-sum game theory is Robert Wright, author of *Nonzero: The Logic of Human Destiny* (New York: Pantheon, 2000).

45. David Cohen, "The Role of the State in a Privatized Regulatory Environment," Chapter 2, below.

46. These motivations are variously explored in the chapters of this volume. Professor Wes Cragg of the Schulich School of Business (York University) has suggested that investor-owned corporations, by virtue of their status as legal creations, have a fiduciary obligation to shareholders to advance both public and private interests, which encompasses an obligation to enhance share value but also an obligation to work within the framework of law and prevailing moral standards to advance public as well as private interests. In so doing, Cragg provides the foundation for corporate social responsibility activities (in the form of codes of conduct) that extend beyond mere compliance with laws and simple profit maximization. See W. Cragg, *Business Ethics and Stakeholder Theory*, unpublished manuscript available from the author (November 2001).

47. As discussed in many of the chapters.

problems, it seems evident that the lines separating the public and private spheres are blurring, representing, as one commentator called it, a "hybridization of law and market, state and non-state."[48] This has led some commentators to suggest that a new conception of "government" is needed, capable of encompassing "the entire complex of ideals, goals, rationales, techniques, procedures and programs by which a diversity of state and non-state authorities seek to shape human conduct to desired ends."[49] In this broader conception of government, it is possible for non-State actors such as industry associations and NGOs to use "governmental technologies"[50] such as codes and standards to achieve their aims, alongside government use of such instruments.

Some might argue that voluntary codes and standards depoliticize important environmental, health and economic issues, replacing them with technical and managerial devices and instruments driven by industry.[51] With their emphasis on procedure, formality and technical expertise, the argument goes, voluntary codes mute the struggles over risks, harms, jobs and profits inherent in decision making concerning environmental, human rights, consumer protection and worker safety issues. Debates about "justice, poverty, racism, ecological integrity, animal rights, the intrinsic value of nature" are transformed through the use of codes and standards into "matters of managerial expertise and market preference," thus enabling inequality and repression to be perpetuated, and disguising their own role in that perpetuation.[52]

While this muting of significant political issues and perpetuating of inequalities is a distinct possibility — particularly when civil society and governments have no opportunity to meaningfully participate in code development and implementation[53] — an equally plausible scenario is that voluntary codes can act to operationalize vague and

---

48. S. Wood, "Green Revolution or Greenwash? Voluntary Environmental Standards, Public Law and Private Authority in Canada," in *New Perspectives on the Public-Private Divide* (Vancouver: UBC Press, 2004). Note that Professor Wood was speaking specifically about the use of the ISO 14001 standard environmental management system standard.

49. Wood, ibid., drawing on, among others, M. Foucault, "Governmentality," in G. Burchell, C. Gordon and P. Miller, eds., *The Foucault Effect* (Chicago: Chicago University Press, 1991), pp. 87–104; N. Rose and P. Miller, "Political Power Beyond the State: Problematics of Government," *British Journal of Sociology* 43 (1992), p. 173.

50. Wood, ibid.

51. The following is a paraphrase of discussion found in Wood, ibid., which was specifically addressing the ISO 14000 environmental management system standard. It may be that the arguments concerning the effects of management-oriented standards would not apply with equal force to NGO-led or -supported codes that may or may not have the same degree of technical, management orientation.

52. Wood, ibid.

53. A key issue is how the public interest is factored into non-governmental voluntary code activity. One technique is to ensure that a full range of stakeholders has a meaningful opportunity to participate in code development and implementation. Discussion in several chapters in this volume suggests that, for reasons of enhanced credibility, as well as to improve the quality of decisions, this is increasingly considered essential (see, e.g., discussions on this issue in the chapters on Responsible Care, Gap Inc.'s code of conduct, sustainable forestry practices, and Canada's eco-labelling program and helmet standards and regulations, below). In Canada, formal standards bodies must have a balanced matrix of representation on their standards development committees (on this point, see particularly discussions in the sustainable forestry practices and helmet standards and regulations chapters, below). A second technique is to structure voluntary code activity within a greater framework of law. The multiple ways in which the law structures voluntary codes are discussed in greater detail in Webb and Morrison, "The Law and Voluntary Codes," Chapter 5, below.

general policy objectives, thus providing all parties with practical guidance on how to structure potentially harmful activities and behaviours, in the process moving discussions from high-level policy rhetoric and slogans to more mundane, nitty-gritty action. The fact that leading, high-profile NGOs with conventional advocacy and political orientations are now championing use of such instruments is evidence that, even in the eyes of these consummate political players, there is no perceived incompatibility between, on the one hand, engaging in political discussions about issues of societal concern and, on the other, attempting to devise instruments to address these issues. Indeed, one can argue that the ability of NGOs to be effective in their political activities will be enhanced through the knowledge gained developing and implementing codes.

Voluntary Codes and Innovation

The final concept in the title of this volume, innovation, is as vast in scope as private governance and the public interest. In its most basic form, innovation is any process through which new means and/or ends are developed.[54] Innovation can be focussed on the private sector (with new products or services, new ways of making those products, new ways of marketing and distributing them, etc.), the public sector (new policies, new ways of delivering policy, new ways of funding) or the not-for-profit sector (in the delivery of an organization's mission, in funding and in administration).[55]

The focus of attention here is on voluntary codes as a form of *rule innovation,* with significant market and social (including public policy) implications. The concept of rule innovation draws for inspiration on the recent work of Harvard Business School Professor Clayton Christensen concerning breakthrough innovations in the "connected economy."[56] A key characteristic of breakthrough innovations is that they typically *enable a larger population of less skilled people to do things previously performed by specialists in less convenient, centralized settings,* and usually facilitate *empowered participation.* He gives as an example the computer, which in its early forms was a very large, expensive mainframe device used only by experts for sophisticated problem solving, but then with the advent of the personal computer, became something that, while not as powerful as mainframes, was suddenly accessible to many, and hence capable of application to a much wider variety of situations than ever before. Innovations such as

---

54. For good discussions of the nature of innovation, see P. Kelly and M. Kranzburg, eds., *Technological Innovation: A Critical Review of Current Knowledge* (San Francisco: San Francisco Press, 1979). See also Editorial Board of the *Innovation Journal*, "Some Thoughts on Definitions of Innovation," *The Innovation Journal* 4:3 (September–December 1999), available at <www.innovation.cc/discussion-papers/thoughts-innovation.htm>.

55. See, generally, ibid., and P. Griffith, "Innovation in Not for Profits and Government," *The Innovation Journal* 4:2 (May–August 1999), available at <www.innovation.cc/discussion-papers/not-for-profits.htm>; and Public Policy Forum, "Innovation in the Federal Government: The Risk Not Taken," *The Innovation Journal* 4:2 (May–August 1999), available at <www.innovation.cc/discussion-papers/risk2.htm>.

56. See generally, C. Christensen, *The Innovator's Dilemma: When New Technologies Cause Great Firms to Fail* (Boston: Harvard Business School Press, 1997), and more particularly C. Christensen and T. Petzinger, "Innovation in the Connected Economy: A Conversation with Clayton Christensen," *Perspectives on Business Innovation,* Issue 5: The Connected Economy (September 2000). Note that Christensen's conception focussed exclusively on *commercial* applications.

the introduction of the personal computer tend to distribute expertise and access, and to decentralize power.[57]

The position taken here is that voluntary codes are a form of breakthrough *rule* innovation with significant public policy implications: clearly, public organs of rule making, administration and adjudication are and will remain the "mainframe computers" of society, controlled and used by experts (elected members of legislatures, government regulators, judges, etc.) for sophisticated problems. Voluntary code rule systems, on the other hand, are the comparatively inexpensive personal computers of societal rule development and implementation — they are perhaps not as powerful as "mainframe" rule approaches, but they are accessible to a much wider group of players and may be nimbler and more portable. While laws are imposed in a top-down fashion, have a coercive base and are the product of centralized rule systems, voluntary codes are inherently bottom-up, cooperative and consent-based, working only when agreed to by the appropriate attentive publics. Through use of voluntary codes, NGOs, firms, industry associations, multistakeholder groups, and others are in an empowered position[58] to create and operate their own rule systems, to engage in "norm conversations" directly with various publics, as opposed to exclusively through the intermediary of the State, and in so doing societal opportunities for norm development and implementation are enriched and vitalized.

Just as the introduction of personal computers did not obviate the need for mainframes, so too voluntary code rule systems will not replace the conventional rule systems of the State — indeed, voluntary codes function within an overarching framework of law. Voluntary codes are an additional instrument for rule development and implementation, operating alongside legislative techniques and processes, and as such increase and enrich the possibilities for effective norm development and implementation. In addition to acting as innovative voicing mechanisms for NGOs, industry associations and hybrid multistakeholder groups, codes can act as incubators for new legal approaches by testing out what does and does not work, refining and enhancing legal approaches, addressing activities not easily controlled through legislative techniques, helping define what constitutes legally acceptable conduct, assisting in addressing some of the weaknesses of laws, being incorporated into the terms of legal instruments, extending the reach of legislative techniques, stimulating "beyond legislative compliance" behaviour, and enhancing the enforcement capabilities of governments.[59]

Some might be concerned that the proliferation of codes can be confusing — for consumers and citizens, as well as for governments and industries — as each code competes for attention. There is, of course, this possibility. But this potential confusion

---

57. Christensen and Petzinger, ibid.

58. Of course, whether voluntary codes are tools for empowering disadvantaged groups depends to a large degree on the code and context under consideration. A trade association may purposely shield its code development and implementation from input by affected parties, and in so doing fail to be empowering. However, failure to meaningfully involve these affected parties could negatively affect a code's credibility and legitimacy. See, particularly, discussion of the sustainable forestry standards and apparel worker code standards in this volume for examples of this.

59. These points are all discussed in Webb and Morrison, "The Law and Voluntary Codes," Chapter 5, below.

may be overstated. At the level of individual behaviour, consumers seem to have a highly developed ability to sort through diverse products and services in order to select those that meet their needs — whether it be fair trade coffee, organic food, merchants that are members of the Better Business Bureau, products that meet Canadian Standards Association or British Standards Institute standards, garages that are approved by the Canadian Automobile Association or American Automobile Association, and so on. As long as codes and claims made about them are not misleading or otherwise anti-competitive (in which case they are open to legal action), it is difficult to see how diversity of codes is, in the final analysis, a troubling development for consumers, worthy of government constraint. From a market standpoint, there is the potential that code diversity will lead to improvements (see, for example, discussion of the seemingly positive impacts flowing from competition between the Canadian Standards Association and Forest Stewardship Council sustainable forestry initiatives, later in this volume). Moreover, it is not unreasonable to anticipate that, from time to time, early code diversity in a particular area (e.g. code initiatives pertaining to consumer protection in the area of electronic commerce) will lead to "market shakedowns," with only a small number of such initiatives emerging as the most prominent. Thus, sudden, riotous and confusing proliferations of codes pertaining to a particular topic are likely to be only temporary conditions. Fourth, when governments are concerned about code confusion and proliferation, they can introduce their own code initiatives (see discussion of the Environmental Choice Program in Chapter 10 of this volume), support and endorse those they feel are worthy (as is the case with the Apparel Industry Partnership/Fair Labor Association and scanner accuracy code initiatives discussed in chapters 7 and 13 of this volume), draw on voluntary initiatives to create legislative approaches (as was the case with the development of the Canadian federal personal information protection law, which is based on a Canadian Standards Association code, as discussed in Chapter 8 of this volume), and constrain those who act in a manner considered contrary to public policy (e.g. contrary to anti-trust/competition or misleading advertising provisions and guidelines, as discussed in Chapter 5 of this volume). In short, code diversity would appear to be a positive development in most circumstances, and when it is not, governments have the tools at their disposal to address problematic aspects (and have so used these tools).

Voluntary Codes as Voicing Mechanisms

When NGOs take leadership roles in the development of voluntary codes (as in the case of the Forest Stewardship Council, Fair Labor Association and Web Trader initiatives discussed in this volume), the codes can act as aggregate voicing mechanisms for demand-side interests of the economy.[60] Before NGOs began regularly using voluntary codes in this manner, publications and consumer boycotts were virtually the

---

60. See Bendell (footnote 22) for discussion of the increasingly important role that organizations of civil society will have in setting the standards for business behaviour in the 21st century.

only way for voicing to be undertaken by the demand side of the economy,[61] and industry — through use of techniques such as surveys, focus testing, and advertising campaigns — had a virtual monopoly over the organized definition of consumer needs.[62] In contrast with boycotts (the main techniques for demand-side voicing used in previous eras), voluntary codes are information-rich, targeted, proactive and practical. While boycotts essentially tell the marketplace that some aspect of private sector behaviour is unacceptable (and do so in a rather blunt, approximate manner), voluntary codes can be more constructive, providing detailed prescriptive information on what commercial behaviour is considered proper and improper, and how firms can operate in an acceptable manner. When a code is operated in conjunction with a labelling scheme, a practical system is in place for businesses to demonstrate good behaviour and for consumers to identify and reward that good behaviour.

In many circumstances, the ability of NGOs to act as demand-side voice aggregators has been enhanced considerably through use of the Internet. The opportunity for NGOs to gather information concerning a particular activity or firm, to share that information with their partners in code development, and to communicate and promote code initiatives to the broader community is improved through the use of Web sites, e-mails and search engines. Members of the public also have an enhanced ability to conduct their own Internet-based research on code issues as they see fit, and not rely solely on what supply-side advertising or mainstream media might choose to say about an issue. While in the past it has been governments and industry sectors that have had significant strategic informational advantages in terms of networking and communications, the Internet is now offering the possibility of a more "level playing field" for demand-side interests. In short, as access to the Internet becomes more pervasive, the information asymmetries between supply-side and demand-side interests may lessen, and information-related transaction costs associated with demand-side voice aggregation and organization may diminish. This would appear to be a significant contributing factor in the rise to prominence of NGO-led voluntary code initiatives. (In the next section, another possible contributing factor in the rise to prominence of NGO-led voluntary code initiatives is discussed — the high public credibility of NGOs, and the associated, considerably lower levels of public confidence in government and industry representatives.)

NGOs that take on the role of championing demand-side needs and wants through use of voluntary codes may be able to work with others to transform an ambiguous consumer attitude toward a particular behaviour[63] (which due to its generality

---

61. For a good discussion of the history and evolution of boycotts, see N. C. Smith, *Morality and the Market: Consumer Pressure for Corporate Accountability* (London: Routledge, 1990). Cooperatives have long been used for aggregate demand-side purchasing, but not primarily as a voicing mechanism.

62. Of course, the *threat* of consumer boycotts can still exist behind the comparatively benign face of an NGO-led voluntary code, and it is possible that the potential for exercise of that threat is increased once a voluntary code has been developed (since there is a peak organization to promote it that one can join, and presumably there is a constituency that can be called on to support the cause). Members of NGOs can also participate in protests of merchants that are not adhering to their (or an acceptable) voluntary code, and in this way "encourage" businesses to adhere to their code. See, generally, Gereffi, Garcia-Johnson, and Sasser (footnote 25).

63. See, e.g., Environics International (footnote 24).

might not otherwise manifest itself at the cash register[64]) into focussed, actionable changes in marketplace behaviour. Thus, for example, generalized public concern about clear-cut forest activities is operationalized through the World Wild Fund for Nature-supported Forest Stewardship Council that, as the result of the work of its affiliated certification partners, has now certified 24 million hectares of forests around the world as being sustainably harvested. Similarly, the Fair Labor Association's apparel-related code (whose founding members include consumer, faith-based and human rights NGOs, as well as businesses), transformed generalized consumer concerns with the working conditions of labourers in factories into commitments from major brand-name apparel retailers to comply with its workplace code of conduct. And the Web Trader program in the U.K. and other European countries responded to generalized consumer concerns with online merchants through a code of conduct and seal program that attracted more than 3,000 participating merchants. Note that with respect to both the Forest Stewardship Council and Fair Labor Association initiatives, a key to success was recognition and support by certain retailers of the value of the initiative, and agreement from them to work with NGOs to change behaviour. These retailers, as major buyers (on behalf of their consumers) were then in a position to push for change from producers. This sort of NGO-retailer-producer leveraged influence relationship is discussed in greater detail below.

A slight variation on the theme of voluntary codes as innovative voicing mechanisms in the marketplace occurs when businesses *lead* in the development of voluntary codes. Here, businesses are attempting to respond to, or anticipate, demand-side interests in some aspect of their products and services by articulating how their businesses address the perceived demand-side interest (or they are attempting to anticipate or respond to government demands). However, it is increasingly clear that industry voluntary initiatives developed without meaningful consultations with NGOs, affected communities and other civil society stakeholders may lack credibility. While NGO-led initiatives can be described as *push* mechanisms for "voicing," industry-led initiatives are more like *pull* mechanisms, attempting to "tell" consumers, communities, governments and other attentive publics what businesses think those attentive publics want to hear (and then responding on the basis of what they hear).

In either case, once an NGO or industry group makes public its intention to create a code, and thereafter as the code is developed, there are frequently replies from other interests, and so as the initiative evolves, and as several voices variously make themselves heard, a form of "norm conversation" — sometimes an argument — takes place. Not too surprisingly, the shape of initiatives may change as the conversations and arguments progress.[65]

---

64. See, e.g., a recent U.K. study that has labelled the phenomenon the "30:3 syndrome," due to the fact that while more than 30 percent of consumers express support for corporate social responsibility, ethical products hold only 3 percent of the market. Per R. Crowe and S. Williams, *Who are the Ethical Consumers?* (London: The Cooperative Bank, 1999). For discussion of a similar phenomenon in Canada (the Environmental Choice Program), see K. Harrison, "Canada's Environmental Choice Program," Chapter 10, below.

65. Thus, for example, Gap Inc.'s original code for El Salvador supplier factories was not subject to third-party monitoring, but now is, following NGO criticism, as discussed in greater detail later in this volume.

Voluntary Codes and Leveraged Influence

Research in this volume suggests the importance of recognizing the potential for voluntary codes to be used to influence behaviour beyond the direct parties involved. NGOs have been able to develop alliances with retailers, who in turn are in a position (as proxy, aggregated consumers with buying power) to demand significant changes from supplier-producers (e.g. in the context of sustainable forestry and apparel worker codes).[66] In this way, NGOs may be able to exercise, on behalf of consumers, a degree of market influence beyond what would be expected based on their membership base. On the industry side of the ledger, chemical producers are also now beginning to extend their Responsible Care model to bring about change in conduct from downstream commercial chemical users, and thereby leverage their influence over these users. Research in this volume also suggests that the Responsible Care model has been widely emulated by other industry sectors, tacitly becoming a benchmark for a number of non-chemical-related industries wishing to put in place a voluntary program. Large automobile manufacturers are requiring their suppliers to comply with the voluntary International Organization for Standardization (ISO) environmental management standard, in a kind of supply-chain domino effect. Shareholders, investors and pension funds are using governance and social responsibility guidelines as measures of acceptable and unacceptable levels of risk management behaviour by corporations, and are thereby influencing firms to change their behaviour with a view to becoming more attractive to the investment community. Insurers are reducing premiums for companies that comply with recognized environmental programs.

Several years ago, the suggestion was made by Mancur Olson in *The Logic of Collective Action*[67] that, for reasons mainly pertaining to organizational dynamics, smaller, tightly knit groups might be more successful in getting changes made to public policy than would less tightly knit groups. Olson's attention was focussed on the behaviour of non-State actors vis-à-vis State rule-making institutions, but it would appear that a similar phenomenon and dynamic may be at work with respect to voluntary codes and market behaviour. In effect, a comparatively small but well-organized NGO, retailer, industry association or multistakeholder body may be able to stimulate widespread market behavioural change beyond its membership aided by the use of voluntary codes. Needless to say, those industry sectors, such as the mining sector, that do not have an identifiable retail exposure may be less vulnerable to consumer pressure than are others, but they may nevertheless be stimulated to respond as the result of pressure from other demand- or supply-side actors, such as retail-exposed shareholders, investors, pension fund managers and insurers, with which they have commercial and other relations.

To be successful, code proponents must target multiple potential supporters (ultimately, the consuming public), perhaps via proxy intermediaries such as retailers, while those wishing to influence the shape and content of laws may have their eye on the electorate, but tend to target their lobbying efforts on a small group of key ministers, the Cabinet and government officials. Unlike lobbying efforts concerning laws, an industry-

---

66. All of the examples in this paragraph are from research described in the volume.

67. M. Olson, *The Logic of Collective Action* (Cambridge, Mass.: Harvard University Press, 1965).

initiated code can be countered by an NGO-initiated code (and vice-versa), so that an open, pluralist, market-based "rule competition" for the hearts and bank accounts of consumers is possible. Good examples of this are the competing NGO- and industry-led code and labelling initiatives pertaining to sustainable forestry and treatment of apparel workers, and similar competitions between NGO- and industry-led merchant reliability programs in the area of electronic commerce (as discussed in this volume). Concerns that codes can be wielded by powerful industrial interests (who have money, access to critical information, and influence) against those less powerful are being put to the test when NGOs develop their own initiatives, and are supported in their efforts by a range of consumer and other interests.

NGOs and industry interests that have developed voluntary codes may also attempt to use codes in efforts to influence public lawmaking. Thus, for example, an NGO or industry association could argue that the voluntary code that it developed, supported and/or implemented demonstrates the workability and indeed popularity of the initiative, so that it should be the basis for a law (as in the case of the support by the Canadian Marketing Association for the CSA privacy code becoming the basis for federal and provincial privacy laws). Or an industry association might argue that there is no need for a new law because a voluntary initiative is already addressing a particular problem (the spectre of this has been raised by NGO interests vis-à-vis the Responsible Care program). Or, an NGO could argue that a failure of a particular code initiative proves the need for a law.

In so acting, these interests would essentially be behaving in a manner entirely consistent with Olson's original observation focussed on the potential enhanced capability of a comparatively small set of private actors to affect public policy, with the slight variation that the private organizations in question would be using market-oriented codes to bolster their public policy arguments. Some might argue that use of codes by industry associations and NGOs to influence public policy demonstrates the dangers of codes to public policy and thereby undermines democratic processes. There is always this possibility. But at least the basis for their lobbying efforts would be an operating rule regime, voluntarily agreed to by a range of supply- and demand-side interests (as the case might be), and not simply a more or less persuasive argument for why there should or should not be a law (the more conventional basis for lobbying). There would also be the possible existence of other, rival code initiatives for legislators and government officials to consider in their public policy decision making. Codes-based public policy lobbying is lobbying based on some degree of experience with rules in action, and in that regard at least offers the opportunity for all parties to reach their own conclusions about the merits of a public policy proposal based on operating code regimes.

Credibility, Commodification and Codes

Scholars such as Professor Benjamin Cashore of Yale University's School of Forestry and Environmental Studies have begun to turn their attention to the importance of credibility or legitimation in understanding the use and effectiveness of code initiatives.[68] Drawing on his research concerning forestry management initiatives, Cashore suggests that voluntary code systems have four distinctive governance characteristics: no use of State sovereignty to force compliance, authority granted through external audiences, authority granted through a supply chain, and verified compliance. According to Cashore, there are a variety of types of legitimacy that can be granted by a code's audience: *pragmatic legitimacy*, which rests on the self-interested calculations of an organization's most immediate audience (e.g. certification will give a particular forestry company a competitive advantage), *moral legitimacy*, which reflects a calculus based on what is "the right thing to do" (more likely to be granted by supportive NGOs), and *cognitive legitimacy*, which may flow from conforming to established modes or standards (e.g. building a Canadian Standards Association forestry standard on an existing ISO 14000 platform). The voluntary codes examined in this volume reveal the wide number of legitimacy-enhancing activities engaged in by business-, NGO- and government-supported voluntary code regimes.[69]

Recently, Canadian provincial and American state governments announced that they were having their regulatory regimes for the management of forestry and fisheries resources certified by NGO-spearheaded voluntary code initiatives.[70] Such actions seem to show government recognition that their regulatory programs are lacking in public and market credibility, and that NGO-led certification might assist them in providing that needed credibility.[71] In doing so, they join the line already formed by commercial

---

68. See, e.g., B. Cashore, "Legitimacy and the Privatization of Environmental Governance: How Non State Market-Driven (NSMD) Governance Systems (Certification Eco-labelling Programs) Gain Rule Making Authority," *Governance: An International Journal of Policy, Administration and Institutions* 15:4 (October 2002), pp. 503–529; S. Bernstein and B. Cashore, "Globalization, Four Paths of Internationalization and Domestic Policy Change: The Case of Eco-forestry Policy Change in British Columbia," *Canadian Journal of Political Science* 33 (2000) pp. 67–99.

69. See particularly discussions in Rhone, Stroud and Webb, "Gap Inc.'s Code of Conduct," Chapter 7, below; Rhone, Clarke and Webb, "Sustainable Forestry Practices," Chapter 9, below; Harrison, "Canada's Environmental Choice Program," Chapter 10, below; Webb and Clarke, "Other Jurisdictions," Chapter 13, below.

70. For example, the State of Alaska's commercial salmon fisheries management program has been certified as sustainable by the non-governmental Marine Stewardship Council, pursuant to its sustainable fishery standards: see Office of the Governor of Alaska, *Alaska's Salmon Fishery Certified as Sustainable*, press release, September 5, 2000. Professor E. Meidinger (footnote 13), p. 10169, reports sources indicating that the agencies responsible for managing state-owned lands in Minnesota, New York and Pennsylvania have either achieved Forest Stewardship Council certification or announced they intend to do so. In March 2001, the Ontario Minister of Natural Resources announced that the province was initiating a bilateral process with the Forest Stewardship Council (FSC) to obtain FSC certification of all Crown-owned forests managed in compliance with Ontario law and the products derived from those forests. Per Ontario Ministry of Natural Resources (footnote 13).

71. In *Group Politics and Public Policy*, 2nd ed. (Toronto: Oxford Press, 1992), Paul Pross articulates a nuanced and useful concept to describe the actors who have acquired a dominant voice in determining government decisions in a field of public activity, which he refers to as the *policy community* (see, e.g., p. 119).

interests wishing to have their actions NGO-approved. The success of these NGO-supported initiatives, as well as those of standards such as ISO 14000, and the popularity of "ethical citizen" businesses such as Ben and Jerry's and The Body Shop provide more evidence that social, ethical and environmental values have entered the marketplace, and are capable of commodification.

An argument can be made that values-based NGOs that spearhead the development of voluntary codes are attempting to parlay or transform their credibility as critics of government and private sector activities into arbiters of good government and good business behaviour through market-oriented voluntary code "rule commodities." Prior to this point, NGOs were usually in the luxurious (if frustrating) position of never having the responsibility of regulating an activity.[72] This allowed them to develop their skills in pointing out the weaknesses of others, but otherwise kept them above the fray. Now, it may be that the tables will be turned. They will likely face the same barrage of critical and skeptical questions that in the past they themselves have asked of government: for example, just how accountable and transparent are their decision-making processes? Are there meaningful opportunities for all affected parties to participate? What is the basis for their decisions? Indeed, the suggestion has been made that NGOs should themselves be the subject of a voluntary code of accountability.[73] At an operational level, it is reasonable to assume that NGO-spearheaded voluntary code administrations will be susceptible to the usual litany of problems faced by those that regulate (e.g. incompetence, corruption, conflict of interest, unfair treatment, etc.). In short, the real test of the credibility of NGOs as rule makers and implementors is just beginning. The advocacy activities of NGOs may be enriched through the knowledge gained in assuming rule-making and implementation responsibilities, but their reputation as observers above the fray is likely to be challenged.

In sum, in this volume, voluntary codes are considered to be innovative approaches to rule making and implementation, providing new competition to existing players and processes, both in the context of the market and concerning public policy. Codes offer a new and different model for framing, voicing and implementing market and public policy rules — a model potentially allowing more parties into the rule-making process. Codes compel a re-examination of how market and public interest rule making and implementation have to date been undertaken. But, on the other hand, codes that are not properly designed and implemented can cause problems for all parties concerned. These themes are variously illustrated and explored in the chapters that follow.

[handwritten notes]

In a diagram on p. 123 that sets out the concentric rings of influence in a typical policy community, government agencies are at the centre. When non-State public policy-oriented voluntary codes are in use, and government regulatory credibility is threatened, it could be that a different conception of policy community is required, in which government agencies are circling NGO-led code institutions that occupy the central position.

72. It perhaps goes without saying that in light of the fact that NGOs are not government entities, the only opportunities they will have to regulate is through private regulatory mechanisms.

73. A. Adair, *A Code of Conduct for NGOs: A Necessary Reform* (London: Institute of Economic Affairs, 1999).

The volume is organized into several parts. Part One consists of this chapter's introduction to the concepts and themes. Part Two is devoted to broad, cross-cutting examinations of basic issues that underlie the use of voluntary codes. The main objective is to provide readers with some idea of the intellectual and practical contextual background within which voluntary codes operate. In Part Two, the role of the State in a privatized regulatory environment is explored, as are the public administrative, political economy and legal aspects of voluntary codes. Part Three then consists of six case studies of existing voluntary code initiatives. The chemical producers' Responsible Care environmental program, Gap Inc.'s code of conduct for the treatment of overseas workers, a variety of privacy self-regulatory initiatives, two sustainable forestry initiatives, and the Canadian Environmental Choice Program are all reviewed. A comparison of voluntary bicycle helmet standards and hockey helmet regulations is also provided. Part Four is devoted to analysis of voluntary code experiences outside of Canada, with the Australian, American, European and developing country experiences all examined. Finally, in Part Five, a concluding chapter looks at the future of voluntary codes.

Part Two begins with David's Cohen's chapter, "The Role of the State in a Privatized Regulatory Environment." Cohen traces the movement towards regulation by private rather than public institutions. He describes voluntary codes as part of a transformation of our historical conceptions of government, to encompass activities of both State and non-State actors in the face of the growing economic, social and political importance of multinational and non-governmental organizations. In this new regulatory environment, the State and laws still have a place, but their roles are very different from (and of less central importance than) those considered appropriate for much of the 20th century.

In support of the idea that voluntary codes are a form of rule innovation, Cohen characterizes voluntary codes as decentralized contractual bargains between various stakeholders, replacing the centralized production of regulations by governments. When designed properly, voluntary codes can represent an effective regulatory instrument providing for a multiplicity of interests and values to be heard and reflected in the output of markets. Ideally, voluntary codes can provide a mechanism for industry to take an enlightened view of its self-interest, for NGOs to be more effective, for small business to be heard, and for labour to be represented, with government acting as a form of mediator. Moreover, voluntary codes can potentially avoid many of the constitutional limitations that constrain the legal authority of the State.

But there is no guarantee that voluntary codes will fulfil this promise. Cohen describes another, less positive vision of voluntary codes, one in which the instrument simply permits the most knowledgeable and powerful actors in the markets to dominate not only the production of private goods, but also the definition and creation of public goods. Codes may simply be a strategy to deflect the energy of interest groups away from the political process and permit firms to avoid more effective and rigorous public regulation.

Cohen concludes that perhaps both visions are true, and withholds judgment at this time on the utility of voluntary codes. Codes are neither inherently good or bad. What is certain is that underlying the use of voluntary codes is a complicated relationship of private and public regulation in shaping behaviour. And while the State is being transformed, it is still present, with laws and governmental action stimulating and shaping the form and content of voluntary codes. He speculates that the utility and impact of voluntary codes is likely to vary depending on the context, their design and implementation, and their relation to legal regimes.

In "Institutional and Public Administrative Aspects of Voluntary Codes," G. Bruce Doern explores the application of the concept of accountability to the use of voluntary codes. He divides his analysis into five interrelated themes: accountability to the democratic State and Parliament, internal accountability within the groups that develop and administer codes, the characteristics of voluntary codes as public policy instruments, the impact of budgetary cutbacks on the ability of the State and others to carry out their tasks, and the nature of overlapping regimes of regulation and their relevance to voluntary codes. In contrast to conventional command-and-control regulation, which is subject to an upward and inward accountability to Parliament, voluntary codes have more of a downward and outward accountability to the broader collective.

Doern cautions against characterizing a world of greater reliance on voluntary codes as a world that is a full or sharp break from one with conventional regulation, noting that even with conventional regulation there is an important aspect of activity that is "relational," involving ongoing persuasion, education and information between regulators and regulated. Much of voluntary codes activity has a strong relational component. With budget cuts, the ability of regulators to understand and properly respond to voluntary codes activity may be negatively affected.

Doern suggests that use of voluntary codes is likely to focus attention more on exactly what associational, corporate and intergroup democracy and accountability really involves. In a way, Doern observes, these organizations become "surrogate States," leading to the legitimate question, what capacity do they have to carry out all of the rule functions that we currently associate with public institutions? Voluntary codes may mean fewer *public* bureaucrats, but not necessarily fewer bureaucrats. In this regard, the adequacy of accountability mechanisms within organizations that develop and implement voluntary codes will be of central importance — mechanisms such as reporting, compliance verification processes and public involvement.

In conclusion, Doern suggests that perhaps the largest institutional and public administrative picture to emerge from his analysis is that of a government presiding over two broad clusters of rule makers and compliance organizations: one that the government regulates itself and one in which it oversees, in some less clear and less direct fashion, a set of self-regulators and code administrators that has the direct relationship with the persons and interests affected by the code. In this regard, the growing number of voluntary codes regimes can be seen as a natural "bottom-up" construction of systems of rules and guidelines that complement the more formal State-centred regime. Concerns about accountability, especially democratic accountability and administrative capacity of organizations that develop and implement voluntary codes, are likely to be of increasing importance.

Bryne Purchase's chapter, "The Political Economy of Voluntary Codes," explores the competitive advantages of States and non-State actors as rule-making and implementation institutions. Democratic governments have a monopoly on the legitimate use of incarceration in support of laws, and have the ability through taxation to raise funds to support regulatory programs. As a result, the State has a key competitive advantage in terms of its ability to impose obligations on those who would otherwise not comply, and effectively ensure compliance with them. But States have difficulty addressing problems that extend beyond their boundaries, their financial capacities are not unlimited (and indeed are increasingly under pressure), their legitimacy as rule makers is increasingly being challenged, and their primary instrument of public policy (conventional command penalty regulations), because of its formality and comparative inflexibility, can stifle innovation.

Purchase notes that modern developments in the areas of voluntary standards, certification approaches, alternative dispute mechanisms and voluntary codes should be viewed as a continuation of non-governmental efforts to establish credibility in the marketplace. Non-State actors who develop voluntary codes cannot rely on the threat of coercion to support of their rule-making activity. Instead, their rule-making activity is inherently consent-based. In Purchase's analysis, this is both a strength and a weakness. On the one hand, non-State actors have considerable difficulties addressing the behaviour of free riders who choose not to comply with their rules. But on the other, non-State actors are not constrained by jurisdictional boundaries, and so are capable of developing consent-based voluntary codes that extend across the globe. Their rule-making activities can be sector-specific, flexible and outcome-oriented.

Although the consent basis of private regulatory activity can be viewed as a disadvantage when compared with conventional command-penalty regulation, Purchase points out that consent is the most effective form of governance, since it is most likely to lead to controlled behaviour, even when formal monitoring and enforcement mechanisms are weak. Participation and effective voice in the rule-making process is one way to increase the likelihood of consent being provided. While difficult to achieve, the wider the coverage of a code (e.g. within an industry), the more credible it is likely to be in the eyes of other stakeholders. A central challenge is to develop highly consensual processes that will attract parties to join. Credibility and legitimacy will also be enhanced if external stakeholders are meaningfully involved, although this is clearly not an easy task. Purchase points to the possible value of principled negotiation as a way of developing consensus, a process that separates people from problems, focusses on interests not positions, searches for commonly agreed benchmarks, and has a problem-solving orientation.

Purchase explores the interrelation between State and non-State actors, and the ability of State actors to influence the shape or content of voluntary initiatives. In particular, the question of the role of the threats of State action as a stimulus for voluntary activity is discussed. While the certainty of State action may be beneficial in producing voluntary agreements, the more predictable the State's actions, the more likely it will have to act. Purchase suggests that the State adopt a poker player's stance, and keep non-State actors guessing as to whether they will resort to regulation: the more uncertainty there is about how the State will act, the more likely there will be "voluntary" agreement. In addition to influencing the shape and content of voluntary codes through threats of new regulations, States can also "steer rather than row," by publishing guides, assisting non-governmental organizations in their participation, and giving positive publicity to good codes.

Voluntary Codes: Private Governance, the Public Interest and Innovation

Kernaghan Webb and Andrew Morrison's chapter, "The Law and Voluntary Codes: Examining the 'Tangled Web'," suggests that, while voluntary codes are non-legislatively required commitments, they nevertheless are strongly influenced by legal factors, and often have significant legal implications. Voluntary codes and standards can be referentially incorporated in regulations, with or without the approval of the original authors, and such codes can elaborate and refine upon the generality of regulatory requirements. Courts can draw on the terms of voluntary codes as evidence of the appropriate legal standard of care for an industry. The contract basis of voluntary codes can allow industry associations to impose sanctions on member companies. Codes — particularly when they are agreements among firms — can conceivably have competition law and trade law implications.

Compared with laws, the main advantages of voluntary rule systems centre around their flexibility and lower costs, speed in developing and amending rules, avoidance of jurisdictional concerns, potential for positive use of market, peer pressure internalization of responsibility, and informality. Compared to laws, typical drawbacks of voluntary codes include generally lower visibility, credibility, difficulty in applying the rules to free riders, less likelihood of rigorous standards being developed, uncertain public accountability, and a more limited array of potential sanctions.

In practice, laws and voluntary codes frequently work in tandem, often with positive effects. For example, in spite of their consent-based origins, voluntary code arrangements can be used by courts to impose standards and liability on parties who did not necessarily agree to be bound by the original voluntary code arrangement. In this way, free riders, who avoided joining a voluntary code system, may nevertheless have it imposed on them. At the same time, voluntary codes can help to "flesh out" legal regimes, such as providing detail on what constitutes due diligence in a particular context. A vigilant and consistent regulatory enforcement presence can provide strong encouragement for industry to engage in voluntary initiatives. The chapter concludes by noting that, even though voluntary codes may be developed for reasons that do not relate directly to the law or government, the legal system can play an important role in stimulating the development of voluntary initiatives, reinforcing the effectiveness of such measures, or constraining unacceptable code behaviour. Law and voluntary codes are inextricably intertwined, engaged in an ongoing conversation. As a result, all stakeholders need to carefully consider the legal implications of voluntary codes before participating in or supporting such initiatives.

Part Three begins with "Responsible Care: A Case Study of a Voluntary Environmental Initiative" by John Moffet, François Bregha and Mary Jane Middelkoop. The authors trace the evolution of the Canadian Chemical Producers' Association's Responsible Care initiative from its earliest days to its present form as one of the most advanced and emulated industry self-regulatory environmental protection regimes in the world. In its original form, Responsible Care was largely a reaction to negative public image associated with chemical disasters, as well as an attempt to forestall the introduction of new environmental regulations. What began as a set of basic principles, soon grew to extensive codes, a formal multistakeholder advisory panel, community consultations, public reporting and a unique verification process that involves peers and community representatives. Statistics show reductions of many key substances, but it is difficult to ascertain with certainty how much is because of Responsible Care, and how much is stimulated by other factors. The authors note the importance of several factors in the program's success, including strong leadership shown by some of the players in the large chemical companies, the value of information-sharing sessions and peer pressure, and technology sharing. The authors note that both community relations and relations with government seem to have improved since the introduction of the program, but there are also criticisms that the Canadian Chemical Producers' Association has been able to soften certain legislative initiatives.

In "Gap Inc.'s Code of Conduct for Treatment of Overseas Workers," Gregory T. Rhone, John Stroud and Kernaghan Webb describe how one clothing retailer has used its contracting power to exert control over the working conditions in supplier factories located around the world. It is also the story of the power of negative publicity, and the susceptibility of large image-conscious firms to such negative publicity, as workers from one of its plants in El Salvador, flown to North America to expose their working conditions, effectively compelled Gap Inc. to rewrite its code and introduce third-party monitors into its El Salvador factories. The authors describe Gap Inc.'s experience and the evolution of its code as a possible example of the "roach motel" syndrome,[74] since the initial commitment to abide by a code is comparatively easy, but after that point, exit is very difficult: any public exposure of foot dragging or reneging on commitments may compel the firm to shamefacedly agree to more aggressive terms. Clearly, continued NGO, consumer or other watchdog scrutiny is necessary to ensure the continued effectiveness of the code.

Colin J. Bennett's chapter, "Privacy Self-Regulation in a Globalized Economy: A Race to the Top, the Bottom or Somewhere Else?" describes a complex and ongoing dialogue among self-regulatory and regulatory policy instruments (and their various champions) designed to protect personal information in the global economy. Like personal information itself, the dialogue takes place across borders, and between both State and non-State actors. Bennett articulates a useful typology of interrelated self-regulatory instruments, from commitments to privacy codes, standards and privacy seals. Bennett describes the evolution from voluntary to legislated approaches in Canada, the influence of external factors to this evolution, and the distinctive mix of public and private instruments underlying the development of the "safe harbour" agreement in the United States. He concludes that there is an overall move toward integration at the global level, with the resultant level of protection being neither a race to the top nor the bottom. In Bennett's opinion, the proliferation of self-regulatory instruments, and their broadening scope, means that the overall trajectory and dynamics constitute, if not a race to the top, then at least a steady walk. Even though many self-regulatory tools are designed to stem this process and avoid regulation, overall the bar has been raised, and self-regulation, along with legislative and technological instruments, has contributed to that process.

---

74. Roach motels are devices used to rid dwellings of unwanted insects. They consist of small boxes with several holes and an attractive scent. The scent lures insects in, and they are subsequently killed by an insecticide. Hence, insects can check into a roach motel, but they can never leave.

Voluntary Codes: Private Governance, the Public Interest and Innovation

As described earlier, Gregory T. Rhone, David Clarke and Kernaghan Webb's chapter, "Two Voluntary Approaches to Sustainable Forestry Practices," provides a comparative exploration of the evolution and development of an industry-led and an environmental group-led sustainable forestry initiative. While the two programs are not identical in function or content, nor in their process of development, it is clear that they are vying for the same goal: credibility in the marketplace as legitimate and effective mechanisms for ensuring that forests are harvested in a sustainable manner. Particularly interesting are the efforts of the environmental organization-led initiative to cope with unexpected popularity, and that of the industry-led initiative to demonstrate its credibility in the face of criticisms. Both programs have undergone considerable evolution, and no doubt will continue to do so.

Kathryn Harrison's chapter, "Promoting Environmental Protection Through Eco-Labelling: An Evaluation of Canada's Environmental Choice Program," reveals a government program whose mode of operation has changed significantly over time. Government has essentially delegated program administration to a private firm. The orientation of the program has become considerably more business-oriented with the passage of time. As a result, many of the least popular product categories have fallen by the wayside, and the process for reviewing applications has been streamlined to be quicker and less expensive. A key point raised by Harrison is the selective nature of eco-labelling programs, whose objective is to raise the ceiling as opposed to setting a floor of minimum standards. Rather than encouraging participation by all members of an industry, eco-labelling programs quite intentionally restrict participation to a subset of leaders. Free riding is not an issue, but eco-labelling programs must confront the potential for intra-industry competition. As such, third-party leadership is essential and an objective of consensus in standard setting is quite inappropriate. However, the resistance to eco-labelling by firms who fear a loss of market share may offer a cautionary lesson concerning other voluntary codes as well. Differences in the ability and willingness of individual firms to pursue social goals is an issue that must be confronted by other types of voluntary codes. The evidence from this case study that firms within an industry will resist standards that they cannot meet provides cause for concern more generally about the leadership potential of voluntary codes based on industry-wide consensus.

In "Bicycle Helmet Standards and Hockey Helmet Regulations: Two Approaches to Safety Protection," Andrew Morrison and Kernaghan Webb explore why the standard for the safety of bicycle helmets is voluntary, while that for hockey helmets is mandated in regulation. The study suggests that it is wrong to view selection of regulatory and non-regulatory approaches as an either-or proposition. In practice, the two work in tandem. Thus, for example, there are federal regulatory product standards for the manufacture of hockey helmets, yet use requirements are (with the exception of in Quebec) implemented through non-regulatory means. In the case of bicycle helmets, performance standards for the manufacture of helmets are not set out in law, but several jurisdictions have use requirements enshrined in law. In both contexts, the mix of regulatory and voluntary techniques operates against a backdrop of tort liability. As to why a regulatory measure was used for hockey helmets and a voluntary approach for bicycles, a combination of factors seems to be at play, including the distinctive nature of the activity, varying government attitudes toward regulations over time, divergent market conditions, jurisdictional issues, and the increasing credibility of standards bodies.

Part Four begins with Neil Gunningham's chapter, "Codes of Practice: The Australian Experience." Gunningham describes the development and content of Australia's guide to fair trading codes of conduct, as well as several examples of voluntary codes operating in Australia. Gunningham provides the example of a code for supermarket scanners as an effective voluntary code. Notable features include the fact that customers get the product for free when the price at the cash register does not match that on the shelf. The effect of this commitment to a free product when errors are found is to create a strong incentive for consumers to be vigilant, and an even stronger incentive for businesses to train and closely monitor their employees so that errors do not occur. On the basis of his research, Gunningham concludes that there is no doubt that codes of practice, properly designed and administered, in appropriate circumstances, with appropriate government oversight, can provide important benefits to consumers and others. Central to their success are a clear statement of code objectives, a mechanism for administration involving outside representation, membership covering a large portion of the industry, independent complaints handling, commercially significant sanctions, good code publicity, adequate training, good data collection, monitoring and reporting, and a regular review to ensure the standard meets community expectations.

In "Voluntary Codes in the United States, the European Union and Developing Countries: A Preliminary Survey," Kernaghan Webb and David Clarke examine environmental, human rights/worker protection and consumer protection (conventional and e-commerce) initiatives in the United States, Europe and developing countries. The research reveals that voluntary initiatives are flourishing in each of these jurisdictions, but that the process, form and content of initiatives vary significantly from one jurisdiction to another. In Europe, there seems to be less resistance to the idea of government playing a lead role in the development and supervision of voluntary initiatives. In the United States, there appears to be a predisposition in favour of letting voluntary codes develop with little or no direct government assistance. In developing countries, voluntary approaches are used to supplement weak regulatory regimes, but also have flourished upon the introduction and implementation of new, aggressive legislation. In all three jurisdictions, there are examples of government, industry and non-governmental organizations leading in the development of voluntary initiatives. The European "hands-on" approach to voluntary approaches, particularly at the European Union level, shows considerable willingness to integrate, coordinate and rationalize voluntary instruments with regulatory instruments in a systematic and effective manner. As such, the approach provides an intriguing model for other jurisdictions on how voluntary code rule innovation can be fostered.

Part Five consists of Kernaghan Webb's concluding chapter, "Voluntary Codes: Where To From Here?" Webb suggests that all stakeholders need to embrace a new conception of governing, one that brings together the use of a wide range of instruments, and harnesses the energies and potential of a broad range of actors, including the private sector and civil society, in a global context. In this new conception of governing, called *sustainable governance*, the State neither retreats nor expands, but rather acknowledges and makes room for other players and instruments to play a role in protecting the public interest. This new concept is likely to be particularly useful in addressing cross-jurisdictional issues, and is capable of adjusting to different operating conditions (e.g. differences in regulatory, social and economic environments between developed and developing countries). The final issue discussed is the trend towards companies using corporate social responsibility codes to address the full range of effects that companies have on employees, their families, the local community, the environment and society at large. The corporate social responsibility code movement is seen to be an excellent example of the type of evolving voluntary initiative that can emerge from adopting the sustainable governance model.

PART TWO

Four Perspectives

Chapter 2
The Role of the State in a
Privatized Regulatory Environment

David Cohen

Introduction

Regulation can be defined as an organizational system that determines the production and distribution of goods and services in society. Markets, the common law, constitutions, social conventions and cultural norms, as well as more recognizable regulatory instruments, such as tax policy, information, regulation, and penalties and fines imposed by governments, are all social systems that determine what is produced both as private and public goods, in what amount and at what price. Voluntary codes are one example of a private regulatory instrument — a system involving a set of non-legislatively required commitments agreed to by one or more private firms that are designed to influence firm behaviour, and are to be applied in a consistent manner by all signatories.

In the new industrial world of the 19th century, liberal notions of market economies and the role of governments led most to think of the question of the markets and regulation in a dichotomous paradigm. Markets (the non-State) were to be free to organize themselves in order to maximize the efficient production of goods and services. The role of governments was to tax the economic output of markets, in some cases to tax market transactions themselves, and to regulate the market when it failed. The revenues from the taxation of market outputs and market transactions would then be redistributed. Sometimes this redistribution would be in kind, but more often it would be mediated through public bureaucracies, to deliver public services — police, medical care, education, housing, transportation, criminal justice — that were either underproduced in private markets, or distributed in private markets in a way that offended popular conceptions of equity in a modern liberal society.

Leaving tax policy aside, the regulation of markets was the purview of lawyers and others familiar with criminal justice. Offensive behaviour was defined by law, and transgressions were punished by sanctions. Perhaps at one time that regulatory model was perceived as effective. When the number of offences was relatively small, when industry participants could be expected to know or to be able to acquire knowledge of the legislation that defined permissible behaviours, when obedience to law was a commonly held norm of behaviour, when social stigma existed in local markets and could be trusted to impose magnified costs for transgressions of legal norms of conduct, and when firms were more local than transnational, the criminal justice model of regulation may have worked. As well, in liberal societies, "law" was a symbol of the appropriate role of the State — its process was conceived of as neutral, it left the market to work its wonders within the parameters set by the law, and the costs of the system were relatively low and largely private.

Kernaghan Webb, Editor, *Voluntary Codes: Private Governance, the Public Interest and Innovation.*
This chapter ©2004 David Cohen, pages 35–56.
Published by the Carleton Research Unit for Innovation, Science and Environment, Carleton University, Ottawa, Canada.

Voluntary Codes: Private Governance, the Public Interest and Innovation

Perhaps 20 years ago, many Western governments began realizing that the model was breaking down. Law as a solution to social ills became increasingly expensive. As we once had police to monitor blatant and notorious anti-social conduct, we now had much more complicated and perhaps less effective compliance and enforcement policies — involving information disclosure, reporting systems, investigatory and monitoring bureaucracies, and more. Firm behaviour became decentralized, transnational and much less susceptible to the traditional coercive role of the nation-state. As a result, for 20 years we have been reading about alternatives to command-and-control models of regulation — most commonly referred to as "economic instruments" — as more effective vehicles to achieve regulatory objectives.

However, many writers have concluded that economic instruments, while they may avoid the most expensive aspects of traditional coercive models of regulation, do not avoid the most intractable problem — how to set standards that will achieve our regulatory objectives in the most cost-effective way. Economic instruments can be used to create incentives to meet or exceed centrally mandated standards. They can perhaps reduce the enforcement and compliance costs associated with criminal justice models of regulation. But they did not transform regulation in the way that their original proponents hoped and believed. Most economic instruments require the State to set standards, with the difference between this instrument and command-and-control regulation being that incentives and markets were used to move firms towards compliance. And while levels of compliance were perhaps higher than those achieved with command-and-control regulation, economic instruments still required public bureaucracies to monitor and ultimately to enforce the standards.

Today we are seeing a rapid evolution of regulation towards private rather than public institutions — the private institution is the "voluntary code" that is being examined in this volume. Voluntary codes are part of a transformation of our historical conceptions of the modern liberal State. In the face of the growing economic, social and political importance of transnational firms and non-governmental organizations relative to formal legal authority, the 20th-century conception of government — which focusses on State institutions and instruments — is now giving way to a more nuanced and inclusive notion of governance, which is sufficiently broad to encompass the activities of both State and non-State institutions and actors (this point is explored in greater depth in the conclusion to this volume). Support for voluntary codes flows from the increasing relative importance of international trade to many firms and indeed to many nation-states. The breaking down of nationally mandated barriers to trade is rapidly accelerating — experience with the General Agreement on Tariffs and Trade educated some national governments about the benefits of freer trade, but more importantly, it left recalcitrant governments with no option but to look to international trade as the next engine of economic growth. It also provided a model for bilateral and multilateral trade agreements that are rapidly proliferating. One result of the growth in international trade is that governmental standards can be challenged as tariff barriers to trade,[1] and at a minimum

---

1. This point is made by the authors of the bicycle and hockey helmet case study as one explanation for the federal government's withdrawal of an initial proposal to regulate bicycle helmets, and the adoption of a voluntary national code strategy in its stead. See Andrew Morrison and Kernaghan Webb, "Bicycle Helmet Standards and Hockey Helmet Regulations: Two Approaches to Safety Protection," Chapter 11, below.

engender opposition as barriers to economic growth that are easily avoided by firms that can raise capital in international capital markets, employ labour in component enterprises in countries around the world, and sell to consumers in any one of dozens of rapidly growing markets. Firms that produce goods in one domestic market for distribution in dozens of others demand standards that are harmonized across national boundaries — voluntary codes are one method to facilitate consistency of standards in international trade.

The impact of the internationalization of product and service markets, labour markets and capital markets has been magnified in many Western liberal democracies, and certainly in most Canadian political jurisdictions, by the deficit reduction strategies adopted by or forced upon federal and provincial governments — privatization of regulation is one way to reduce the public (but perhaps not the net) costs of regulation. The privatization of regulation at a minimum reduces governmental expenditures on regulatory development and enforcement activities. It may also increase economic activity, tax revenues and employment.

The impact of internationalization and deficit reduction strategies has been accelerated by the diminution in relevance and stature of the federal government in Canada. While once Quebec and British Columbia may have been at the extreme — arguing for a fundamental decentralization of political authority in Canada — they have recently been joined by Ontario and Alberta, the two other major economic, political and population centres in Canada. The poorer, less populated and less powerful provinces may not be able to withstand the power of the four most influential provinces in the long run. As political power shifts away from Ottawa, it flows not necessarily to provincial governments but is transformed into economic and social authority and is transferred as well to private entities — both to firms and perhaps to non-governmental organizations — precisely those groups that contribute to and perhaps support the development of voluntary codes as a private alternative to traditional regulation.

The prevalence of voluntary codes in Canada and Australia may represent the interest of firms in federal states with strong decentralized provincial and state governments to avoid a fragmented, conflicting and confusing welter of provincial/state legislation in favour of uniform "national" or international voluntary codes rather than provincial/state mandatory standards. Voluntary codes — perhaps the Canadian Standards Association's Sustainable Forest Management Certification System is the best example[2] — may permit national standards to be developed when neither federal standards nor provincial standards would pass constitutional review if they were applied to forest lands owned or controlled by both federal and provincial governments, private firms and native peoples across Canada. Voluntary standards, because they are a form of private rather than public ordering, are not subject to constitutional constraints that apply to central or provincial governments. As Kernaghan Webb and Andrew Morrison point

---

2. Gregory T. Rhone, David Clarke and Kernaghan Webb, "Two Voluntary Approaches to Sustainable Forestry Practices," Chapter 9, below.

out, this advantage of codes is a general trait that potentially makes private regulation superior to public regulation in Canada.[3]

If this is an accurate (if somewhat overstated) description of governing in the modern world, then regulation as we have known it may be itself a legacy of a century past. The Canadian State is facing choices unlike those seen since Confederation. As the nation-state recedes or changes, its role as a primary source of social ordering is taken on or shaped by business enterprises, religious groups, professional associations and non-governmental organizations. Some operate at a very local level, others are organized on an international scale. Their commonality is that they rely on domestic law only to establish their legal existence, and to permit and facilitate market activity between and among them. Voluntary codes represent decentralized contractual bargains between these entities — replacing or adding to centralized production of regulation by governments. Governments still have a place in this new world, but it is very different from that with which we are familiar.

Supporters of voluntary codes argue that they represent an efficient regulation instrument that, if designed properly, will provide a vehicle for a multiplicity of interests and values to be heard and reflected in the output of markets. Voluntary codes represent the outcome of decentralized autonomous bargains between collective interests — consumers and service providers, labour and management, firms, employees, local communities and environmental groups who, absent impacts on parties excluded from the bargaining, should perhaps be free to negotiate arrangements that maximize their joint welfare rather than be subjected to centralized regulatory control by a remote government.[4] Codes are a mechanism for industry to take an enlightened view of their self-interest; for non-governmental organizations associated with the production of public goods to be more effective in their articulation of how product safety, sustainability, economic justice or human dignity can be achieved within a market environment; for small businesses to be heard in public policy formation; for labour to be represented in management decisions; and for governments to continue to represent our ideal of the mediator of private interests. However, the opposite may unfortunately be true. Voluntary codes may simply permit the most knowledgeable and powerful actors in market economies to dominate not only the production of private goods but our definition and creation of public goods as well. While codes may be generated by market demand for public goods — privacy, sustainable forestry, public safety — they may at the same time be simply a strategy to deflect the energy of interest groups away from the political process, and permit firms to avoid more effective and certainly more rigorous public regulation.

Perhaps both are true. In this chapter I will offer some thoughts on what we might learn from the voluntary codes discussed in this volume. The range of application is remarkable. Today, voluntary codes are being proposed or are in place that purport to regulate the protection of personal information, product safety, sustainable forests, labour

---

3. Kernaghan Webb and Andrew Morrison, "The Law and Voluntary Codes: Examining the 'Tangled Web'," Chapter 5, below. One point that is discussed is that non-State voluntary codes, again because they are private, are not subject to the *Canadian Charter of Rights and Freedoms*. This characteristic of voluntary codes may make them easier to develop and, in that sense, superior to efforts by the State to regulate in a number of areas.

4. A. Ogus, "Rethinking Self-Regulation," *Oxford Journal of Legal Studies* 15 (1995), pp. 97–108, p. 99.

practices, environmental activities of manufacturers and electronic commerce. However, as we examine recent experience under these voluntary codes we must be aware of the complicated relationship of private and public regulation in shaping firm behaviour. The State, while it is being transformed, is still present, and voluntary codes exist and operate surrounded by threats of State action, can be facilitated by government-mandated programs (which can affect participation in voluntary code programs) and can influence both private legal action and the enforcement of command-and-control legislation.

As to the utility of voluntary codes, the answer will likely come from experience with voluntary codes in operation over time. And I suspect that it will not be uniform — as with so many other regulatory instruments, voluntary codes will work more effectively in some contexts than in others. Much will depend on how voluntary codes are designed and implemented. And in many cases, the success of voluntary codes may depend on complementary legislative initiatives.[5]

I begin with the obvious: voluntary codes are the essential means by which social and economic relations are defined and ordered in a liberal, democratic society that uses a market economy to produce goods and services. Firms — their internal structures, their accountability mechanisms, their information flows and their internal economic order — are largely defined by voluntary codes. Corporate constitutions, bylaws, corporate structures, policies and operational manuals are all "voluntary codes" that define what is produced by the firm, where and how it is produced, how it is priced, marketed and distributed, and so on. No one could seriously imagine that the production of private goods and services could be carried out effectively except by voluntary codes — corporate structures and contracts among and between firms that define, monitor and sanction the behaviour both of internal actors and external contractual parties.

The differences between these voluntary codes and the codes examined in the case studies in this volume are important, because it is those differences that give us pause. Voluntary codes are often perceived as designed to achieve public rather than private purposes. They appear, therefore, unnatural to those who see firms as engaged in conduct solely to generate profits or power for owners. To a certain degree, and in a certain way, that is true, but the motivations for voluntary codes are complex and diverse. In many cases, the public good is simply a way to further private gain, or is perhaps a fortunate concomitant to efforts to generate profits. When this is so, then voluntary codes become just one more management tool that, perhaps fortunately, generates positive externalities for third parties. If this is so, then, as in the case with positive externalities generally, the role of the government should be to encourage and facilitate behaviour that would otherwise likely produce less than the optimal amount of the public good at issue.

The characteristics of, and experience with, the voluntary codes presented and examined by the authors of the following chapters permit us to begin to identify whether there are critical attributes of this regulatory instrument of which we must be cognizant if we are to transform our regulatory regimes successfully. In this chapter I will make an effort to draw together these various issues that must be understood and addressed if we

---

5. This point is made most persuasively by Morrison and Webb in their chapter on bicycle and hockey helmets (Chapter 11, below). The authors point out that the success of the voluntary code in the case of bicycle helmets may well be a product of an effective voluntary product safety standard, coupled with mandatory use requirements enacted by municipal and provincial governments.

are to make appropriate decisions to support, regulate or interfere with the continued development of voluntary codes as regulatory instruments in Canada. In each case, I will make an effort to reflect on the possible and continuing role of governments in voluntary code and standard-setting processes, implementation and review.

The Process of Voluntary Code Development

It is notoriously difficult for regulators to assess the substantive benefits of voluntary code initiatives. Accordingly, considerable attention is focussed in this volume on the standard-setting processes associated with the development of voluntary codes. In one sense, this focus on process comfortably avoids the issue of public scrutiny of the substance of codes and whether they, in fact, have moved or will move industry in the direction that we want it to go. It is also consistent with a contractarian philosophy that posits our inability to judge the substantive social justice of these bargains, and asks only that the bargaining process be fair. At the same time, there is a sense — but only a sense — that a focus on process will increase the legitimacy of the voluntary code system, will provide better information to code developers on the values of diverse groups whose welfare may be affected by the code, and will enhance compliance with voluntary code standards through education of both industry and the marketplace.

Several of the case studies offer important insights into the fairness of code development procedures, focussing first on the participants in the bargaining process. This is evident in the description of the multisectoral advisory panel in the case study of the Canadian Chemical Producers' Association's Responsible Care program; the constitution of the Environmental Choice Advisory Board establishing "seats" for academics, consumer representatives, environmentalists and industry; and the multistakeholder standard-setting process in Gap Inc.'s code of conduct. It is also reflected in the description of the Canadian Standards Association's Sustainable Forest Management Certification System code development process. Here some 32 members of the standard-setting task force were selected to ensure representation of forestry experts, small private woodlot owners, environmental groups, government, the forest industry, academics and others.[6]

However, not all code development processes are as multisectoral as those described above.[7] The use of academics, consumers, labour representatives, small business and geographically representative firms in the standard-setting process apparently, and in the immediate term, lends legitimacy to the process. In the best of worlds, the interests and values of those groups will be embedded in the substantive content of the voluntary standard.

---

6. However, First Nations representatives, international environmental groups and some consumer groups ultimately opted out of the process. What no one tells us is how to respond satisfactorily to the problem of regulatory "vetoes" and strategic bargaining conduct, when every party is able to veto proposals for voluntary code provisions.

7. See, e.g., Gregory T. Rhone, *Canadian Tobacco Manufacturers' Council Tobacco Industry Voluntary Packaging and Advertising Code*, a draft case study prepared for the Voluntary Codes Symposium, Ottawa, 1996, available in summary at <http://strategis.ic.gc.ca/epic/internet/inoca-bc.nsf/en/ca00800e.html>, which notes that no consumer, environmental or health interest groups were consulted in the development of the code.

Unfortunately, few of the case studies tell us very much about the detail of this code-development process:

- How were the academic, professional and interest-group representatives selected? The academic and non-governmental organization communities are not homogenous, and the developers of voluntary codes may be able to choose participants selectively with a view to obtaining cooperative independent participants in the code-development process. Are these independents captured themselves by the association/code-development firms?
- How were non-governmental groups funded? As provincial and federal government core funding support for the non-governmental community suffers drastic reductions is it realistic to expect that this sector will be able to take on expanded regulatory responsibilities?
- When were the interest groups involved in the process? Were they involved in issue identification, and in articulating alternative approaches to the design of the code?
- Was the process transparent? Was it publicized, and were background studies and draft codes widely circulated?[8]

Most important, how was conflict resolved and consensus achieved in the code-development process? It is insufficient to state that a code was developed by "consensus" of the groups involved in the process. Much more detailed information about how consensus was achieved is necessary before one can fully understand how conflicting values were adjusted and ultimately incorporated or ignored in the resulting code.

Voluntary codes, if conceived of as Coasian bargains between firms, non-governmental organizations, the government and other actors, can be defended only when one is relatively comfortable with the adequacy of the information available to all of the groups negotiating the code, with a sense of balance among the relative bargaining strengths of the parties, and with the existence of real options available to the parties if the negotiations collapse. In other words, we have to be able to assess the fairness of the bargaining process if we are to support the outcome of the bargain itself represented by the voluntary code.

This focus on process does suggest a role for the government if voluntary codes are to become an effective and defensible regulatory tool in the future. Perhaps the government can provide incentives to voluntary code developers to ensure that independent mediators and conciliators are involved in the code-development process. The independent mediator might increase the likelihood that all relevant groups are identified early in the code-development process, and are able to participate effectively in the bargaining that leads to the development of the code. The mediator's role might include ruling on the legitimacy of a complaint or concern, and developing decision-making processes that give real meaning to consensus. However, it would be naive to believe that the involvement of an independent mediator will, of itself, ensure bargaining fairness.

---

8. Rhone, Clarke and Webb, in "Sustainable Forestry Practices," Chapter 9, below, do provide extensive detail on the public consultation involved in the Canadian Standards Association's standard-setting process — not only the circulation of draft standards to hundreds of groups, but also large public consultations held in major urban areas across the country.

The Role of Information in the Development of Voluntary Codes

Most analyses of the process of voluntary code formation identify and assess the constituencies represented in the code-development process. In some cases, we can determine whether those groups are able to participate effectively in code development. Equally important, however, to an assessment of the voluntary code process is an evaluation of the information base upon which the standard is founded. The chapter in this volume dealing with Canada's "EcoLogo" program provides an example: the standard-setting body, chaired by an independent, credible person selected by government, was able to produce independent analyses of existing data on which to base its standards.[9]

The standard-setting process requires information, but the information on which the voluntary code is developed can be generated by industry, or it can be generated by an independent agency answerable to the collective membership of the group designing the voluntary code. For bargaining to be defensible as a model for public governance, the code-development process must ensure that the severe informational asymmetries between industry and others are corrected.

Free Riders and Voluntary Codes

The effectiveness of voluntary codes depends critically on managing effectively the risk that some significant proportion of firms in the relevant industry will "free ride" on the benefits of the voluntary code, refuse to participate or purport to comply and either defect or comply only reluctantly, and in either case gain substantial cost advantages over their competitors.[10] If the government or industry association is not granted monopoly powers to mandate conduct of all industry participants, some competitors might make rational decisions to not comply with the voluntary standard.

The literature suggests that concern with free riders is most evident in industries consisting of numerous, geographically dispersed, relatively unsophisticated, small businesses. The problem is one of increasing coordination and monitoring costs, coupled with the inability of the major firms in each case to confirm that the assurances of unknown firms are reliable.

---

9. See Kathryn Harrison, "Promoting Environmental Protection through Eco-Labelling: An Evaluation of Canada's Environmental Choice Program," Chapter 10, below.

10. The existence of free riders is the most common argument that political economists present for the position that voluntary codes ultimately fail as governance systems. Each individual firm, although it might benefit from collective action if all competitors were obliged to comply with voluntary standards, will benefit even if it does not participate. Thus, as Mancur Olson argues, each firm will make a rational decision not to participate, or perhaps to feign participation, and, at the very least, minimize the investment it chooses to make in complying with voluntary self-regulation. Ultimately, Olson argues, collective goods will be provided only through coercion or other external inducement. See M. Olson, *The Logic of Collective Action* (Cambridge, Mass.: Harvard University Press, 1965). The failure of trade associations to organize collective action successfully is described in detail in J. Q. Wilson, *Political Organizations* (New York: Basic Books, 1973), Chapter 8.

Possible responses to the free-rider problem, other than seeking government regulation,[11] are varied. Some associations, such as the Canadian Chemical Producers' Association, attract potential free riders by offering significant benefits — information, management expertise and technology — to those firms that participate in the voluntary codes.[12] These benefits are perhaps especially important to those smaller firms facing competitive pressures that may force them into short-term planning strategies. In other cases, such as the Ontario government's self-management initiative, operating within a statutory framework, industry associations, with government and consumer group representatives on their boards, have been given lawful authority to license particular firms to do business in Ontario, pursuant to mandatory standards.[13] In the case of codes promoted to increase public/consumer confidence in the industry, or to impose a level playing field among firms in the industry,[14] there may be some evidence that the more responsible firms in an industry will themselves "self-police" potential free riders by publicly sanctioning those who do not participate in the self-regulatory program.[15] Free riders may also be controlled by markets, especially in cases of standards driven by consumer demand. Here, the costs of non-participation in the voluntary code — loss of market share and an inability to compete on price — may exceed compliance costs, thus creating economic incentives for firms to participate voluntarily in the code or standard.

Market-based code programs, such as those pertaining to labour practices in the apparel industry, and sustainable forestry and environmental labelling programs, suggest

---

11. The argument is made that the U.S. pharmaceutical industry sought Food and Drug Administration-mandated regulation of tamper-proof packaging because no single firm was willing to engage in the expense of such packaging without assurances that its competitors would do the same. See S. B. Foote, "Corporate Responsibility in a Changing Legal Environment," *California Management Review* 26 (1984), pp. 217–228. This argument is made as well by Gregory T. Rhone in *Investment Funds Institute of Canada Draft Code of Sales Practices for the Mutual Fund Industry*, a draft case study prepared for the Voluntary Codes Symposium, Ottawa, 1996, available in summary at <http://strategis.ic.gc.ca/epic/internet/inoca-bc.nsf/en/ca00880e.html>. Rhone points out that several firms had argued for a mandatory code in order to "ensure a fair, level playing field," and that if the code was not made mandatory, compliance on a voluntary basis would be short-lived.

12. See John Moffet, François Bregha and Mary Jane Middelkoop, "Responsible Care: A Case Study of a Voluntary Environmental Initiative," Chapter 6, below.

13. Examples of Ontario self-management program include the Ontario Motor Vehicle Industry Council, regulating the province's automobile dealerships and salespersons (<www.omvic.on.ca>); the Travel Industry Council of Ontario, regulating travel agencies (<www.tico.on.ca>); the Real Estate Council of Ontario, regulating real estate agents (<www.reco.on.ca>); the Technical Standards and Safety Authority, responsible for administering seven provincial safety statutes (<www.tssa.org>). For a discussion of Ontario's self-management program, see Z. Lonti and A. Verma, *Industry Self-Management as a Strategy for Restructuring Government: The Case of the Ministry of Consumer and Commercial Relations (MCCR) and the Technical Standards and Safety Authority (TSSA) in Ontario* (Ottawa: Canadian Policy Research Networks, December 1999), available for download from the Networks' Web site (<www.cprn.com/en/doc.cfm?doc=726>). Similar programs are apparently the practice in Japan, where every firm is required to be a member of a "peak" organization, thus dramatically reducing the risk of free riders. See E. Vogel, *Japan as Number 1* (New York: Harper Colophon, 1979), p. 112.

14. This rationale for voluntary codes is presented in the examination of the history of Responsible Care in Moffet, Bregha and Middlekoop, "Responsible Care," Chapter 6, below.

15. The Canadian Marketing Association attempts to address the problem with marketers even though they are not part of the association. See David Clarke and Kernaghan Webb, *Market-Driven Consumer Redress Case Studies and Legal Issues* (Ottawa: Office of Consumer Affairs, Industry Canada, 2002), available at <http://strategis.ic.gc.ca/epic/internet/inoca-bc.nsf/enca01643e.html>.

that the codes can employ the power of the free market to reduce the risk of free riders.[16] Non-participants may suffer loss of market share or a reduction in price when their product or service is identifiable as non-complying with voluntary standards.

Here again, governments can play a major role in addressing free-rider concerns. They can do so by supporting advocacy groups that can trigger market behaviour that will influence firm conduct.[17] Similarly, governments can engage in education programs that will shape consumer demand and thus reduce the risk of firms making decisions to free ride on the voluntary code — but again, only in the case of codes generated by market demand for either public or private goods.

They can also consider, as proposed in the Ontario government's self-management initiative, recognizing industry associations as entitled to license and discipline members. This model is taken directly from the traditional role of the State in vesting regulatory authority in professional associations — those in the areas of accountancy, law and medicine come immediately to mind. The model privatizes a substantial proportion of regulatory costs. It also ensures that regulation — performance standards, insurance requirements, ethical codes of conduct — is designed by experts. It does, however, raise concerns about barriers to entry, and self-dealing to protect industry rather than public interests.

The concern with free riders is met not by a simple rejection of the possibility of collective action without State regulation, but rather by providing mechanisms to ensure that firm assurances of cooperation are credible[18] — the assurances can come from self-policing, as well as from the tangible benefits associated with membership in the voluntary association, and finally from the threat of market sanctions by consumers and other third parties. Where the industry is highly competitive, with large numbers of dispersed smaller firms, and where there are no effective market sanctions that might be applied by consumers, then one must remain sceptical of the efficacy of voluntary codes as a coordinating mechanism to achieve public goals.

---

16. See Gregory T. Rhone, John Stroud and Kernaghan Webb, "Gap Inc.'s Code of Conduct for Treatment of Overseas Workers," Chapter 7, below, and Harrison, "Canada's Environmental Choice Program," Chapter 10, below.

17. The Canadian Care labelling program apparently has few free riders — due in part to low compliance costs but also to an active lobbying effort by consumer groups formally funded by the federal government. See Gregory T. Rhone, *The Canadian Care Labelling Program*, a draft case study prepared for the Voluntary Codes Symposium, Ottawa, 1996, available in summary at <http://strategis.ic.gc.ca/epic/internet/inoca-bc.nsf/en/ca00880e.html>.

18. The "assurance" argument is made by Ian Maitland in "The Limits of Business Self-Regulation," *California Management Review* 27:3 (1985), pp. 132–147.

The Anti-Competitive Risks of Voluntary Codes

While voluntary codes among firms normally in competition with one another may present to many commentators an example of collusive, cooperative arrangements among firms designed to create barriers to entry by competitors,[19] they may nevertheless be supported by governments who are interested in creating non-tariff barriers to trade. We are not generally concerned with collusive anti-competitive behaviour when a car manufacturer purchases parts from a small or indeed larger firm. We should be and are concerned when several car manufacturers agree with one another that they will employ a particular kind of safety glass standard, or when members of the forest sector establish expensive and complex forest management systems with which all of their members must comply. The literature on rent-seeking by firms looking for government approval of self-regulatory powers is extensive and well respected.[20]

This volume points out that collusion is perhaps less likely[21] when the code development process includes both large and small firms, and when non-firm participants (e.g. consumer organizations) are involved effectively. But that is not necessarily the case. The inclusion of small firms may represent capture of those firms by the larger corporate actors. Other smaller firms may be substantially prejudiced by the voluntary standard. It is facile to argue that collusion is less likely when "all of the interested parties" are involved in code development. That simply will never be the case. The inclusion of consumer representatives in the code-development process is meaningful, as many authors point out, only when they have access to technical expertise that permits them to engage in meaningful dialogue with the major firm actors.

Voluntary codes for public purposes, like their counterparts used by firms for private purposes, need not always be multilateral or bilateral contracts with attendant anti-competitive risks. Firms can also adopt internal management systems — like Gap Inc.'s *Code of Vendor Conduct*[22] — that are unilateral voluntary codes and are motivated perhaps both by private gain and public citizenship. Here the anti-competitive risks are very different. Internal voluntary codes present us with cases in which markets are shaped not only by decisions of firms motivated by private gain, but also by public interest — in this case a concern with labour standards in less developed countries. In this case, the allegedly morally neutral imperatives of the market, wealth maximization and efficiency, are replaced by political and social policy motives, and perhaps by motives to unfairly discriminate against certain firms.

On balance, the risk of rent-seeking through the development of voluntary codes leads to two recommendations. First, it supports a requirement that code-development processes include not only consumer representatives, but also small and large firms in a particular industry, and, as well, that firms supply goods and services to, or purchase

---

19. See A. Shaked and J. Sutton, "The Self-Regulating Profession," *Review of Economic Studies* 48 (1981), pp. 217–234.

20. See Ogus (footnote 4), and C. K. Rowley, R. D. Tollinson and G. Tullock (eds.), *The Political Economy of Rent-seeking* (Boston: Kluwer Academic Publishers, 1988).

21. See Webb and Morrison, "The Law and Voluntary Codes," Chapter 5, below.

22. See Rhone, Stroud and Webb, "Gap Inc.'s Code of Conduct," Chapter 7, below.

goods and services from, the industry whose members are developing the code. It also means that ministries of justice and an independent bureau of competition policy (government departments independent of industry and sectoral lobbying and influence) must continue to play a central role in monitoring anti-competitive behaviour associated with voluntary codes. A concern, of course, is that the resources of the anti-trust divisions of most governments are limited — and it is very difficult to tease out *ex ante* the anti-competitive impacts of voluntary standards.

The future of voluntary codes as important components of public policy in Canada depends, as Kernaghan Webb and Andrew Morrison point out, on the ability of the federal government to examine closely the anti-competitive impacts of voluntary codes, and to provide exemptions to voluntary codes only after close scrutiny of the purposes of the voluntary agreement, and an assessment of the net benefits of the self-regulatory scheme taking into account the risks of its anti-competitive consequences.[23] It is not clear that the current *Competition Act* is drafted to permit this to be so.

The Relationship of Voluntary Codes to Regulatory Initiatives

Perhaps the most complicated issue that is presented by examination of voluntary codes is their relationship to governmental and legal regulatory regimes.[24] At a minimum, most if not all voluntary codes require compliance with legislative standards when they exist. For example, the Canadian Standards Association's Sustainable Forest Management Certification System requires compliance with applicable forest legislation.[25]

The question that must be answered is how the existence of codes is related to the governmental regime that does, or might, regulate the same or similar corporate conduct. The absence of legislation is at once explained as the reason for the development of voluntary codes; at the same time, the existence of the voluntary codes is interpreted as one reason for the absence of government action.[26]

Certainly, in several chapters of this volume, the authors' interpretation of the political environment surrounding the development of the voluntary codes suggests that one, albeit not the sole, private benefit of voluntary codes is the avoidance of even more costly (and more intrusive) governmental regulation.[27] However, public political demand for regulation, which might be avoided by voluntary codes, is often coupled with

---

23. See Webb and Morrison, "The Law and Voluntary Codes," Chapter 5, below. See also *Competition Act*, R.S.C. 1985, c. C-34, s.45 (as amended), and Director of Investigation and Research (Canada), *Strategic Alliances Under the Competition Act* (Hull, Que.: Ministry of Supply and Services, 1985).

24. This aspect of voluntary codes is extremely well developed in Webb and Morrison, ibid.

25. See Rhone, Clarke and Webb, "Sustainable Forestry Practices," Chapter 9, below.

26. As I point out later in this chapter, many authors explain the primary motive for voluntary code development as the avoidance of more stringent regulation.

27. For example, the Responsible Care initiative is in part intended to reduce the need for more government regulation. See Moffet, Bregha and Middelkoop, "Responsible Care," Chapter 6, below.

consumer demand for corporate behaviour that is met by the same voluntary codes. If that is so, then both free-rider concerns and compliance costs are significantly reduced through the adoption of voluntary codes. It is simply unknowable whether the net regulatory benefits of the voluntary codes — taking into account not only the regulatory standards but compliance and enforcement practices — are more or less than those that might have been generated by more traditional government action.

The "voluntariness" of codes is also the subject of considerable debate as proposals are made that self-regulating organizations be recognized by governments as having "licensing powers" and thus be able to control entry into the industry and the behaviour of industry participants, much like the regulatory authority now enjoyed by professional associations and some stock exchange authorities.

In addition, analyses by Webb and Morrison and the authors of the Responsible Care case study point out that the industry standards that are represented by "voluntary" codes may in fact establish both the standard of care expected of firms in product liability litigation, and due diligence standards in the enforcement of traditional command-and-control legislation. In these cases the voluntary code becomes the *de facto* legal standard, and thus in effect imposes mandatory standards of conduct on firms, enforceable by private action. In some cases, the nature of the voluntary code results in the "enforcement" of the voluntary standards by the government.

The point here is that the case studies confirm that there is no clear demarcation between voluntary codes and legislative action — and, in most cases, there are a variety of linkages and connections between the voluntary code and legislative and regulatory action. The lesson is that regulatory benefits will likely be maximized when we are able to develop creative policy instruments that coordinate the actions of public and private institutions. In the conclusion of this chapter I suggest, tentatively, some preliminary policy directions that take into account the complicated relationship that voluntary regimes can have to State action.

Voluntary Codes as Performance/Design Standards and Management Systems

The voluntary codes that have been developed to date in Canada incorporate and employ, in many cases, the same array of substantive regulatory techniques as those employed by governments engaged in traditional regulation. Bicycle helmet codes incorporate performance standards for manufacturers, for instance — they are not qualitatively distinct from hockey helmet regulations.

However, it seems that a clear distinction can be drawn between many voluntary codes and traditional forms of regulation. In general, many voluntary codes appear to be a complex mix of traditional standards — albeit with the flexibility and economic efficiencies associated with performance standards — but at the same time they incorporate very specific provisions and operational manuals that purport to micromanage the firm in a way that is not often seen in legislation and regulations. This is perhaps a surprise, since many political economists describe "self-regulation" as the least intrusive regulatory instrument available to governments. However, while the absence of State coercion may make that classification accurate in a sense, the evidence in these case studies suggests that, substantively, codes are likely to impose management systems on firms to a degree that governments neither would nor could. If the private enforcement and compliance systems that operate in the case of voluntary codes are even partially effective, the regulatory benefits of voluntary codes — taking into account this management system characteristic — may be substantial.

The willingness of firms to consent to this degree of control suggests that a popular argument in favour of codes — that they reflect the substantial informational advantages of the private sector in understanding and regulating firm behaviour — is true. It also suggests that firms perhaps perceive the threat of regulatory oversight to be far less intrusive, and less costly in terms of firm productivity and profits, in the case of voluntary codes than they would be in the case of traditional regulation.

Flexible and Responsive Regulation

Many of the authors of the case studies point to the theoretical enhanced adaptability and flexibility of voluntary codes. The Canadian Standards Association's Sustainable Forest Management Certification System is presented as flexible enough to apply differently to different types of forests.[28] The merits of permitting regulatory objectives to be achieved by firms through the most efficient means possible are incontrovertible. The risks, however, are very real, demanding centralized oversight that is not readily apparent in all codes.

Related to sectoral adaptability is the argument that voluntary codes are perhaps well suited to industrial sectors characterized by rapid change — technological, social, informational, and so on. The EcoLogo program represents an example of flexibility. Here, the voluntary environmental standards were designed to be "ratcheted up" as an increasing percentage of a particular market/industry came into compliance with the voluntary standard.[29] The Canadian Standards Association's Sustainable Forest Management Certification System is designed to be modified rapidly as changes in environmental information and impacts become available to the forest industry.[30] In both cases, the argument is made that voluntary codes are perhaps better able to be adapted to rapid changes in information, tastes, technology and markets than are legislated standards.[31] However, this is not a necessary characteristic of voluntary codes.

---

28. See Rhone, Clarke and Webb, "Sustainable Forestry Practices," Chapter 9, below.

29. See Harrison, "Canada's Environmental Choice Program," Chapter 10, below.

30. This is an explicit requirement of the code: a forest management system will be approved only when it, *inter alia*, establishes a continual improvement loop to maintain and improve firm performance.

31. The distinction, however, is not that clear. For example, in "Helmet Standards and Regulations," Chapter 11, below, Morrison and Webb point out that the federal *Hazardous Products Act* establishes a product safety standard by reference to a "voluntary" standard "as amended from time to time." Some would argue that this technique is impermissible as an attempt to delegate legislative authority to the private sector. Nonetheless, it has permitted, as the authors point out, four revisions to the standard since 1973.

We do not have data, and it is not certain whether they could be developed, that compare the rate of change between voluntary and regulatory standards. Impressionistic and experiential reports do suggest, however, that voluntary codes can be modified to meet changing conditions in a far more cost-effective and timely fashion than can regulations.[32] One concern, of course, is that the potential benefits associated with the relative speed of development and modification of voluntary codes are offset by the failure of some voluntary code development processes to incorporate any serious consultative mechanisms.

Nonetheless, it is important to understand why it is that voluntary codes appear to be more readily modifiable to meet changing information, technologies or market conditions. Assuming that the process concerns described above are met, this is an important attribute of voluntary codes in times of rapid transformation in most industry sectors. As well, the design of voluntary codes to permit tailoring to specific industry and perhaps even firm conditions is likely to generate considerable efficiencies in operation. With the proper oversight — described in the conclusion of this chapter — this too can be an important advantage of voluntary codes not usually achieved through traditional regulatory action.

Compliance and Enforcement: Monitoring and Modifying Firm Behaviour Under Voluntary Codes

All regulatory systems, including legitimate and credible voluntary codes, require that firm behaviour be monitored to assess compliance and thus the effectiveness of the regulatory scheme. As described in the chapter on the Responsible Care program, one of the alleged effects of the program has been to transform the corporate culture of firms involved in the program.[33] As Christopher Stone puts it, it is far better when the public values of a regulatory system are internalized as the private values of the firm managers — that they act in accordance with the voluntary code's directions because they think it is the "right thing to do."[34] While that might be true, it is difficult to verify, and may not be as widespread as one might naively hope. More focussed monitoring of firm behaviour is a necessary prerequisite to the implementation of a voluntary code. The risk that firms might feign compliance or invest only to a minimum standard of compliance is simply too great a risk to ignore when the "governing body" is not the State.

However, even before monitoring of firm behaviour comes education. In some cases the voluntary code itself can enhance compliance through the incorporation of management systems that improve knowledge of the voluntary code and the ability of the firm's employees to conform to the code's requirements.

Monitoring follows education. Monitoring of firm compliance can be undertaken by consumers and more generally by non-governmental organizations

---

32. However, the Canadian Care Labelling standard task force apparently took six years to develop its original standard. See Rhone, *The Canadian Care Labelling Program* (footnote 17).

33. See Moffet, Bregha and Middelkoop, "Responsible Care," Chapter 6, below.

34. C. Stone, *Where the Law Ends* (New York: Harper, 1975), p. 112.

operating in the marketplace. For example, in the chapter on bicycle and hockey helmets, the authors argue that the almost perfect compliance with voluntary standards in the case of bicycle helmets is related to the fact that consumer awareness of the safety codes is quite high. Since consumers desire safe helmets and associate the logos with safety, manufacturers are compelled to ensure that their helmets meet these standards.[35]

In these cases, governments can fund non-governmental organizations to develop education programs, or perhaps fund education programs themselves, that will shape consumer preferences and thus enhance the compliance of firms in the case of standards generated by market demand for either public or private goods and services. The benefits are beyond argument. Using markets means that the voluntary code's benefits are in fact being demanded by citizens. Measuring demand for public goods is notoriously difficult for regulators, and using markets to influence firm behaviour means that enforcement costs are entirely privatized to the industry and its consumers.

However, as is pointed out in the eco-labelling chapter, using markets to enforce compliance with voluntary standards generates its own controversies. Demand for products or services that are manufactured or developed in compliance with voluntary codes will provide strong incentives for industry to comply, incentives that do not impose costs on public revenues. However, the shift in market share associated with incentives imposes substantial costs on other private firms, leading to strategies that run from efforts to delay the development and implementation of voluntary codes, to attempts to influence political decisions associated with code promulgation. Monitoring and compliance of firm behaviour can also take place through effective individually initiated complaint procedures.

Perhaps the single most important element of monitoring and compliance strategies that characterizes some, but certainly not all, of the case studies in this area is the role of ongoing independent third-party verification of firm behaviour. This is, by all accounts, a major transformation of the relatively close relationship among government and firms that makes monitoring and compliance in the public sphere a comfortable and often secret arrangement in many sectors.[36] Independent third-party verification is likely to be far more systematic and comprehensive than relying on individual complaints to monitor and enforce firm behaviour. Some codes can and do require annual or at least periodic monitoring of firm behaviour in order for the firm to remain in compliance with voluntary code requirements.[37]

---

35. See Morrison and Webb, "Helmet Standards and Regulations," Chapter 11, below. One could argue, however, that Canadian consumers receive complying products because manufacturers must comply with mandatory U.S. standards that are equivalent to the Canadian voluntary standard. It would not seem to make economic sense for manufacturers who distribute in the North American market to produce two classes of helmet, one that complies with safety standards for the American market and one that does not for the Canadian market. As well, one can imagine the product liability risks associated with such a strategy should a child or adult suffer personal injuries associated with a non-complying helmet in Canada.

36. However, it is a direct relative of the traditional role of independent auditors who, in the case of most provincial companies legislation, are required to be appointed, to report to an independent audit committee, and to represent the interests of shareholders in the case of firms whose shares are held widely by members of the public.

37. For example, the Sustainable Forest Management Certification System requires an audit three years after the original certification and every five years thereafter. See Rhone, Clarke and Webb, "Sustainable Forestry Practices," Chapter 9, below.

The public accountability represented by third-party monitoring of firm compliance with the Responsible Care program is remarkably different from the relative absence of public information and accountability associated with monitoring of the private sector by public bureaucracies.[38] Similarly, multisectoral independent third-party monitoring of compliance is a central characteristic of Gap Inc.'s *Code of Vendor Conduct*. In this case monitoring is carried out by grassroots church and labour activists drawn from local communities.[39] These examples of monitoring by "volunteer" public interest groups can be compared with the requirement under the Canadian Standards Association's Sustainable Forest Management Certification System that firms have their management practices "audited" by professional organizations.[40]

There are two factors that influence the choice to use either individual complaint procedures or third-party auditing/monitoring systems in voluntary codes. The first is an expert assessment of which system will ensure, in a cost-effective manner, the highest level of compliance with voluntary code requirements. The second, and perhaps more important factor to the industry participants in the voluntary code processes, is public legitimacy associated with the auditing system — certainly, the Canadian Standards Association's Sustainable Forest Management Certification System is premised on industry awareness that national and international market forces demand independent, reliable certification systems.

There remain important roles for government in the area of monitoring and compliance. First, the government can require publication of the results of individual complaints and/or audit reports as a prerequisite for support of the standards-development process or indeed of the standard itself. Second, as in the case of the bicycle helmet standard, the government can undertake that it will itself monitor compliance and threaten to regulate at a later time if its review of the efficacy of the voluntary code suggests that positive government regulation is necessary. Of course, this latter strategy is only effective when the continued threat of government regulation is credible. When the driving force behind the privatization of regulation is the inability of governments to regulate effectively due to budget restraints,[41] then compliance with voluntary codes becomes increasingly problematic. Education, the modification of firm behaviour and monitoring compliance with voluntary code standards are, of course, only the beginnings of an effective compliance and enforcement strategy. Enforcement of standards by institutions that do not enjoy the authority of the State is perceived by some as the critical weakness of voluntary codes. Obviously, associations and firms do not have the legal authority of the State to impose fines and penalties under the threat of force.

---

38. See Moffet, Bregha and Middelkoop, "Responsible Care," Chapter 6, below.

39. See Rhone, Stroud and Webb, "Gap Inc.'s Code of Conduct," Chapter 7, below.

40. See Rhone, Clarke and Webb, "Sustainable Forestry Practices," Chapter 9, below. As well, the Sustainable Forest Management Certification System establishes general environmental auditing principles that the auditing firm must apply in conducting its review. It is not clear whether the auditor reports are public, although they must be included in the firms' performance appraisals.

41. For example, Rhone, in *Investment Funds Institute of Canada* (footnote 11), describes an Ontario Securities Commission that was operating under increasingly unworkable conditions due to funding cuts, and that was therefore not likely to take on the additional and costly regulatory responsibilities of supervising investment fund dealers.

As well, subject to anti-trust laws, associations can impose penalties through contract. Properly drafted voluntary codes can provide, as contractual terms, that the offending firm pay damages in a specified amount to the association upon demonstration of a violation of the code's provisions. Similarly, properly drafted voluntary codes can insist on remedial measures being undertaken by the offending firm to publicize its non-compliance, educate the public or remedy environmental damage. Although enforceability is an issue here, it can be straightforwardly dealt with by requiring the offending firm to pay the costs of remedial measures as damages to the association. Finally, voluntary codes can provide for "delicensing" (the removal of the offending firm from membership in the industry trade association),[42] public notification of a breach of the code or (in the case of internal management codes)[43] a refusal to do business with the offending supplier firm.

However, several of the voluntary code case studies — and in particular the description of the Responsible Care program and the analysis of Gap Inc.'s *Code of Vendor Conduct* — reveal that those responsible for the enforcement of voluntary codes are well aware that penalties are not the most effective enforcement tool, since these traditional enforcement measures may not ultimately work to achieve the public purpose behind the code. Moreover, as with traditional regulation, enforcement has a cost not only to the regulatee but also to the regulator — delicensing and fines are public confirmation that the regulatory regime has failed. These draconian measures may have significant negative externalities, particularly on employees and on third parties such as firms doing business with the regulated firm.

The lesson that we learn from the codes examined in this volume is that the threat of penalties may be a poor substitute for education and training of non-conforming firms. Certainly, the imposition of financial penalties (contract cancellation, payment of damages, exclusion from the industry association) will not achieve the "regulatory" objectives embodied in these codes. The risk of significant loss of market share or revenues and the damage to a firm's business reputation may, when combined with more constructive sharing of information, management expertise and technology, be a far more effective set of enforcement tools than those traditionally available to and employed by governments.

---

42. Harrison, in "Canada's Environmental Choice Program," Chapter 10, below, describes this sanction as a component of the Environmental Choice Program's licensing contract.

43. See, for instance, Webb and Morrison, "The Law and Voluntary Codes," Chapter 5, below.

Do Voluntary Codes Achieve their Regulatory Objectives?

The codes examined in this volume point to the absence of conclusive evidence, or even of experiential reports, that the public good objective of voluntary codes has been achieved. While voluntary codes may be criticized on these grounds, it is a failing shared by public regulation as well. It is difficult to assess, let alone quantify, the marginal impact of a voluntary code on the reduction of environmental degradation, for instance. The alleged benefits of the voluntary code are often not quantifiable, they are difficult to isolate from other exogenous factors, and, of course, one has to choose a reference point from which to assess the benefits of the standard. The analysis of the Responsible Care program[44] suggests that there have been environmental benefits associated with the implementation of that program. But even here, one must look closely at the experience of industry and government before reaching conclusions about "regulatory effectiveness." How does one define the benefits associated with a code? Are they due to the standard or to other regulatory and market mechanisms? For example, the alleged 100 percent compliance with the care labelling voluntary code[45] might very well be the product of our relationship to the American market, where equivalent codes are mandated by legislation. What would have been the environmental costs and benefits of alternative regulatory instruments?

Finally, many of the studies point out that the benefits of voluntary codes must be examined with a lens that looks outside of the immediate short-term modification of firm behaviour. Here, we may be able to identify systemic and long-term changes in corporate culture that will generate substantial regulatory benefits — a positive externality that may go unnoticed in many cases. This is the argument made by the Responsible Care case study. It certainly deserves further critical examination. In the end, this is the most problematic aspect of the case studies presented in volume. In the introduction to this chapter, I argued that while contractarian models of governance pointed to the importance of fairness in the bargaining processes that led to the development of particular codes, that does not eliminate an obligation to assess the substantive outcome of the implementation of the code in practice. Of course, in several cases, it is far too early in the life of the codes to expect that reliable data on the code's impact on the marketplace are available. Yet in several of the case studies the codes have been in place for some time, and even here, data are not presented by the authors to support a conclusion that the voluntary code "is working."

At a minimum this leads to one inexorable conclusion. If one is going to support voluntary codes as a regulatory instrument then guidelines for code development must require code developers to design and fund an ongoing evaluative mechanism that will provide reliable public data and analyses of the impact of the code on firm behaviour and on the production of the public good sought through the development and implementation of the code on an industry-wide basis. And the review process must be carried out on an ongoing basis. While the Responsible Care program and the Canadian Standards Association's Sustainable Forest Management Certification System both

---

44. See Moffet, Bregha and Middelkoop, "Responsible Care," Chapter 6, below.

45. See Rhone, *The Canadian Care Labelling Program* (footnote 17).

provide for ongoing review, in both cases the periodic compliance assessment is carried out on individual firms. While this is a salutary characteristic of both codes, it is only a partial solution to this problem.

Conclusion

The codes examined in this volume provide some evidence of the growth and maturation of voluntary codes as regulatory instruments in Canada. Therefore, perhaps the most difficult task we face in evaluating such codes is determining whether the public good that is being sought to be achieved through them should be supported by the State. The abstractions articulated in most codes — public safety, consumer protection, environmental sustainability, child welfare — are ill-defined and largely immeasurable. While attractive in their apparent simplicity, they overlay a complicated subset of outcomes that we must tease out and be able to assess before making a decision to support particular code processes.[46]

Governments cannot avoid their responsibility to identify, monitor, assess and ultimately support or withdraw support of a voluntary code initiative based on their independent oversight of the public purpose underlying the code.[47] These kinds of voluntary codes — when an industry's market behaviour is motivated by environmental, social or other public goals — present governments with the invidious task of deciding which of the goals are in accord with the State's conception of the public interest.

The role of governments must be to assess independently the public purpose to which the market is being put. If the government is to play a mediating or facilitating role in voluntary codes, it cannot avoid having to identify and evaluate the public benefits of voluntary codes, and then ultimately support or deny support to industry sectors based on its independent view of the public interest being pursued through the voluntary code, an assessment of the process used to develop the code, and ongoing monitoring of the public goods produced by the code.[48]

One approach that meets this test is to have governments establish — either formally through legislation or informally through policy documents — a set of broadly articulated regulatory objectives that may be pursued through the development of a voluntary code. Governments would be consulted during the code's development process and might even produce a voluntary code development guideline that the code developer would be encouraged, through financial incentives, to adopt and implement. Once the code was developed, the government would evaluate the code to determine whether and

---

46. More problematic are components of voluntary codes — say, a prohibition on advertising by lawyers — that, while not necessarily designed to achieve illegal ends, are antithetical to the government's assessment of the public good.

47. Imagine the response of the Canadian government to a self-regulatory initiative of a Canadian subsidiary of an American firm that developed an internal ethical code of conduct that led it to refuse to buy or sell from a Canadian firm engaged in business dealings with Cuba, or because the Canadian firm failed to implement forest management practices that were in accord with the values of the American purchaser.

48. This governmental role is proposed, for example, by Neil Gunningham in "Codes of Practice: The Australian Experience," Chapter 12, below, and in E. Bardach and R. A. Kagan, *Going by the Book: The Problem of Regulatory Unreasonableness* (Philadelphia: Temple University Press, 1982).

to what extent the code's provisions are consistent with the policy document/legislation pursuant to which it was developed. To the extent that they were, the government would then decide to support the code — through tax incentives, *ex post facto* compensation for some portion of the code's development costs, or perhaps through "certification" of the code through an independent certification system. Subsequently, the government would periodically evaluate the intended and unintended impacts of the voluntary code and make ongoing decisions to continue support of the code in operation.[49]

As with so many other regulatory phenomena, the development of private voluntary codes is neither inherently good nor evil. Ideology does not answer the question that I posed at the outset. Rather, an examination of how codes work — what they can and have achieved, at what cost, and to whose benefit — is an ongoing process. There is no reason to believe that there is one answer to those questions. But there may be patterns that will be revealed upon further study.

Those patterns and themes will permit us to reach preliminary conclusions as to how industry, governments and the non-governmental organization community should involve themselves in the ongoing development of these regulatory phenomena in the future. There is no neutral stance than can be taken by any of us — professional, academic, corporate player, public interest group or government. We will all play a role that will shape the future of voluntary codes. Our task, then, is to define how we should contribute to this very exciting future.

At a minimum, from the work presented in this volume, we should be able to identify both the endogenous characteristics of voluntary codes — development processes, application, enforcement and outputs — as well as the exogenous characteristics of industry sectors regulated by the voluntary code. Having identified these characteristics, we can then make decisions as to when and how to ensure that voluntary codes contribute to the pursuit of the public interest.

---

49. There is no reason to believe that the law of unintended effects that plagues public regulation will be avoided as regulation is partially or wholly privatized through voluntary codes.

Chapter 3
Institutional and Public Administrative Aspects of Voluntary Codes

G. Bruce Doern

Introduction

The purpose of this chapter is to examine selected institutional and public administrative aspects of voluntary codes as an alternative to, or complementary feature of, traditional regulation.[1] Voluntary codes are a class of rules that are crafted by and agreed to by private parties and organizations without being directly promulgated by the State. The selected institutional aspects are examined in two ways, first conceptually and then in relation to the case studies prepared for this volume.

The terms *institutional* and *public administrative* are used more or less interchangeably throughout the chapter. They both evoke values and procedural concerns rooted in democratic political institutions in Canada and deal with how public bureaucracies function (or ought to function) in devising and implementing public policy. Such an institutional focus is presented as a complement to the legal and political economy perspectives provided in other chapters.

Five institutional and public administrative aspects of voluntary codes are examined:

- accountability to the democratic State and to the electorate, particularly in terms of Cabinet-parliamentary government;
- internal accountability and democracy regarding interest groups, associations and firms, particularly since these are the arenas in which voluntary codes would be developed and "administered";
- the nature of policy instruments (taxation, regulation, spending, persuasion) as relates to implementing public policies and understanding the actual mix of functions involved in regulation and the use of voluntary codes;
- the impact of budget and personnel cuts and capacities in carrying out tasks both in the State sector and the private associative democracy sector; and
- the nature of overlapping regimes in regulation (e.g. social-versus-economic or framework-versus-sectoral regulation), such as in the regulation of competition, the environment and the services delivered by the professions.

Each institutional aspect is briefly sketched out and examined. Since each aspect is complex and cannot be fully covered in the space available, the style of analysis has to be basic and suggestive. Thus the approach taken is to compare and contrast, where feasible and appropriate, each aspect as it applies to "normal regulation" compared to voluntary codes. There are of course dangers in casting something as normal regulation,

---

1. Special thanks are owed to Kernaghan Webb, David Cohen and Derek Ireland for helpful comments on an earlier draft of this chapter.

Kernaghan Webb, Editor, *Voluntary Codes: Private Governance, the Public Interest and Innovation.*
This chapter ©2004 G. Bruce Doern, pages 57–76.
Published by the Carleton Research Unit for Innovation, Science and Environment, Carleton University, Ottawa, Canada.

since there are many kinds and degrees of regulation.[2] However, it is necessary to do so because, in broad terms, the use of voluntary codes is seen as a potentially better or necessary alternative or complementary way of achieving certain kinds of "public purpose." Thus, for the purposes of this chapter, normal regulation implies that we are dealing with more direct regulation by the State in which rules are promulgated through democratic, elected institutions and implemented by State agencies and departments that have reasonable staffs to enforce and ensure compliance. Voluntary codes, in contrast, imply that rules are being crafted and implemented by private parties without the direct presence of the State and its bureaucracies or with an extremely limited such presence.[3] More specifically, voluntary codes can be defined as a set of non-legislatively required commitments that are agreed to by one or more individuals, designed to influence, shape, control or benchmark behaviour, and are to be applied in a consistent manner or to reach a consistent outcome.[4]

Both the conceptual literature and decades of practitioner experience (by regulators and the regulated) teach that there are ~~numerous~~ gray zones between normal regulation and voluntary codes, hence the use of such potential or actual oxymorons as "self-regulation," "enforced self-regulation" or "symbolic regulation."[5] This means that there are many shades of "publicness" and "privateness" and of government and governance.[6] The discussion of each institutional aspect will be alert to these realities but for purposes of raising the issues and discussing the five institutional aspects, the section will take normal regulation and voluntary codes to be stylized polar opposites. When we apply the discussion of the five aspects to the selected case studies the gray zones of reality reappear in at least some of the cases.

The voluntary codes discussed here will serve as a basis for commentary and analysis rather than a full-scale comparative project.[7] This is because the code analyses undertaken in this volume were not explicitly written with this chapter's five-point institutional framework in mind and hence not all relevant information is available to fill in all the analytical spaces. But the codes discussed in the volume do supply a rich base for illustrative commentary. Hence, at the end of each section in the five-point institutional framework, I will draw on these to illustrate key points and/or for further complementary insight. However, the basic task is to highlight each aspect first, by

---

2. I. Ayres and J. Braithwaite, *Responsive Regulation: Transcending the Deregulation Debate* (New York: Oxford University Press, 1992).

3. P. N. Grabosky, "Using Non-Governmental Resources to Foster Compliance," *Governance: An International Journal of Policy, Administration and Institutions* 8:4 (1995), pp. 527–550.

4. Office of Consumer Affairs and Regulatory Affairs Division, Treasury Board Secretariat (Canada), *Voluntary Codes: A Guide for Their Development and Use* (Ottawa: Industry Canada and Treasury Board Secretariat, 1998), p. 2, available at <http://strategis.ic.gc.ca/epic/internet/inoca-bc.nsf/en/ca00880e.html>.

5. J. Braithwaite, J. Walker and P. N. Grabosky, "An Enforcement Taxonomy of Regulatory Agencies," *Law and Policy* 9 (1987), pp. 323–350.

6. P. Aucoin, *The New Public Management: Canada in Comparative Perspective* (Montréal: McGill-Queen's University Press, 1997); C. Hood, *Administrative Analysis* (London: Harvester Wheatsheaf, 1986), Chapter 3.

7. See the case study chapters in this volume, below, and those from the symposium on voluntary codes held in Ottawa in September 1996, available in summary at <http://strategis.ic.gc.ca/epic/internet/inoca-bc.nsf/en/ca00880e.html>.

discussing the institutional aspect in general, then by relating it to "normal regulation" and, finally, by drawing out its implications and meaning for voluntary codes.

Public Accountability and the Democratic State

The first institutional aspect is public accountability. Accountability in its broadest form under Westminster-based systems of Cabinet-parliamentary government involves a set of processes whereby elected ministers are held accountable to Parliament and officials are accountable to ministers.[8] The Cabinet and its ministers are responsible for policy and, in addition, ministers are accountable for all decisions made within the ambit of such policies. Accountability for individual decisions is supposed to apply even though officials have been the *de facto* decision makers in many individual situations. Thus, in theory, ministers would resign over major errors of omission or commission.[9]

Accountability in the above system tends to centre on the notion of "answerability" or having to account for what is being done. The occasions for giving an account are numerous and can include parliamentary question period, scrutiny before parliamentary committees, supplying information to the Auditor General or provincial equivalents, internal reporting to the central fiscal and political agencies of the government, and specialized reporting on matters such as language policy, human rights, and privacy (to name only a few).[10] Ultimately, however, these systems of accountability are underpinned by the larger imperative that a government can be defeated if it does not command the confidence of the House of Commons.[11]

In the above context, accountability is cast in terms of only one central constitutional feature of Canadian government, parliamentary government. Accountability, however, is further complicated by federalism and by the *Canadian Charter of Rights and Freedoms*. But, in itself, this central parliamentary aspect of accountability does not answer all the questions that many ask about the concept of accountability.[12] These questions include *accountability to whom? accountability for what?* and *accountability over what time frame?* The question of *to whom accountability is owed?* can elicit varied responses in that many players think that accountability should also be to the citizens or interests most affected by a policy. The question of *accountability for what?* raises difficult concerns about whether the "what" refers to

---

8. S. L. Sutherland, "Responsible Government and Ministerial Responsibility: Every Reform Has Its Own Problem," *Canadian Journal of Political Science* 24 (1991), pp. 91–120.

9. K. Kernaghan and D. Siegel, *Public Administration in Canada,* 2nd ed. (Toronto: Nelson Canada, 1991).

10. G. B. Doern and S. Sutherland, *Bureaucracy in Canada: Control and Reform 1985* (Toronto: University of Toronto Press, 1985); G. Osbaldeston, *Keeping Deputy Ministers Accountable* (London: National Centre for Management Research and Development, 1988).

11. M. Atkinson, *Governing Canada: Institutions and Public Policy* (Toronto: Harcourt Brace Jovanovich, 1993).

12. P. Burton and S. Duncan, "Democracy and Accountability in Public Bodies: New Agendas in British Government," *Policy and Politics* 24:1 (January 1996), pp. 5–16; G. B. Doern, *Political Accountability and Efficiency*, Government and Competitiveness Discussion Paper Series (Kingston, Ont.: School of Policy Studies, Queen's University, 1993), pp. 1–36; K. Kernaghan, "Reshaping Government: The Post-Bureaucratic Paradigm," *Canadian Public Administration* 36:4 (Winter 1993), pp. 636–645.

precise and measurable performance criteria, or criteria related to democratic processes, or to some combination of both kinds of criteria. The issue of the *relevant time frame* is important because accountability time periods can be annual or even monthly and thus short-term accountability reporting regimes may distort accountability simply because many policies are by their nature long-term in their consequences and in the time needed to achieve mature implementation.

One does not have to ask too many basic questions before it is realized that in practice there are many "accountabilities" within the overall Canadian or other versions of the Westminster model of Cabinet-parliamentary government.[13] What happens, then, when we add the dual questions central to this chapter, namely, how does this institutional element relate to normal regulation and to "voluntary codes"?

With regard to normal regulation, it is apparent from both the literature and from practice that there are at least three kinds of regulatory mode in which basic accountability systems differ: the regular department as regulator headed by an elected minister; the independent multimember commission as regulator; and the designated statutory person as regulator.[14] Arguably, the first of these can be seen to be located closely within the core traditions of the parliamentary model, in that regulators such as the Department of the Environment or the Department of Agriculture and Agri-Food carry out their tasks under such a basic system.

The commission and statutory person models are, by definition, at least one step further removed in the accountability continuum. They are given forms of independence from the minister and from Parliament. Thus, the National Energy Board is a regulatory commission independent from the Minister of Natural Resources, and the Commissioner of Competition functions under the *Competition Act* in a manner that gives him independence from the Minister of Industry.[15] The independence is never total but it is more established than it is for the regular department. And the more distant these arrangements are from ministers, the more likely it is that the regulator, and the regulated, will see accountability as a broader democratic concept with accountability owed as well to those being regulated or to those citizens and interests that are the beneficiaries of the regulations.

The greater the distance from the central parliamentary concepts, the more that accountability is less clear and perhaps the more difficult it is to know who to blame when things go wrong or, indeed, who to praise when things go right. The greater the distance the less that accountability is also a system of control. But this argument can only be taken so far, in that many commentators have been critical for decades of the "pure" accountability claims of parliamentary government.[16]

---

13. Kernaghan and Siegal (footnote 9); P. Day and R. Klein, *Accountabilities* (London: Tavistock Publications, 1987).

14. M. Hill, *The Choice of Mode For Regulation: A Case Study of the Canadian Pesticide Registration Review 1988–1992*, unpublished doctoral thesis (Department of Political Science, Carleton University, Ottawa, 1994); G. B. Doern, M. Hill, M. Prince and R. Schultz, *Changing The Rules: Canada's Changing Regulatory Regimes* (Toronto: University of Toronto Press, 1999).

15. G. B. Doern, *Fairer Play: Canadian Competition Policy Institutions in a Global Market* (Toronto: C. D. Howe Institute, 1995).

16. Kernaghan (footnote 12); Obaldeston (footnote 10).

In principle then, the development of voluntary codes to deal with some aspect of public concern moves the accountability circumference one step further from basic views of elected parliamentary government. Indeed, it may have no connection whatsoever in terms of anything like what normal accountability occasions to elected ministers or members of Parliament. Accountability regimes will almost by definition be seen, under a codes regime, not as relationships that go "upward and inward" towards parliamentary government and executive authorities but rather radiate in a broad "downward and outward" direction to interests, communities, clients and the like. Whether this is good or bad, or merely inevitable, further depends on how we assess the other institutional aspects that follow.

My reading of the case studies suggests that at least half of them undoubtedly involve some form of traditional basic accountability, but these cases also show that the accountability chains are quite diverse in both the "upward and inward" and "downward and outward" directions. For example, the hockey helmet case and its comparison with bicycle helmets[17] seems to be a relatively simple case in that over a two-decade period, the safety concerns of hockey helmets were dealt with as a regulation under the *Hazardous Products Act*. Amendments occurred over the years through a process led by the Product Safety Branch of the then-Department of Consumer and Corporate Affairs and hence with a direct line of accountability to the minister of that department. But clearly, this case also involved a considerable parallel and complementary use of an independent standards-writing organization, the Canadian Standards Association, which in turn involved a broader stakeholder committee in its processes. The Canadian Hockey Association (formerly the Canadian Amateur Hockey Association) also became a crucial player through its own reinforcing rules. Looking back, the case seems to be one in which reasonable success was achieved among several stakeholders but in a situation in which no significant voluntary codes *as such* were involved. The case (or the consumer product involved) was also one that was relatively simple compared to other cases of consumer product safety that might occur in consumer regulation.

This example does not capture all of the kinds of broader political, legal and marketplace accountability that exist. For example, the practice of voluntary codes involves potential review under the *Competition Act* by the Competition Bureau and the Commissioner of Competition. This would arise if such codes in their particular design were deemed to be anti-competitive in their intent or effect. Legal accountability concerns can arise out of the limits of delegated authority in the government's endorsement of code arrangements.[18] As for broader marketplace accountability, the EcoLogo and Gap Inc. code cases suggest that ultimate consumer reactions are the true disciplining factor.[19]

---

17. See Andrew Morrison and Kernaghan Webb, "Bicycle Helmet Standards and Hockey Helmet Regulations: Two Approaches to Safety Protection," Chapter 11, below.

18. See Kernaghan Webb and Andrew Morrison, "The Law and Voluntary Codes: Examining the 'Tangled Web'," Chapter 5, below.

19. See Kathryn Harrison, "Promoting Environmental Protection Through Eco-Labelling: An Evaluation of Canada's Environmental Choice Program," Chapter 10, below; Gregory T. Rhone, John Stroud and Kernaghan Webb, "Gap's Code of Conduct for Treatment of Overseas Workers," Chapter 7, below.

In general, the discussion above of accountability concepts suggests that the use of voluntary codes pushes the accountability circumference further and further away from the State and its branches. However, it also shows that even in the realms of traditional regulation these accountability chains had already become extremely varied and elongated. The analysis also suggests that accountability regimes deal with crucial questions regarding accountability *for what?* and not just *to whom?* Since there are many aspects of such substantive performance criteria, it follows that voluntary codes can aid in ensuring that particular kinds of performance are carried out in ways that more traditional kinds of regulation may not.

Accountability in Interest Groups, Firms and Associations

The second institutional element to be highlighted is the parallel issue of accountability within and among interest groups, firms and associations of many kinds. If the State is not to directly regulate but rather some set of "private" or "non-State" institutions are to be the location for the development and implementation of voluntary codes, then one key issue is what kinds of democratic accountability, if any, do such associations have within any given organization and also between and among them?[20] Freedom of association is itself a democratic right and a principle of great importance but there are many conceptual and practical issues involved in the overall world of associative democracy and politics.[21]

Accountability in this realm must first be seen in terms of long-argued beliefs about the nature of a broader representative democracy that goes well beyond parliamentary democracy. A recent analysis concludes that advocates of such extended forms of political organization see three principles as being central:

- that voluntary, self-governing associations gradually and progressively become the primary means of democratic governance of economic and social affairs;
- that power should as far as possible be distributed to distinct domains of authority, whether territorial or functional, and that administration within such domains should be devolved to the lowest level consistent with the effective governance of the affairs in question — these are the conjoint principles of State pluralism and of federalism; and
- that democratic governance does not consist just in the powers of citizen election or majority decision but in the continuous flow of information between governors and the governed, whereby the former seek the consent and cooperation of the latter.[22]

20. S. Phillips, "How Ottawa Blends: Shifting Government Relationships With Interest Groups," in F. Abele, ed., *How Ottawa Spends 1991–92* (Ottawa: Carleton University Press, 1991), pp. 183–227; M. Taylor, "Between Public and Private: Accountability in Voluntary Organizations," *Policy and Politics* 24:1 (January 1996), pp. 57–72.

21. P. Pross, *Group Politics and Public Policy* (Toronto: University of Toronto Press, 1986); P. Hirst, *Associative Democracy: New Forms of Economic and Social Governance* (Cambridge: Polity Press, 1994).

22. Hirst, ibid., p. 20.

There can be no denying that these long-held beliefs are a crucial part of the accountability and implementation of many current policies of government (regulatory and non-regulatory), but they also raise several issues about the exact nature of governance regimes and of what constitutes "effective governance."

The first issue to note is simply the wide variety of mechanisms adopted internally in each associative realm. The internal governance systems of labour unions, churches, corporations, business and social interest groups, and voluntary organizations vary enormously. Some have processes for annual accountability and others for more frequent avenues of joint decision making with member or delegate voting. Some interest groups are continually polling their members for their views while others scarcely know who their members are. Some have their democratic governance determined quite extensively by the State through laws or regulations while others are more truly "self-regulating."

A second feature of the associative or interest-group realm is that such entities have diverse internal dynamics regarding the extent to which they exist, a) to deliver practical services to their members (magazines, travel discounts, information) or b) to lobby the State for favourable laws and policies. The rest of the State-centred political system may well see them largely in terms of the second or lobby role whereas the larger portion of their members may see them in more day-to-day, service-oriented terms.[23] Often this is because the capacity to extract membership dues from the attentive but not passionately attentive adherent turns on quite utilitarian views of value for money by individual members. These choices of relative emphasis within the association vary widely across the economic versus social clusters or groups but each association faces them to some extent.[24] Accordingly, the potential addition of more voluntary code activity by an association will be filtered through a dual lobby-versus-service role lens not just through the singular lens of a lobby role.

A third issue flows inexorably from the first two. If policy efficacy is a concern, then the nature of the association's own bureaucracy will be of considerable import. Bureaucracy here has a dual meaning. It means first the staff of the association (if there is a staff) and its particular kinds of expertise and experience. But bureaucracy also means its capacity to develop procedures and records for the exercise of discretion (either on its own or in some shared manner with other associations). This point is important because a world that puts greater reliance on voluntary codes will be a world with possibly less for the State to do but *not* a world of less bureaucracy in both of the above senses. When there is discretion, there is bureaucracy, because without it, discretion becomes only random or arbitrary power.[25] And however "voluntary" a "code" might be, it is presumably not being agreed to so that it can "be administered" arbitrarily.

In what other ways does a stylized world of traditional regulation versus voluntary codes relate to these brief points about associative democracy and accountability? Traditional regulation has certainly had to encompass all of these realities to some degree at least. When assessing written briefs for change in laws and regulation,

---

23. Pross (footnote 21); Taylor (footnote 20).

24. P. Dunleavy, *Democracy, Bureaucracy and Public Choice: Economic Explanations in Political Science* (London: Harvester Wheatsheaf, 1991).

25. Hood (footnote 6).

regulators must constantly assess the degree to which they think various groups are representative and legitimately "speak" for their members. Most regulators, moreover, are saved enormous amounts of work in information gathering and compliance simply because there are interest groups they can work with or through. Regulatory compliance and inspection activity is crucially dependent upon the professionalism and "bureaucracy" of the corporation or the union, since it often does the larger part of the real inspecting of the behaviour that regulators want to control or promote.[26]

A world of greater reliance on voluntary codes is therefore not a world that is a full or sharp break from normal regulation. But it is likely to put a new, more focussed searchlight on exactly what associational, corporate and intergroup democracy and accountability really involve. Indeed, the above discussion has been mainly about accountability within associations rather than among them.

The case studies vary in the degree to which some of these issues are examined, but glimpses of their importance are nonetheless present in some of them. One such case is certainly the chemical industry's Responsible Care program, as examined by Moffet, Bregha and Middelkoop.[27] The Canadian Chemical Producers' Association (CCPA) introduced its environmental Responsible Care program in the early 1980s and its member companies must commit formally to it if they are to be members of the association. Accordingly, several features of the CCPA's internal democracy and accountability arise.

It is not clear from the case exactly what internal, real trade-offs were made behind the scenes among member companies as to what Responsible Care principles or standards were tolerable or feasible among its members. The differences between big and small firms are hinted at in the case but, despite some consultation processes, it cannot be said that the processes of arriving at this private form of public policy are as open as they might be under direct government auspices.

Moffet, Bregha and Middelkoop's account of the association's other internal accountability mechanisms centres on three mechanisms: reporting, a compliance verification process and public involvement. While the authors commend progress on each of these mechanisms relative to the previous period prior to the program, they also raise issues about the inadequacies of each mechanism as well. These concern such issues as whether the reporting information on member firms deals with particular pollutants as opposed to some overall environmental performance. Concerns about whether third-party involvement through advisory committees and other mechanisms are adequate for sustained pressure on the industry are also raised.

With respect to voluntary codes and accountability within and among interest groups, firms and voluntary associations, the most basic overall conclusion is that this is the realm that we know least about. In terms of basic capacity to act as a surrogate State or series of mini-governing realms, these associations have some strengths and many weaknesses. While voluntary codes are often seen as a way to reduce the role of

---

26. J. Clifford and K. Webb, *Policy Implementation, Compliance and Administrative Law* (Ottawa: Law Reform Commission of Canada, 1986); G. B. Doern, *The Road To Better Public Services: Progress and Constraints in Five Federal Agencies* (Montréal: C. D. Howe Institute, 1994).

27. John Moffet, François Bregha and Mary Jane Middelkoop, "Responsible Care: A Case Study of a Voluntary Environmental Initiative," Chapter 6, below.

bureaucrats, they are unlikely to be avenues that reduce the need for bureaucracy in the sense of having reliable procedures and competences to underpin the administration of the codes.

The Nature of Policy Instruments and *de facto* Implementation

The third institutional element involves the actual interplay among the practical nature of *implementation* (including enforcement, compliance and service delivery), basic policy *instruments* (such as regulation, spending and persuasion) and the actual *mix of functions* that an agency carries out. For the purposes of this section, policy implementation can be portrayed as the overarching activity of operational agencies of government within which there is a continuum of actions variously viewed as compliance, enforcement and service activities.[28] Implementation is the process of carrying out and realizing the intent of public policy established by laws and the decisions of elected politicians. Accordingly, it involves the values and processes through which laws and programs are carried out through discrete decisions on "cases" (firms, individuals, projects) involving action and decisions not to act. It inevitably also involves the exercise of detailed decision making and discretion by both officials and private citizens and interests. And it involves processes through which that discretion is subject to review, grievance handling, appeal and actual redress by governmental agencies or the courts.

The notion of compliance, enforcement and service provision being a subset of implementation can be seen through any reasonable understanding of the basic policy instruments available to government to get things done.[29] Such instruments are variously categorized and sub-categorized but usually in the aggregate include outright State ownership, regulation, taxation, spending and persuasion. Clearly, how compliance, enforcement and service realms are viewed depends upon how agencies and their programs are nested amidst a specific set of instruments and attitudes towards their use.[30]

For example, Clifford and Webb's study for the Law Reform Commission of Canada demarcates the "compliance" realm of implementation.[31] Compliance "refers to a measure of private action or inaction, insofar as it conforms to a standard of conduct requested or commanded by government."[32] Thus, compliance implies some direct coercion, but the rest of the study then goes on to show how, *within* the compliance spectrum of activities, there are many service-oriented elements. This is so simply because persuasion, education and information gathering are key aspects of what is

---

28. See Hood (footnote 6); Doern (footnote 26); A. Ogus, *Regulation: Legal Form and Economic Theory* (Oxford: Clarendon Press, 1994).

29. G. B. Doern and R. W. Phidd, *Canadian Public Policy: Ideas, Structure, Process* 2nd ed. (Toronto: Nelson Canada, 1992), chapters 7 and 12; S. Linder and G. Peters, "Instruments of Government: Perceptions and Contexts," *Journal of Public Policy* 9:1 (1989), pp. 35–58.

30. Linder and Peters, ibid.

31. Clifford and Webb (footnote 26).

32. Ibid., p. 10.

involved in the compliance-implementation process. In other studies of implementation, enforcement is used as a term that directly involves sanctions or the harder edge of the State's powers and authority. Often, of course, enforcement and compliance are used together.[33]

Because of these key features, most studies of implementation show that the real nature of implementation is "relational" and thus "stands in sharp contrast to the discrete isolated incident approach to law or to there being a distinct public and private sector."[34] Clifford and Webb's three-part framework shows compliance as consisting of *relations*, *instruments* and *activities*. Compliance implementation is *relational* because the parties involved include administrators, "administrés" and third parties. *Instruments* refers to the basic command-penalty, incentives and persuasion choices already noted above. And *activities* refers to an even finer set of actions and processes that concretely occur in compliance situations. These include inspecting, investigating, negotiating, observing, information gathering, coaxing, cajoling, warning and the like. It is less a world of discrete products or actions cascading down a hierarchy and much more a world of continuous interactions and negotiations, embedded in both service and compliance activity of the most detailed, disaggregated kind.

When considerations of instrument choice and implementation are brought to bear on what I am labelling "traditional" regulation or on regulatory agencies, one must look for similar mixes of activity. For example, a crucial question is to determine what *de jure* and *de facto* mix of functions the "regulator" carries out.[35] In an even more detailed list, these functions can include regulation making (in the sense of delegated legislation), rule making (e.g. about the agency's own procedures or hearings), quasi-judicial decisions, for which norms and processes akin to court procedures must be practised, quasi-political allocative tasks, in which licences or approvals are determined or negotiated, the complementary administration of spending grants or subsidies, policy advisory functions, either *de facto* or mandated by law, and broad leadership, educational or exhortative tasks, in which the regulator is expected to lead, guide and persuade.[36]

Literally dozens of studies from the legal, political and even economic disciplines point to the crucial nature of the mix of functions when regulatory (and other) organizations are looked at closely and seriously. There is, however, often only limited agreement as to how one can often distinguish, say, a quasi-judicial decision from a quasi-political or administrative decision.[37] Since few if any regulators are unifunctional and engage only in regulation, it follows that regulators are more than just rule makers.

---

33. M. K. Sparrow, *Imposing Duties: Government's Changing Approach To Compliance* (London: Praeger 1994); *Responsible Regulation*, (Ottawa: Economic Council of Canada, 1979); *Reforming Regulation*, (Ottawa: Economic Council of Canada, 1981).

34. Clifford and Webb (footnote 26), p. 6.

35. Doern, Hill, Prince and Schultz (footnote 14); Linder and Peters (footnote 29); Clifford and Webb, ibid.; Ayres and Braithwaite (footnote 2).

36. L. Susskind and G. McMahon, "The Theory and Practice of Negotiated Rulemaking," *Yale Journal of Regulation* 3 (1985), pp. 133–165.

37. See Hood (footnote 6); E. Ratushny, "What are Administrative Tribunals? The Pursuit of Uniformity in Diversity," *Canadian Public Administration* 30:1 (1987), pp. 1–13; M. Trebilcock, "Requiem for Regulators: The Passing of a Counter-Culture?" *Yale Journal of Regulation* 8:2 (Summer 1991), pp. 497–510.

They are also unelected politicians and administrators engaged in numerous acts of discretion and political choice in partnership with private sector players whose voluntary and involuntary involvement is essential for success.

If one takes these points about implementation and instruments further, how do they relate to the theoretically opposite situation of voluntary codes? In the realm of voluntary codes, the notion of enforcement is presumably a non-issue in the sense that the State is not directly a player and hence the legitimate coercive powers of the State are not being exercised. But the threat of such powers may well be a part of the calculus that is inducing key interests to "volunteer" themselves for involvement in the "administration" of the code. In short, there is a veiled view that "if we do not act, the government will."

It is also presumably the case that in the realm of voluntary codes, the implementation of the code relies much more on the softer instruments such as information provision and education, perhaps with some basic capacity for dealing with controversial cases through ombudsman-like or mediation processes. The reporting of cases in some public form may also be utilized. As experience with codes is acquired, pressure may well increase to routinize the code and to convert it into direct regulation. This could easily happen if cases were taken to the courts despite the fact the whole regime is supposed to be "voluntary."

What do the case studies show regarding this third institutional aspect? In essence, several of them show the detailed density and embeddedness of real implementation and thus lend credence to those who argue that traditional regulation and voluntary codes are more alike than they are different. In essence, they show that achieving desirable or publicly desired changes in human behaviour is indeed characterized by many kinds of concrete actions by public and private implementors. They also show that the key terminology used — regulations, guidelines, standards, codes — may in fact involve many kinds of norms and rules. A "regulation" may in fact be implemented as if it was a softer guideline. A "guideline" may in fact be implemented with a regulation-like hard edge of enforcement. Moreover, the range and mix of policy instruments must be situated in a realistic "bottom-up" mapping of the inherent scope of the terrain to which the regulations/codes are purporting to apply.

Consider, for example, the Canadian Standards Association's Sustainable Forest Management Certification System, addressed by Rhone, Clarke and Webb.[38] What strikes the novice reader of this case is first the mind-boggling scope of the enterprise when seen from the perspective of the inherent physical spread of Canada's forest resources. To this picture, one adds the 450 organizations involved in the consultation process, the various ecological criteria at the heart of sustainable forest management, and the fact that one is concerned about long time frames and thus intergenerational behaviour. And all of this is nested in a set of current, largely provincial, laws, regulations and programs already governing the forestry sector.

It is little wonder, given the many multiple behaviours that it is hoped will be changed, that the case refers to the initiative as basically a guidelines approach that is voluntary, national in scope and consensus-based. But it also involves a certification

---

38. See Gregory T. Rhone, David Clarke and Kernaghan Webb, "Two Voluntary Approaches to Sustainable Forestry Practices," Chapter 9, below.

system with an auditing process that suggests something closer and more specific and that, accordingly, sounds like regulation. Meanwhile, all the organizations and firms that might voluntarily seek to be recognized as a certified practitioner of the new code already function within a system of real legislation and regulations.

The point to be emphasized in painting the above portrait of the sustainable forestry case is not to be critical of the initiative, as such. Anything of such an immense policy scope cannot help but take such a multi-instrument, multistakeholder approach and then seek to advance the cause of sustainable development in many ways.

A key feature of the forestry case and its implementation issues is that we are looking at the case in its early days and attempting to visualize what might happen in a longer term future. A general conclusion to emerge from a discussion of instruments and implementation is that the private institutional administrator of codes is likely to have, in the first instance, a similar array of instruments to that of the traditional regulator. But this does not mean that it can or will behave like a traditional regulator. For example, with respect to sanctions and therefore actual legitimate coercive powers, the private administrator is likely to be weaker, in part because it will find it hard to bring actions against its own members. In the final analysis this is because it is not a part of the State.

Budget and Personnel Cuts and Technical Capacity

The relationship between budget and personnel cuts and the technical capacity to carry out agreed public tasks presents a "catch-22" situation regarding voluntary codes and traditional regulation. This is because the severity of public sector budget and personnel cuts in the last decade is one of the key factors why voluntary codes and other types of "reinvented regulation" are being advocated.[39] In other words, it is simply the case that the State can no longer do it alone and hence partnerships are essential. The "catch-22" is that many elements of the associative and interest group sector are also facing budget and personnel cuts. Indeed, in the case of the social interest group sector and the voluntary sector, these associations may not have had many staff to begin with and, moreover, what funds they had often came in crucial proportions from the State itself.[40] Thus, the fourth institutional aspect of budget and personnel cuts needs to be looked at in quite a careful way. Consider first some basic features of this aspect when applied to traditional regulation.

Internal regulatory agency capacity — that is, the ability to carry out regulatory tasks (its actual mix of functions) — is crucially a function of personnel. Regulatory agency budgets are not typically large but they are personnel-intensive. In the case of staffing, real capacity in turn depends also upon the availability of appropriate technical knowledge and the ability to attract people and maintain up-to-date competences. Hiring twice as many staff does not mean that a regulator can be twice as good at its job or catch

---

39. Phillips (footnote 20); J. Martin, *Regulating the Regulators: The Canadian Approach to Implementing Government-wide Regulatory Reform Strategies*, paper presented to the New South Wales Regulatory Review Conference, Sydney, Australia, June 20, 1995; R. Pildes and C. Sunstein, "Reinventing the Regulatory State," *The University of Chicago Law Journal* 62:1 (1995), pp. 1–129.

40. Phillips, ibid.

or prevent twice as many offences. But equally, any regulatory body requires some minimum basic capacity or it simply lacks credibility and a capacity to act.

A further crucial and long-known aspect of regulatory institutional behaviour is the importance of asymmetrical knowledge and information between the regulatory staff and the industries and associative communities being regulated.[41] This asymmetry almost always produces an enormous political advantage for the regulated. The regulator can simply never know as much as the regulated and this becomes a crucial basis for possible capture. Information asymmetry can also come in the form not just of technical superiority but also a capacity to inundate the regulator with information if need be. For the regulator, the only counterweight to this kind of *de facto* power of knowledge may well be the agency's capacity to exercise discretion and hence to wield the power inherent in the presence of such uncertainty. The regulator has this capacity by virtue of its legal ability to exercise the "authority" of the State.

Accordingly, the design of a regulatory body can involve situations in which ministers can confer on the regulator extensive authority but limited resources, more limited powers but quite extensive resources, and various combinations in between. These combinations can be altered as time goes on and thus represent the ability of Cabinets to "discipline" or "enable" the regulator, depending upon political judgments of the regulator's performance. For example, there are often serious constraints placed upon regulators in their ability to launch legal action when needed. Regulators and governments know that legal costs can be enormous, even when budgetary times are good, and that on an annual basis a small handful of cases could potentially "exhaust" their legal war chest.

While the above discussion has stressed the staffing side of the capacity equation, it should not be implied from this that budgets do not matter. Budget cuts can affect the ability of the regulator to do or commission research and to obtain information, as well as the capacity to hold hearings and obtain public input. The ability to transparently report case experiences and trends in a publicly accountable fashion can also be greatly harmed when budget cuts get too close to the bone.

When applied to a hypothesized greater reliance on voluntary codes administered by associative bodies of various kinds, the budgets and staffing issues suggest both advantages and problems. In principle, one might have access to a wider array of expertise from the associations involved. However, such expertise is unlikely to be engaged in any concerted way with only the work involved in ensuring that the code is implemented. The array of associative bodies will have their staff engaged primarily on those activities most crucial to their membership. The likelihood is strong that "voluntary code" administration will not only be voluntary but also that it will be implemented on a part-time or overtime basis.

The associative sector does of course vary in its capacities. Larger business groups and certainly many large firms may well be able to attach their new involvement in a code to their already large involvement in other traditional regulatory realms. For

---

41. M. Bernstein, *Regulating Business By Independent Commission* (Princeton, N.J.: Princeton University Press, 1955); T. Makkai and J. Braithwaite, "In and Out of the Revolving Door: Making Sense of Regulatory Capture," *Journal of Public Policy* 12:1 (January–March 1992), pp. 61–78; S. Harris, *The Political Economy of the Liberalization of Entry and Ownership in the Canadian Investment Dealer Industry*, unpublished doctoral dissertation (Department of Political Science, Carleton University, Ottawa, 1995).

associations without such a built-in capacity, the addition of the voluntary code simply adds one more impossible job to others with which it is already struggling to cope.

With regard to the case studies, it must first be said that their authors did not systematically focus on these budgetary and staffing cutback issues. However, some of the cases do contain observations that suggest that such cutbacks and issues of administrative capacity are important.

The case studies supply glimpses into just how far one must go to get an accurate picture of what administrative capacity means and what kind of a public/private implementation chain of relations is actually involved in regulation as compared to voluntary codes. For instance, in the case of Gap Inc.'s *Code of Vendor Conduct*, the *de facto* implementation and compliance chain stretches across the globe to Third World factories, intermediate suppliers, workers and unions, and associated "whistle blowers."[42]

A further aspect of budgets and voluntary codes is that costs may be spread differently in the separate realms of rule making and compliance. In the latter function, codes lead to costs being met more by affected parties than by general taxpayers. Thus, in the Responsible Care case study, each company paid for its own third-party compliance verification.[43]

The issue of budgets, personnel and technical capacity produces overall conflicting points regarding voluntary codes. On the one hand, the pressures of governmental budget cutting are among the more powerful reasons why codes are seen as necessary. On the other hand, the spending, personnel and other aspects of inherent technical capacity that private associations must have but often do not are too often ignored.

Overlapping Regimes in Regulation

The fifth and final institutional aspect is that of recognizing and dealing with the growing overlapping regimes of regulation inherent in the total world of the Canadian regulatory system.[44] The kind of overlap envisaged here is that which arises from the interactions that a traditional sectoral regulatory agency such as the Canadian Radio-television and Telecommunications Commission or the National Energy Board may have with an array of regulators whose mandates are horizontal or framework-oriented and that therefore in principle are intended to cut across sectors and not discriminate between sectors. Such realms are rarely as pure as this description suggests, but there is little doubt that these overlaps are of growing importance.

Again, one of the reasons why both firms and citizens are pushing for a greater reliance on voluntary codes and flexible regulation is that they have for a long time experienced regulation as a confusing morass.[45] They do not see their world as being one in which they face a neat, clear relationship with one or even two principal regulators.

---

42. See Rhone, Stroud and Webb, "Gap's Code of Conduct," Chapter 7, below.

43. See Moffet, Bregha and Middelkoop, "Responsible Care," Chapter 6, below.

44. Doern, Hill, Prince and Schultz (footnote 14).

45. Martin (footnote 39); T. O. McGarity, *Reinventing Rationality: The Role of Regulatory Analysis in the Federal Bureaucracy* (New York: Cambridge University Press, 1991).

Rather, they have experienced a plethora of regulators and rules emanating from several levels of government within Canada and increasingly from international bodies and agreements as well.[46] Several examples can be cited here, but the nature of the dynamics can be illustrated in three areas: competition regulation, environmental regulation, and the regulation of the professions and service quality.

Competition law and environmental regulation are arguably the most important recent manifestations of the broad overlap between sectoral and framework regulation, but there are other areas that many would include, such as tax laws and rules, trade and investment, consumer and product quality and safety, and banking and financial probity.[47] Both competition and environmental regulatory realms have crossed paths with sectoral regulatory realms, often in conflict and sometimes cooperatively.[48]

Competition regulators have often been restrained by statutory provisions that exempted several sectors from their jurisdiction. But a decade or more of privatization and deregulation has itself made more compelling the case that competition law should take precedence over sectoral regulators who may have only limited pro-competitive instincts or mandates.[49] On the other hand, the particular tools and time frames that might be applied by competition regulators might be quite inappropriate for the technical and political-economic realities of sectors such as energy or telecommunications.

Environmental regulators have been similarly restrained in the past and have often crossed swords with their sectoral brethren (and aligned interests). But the gradual articulation of sustainable development mandates in many governments has meant that the horizontal reach of green regulators is expanding, albeit in numerous particular forms and degrees in different countries.[50]

At this point one can simply observe that in these areas alone firms, citizens and the various regulators are dealing with multiple laws and rules that are intersecting in ways that governments are trying to sort out, or that firms and citizens are sorting out for them through court cases and myriad case-by-case compromises. Some of these responses may already be "code-like" in nature, in that the regulations range from hard rules to published guidelines to circulars suggesting how firms or people might behave.

At a quite different level, consider the overlap issues inherent in the regulation of professions and the public services they deliver. The extensive literature on the professions and on the regulation of quality suggests that there are four central cross-

---

46. D. Vogel, *Trading Up: Consumer and Environmental Regulation in a Global Economy* (Cambridge, Mass.: Harvard University Press, 1995); G. B. Doern, "A Political-Institutional Framework for the Analysis of Competition Policy Institutions," *Governance* 8:2 (April 1995), pp. 195–217.

47. J. Francis, *The Politics of Regulation: A Comparative Perspective* (Oxford: Blackwell, 1993); G. B. Doern and S. Wilks, eds., *Changing Regulatory Institutions in Britain and North America* (Toronto: University of Toronto Press, 1998).

48. P. Vass, "The Accountability of Regulators," in *Regulatory Review 1994* (London: Centre for the Study of Regulated Industries, 1994).

49. Doern and Wilks (footnote 47).

50. G. B. Doern and T. Conway, *The Greening of Canada: Federal Institutions and Decisions* (Toronto: University of Toronto Press, 1992); T. S. Gray, *UK Environmental Policy in the 1990s* (London: MacMillan, 1995); A. Weale, *The New Politics of Pollution* (Manchester: Manchester University Press, 1992); and G. Hoberg, *Pluralism By Design: Environmental Policy and the American Regulatory State* (New York: Praeger, 1993).

cutting socioeconomic principles or questions involved.[51] The first centres on the nature of the service involved. Professional/client relationships involve a highly individualized form of service geared to the client's specific needs and circumstances. The service also involves a technically sophisticated base of knowledge. And it involves extensive realms of professional judgment applied to specific case situations. Other key dilemmas of regulation flow from these service and relational characteristics.

The second question regarding professional services is that normal competitive markets as a "regulator" and traditional direct regulation by the State are both virtually impossible to employ in these circumstances.[52] Normal markets are difficult because there is no homogeneous product the price of which will provide appropriate market relations and signals. Each output or service is unique. For the same reason no regulator or regulatory commission can easily specify outputs and standards as a basis of direct regulation. It follows as well that clients of the professional service provider must place a considerable amount of social trust in the integrity and competence of the professional. Society, on the other hand, through its political institutions, will not likely allow unfettered trust. Trustworthiness will somehow have to be shown — i.e., "regulated."

A third issue of principle flows out of the trust relationship. It is that a professional culture and set of entrenched norms and principles (codes?) must be developed collectively by the profession though education and other ongoing mechanisms.[53] But individuals, and individualism, may break these norms. The client meanwhile must have almost perfect information about professional suppliers, a condition that rarely applies, and that therefore supplies one of the most broadly supported rationales for government regulation, rather than just codes or guidelines.

A fourth principled concern goes beyond service outputs and relates to the *quality* of outputs. Quality is not a simple concept. While it could simply be an attribute related to price or the basic presence or absence of value for money, quality can also extend to characteristics of technical ability, including such things as the ability to provide clear explanations to a layperson.[54]

Given these characteristics, only certain kinds of regulatory mechanisms or models become available and these initially involve choices about regulating inputs versus outputs and then choices about the extent of State regulation versus so-called self-regulation. Each has different advantages and disadvantages. Even the model referred to as "self-regulation" is in fact a form of delegated regulation. The key here, not surprisingly, is that in professional knowledge and service-delivery realms, the central

---

51. M. Trebilcock, "Regulating Service Quality in Professional Markets," in D. Dewees, ed., *The Regulation of Quality* (Toronto: Butterworths, 1983), pp. 83–108; R. D. Blair and S. Rubin, *Regulating the Professions* (London: DC Heath, 1980); T. Stevenson, "Regulation, Deregulation, Self-Regulation: The Case of Engineers in Ontario," *Journal of Business Ethics* 4 (August 1985), pp. 253–267.

52. D. Dewees, ed., *The Regulation of Quality* (Toronto: Butterworths, 1983), Chapter 1.

53. J. Shapland, *Self-Regulation of the Professions: Coercion or Free Choice*, paper presented to the Conference on Regulating the Professions, University of Strathclyde, Glasgow, April 20–21, 1995; C. Tuohy and A. Wolfson, "Self-Regulation: Who Qualifies?" in P. Slayton and M. Trebilcock, eds., *The Professions and Public Policy* (Toronto: University of Toronto Press, 1978), pp. 111–122.

54. Trebilcock (footnote 51); R. Dingwall, *A Respectable Profession? Sociological and Economic Perspectives on the Regulation of Professional Services*, paper presented to the Conference on Regulating the Professions, University of Strathclyde, Glasgow, April 20–21, 1995.

relationships of "agency" are dual in nature: first between the professional and the client, and second between the profession and the State.

The overlap of these regimes — framework-versus-sectoral and social-versus-economic regulation — produces their own further version of a regulatory paradox. They have already produced the need for arrangements that often look like voluntary codes but are not necessarily called that. And they have led to various forms of partial enforcement and a search for new compliance approaches. But equally, they make the task of adding new or partial voluntary codes more and more complicated. They also produce probable losses in accountability, certainly in the sense that there will be no voters and parliamentary government involved, but also in that interest groups and associations will be hard pressed to figure out how their public and private responsibilities are connected and entangled.

Some of the case studies reflect the presence of overlapping regulatory regimes but not necessarily in the form of a head-to-head collision with two sets of rules — one framework and the other sectoral. Rather, several of the cases involve the application of a framework regulatory regime that then confronts facts and complexities that are either peculiar to a specific sector or are simply resisted or amended by that sector's interests and views. This can occur either at the stage at which rules are being established or amended or through various kinds of accommodation during implementation.

A high proportion of the voluntary codes examined in this volume involve consumer regulation and issues.[55] In broad terms, the various kinds of consumer law are framework in nature, in that they are intended to ensure that all sectors of the economy are characterized by fair and open market practices, adequate information and forms of redress for consumers when things go wrong. But while designed to be sector-neutral, the practical politics of each application of the law or the regulations may be sector-specific. For example, there are specific regimes for helmets and for privacy.

Inevitably, each sector will have its own peculiarities and special circumstances, not only among the producer interests but also among the various kinds of consumers. The practical technical/physical features of the consumer end product or the production process that produces it will also be different. Many of the voluntary codes examined in this volume bring out some of these basic sectoral features, which must inevitably "bend" the nominal framework or horizontal nature of rules into a series of regulatory pretzels.

But there is even more to the overlap than this. The case studies tell the story from the starting point of a particular statute, regulation or voluntary code (in these cases, consumer-related). But, because of their brevity, the authors of the case studies cannot possibly fill in the rest of the real-world picture, which is that these sectors already, or in addition, have several other aspects of governmental regulation impacting upon them, some directly sectoral, and others still *other* kinds of framework law.

---

55. See Rhone, Stroud and Webb, "Gap's Code of Conduct," Chapter 7, below; Colin J. Bennett, "Privacy Self-Regulation in a Global Economy: A Race to the Top, the Bottom or Somewhere Else?" Chapter 8, below; Rhone, Clarke and Webb, "Sustainable Forestry Practices," Chapter 9, below; Harrison, "Canada's Environmental Choice Program," Chapter 10, below; Morrison and Webb, " Helmet Standards and Regulations," Chapter 11, below.

Conclusions

This chapter has examined a set of five institutional and public administrative aspects of the use of voluntary codes. These institutional aspects must be considered along with the legal, economic and other aspects of codes examined in other chapters. The five selected institutional aspects are by no means the only ones that could have been selected but anyone seeking to understand the actual or potential role of voluntary codes does need to appreciate each of the five aspects. Parliamentary accountability, the democratic basis of associational politics, the nature of policy implementation and mixes of policy instrument choice, the impact of budget and personnel cuts, and the effects of overlapping regulatory regimes are each important in their own right.

It must also be said that it is not difficult to see that it is at times quite artificial to analyze each of the five institutional elements separately. They are not entirely watertight categories of analysis or of the expression of important democratic values. Moreover, the chapter has necessarily discussed them in a somewhat polarized manner by differentiating between stylized notions of traditional regulation versus voluntary codes. The case studies are a useful antidote for any such analytical tendencies. Though not fully designed to fit the particular questions posed by this chapter, the case studies do offer important insights into some of the issues raised above, as well as others that were not the focal point of this chapter but that other academic and practitioner perspectives are concerned about.

Perhaps the largest institutional and public administrative picture to emerge from the chapter as a whole is that of a government presiding over two broad clusters of rule makers and compliance organizations: one that the government regulates itself and in which it has direct contacts with regulatees, and one in which it oversees, in some less clear and indirect fashion, a set of self-regulators and code administrators that have the direct relationship with the persons and interests affected by the code. In this regard the growing voluntary codes regime can be seen as a natural "bottom-up" construction of systems of rules and guidelines that simply complements the more formal State-centred regime. Hence, according to this view, a voluntary codes regime is desirable and necessary in an increasingly complex society and economy.

However, it is inappropriate to leave the issues involved at this level of approving generality. The questions that need constantly to be posed and empirically examined all centre on the key middle-level aspects explored in this chapter.

Concerns about accountability are crucial, but both the conceptual analysis and the case studies show that there are many competing notions of accountability, including those informed by traditions of parliamentary government and those that see accountability extending outwards to interest groups, citizens and markets.

The more extended the accountability chain to private or quasi-private realms of "governance," the more likely the spotlight will fall on the nature of associational democracy and, eventually, on the administrative capacity and fairness of firms, associations and groups of associations acting in concert. Thus a greater use of voluntary codes may well suggest a world of fewer State bureaucrats, but it is unlikely to be a world of less bureaucracy if bureaucracy is understood to be rule-based governance.

The nature of actual implementation and the mix of policy instruments involved in both a world of regulation and a world of voluntary codes is often the institutional aspect least appreciated, or at least most overstereotyped. There is simply no avoiding in most realms of public policy a confusing but necessary multilayered set of instruments that range across a wide spectrum of enforcement and compliance. Such instruments include incentives, education, persuasion and voluntarism galore, but they also include actual enforcement and penalties or the fear of such actions. Voluntary codes may have strengths in the use of some of these instruments and hence help solve real problems, but they are likely to prove weak in other respects because associations will find it difficult to apply real sanctions to their own members.

The issue of budgetary and staffing cuts and capacities is important in the last decade because it is obvious that some suggestions for the greater use of voluntary codes and self-regulation are a direct result of the shrinking of the real State and hence the need to form a larger, para-public, quasi-State apparatus. However, budgetary and staffing capacities are in fact a larger issue in that the private sector writ large will be the "administrators" of the elongated voluntary code chain of behaviour. Thus, not only the size of the resource commitment private interests make but also its detailed competence and procedural capacity will assume greater importance.

And finally, the overlap of regulatory regimes is important in any rigorous account of governance through codes. Many of the case studies in fact dealt with framework regulatory starting points and concerns, but the actual implementation of these rules runs headlong into the specific features of sectors, with sectors themselves being as broad as the forestry industry or as narrow as the hockey helmet industry. These interlocking worlds make the demand for more voluntary codes perfectly understandable. But equally, they make the prospect of clear, narrowly defined accountability utterly impossible.

Chapter 4
The Political Economy of Voluntary Codes

Bryne Purchase

Introduction

Aristotle noted that humans are political animals. Adam Smith, on the other hand, saw that individuals have a propensity to "truck, barter and exchange."[1] Both manifestations of human existence imply social interaction, with the former oriented to collective or group action and the latter focussed on bilateral exchange from an individualist perspective. The study of human civilizations might then proceed as the specialist study of politics or of economics. And in large measure it has done so. The study of political economy, however, acknowledges the close interrelation of the two.

Indeed, Thomas Hobbes argued that life in a state of nature, without the rule of law, would be "nasty, brutish and short."[2] The same might be said of markets without rules. Hence a role for the nation-state. Accordingly, many, if not most, of the rules governing private exchange are now supplied through the collective apparatus of the State and are maintained by the State's continuing political legitimacy. The rules, and the processes for making and enforcing them, are a public good.[3]

It has been a long, evolutionary process, but this formalized, government-supplied framework of law has proven to be enormously productive. Whatever their pitfalls and frailties, the rules governing private property, liability and contract are central to the growth of market societies.[4] It is this formal institutional infrastructure that formerly communist and other bureaucratic and autocratic societies now hope to emulate.

Where then does the political economy of voluntary codes enter the picture? There are two broad issues. The first is the question of the degree to which voluntary codes are a good substitute for — and perhaps even to be preferred to — the more formal rules produced by the State. Or, to put it more prescriptively, what set of circumstances and procedures gives legitimacy and efficacy to a set of rules by which otherwise free individuals or organizations will voluntarily consent to be governed? Most of this chapter is directed at examining the answers to this question.

---

1. Aristotle, *Nicomachean Ethics*, T. Irwin, trans. (New York: Hackett Publishing Company, 1985), Book 1, Chapter 7, 1.1097b10; A. Smith, *An Inquiry into the Nature and Causes of the Wealth of Nations* (1776) (London: Oxford University Press, 1997), Book 1, Chapter 2.

2. T. Hobbes, *Leviathan* (1651), R. Tuck, ed., (Cambridge: Cambridge University Press, 1996), Part i, Chapter xiii.

3. Laws and regulations and their enforcement provide a general benefit in that they reduce transaction costs and facilitate production and exchange. They are a public good in the formal sense that, once supplied, they are *non-rival* and *non-exclusive*. *Non-rival* refers to the fact that their consumption by one person leaves no less available to another. (This ignores the congestion problem in the courts.) *Non-exclusive* refers to the fact that once the public good is produced, it is technically impossible or prohibitively expensive to exclude anyone from consuming it.

4. See, e.g., N. Rosenberg and L. E. Birdzell, *How The West Grew Rich* (New York: Basic Books, 1986).

Kernaghan Webb, Editor, *Voluntary Codes: Private Governance, the Public Interest and Innovation.*
This chapter ©2004 Bryne Purchase, pages 77–96.
Published by the Carleton Research Unit for Innovation, Science and Environment, Carleton University, Ottawa, Canada.

The second issue is the degree to which State intervention might be invoked in any case. This consideration is somewhat more in the vein of traditional theories of political economy. Of course, such theories are usually meant to explain, not prescribe. But we might still take a normative perspective to outlining the ways in which the State can support the development of effective voluntary codes. The last section of this chapter addresses the role of government as a catalyst to private code formation. It also acknowledges that, inevitably, voluntary codes are not simply a substitute for more formal government action, but also a complement to the existing framework of law.

Voluntary Codes as a Substitute for State Rules

The Efficacy of State Supply

The State's Competitive Advantage

The efficiency and effectiveness of a group in supplying rules to its members or constituents typically depend on its abilities to both accurately determine group preferences on the one hand, and to efficiently administer to or serve those interests on the other. In short, there is both a demand-side and a supply-side measure of group efficiency and effectiveness. The key issue, with both demand- and supply-side implications, is the group's ability to cope with free-rider problems.[5]

The free rider can benefit without paying, or impose costs on others without giving compensation. It is the same generic problem as that which afflicts commonly held resources. But it is a more widespread phenomenon than many would recognize. It is not restricted to the uses of air, water or fish. For example, we are all "known by the company we keep." The dishonest businessman gains from the credibility established by his honest competitors, but does not compensate the group for its loss of credibility as a result of his own dishonesty. And, in the current context, the chemical companies that developed the Responsible Care[6] program recognized that they all suffered a loss of public confidence as a result of the environmentally irresponsible actions of the few. Rules are usually meant to restrain such behaviours — "externalities" in the lexicon of economics — and lead to more efficient markets and, in general, more productive human relations.

Democratic governments have been preferred suppliers of rules and regulations (laws) because they have a monopoly on the legitimate power to incarcerate those who do not comply with them. And, at least until recently, they have been able to raise the financial resources necessary to undertake monitoring and to enforce compliance when necessary.[7] As well, nation-states typically span wide geographic areas and encompass

---

5. Free riding, the ability to benefit without paying, is always possible when public goods, as defined above, are concerned. Free riders can exploit the non-exclusive properties of such goods to gain access to the benefits and avoid the costs. They do this by simply cheating or not revealing their true preferences.

6. See John Moffet, François Bregha and Mary Jane Middelkoop, "Responsible Care: A Case Study of a Voluntary Environmental Initiative," Chapter 6, below.

7. The ability to tax so effectively stems, in part, from the same legitimized coercive potential.

large populations. The result is a significant competitive advantage, compared to other groups, in dealing with free riders. And that, in turn, has led to a remarkable expansion of State regulatory activities over the past 50 years.

Limitations to State Supply

On the other hand, nation-states, or their responsible sub-jurisdictions, are limited in their regulatory range to their own geographic areas. If the perceived problems (for example, environmental degradation or abuse of human, labour or animal rights) extend beyond these boundaries, then governments must negotiate treaties or other institutional arrangements to address them. These formal agreements between governments, in whatever bilateral or multilateral context, can be time-consuming to negotiate, complicated by many other side issues, and expensive to implement. Non-governmental initiatives, however, might be quickly extended across national boundaries and focussed on a single behaviour, product or set of producers. Examples are found in the case studies on Responsible Care, Gap Inc.'s support of certain international labour standards and the Canadian forest industry's response to European boycott initiatives.[8]

The financial capacity of the State is now also constrained in a manner that significantly reduces its competitive advantage in monitoring and enforcement. Most governments are less inclined to employ the resources necessary for effective monitoring of a huge regulatory structure. And the State is equally less inclined to commit the investigative and legal resources necessary to enforce regulations in the courts, or even to supply the judicial apparatus. And lack of enforcement has opened the door to liability suits against government. To some degree this has been offset by the increased use of direct user fees and charge-backs. On the other hand, the voluntary code represents the potential to move all regulatory costs onto those being regulated.[9]

At the same time, the State has in general suffered a secular decline in its legitimacy or credibility in dealing with collective problems. In Canada, the evident dissatisfaction of voters with incumbent governments, the wide ideological swings in voting patterns, the growth of tax evasion and avoidance and, in terms of public opinion, the steady decline in the perceived trustworthiness of politicians, all point to this conclusion. The implication of declining legitimacy is that the State now gets less voluntary compliance, whereas the efficacy of the voluntary code is premised on a high level of voluntary compliance.

Moreover, the form of regulation most frequently chosen by the State (command and control) stifles innovation, imposes unnecessary costs and is not well suited to an environment of rapid technological or economic change. This has also helped to undermine the apparent efficacy of regulation by the State. To the degree that voluntary code arrangements are more outcome-oriented and more flexible over time, they may prove a superior alternative. Similarly, State regulation of general application,

---

8. See Moffet, Bregha and Middelkoop, "Responsible Care," Chapter 6, below; Gregory T. Rhone, John Stroud and Kernaghan Webb, "Gap's Code of Conduct for Treatment of Overseas Workers," Chapter 7, below; Gregory T. Rhone, David Clarke and Kernaghan Webb, "Two Voluntary Approaches to Sustainable Forestry Practices," Chapter 9, below.

9. As is well known, the vast bulk of regulatory cost is already borne by the regulated.

for example in respect of information privacy, is a compromise that may not fit the needs of each industry sector precisely. By contrast, the voluntary code can be tailored to fit the unique circumstances of each sector.[10]

All of these things suggest that non-State collective action may reassert itself as a more efficient and effective alternative, at least under certain circumstances. Much depends, as before, on the ability of these new collectives to discern a "group" preference and to control free riding. It is to these issues that we now turn.[11]

Alternatives to the State

Notwithstanding the pervasiveness of the modern regulatory State, the State has never supplied all the rules in any area of human interaction. There have always been private groups, clubs, cooperatives, leagues or associations in which people voluntarily submit to a code of conduct, whether formal or informal, governing the group. And, for the most part, these are legitimate and viable alternatives to government action. For example, the cooperative movement is, at least in part, a non-governmental response to the problem of monopoly power.

In terms of commercial rules governing exchange, sellers and traders have historically been quite prepared to restrict their behaviour in order to enhance their market. The craft guild — the medieval precursor to the modern professional association — provided the buyer with a certain measure of quality assurance.[12] The *lex mercatoria* was a private system of commercial law and dispute resolution (outside the established church law) established by merchants and administered by independent judges.[13]

The modern development of product standards organizations, bonding and certification procedures, alternative dispute resolution mechanisms and voluntary codes for regulatory purposes should be seen as a continuation of a long historical evolution of non-governmental efforts to establish credibility in the marketplace. Even if they are far from perfect institutions, markets are capable of producing some of their own self-governing mechanisms.

---

10. See, for example, Colin J. Bennett, "Privacy Self-Regulation in a Global Economy: A Race to the Top, the Bottom or Somewhere Else?" Chapter 8, below.

11. If there is a broad general literature that is applicable to the process of negotiating voluntary codes and of implementing them, it is perhaps that related to the general workings and processes of democratic governments. While it is not governments that are to supply the rules in these circumstances, much can be learned from the experience of governments as alternate suppliers. Potentially relevant literature is that related to the theory of clubs, game theory and the origins of the State.

12. In fact the rules of the typical guild went far beyond prescribing the standards of training and technology to be employed by the craft members. They often prescribed detailed standards of personal behaviour as well. See R. Heilbroner, *The Making of Economic Society,* 4th ed. (Englewood Cliffs, N.J.: Prentice Hall, 1972).

13. See P. Milgrom, D. North and B. Weingast, "The Role of Institutions in the Revival of Trade: The Medieval Law Merchant," *Economics and Politics* 2 (March 1990), pp. 1–23.

The Viability of Voluntary Codes

Introduction

This section outlines two sets of considerations for assessing the viability of voluntary codes. The first is simply to consider those industry circumstances that are most conducive to the effective formation and operation of a voluntary code regime. The second is to outline the types of institutional structures that will enhance the operation of the voluntary code, both with respect to making codes and to enforcing them.

General Considerations

Why do industry groups form to agree to restrain their individual behaviours — that is, to produce voluntary codes? One thing is certain: it is always a commercial benefit that is anticipated. Usually it is some benefit that cannot fully or satisfactorily be achieved by each acting alone. One or more of the following purposes typically play a role:

- to gain consumer confidence and trust;
- to forestall consumer collective actions (boycotts);
- to forestall adverse, or to promote desired, political interventions; and
- to restrain trade.

As noted above, a key determinant of group effectiveness is the group's ability to control free riders. How is that achieved? On the one hand, it is best pursued by employing strategies designed to enhance voluntary compliance and, on the other, by having effective monitoring and enforcement mechanisms to deal with non-compliance. Both are reviewed below.

In general, free-rider problems grow as the size of the group necessary for effective action grows (in terms of numbers of firms or persons to which the rules apply). There are two reasons for this.[14] One, as noted above, is that there are more diverse opinions on the appropriate content of the rules and therefore greater difficulty in reaching consensus. In addition, however, as the group increases in size there are increased opportunities and/or incentives to cheat.[15]

---

14. M. Olson, *The Logic of Collective Action* (Cambridge, Mass.: Harvard University Press, 1965). See also, P. Dunleavy, *Democracy, Bureaucracy and Public Choice: Economic Explanations in Political Science* (London: Harvester Wheatsheaf, 1991); D. C. Mueller, *Public Choice II, A Revised Edition of Public Choice* (Cambridge: Cambridge University Press, 1989); J. M. Buchanan, "An Economic Theory of Clubs," *Economica* 32 (February 1965), pp. 1–14; J. M. Buchanan and G. Tullock, *The Calculus of Consent* (Ann Arbor, Mich.: University of Michigan Press, 1962); A. O. Hirschman, *Exit, Voice, and Loyalty* (Cambridge, Mass.: Harvard University Press, 1970).

15. Large group size produces anonymity and makes monitoring more difficult. It also diminishes the incentive to cooperate, since each individual's contribution is not essential to the group's effectiveness (thereby increasing the perceived opportunities to free ride).

Conversely, the ability to control free riding, and therefore the efficacy of voluntary codes, increases as on the supply side:

- there are fewer industry players;
- they are aware of each other's behaviour and can detect non-compliance;
- they have a history of effective cooperative action;

while on the demand side:

- consumers value compliant behaviour;
- consumers can identify compliant firms;
- there are many repeat transactions; and
- non-compliant behaviour can be punished.[16]

In short, much depends on the ability of peers or consumers to identify and to punish non-compliant behaviour or to reward compliance.

Stakeholder Participation

Legitimacy Through Consent

Despite the considerable coercive power of democratic governments, they rely heavily on consent and voluntary compliance. Such governments must continuously legitimize their power by keeping coercion to a minimum. This requires accurately gauging the public preference. Democracies employ a number of institutional devices to ensure this reading of the public will — for example, free speech, universal suffrage, elections, one-person-one-vote, majority rule, parliament and political competition.[17]

Even in their activities between elections, governments are cognizant of the demand side of their operations. For example, consensus mechanisms and widespread public consultations are now considered an essential part of good regulatory practice. The Canadian federal government has produced an extensive range of guidebooks to assist departments with regulatory functions.[18] They are highly informative on the basics of the efficient and effective supply of regulation by government agencies. Public consultation and feedback and the development of consensus is an essential service quality.

Effectiveness Through Consensus

Consent is the most effective form of governance, since it is most likely to lead to controlled behaviour, even when formal monitoring and enforcement mechanisms are weak or ineffectual. By contrast, non-consensual decision making, while technically possible for governments, increases the potential for grievance. And the more widespread

---

16. Of course, the potential for government action can, in part, be substituted for these conditions.

17. This is not to imply that there is anything about these institutions that is perfect, either in part or in whole, or that cannot be improved. But that is not the issue here.

18. See, e.g., Treasury Board of Canada Secretariat, *Federal Regulatory Process Management Standards Compliance Guide*, available at <www.pco-bcp.gc.ca/raoics-srdc/docs/publications/rpms_e.pdf>.

and the more intense the feelings of grievance, the more difficult it is to control behaviour. As democratic theory and institutional practice imply, participation and effective voice in the rule-making process is one way to increase the likelihood of consent.[19]

Therefore, consent is also highly cost-effective, once it has been achieved. There are, of course, potentially large up-front costs in this approach, especially when there are a large number of players with widely differing perspectives. But these development costs have to be balanced against the higher operating costs of monitoring and enforcing rules when consensus has not been achieved.

Industry Participation

Who then should be involved in the production of voluntary codes?[20] Perhaps the only definitive conclusion is that, at a minimum, participation should include all those without whom the code would be inoperative or ineffectual. That is something of a truism. But it is a useful reminder of the need for flexibility in each specific circumstance.

Effectiveness is a function of both coverage and credibility. The two are interrelated but each can be examined in turn. For example, if a code dealing with industry environmental or selling practices does not involve a large part of an industry, then it is unlikely to be judged a viable regulatory effort. Therefore, participation representing a substantial industry market share would seem to be a precondition of success.

This precondition in turn demands that the process of setting the codes and determining their enforcement procedures must be highly consensual among producers — that is, among those whose behaviour is to be modified. In the case of Responsible Care, unanimity was required for the large players in the industry association (at least at the beginning).[21] Of course, unanimity is a demanding decision rule, even among producers. It would become totally impractical as more external interests and perspectives were involved in code development.

How then should one proceed? Again, the key determinant is effectiveness. Even governments do not operate on the basis of unanimity. But neither can they always be operating with 51 percent majorities. The balance must be struck somewhere between a simple majority and unanimity — perhaps 75 percent.[22]

---

19. See D. T. Miller, *Psychological Factors Influencing Compliance: Final Report*, Study for the Federal Statutes Compliance Project, Department of Justice Canada (Vancouver: Vancouver Psychology and Law Institute, Simon Fraser University, 1985).

20. See, e.g., *Building Consensus for a Sustainable Future: Guiding Principles, An Initiative Undertaken by Canadian Roundtables* (Roundtables on the Environment and Economy in Canada, August 1993). This guide sets out 10 principles for consensus processes: purpose driven, inclusive not exclusive, voluntary participation, self-design, flexibility, equal opportunity, respect for diverse interests, accountability, time limits and implementation.

21. See Moffet, Bregha and Middelkoop, "Responsible Care," Chapter 6, below.

22. This is simply offered as a numeric benchmark, not a rule. When it comes to producers this need only apply to the share of the market they represent, if the primary purpose is to serve the need for wide coverage.

External Stakeholders

The wider the interests represented in the development of a code, the greater the credibility and legitimacy the code is likely to acquire. Each group added may bring a different element of credibility to the table. For example, academics and others may add an "independent perspective," whereas still other participants will represent the view of specific interests or constituencies — such as consumers, labour, environmentalists and rights activists. This broader representation, or multistakeholder participation, is particularly crucial if the code is being developed to forestall punishing retaliations by others, such as consumer boycotts or draconian State intervention (domestic or foreign).

If a group is intent on forestalling government action, then obviously it would be wise to include all groups that have political salience on the issue at hand. At times, the State itself may strongly recommend the involvement of outside interests.[23] And, inevitably, if governments actively promote the use of voluntary codes, they will, to satisfy their own imperatives, have to *ensure* the involvement of a wide range of interests.

For example, in the forest industry case, external credibility is absolutely essential to the industry purposes. The Canadian Standards Association's involvement in, and its use of, multistakeholder consensus mechanisms to develop codes of conduct for sustainable forest development, with credible enforcement procedures, is all an attempt to forestall commercial penalties.[24] Hence the degree of non-industry group participation and the level of enforcement contemplated is well beyond what even most State regulations would entail. To some extent the Gap Inc. case is similar in that there was a need to gain credibility with a wide audience — although the code and its enforcement procedures are much less fully developed than they are in the forest industry case.[25]

In other cases, neither consumers nor the State may be involved. Consumers, for example, may not represent a credible collective threat either economically or politically.[26] In some instances external advocacy groups may be impossible to involve, since they are opposed to the product or industry itself — as would be the case for some groups in respect of codes pertaining to the tobacco industry or animal fur industry.

As a practical matter, the more perspectives and interests that have to be accommodated, the more time consuming and costly the process. This is the balancing factor that has to be considered. Credibility comes from a more encompassing group, but it is purchased at the price of a more time-consuming and demanding process. There is an optimum number of disparate interests, but it will surely vary from situation to situation.

---

23. See Neil Gunningham, "Codes of Practice: The Australian Experience," Chapter 12, below.

24. See Rhone, Clarke and Webb, "Sustainable Forestry Practices," Chapter 9, below.

25. See Rhone, Stroud and Webb, "Gap's Code of Conduct," Chapter 7, below.

26. See Gunningham, "The Australian Experience," Chapter 12, below; Gregory T. Rhone, *Canadian Tobacco Manufacturers' Council Tobacco Industry Voluntary Packaging and Advertising Code*, a draft case study prepared for the Voluntary Codes Symposium, Ottawa, 1996, available in summary at <http://strategis.ic.gc.ca/epic/internet/inoca-bc.nsf/en/ca00880e.html>.

Moreover, the development of a voluntary code initiative does not have to begin as an all-encompassing exercise. Group participation may expand over time to reflect the need for greater credibility as the ambitions of the group expand. Similarly, the group may contract as participants self-select on the basis of their continuing contributions or interests.

Procedural Rules and Processes

The literature on voluntary agreements suggests that there is no one right procedure. Typically it will involve face-to-face negotiations. And, in general, the procedures should be designed by the participants, and the process should be subject to time limits.[27] The multistakeholder group should also begin with clear objectives. But from there, many suggest using the techniques of "principled negotiation" to hammer out an agreement.[28] Principled negotiation is based on the following principles:

- separate the people from the problem;
- focus on interests not positions;
- search for commonly agreed external benchmarks; and
- problem solve.

Another procedural complication may be the question of designating individuals who are duly empowered to negotiate on behalf of a group. No particular rules arise here, except that conventional practice would provide the designate with a basic mandate to negotiate, with frequent recourse back to the group for debriefing and further instruction. And normally the group would wish to reserve the right to vote on any code at the completion of the code development phase.

The building of consensus must move from shared information to shared understanding to shared goals. This is not always easy. It requires convergence of perspective. That in turn will often require that groups be willing to be "educated" together. For example, they may need to compile some basic data and assess certain "factual" information. And they will have to establish a process by which this is to be accomplished. Very often even so-called scientific information is contentious, with respect to both the frequency of an occurrence and its impact. For example, the standards of epidemiological studies are constantly being contested as an insufficient basis for decision making. And it is easy, as the courts and tribunals have demonstrated, to fall into the trap of the "duelling experts."

There are also differing attitudes towards assessments of risk.[29] People have differing tastes for risk and differing perceptions of both the frequency and the consequences of an event. They also have different perspectives on risks they willingly assume and the same quantum of risk that is imposed upon them. But very often there is

---

27. See L. E. Susskind and J. Cruikshank, *Breaking The Impasse: Consensual Approaches to Solving Public Disputes* (New York: Basic Books, 1987).

28. See R. Fisher and W. Ury, *Getting to YES: Negotiating Agreement Without Giving In* (Markham, Ont.: Penguin Books, 1981).

29. See, e.g., W. Leiss and C. Chociolko, *Risk and Responsibility* (Montréal: McGill-Queen's University Press, 1994).

not enough experience to even measure risk. Or, the interplay of human and technological factors that are involved is so complex as to make an objective assessment impossible.[30]

Issues dealing with health and safety are particularly subject to deeply divided perspectives. Even for formal political institutions, life and death issues such as capital punishment, euthanasia and abortion continue to be the most fundamentally divisive and potentially destructive to the collectivity. It is extremely difficult to gain a high level of consensus on these issues. Nonetheless, more and more experiments are being conducted to determine "public" preferences involving risk to health and life. These public preferences have been used to operationalize government budget constraints in such areas as publicly funded health insurance coverage. The most commonly cited are those in Oregon.

The use of outside or independent professional services is sometimes required to assist in establishing the code. This may take the form of a facilitator or mediator, or even an arbitrator. They not only facilitate negotiation but also may add credibility to the process. The services and procedures of a standards organization may be particularly useful in this regard.[31] No doubt this is what attracted the forest industry to this route. A facilitator was also useful in the early development of Responsible Care.[32]

Compliance

Obviously, for a rule-making body to be effective requires an effective compliance strategy. This section reviews some considerations with respect to monitoring, enforcement and dispute resolution.

Monitoring

For most programs it can be expected that voluntary compliance is the primary form of compliance. In short, the participants will engage in self-monitoring and self-restraint. Again the effectiveness of this depends very much on the degree of commitment that can be generated around the code and the effectiveness of the deterrents to free riding outlined above. In general, voluntary compliance is increased if regulatees:[33]

- perceive rules to be fair;
- perceive monitoring and enforcement to be fair;
- know and understand the rules; and
- are committed and feel personally responsible.

---

30. J. Martin and C. Iwankow, *The Canadian Government Perspective on Cost-Effective Regulation* (Fredericton, N.B.: Joint Meeting of the Canadian Nuclear Association and the Canadian Nuclear Safety Society, June 1996).

31. See Rhone, Clarke and Webb, "Sustainable Forestry Practices," Chapter 9, below.

32. See Rhone, Clarke and Webb, ibid.; Bennett, "Privacy Self-Regulation," Chapter 8, below; Moffet, Bregha and Middelkoop, "Responsible Care," Chapter 6, below.

33. This list draws on the study by Miller (footnote 19).

However, code enforcement will be more effective, and therefore more credible, the more easily compliance can be monitored by others. This can be assured by having independent groups monitor compliance. Again, the effectiveness of monitoring is enhanced if non-compliant behaviour is easily detected. The more information and transparency there is with respect to the actions of the regulatee, the easier it is to detect non-compliance.

Monitoring is also more effective if there is a self-interest in effective monitoring. For example, consumers can be effective monitors. However, there are two conditions for this to apply. Consumers must be able to identify non-compliance and there must be a clear benefit to consumers from compliant behaviour by the producer. In the case of Gap Inc.'s stores, the labour union was an effective monitor, at least to a point, since it wanted to protect the jobs of American workers.[34] Competitors can sometimes be effective monitors (if they fear some adverse effect of non-compliance on them). And non-governmental organizations or interest groups may also participate actively in monitoring compliance.

Enforcement

Individual compliance is typically enhanced if the regulatee perceives that there are costs to non-compliance and benefits for compliance. Accordingly, the effectiveness of a voluntary code is enhanced when there are clear benefits that accrue only to those conforming to the code — that is, when there are "private" benefits. It is further enhanced if there are greater private benefits that accrue only to the most active or diligent members.[35] In each instance the opportunity and/or incentive to free ride is reduced.

The ability to identify good (compliant) behaviour and target rewards or penalties is very often a critical element to effective enforcement. Most strategies for the development of effective voluntary codes focus on these issues. For example, firms comply with various international or national industrial standards, even when they are not government-mandated, because there are commercial benefits to doing so. It is a form of product differentiation. The benefits accrue principally to the producers who abide by the code (provided that the added costs of compliance are less than the net revenues from increased sales).

But, as emphasized above, for this to happen consumers have to be able to distinguish between those products that comply and those that do not. This implies some identification mark. As noted above, consumers also have to be aware of the benefits to them of a product's compliance with the standard. And they have to value these benefits sufficiently to buy only the compliant products. Hence the need for a publicity campaign to increase consumer awareness.

---

34. See Rhone, Clarke and Webb, "Sustainable Forestry Practices," Chapter 9, below.

35. The Canadian Chemical Producers' Association (CCPA) has done some work on the commercial benefits that accrue to firms that comply with the Responsible Care code. See CCPA, *Does Responsible Care Pay? A Primer on the Unexpected Benefits of the Initiative* (Ottawa: CCPA, 1996).

The same logic can be applied to the voluntary code. This is why the development of well-publicized logos or other identification marks is so important.[36] There are important advantages in this approach. For example, it can facilitate the consensual development of very stringent standards, often more stringent than could otherwise be achieved. If there are commercial benefits from these they are then available only to those who comply. For example, the development of a certification process for a designated forest allows a firm to differentiate its products in the marketplace. This reduces the free-rider potential in such initiatives. Publicity campaigns enhance the value of the logo and further reduce free riding.

There are other ways to target non-compliance. For example, there is the threat of commercial loss from boycotts and negative publicity targeted at a single distributor. The target may, in turn, expand the coverage to its suppliers. To ensure supplier compliance, Gap Inc., for example, is prepared to cease buying from an offending factory.[37] Non-compliance with a voluntary code may also open a firm to legal liability from lack of due diligence, or to increased insurance costs.[38] It is common practice for insurance companies to require certain conforming behaviours in order to be eligible for lower premiums or even to get coverage. If so, this could enhance the effectiveness of voluntary codes because it implies a targeted penalty for non-compliance.

Mass boycotts can be an effective penalty if there are a large number of like-minded consumers. Of course, collective consumer action in the form of a boycott gives rise to the same generic problems as collective action among producers. In the case of consumers, however, this is compounded by their typically larger numbers. Moreover, consumer boycotts are not a wholly effective way to pursue environmental or "rights" objectives.[39] They imply that some consumers would be willing to pay to avoid environmental degradation or the abuse of "rights," while others might free ride.[40]

A more effective incentive may be the threat of government action. But now the producer group still has to overcome a free-rider problem — since some firms may not comply, but still benefit from the absence of government action. In the case of Responsible Care, they appear to have done this very much through the effect of peer pressure.[41]

---

36. See Kathryn Harrison, "Promoting Environmental Protection through Eco-Labelling: An Evaluation of Canada's Environmental Choice Program," Chapter 10, below.

37. See Rhone, Clarke and Webb, "Sustainable Forestry Practices," Chapter 9, below.

38. See Kernaghan Webb and Andrew Morrison, "The Law and Voluntary Codes: Examining the 'Tangled Web'," Chapter 5, below.

39. See Harrison, "Canada's Environmental Choice Program," Chapter 10, below.

40. There is an obvious tension here between the notion of a free rider and the individual who simply has a different set of values or a different perspective. It may be difficult to be certain when controlling free riders is not simply an exercise in coercion.

41. See Moffet, Bregha and Middelkoop, "Responsible Care," Chapter 6, below. Membership in the Canadian Chemical Producers' Association is now also conditional on compliance with Responsible Care. To the degree that there are private benefits from participation in the Association, this will act as a deterrent to non-compliant behaviour.

Indeed, peer pressure is a powerful motivating and disciplining force. In fact, peer pressure is the dominant compliance technique of most non-governmental groups.[42] It is only in comparison with the right to incarcerate people that it seems ineffectual. In this regard, there are many similarities between the formation of voluntary codes for business and effective religious organizations or movements. Indeed, adherence to the code may become almost a secular religion.[43] And its proponents often exhibit a missionary zeal. This zeal is typically reinforced by education and training programs to ensure that company staff and procedures are in accordance with the letter and spirit of the code.

Almost all group action is catalyzed and dominated by a few individuals with strong entrepreneurial or leadership qualities. Their entrepreneurship is not necessarily with respect to their commercial abilities but rather their abilities to mobilize collective activities. The entrepreneurs are very often deeply committed, articulate and charismatic leaders. Peer pressure may also be enhanced in the context of strong leadership from key individuals in a group.

Dispute Resolution

Rules inevitably lead to disputes. Accordingly, to implement voluntary codes, groups will need a process for settling disputes. There are numerous dispute resolution alternatives, including ombudsmen, mediation, arbitration and adjudication. Each has strengths and weaknesses. But the overriding consideration for institutional effectiveness is credibility. Again, credibility is enhanced to the degree that the process is independent, accessible and transparent. Independence would place the adjudication in the hands of a non-partisan judge or panel. Accessibility would increase to the degree that any group could bring a complaint. Transparency would ensure that reasons are published to explain the decisions of the adjudicators.

Furthermore, democratic theory and practice also suggest that dispute resolution procedures should conform to the standards of due process. In addition, compliance is most likely to be enhanced if the adjudication process attempts to fit the penalties to the offence and takes into account previous behaviour and the motivations of the regulatee.[44]

Financing

There is also the issue of financing for the administrative, monitoring and enforcement expenses of the group. Traditionally, regulatory activities of the government in Canada are financed, in terms of the government's costs, from the Consolidated

---

42. The threat of punishment in another life is frequently employed by religious organizations. For believers, the effectiveness may vary with one's life expectancy and time discount rate. "Enlarging the shadow of the future" is a way to increase compliance. For example, if there will be future interactions (repeat transactions), a player is less likely to cheat. This is also reinforced the more certain is retaliation (but not endless retaliation — only that which matches the offence). See R. Axelrod, *The Evolution of Cooperation* (New York: Basic Books, 1984).

43. See B. Wastle, *Are We There Yet? The Responsible Care Ethic as an Evolving Secular Religion*, speech given at the University of Ottawa, March 1996.

44. See Miller (footnote 19).

Revenue Fund. Increasingly, however, it is acknowledged that regulatory activities are "local" public goods that benefit primarily those involved in consuming and producing the particular product or service. Financing from the Consolidated Revenue Fund, therefore, often implies a subsidy in respect of government-supplied regulation. As a result, governments are now implementing user fees that are designed to recover these costs. In this instance there is an increase in economic efficiency, although the government may act as a monopolist and impose excessive costs on the regulated sector.

Those implementing voluntary codes obviously have to absorb the costs of developing and administering the codes. This raises the issue of the division of costs. Who will pay? How will the group deal with free riding on the financial contributions of others? In most instances, the participating groups will differ in terms of their motives, the salience of the issue, their resources and their strategies in negotiation. This imbalance of resources is perhaps one of the more contentious issues. Yet it is misleading to focus only on financial capacity. Resources include not only financial resources, but also factors relating to the size of the group, its cohesiveness, its moral commitment or the ability to tie-in its membership, its public profile, its options, its legitimacy and history, its leadership and its alliances.

Therefore, it is simplistic to argue that financially weaker interests will not be heard. Other factors are important. The forest industry example best illustrates the point.[45] The industry paid for the participation of other groups. It made economic sense to do so in order to gain credibility. Even then it is not a sure-fire investment for the industry, as the exit of some influential groups attests.

Sustainability and Changing Rules

In general there are certain standards that can be used to assess the viability of voluntary codes over time. These are its *fairness*, its *efficiency* and its *stability*.[46] Fairness, of course, is in the eye of the beholder. But it does speak to issues of equal access, transparency and balanced consideration of all relevant information and all points of view. Perhaps this is the place for wisdom as well. Fairness typically implies a judicious balancing of all relevant considerations. It is not necessarily a rigid application of concepts such as equality. When codes are perceived to have been fairly developed and applied they are more likely to be both effective and to persist over time.

A second test is technical efficiency. This implies that in the give and take of setting standards, participants have taken advantage of all the gains from trade that are available. The techniques of *principled negotiation* are particularly useful in this regard, since they clearly promote an active and innovative canvassing of trading possibilities. That is the meaning of focussing on interests rather than positions. Moreover, when clear performance or outcome standards have been established, a code is likely to be efficient

---

45. See Rhone, Clarke and Webb, "Sustainable Forestry Practices," Chapter 9, below.

46. Susskind and Cruikshank (footnote 27) set out four conditions: fairness, efficiency, wisdom and stability. *Effectiveness* is a term much favoured by management consultants and auditors to mean "right action" as opposed to "least-cost action." In economics, the term *efficient* includes the notion of effectiveness. A situation cannot be efficient and yet be ineffective. In any case, it is unlikely, in the current context, that an agreement could be fair, efficient and sustainable but at the same time ineffective.

when those to whom it applies are given the flexibility to find the least expensive ways to meet the standards.

The third criterion is stability. Fairness at the outset adds to stability, but it is inevitable that circumstances will change. Effective regulatory regimes allow rules to be revisited. Shifts in tastes, technologies and the numbers of buyers or sellers and/or their sophistication can make rules obsolete and in need of elimination or redrafting. Many of the regulatory battles of the last 20 years might be understood in the context of the need to adjust regulation to a dramatically changing global marketplace. Sharp reversals of policy are most likely when strong trends and interests are, at least temporarily, overridden or forestalled. Voluntary codes will be more stable, as will State-supplied regulation, to the degree that they can accommodate gradual change.

The Continuing Role of the State

Traditional Political Economy

There is a very large literature in political economy that deals with the implications for economic policy and economic performance when various interest groups succeed in "capturing" politicians or bureaucrats in the tax-expenditure or regulatory processes of government. This is the more traditional political economy, as exemplified by the various "public choice" theories of regulation.[47]

In fact, however, not only are regulatory agencies subject to capture, but also their initial configuration inevitably reflects the political environment at their inception. In short, relative political strengths determine the initial administrative structures and forms of regulation as well as any bias in their subsequent operation. Therefore, one could apply the traditional tools of political analysis to each case of voluntary code formation to explain this particular instrument choice.

On balance, it is reasonable to presume that, whether formally at the table or not, the State is always a potential presence in the formation of voluntary codes. Each potential participant has to assess the costs and benefits of the legal and political alternatives that are open to them to achieve their objectives. For example, legal action was actively considered in the Gap Inc. case.[48] In particular, each potential participant must assess carefully the possibility that the State may be encouraged to act on its own, and the nature of that action. In general, the consensus view strongly asserts that the formal threat of State intervention is the only way to get closure on a "voluntary" agreement. Otherwise the negotiation process drags on and on.

Yet there must be a caveat. While the certainty of State action may be beneficial in producing voluntary agreements, the more predictable the State's actions, the more likely it will have to act. The reason is straightforward. Think of the State in this instance as a form of compulsory arbitration. If the outcome of the "voluntary" negotiation is

---

47. See, e.g., S. Peltzman, "Towards a More General Theory of Regulation?" *Journal of Law and Economics* 19 (August 1976), pp. 211–240; G. J. Stigler, "The Theory of Economic Regulation," *Bell Journal of Economics and Management Science* 2 (Spring 1971), pp.137–146; G. S. Becker, "A Theory of Competition Among Pressure Groups for Political Influence," *Quarterly Journal of Economics* 98 (August 1983), pp. 371–400.

48. Rhone, Stroud and Webb, "Gap's Code of Conduct," Chapter 7, below.

anything less than the State is known to prefer, State action will be invoked by the party that perceives itself most likely to benefit. No group will settle for less in a negotiation than they know for certain they could get from a State-imposed solution. It is only when the State's preferences are not clearly understood that groups may be inclined to settle. Therefore, the more uncertainty there is about how the State will act, the more likely there will be "voluntary" agreement.

Therefore, the State, acting self-consciously, can guide the process of negotiation and implementation of voluntary codes. To what end it will do so, we cannot be certain. Rules are not value-free. They inevitably give some interests an advantage and put others at a disadvantage.[49] What we must trust is that the State will choose wisely in terms of national objectives.[50]

The State as Catalyst

In a bestselling book on reinventing government in the United States, Osborne and Gaebler suggest that governments are now acting more to "steer rather than row."[51] In this capacity they can act as a catalyst to the collective actions of others. In fact, of course, this is a governing tactic already much in use. For example, governments have supplied legislation that permits effective formation of labour unions for purposes of collective bargaining. Automatic check-off of dues allows the union to overcome the free-rider problem implicit in collective bargaining when union membership is not mandatory. Similarly, governments supply the legislative framework that allows self-regulation of a wide range of professions.

In the case of voluntary codes the idea is to stop short of a formal legislative action. However, the government might still act as a catalyst to group formation. It may give technical assistance to those contemplating such actions. For example, Australia, New Zealand and Canada have published guides on the process of voluntary code formation.[52] It could also act as a facilitator and coordinator of a group's activities and as

---

49. Political events can be forecast. See, e.g., B. B. DeMesquita, D. Newman and A. Rabushka, *Forecasting Political Events: The Future of Hong Kong* (New Haven: Yale University Press, 1985). In predicting the actions of the State, one now has to take into account its impecunious circumstances and hence its interest in voluntary codes in the first place. But there are a variety of other considerations. Predicting the "net" preference of a government cannot be attempted except by analysis of each specific situation. And a large consideration in each circumstance is likely to be the efficacy of voluntary codes applied to the particular purpose (for example, environmental standards) and in the context of a specific market structure.

50. In traditional political economy, the consequences for the economy of this sort of interface between State and interest group are typically negative. See, e.g., M. Olson, *The Rise and Decline of Nations: Economic Growth, Stagflation, and Social Rigidities* (New Haven: Yale University Press, 1982). But there is no particular ideology attached to the study of political economy. It has strong roots in both the left and right of the political spectrum, although on the right it tends now to go under the title of the study of "public choice" and is more closely associated with the work of economists. In fact, it is arguably the case that both ends of the political spectrum harbour the same fear and suspicion — that the State is potentially, and actually, the servant of the other.

51. D. Osborne and T. Gaebler, *Reinventing Government* (Don Mills, Ont.: Addison-Wesley, 1992).

52. Gunningham, "The Australian Experience," Chapter 12, below.

a formal participant in negotiations.[53] It may also assist financially the participation of some non-governmental organizations. Once the code has been established, the government may strengthen the group by recognizing and giving positive publicity to the group's activities or giving awards for its accomplishments. Some suggest that government procurement could even be used in this manner to reinforce commercial penalties against those who do not comply.[54]

Whenever the State encourages collective actions by producers it has to be aware of the potential anti-competitive purposes of such organizations. Obviously, some of the industry attributes that signify good candidates for voluntary codes are also conducive circumstances for anti-competitive behaviours. And in fact there is a tension between the ability of voluntary codes to serve the interests of consumers in terms of information about product qualities and after-sales service guarantees on the one hand, and their use to restrain competition by limiting service or quality variations on the other. It is the same tension found in the self-regulation of professional groups. It also adds a reason why the participation of consumers in the development and ongoing operation of codes is desirable.

However, at least in respect of adverse environmental effects, anti-competitive activities that restrict output are beneficial. In this instance, the two opposing implications for social welfare have to be netted against one another. It is theoretically possible that the environmental effects would be quantitatively more important. As is the case with respect to unions and self-regulating professional bodies, the balance of positive and negative effects has to be considered. Ideally, the State would consider, and be able to evaluate, in quantitative as well as qualitative terms, all such possibilities.

The State as a Complement

The development of voluntary codes should not be seen strictly in terms of a substitute for government regulation. It is not necessarily part of some larger initiative to downsize or right-size government. Indeed, voluntary codes might simply be seen as one of a list of alternative possible arrows in the government's regulatory quiver. There is a well-articulated continuum of governing instruments that may be employed to achieve a given public policy objective. Each has strengths and weaknesses. And this particular alternative should be evaluated as part of a best-practice approach to the supply of regulation by government.[55]

---

53. See Y. Giroux and D. Waite, *Electronic Funds Transfer Code*, a draft case study prepared for the Voluntary Codes Symposium, Ottawa, 1996, available in summary at <http://strategis.ic.gc.ca/ epic/internet/inoca-bc.nsf/en/ca00880e.html>.

54. See C. Ferguson, *Voluntary Industry Self-Management in Ontario*, a draft case study prepared for the Voluntary Codes Symposium, Ottawa, 1996, available in summary at <http://strategis.ic.gc.ca/ epic/internet/inoca-bc.nsf/en/ca00880e.html>.

55. See Treasury Board of Canada Secretariat (footnote 18). The Canadian Radio-television and Telecommunications Commission has used the voluntary code, in part, to substitute for its own more formal regulatory apparatus in the case of the cable television industry.

However, even in aiding in the development of voluntary codes, the government is not surrendering its overarching responsibilities or its powers. Voluntary codes are obviously framed against a legislative background of laws of general application.[56] This is true in terms of consumer protection, environmental protection and the protection of labour or capital.

For example, wearing a helmet is a rule of the Canadian Hockey Association (formerly the Canadian Amateur Hockey Association) for league play. But that helmet must comply with a safety standard that is a regulation of the government.[57]

Conclusions

The State has an important competitive advantage in the supply of regulation to the marketplace. Democratic governments have been preferred suppliers of rules and regulations because they have a monopoly on the legitimate power to incarcerate those who do not comply with the law. And, at least until recently, they have been able to raise the financial resources necessary to undertake monitoring and to enforce compliance if necessary.

Yet that advantage is constrained in some circumstances and is under increasing financial pressure. The traditional command-and-control model of government regulation is increasingly costly to enforce, difficult to apply across national boundaries, inflexible and inefficient. In certain circumstances, the voluntary code may offer some opportunity to reduce these costs without sacrificing actual effectiveness.

This chapter has argued that private individuals have historically sought to provide rules and discipline to the marketplace. The promotion of voluntary codes for regulatory purposes should be seen as a continuation of a long historical evolution of non-governmental efforts to establish credibility in the marketplace. Industry groups will form and their members agree to restrain their individual behaviours when a commercial benefit is anticipated. That benefit often cannot fully or satisfactorily be achieved by each acting alone. The ability to achieve this benefit, however, will typically depend on the group's effectiveness in controlling free riders. The free rider can benefit without paying, or impose costs on others without compensation.

In this regard, this chapter outlined the general industry characteristics on both the supply side and the demand side that increase the ability to control free riding and therefore favour the development of voluntary codes. But the control of free riding is also enhanced when the institutional structure producing the rules has legitimacy. Accordingly, we reviewed the organizational and procedural principles that are conducive to greater efficiency and effectiveness. They draw heavily on the principles and institutional practices of democratic governments seeking to attain consent, consensus and thereby greater voluntary compliance.

---

56. See Webb and Morrison, "The Law and Voluntary Codes," Chapter 5, below.

57. See Andrew Morrison and Kernaghan Webb, "Bicycle Helmet Standards and Hockey Helmet Regulations: Two Approaches to Safety Protection," Chapter 11, below.

Consensus is expensive to achieve in the context of widely disparate views. But, once achieved, it is cost-effective in terms of monitoring and enforcement because it increases voluntary compliance. Therefore, one must balance the high costs of negotiating consensus with the resource savings from a higher level of credibility and voluntary compliance. When very disparate interests are concerned, the techniques of "principled negotiation" are recommended.

Notwithstanding greater voluntary compliance, all regulatory activities require some capacity to monitor and to enforce the rules. The credibility of compliance is essential to effectiveness. Credibility is, in general, increased by the degree to which the code participants surrender their freedom to act in their own exclusive interests. For example, credibility of the rules will depend upon the degree to which monitoring and enforcement activities are transparent and stand at arm's length from the regulated entity. Therefore, annual reports on compliance, periodic independent audits and an independent dispute resolution machinery greatly enhance the likely compliance to, and effectiveness and credibility of, the codes. Moreover, due process and fair redress are important principles to be applied to the dispute resolution process. Overall, the performance tests of voluntary codes will be whether they are fair, efficient and sustainable.

All of this is in addition, of course, to the ever-present possibility of State intervention. The participants in every voluntary code are constantly gauging the costs and benefits of alternative courses of action, either with respect to the courts or to the government. While the certainty of State action may be beneficial in producing voluntary agreements, the more uncertainty there is about how the State will act, the more likely there will be "voluntary" agreement.

As well, governments can act to reinforce "private" collective actions, either very formally through legislation or more informally by simply giving acknowledgment and public support. Moreover, the voluntary code is not simply a substitute for direct government action. It is also a complement. Voluntary codes are inevitably encased within a larger framework of law and regulation supplied by and maintained by the State. The existence of the voluntary code may strengthen the broader legal framework in the context of due diligence considerations. And, in turn, the broader legal recourse may act to give greater effect to the voluntary code.

Chapter 5
The Law and Voluntary Codes:
Examining the "Tangled Web"[1]

Kernaghan Webb and Andrew Morrison

Introduction

Even though firms may agree to adhere to the rules of voluntary code initiatives without being required to do so by legislation or regulations, there are nevertheless many ways that the law and voluntary initiatives are closely interconnected — so many that one could describe the linkages as creating a "tangled web." The Scottish novelist and poet Sir Walter Scott once said, "Oh, what a tangled web we weave/When first we practice to deceive."[2] While it may be appropriate to characterize the law-codes relationship as tangled, the position put forward here is that, on the whole, it is a positive and mutually reinforcing relationship. There is, nevertheless, potential for *self*-deception, for those who fail to appreciate the significant legal issues surrounding the development and use of voluntary initiatives. A more systematic, less tangled approach to law-voluntary code relations holds considerable promise for enhancing the effectiveness of both instruments, for the benefit of all parties concerned. These themes are explored in greater detail in the chapter. We begin here with some examples of how law and voluntary codes are interlinked:

- the impetus for industry sectors adopting voluntary initiatives is not infrequently the perception that, if action is not taken by the sector, then government regulation is likely to follow;[3]

---

1. This chapter draws substantially on earlier explorations on this topic, particularly K. Webb and A. Morrison, "Voluntary Approaches, the Environment and the Law: A Canadian Perspective," in C. Carraro and F. Lévêque, eds., *Voluntary Approaches in Environmental Policy* (London, U.K.: Kluwer Academic Publishers, 1999), pp. 229–259; K. Webb, "Voluntary Initiatives and the Law," in R. Gibson, ed., *Voluntary Initiatives: The New Politics of Corporate Greening* (Peterborough, Ont.: Broadview Press, 1999), pp. 32–50; K. Webb, "Government, Private Regulation, and the Role of the Market," in M. MacNeil, N. Sargent and P. Swan, eds., *Law, Regulation and Governance* (Don Mills, Ont.: Oxford University Press, 2002), Chapter 12.

2. Sir Walter Scott, from the poem *Marmion* (1808).

3. In some cases, there are communications from regulators that regulation will be forthcoming if voluntary action is not taken. For example, the Canadian cable television industry assumed self-regulation responsibilities over customer service activities following suggestions from the Canadian Radio-television and Telecommunications Commission (CRTC) that if the industry did not take on these responsibilities the CRTC would. See David Clarke and Kernaghan Webb, *Market-Driven Consumer Redress Case Studies and Legal Issues* (Ottawa: Office of Consumer Affairs, Industry Canada, 2002), available for download at <http://strategis.ic.gc.ca/epic/internet/inoca-bc.nsf/en/ca01643e.html>. In 1999, in the context of discussions about regulation of certain toxic chemicals, the Canadian Minister of Environment was reported as having said she was prepared to regulate the release of 18 chemicals "unless more companies took voluntary action against them." She is then quoted as saying, "We have made some good progress with voluntary measures. But if some make the effort and others don't, you have unfair competition." (See A. Duffy, "Industry Told its 'Free Ride' on Pollution About to End," *Ottawa Citizen*, March 20, 1999.) In other cases, the likelihood of regulations being

- voluntary initiatives may pave the way for legislation, with industry and others calling on governments to pass legislation based on voluntary initiatives;[4]
- voluntary standards can be referentially incorporated in law, with or without the approval of the initiators of the voluntary standard;[5]
- voluntary code initiatives may elaborate on and refine the generality of legislative requirements;[6]
- voluntary initiatives may be explicitly created pursuant to legislative instruments;[7]
- governments may support the development of voluntary initiatives that have extraterritorial application when it might be difficult to directly legislate these non-domestic operations;[8]

---

promulgated may not be communicated by government officials directly, but is nevertheless understood by industry. In the United States, the vice-president of one supermarket chain that has adopted a voluntary third-party audited food safety program for its suppliers has stated, "If we don't give them internally generated voluntary programs, we're going to get it from regulatory agencies." See R. Vosburgh, "Produce Safety Audits are Consumer Driven," *Supermarket News*, March 6, 2001, available at <www.primuslabs.com/ap/ SN_0300.htm>; see also discussion of the origins of the Canadian Chemical Producers' Association's Responsible Care program, in John Moffet, François Bregha and Mary Jane Middelkoop, "Responsible Care: A Case Study of a Voluntary Environmental Initiative," Chapter 6, below.

4. See, for example, the origins and development of Canadian federal legislation on personal information collected and used for commercial purposes, which started life as the voluntary *Model Code for the Protection of Personal Information* developed by governments, the private sector and consumer groups through the Canadian Standards Association. When the Code was finalized, the Canadian Marketing Association (which participated in drafting of the Code) urged the federal government and the provinces to develop legislation based on the Code. See Canadian Marketing Association, *Direct Marketing Industry Welcomes Federal Privacy Bill*, October 1, 1998. See also Colin J. Bennett, "Privacy Self-Regulation in a Global Economy: A Race to the Top, the Bottom or Somewhere Else?" Chapter 8, below. In the environmental area, the vice-president of the Canadian Chemical Producers' Association, speaking in the context of discussions to move control of certain toxic chemicals from a voluntary program to government regulation, was quoted as saying, "We don't have any problem with having regulations when voluntary programs don't work. When they don't work, they have to be backed up by a government willing to regulate, or else you will have free riders — companies that don't take care of their problems." (Cited in Duffy, footnote 3.) See also discussion in Moffet, Bregha and Middelkoop, "Responsible Care," Chapter 6, below.

5. See such examples as hockey helmet, toy safety, sustainable forestry management, environmental management, and health and safety standards incorporated into legislation, discussed later in this chapter.

6. For example, the Canadian Competition Bureau is currently considering adopting as guidelines the ISO 14021 standard on environmental claims, to help interpret the deceptive marketing provisions of the federal *Competition Act*. See <http://cb-bc.gc.ca/epic/internet/incb-bc.nsf/vwGeneratedInterE/ct02206e.html>.

7. For example, the European Eco-Management and Audit Scheme is a voluntary scheme established by law. See *Council Regulation (EEC) No. 1836/93 of 29 June 1993*, superceded by *Regulation (EC) No. 761/2001 of the European Parliament and of the Council of 19 March 2001*. See also the Canadian Environmental Choice Program, with draft guidelines published in the *Canada Gazette*, pursuant to s. 54(3) of the *Canadian Environmental Protection Act. 1999* (as amended). The Environmental Choice Program is discussed in Kathryn Harrison, "Promoting Environmental Protection through Eco-Labelling: An Evaluation of Canada's Environmental Choice Program," Chapter 10, below.

8. For example, the U.S. Department of Labor has provided financial support to the Fair Labor Association, which operates a voluntary apparel code of conduct and monitoring system used by American retailers dealing with their overseas suppliers. See, e.g., Fair Labor Association, *Fair Labor Association Awarded $750,000 Grant as Part of the Department of State Anti-Sweatshop Initiative*, press release, January 16, 2001, available at <www.fairlabor.org/html/press.html#Press011601>. For reasons of limits on State sovereignty (and due to trade conventions), it would be difficult for most jurisdictions to develop and enforce command-and-control legislation that has this degree of effective extraterritorial application.

- regimes for the development of voluntary standards by non-governmental parties may be the subject of legislation;[9]
- in the context of regulatory enforcement activities, regulators may offer incentives for firms to use voluntary programs that reduce the likelihood of violations taking place; moreover, non-compliance with voluntary standards can be a factor used by judges in determining liability, compliance with voluntary standards can aid firms in avoiding penal liability or reducing penalties, and the terms of voluntary programs can be judicially imposed on firms as part of sentencing;[10]
- consumers or affected members of a community may be able to use the commitments made in voluntary initiatives in legal actions to assist in establishing liability against individual firms[11] and against those who develop voluntary standards;[12]
- affected members of the public may be able to use voluntary standards to assist in establishing liability against public bodies in certain circumstances;[13]
- disciplinary actions by code administrators against participating firms may be undertaken through contractual actions;[14]
- the fairness of disciplinary actions taken by code administrators toward participating firms may be reviewed by the courts and, if found wanting, the actions can be overturned;[15]
- governments may   "beyond regulatory compl

---

9. In Canada, the national   plementation system with both rule-deve   d non-governmental interests use   uncil of Canada, a Crown corporation establ   *ds Council of Canada Act*, R.S.C. 1985,   opment organizations such as the C   levoted to conformity assessment acti

10. See discussion of use o   ernments and the courts, later in this chapter.

11. See discussion of legal suit against Nike, later in this chapter.

12. See discussion of legal suits against the National Spa and Pool Institute, later in this chapter.

13. Recently, following the introduction of a revised voluntary playground equipment safety standard, school boards in some Canadian municipalities dismantled their existing structures out of fear that they would not meet the revised standard, and that the municipality could be held liable. This is discussed in greater detail later in this chapter.

14. See discussion of *Ripley v. Investment Dealers Association* and other legal suits by industry associations against members over issues of code non-compliance, later in this chapter.

15. See discussion of legal suits by code members against code administrators, such as *A.A.A. Khan Transport Inc. v. Bureau d'éthique commerciale de Montréal Inc.*, later in this chapter.

16. See discussion of beyond compliance environmental programs, later in this chapter.

- governments may develop or support voluntary programs to avoid trade restrictions that apply to regulatory programs;[17]
- firms can incorporate legislative and regulatory requirements into the terms of voluntary codes that apply to participating firms in other jurisdictions;[18]
- governments may have their regulatory regimes certified as meeting the terms of non-governmental voluntary codes;[19] and
- anti-competitive aspects of voluntary code arrangements may be restricted through competition law.[20]

As even this summary listing illustrates, the relationship between voluntary initiatives and law is complex and varied. In light of this, it might be fruitful at the outset to examine the relationship from two perspectives: that of the impact of law on voluntary codes, and that of voluntary codes' impact on the law.

Looking first at the *impact of law on voluntary codes*, and drawing on the above-noted examples, there appear to be four main aspects to this relationship.

- *Enabling.* When parties draw on contract and intellectual property law, or a standards system that has a statutory basis to assist them in structuring their voluntary arrangements, the law facilitates development of voluntary codes. In this respect, there is an *enabling* relationship between law and codes (i.e. law provides some of the tools for code development).

---

17. For example, a voluntary labelling standard for foods containing genetically modified ingredients is being developed in Canada, whereas mandatory regulatory requirements on such issues may contravene restrictions contained in trade agreements, as discussed later in the chapter.

18. For example, as part of its apparel workers code, Nike has committed that all Nike supplier factories meet certain U.S. Occupational Safety and Health Administration indoor air quality standards. For discussion of these provisions, see T. Connor, *Still Waiting for Nike to Do It* (San Francisco: Global Exchange, 2001), p. 1, available at <http://store.globalexchange.org/nike.html>. According to Connor, "Health and safety is one area where some improvement has occurred. But even here the company is not willing to put in place a transparent monitoring system involving unannounced factory visits." (Ibid., p. 5.)

19. For example, the State of Alaska's commercial salmon fisheries management program has been certified as sustainable by the non-governmental Marine Stewardship Council, pursuant to its sustainable fishery standards. (See Office of the Governor of Alaska, *Alaska's Salmon Fishery Certified as Sustainable*, press release, September 5, 2000.) Professor E. Meidinger, in "Environmental Certification Programs and U.S. Environmental Law: Closer Than You May Think," *Environmental Law Reporter* 31 (2001), pp. 10162–10179, p. 10169, reports sources indicating that the agencies responsible for managing State-owned lands in Minnesota, New York and Pennsylvania have either achieved Forest Stewardship Council certification or announced they intended to do so. In Canada, the Ontario Technical Safety Standards Authority (TSSA), an independent non-profit agency formed by the Ontario government in 1997 to administer Ontario safety legislation, is "moving towards ISO 9001/2000 certification." (ISO 9001 is a non-governmental quality management system.) See TSSA, *Consolidated TSSA 2005 Strategy and 2001/2002 Plan* (Ontario: TSSA, 2001), p. 5, available at <www.tssa.org/about_tssa/pdf/tssa_plan.pdf>.

20. Competition law implications are discussed later in this chapter.

- *Negative stimulus.* When voluntary codes are developed in tacit or clear recognition that failure to do so may lead to legislation or regulation, it is not inaccurate to say that there is, in essence, a *threat-based* relationship between law and voluntary codes (i.e. the prospect of new legislation or regulations is used as a negative stimulus for voluntary codes, so that the codes operate "in the shadow of the law"[21]).
- *Positive stimulus.* When governments expressly use legislation to encourage the use of voluntary initiatives in furtherance of specific public policy objectives, it could be said that there is a *positive stimulus* relationship between law and voluntary codes (i.e. to some extent, in this respect, voluntary initiatives "stand on the shoulders" of a particular legislative structure).
- *Constraining.* When, through competition law, fairness requirements associated with contracting or the provisions of trade agreements, law prevents or restricts the ability of parties to enter into or operate voluntary code-type arrangements, there is a *constraining* relationship between law and codes (i.e. law sets limits on what can be accomplished through voluntary codes, and how it can be accomplished).

In all of these respects, although in different ways, the law provides a framework within which voluntary codes are developed.

Looking at the *effect of voluntary codes on the law*, there appear to be six main aspects to this relationship.

- *Modelling.* Voluntary codes can act as precursors of laws, demonstrating the practicality of a particular approach, and showing areas in which multiparty consensus can be found. In this sense there can be a *modelling*[22] relationship between voluntary arrangements and the law.
- *Supplementing.* Voluntary codes can refine or elaborate on or operationalize vague legislative or judicial concepts, and in this sense have a *supplementing* relationship with the law.
- *Jurisdiction extending.* When the ability of a State to directly legislate or regulate is constrained for reasons of limits on State sovereignty, voluntary codes can in some cases act to *extend* the reach and influence of governments through non-regulatory means.
- *Interoperability.* Voluntary codes can be used by legislators, regulators and courts as component parts of legal regimes and, as such, there can be a relationship of *interoperability* between voluntary approaches and the law.
- *Substitutability.* In some cases, the promulgation of legislation and regulations, or effective enforcement thereof, is not possible (e.g. by reason of restrictions found in constitutions or trade agreements). In such circumstances, there may be occasions when voluntary codes can act as *substitutes* for or alternatives to laws.

---

21. The expression "in the shadow of the law" has been used by legal commentators for some time. See, e.g., R. H. Mnookin and L. Kornhauser, "Bargaining in the Shadow of the Law: The Case of Divorce," *Yale Law Review* 88 (1979), pp. 950–997.

22. The notion of rule modelling is discussed extensively in J. Braithwaite and P. Drahos, *Global Business Regulation* (Cambridge: Cambridge University Press, 2000).

- *Performance- and credibility-enhancing.* In some situations, adherence by government bodies or government regulatory programs to the terms of voluntary arrangements may actually improve the operation of those government bodies or programs, their public image or both. In this sense, voluntary codes can be seen to enhance the performance and credibility of laws.

It is probably apparent that, in many of these aspects, there can be a close and oft-times mutually reinforcing relationship between the law and voluntary codes. The weaknesses of a legal instrument may to some extent be "covered off" through use of a voluntary approach, and vice-versa. To take an example of public sector actors using voluntary approaches to supplement legal regimes, a government environmental protection agency may choose to support or develop market-driven voluntary programs specifically to stimulate regulated actors to undertake innovative action that goes beyond regulatory compliance; it may use voluntary programs to address harmful behaviour outside its regulatory authority (e.g. behaviour that would be difficult to address directly due to limitations applying to its legislative initiatives); it may develop voluntary programs to quickly obtain reductions of particular pollutants that cannot be addressed so expeditiously through regulatory action (because of the ponderous, careful, expensive and slow process of regulatory development); or it may seek the endorsement or approval of those operating market-based sustainable forest or fish management programs for its activities (in an effort to enhance the perceived public acceptability or legitimacy of its regulatory practices). By the same token, voluntary programs for toxic reductions that, on their own, may be vulnerable to criticisms about how much actual progress is being made may benefit from use of government-mandated information disclosure programs, to enhance transparency and accountability of the voluntary programs.

Similarly, business and civil society organizations that develop voluntary initiatives often buttress or reinforce their programs through legal instruments. Voluntary certification initiatives developed by private sector interests or public interest-oriented non-governmental organizations (NGOs) typically rely on contract law to implement the terms and conditions of operation; the benchmarks of acceptable and unacceptable behaviour articulated by industry associations or standards bodies through their voluntary codes and standards initiatives may be recognized by courts in regulatory actions or private law negligence actions as constituting the accepted "standard of care" for that activity, and, as such, the ability of the industry associations or standards organizations to stimulate compliance with those codes or standards may be enhanced (particularly against "free riders" who may be resisting efforts to comply with the code or standard). From these examples, one can see the potential for symbiotic, constructive interaction between laws and voluntary initiatives, in which some combination of the two types of instruments may work better than either could on their own.[23]

Of course, this degree of reinforcement of one type of instrument by the other need not always occur: indeed, there are situations in which operation of the one type of instrument may be perceived as detracting from the operation of the other. For example, some have claimed that the existence of voluntary programs can be used by the private sector to stave off needed legislative or regulatory initiatives, and that support by a

---

23. The strengths and weaknesses of the two instruments are discussed below.

government agency for a voluntary measure might restrict its ability to act in the future.[24] There is always this potential. But when from the outset parties understand the nature of the impacts voluntary instruments can have on the law, and vice-versa, there is good potential for the two instruments to be developed in a positive and complementary manner.

This chapter explores these and other themes in greater detail. It is divided into two main parts. The first consists of a functional comparison of voluntary code and command-and-control regulatory approaches as rule systems. Analysis suggests that regulatory approaches tend to be advantageous in terms of visibility, credibility, accountability, compulsory application to all, greater likelihood of rigorous standards being developed, sharing of costs of operationalization, and diversity of sanctions. However, regulatory approaches also tend to be highly formal, and expensive to develop and operate, may foster legalistic, adversarial relations between regulator and regulated, have limited scope (i.e. governments have jurisdictional limits), may not encourage innovation and "beyond compliance" behaviour, and are usually difficult to develop and amend (i.e. the rule-making and amendment process is slow and expensive).

Examination of voluntary code initiatives suggests that their main advantages centre around their flexibility, lower cost (i.e. the taxpayer may not directly assume any costs, and the institutions of rule-making, implementation and dispute resolution may be less expensive to operate), speed in establishing and amending rules and structures, minimization of jurisdictional concerns (e.g. it is less difficult to devise systems with multijurisdictional application), potential for harnessing non-State, non-coercive energies (e.g. positive use of market and peer pressure and internalization of responsibility), informality and accessibility to government, private sector and civil society actors. Typical drawbacks of voluntary approaches include generally lower visibility and credibility, difficulty in applying the rules to those who do not wish to participate in the program, the possibility of less rigorous standards being developed, uncertain public accountability and potentially weaker enforcement capacity.

It is also important to recognize at the outset the tremendous variety of voluntary code approaches in operation: some are initiated at the behest of government, others independently of government; some are adjuncts and refinements to statutory regimes, others have no direct connection to legislation; some apply to only one firm, others apply to many (even across jurisdictional boundaries); some are market-based; and some have no market dimensions. In light of this variety, it is useful to view voluntary codes on a continuum, with some having formal rule-making, implementation and adjudication institutions and processes, and others being less formal and elaborate.[25] The reader should also bear in mind that with such a wide variety of voluntary arrangements in existence, the general observations made in this chapter may apply more to some types of codes than others.

---

24. See J. Moffet and F. Bregha, "Non-Regulatory Environmental Measures," in R. Gibson, ed., *Voluntary Initiatives: The New Politics of Corporate Greening* (Peterborough, Ont.: Broadview Press, 1999), pp.15–31, footnote 7.

25. See M. Priest, "The Privatization of Regulation: Five Models of Self-Regulation," *Ottawa Law Review* 29 (1998), pp. 233–302, p. 236.

The second part of the chapter focusses on the legal implications of the use of voluntary codes. An examination of the applicability of contract law to voluntary code arrangements highlights the consensual nature of such systems, and suggests that actions based in contract law may be used by consumers, standards organizations, individual firms and associations to require that voluntary code commitments are kept. A potentially significant conclusion emerging from the tort law analysis is that, in spite of their consensual nature, voluntary code arrangements can be used by courts to impose standards and impose liability on those who develop the code and on parties who did not participate in the original voluntary code arrangement. Legislation prohibiting deceptive practices can be used to address failure to meet commitments contained in voluntary codes. Regulatory legislation concerning consumer, environmental and worker health and safety protection can draw on voluntary codes and standards particularly with respect to determinations of due diligence and in sentencing. Analysis of the legal effects of government support of voluntary initiatives on enforcement suggests that such support can assist compliance activities but it can also undermine enforcement capacity through claims of abuse of process or officially induced error. The impact of trade agreements on voluntary initiatives is explored and the suggestion is made that such agreements indirectly create incentives for governments to support properly framed voluntary standards, since voluntary standards are less constrained by such agreements than are regulatory approaches. A review of antitrust (competition) law reveals that this type of law can restrict the operations of voluntary codes when they decrease the ability of non-participating competitors to gain access to a market and sell their products and services, or increase prices.

Taken together, this analysis suggests that individuals, firms, industry associations, non-governmental organizations and governments need to thoroughly explore and understand the legal implications of voluntary code arrangements before undertaking or participating in such initiatives. It is possible to devise and operate voluntary code regimes that serve *both* the public and private interests involved, but failure by all parties to properly consider the legal implications and act accordingly could potentially result in problems for all concerned. The final section of the chapter explores how the legal system and voluntary codes could be designed to operate in a more systematic, less haphazard way.

Comparison of Regulatory and Voluntary Code Regimes as Rule Systems

As understood for the purposes of this chapter, both regulatory and voluntary code regimes consist of groupings of institutions, mechanisms and processes created to carry out the functions of rule creation, administration/implementation and adjudication,[26] which are designed to affect the behaviour of a defined population. In view of the tremendous variation possible from one regulatory or voluntary regime to another, the comparison of the two types of rule systems that follows is at quite a high level of generality. However, the comparative charts set out in the following pages, while only a summary, can be used to test specific regimes. Indeed, an attempt has been made to refer for illustrative purposes to aspects of particular codes whenever possible.

Rule Creation

As the following chart demonstrates, the rule-creation function can be considered from a number of perspectives. Generally speaking, the public law, regulatory rule-creation function, which develops statutes, regulations and related instruments, is carried out by well-known, pre-existing institutions[27] possessing a high degree of credibility and visibility. It is, of course, possible for government to create new regulatory rule-making bodies, and indeed governments have done so from time to time. For example, prior to the 1970s, most jurisdictions had no separate government agencies responsible for environmental protection, whereas now such regulatory agencies are commonplace.[28]

---

26. This tripartite discussion of rule systems is in basic agreement with definitions of the constituent components of legal systems, such as those described by J. Raz, *The Concept of a Legal System: An Introduction to the Theory*, 2nd ed. (Oxford: Oxford University Press, 1980). Although Raz speaks specifically of State-based legal systems, the basic functions are the same for voluntary codes.

27. For example, legislative bodies variously named "Parliament" or "Congress" or "Legislative Assembly," executive delegated authority rule-making bodies such as Cabinet and the "Governor General in Council," and statutorily delegated rule-making bodies such as regulatory agencies, including the Canadian Radio-television and Telecommunications Commission and the U.S. Federal Trade Commission.

28. In Canada, environmental protection has in general been entrusted to government departments or ministries, and not independent agencies. See discussion of evolution of Canadian federal environmental protection regimes in K. Webb, *Pollution Control in Canada: The Regulatory Approach in the 1980s* (Ottawa: Law Reform Commission of Canada, 1988), pp. 3–15. In the United States, a separate, independent agency with rule-making powers for environmental protection (the Environmental Protection Agency) was established in 1970 (see <www.epa.gov/history/topics/epa/15c.htm>).

Rule Creation: Comparison of Regulatory and Voluntary Code Regimes		
Characteristics	**Regulatory Regimes**	**Voluntary Codes**
Rule-making institutions	Pre-established by State: well-known, highly credible. State controls process, access.	May be newly established: less credible, at least at outset. Government, business or non-governmental organizations can create.
Visibility of process	Generally high, particularly in the democratically elected rule-making organs of State.	Generally lower, but not necessarily so.
Cost	High, but usually spread across society.	Lower, but borne by a smaller group.
Development process	Difficult: highly formal, expensive, democratic (in primary rule-making bodies). Theoretically open to all.	Possibly easier: less formal, less expensive. May not be open to all.
Ability to make amendments	Difficult (see above).	Easier (see above).
Sanctions that can be attached	Can include coercive and liberty-depriving sanctions, including imprisonment.	Primarily market-based. May be tort and contractual liability implications.
Scope of application	Can be imposed on free riders. Not based on contractual consent.	Difficulty with free riders. Based on contractual consent.
Constraints on rule development/implementation	Considerable: constitutional and procedural.	Few: may apply across national and provincial boundaries.
Likelihood of rules being developed through the process	Political process makes outcomes difficult to predict.	Closed, limited process may make outcomes easier to predict.
Likelihood of rigorous obligations being developed	High: obligations developed by parties other than those who will be directly affected, less chance for bias to affect obligations being developed.	Low: obligations often developed by parties whose interests are directly affected, greater chance for bias to affect obligations being developed.

Voluntary Codes: Private Governance, the Public Interest and Innovation

The function of rule making in a voluntary code context may necessitate creating new bodies (e.g. the formulation of a new organization tasked with the rule-making responsibility),[29] or it may be undertaken by an existing body, be it an individual firm,[30] an association of firms,[31] a non-governmental organization,[32] a multistakeholder group[33] or a standards organization.[34] Typically, these types of bodies do not have the visibility, credibility or legitimacy[35] of pre-established governmental institutions, but in some respects this can be considered advantageous: first, businesses, NGOs or others are largely free to create these new bodies and operate them as they choose (subject to certain legal restraints as discussed in the second part of this chapter), and so there is a climate conducive to considerable rule innovation. Unlike public rule-making organs, such as legislatures or regulatory agencies, government does not "set all the rules" pertaining to the operation and access to the process.[36] Second, because they are not normally well-established bodies with known reputations, non-governmental voluntary code rule-making bodies may be stimulated to engage in credibility-, visibility- and legitimacy-enhancing activities. Thus, for example, as in the case of sustainable forest certification programs, there may be open competition among rival certification initiatives, with each pointing out their strengths and their counterparts' weaknesses.[37]

---

29. For example, the Cable Television Standards Council created by the Canadian Cable Television Association, as discussed in Clarke and Webb (footnote 3); see also the Assembly created as part of the multistakeholder Forest Stewardship Council, as discussed in Gregory T. Rhone, David Clarke and Kernaghan Webb, "Two Voluntary Approaches to Sustainable Forestry Practices," Chapter 9, below.

30. See, e.g., Gregory T. Rhone, John Stroud and Kernaghan Webb, "Gap's Code of Conduct for Treatment of Overseas Workers," Chapter 7, below.

31. See, e.g., Moffet, Bregha and Middelkoop, "Responsible Care," Chapter 6, below.

32. For example, the Web Trader consumer electronic commerce regime, developed by the U.K Consumers Association, discussed in Kernaghan Webb and David Clarke, "Voluntary Codes in the United States, the European Union and Developing Countries: A Preliminary Survey," Chapter 13, below (hereafter "Other Jurisdictions").

33. For example, the multistakeholder Fair Labor Association, which has established rules for proper treatment of apparel workers, as discussed in Rhone, Stroud and Webb, "Gap's Code of Conduct," Chapter 7, below.

34. For example, the Canadian Standards Association, as discussed in Andrew Morrison and Kernaghan Webb, "Bicycle Helmet Standards and Hockey Helmet Regulations: Two Approaches to Safety Protection," Chapter 11, below; Rhone, Clarke and Webb, "Sustainable Forestry Practices," Chapter 9, below.

35. For discussion of the importance of legitimacy in the context of voluntary sustainable forestry certification schemes, see B. Cashore, "Legitimacy and the Privatization of Environmental Governance: How Non State Market-Driven (NSMD) Governance Systems (Certification Eco-labelling Programs) Gain Rule Making Authority," *Governance: An International Journal of Policy, Administration and Institutions* 15:4 (October 2002), pp. 503–529.

36. This can allow for considerable innovation in terms of how rules are developed. Perhaps the most effective restraints on this rule-creation capability are member- and market-driven, not legal.

37. See discussion of the activities of the proponents of the Canadian Standards Association and Forest Stewardship Council sustainable forestry initiatives in Rhone, Clarke and Webb, "Sustainable Forestry Practices," Chapter 9, below. As pre-established organs of the State, regulatory bodies in normal circumstances do not have to engage to the same extent in such credibility-enhancing activities. This is not to suggest that regulatory agencies, and indeed, States, do not engage in competition with their counterparts elsewhere, but this form of competition is largely interjurisdictional in nature (e.g. each regulatory agency has a monopoly over the management of a particular resource within its jurisdiction). In apparent recognition of the fact that governments, too, are increasingly being required to earn and maintain marketplace credibility, we now have the

With respect to public sector regulatory regimes, in keeping with the democratic nature of rule-creation processes in most industrialized countries, the development of statutes and regulations is normally characterized by a high degree of formality and attempts to ensure that the process is accessible, fair and transparent, and is perceived as such. On the one hand, this undoubtedly adds to the credibility and visibility of public sector regulatory regimes. On the other, it also contributes to the expense and slowness of statute and regulation development. The costs of developing statutes and regulations are generally[38] borne by all taxpayers, and thus there is a "cost-spreading" effect at work. There is also a high publicity value associated with use of the formal and transparent lawmaking processes.[39]

In contrast, the rule-development process for voluntary codes may be considerably quicker and less expensive than for regulatory regimes. The process may be quite informal, but also may not be accessible to all who are affected, nor may its mode of operation be very visible or well understood.[40] This, of course, may affect the credibility of the rules developed, since it would be easy for those who were not given the opportunity to participate, or not given an explanation of its mode of operation, to assume that an inadequate *fait accompli* was devised among like-minded insiders.[41]

This need not be the case, however, since it is possible for firms, associations, NGOs, multistakeholder organizations and standards organizations to engage in transparent, accessible, fair and easy-to-understand rule-development processes.[42] It

---

spectre of governments seeking out the approval and certification of non-governmental organizations for their regulatory and administrative programs. For example, the State of Alaska has successfully obtained certification for its salmon fishery management system through the non-governmental Marine Stewardship Council, as discussed above (footnote 19).

38. In some jurisdictions, there is experimentation with forms of co-regulation, where new quasi-autonomous but accountable entities are established by government to administer or "manage" legislative regimes. These entities may be given a modicum of authority to develop some of the rules associated with the implementation of the regime, and may operate on a cost-recovery basis. See, for example, in Ontario, the experience with the Technical Safety Standards Authority, as discussed above (footnote 19).

39. For example, laws are debated in publicly accessible fora, frequently with television coverage, and regulation development can be the subject of extensive public consultations.

40. That is, the process of rule development for voluntary codes may not follow such well-known techniques as consensus, majority rule, draft versions circulated for comments, etc. It should be noted that formal standards development processes used to devise voluntary initiatives, such as those employed by the Canadian Standards Association, do use consensus decision-making techniques, and have formal notice and comment processes.

41. See, e.g., discussion of criticisms levelled at the Canadian Chemical Producers' Association's Responsible Care program in Moffet, Bregha and Middelkoop, "Responsible Care," Chapter 6, below, and discussion of the Canadian Standards Association's processes concerning development of the sustainable forestry management standards, in Rhone, Clarke and Webb, "Sustainable Forestry Practices," Chapter 9, below. For insights on the perspective of environmental non-governmental organizations concerning voluntary standards development, see, e.g., T. Burrell, *CSA Environmental Standards Writing: Barriers to Environmental Non-Governmental Organizations Involvement* (Toronto: CIELAP, 1997).

42. See, e.g., the discussion of rule-development processes associated with the Responsible Care program (Moffet, Bregha, and Middelkoop, "Responsible Care," Chapter 6, below), sustainable forestry initiatives (Rhone, Clarke and Webb, "Sustainable Forestry Practices," Chapter 9, below), helmets (Morrison and Webb, "Helmet Standards and Regulations" Chapter 11, below), privacy (Bennett, "Privacy Self-Regulation, " Chapter 8, below), apparel (Rhone, Stroud and Webb, "Gap's Code of Conduct," Chapter 7, below), and e-commerce (Webb and Clarke, "Other Jurisdictions," Chapter 13, below). See also discussion of the cable television rule-development process and that associated with advertising standards, in Clarke and Webb (footnote 3).

perhaps goes without saying that the more transparent, accessible, fair and easy-to-understand the rule-development process is, the more expensive it tends to be. Thus, although voluntary code rule making may be considerably less costly than regulatory rule making, it can still be an expensive proposition. And since costs are borne principally by the rule makers (e.g. a firm or group of firms, an NGO), and not all taxpayers, there is less of a "cost-spreading" capability than there is with regulatory decision making. As long as markets are adequately competitive, most costs borne by voluntary code rule makers are likely to be passed on to the ultimate consumers of products and services, in the form of higher prices. Thus, the discipline of the market is likely to push firms to attempt to minimize rule-making costs and cut corners. In the long run, however, it may be a worthwhile investment for code developers to be as open, accessible and thorough as possible in voluntary code rule making, since this will usually serve to decrease the likelihood of criticisms and problems arising later on.

In this regard, for the task of rule making, drawing on the services of established standards development organizations, such as the Canadian Standards Association, the British Standards Institution, the American National Standards Institute and Standards Australia, may represent an attractive option in some situations.[43] The credibility and experience of these organizations in developing standards, their use of matrix models to ensure balanced representation, and their employment of public consultation strategies can help answer the need for transparent, fair, accessible and understandable rule making.[44] In a sense, standards development organizations could be described as professional "rent-a-rule-makers."

With respect to sanctioning options, the State is the exclusive organ in Canadian society to have the authority to deprive individuals of their life, liberty or security (e.g. through capital punishment, imprisonment, probation), and can only do so in a manner compatible with principles of fundamental justice.[45] However, a wide variety of sanctions short of capital punishment and imprisonment are available to non-State bodies, including fines, withdrawal of association privileges, membership and use of logos, and adverse publicity. These sanctions are discussed in greater detail later in the chapter in the examination of dispute resolution.

A key distinction between public law regulatory regimes and non-governmental voluntary code rule making is the ability of public law-making organs to develop a specialized form of rule (laws) that apply to *all* actors in a sector, *whether or not those actors agree to the rules*. When developing consumer, environmental, or health and safety regulatory regimes, the elected members of democratic organs of the State

---

43. See descriptions of bicycle and hockey helmet standards developed through the standards process in "Helmet Standards and Regulations," Chapter 11, below; privacy standards in Bennett, "Privacy Self-Regulation," Chapter 8, below; and sustainable forestry management standards in Rhone, Clarke and Webb, "Sustainable Forestry Practices," Chapter 9, below.

44. Ibid. However, it should be noted that the rule-making processes of standards organizations have not been without criticism, as is discussed in Rhone, Clarke and Webb, "Sustainable Forestry Practices," Chapter 9, below, and in T. Burrell (footnote 41).

45. Section 7 of the *Canadian Charter of Rights and Freedoms* stipulates that everyone has the right to "life, liberty and security of the person and the right not to be deprived thereof except in accordance with the principles of fundamental justice." As discussed later in the chapter, the ability of the State to implement penalty regimes may be constrained by principles of natural justice in ways that do not so constrain non-State regimes.

(e.g. members of Parliament, members of Congress, members of legislative assemblies) are typically *not* the very parties who will be the subject of the regulatory regimes, and nor is the consent of those regulated industries necessary before such laws are passed.[46] The reverse is true with voluntary code regimes developed by industry, for industry. As Bryne Purchase notes in his chapter in this volume, ultimately, a voluntary code regime is a consensual arrangement. It is therefore not possible for a group of firms *by itself* to compel a firm that has not agreed to participate in a voluntary code arrangement to comply with the code. As a result, there is a potential problem in voluntary code regimes with free riders (firms that do not participate in the code, but nevertheless benefit from the perception of others that they are part of it, without paying the cost). As discussed earlier in the chapter, it *is* possible that the standards contained in a voluntary code regime could be incorporated into legislation or regulations (and thus apply to all firms in a sector), or be applied by a court to a non-participating firm through an action in tort or through a regulatory offence prosecution (examined in greater detail in the second part of this chapter), but the voluntary code makers cannot *on their own* compel non-members to comply with a voluntary code.

Governments can only establish laws to the extent of their authority to legislate on any particular subject matter. They cannot create a set of rules when they do not have the constitutional authority to do so. In Canada, for example, a province cannot normally create a regulatory regime applying specifically to banks, because banks are a federal responsibility.[47] Moreover, it is difficult for governments in one jurisdiction to create legislation designed to apply to companies in another jurisdiction. For example, it is not possible, in a direct manner, for a Canadian government to require a company in El Salvador to meet Canadian labour or environmental standards.

In contrast, through a non-governmental voluntary code, there is no constraint for a private actor such as a Canadian company stipulating that its El Salvadorian suppliers meet Canadian standards, as a term of contract.[48] Of course, if an El Salvadorian supplier does not wish to meet the conditions stipulated by its potential Canadian business partner, it can simply choose to not enter into a contract with that company. The contract is voluntarily entered into. A foreign or domestic government legislatively imposing a particular standard faces constitutional and legislative constraints that typically do not affect private consenting commercial parties. Similarly, a group of firms operating in several countries can establish a voluntary code that applies in multiple jurisdictions (as long as competition and other domestic legislation is not being violated). For example, versions of the Responsible Care program operate not only in Canada, but also in more than 40 other countries.[49] Similarly, voluntary code regimes such as the

---

46. This is not to suggest that governments do not expend considerable resources consulting with regulated industries and others in an effort to ensure that the rules are practical and effective, in an effort to increase the cooperation and compliance of those industries to the new legislation and regulations. And, of course, industry associations spend enormous sums of money on lobbying efforts aimed at legislators, regulators and the attentive public.

47. For example, Quebec's *An Act respecting the protection of personal information in the private sector*, L.Q. P-39.1, does not apply to banks.

48. For example, the clothing company Gap Inc. requires its suppliers to meet particular standards for working conditions. See Rhone, Stroud and Webb, "Gap's Code of Conduct," Chapter 7, below.

49. Moffet, Bregha and Middelkoop, "Responsible Care," Chapter 6, below.

Forest Stewardship Council can also operate in multiple jurisdictions, as can formal standards initiatives such as ISO 9000 (quality management) and ISO 14000 (environmental management).

From a predictability standpoint, because of the formal, lengthy nature of legislative and regulatory rule making, with its many checks and balances, there are considerable opportunities for legislative and regulatory projects to be derailed. Frequently, we hear of legislative projects that have not been passed before the closing of legislative sittings, and often the "death" of these bills reflects successful lobbying by particular interest groups.

In contrast, once there is agreement to establish a voluntary code arrangement — be it through an industry association, standards body, NGO, or otherwise — there would appear to be fewer obstacles preventing those rules from being promulgated.

A final but crucial point concerning rule making pertains to the content of the rules themselves. All other things being equal, one can generally expect greater rigour in the substantive obligations imposed by legislation and regulations on industry than in the substantive obligations imposed on firms by firms, by multistakeholder groups and, to some extent, even by NGOs. Decisions about the content of particular rules made by legislators or civil servants on the one hand and by representatives of private firms or NGOs on the other tend to reflect their respective constituents. As mentioned earlier, although members of Parliament, members of legislative assemblies and civil servants may all have particular viewpoints, and may be influenced by the views of others through lobbying, in the final analysis the one essential fact is that they are not employees or representatives of particular firms, and are not directly beholden to those firms.[50] Moreover, they are accountable, directly in the case of elected members, and indirectly in the case of civil servants, to the broad electorate they serve, and not simply to a narrow set of interests.

In contrast, individuals in the private sector with responsibility for drafting voluntary codes are paid by firms, and these firms are accountable ultimately to their shareholders and to their customers. When voluntary codes to control industry conduct are developed by public interest-oriented NGOs,[51] one can perhaps expect greater rigour in the obligations than one would expect from voluntary codes developed by industry. However, because ultimately the codes developed by consumer, environmental or worker NGOs are to be applied by industry, the obligations contained in such voluntary codes cannot be so rigorous as to repel industry "clients." Voluntary code approaches that employ multistakeholder rule-development processes (e.g. standards developed through formal standards development processes) are perhaps the most likely to develop rigorous yet practical substantive obligations, yet even with these it is possible for individual firms or stakeholders to "leave the table" (and, to some extent, to thereby stymie the process) when they do not like the obligations being developed. No such avenue is open to parties

---

50. Of course, in practice, monied interests are often in a position to influence in any forum, but even this is indirect influence.

51. The Web Trader e-commerce regime developed by the U.K. Consumers' Association is a good example of such a scheme. It is discussed in Webb and Clarke, "Other Jurisdictions," Chapter 13, below. The Forest Stewardship Council was spearheaded by environmental non-government organizations, and is discussed in Rhone, Clarke and Webb, "Sustainable Forestry Practices," Chapter 9, below.

subject to legislation or regulations (i.e. the rules will be developed and imposed regardless of whether these parties "leave the table").

There is another way in which legislative and voluntary code approaches to rule-making content may be different. Typically, laws must be written in precise, detailed language. If they are not, it is possible that the laws would be held void for vagueness, and therefore unconstitutional.[52] On the other hand, voluntary codes can be written in considerably more general language. This can be advantageous when the activity to be addressed is highly variable and defies easy definition. For example, Advertising Standards Canada has established rules concerning advertising that is in "bad taste."[53] It would probably be very difficult, and perhaps not desirable, for governments to attempt to discourage "bad taste" through laws, but businesses, concerned with upholding a certain image, may be in a better position to address such behaviour of their peers.

In the United Kingdom, a voluntary regime for controlling the acquisition of publicly listed companies has existed for many years.[54] The regime sets out general principles rather than detailed provisions. In reviewing the regime, judges have remarked on the apparent effectiveness of this approach.[55] Of course, lack of precision can also become an excuse for non-compliance, when variable interpretations are possible, and no one can agree on the correct interpretation. Therefore, the possibility of establishing less precise obligations for voluntary codes than for laws is not necessarily advantageous.

It is also worth pointing out that, in the short run, the existence of a voluntary code arrangement may decrease the likelihood of legislation or regulations being introduced. In some cases, industry may develop a voluntary code in the hope of delaying or preventing the passage of perceived burdensome legislation.[56] While there is undoubtedly a need for governments and others to be wary of this type of strategy, it is also possible that the rules developed through voluntary code arrangements can become the basis for legislative action, with support from industry,[57] or that government will specifically give industry the opportunity to regulate itself in lieu of government-imposed regulations.[58]

---

52. A law must not be so vague that a court cannot give "sensible meaning" to its terms. See *Re: ss. 193 and 195.1 of Criminal Code (Prostitution Reference)* [1990] 1 S.C.R. 1123 at 1160.

53. Clarke and Webb (footnote 3).

54. *R. v. Panel on Take-overs and Mergers* [1987] 1 All E.R. 564.

55. Ibid., p. 567.

56. This was one of the motivations for development of the Responsible Care program, discussed in Moffet, Bregha and Middelkoop, "Responsible Care," Chapter 6, below.

57. In Canada, the Canadian Standards Association's *Model Code for the Protection of Personal Information* became the basis for federal privacy legislation, in the *Personal Information Protection and Electronic Documents Act*, S.C. 2000, c-5, as discussed earlier.

58. For example, the Canadian Radio-television and Telecommunications Commission (a federal agency), specifically provided the Canadian cable industry the opportunity to self-regulate certain aspects of its activities, subject to review by the Commission. See discussion in Clarke and Webb (footnote 3).

Rule Administration

The comparative chart on page 115 summarizes the main characteristics of command-and-control regulatory regime and voluntary code regime administration. Many of the same factors in play in rule creation are in play for rule administration.

Although there is a school of thought that holds that enforcement of rules is not always necessary to achieve compliance,[59] it can generally be said that without effective rule implementation, there is strong potential for voluntary codes to become little more than "window dressing," and as such mislead the public and government and put competitors at a disadvantage. A voluntary code that is not fully implemented is susceptible to legal actions (as discussed in the second part of this chapter), public exposure and embarrassment. This scenario materialized with respect to Gap Inc.'s initial code of conduct for apparel workers. As discussed in Chapter 7, in the face of public criticism, Gap Inc. eventually agreed to a more rigorous code with implementation monitored by civil society non-governmental organizations.[60]

It is worth pointing out that regulatory regimes, like their voluntary counterparts, can also be less than fully enforced. This strategy can backfire on regulators just as limited implementation of voluntary code initiatives can backfire on firms.[61] Formal accountability mechanisms, such as annual reports, Auditor General reports, inquiries, questions in legislative assemblies to the elected officials responsible for program administration, and legal actions, can all go some way toward revealing regulatory enforcement inadequacies. By the same token, voluntary code administrators can issue annual reports, and include community, academic and NGO representatives in compliance verification activities.[62] Non-affiliated academics[63] and non-governmental organizations[64] can also conduct investigations and release public reports on voluntary code compliance. Commentators have suggested that information sharing, transparency and general public access to information are the most important mechanisms available to

---

59. J. Braithwaite and P. Drahos (footnote 21), p. 554, following Chayes and Handler Chayes, *The New Sovereignty: Compliance with International Regulatory Agreements* (Cambridge, Mass.: Harvard University Press, 1995) and O. Young, *Compliance and Public Authority: A Theory with International Implications* (Baltimore: Johns Hopkins University Press, 1979). The theory is that enforcement in some cases is a secondary consideration because it is dialogue that redefines interests, delivers the discipline of complex interdependency, and persuades parties to normative commitment.

60. See Rhone, Stroud and Webb, "Gap's Code of Conduct," Chapter 7, below.

61. For example, the 1992 Westray mining disaster (Nova Scotia, Canada) could be described as an example of regulatory non-enforcement, with tragic results. See Justice K. Peter Richard, Commissioner, *The Westray Story: A Predictable Path to Disaster* (Report of the Westray Mine Public Inquiry, 1997).

62. See discussion of the public reporting and compliance verification activities used in Responsible Care administration in Moffet, Bregha and Middelkoop, "Responsible Care," Chapter 6, below.

63. See, e.g., D. Rourke, *Monitoring The Monitors:A Critique of Pricewaterhousecoopers (PWC) Labor Monitoring* (Boston: Massachusetts Institute of Technology, 2000), available at <http://web.mit.edu/dorourke/www/PDF/pwc.pdf>.

64. See, e.g., Connor, *Still Waiting for Nike to Do It* (footnote 18), p. 1.

address criticisms concerning the legitimacy, independence and objectivity of voluntary code enforcement, that pressures are growing for code administrators to use these mechanisms, and that it is likely they will respond to them over time.[65]

In the final analysis, a key factor when considering rule implementation is an intangible factor that could be called a "compliance ethos." In Canada, as in most Western developed countries, laws are generally held in high regard. For the most part, few wish to be seen to be in non-compliance with laws. There may be no similar ethic or aura surrounding voluntary codes. As a result, there may be less perceived societal pressure for firms to comply with voluntary codes. This is not to suggest that there are not other incentives at work that will tend to encourage compliance with voluntary codes. There undoubtedly are. One is peer pressure. When the rules are developed by firms, there may be considerable pressure from other firms to preserve the good image of the code and the industry.[66] There is potential for an internalization of responsibility to take place when voluntary codes are employed "by industry for industry" that may be missing when rules are externally imposed on industry by government. There may also be market pressure to comply — bad publicity may harm sales — and representations that one is meeting high standards may be rewarded (particularly when third parties attest to compliance with the standards).[67]

A 1985 study by Dale T. Miller of Simon Fraser University's Psychology and Law Institute, entitled *Psychological Factors Influencing Compliance*,[68] suggests that, when those who are the subject of regulations:

- initially propose the standards;
- acknowledge the social value of the goal the regulations promotes and the means of achieving that goal;
- make a public commitment to the standards and the goals of the standards;
- feel that the regulations are clear and feasible and take into account the circumstances of the regulated;
- introduce their own sanctions;
- feel responsible for their own compliance records; and
- are subject to positive economic incentives and sanctions in instances of non-compliance,

they are more likely to feel that the regulations are fair and therefore accept a constraint on their freedoms and resources, and are more likely to conform to the standards. All of these factors would appear to apply with equal force to voluntary code regimes. Thus, as Bryne Purchase suggests in his discussion of consent in his chapter in this volume, while it is not the same as the compliance ethos associated with laws, there may nevertheless be

---

65. E. Meidinger (footnote 19), p. 10164. Although Meidinger was speaking specifically about environmental certification schemes, his remarks would appear to apply with equal force to voluntary code administration in other policy contexts.

66. See Moffet, Bregha and Middelkoop, "Responsible Care," Chapter 6, below.

67. See Rhone, Stroud and Webb,"Gap's Code of Conduct," Chapter 7, below.

68. D. T. Miller, *Psychological Factors Influencing Compliance: Final Report*, Study for the Federal Statutes Compliance Project, Department of Justice Canada (Vancouver: Vancouver Psychology and Law Institute, Simon Fraser University, 1985).

a powerful compliance ethos in play for firms complying to voluntary codes, since voluntary codes are inherently consensual instruments, involving the close cooperation of the "regulated" in the development of (and public commitment to) the rules and incentives and sanctions.

Rule Administration: Comparison of Regulatory and Voluntary Codes Regimes		
Characteristics	**Public Laws**	**Voluntary Codes**
Institutions of rule administration	Primarily pre-established institutions.	May use newly developed institutions or existing bodies.
Visibility of rule implementation process	High: public reporting requirements.	Lower: can have procedures to ensure visibility such as public reporting requirements.
Cost	High: due to need to adhere to due process considerations and transparency obligations, but cost spread across society.	Lower: may be lesser concerns with transparency but cost borne by a small group.
Accountability	High: scrutiny by Auditor General, responsible ultimately to Minister/Parliament.	Lower: depends on reporting requirements; the market, public and media are important.
Constraints on rule administration	Considerable: constitutional and procedural.	Few: varies by institution.
Credibility	High.	Tends to be lower.
Investigation and inspection capabilities	Subject to constitutional constraints: may have extensive powers.	Subject to consent of parties: may have extensive powers.
Sanctions for non-cooperation in administration of rules	May include coercive measures.	May be more limited: consensual system.
Formality	Normally high.	Variable.
Likelihood of rules being followed	High: in a law abiding society few wish to be seen in violation.	Lower: pressure to comply is derived primarily from peers and market perceptions.

Adjudication

The chart below summarizes the main points of distinction between regulation and voluntary code dispute resolution.

Adjudication: Comparison of Regulatory and Voluntary Code Regimes		
Characteristics	**Public Laws**	**Voluntary Codes**
Institutions of rule adjudication	Both pre-established (courts) and new (e.g. regulatory tribunals).	Primarily newly established bodies, indirectly supported by courts.
Authoritativeness of determinations	High.	Variable.
Ability to enforce judgments	High: can draw on State-approved coercion.	Variable: limited ability to use coercive force; can use market-based sanctions.
Structure of adjudication	Tends to be centralized.	Variable centralization.
Application	Wide: applies to all parties, can compel attendance, impose penalties on parties who do not attend.	Variable: dependent ultimately on consent; difficulty applying sanctions to those who do not wish to participate.
Cost	High: spread across society.	Variable: borne by a small group.
Formality	Tends to be high.	Variable: may be formal or informal.
Credibility	High.	Variable,
Visibility	High.	Variable.
Constraints	Considerable: constitutional and procedural.	Variable.

It is worth noting that governments, the courts, the private sector and individuals are increasingly turning to private adjudicative mechanisms, methods and institutions, in light of their advantages in terms of speed, cost and their perceived fairness and effectiveness.[69] These private dispute resolution approaches — mediation, ombuds-services, arbitration, tribunals and others — depend to some extent for their success on the existence of court systems as a backstop final resort. Thus, parties may engage the services of a private dispute resolution service because they wish to avoid the expense, slowness, uncertainty, adversarial nature and formality of the courts. Yet, in most cases, those same parties may have some comfort in knowing that formal litigation remains a

---

69. S. Henry, *Private Justice: Towards Integrated Theorising in the Sociology of Law* (London: Routledge & Kegan Paul, 1983).

viable option of last resort, should alternative techniques be considered inappropriate, unless the parties agree in advance that the decision is final.[70] Furthermore, decisions reached through alternative dispute resolution approaches may ultimately be imposed through the formal legal processes.

In voluntary code regimes, a wide range of approaches have been used to encourage compliance. Canadian Automobile Association (CAA) members can make use of CAA arbitration services for consumer disputes concerning Approved Automobile Repair Service garage owners.[71] The Canadian Bankers Association has established a consumer ombudsman service to complement those in place for individual banks.[72] For consumer disputes about cable television, the Canadian Cable Television Association has established a formal tribunal as a dispute resolution mechanism, which includes representatives from the cable industry and from a public interest or consumer group.[73] Decisions from this tribunal (including dissenting opinions) are made public.

Formal and transparent approaches, including the use of non-business-affiliated third parties (e.g. consumer or environmental group representatives, retired judges, experienced arbitrators), would appear to have the most credibility in the eyes of the public, and with non-governmental organizations and governments.[74] However, they may also be the most expensive, and are not necessarily the most effective.

Private adjudicative bodies may be able to employ decision-making processes that reverse burdens of proof so that firms accused of wrongdoing must demonstrate that their practices were in compliance with the terms of the voluntary code. While such processes are more likely to protect the consumer interest, it would be difficult for public courts or tribunals to operate in this manner.[75] For example, the private, independent, U.K. Advertising Standards Authority (ASA) notes that "in many instances the Codes go further than the law requires. Under the Authority's system of control, the normal judicial burden of proof is reversed: advertisers must prove to the ASA that their claims are true. Another distinction is that the Codes are applied in the 'spirit' as well as in the letter."[76] The ASA's adjudicative methods have been the subject of legal challenge, with U.K. courts declaring that the procedures were "perfectly proper and satisfactory."[77] The

---

70. In consumer-business contexts, in the authors' opinion, efforts to contractually foreclose the option of resort to courts when some other mechanism of resolution is provided should generally be discouraged because of the imbalance of power between the parties.

71. Approved Automobile Repair Service garages must, as a term of participation in the CAA's program, agree to meet CAA service standards and submit to random inspections. As described in Clarke and Webb (footnote 3).

72. Ibid.

73. Ibid.

74. The Government of Quebec and a Quebec automobile protection association (an NGO) only agreed to approve operation of a Quebec version of the non-statutory Canadian Motor Vehicle Arbitration Plan after there was improved transparency and public disclosure concerning the results of arbitrations. See Clarke and Webb (footnote 3).

75. This point is discussed in greater detail in the second part of this chapter.

76. Advertising Standards Authority, *Misleading Advertisements: The Law*, available at <www.asa.org.uk/issues/background_briefings>.

77. Lord Justice Glidewell, in *R. v. Advertising Standards Authority, ex parte The Insurance Service plc*, Queen's Bench Division, 9 Tr L 169, July 6, 1989.

ASA's processes have also been the subject of government review (most recently in 1999). According to the 1999 review, "the Government strongly supports the self-regulatory controls on advertising in the UK run by the Advertising Standards Authority."[78] The point here is that private adjudicative bodies may be able to operate in a more flexible manner than do public adjudicative bodies, to the advantage of public interests such as those of consumers.

Although it is not possible in the context of a voluntary code regime for a private body to impose penal sanctions such as imprisonment on recalcitrant members, a full panoply of other potentially effective techniques are available and are used, including fines,[79] publicity,[80] withdrawal of privileges such as access to certain databases or services[81] or use of logos,[82] orders of restitution and rectification[83] and banishment from an association.[84]

Significance of the Differences in Rule Creation, Administration and Adjudication

What emerges from the foregoing comparison of command-and-control regulatory regimes and voluntary codes as rule systems is that each approach has strengths, weaknesses and distinctive features. Clearly, the public organs of rule making, implementation and adjudication are powerful, credible, open, democratic and generally effective, although they tend to be formal, expensive and slow. Voluntary code rule systems tend to have less visibility and credibility, less ability to deal with those who do not wish to join the program and reduced options for stimulating compliance, but they

---

78. U.K. Department of Trade and Industry, *Modern Markets, Confident Consumers* (July 1999), available at <www.dti.gov.uk/consumer/whitepaper>. In the late 1980s, regulations were introduced that provided the ASA with an additional sanction whereby the Director General of Fair Trading could be asked by the ASA to initiate legal action (an injunction) against advertisers for serious or persistent breaches of the Codes. The *Control of Misleading Advertisements Regulations 1988* recognized the ASA as an "established means" for controlling the content of non-broadcast advertising. Since 1988, there have been 10 referrals to the Office of Fair Trading. See ASA (footnote 76). Note that the ASA remains an independent, privately funded body.

79. For example, some real estate boards discipline their members by imposing fines.

80. The Canadian Marketing Association (CMA) publishes the names of companies found to be in non-compliance with its voluntary standards. See the CMA's Web site, <www.the-cma.org>. See also Clarke and Webb (footnote 3).

81. For example, some real estate boards refuse access to Multiple Listing Services when a member is non-compliant.

82. This is the case with the Better Business Bureau in Canada. See Clarke and Webb (footnote 3).

83. This is so in the cable television industry in Canada. See Clarke and Webb (footnote 3).

84. The Canadian Chemical Producers' Association requires adherence to the Responsible Care program as a condition of membership. See Moffet, Bregha and Middelkoop, "Responsible Care," Chapter 6, below.

can be more flexible, less expensive and faster, avoid certain jurisdictional limitations attached to public organs, allow non-State parties the freedom to create their own rule structures, and be effective in harnessing the energies of non-State actors.

As discussed in the introduction to this volume, Harvard Business School Professor Clayton Christensen has articulated the idea of "breakthrough innovations" to describe new approaches or processes for developing products that typically enable a larger population of less skilled people to do things previously performed by specialists in less convenient, centralized settings.[85] As with the introduction of personal computers into a world of mainframe devices, voluntary codes open up the possibility of societal rule development and implementation to a much wider group of players than do conventional public law organs such as legislatures and the courts. Non-governmental organizations, firms and multistakeholder groups can establish and operate their own rule systems and engage in "norm conversations" without need for a government intermediary. These voluntary code rule systems are not a replacement for those of the State, and indeed they operate within a broader State legal framework. Seen in this light, voluntary rule systems are an addition to conventional legal processes, with concomitant increased, enriched possibilities for effective norm development and implementation.

Legal Implications of Voluntary Codes

Contract Law and Voluntary Codes

As observed above, a key point of distinction between command-and-control regulatory regimes and voluntary codes is that regulations are imposed on a particular set of actors, whether or not those actors desire it or agree to the terms, while voluntary codes are in essence consensual regimes, so that at first instance, only those parties who agree to participate are subject to them. In legal terms, a formalized consensual arrangement typically takes the form of a contract. A contract is formed when one party makes an offer that is accepted by another party and consideration is exchanged.[86] The existence of a contract has legal implications for the parties involved — implications that translate into rights and obligations ultimately enforceable in court. Many voluntary code arrangements are structured through contracts,[87] particularly market-driven initiatives that employ certification schemes and logos (e.g. those pertaining to apparel production, worker-friendly and environmentally friendly food, organic food, pesticide-free food,

---

85. See, generally, C. Christensen, *The Innovator's Dilemma: When New Technologies Cause Great Firms to Fail* (Boston: Harvard Business School Press, 1997) and, more particularly, C. Christensen and T. Petzinger, "Innovation in the Connected Economy: A Conversation with Clayton Christensen," *Perspectives on Business Innovation*, Issue 5: The Connected Economy (September 2000).

86. Consideration has been defined by the courts as "some right, interest, profit or benefit accruing to the one party or some forbearance, detriment, loss or responsibility, given, suffered or undertaken by the other": *Currie v. Misa* (1875) L.R. 10 Exch. 153. Typically, consideration takes the form of a payment for goods received or services rendered.

87. Licensing agreements, which authorize the use of logos on products and representations in advertising and company literature, are an example of a contractual arrangement that is common in market-oriented voluntary code regimes. As discussed below, there may also be contracts between code administrators and compliance verification bodies, between firms and their suppliers, and between industry associations and members.

sustainable forestry and fishery practices, humane treatment of animals, consumer friendly e-commerce merchants, ethical businesses, privacy, and quality and environmental management). There are also issues of intellectual property associated with many voluntary code regimes (e.g. copyright of standards and trademarks of logos and names of programs), but since these are generally straightforward and non-controversial, we will not discuss them further in this chapter.

For purposes of voluntary code analysis, key issues in contract law revolve around when a contract is made, what its terms are, and who the parties to it are.[88] Parties to a contract who fail to comply with contract terms may be liable for restitution, damages or specific performance requirements. As with all legal instruments and actions, there must be sufficient precision in the terms of the commitment (e.g. the provisions of the voluntary code) before there are grounds for action. The use of contracts in voluntary code regimes can take many forms, and involve a number of different parties. These issues are discussed below.

Contracts, Code Administrators and Participating Firms

Perhaps the most obvious contractual relationship created by voluntary code regimes is between code administrators and those participating in the code program. Typically, when member firms join a voluntary codes body, they must pay a membership fee and agree to abide by whatever rules and standards are imposed by the codes body. In exchange, the member firms can advertise their affiliation with the body, and have access to services provided by it. The failure of a member firm to abide by agreed-upon standards set by the codes body may be actionable in contract by the body, just as a failure on the part of the body to provide agreed-upon services could result in an action against the body. "Disciplinary actions" by industry associations,[89] non-governmental organizations,[90] multistakeholder organizations[91] and standards organizations are common.

A 1991 Nova Scotia Court of Appeal decision[92] dealt with a member of the Investment Dealers Association who had breached its standards and was subsequently disciplined by the Association's Business Conduct Committee. Although the plaintiff member acknowledged that he was familiar with the standards set by the organization and the penalties for breaching them, he argued that the Association should not be

---

88. For more information on contract law see, generally, G. Fridman, *The Law of Contract in Canada* (Scarborough, Ont.: Thomson, 1994).

89. See discussion of the Investment Dealers Association and Better Business Bureau (Quebec) cases below.

90. For example, the U.K. Consumers' Association's Web Trader consumer e-commerce regime has withdrawn membership of merchants who were not complying with the terms of the program. See discussion of dismissal of Jungle.com from Web Trader in E. Taylor, "E-tailers Seek Seal of Approval To Reassure Cautions Customers," *Wall Street Journal Europe*, March 1, 2001. Following extensive improvements, Jungle.com was reinstated.

91. For example, the multistakeholder group Forest Stewardship Council has suspended activities of the Europe-based Skal Certification body; see Forest Stewardship Council, *Forest Stewardship Council Suspends Activities of Europe-Based Certification Body*, press release, March 30, 2001.

92. *Ripley v. Investment Dealers Association (Business Conduct Committee)* [1991] 108 N.S.R. (2d) 38 (N.S.C.A.).

permitted to discipline him since this would violate his Charter rights under sections 7 and 11. The Nova Scotia Court of Appeal ruled against the member, noting that:

> It may be inferred that members of the securities industry contract to regulate themselves because it is to their advantage to do so. An obvious benefit is the avoidance of the need for government regulation in a field where the need for protection of the public might otherwise attract it. A party to such a contract cannot have it both ways; if he enjoys benefits from a contract which excludes government intervention from his profession, he cannot claim *Charter* protection when he is accused of breaching the conditions of his contract.[93]

The effect of the decision is to uphold the right of industry associations to enforce agreed-upon standards on members. While the right of industry associations to discipline their members, and to not be constrained by the Charter in doing so was confirmed in the Investment Dealers Association case,[94] this is not to suggest that such disciplinary actions, even though part of private, contractual regimes, are not subject to basic notions of fairness. The 1998 Quebec case pertaining to disciplining actions of the Quebec chapter of the Better Business Bureau[95] is judicial authority for the proposition that, even with private rule initiatives, code administrators must meet basic notions of procedural fairness, such as providing a member being disciplined with notice that a complaint has been laid against that member, and giving the member an opportunity to respond to the complaint before being removed from the organization.

In the sense that code administrators can impose penalties and discipline members, yet must do so in a fair manner, the contractual enforcement actions of code administrators resemble in many ways the enforcement actions of regulatory agencies against regulated parties. The key difference is that, in private rule contexts, a code administrator can bring a contractual enforcement action only against a party who has previously agreed to participate in the voluntary code arrangement. Those firms or individuals who choose not to join the program are beyond the reach of code administrators through contract litigation, even though the reputation of all the firms in a particular sector may be sullied by the activities of the non-participating firm.[96]

---

93. Ibid.

94. Note that unlike private voluntary code administrators, governments are subject to the Charter, as discussed later in the chapter.

95. *A.A.A. Khan Transport Inc. v. Bureau d'éthique commerciale de Montréal Inc.* [1998] Q.J. No. 226, Quebec Superior Court (General Division) (Q.L.). In a curious side note, an Ontario court has recently ruled that it would *not* interfere with a dispute between a company that produces and sells kosher meats and three rabbis who were senior members of a council that supervised the production and distribution of kosher food, on the grounds that the matter was more properly to be addressed through a rabbinical court. As result, the legal action for, among other things, breach of contract, was stayed: *Levitts Kosher Foods Inc. v. Levin* [1999] 45 OR (3d) 147 (Ont. Superior Ct.). In the United States, state attempts to create statutory provisions that explicitly protect consumers against false labelling of food as kosher have been ruled unconstitutional, as a violation of the First Amendment because they were interpreted as endorsing and advancing religion: see discussion later in this chapter.

96. It is worth noting that although compliance with voluntary arrangements cannot be compelled on firms not party to the agreement through an action in contract, other legal pressures, particularly tort or regulatory law, can lead a non-member to comply. These aspects are discussed later in this chapter.

Contracts, Codes, Firms and Suppliers

Firms can require that suppliers meet certain criteria as a term of contract. While regulatory regimes are, in most circumstances, limited in application to the jurisdiction in which the laws are made, there are few such constraints in private law contracts between, for example, retailers in one jurisdiction and suppliers in other jurisdictions that agree to abide by the terms of a voluntary code program. Through such arrangements, voluntary codes can have multijurisdictional application, so that, for example, Nike Inc. can require by contract that its suppliers located around the world meet certain U.S. Occupational Safety and Health Administration standards for indoor air quality.[97] In the event of non-compliance with code obligations, these supplier-factories risk termination or suspension of contracts.[98] An interesting variation on this theme is the agreement of Gap Inc. to hire local union, religious and academic leaders as independent monitors of their code of compliance for some of their supplier factories. The monitors meet regularly with workers to hear complaints, investigate problems and look over the books.[99] This monitoring arrangement represents another layer of contractual relationship developed as part of voluntary code implementation.

Contracts, Codes, Consumers and Retail Firms

Although there are practical obstacles that discourage such actions,[100] it is possible for consumers to bring actions in contract law over issues pertaining to voluntary codes. From the standpoint of consumers, a firm or group of firms that boasts that it is complying with a voluntary code is making a commitment to consumers that it will meet certain obligations. It has long been established in contract law that an offer made to any member of the public, if accepted, must be honoured.[101] If the terms of the offer are not met, actions can be brought in contract,[102] or can be based on legislative protections prohibiting unfair business, deceptive labelling and advertising practices.[103] If a retailer falsely claimed that a product or service had certain attributes, and the retailer knew that the representation was false, and intended to deceive — for example, that it

---

97. See, e.g., Connor (footnote 18).

98. In one well-documented case concerning supplier-factory Mandarin International (now called Charter) in El Salvador, following NGO-assisted public exposure of worker abuse, two of four retailers terminated contractual relations with Mandarin (including J. C. Penney), one suspended its contract (Eddie Bauer, a unit of Spiegel Inc.) and a fourth (Gap) stayed after deciding that all groups — workers, labour activists and factory owners — were willing to make changes. See Rhone, Stroud and Webb, "Gap's Code of Conduct," Chapter 7, below, and L. Kaufman and D. Gonzalez, "Labor Standards Clash with Global Reality," *New York Times*, April 24, 2001.

99. Gap itself made changes as well — reformulating and improving its suppliers' code of conduct, as discussed in Rhone, Stroud and Webb, "Gap's Code of Conduct," Chapter 7, below.

100. See "Drawbacks of Contractual Actions," below.

101. *Carlill v. Carbolic Smoke Ball Co.* [1893] 1 Q.B. 256 (C.A.).

102. Fridman (footnote 88), p. 694.

103. See explorations of the relation between misleading advertising regulatory prohibitions and voluntary codes later in the chapter.

was a Canadian Automobile Association-approved garage, a Better Business Bureau-approved merchant, or that it was selling a Forest Stewardship Council-approved sustainable forestry product, a Fair Labor Association-approved garment, or a Canadian Standards Association-certified product or service, when it was not — a consumer (or the body that grants approvals of these sorts of merchants or products) could potentially bring a contractual action for fraudulent misrepresentation.[104]

Contracts, Codes, Consumers and Manufacturers

In most cases consumers do not purchase goods directly from the manufacturer, but rather from a retailer. In this scenario a contract exists between the consumer and the retail vendor, but no contract exists between the consumer and the manufacturer. However, this does not necessarily prevent the consumer from suing the manufacturer for breach of contract. Using a doctrine known as "collateral contracts," the court can find that an implied contract exists between the manufacturer and the consumer in which the manufacturers make claims concerning their products or services that cannot be fulfilled. For example, a manufacturer could claim that a product meets certain environmental standards when it does not. If a court finds that a manufacturer's statements about a product constitute a binding promise or contractual undertaking, the court can rule that a "collateral contract" exists between the manufacturer and the consumer, and should the claim not be substantiated, provide a remedy for any breach.

A case that illustrates the application of this principle is *Murray v. Sperry Rand Corporation.*[105] The manufacturer of farm machinery published a brochure that contained statements about the quality of the machine. The brochure was highly promotional and was not merely a description of the machine. The court found that anyone reading the brochure would reasonably conclude that the manufacturer was promising that the described performance was the actual performance of the machine. Even though the product was purchased through a distributor, the manufacturer was found liable to the consumer in contract, since through its promises it had induced the consumer to purchase the machine.

Drawbacks of Contractual Actions Concerning Codes

There are a number of factors that tend to mitigate against individual consumers bringing actions in contract against retailers or manufacturers for violations of the terms of voluntary codes. Most focus on the uneven power relationship between the two parties: firms tend to have the expertise to know when a contractual term is being violated, whereas individual consumers may not. Firms may also have the know-how to successfully fight a contract action in court, while individual consumers may be intimidated by court processes and not knowledgeable about court rules and procedures. Firms are more likely to have the resources to hire lawyers than are individual consumers and their representatives. And finally, the individual damage to any one consumer in

---

104. Fridman (footnote 88), p. 295.

105. (1979) 23 O.R. 456 (H.C.).

instances of code non-compliance may be so small that the consumer may simply decide not to bother with the action (and the court may also find the damages to be negligible). With respect to the latter point, this may be particularly troubling since, while the damage to any one consumer may be inconsequential, the cumulative or aggregate damage to all affected consumers and to the marketplace may be quite large.[106]

For all of these reasons, legislators in certain jurisdictions have developed class action legislation.[107] Here, one consumer or a small group of consumers can bring an action on behalf of all affected consumers. Even though an individually aggrieved consumer might not feel he or she has been harmed to such a degree as to warrant bringing an individual action, and also might not have the resources or stamina to bring a legal action, a group of consumers acting together is in a considerably stronger position to bring such actions. In the Canadian jurisdictions that have modern class action legislation (e.g. Ontario, British Columbia and Quebec), there are a number of procedures and mechanisms in place that go a long way toward levelling the playing field between the parties, and in turn increase the likelihood that mass contractual voluntary code breaches can be remedied.

Tort Law and Voluntary Codes

Although the consensual nature of many voluntary code arrangements makes the contract law aspects of codes particularly self-evident, tort law and voluntary codes can also be closely linked. Torts are "civil wrongs" characterized by breach of legal duties when there are no necessary pre-existing contractual relations between the litigating parties. Determinations of what constitute "legal duties" can include drawing on the existence of voluntary codes as evidence of both the nature of the duty and to whom it is owed. We will look here at two types of torts, nuisance and negligence.

The Tort of Nuisance and Codes

Nuisance has been described as "an unreasonable interference with the reasonable use and enjoyment of land by its occupier or of the use and enjoyment of a public right to use and enjoy public rights of way."[108] The basic premise underlying the tort of nuisance is that people should be free to use their own land in any manner they wish, so long as their actions do not interfere with the proper use of their neighbour's land. In recent years, suits in nuisance have tended to be related to the environment, addressing nuisances such as noise, vibration and pollution. Voluntary standards can assist courts in determining what constitutes a nuisance. For example, in *340909 Ontario*

---

106. It is for all these reasons that consumer regulatory agencies have been created. Using legislative prohibitions against unfair, deceptive and misleading business practices, such agencies can act on behalf of individual consumers, and (in theory at least) they have the expertise, time and resources to see such actions through to fruition. See explorations of the relation between deceptive practice prohibitions and voluntary codes later in the chapter.

107. For more information on class actions, see M. Cochrane, *Class Actions in Ontario: A Guide to the Class Proceedings Act 1992* (Toronto: Canada Law Book, 1992).

108. A. Linden, *Canadian Tort Law* (Toronto: Butterworths, 1988), p. 503.

Ltd. v. Huron Steel Products Ltd.,[109] International Organization for Standardization (ISO) standards were used to determine whether vibrations caused by a plant constituted a nuisance. Expert witnesses testified that, at the time, there were three different ISO standards for vibration levels. The vibrations caused by the plant exceeded these levels by two, two-and-a-half, and seven times. The court found that the vibration levels were so severe that they interfered with the plaintiff's reasonable use and enjoyment of the land, and thus awarded judgment for the plaintiff.

The Tort of Negligence and Codes

A key feature of tort actions in negligence is that, if the court accepts that the standard of care embodied in a voluntary code represents the "accepted industry standard," such codes may in effect impose liability on parties even if those parties never directly participated in the voluntary code arrangement in question. In this way, it is possible for voluntary code arrangements, through judicial endorsement in tort actions, to have application beyond the members who participated in the voluntary code regime to parties who did not agree to participate in the regime, but may nevertheless be benefiting from the good name and reputation associated with the regime (free riders). Affected individuals and communities who are in a non-contractual relationship may be able to make use of voluntary codes in negligence actions. For example, if citizens of a town downwind from a polluter suffer certain harm, it is possible that they can bring an action in negligence, and make use of the existence of a voluntary code concerning emissions as evidence of an accepted industry standard, even though those citizens may have never entered into any type of formal arrangement with the polluter.

To establish a cause of action in negligence, the aggrieved party must demonstrate three factors: the existence of a duty of care owed by the defendant to the plaintiff, a breach of the duty caused by the defendant failing to meet an acceptable standard of care, and actual harm ensuing from the breach.[110]

Standard of Care in Negligence Actions

In general, the standard of care used by courts in tort cases of negligence is "that degree of care which a reasonably prudent person should exercise" in the circumstances.[111] However, when negligence occurs in the course of a specific function, the standard of care changes. For example, when a doctor is accused of medical negligence, the standard becomes that of the reasonable *doctor* in like circumstances (and not just any "reasonable person"). When allegations of negligence are made against a corporation, the standard generally used is that of the particular industry. For example, if a chemical company were accused of negligence, its conduct would be judged against the industry practice. If the company's conduct deviated from the industry practice and this was demonstrated to the satisfaction of the judge, in practice there would be a strong presumption of negligence. Although the industry standard does not alone determine

---

109. [1992] 9 O.R. (3d) 305 (Ont. C.A.).

110. Linden (footnote 108), p. 92.

111. J. R. Nolan and J. M. Nolan Haley, eds., *Black's Law Dictionary* (St. Paul, Minn.: West, 1990).

negligence, proof of deviation from the industry standard may be a difficult burden for a defendant to overcome.[112]

Often, courts find the accepted industry practice indicative of what is reasonable in the circumstances. Furthermore, it has been suggested that it would be unfair to demand that the defendant in a negligence action be required to know of safeguards beyond those used in his or her profession.[113] For these reasons, negligence actions are often mainly concerned with the question of what constitutes the agreed-upon industry standard. Voluntary codes can be viewed by the courts as having the effect of establishing, documenting and/or raising the standard for a particular industry. In addition, those who are not adherents to a voluntary code may nevertheless be judged by the standard specified in the code, when it is the accepted industry norm. From a public standpoint, this could have a beneficial effect on firms that have refused to directly participate in voluntary code arrangements (i.e. free riders). American judge A. David Mazzone sees the deterrence of free riders through increased potential liability as one of the main benefits of voluntary standards. Speaking about the ISO 14001 environmental standards, Mazzone commented, "This [reduced chance of liability] is the carrot. If companies fail to adopt a compliance program and commit an environmental offence, we will essentially be giving them the stick."[114]

However, the use by courts of voluntary codes as an indication of the standard of care for a particular sector can in a sense make such codes compulsory, since courts can measure the behaviour of a firm that decides not to adhere to a particular standard and find the firm's conduct unacceptable. While this can have a beneficial effect when the result is increased safety or environmental protection, there is also the theoretical potential for judicial recognition of such standard to have inefficiency or anti-competitive effects. For example, a voluntary standard could be set at a level that is costly to meet and offers few tangible safety or environmental benefits. Nonetheless, organizations could feel obliged to comply with it since it may be used by the court as the basis for determining what constitutes industry practice.[115] In addition, standards that are set very high and are expensive to meet could force smaller companies out of the marketplace and thereby indirectly establish a barrier to entry into the marketplace. By the same token, a voluntary code standard could be set at an artificially low level, below the standard that the industry is capable of achieving. In either circumstances, if the voluntary code was inadequate as the basis for an industry standard, it would be open to an individual firm or organization that is the subject of the negligence action or a plaintiff that is bringing the legal suit to point out the inadequacies or inappropriate aspects of a standard to a court

---

112. *Clark v. MacLennan* [1983] 1 All E.R. 416 (Q.B.).

113. Linden (footnote 108), p. 162.

114. "Reducing Legal Liability With an ISO 14001 EMS," *Standards New Zealand Environmental Newsletter* (February 1996), p. 1. While Mazzone's comments refer specifically to the use of an *offence* as a "stick," the same argument can be made with respect to private negligence actions.

115. "In a controversial demolition binge last summer, hundreds of playground structures were levelled ... because they did not meet new specifications set by the Canadian Standards Association. Engineering student Alfredo Montenegro says the revised standards were not intended to be applied to existing equipment that could, perhaps, have been modified to make it safer. Erring on the side of caution, many school boards and regional governments decided to demolish the structures ... ." (V. Galt, "Child's Play a Challenge for Engineers," *The Globe and Mail*, December 4, 2001).

considering the issue. And anti-competitive aspects would be open to challenge under competition or antitrust laws (as discussed later in this chapter).

There are a number of examples of actions in negligence that turned on whether a voluntary standard was followed. For example, in *Visp Construction v. Scepter Manufacturing Co.*,[116] a pipe manufactured to meet Canadian Standards Association (CSA) standards burst. The plaintiff sued the defendant manufacturer arguing that the pipe was defective in its construction. The court ruled that the defendant had exercised due diligence in ensuring that the pipe was properly produced. Judge Anderson emphasized the merits of adhering to the CSA standard, stating, "I find and conclude that the CSA specification was a reasonable standard for the defendant to have adopted, and that [the defendant] took reasonable steps to ensure that its product met that standard."[117]

Another case in which a manufacturer demonstrated due diligence through its adherence to a voluntary standard was *Meisel v. Tolko Industries Ltd.*[118] In this case a construction worker who fell through a roof constructed with wood supplied by the defendant sued the defendant for the injuries he sustained. The plaintiff attempted to use the voluntary standard for lumber companies to his advantage, arguing that the wood was improperly graded according to the National Lumber Grades Authority (NLGA) standard. The defendant disagreed and used expert testimony to demonstrate that the NLGA standards were followed in a manner common in the industry. Since the defendant followed both the industry practice and the NLGA standards in assessing the wood, the court concluded that it had exercised due diligence.

Just as evidence that one has followed voluntary standards can be used by a defendant to assist in establishing that he or she has exercised due diligence, failure to adhere to commonly accepted standards can be used by a plaintiff as evidence of negligence. For example, in *Reed v. McDermid St. Lawrence Ltd.*,[119] the plaintiff, an investor, sued her broker, arguing that he was negligent in failing to warn her of the volatility of her investment. At trial, the court found for the plaintiff, emphasizing that "the root of the basic ethic of the Investment Dealers Association [is] that a broker know his client. In this case, the form is evidence that the broker did not know his client. Among other things, the assessment to be made by the broker of the plaintiff's 'investment knowledge' was left blank."[120] Thus, the form, developed by the Investment Dealers Association, was taken to have codified industry standards, so that failure to fill out that form could be considered evidence of non-compliance with the standard of care.

While adherence or non-adherence to voluntary standards can provide vital evidence in negligence cases, it does not alone determine the result. Typically, the judicial approach to voluntary codes is that such codes are useful for determining industry practices and providing a comparison between a practice known to be safe and the practice used in a particular case. The approach of the Australian judiciary was

116. (1991) 45 Const. L. Rep. 170 (Ont. Court Gen. Div.).

117. Ibid., pp. 29–30.

118. [1991] B.C.J. No. 105 (SC).

119. (1991) 52 B.C.L.R. (2d) 265 (CA).

120. Ibid. This judgment was reversed on appeal, with the court ruling that the basic duty of the broker is to carry out the instructions of his or her client. Nonetheless, the decision is important because it demonstrates the potential value of voluntary codes to consumers.

summed up by Justice Duggan in *Benton v. Tea Tree Plaza*: "Care must be taken not to attach too much importance to standards in cases such as the present. Failure to follow a standard does not, without more, establish negligence."[121]

The presumption of the court that breaching a voluntary standard does not in itself prove negligence is not unique to Australia. In a recent British case, the court ruled that a breach of the Professional Code of Solicitors is not by that fact alone synonymous with negligence.[122] The action of the plaintiffs, based largely on the lawyer's breach of the Code, was defeated. Common-law Canadian courts approach voluntary codes in much the same way as their common-law Australian and British counterparts. In *Murphy et al. v. Atlantic Speedy Propane Ltd.*,[123] the defendant installed a gas dryer and propane tanks at the plaintiff's house. The dryer later started a fire that destroyed the house. The defendant argued that he had followed the industry norm described in the *Code for Propane Burning Appliances* and that the dryer met CSA standards. Despite the defendant's compliance with the voluntary code followed by the industry, the judge found the industry practice unsafe, ruling in favour of the plaintiff and stating that the defendant "cannot hide behind the industry practice."[124]

A recent regulatory case pertaining to the issue of appropriate standards of care from New Zealand adds a new wrinkle to the way in which courts will use voluntary codes as evidence of due diligence. In *Department of Labour v. Waste Management N.Z. Limited*,[125] the defendant company was defending a charge under the *Health and Safety in Employment Act* after an employee died while using a machine leased by the defendant. The case turned on whether the machine was unsafe. In its defence, the company argued that its machine met the American standard for such machines. However, the judge ruled that meeting the American standard was insufficient, since the American standard may have been inferior to the New Zealand standard as a result of the way it was developed, or the circumstances surrounding its development.[126] Although the specific reasoning adopted by the New Zealand court in this case has not been applied in Canada, it does raise several interesting issues. For instance, should Canadian courts give preference to Canadian standards over American or international standards? Should the courts consider the development process of the particular standard? Should the courts consider the context (political and social) in which the standard was developed? These issues are discussed later in this chapter.

---

121. *Benton v. Tea Tree Plaza* (1995) No. SCGRG 94/417, Judgment No. 5144 (SC of South Aus.), p. 30. In this case, the plaintiff had fallen over a curb that was 50 millimetres higher than the Australian Standards Association (ASA) standard. The court used the standard as a yardstick to compare the curb in question with a curb height it presumed safe. Had the curb in this case exceeded the ASA standard by only a few millimetres, the court might have reached a different result. The verdict was not based on the fact that the curb exceeded the height mandated by the ASA, but that it exceeded that height by a large amount.

122. *Johnson v. Bingley and Others, The Times* (London), February 28, 1995 (QB).

123. (1979) 103 D.L.R. (3d) 545 (NSSC).

124. Ibid., p. 555.

125. [1995] CRN No. 40040511262 (Dist. Ct. — Auckland).

126. Ibid., p. 9.

In certain circumstances, it may be possible to bring tort actions in one jurisdiction to address corporate activities that have occurred in another jurisdiction. Recently, there has been a flurry of legal actions in the United States and the United Kingdom pertaining to alleged wrongful corporate activity in developing countries. Voluntary codes and standards can play important roles in such litigation, as part of court explorations of what constitutes "reasonable care." Codes of conduct can play key roles in both demonstrations by corporations that they are living up to appropriate standards of care or, alternatively, in judicial determinations of liability against those corporations that fail to meet them. In the United States, the key instrument for such actions has been the *Alien Tort Claims Act*[127] of 1789. Pursuant to this Act, non-American plaintiffs (aliens) can bring actions against parties with affiliations to the United States in American courts for civil wrongs that are violations of customary international law or a treaty of the United States. Although originally the Act was used primarily to address actions of individuals who were State actors (and thus subject to international treaties and customary law), courts in recent years have adopted a more broad interpretation, leading to litigation against corporations on grounds of complicity in human rights violations.[128]

In the United Kingdom, several court actions have led to multimillion dollar settlements by multinationals with subsidiary operations in developing countries.[129] A leading U.K. litigator involved in some of the key decisions to date has stated, "In the light of the House of Lords decision ... multinationals would be well advised to take active measures to ensure that the working conditions at their worldwide operations comply with the standards they would be expected to meet at home or with international standards." In an article concerning the use of the *Alien Tort Claims Act* to address corporate responsibility, Professor Ralph Steinhardt of the George Washington University Law School brings together codes of conduct and interjurisdictional tort litigation as follows:

> ... corporations have demonstrated that they are willing to adopt voluntary codes of conduct and to exploit those segments of the markets that make consumption and investment decisions on the basis of a company's perceived commitment to human rights. ... [M]arket incentives and ... liability litigation are not mutually exclusive and ... can actually reinforce one another. ... [I]t does seem clear that the prospect of litigation may have accelerated the voluntary, marketplace initiatives and that litigation will define the primitive minimum beneath which the market will not operate.[130]

---

127. USC (Annotated) § 1350.

128. See, e.g., discussion of *Doe v. Unocal* (2000) and *Wiwa v. Royal Dutch Petroleum Company* (2000) in R. Steinhardt, *Litigating Corporate Responsibility* (2001) at <www.lse.ac.uk/collections/globalDimensions/seminars/humanRightsAndCorporateResponsibility/steinhardtTranscript.htm>.

129. See, e.g., discussion of litigation against Thor Chemicals, RTZ Corporation, and Cape plc, in R. Meeran, "Victims of Multinational Corporations: What Avenues are Available?" *Mealey's Litigation Report: Asbestos*, March 23, 2001.

130. Steinhardt (footnote 128).

Initiatives such as the Mining Minerals and Sustainable Development Project,[131] the U.S./U.K. Voluntary Principles on Security and Human Rights[132] for resource-based companies, and the International Code of Ethics for Canadian Businesses[133] can all be seen as industry-driven efforts to articulate global standards of care, and, as Steinhardt suggests, they may in part be stimulated by the ~~type of interjurisdictional tort litigation~~ that has become increasingly common in the United States and the United Kingdom.[134]

In summary, it is clear that voluntary codes can be useful to courts in tort actions, both as examples of safe or appropriate practices and as evidence of typical industry practices. While voluntary codes are important factors in any tort action, they alone do not determine the outcome. The increasing prevalence of voluntary codes might have the effect of stimulating improvements in industry practice in a particular sector. This can occur in two ways. First, if the voluntary standard is adopted by a significant portion of the sector, this may assist the court in reaching the conclusion that it is the standard of care for the sector. Members of industry who ignore the standard may have difficulty defending a tort suit. Since, in many instances, the cost of defending oneself or obtaining a court award is greater than meeting the voluntary standard in the first place, it may induce many organizations to comply with the standard. Second, a voluntary standard that is not adopted by the sector may still be useful for courts as a benchmark for comparison. Judges may make a tacit assumption, for example, that a voluntary standard illustrates a safe practice in a particular situation. Even when the actual sector practice is different (and seems adequate), the court may refer to the voluntary standard to demonstrate that the company did not use due diligence when ensuring that the public was safe. Since firms or organizations may risk liability when they do not adhere to the standard in question, some may conform to the higher standard even when they are satisfied that the current practice is safe.[135]

Negligence Liability of Code Development and Implementation Bodies

The second issue that arises when considering the connection between negligence and voluntary codes is whether bodies entrusted with developing codes and ensuring compliance with them could be held negligent if they fail to keep the code up to date, neglect to adequately notify affected parties of changes to its terms or otherwise fail to ensure its effective implementation, or if the code itself is not adequate. Unless shielded from liability by statute, code bodies can be held to the same standard of care as

---

131. For more information about this initiative go to <www.iied.org/mmsd>.

132. For more information about this initiative go to <www.state.gov/g/drl/rls/2931.htm>.

133. For more information about this initiative go to <www.cdp-hrc.uottawa.ca/globalization/busethics/codeint.html>.

134. The United States and the United Kingdom would appear to be magnets for such litigation, in part because many large multinationals have headquarters or significant operations in these jurisdictions (i.e. the corporate structures are not just empty corporate shells with no funds available, as in some developing countries). Nevertheless, a significant threshold to meet in bringing such actions is establishing that American and U.K. courts are appropriate fora for such litigation, when compared with the courts in the developing countries. This point is discussed by both Steinhardt (footnote 128), and Meeran (footnote 129).

135. See, e.g., the reaction of several school boards to the introduction of revised playground safety standards, as discussed earlier.

anyone else and can be held liable if their negligence leads to injury.[136] For example, liability was imposed on the company that developed and implemented the *Good Housekeeping* Seal of Approval (the Hearst Corporation) in a case involving injury from negligently manufactured shoes bearing the Seal. The court emphasized *Good Housekeeping*'s voluntary involvement in the marketing process for its own gain, the loan of its reputation to the product through its endorsement, and the consumer's reliance upon this endorsement.[137]

Industry associations can also be liable when the codes they develop are considered inadequate. In *King v. National Spa and Pool Institute Inc.*,[138] the estate of a man who died after diving into a swimming pool sued the trade association that promulgated the standards that the manufacturer and installer of the pool relied on. The Supreme Court of Alabama found that the trade association owed a duty of care to the user of the pool, since it was aware that manufacturers and installers relied on its standards. The court stated, "It is well settled under Alabama law that one who undertakes to perform a duty [that it] is not otherwise required to perform is thereafter charged with the duty of acting with due care."[139] The National Spa and Pool Institute's voluntary undertaking to promulgate minimum safety design standards "made it foreseeable that harm might result to the consumer if it did not exercise due care."[140]

In a later case, *Meneely v. S. R. Smith, Inc.*[141] the State of Washington's Court of Appeals held that a trade association such as the National Spa and Pool Institute owes a duty of care when formulating its safety standards and a duty to warn the ultimate consumer about the risk of injury. "By promulgating industry wide safety standards that pool and board manufacturers relied upon, [the National Spa and Pool Institute] voluntarily assumed the duty to warn Mr. Meneely and other divers of the risk posed by this type of board. ... It failed to exercise reasonable care in performing that duty, when it did not change the standard after it knew that studies showed the pool and board combination was dangerous for certain divers."[142] The Court also stated that the National Spa and Pool Institute assumes a duty of care "when it undertakes the task of setting safety standards and fails to change those standards or issue warnings after it becomes aware of a risk posed by the standards."[143] According to the Court, the National Spa and Pool Institute's duty of care "arose from its voluntary assumption of the task of

---

136. Some code development bodies may be protected by statute from negligence suits, such as certain government-operated standards development bodies.

137. *Hanberry v. Hearst Corp.*, 81 Cal. Rptr. 519 (Cal. Ct. App. 1969). The foregoing taken directly from P. Schuck, "Tort Liability to Those Injured by Negligent Accreditation Decisions," in C. Havighurst, ed., "Private Accreditation in the Regulatory State," *Law and Contemporary Problems* 57:4 (Autumn 1994), p. 192.

138. 570 So. (2d) 612 (Ala. 1990).

139. Ibid., p. 614.

140. Ibid., p. 616.

141. [2000] WA-QL 1055 No. 18036-1-III (August 3, 2000) Court of Appeals, State of Washington.

142. Ibid., para. 44.

143. Ibid., para. 5.

formulating safety standards, knowing that the pool industry would conform its products to those standards."[144]

It is difficult to say at this point exactly what effect the National Spa and Pool Institute cases will have on voluntary codes activities of industry associations in the United States, but it is reasonable to assume that it should discourage such activities unless they are undertaken with great care. Some American commentators have suggested that multistakeholder standards organizations, such as the American National Standards Institute (ANSI) (i.e. *not* industry associations) that follow specified operational "game rules" (i.e. the ANSI procedures, including those pertaining to openness, balance of stakeholders, consensus and regular revision), may be in a good position to defend against such negligence actions.[145]

Negligence Class Actions and Codes

Even when a code is in place and appears to set an appropriate standard of care for a particular sector or activity, there may still be significant obstacles facing those injured by the negligence of others as they attempt to bring legal actions to protect their rights. These obstacles often revolve around inadequate time, resources and expertise to see such actions through to completion. Moreover, as with contract actions by consumers, any one individual may be harmed to such a relatively minor extent that he or she might feel that a legal action would not be worth the trouble. Yet, when taken together, many individual instances of harm might reflect significant damage to a community or segment of the population. As discussed earlier, when modernized class action laws are in place, negligence actions by a small number of individuals on behalf of a larger group become more feasible.[146]

Government Regulatory Regimes and Voluntary Codes

Government regulatory regimes and voluntary codes are intertwined in a wide variety of ways. In this section of the chapter, several of the key aspects are discussed. First, an examination of the relation between laws prohibiting deceptive practices and voluntary codes is provided. Then, the roles of voluntary codes in regulatory enforcement are explored. The regulatory implications of use of voluntary codes for business, non-governmental organizations and governments are examined. With respect to governmental implications, the legal effects of regulator participation in voluntary codes, regulatory incorporation of voluntary codes, the use of voluntary codes as supplements to regulatory enforcement, the use of compliance information from voluntary codes in regulatory enforcement, and government support of "beyond compliance" voluntary codes are each discussed.

---

144. Ibid., para. 29.

145. A. Marasco, *Standards Development: Are You At Risk?* (1999), available at <www.ansi.org/ news_publications/other_documents/risk.aspx?menuid=7>. See also J. Q. Smith, J. P. Bolger and A. Marasco, *Products Liability Claims Against Voluntary Standards Developers: An Update on Recent Developments*, (1996).

146. See Cochrane (footnote 107).

Regulatory Prohibitions of Deceptive Business Practices and Voluntary Codes

Most jurisdictions have laws in place prohibiting firms from engaging in deceptive or misleading business practices.[147] Deceptive claims made by firms about their activities and products as they relate to voluntary codes and standards have led to courts imposing legal liability in a number of circumstances.[148] In the United States, laws have been put in place that allow individuals to bring actions concerning allegedly deceptive business practices.[149] In one such case, still before the courts, a private attorney general lawsuit was brought against Nike Inc. and five of its corporate officers, alleging that, in the course of a public relations campaign that revolved around its code of conduct, Nike made misrepresentations regarding its labour practices in its Asian contractor factories.[150] In other cases, apparel firms have settled out of court.[151]

147. In Canada, see *Competition Act*, R.S.C. 1985, c. C-34, s. 52; *Ontario Business Practices Act*, R.S.O. 1990, c. B. 18, s. 2. In the United Kingdom, see the *Trade Descriptions Act, 1968*, s. 14. In the United States, see *Federal Trade Commission Act* 15 USC, s. 5(a), and the unfair competition and false advertising law provisions within the California *Business and Professions Code*, para 17200 et seq. In Australia, see the *Trade Practices Act*, 1974, ss. 52 and 53. In Europe, see the European Union's *Misleading Advertising Directive* 84/450.

148. See discussion of American court actions below. Examples from Australia of such actions include *Re: Robert George Quinn and Brian Alexander Given*, (1980) 41 F.L.R. 416, in which a company falsely represented that its fire extinguishers met Australian standards. Other examples from Australia include *Re: Evaline Jill Hamlyn and Moppet Grange Pty. Ltd.* (1984) Nos. G375-377 of 1983 (Fed. Ct. of Aus.), in which the manufacturer of children's night garments incorrectly represented that the garments met Australian flammability requirements; *Re: Malcolm David Lennox and Megray Pty. Ltd.*, (1985) Nos. VG23 to VG28 of 1985 (Fed. Ct. of Aus.), in which the manufacturer affixed Australian Standards Association (ASA, now Standards Australia) labels to bicycle helmets that were not yet ASA-approved.

149. The federal *Lanham Act* provides a civil action to anyone who is or is likely to be damaged by a commercial misrepresentation of goods or services:

> Any person who, on or in connection with any goods or services, or any container for goods, uses in commerce any word, term, name, symbol, or device, or any combination thereof, or any false designation of origin, false or misleading description of fact, or false or misleading representation of fact, which is likely to cause confusion, or to cause mistake, or to deceive as to the affiliation, connection, or association of such person with another person, or as to the origin, sponsorship, or approval of his or her goods, services, or commercial activities by another person, or in commercial advertising or promotion, misrepresents the nature, characteristics, qualities, or geographic origin of his or her or another person's goods, services, or commercial activities, shall be liable in a civil action
> ... .

Per 15 U.S.C. para. 1125(a)(1). See Meidinger (footnote 19), for discussion of use of the *Lanham Act* in the context of environmental certification programs. In California, private attorney general actions can be brought to address incidents of consumer deception pursuant to the unfair competition law provisions within the *Business and Professions Code*, para. 17204.

150. *Kasky v. Nike Inc.* 27 Cal. 4th 939 (California Supreme Court, 2002). Nike has maintained that the action curtails its rights to freedom of expression. See discussion of the case focussing on its constitutional aspects later in the chapter.

151. In 1999, lawsuits were launched that alleged that several large U.S. garment retailers were engaging in unfair and deceptive business practices contrary to the California *Business and Professions Code* by advertising their garments as being "Sweatshop Free." This legal action led to several financially significant settlements in 2002, and agreements by the retailers that their contractors will comply with a new code of conduct, with independent monitoring. See R. Collier and J. Strasburg, "Clothiers Fold on Sweatshop Lawsuit," *San Francisco Chronicle*, September 27, 2002.

In a number of ways, governments are explicitly linking their regulatory regimes prohibiting deceptive business practices with voluntary code programs. In 2002, the Canadian Competition Bureau announced that it was considering adopting a voluntary standard on environmental claims developed through ISO (ISO 14021) as a guideline to assist in interpreting the *Competition Act's* deceptive advertising provisions as they apply to environmental claims.[152] Some governments have developed regulatory offences prohibiting deceptive practices associated with misuse of voluntary religious food certification and labelling programs. Several American states have passed legislation specifically prohibiting false labelling of food as halal (i.e. in compliance with Islamic food preparation standards) or as kosher (i.e. in compliance with Jewish food preparation standards).[153] In essence, these laws can be considered as supplements to the non-governmental halal and kosher voluntary food preparation certification regimes.[154] Under 1988 regulations promulgated by the U.K. government, the Advertising Standards Authority (a non-statutory, privately funded, voluntary organization devoted to maintaining high standards in the advertising industry) was explicitly recognized as an "established means" for purposes of controlling the content of non-broadcast advertising.[155] This is an example of two programs devoted to reducing the instances of deceptive business practices — one a governmental program employing a conventional regulatory prohibition approach, the other a non-governmental voluntary code program — being formally linked in order to enhance overall effectiveness.

Regulatory Enforcement and Voluntary Codes

Voluntary codes can elaborate on the requirements contained in regulatory legislation, and thereby be used in both in determinations of regulatory liability and sentencing. A good point of departure for understanding the role of voluntary codes in regulatory enforcement is an examination of the nature and operation of regulatory offences. The main type of offence used in Canadian regulatory legislation enforcement is called the strict liability offence.[156] With this type of offence, once the Crown has

---

152. See <http://cb-bc.gc.ca/epic/internet/incb-bc.nsf/vwGeneratedInterE/ct02206e.html>.

153. See, e.g., information at <www.ifanca.org/halal.htm> (halal) and at <www.jlaw.com> (kosher).

154. However, in a July 2000 judgment, the New York Eastern District Court ruled that statutory provisions designed to protect New York consumers against false labelling of food as kosher were unconstitutional, as a violation of the First Amendment because they were interpreted as endorsing and advancing religion. See discussion on this point later in this chapter.

155. *Control of Misleading Advertisements Regulations 1988* (SI 1988 No. 915), passed pursuant to the *Trade Descriptions Act, 1968*.

156. For more detailed discussion of regulatory offences in Canada, see K. Webb, "Regulatory Offences, the Mental Element, and the Charter: Rough Road Ahead," *Ottawa Law Review* (1989), p. 419. The due diligence defence is also widely available in U.K. and New Zealand regulatory legislation, and to a lesser extent in Australia. In the United States, the due diligence defence is generally *not* available for strict liability offences. See K. Webb, *Regulatory Offences: The Quest for a Non-Criminal Approach to Penal Liability* (Doctor of Laws thesis, University of Ottawa, 1999). For a discussion of U.S. strict liability offences in the environmental context, with a focus on the use of ISO 14001, see S. W. Rosenbaum, *ISO 14001 and the Law* (California: AQA Press, 1998), p. 26. However, even in jurisdictions where no due diligence defence exists, companies that have put in place voluntary compliance programs, such as ISO 14001, are less likely to run afoul of the law and, when they do, may be able to use adherence to the terms of the program to mitigate the severity of sentences

proven the facts of the offence beyond a reasonable doubt, the accused will be convicted unless he or she establishes on a balance of probabilities that every reasonable action was taken to avoid the commission of the offence.[157] This is often referred to as a "due diligence" or "reasonable care" defence.

The process of determining what constitutes reasonable care in the circumstances, and whether reasonable care has actually been exercised, is not unlike the process of determining liability in a civil action of negligence. In fact, the strict liability offence has been referred to as an offence of negligence for this reason.[158] As with negligence actions, courts look to evidence of industry standards when considering due diligence defences. The existence of a voluntary code or standard, prepared and applied by industry, can be of considerable assistance in the court's determinations of reasonable care.

In *R. v. Domtar*,[159] the defendant was charged with a violation of the *Ontario Health and Safety Act* after a Hudson's Bay Company employee was killed while using a compactor leased by the accused to the Hudson's Bay Company. The compactor lacked a safety mechanism required by the standard established by ANSI that would have prevented the death of the employee. Justice of the Peace McNish concluded that non-compliance with the ANSI standard constituted evidence of a lack of due diligence on the part of Domtar. However, Domtar was ultimately acquitted because the nature of the accident was unforeseeable and stemmed from factors other than the unsafe machine. Nevertheless, judicial acceptance of use of the ANSI standard in this case illustrates how voluntary industry benchmarks of acceptable conduct can be employed in regulatory enforcement actions.

The New Zealand case of *Department of Labour v. Waste Management N.Z. Limited*[160] (discussed earlier) provides further insight into the issue of regulatory liability. The accused company was charged under an employment health and safety statute after one of its garbage compactor machines crushed the user of the machine. The compactor complied with an American standard. However, as noted above, the court ruled that meeting the American standard was insufficient, since an American standard may have been less stringent than the New Zealand standard. In his decision Justice O'Donovan stated:

> It seems to me that political and other factors may very well determine the nature of a standard. ... A standard formulated in the United States against the background of legislation in that country might very well be different from one which needs to be formulated in this country having

---

imposed. See, e.g., J. Kaplan, "The Sentencing Guidelines: The First Ten Years," *Ethikos* (November–December, 2001). See also the draft U.S. environmental sentencing guidelines, discussed below.

157. For example, in an environmental context, the facts to be proved might be that emissions emanating from the accused's factory caused or potentially caused harm to the environment. In a consumer setting, the Crown might have to prove that a representation concerning a product or service was made, that it was misleading or potentially misleading, that it was made by the accused, and that there was ensuing harm or potential harm to consumers.

158. Justice Dickson in *Strasser v. Roberge* (1979) 103 DLR (3d) 193, p. 202.

159. [1993] O.J. No. 3415 (Ont. C.J. — Gen. Div.).

160. [1995] CRN No. 40040511262 (Dist. Ct. — Auckland).

regard to our legislation. ... I am not satisfied in this case that adherence to the American standard on the part of this defendant serves to discharge the defendant's obligations under the New Zealand statute.[161]

Although this case has not as yet been applied in Canada, it does raise some interesting issues. When several standards exist, should a Canadian court give more weight to a domestic standard (e.g. CSA) as compared to that of ANSI or the American Society for Testing and Materials, for instance? Perhaps more importantly, it suggests that courts might begin to look more carefully at how standards were made, and by whom. For example, in the development of the standard, were Canadian consumer, environmental or other affected groups able to participate on an even footing with those of industry? Who made the final decision, and how?[162] As a final point, if government has participated in the development of a voluntary code standard, this may have implications for regulatory enforcement (discussed in greater detail below).

Industry-developed standards can also play a role in regulatory sentencing. Recently, some Canadian courts have required compliance with ISO 14001 environmental management system (EMS) standards as a term of sentence in several regulatory enforcement actions.[163] One commentator has suggested that programs such as ISO 14001 — which can involve independent certifications that a firm has successfully passed an EMS audit — may be of particular use in sentencing by "judges who may be lacking the experience and time to devise an appropriate organizational structure for environmental compliance."[164] In apparent recognition of the potentially constructive role that voluntary environmental management systems can play in furthering the objectives of legislation, the *Canadian Environmental Protection Act, 1999*[165] now specifically requires that, in imposing a sentence, a court is to take into account "whether any remedial or preventive action has been taken or proposed by or on behalf of the offender, including having in place an environmental management system that meets a recognized Canadian or international standard."[166] The same legislation now also expressly authorizes the court to make orders "directing the offender to implement an

---

161. Ibid., p. 9.

162. For example, the North American bicycle helmet industry uses four major standards that vary in how they are developed and how stringent they are. See Morrison and Webb, "Helmets Standards and Regulations," Chapter 11, below.

163. In *R. v. Prospec Chemicals* (1996) 19 CELR (NS) 178 (Alta. Prov. Ct), following a finding of guilt for exceeding sulphur emission limits contrary to Alberta environmental legislation, defence counsel proposed that Prospec be permitted to seek ISO 14001 certification as part of the court-ordered sentence. The judge agreed, ordering Prospec to complete the ISO program and post a letter of credit for $40,000, subject to forfeiture if the company failed to comply with the certification order. Other similar cases include *R. v. Van Waters & Rogers Ltd.* (1998) 220 AR (315) (Alta. Prov. Ct); *R. v. Calgary (City)* (2000) 272 AR 161, 35 CELR (NS) 253 (Alta. Prov. Ct); *R. v. Corotec (formerly PCI Inc.) and Zadeh* (1998) (Ont. Prov. Ct.), as reported in Environment Canada, *Court Orders Unique Environmental Penalties*, press release, August 20, 1998, available at <www.ec.gc.ca/press/pen0898_n_e.htm>.

164. Environmental lawyer Diane Saxe, as reported in J. Melnitzer, "Fix Environmental Snags Before Seeking ISO 14000 Certification," *Law Times*, June 16–22, 1997, pp. 14–15.

165. S.C. 1999, c. 33.

166. S. 287 (c).

environmental management system that meets a recognized Canadian or international standard."[167] In the United States, draft sentencing guidelines stipulate that adherence to the terms of environmental compliance programs can considerably reduce the penalties imposed.[168]

The fact that courts can draw on the existence of voluntary codes and standards in determining regulatory (or tortious) liability and in imposing sentences is of considerable significance to industry, government, non-governmental organizations and others in the community. Most notably, it suggests that all parties must recognize the importance of voluntary initiatives (i.e. parties need to seriously consider the implications of participating or not participating in the development of such initiatives, and of complying with them), since, on the one hand, adherence to the terms of such programs can reduce the likelihood of regulatory (or tortious) liability and, on the other, failure to abide by the terms of such programs could assist in court determinations of liability.

Implications for Industry

At an industry level, firms considering developing voluntary programs need to be aware from the outset that their efforts could have regulatory implications. A voluntary industry program may through creation of a benchmark standard of care expose member companies to legal liability.[169] At the same time, a firm that does *not* participate in an industry voluntary code or standard regime may nevertheless have the code or standard imposed on it by a court through a regulatory enforcement action or tort lawsuit. In this way, the management of firms who believe they can take a "free ride" on the positive industry image produced by others who adhere to a voluntary program without actually complying themselves may have an unpleasant surprise awaiting them when their non-compliance with the terms of the program subsequently plays a role in a court's determination of regulatory or tortious liability or as part of sentencing.

In one way, the prospect of a voluntary program establishing a benchmark that can, in effect, be imposed by the courts on free riders may create an incentive for reluctant industry members to participate in such programs. After all, involvement in

---

167. Subs. 291 (1) (e).

168. The draft guidelines are available at <www.ussc.gov/publicat/environ.pdf>. For a discussion concerning them, and the role of environmental management systems, see E. Orts, "Reflexive Environmental Law," *Northwestern University Law Review* 89 (1995), pp. 1227–1340, especially pp. 1281–1283. The environmental compliance programs must involve a commitment of resources and a "management process" that is reasonably calculated "to achieve and maintain compliance with environmental requirements." (p. 1282)

169. Brian Wastle, vice-president, Canadian Chemical Producers' Association, has indicated that in the initial phase of development of the Responsible Care voluntary initiative, legal counsel had noted the potential liability flowing from adoption of the Responsible Care principles (personal communication with the author, September 1996). The fact that a firm or sector would develop or comply with a voluntary program in spite of potential liabilities suggests that there may be strong "non-regulatory" motivations for such programs. A recent survey of 580 U.S. manufacturing plants suggests that, while regulatory compliance was an important motivator for adopting environmental management systems such as ISO 14001, so was the prospect of cost savings, improved business performance and responding to community, worker and customer concerns. See R. Florida and D. Davison, "Why Do Firms Adopt Advanced Environmental Practices (and Do They Make a Difference)?" in C. Coglianese and J. Nash, eds., *Regulating From the Inside: Can Environmental Management Systems Achieve Policy Goals?* (Washington: Resources for the Future, 2001), Chapter 4.

program design will at least give a firm some ability to influence the terms of the standards. The prospects of free riders being held liable at least in part because they are not complying with a voluntary program is perhaps some solace to firms who participate in the formulation and implementation of such programs. In short, the possible imposition by the courts of a voluntary code or standard on a non-participant may represent a counterargument to those who maintain that voluntary programs fail to address the free rider problem.

The question can legitimately be asked, How voluntary is a code or program if it can be imposed by a court on a firm against its will? A code or program is voluntary in the sense that legislation or regulations (and the tort of negligence) do not *require* compliance with the terms of the voluntary program, and courts are generally not *required* by legislation or regulations or common law to accept a voluntary code or standard as the benchmark of acceptable industry behaviour, or to use such codes or standards in sentencing.[170] Indeed, from one case to another, a court can choose to draw on the existence of a pre-established voluntary program or not. A voluntary measure developed by an industry association is one way of attempting to meet the reasonable care/due diligence standard, but individual firms are free to articulate and implement their own systems. As long as the individual firm can demonstrate to the satisfaction of the court that the approach developed by that firm constitutes reasonable care or due diligence, there is no need to use an existing code program developed by an industry association. Similarly, with respect to sentencing, a court may devise its own requirements that a firm must meet as part of a sentence, and need not rely on an existing code or standard developed by industry. Thus, at first instance, a firm can decide against using an existing industry voluntary code or standard, if it has the documentation to demonstrate to a court that its own approach constitutes reasonable care.

Implications for Non-governmental Organizations

Non-governmental organizations need to seriously consider the merits of initiating or participating in the development and implementation of voluntary programs in light of the considerable role such programs can play in stimulating good conduct from industry, and in influencing judicial interpretations of regulatory and tortious liability and sentencing. NGO involvement can help encourage adoption of more rigorous standards and stronger inducements for implementation.[171] At the same time, NGOs need to

---

170. Even the *Canadian Environmental Protection Act, 1999,* discussed above, only requires courts to "take into account" environmental management systems, and in sentencing, merely authorizes (but does not require) courts use environmental management standards. In both cases, these are discretionary powers.

171. In J. Braithwaite and P. Drahos, *Global Business Regulation* (footnote 22), the authors acknowledge the perception of many actors in the NGO sector that consider ISO standards to be voluntary, toothless and therefore unimportant. They nevertheless argue that this perception is wrongheaded and that increased NGO participation would be strategic (pp. 282–283). Increasingly, environmental organizations seem to be recognizing the benefits of establishing direct relations with industry through the vehicle of voluntary programs. Mike McCloskey, chair of the American Sierra Club, is reported as saying, "The time is right for corporations and environmentalists to deal directly with each other and not filter everything through government. The companies that sign CERES Principles [a voluntary initiative concerning environmental responsibility] identify

consider how direct involvement in industry programs will be perceived by their members and the broader community.[172]

Implications for Government

For regulators, the potential benefits flowing from initiation of or participation in non-regulatory voluntary initiatives or support of their use may appear to be considerable. The potential of such initiatives includes the following:

- assisting in elaborating on the meaning and operationalization of acceptable regulatory conduct;
- decreasing incidents of non-compliance from taking place;
- assisting enforcers in identifying likely compliant and non-compliant actors;
- stimulating "beyond regulatory compliance" behaviour; and
- assisting courts in structuring the behaviour of firms found in non-compliance.

On the other hand, government involvement in or support of voluntary initiatives that are operated in conjunction with regulatory regimes can raise serious questions about the ability of regulators to remain neutral and effective in enforcement and ready to introduce new legislation or regulations as necessary. These issues are discussed below.

Government Participation in Voluntary Codes Supporting Regulatory Activities

Taken together, the fact that voluntary codes and standards can have the enforcement-oriented benefits listed above would appear to suggest that government participation in developing these initiatives is necessary to ensure that they are as rigorous as possible. Should governments fail to provide such input, there is the risk that the codes and standards produced without their participation will be considered reasonable by judges even though they will be viewed as inadequate by government. Involvement by government in the development of voluntary initiatives can also be seen as providing needed guidance to the private sector about what constitutes reasonable care or due diligence for the purposes of regulatory liability.

At the same time, it is important to recognize that government participation in or support of voluntary initiatives can be taken into account by courts in subsequent legal actions — and not necessarily in ways that governments might want. To illustrate:

themselves as ones that organizations like mine should approach in our desire to forge a new relationship." See J. A. Smith III, "The CERES Principles: A Voluntary Code for Corporate Environmental Responsibility," *Yale Journal of International Law* 18 (1993), pp. 307–317, p. 309.

172. For insights on the perspective of environmental non-governmental organizations concerning voluntary standards development, see, e.g., T. Burrell (footnote 41). On the other hand, Canadian *consumer* organizations appear to have been on the whole more willing to participate in voluntary codes/standards activities, as demonstrated by their involvement in privacy, e-commerce, genetically modified labelling and other non-regulatory initiatives. At the international level, the Consumer Policy Committee has been established within ISO, the International Organization for Standardization. At this point, no parallel ISO environmental or worker policy committees exist.

- As part of a due diligence defence raised by an accused who is adhering to a voluntary standard, the involvement of government in the formulation of the standard could be taken as evidence of its inherent reasonableness, and thus assist the accused in avoiding liability.[173]
- An accused firm known to be complying with a voluntary standard developed with input from government could claim that, because of government involvement, an enforcement action against it is unjustified and therefore the prosecution should not be allowed to continue.[174]
- Depending on the precision of the language used and the nature of commitments made, arrangements between regulators and firms in support of use of particular voluntary programs (e.g. memoranda of understanding or contracts)[175] may raise questions about their potential to fetter or influence enforcement discretion, and the openness, accessibility and fairness of such arrangements (particularly in the eyes of those who were not able to participate), as well as the legal status of such arrangements.[176]
- In the event of harm to the public or the environment stemming from an incident of non-compliance by a firm, involvement of regulators in a voluntary initiative adhered to by that firm could be a factor in a tort action by the affected victims against the government.[177]

---

173. It would be necessary for the accused to demonstrate how compliance with the voluntary standard related specifically to the alleged incident of non-compliance (i.e. adherence in general to a management system approach is not sufficient). As noted earlier, courts are beginning to look more closely at the origins and development of voluntary standards: see, e.g., discussion of the New Zealand *Department of Labour v. Waste Management N.Z. Limited* case, and U.S. *Meneely v. S.R. Smith, Inc.* case. In both decisions, the courts carefully examined who was involved and the process of development of voluntary standards. This laudable judicial scrutiny could very well encompass the roles played by governments in developing and implementing voluntary standards, as evidence of the reasonableness of the standard in the eyes of the participating government.

174. The accused here would be attempting to characterize the enforcement action as constituting an abuse of process (see K. Webb, *Pollution Control in Canada: The Regulatory Approach in the 1980s* [footnote 28], pp. 46–49, or an officially induced error (see, e.g., *R. v. Cancoil Thermal Corp.* (1986) 52 CR (3d) 188). See also North American Commission for Environmental Cooperation (CEC), *North American Environmental Law and Policy* (Cowansville, Que.: Les éditions Yvon Blais Inc., 1998), esp. pp. 51–57.

175. In Canada, memoranda of understanding have been reached between governments and industry on several occasions. See, e.g., discussion of the Ontario Ministry of Environment-Environment Canada-Dofasco memorandum of understanding in L. Lukasik, "The Dofasco Deal," in R. Gibson, ed., *Voluntary Initiatives: The New Politics of Corporate Greening* (Peterborough, Ont.: Broadview Press, 1999), pp. 141–148. In the United States, the state of Wisconsin is in the final stages of operationalizing a contractual "cooperative agreement" program for leading environmental performers and those seeking to make large environmental gains. See discussion in National Academy of Public Administration, *Environment.Gov: Transforming Environmental Protection for the 21st Century* (Washington: National Academy of Public Administration, 2000), pp. 49–50.

176. See discussion in Webb (footnote 174), pp. 44–46. See also CEC, *North American Environmental Law and Policy* (footnote 174), pp. 41–45 and 60–64.

177. In a series of recent cases, Canadian governments have been held liable in situations of mal- or non-enforcement of legislation. If government officials participate in the development of a voluntary code or standard, or otherwise endorse a voluntary code or standard regime once in operation, they could be held liable if an individual or individuals, or an organization, were subsequently injured, and the code or standard deemed inadequate. When the Crown is sued, the court makes a distinction between two types of governmental decisions: policy decisions and operational decisions. As Justice Cory explained in *Just v. British Columbia* [1990] 1 W.W.R. 385 (S.C.C.), "... true policy decisions should be exempt from tortious claims so that

In an indirect manner, the potential for such legal issues to arise reinforces the point that regulators need to act in a publicly accountable and transparent manner when participating in or supporting voluntary programs. In Canada[178] and the United States,[179] some efforts have been made toward providing guidance on federal participation in the development and use of voluntary consensus standards and in conformity assessment activities.[180] In short, just as industry needs to think carefully about the implications of developing non-regulatory measures before becoming involved, so too government involvement in the development and use of voluntary measures having an impact on determinations of regulatory liability should be undertaken only after carefully considering the advantages and possible negative consequences of such involvement. When government participation does take place, effort must be made to ensure that it is done in an open and scrupulously fair manner.

Voluntary Codes Incorporated into Regulatory Law

It is not uncommon for governments to incorporate the terms of non-governmental, voluntary codes and standards into laws, and indeed Canadian, American and other governments have done so for many years.[181] For example, the CSA hockey helmet standard has been referentially incorporated in federal legislation;[182] provisions of the CSA *Model Code for the Protection of Personal Information* are

---

governments are not restricted in making decisions based upon social, political or economic factors. However, the implementation of those decisions may well be subject to claims in tort" (p. 403). The doctrine from *Just* was applied in *Swanson and Peever v. Canada* (1991) 124 N.R. 218. In this case a plane owned by Wapiti Aviation crashed, killing a number of passengers. Because Wapiti Aviation became insolvent, an action was launched against the federal government, since Transport Canada was aware of Wapiti's repeated safety violations and failed to take action to prevent an accident. The court ruled that Transport Canada's decision not to take action against Wapiti was not a policy decision, but one of operation, since the decision was not based on political, social or budgetary factors. When the court finds that the governmental action that is the subject of the lawsuit is an operational decision, the plaintiff must still establish that the Crown owed a duty of care to the injured party, that the Crown breached the duty of care, and that actual harm ensued. These remain significant hurdles to overcome before the Crown will be held liable for enforcement actions when the existence of a voluntary code context is a relevant factor. See also CEC, *North American Environmental Law and Policy,* ibid., esp. pp. 58–59.

178. Industry Canada, *Standards Systems: A Guide for Canadian Regulators* (Ottawa: Industry Canada, 1998), available at <http://strategis.ic.gc.ca/sc_mrksv/regaff/stdguide/engdoc/english.pdf>.

179. For example, Office of Management and Budget, *Federal Participation in the Development and Use of Voluntary Consensus Standards and in Conformity Assessment Activities* (February 19, 1998), available at <www.whitehouse.gov/omb/circulars/a119/a119.html>, as discussed in Meidinger (footnote 19), p. 10170.

180. In Canada, guidance is also provided concerning governmental involvement in voluntary code initiatives that are not part of the standards system. See, e.g., Office of Consumer Affairs and Regulatory Affairs Division, Treasury Board Secretariat (Canada), *Voluntary Codes: A Guide for Their Development and Use* (Ottawa: Industry Canada and Treasury Board Secretariat, 1998), available at <http://strategis.ic.gc.ca/epic/internet/inoca-bc.nsf/en/ca00880e.html>.

181. See, generally, D. J. Lecraw, *Voluntary Standards as a Regulatory Device* (Ottawa: Economic Council of Canada, 1981); Industry Canada, *Standards Systems: A Guide for Canadian Regulators* (footnote 178); R. Hamilton, "The Role of Non-governmental Standards in the Development of Mandatory Federal Standards Affecting Safety or Health" *Texas Law Review* 56 (1978), p. 1329.

182. As discussed in Morrison and Webb, "Helmet Standards and Regulations," Chapter 11, below.

included in federal legislation;[183] firms in several Canadian jurisdictions are required by regulation to establish environmental management systems to the ISO 14001 standard or equivalent;[184] the U.S. Occupational Safety and Health Administration converted a large number of voluntary health and safety standards into regulatory requirements;[185] toy manufacturers and importers in Hong Kong are required to comply with the International Voluntary Toy Safety Standard established by the International Committee of Toy Industries, a European Standard (EN71) or an American Standard (ASTM F963);[186] the Brazilian state of Acre has made certification under the Forest Stewardship Council's sustainable forestry program a requirement for practising forestry in the state;[187] and Zimbabwe has incorporated ISO 14001 into its regulatory system.[188]

In the usual course of events, it would appear that legislative and regulatory incorporation of the terms of non-governmental standards and codes raises few technical issues,[189] as long as the process of incorporation is done in the same open, fair and accessible manner that characterizes the promulgation of normal legislation and regulations. The position taken here is that it really does not matter *where* a legislative or regulatory obligation originally comes from, as long as those obligations are approved through normal legislative and regulatory processes. For example, given that legislative and regulatory obligations must have a rational foundation based on evidence to pass muster under trade agreements,[190] or under domestic requirements,[191] those legislative and regulatory obligations that originated as voluntary standards need to undergo the same stringent review and justification as any other proposed legislative or regulatory obligation. This said, properly developed voluntary standards that are the product of open, accessible and fair rules-based consensus processes should have a certain amount

---

183. The *Personal Information Protection and Electronic Documents Act*, SC 1999-2000, C-5, as discussed in Bennett, "Privacy Self-Regulation," Chapter 8, below.

184. See discussion of Nova Scotia pipeline regulations, New Brunswick gas distributors legislation and Alberta LEAD Program (which will make implementation and maintenance of an environmental management system a licence term and specify the minimum elements of the EMS in the licence), in S. Wood, "Green Revolution or Greenwash? Voluntary Environmental Standards, Public Law and Private Authority in Canada," in *New Perspectives on the Public-Private Divide* (Vancouver: UBC Press, 2004).

185. Meidinger (footnote 19), p. 10170.

186. Pursuant to the 1992 Hong Kong *Toys and Children's Products Safety Ordinance*, available at <www.info.gov.hk/customs/eng/major/consumer/toys_e.html>.

187. See E. Meidinger, "Environmental Certification Programs and U.S. Environmental Law: Closer Than You May Think," *Environmental Law Reporter* 31 (2001), pp. 10162–10179, pp. 10166–10167.

188. See P. Stenzel, "Can the ISO 14000 Series Environmental Standards Provide a Viable Alternative to Government Regulation?" *American Business Law Journal* 37 (2000), pp. 237–279, p. 276 (as reported in Meidinger, ibid., pp. 10166–10167).

189. Technical issues include determining the appropriate limits on the legislative ability to incorporate by reference (e.g. when there is no specific power to do so), and the status of indicating in legislation that the referentially incorporated standard is applicable "as amended from time to time" (is this a proper delegation of legislative authority?). See Industry Canada, *Standards Systems: A Guide for Canadian Regulators* (footnote 178).

190. See, e.g., discussion of trade agreements and voluntary codes, below.

191. In the U.S., when administrative bodies incorporate standards, they are "subject to judicial review and must produce decisional records sufficient to persuade reviewing courts that their decisions were rational and based on adequate evidence." See Meidinger (footnote 187), p. 10170.

of "momentum" when considered for inclusion into legislation or regulations, in the sense that they have already undergone multistakeholder scrutiny and perhaps also have been in operation in the marketplace and found to be practical. It is probably in light of this that legislation has been passed in some jurisdictions that obliges the use of properly developed multiparty standards in legislation and regulation whenever possible,[192] and key trade agreements obligate member countries to use relevant international standards as a basis for technical regulations whenever possible.[193] Presumably, if there were substantive or procedural concerns with to-be-incorporated voluntary standards, these would emerge in the legislative and regulatory promulgation process and be dealt with appropriately. Certainly, the mere fact that an obligation or approach being considered for a statutory or regulatory provision may have originated in a voluntary standard or code should *not* be justification for a *less rigorous* screening than that provided through the regulatory development process applying to any other proposed provision.

Voluntary Codes Supplementing Regulatory Enforcement

Even when they are not made mandatory by incorporation into regulatory law, voluntary programs can still play an important role in regulatory enforcement. Particularly in light of resource constraints faced by many regulatory bodies, government inspectors and other enforcement officials may welcome the use by the private sector of voluntary approaches with the potential to decrease the enforcement burden. In a number of ways, industry adherence to the terms of voluntary programs can reduce government enforcement costs. While monitoring by regulators of all firms is essential, a company that has put in place voluntary programs or systems[194] designed to decrease the likelihood of offences taking place[195] may not need the same degree of attention from inspectors and can hence save investigation, enforcement and remedial corrective action costs.[196]

---

192. For example, see the U.S. *National Transfer and Advancement Act of 1995*, 15 U.S.C. § 3701 (1996). As noted by Meidinger, the statute requires agencies to use voluntary standards, unless doing so would be "inconsistent with law or otherwise impractical," and to report decisions not to use such standards to the Office of Management and Budget. See Meidinger, ibid., p. 10170.

193. See, e.g., the World Trade Organization's *Agreement on Technical Barriers to Trade*, discussed in greater detail below.

194. For example, companies that have put in place effective consumer, worker or environmental protection management systems (particularly those subject to third-party audits).

195. This is not to suggest that firms that adhere to such systems will never find themselves in violation of regulatory requirements, any more than individuals who take their vehicles for service checks before long trips will never subsequently experience car trouble.

196. One of the findings in National Academy of Public Administration, *Environment.Gov:* (footnote 175), was the following:

> The emergence of ISO 14001 and other voluntary, private efforts by firms to identify and manage their environmental responsibilities is likely to raise the level of compliance and create some opportunities for pollution prevention. ... Although third-party registration is not a guarantee of a firm's compliance, state and federal regulators are justified in presuming that certified firms are less likely to pose compliance problems than uncertified firms, and thus less desirable as targets for inspection. That conclusion could change if the integrity of the third-party registration process were to be compromised. (p. 61)

Moreover, self-identification by industry of which firm is complying with voluntary programs, and which is not, can help government target inspection and investigation efforts.[197]

For all of these reasons, and in spite of questions about enforcement even-handedness that may arise,[198] governments are increasingly putting in place programs of regulatory relief or financial incentives to encourage firms to use compliance-enhancing voluntary programs. Although regulatory relief initiatives are not widespread,[199] regulators in the United Kingdom have offered the prospect of reduced inspections to those firms putting in place ISO 14001 environmental management systems.[200] The United States Environmental Protection Agency has announced the Performance Track program that, among other things, will include "a low priority for inspection targeting purposes" for firms with strong compliance records, an environmental management system of some form (not necessarily ISO 14001 or one audited by a third party), appropriate public reporting and outreach, and a commitment to

---

197. This may take many forms, involving both third-party registrars and industry associations. Concerning registrars, when an ISO 14001 registrar finds "significant non-conformances" it must notify the firm immediately. If the firm fails to correct the problem, the registrar would be obligated to suspend or terminate the firm's registration (see NAPA, ibid., p. 41). Because ISO 14001 registration information is public, any removal of a firm's registration status could be a trigger for governmental inspection. With respect to industry associations, in the interests of keeping a good public image, industry associations may come forward with information concerning "bad actors" in their sector. For example, J. Rees, in *Hostages of Each Other: The Transformation of Nuclear Safety Since Three Mile Island* (Chicago: University of Chicago Press, 1994), talks of an industry (the nuclear industry) concerned about its image as a whole, and therefore motivated to develop voluntary programs, monitor compliance and alert authorities to the existence of non-complying parties who could damage the sector's reputation. Similarly, the advertising industry in Canada, the United States and the United Kingdom attempts, through its own voluntary standards and adjudicative systems, to maintain a positive public image, which includes referring cases of non-compliance to authorities. For example, the American Better Business Bureau's National Advertising Division (BBB NAD) referred a file regarding advertisements of the Nuclear Energy Institute to the Federal Trade Commission. The Institute's advertisements touted environmental benefits of nuclear energy that the BBB NAD found questionable. See Better Business Bureau, *Nuclear Energy Advertising Compliance Referred to Government*, press release, May 13, 1999, available at <www.newyork.bbb.org/alerts/19990501.html>. In the U.K., since 1988, there have been 10 referrals from the non-statutory, non-governmental, self-regulatory Advertising Standards Authority (ASA) to the U.K. government's Office of Fair Trading (which has a statutory power to seek an injunction for consistent breaches of the ASA codes). ASA, *Misleading Advertisements The Law*, available at <www.asa.org.uk/issues/background_briefings>.

198. As discussed above, these could translate into legal actions or defences with respect to due diligence, officially induced error, abuse of process, procedural unfairness and tort liability.

199. According to K. Kollman and A. Prakash, "Green by Choice? Cross-National Variations in Firms' Responses to EMS-Based Environmental Regimes," *World Politics* 53 (2001), pp. 399–430, in the United States, "regulators reacted to ISO 14001 with skepticism and have not actively promoted it by offering significant regulatory relief... " (p. 421). While this has generally been the case, see discussion of new EPA performance track and Connecticut initiatives below.

200. "The British government has ... offered firms some limited amounts of regulatory relief by using ... ISO ... as a reducing factor in the risk assessment calculations used to determine frequency of site inspections." Kollman and Prakash, ibid., p. 422. See also J. Cascio, *Implications of ISO 14001 for Regulatory Compliance*, paper presented to the Fourth International Conference on Environmental Compliance and Enforcement, Thailand, 1996, p. 3, available at <www.inece.org/4thvol1/cascio.pdf>.

pollution reduction and compliance.[201] Connecticut regulators are providing benefits such as expedited permit reviews, reduced fees, less frequent reporting, facility-wide permits and public recognition for firms that are registered to ISO 14001, have adopted approved principles of sustainability and have good compliance records,[202] and other states are in the process of setting up similar programs.[203] Some jurisdictions have also offered financial assistance[204] and tax breaks.[205] At the end of the day, rigorous, consistent enforcement that detects and appropriately addresses non-compliant behaviour remains an essential component of and the point of departure for any government strategy designed to encourage the private sector to develop and adhere to voluntary programs.

Use of Compliance Information from Voluntary Codes in Regulatory Enforcement

Encouragement by regulators of industry use of voluntary programs could conflict with the desire of prosecutors to use conformity-related information developed by and disclosed to firms as part of voluntary program implementation (e.g. through the services of private auditors, contracted by the firms) as evidence of non-compliance with laws. Use by prosecutors of this sort of information may discourage companies from engaging in voluntary conformity measurement activities if such conformity-related information could be used against them in enforcement actions.[206] The somewhat uneasy compromise that appears to have emerged is for regulators to refrain from attempts to gain access to such information unless a specific investigation is under way, triggered by

---

201. See NAPA (footnote 196), p. 47. NAPA notes that EPA's performance track programs will succeed only if the agency finds a way to live up to its promises of inspecting participating firms less often, and rewarding high achievers with new regulatory flexibility (ibid.).

202. State of Connecticut, *An Act Concerning Exemplary Environmental Management Systems*, Substitute House Bill No. 6830, Public Act No. 99-226 (1999), available at <www.cga.state.ct.us/ps99/Act/pa/1999PA-00226-R00Hb-06830-PA.htm>.

203. See, e.g., discussion of Wisconsin and Oregon programs in NAPA (footnote 196), pp. 49–51, which were reaching operational stages at the time of writing of the NAPA report.

204. According to Kollman and Prakash (footnote 199), pp. 421–422, in the United Kingdom, regulators "have taken great pains to promote EMS-based policies by linking them to other voluntary initiatives and by offering small and medium-size firms financial help in implementing them."

205. In Canada, one province (Nova Scotia) "offered a corporate income tax credit to assist Nova Scotia companies with costs of achieving ISO 9000 or 14001 certification." See Wood (footnote 184), p. 22.

206. In Environment Canada's *Enforcement and Compliance Policy for the Canadian Environmental Protection Act, 1999*, March 2001, available at <www.ec.gc.ca/CEPARegistry/documents/policies/candepolicy/CandEpolicy.pdf.>), the "power and effectiveness of environmental audits as a management tool" is recognized and encouraged (p. 17). Environment Canada enforcement officers are to conduct inspections and investigations in a manner that will not inhibit the practice or quality of auditing (p. 17). Under the policy, environmental audit reports are not to be requested during routine inspections, but audits may be required when enforcement officers have reason to believe that an offence has taken place and there are no other means to obtain the information (p. 17). In the United States, the Environmental Protection Agency "has not offered an attorney-client type of privilege to third-party auditors. This makes the prospects of using such auditors less appealing to U.S. firms, which face the stiffest environmental liability laws in the world." See Kollman and Prakash (footnote 199), p. 421. At the state level, on the other hand, almost half the states have adopted laws granting some immunity to organizations that carry out environmental audit programs, report violations and take corrective action. Rosenbaum, *ISO 14001 and the Law* (footnote 156), p. 23.

reasonable belief that an offence has taken place.[207] In some jurisdictions, immunity from regulatory action may be granted to firms that carry out approved audit programs and agree to report violations and take corrective actions.[208]

Government Support of "Beyond Compliance" Voluntary Codes

In some circumstances, the careful, slow, formal and scientific nature of regulatory decision making, and the need to develop legal solutions comparable to those being created in other jurisdictions, may impede the ability of governments to respond rapidly to pressing problems.[209] Examples of this from Canada include the backlog of toxic chemicals yet to be fully and appropriately screened as part of the process of review established under the *Canadian Environmental Protection Act, 1999*,[210] and the as yet unrealized efforts of Canadian governments to devise comprehensive regulatory responses to global warming emissions.[211] In both cases, the federal government, working with a range of partners, has played a lead role in developing non-regulatory, voluntary programs that encourage firms to reduce or eliminate the use of certain toxic substances[212] and lessen the levels of emissions causing climate change[213] at an accelerated rate, in advance of regulatory requirements. Similarly, considerable experimentation with "beyond compliance" programs has been undertaken in the United

---

207. This is the Canadian approach, as discussed above.

208. See Rosenbaum (footnote 156), describing the situation in some American states.

209. See generally the summary of the limitations of command and control regulatory approaches in the environmental context, in Orts (footnote 168), pp. 1236–1241.

210. See discussion of this in the report of the Commissioner of the Environment and Sustainable Development, *Managing the Risks of Toxic Substances* (Ottawa: Office of the Auditor General, 1999), Chapter 4.

211. See discussion of this in the report of the Commissioner of the Environment and Sustainable Development, *Responding to Climate Change: Time to Rethink Canada's Implementation Strategy* (Ottawa: Office of the Auditor General, 1998), Chapter 3, available at <www.oag-bvg.gc.ca/domino/reports.nsf/html/c8menu_e.html>.

212. Through the Accelerated Reduction/Elimination of Toxics (ARET) program, and the Voluntary Challenge and Registry initiative pertaining to reduction of Canada's greenhouse gas emissions. See discussion of ARET in report of the Commissioner of the Environment and Sustainable Development (footnote 210), p. 5. According to this report, ARET has been credited with leading to reductions in usage far in excess of what could be established through the regulatory process (see esp. para. 4.91). Two commentators have said "The federal government would not have been able to achieve the reductions realised under ARET by relying on the *Canadian Environmental Protection Act*, which regulates less than 10 per cent of ARET's 117 substances; it has neither the procedural tools to assess quickly the toxicity of so many substances, nor the necessary enforcement capacity to apply a purely regulatory approach." See F. Bregha and J. Moffet, *From Challenge to Agreement? Background Paper on the Future of ARET* (Ottawa: Resource Futures International, December 8, 1997), p. 2. For a more critical perspective, see D. Van Nijnatten, "The ARET Challenge," Chapter 6, and "The Day the NGOs Walked Out," Chapter 7, in R. Gibson, ed., *Voluntary Initiatives: The New Politics of Corporate Greening* (Peterborough, Ont.: Broadview Press, 1999), pp. 93–109.

213. Regarding the climate change issue, although the Commissioner of the Environment and Sustainable Development, in his report *Responding to Climate Change* (footnote 211), was generally highly critical of the lack of progress through legislation and regulations, he was considerably more positive regarding the Climate Change Voluntary Challenge and Registry (VCR) Program. "The VCR Program, launched in early 1995 by federal, provincial and territorial energy and environment ministers, is the single most important new program established under the NACPCC [National Action Plan for Climate Change]" (para. 3.131). More information concerning the VCR program can be found at <www.vcr-mvr.ca>. For a contrary view, see R. Hornung, "The VCR Doesn't Work,"Chapter 10, in Gibson, ibid., pp. 134–140.

States.[214] While both laudable and understandable, the challenge will be to ensure that promotion of voluntary efforts in this regard does not impede the ability and desire of governments to move forward decisively with regulatory approaches and rigorous enforcement whenever this is possible.[215]

Corporate Governance and Voluntary Codes

Laws pertaining to corporate governance have the potential to stimulate corporations to be more open, transparent and accountable in their decision making, to be more accessible to shareholders (if not to a broader range of stakeholders), and to stimulate firms to put in place voluntary codes that demonstrate proactive risk management concerning a range of issues that might affect profitability.

The collapse of Enron and Worldcom and the subsequent promulgation into law of the *Sarbanes-Oxley Act of 2002*[216] in the United States signal the advent of a new era of controls on corporate governance and public disclosures of public corporations in United States, and will undoubtedly have a ripple effect on other jurisdictions and corporations around the world.

Among other things, Section 302 of the *Sarbanes-Oxley Act* requires that the chief executive officer and the chief financial officer of public corporations must each certify, in each annual or quarterly report filed with the Securities and Exchange Commission, that the officer has reviewed the report and that based on the officer's knowledge, the report does not contain an untrue statement of a material fact or omit to state a material fact, and the financial statements fairly present in all material respects the financial condition and operational results of the company. Moreover, the officers are responsible for establishing and maintaining internal controls designed to ensure that material information is made known to the officers in a timely manner, and that the officers have evaluated the effectiveness of those controls and have presented their conclusions in that regard in the relevant report. It remains to be seen exactly how *material fact* will be defined, but it would be reasonable to conclude that failure to disclose problems pertaining to environmental, worker, community, human rights and other issues that might affect the profitability of a corporation could fall within the meaning of *material fact*. Arguably, codes of conduct that proactively address such activities would decrease the likelihood of material fact disclosures becoming necessary.

Under section 406 of the *Sarbanes-Oxley Act*, public corporations are required to disclose whether or not (and if not, why not) the corporation has adopted a code of ethics for its senior financial officers, applicable to all key corporate officers. The code of ethics must cover conflicts of interest, disclosure policies and compliance with governmental requirements. As used within the context of *Sarbanes-Oxley Act,* the notion of *ethics* seems very much to be centred around notions of legal compliance.

---

214. See, e.g., discussion of the Environmental Protection Agency's Project XL (excellence and leadership) and Star Track initiatives, and related state innovations, in NAPA (footnote 196).

215. See comments by environmentalists and labour representatives in Moffet, Bregha and Middelkoop, "Responsible Care," Chapter 6, below.

216. Public Law 107-204, 116 Strat. 745, 15 USCS 7201.

Some might question whether corporate voluntary codes concerning environmental, worker, community, human rights protection and other objectives that extend beyond legal requirements are consistent with the fiduciary obligations of corporate directors to their shareholders. The suggestion here is that such codes are entirely consistent insofar as their use is intended to enhance the profitability of firms, and to demonstrate this to shareholders and other stakeholders. In addition to implementing voluntary codes to proactively address environmental, worker, community and other issues that might otherwise interfere with profitability, corporations may turn to voluntary codes as a way of responding to the desire of shareholders for more open and accessible corporate governance.[217]

Quite apart from the *Sarbanes-Oxley Act*, commentators in the pre-Enron era had noted that the disclosure provisions of the 1934 *Securities Act* (ss. 14(a)) give the Securities and Exchange Commission the authority to require disclosure as "necessary or appropriate in the public interest or for the protection of investors."[218] This provision could easily be interpreted as encouraging firms to put in place codes that would indicate good corporate management and diminish the likelihood of problems arising that would necessitate public interest or investor protection-type disclosures.

In the United Kingdom, since July 2000, trustees of occupational pension schemes have a duty established by regulation to disclose their policy on socially responsible investment in their Statement of Investment Principles.[219] Arguably, these requirements will stimulate corporations to draw on voluntary codes as a means of demonstrating that they are meeting pension law requirements.[220] The shareholder proposal process provided under the *Canadian Business Corporations Act* has recently been amended to give shareholders a limited right to add items to the agendas of annual meetings.[221] This sort of provision has been used by social activist shareholders to stimulate changes to environmental, labour and other practices of corporations.[222] Provisions of this type can be used to stimulate firms to develop codes in response to shareholder proposals.

Taken together, although none of the recent corporate governance reforms *mandates* that firms put in place voluntary codes addressing environmental, worker,

---

217. For example, in the U.S., the Coalition for Environmentally Responsible Economies (CERES) principles, enunciated initially by an association of socially responsible investment firms and public pension funds, which then blossomed into a broader multistakeholder alliance. The 10-point CERES code of corporate environmental conduct has been publicly endorsed by more than 50 companies. See <www.ceres.org>.

218. See, e.g., R. Steinhardt (footnote 128); and C. Williams, "The Securities and Exchange Commission and Corporate Social Transparency," *Harvard Law Review* 112 (1998), pp. 1197–1311.

219. *Occupational Pension Schemes (Investment) Regulations 1996* (SI 1996 No. 3127), which came into force in July 2000.

220. See, e.g., Association of British Insurers, *Investing in Social Responsibility: Risks and Opportunities* (2001), available at <www.abi.org.uk/Display/File/364/csr_Report.pdf>, for an example of Corporate Social Responsibility voluntary guidelines developed to respond (in part) to the new regulations.

221. The *Canada Business Corporations Act*, c. S-11, was amended under the *Act to Amend the Canada Business Corporations Act*, S.C. 2001, c. 14.

222. See, e.g., shareholder activist propositions of the U.S. Walden Asset Management group, which, according to a recent report, have led to significant changes in several U. S. companies. The report is available at <www.waldenassetmgmt.com/social/shareholder.html>.

community and other issues affecting the firms, the reforms do "create the space" for voluntary codes to be used to further statutory obligations oriented at enhancing stakeholder (and, in turn, shareholder) transparency, accountability and accessibility.

Public Law Fairness Constraints on Voluntary Codes

Do public law conceptions of procedural fairness apply to the operation of a voluntary code program so that, for example, disgruntled participants in a voluntary code program can appeal to the courts on the same grounds of procedural fairness as those that would apply to a conventional public regulatory or administrative program in situations of apparent unfair code administration? It should be noted that in Canada, government bodies are subject to common law and Charter obligations of natural justice, procedural fairness and natural justice.[223] A good starting assumption would be that, generally, insofar as a *government*-supported voluntary code program is endorsed, operated and/or funded by a State body, and affects serious interests of individuals, that program might be under a higher obligation to adhere to rules of fairness and "natural justice" than a non-government-supported, private voluntary code program operated by a private body. While it would seem that this is indeed the assumption of many judges, it seems to be overridden in certain cases (more so in some jurisdictions than in others), when courts conclude that there is a significant "public" element to an otherwise privately operated voluntary code regime.

There appear to be two important and difficult thresholds that need to be overcome before public law concerns with procedural fairness and natural justice obligations would be considered to apply to the operations of voluntary code programs. The first requires a determination of whether a "public body" is involved. When a voluntary code is developed directly by government, it is difficult to argue that a public body is not involved. For example, a government-funded and -operated environmental labelling program would seem to be subject to public law obligations of fairness.[224] Use of the government procurement power in support of voluntary code programs could also trigger public law procedural fairness obligations.[225] When government officials only participate in the development of the voluntary code or standard, it is less clear what public law fairness obligations would apply.[226] Use of standards bodies represents

---

223. See generally J. Evans, H. Janish, D. Mullan and R. Risk, *Administrative Law: Cases, Text and Materials*, 4th ed. (Toronto: Emond Montgomery, 1995). For an example, see *Martineau and Butters v. Matsqui Institution Disciplinary Board* [1978] 1 S.C.R. 118.

224. Originally, the Canadian Environmental Choice (EcoLogo) program was administered directly by the federal government. Administration is contracted out, but the draft guidelines for new types of Ecologo products are published in the *Canada Gazette*. For an in-depth discussion of the EcoLogo program, see Harrison, "Canada's Environmental Choice Progam," Chapter 10, below.

225. For example, if the federal government required, for federal contracts over a certain size, contractors to comply with an environmental management system code or standard or a human rights code or standard. For a general discussion of the fairness requirements associated with the federal procurement power, see K. Webb, "Thumbs, Fingers and Pushing on String: Legal Accountability in the Use of Federal Financial Incentives," *Alberta Law Review* 21 (1993), pp. 501–535.

226. Other than the due diligence, abuse of process, officially induced error and procedural fairness considerations discussed above in the context of regulatory enforcement activities.

another area in which there are no clear answers.[227] When an industry association, a non-governmental organization, a group of industry and NGO representatives, or a group of professionals initiates and develops a code, it is more difficult to characterize such bodies as public. The *Ripley*[228] decision discussed above, concerning the refusal of the court to apply the Charter to a disciplinary action of a privately organized investment organization, is indicative of judicial attitudes on such matters.

It is interesting to note that in certain circumstances, U.K. courts have ruled that seemingly private organizations, with no statutory basis, can be subject to public law rules of procedural fairness. One notable example of this is the case of *R. v. Panel on Take-overs and Mergers*,[229] in which the court found that because of the public-oriented function performed by the non-governmental Panel on Takeovers, its long, historically close relationship with government, and the fact that the Panel was referred to in legislation, the body was subject to public law procedural obligations. The case of *McInnes v. Onslow Fane,*[230] concerning the operations of the non-governmental British Boxing Board of Control, is another example of a U.K. court taking special notice of the public character of a private self-regulatory body.[231]

The U.K. Advertising Standards Authority (ASA), a non-statutory, privately funded, voluntary organization devoted to maintaining high standards in the advertising industry, has also been held to be a public body for purposes of procedural fairness. Under 1988 regulations promulgated by the U.K. government, the ASA was explicitly recognized as an "established means" for purposes of controlling the content of non-broadcast advertising.[232] When an advertiser, agency or publisher persistently or deliberately breaches the ASA's codes, the ASA can ask the Director-General of the Office of Fair Trading (a governmental office) to use its discretionary powers to seek an injunction through the courts. In June 1989, a U.K. court declared that, since the ASA was clearly exercising a public law function, its procedures (as distinct from the content of its adjudications) were subject to judicial review.[233] The court tested the ASA

---

227. In Canada, the federal government is the custodian of the standards process through a Crown corporation, the Standards Council of Canada. Standards developers, such as the Canadian Standards Association, are non-profit corporations that are not part of government.

228. See footnote 92.

229. See footnote 54.

230. [1978] 1 W.L.R. 1520.

231. The case is discussed in greater detail later in the chapter. It should be noted that in continental Europe, it is not uncommon to see public law status bestowed on chambers of commerce. This is the case in France, Germany, Italy, Austria, Spain, Luxembourg and the Netherlands, but not in the United Kingdom. See G. Fallon and R. Berman Brown, "Does Britain Need Public Law Status Chambers of Commerce?" *European Business Review* 12 (2000), pp. 19–27, p. 20.

232. *Control of Misleading Advertisements Regulations 1988* (SI 1988 No. 915).

233. See Advertising Standards Authority (footnote 76).

procedures and found them to be "perfectly proper and satisfactory."[234] Here we see an example of a private self-regulatory body evolving into a government recognized body, and its processes being recognized as fair by the courts.

It is difficult to predict whether Canadian courts will, in the right circumstances, follow the U.K. lead in holding public-oriented, private voluntary codes to public law notions of fairness. So far they have not, although there has been some willingness to use notions of fairness associated with private contractual law to much the same effect as those decisions founded in public law. In Canada, generally, as one moves from statutory-required decision making, in which departments, regulatory agencies and administrative officers have principal roles, and decisions pertain directly to the liberty and security of individuals, to instances of voluntary, non-government-led rule making and rule implementation, the potential scope and intensity of public law "fairness" concerns would appear to diminish. In the context of a voluntary code decision-making body, when the "public" threshold can be met (i.e. when it can be determined that a voluntary code administrative body is a public body or is exercising a public function), the second threshold then needs to be addressed.

The second threshold concerns the question of whether an individual's rights, interests, property, privileges, security or liberty have been affected so as to trigger application of public conceptions of procedural fairness. Two possible scenarios in which these might arise are, first, between code administrators and individual members in a disciplinary capacity, and second, between the code administrators or firms that operate codes and the affected public. With respect to the former, the *Ripley* case discussed earlier indicates the Canadian judicial reluctance to characterize private self-regulatory bodies as being subject to Charter protections, even though an argument can be made that such bodies might in some respects be protecting the public through their actions. Concerning public law legal actions by affected citizens against private code administrators or private sector members of a code, one could envisage situations in which citizens might be harmed by action or inaction in a voluntary code context,[235] but so far no such cases have materialized.

At this point, then, the likelihood in Canada of public law concerns with procedural fairness, natural justice or *Charter* protections applying to non-governmental voluntary codes appears comparatively small. However, even though *public law* notions of fairness may not directly apply to private voluntary code administration, we have seen in earlier discussion of the decision of *A.A.A. Khan Transport Inc. v. Bureau d'éthique commerciale de Montréal Inc.* that Canadian courts may find that *private contract law* conceptions of fairness may necessitate that code administrators meet basic procedural obligations, such as providing a member being disciplined with a notice that a complaint has been laid, and giving that member the opportunity to respond to the complaint before

234. Lord Justice Glidewell, in *R. v. Advertising Standards Authority* (footnote 77). Subsequent challenges to the ASA's procedures have also found them to be satisfactory. See, e.g., *ASA Welcomes High Court Victory*, January 17, 2001, available at <www.asa.org.uk/news/show_news.asp?news_id=57&news_section=General>. (See also *SmithKline Beecham plc v. Advertising Standards Authority* [2001] EWJ No. 49 Queen's Bench Division, Administrative Court, 17 January 2001.)

235. For example, when a government-approved or -supported body administering a voluntary code is alleged to have treated an individual complainant improperly, in terms of procedural fairness or a deprivation of security of person.

being removed from the organization. Moreover, the decisions of the U.K. courts with regard to the Advertising Standards Authority indicate that the application of public law notions of fairness to non-governmental code administration bodies are not out of the question, particularly when there is an observable "public" dimension to a non-governmental regime. Synthesizing the foregoing, those voluntary code operators who wish to err on the side of caution might decide to include notice and comment, openness, transparency and other procedural fairness elements in their voluntary code regimes to ensure that their programs operate in a manner consistent with public and private law concepts of fairness, and thereby decrease the likelihood of legal challenge on such grounds.

Constitutionally Protected Freedom of Expression and Voluntary Codes

In both Canada and the United States, freedom of expression is constitutionally protected.[236] Certain forms of commercial communications have been interpreted by Canadian and American courts as being accorded protection as well, although fewer protections than those provided to other safeguarded forms of expression.[237] In view of these interpretations, the question can legitimately be asked: are public statements made by company officials in support of a firm's code of conduct subject to constitutional protections, so that such statements are not actionable under deceptive marketing legislation?

Nike Inc.'s statements and actions concerning the employees of its subcontractors provide an illustration of how the constitutional protections may apply. In the early 1990s, Nike began receiving criticism for sweatshop conditions at its contractors' factories.[238] The company responded by putting in place a memorandum of understanding (i.e. a code of conduct) between itself and its contractors that required its contractors to comply with local minimum-wage laws, overtime regulations, child labour laws, occupational safety and health rules, and other requirements designed to ensure a humane workplace.

In 1996, a *New York Times* columnist wrote two editorials accusing Nike Inc. of exploiting Asian labour. The CEO of Nike replied in a letter to the editor, making various statements in defence of Nike's labour practices. In 1998, Marc Kasky, a California man, brought a legal suit against Nike, claiming that the corporation engaged in misleading advertising contrary to the state's *Business and Professions Code*. California's law permits an individual to sue as a private attorney general on behalf of all the state's residents without having to show that anyone has been injured. Kasky indicated that the CEO's comments in the *New York Times* were misleading in light of subsequent third-party audit reports (leaked to the public through media accounts) that alleged that certain

---

236. In Canada, see s. 2 of the *Canadian Charter of Rights and Freedoms*. In the United States, see the United States Constitution's First Amendment and the Fourteenth Amendment's due process clause.

237. In Canada, see, e.g., *R.J.R. Macdonald v. Attorney General of Canada*, [1995] 3 S.C.R. 1999; in the United States, see *Bolger v. Youngs Drug Products Corp.* (1983) 463 U.S. 60.

238. The following account of the events leading up to the legal action between Marc Kasky and Nike Inc. draws substantially on R. Parloff, "Can We Talk?" *Fortune*, September 2, 2002.

Nike contractors in Vietnam and China were paying less than the minimum wage. When Kasky read about the audit, he is reported to have said, "It struck me as false advertising. The Nike code of conduct is marketing their products. They're marketing it to me under false grounds."[239]

In a decision rendered in May 2002, the California Supreme Court ruled that Nike's statements were commercial speech designed to maintain and increase its sales and profits, and, as such, were subject to only minimal First Amendment protections.[240] Therefore, Kasky was entitled to take Nike to trial, and he could prevail if he were to show that the company's communications were misleading, either in what they asserted or what they left out.[241]

On the face of it, the California Supreme Court's decision appears reasonable: it is clear that a significant reason why firms develop and implement codes that address environmental, labour, consumer, human rights, animal protection and other aspects of their activities, and make communications concerning them, is to maintain or enhance their customer base and commercial opportunities. When firms are not accurate in public communications they make concerning activities addressed in their codes, it is difficult to understand on what basis such inaccuracies should not be subject to laws against deceptive statements. The ruling in now way hinders the ability of corporations to engage in public debate on issues such as the role of corporations in ensuring environmental or worker protection; it only constrains their ability to make misleading assertions about particular corporate practices in the course of public debate. Arguably, the California Supreme Court's interpretation will encourage firms to exercise greater care when making statements about their codes and their activities — for example, by putting in place management systems to ensure that claims are backed up by day-to-day practice. On the other hand, it may have a chilling effect on firms making claims that they cannot support. In this way, the law will reward firms that make accurate statements about their codes and discourage those that do not, thereby maintaining a level, competitive playing field.

Constitutionally Protected Freedom of Religion and Voluntary Codes

In both Canada and the United States, freedom of religion is constitutionally protected.[242] Can such protections affect the operation of commercially oriented voluntary codes that relate to religious practices? Some court interpretations suggest that it can. As part of both the Islamic and Jewish faiths, non-governmental food preparation certification and labelling standards have been established and are administered through religious bodies (halal foods are those prepared in compliance with Islamic standards,

---

239. Ibid.

240. *Kasky v. Nike, Inc.* (footnote 150).

241. At the time of writing, the California Supreme Court's ruling had been appealed to the United States Supreme Court, but had not yet been heard.

242. In Canada, see s. 2 of the *Canadian Charter of Rights and Freedoms*. In the United States, see the United States Constitution's First Amendment.

and kosher foods are those prepared in compliance with Jewish standards).[243] These religious-based food certification and labelling programs operate around the world, typically with little or no government support. In certain American states, legislation has been passed that specifically prohibits false labelling of food as either halal or kosher.[244] In essence, these laws can be considered to be supplements to the non-governmental halal and kosher voluntary code regimes in place. However, in a July 2000 judgment, the New York Eastern District Court ruled that statutory provisions designed to protect consumers against false labelling of food as kosher were unconstitutional, as a violation of the First Amendment because they were interpreted as endorsing and advancing religion.[245] Although the decision throws into question the ability of U.S. governments to regulate halal or kosher food programs, it does not challenge the private operation of such programs. In this regard, it represents another example of how governments may be constrained from regulatory action for some activities in ways that do not constrain private voluntary regimes.

Federated State Interjurisdictional Constraints on Voluntary Codes

One of the reasons why governments in federated states may initiate, participate in or sponsor voluntary measures is to overcome interjurisdictional constraints that hamstring their ability to develop more conventional legal instruments. For example, federal and provincial governments in Canada share constitutional authority over environmental and consumer protection activities. It is frequently difficult for the federal and provincial governments to determine exactly who has what authority in a particular area, and to reach agreement on coordinated legislative action. In such situations, governments may turn to voluntary measures either as transitional instruments (while coordinated, harmonized federal-provincial legislative solutions are being negotiated) or as supplements to legislative approaches. In a federal-provincial setting, such voluntary measures may be more quickly developed and implemented than may legislated measures. Thus, for example, a coalition of Canadian government and other stakeholders has devised and implemented voluntary measures pertaining to the reduction of excess packaging,[246] the protection of personal information,[247] the reduction of toxic

---

243. See, e.g., information at <www.ifanca.org/halal.htm> (halal) and <www.jlaw.com> (kosher).

244. Ibid.

245. See *Commack Self-Service Kosher Meats, Inc. v. Rubin* 106 F. Supp. 2d 445 (U.S. Eastern District Court of New York, 2000).

246. See discussion of National Packaging Protocol in the report of the Commissioner of the Environment and Sustainable Development, *Working With the Private Sector*, (Ottawa: Office of the Auditor General, 2000), Chapter 8, pp. 10–11, available at <www.oag-bvg.gc.ca/domino/reports.nsf/html/C0menu_e.html>. According to the report, the protocol has been successful in meeting its objectives, ahead of schedule.

247. See discussion of the *CSA Model Code of Personal Information* in Bennett, "Privacy Self-Regulation," Chapter 8, below. Provisions of the CSA Model Code have been incorporated into federal legislation (the *Personal Information Protection and Electronic Documents Act*, S.C. 1999-2000, C-5, discussed earlier in this chapter), and may eventually become the basis for provincial legislation.

substances,[248] consumer protection principles for electronic commerce,[249] the reduction of substances contributing to climate change,[250] measures for enhancing biodiversity,[251] and a national financial services ombuds-service.[252] In federated States, these programs, while not necessarily as effective as harmonized legislative initiatives, demonstrate the potential of voluntary initiatives as policy instruments capable of avoiding jurisdictional barriers faced by laws and, in some cases, in responding more rapidly and in a more cost-effective manner to a particular policy problem than can intergovernmental legislated approaches.

Voluntary Codes and Competition Law

Adam Smith wrote that when competitors get together the conversation often ends in a conspiracy against the public.[253] Since many voluntary codes involve competitors coming together to make standards and rules, and to implement them in ways that may affect others, it is no wonder that suspicions arise about such arrangements. There is little doubt that voluntary codes agreed to by some but not all businesses in a particular sector may have the effect of reducing competition and creating barriers to the entry of other players into the marketplace, and thereby reduce market competitiveness. Businesses that do not join a dominant industry association and adhere to its rules may suffer economically by being denied access to essential facilities and otherwise excluded from an activity or industry.[254] This type of injury can adversely affect consumers, since it may reduce competition in a particular industry and prevent new businesses from entering the industry.

There are a number of cases in which courts have held that businesses used voluntary code arrangements with the intent of hurting the commercial viability of rivals. In *Hydrolevel Corp. v. American Society of Mechanical Engineers* (ASME),[255] the jury

---

248. See discussion of the Accelerated Reduction/Elimination of Toxics (ARET) program earlier.

249. Available at <http://strategis.ic.gc.ca/epic/internet/inoca-bc.nsf/en/ca01180e.html>. At the time of writing, an accompanying *Canadian Code of Practice for Consumer Protection in Electronic Commerce* was being finalized.

250. See Canada's Climate Change Voluntary Challenge and Registry initiative, discussed earlier.

251. See description of the Biodiversity Stewardship in Resource Industries (BSRI) initiative at <www.cbin.ec.gc.ca/about/default_e.cfm>. According to the inaugural newsletter of the BSRI initiative, "The BSRI is a multi-stakeholder initiative involving government, industry and conservation groups. It is not a federal government initiative. Federal government departments are participating in order to catalyze action and provide facilitative services. The initiative builds on the fact that there is a strong interest among conservation groups and industry to improve their dialogue in order to develop new conservation initiatives and partnerships. Faced with the 'spongy stick' of the new *Species at Risk Act*, industry needs to do this." Note that the *Species at Risk Act* was passed in 2002, bringing to a close a nine-year legislative process.

252. For more information concerning this initiative, see <www.fin.gc.ca/news01/01-124e.html>.

253. A. Smith, *An Inquiry Into the Nature and Causes of The Wealth of Nations*, 1776 (London: Oxford University Press, 1997), Vol. 1, Bk. 1, Ch. 10, Pt. 2.

254. See R. Heidt, "Populist and Economic v. Feudal: Approaches to Industry Self-Regulation in the United States and England," *McGill Law Journal* 34:1 (1989), p. 41.

255. 635 F. 2d 118 (2d Cir. 1980).

found that the individual defendants, important members of ASME, a standards-setting body, had acted to protect their companies from competition by rivals by suggesting, in the name of ASME, that the competitors' products were unsafe when in fact they were safe.[256]

However, voluntary codes — including standards developed through formal standards bodies — also have the potential to *increase* efficiency. Voluntary codes can more readily allow new small companies to compete with large established companies. For example, a merchant or product that meets standards and receives a logo or label for this can, to some extent, minimize the advantage of more established larger competitors, who can rely on past advertising and reputation. Labels and logos, which are often part of voluntary code schemes, can also help consumers distinguish between companies and products, allowing the consumer to reward those that meet credible standards.

In the context of American antitrust law, judicial treatment of voluntary codes has undergone a remarkable transformation, from hostility in the early years, to qualified acceptance today. Initially, American courts were very reluctant to support the use of voluntary code-type arrangements. In the 1941 case of *Fashion Originators Guild of America. v. Federal Trade Commission,*[257] a unanimous U.S. Supreme Court ruled that even though the Guild was pursuing a legitimate goal, self-regulation was fundamentally unacceptable. The *Fashion* case drew on the 1935 judgment in *Federal Trade Commission. v. Wallace.*[258] In *Wallace*, the court condemned self-regulation in the coal industry aimed at preventing unscrupulous dealers from misrepresenting their coal. The court rejected any attempt at self-regulation as illegitimate in principle, noting "It is not the prerogative of private parties to act as self-constituted censors of business ethics, to install themselves as judges and guardians of the public welfare, and to enforce by drastic and restrictive measures their conceptions thus formed."[259] The court's refusal to allow any industry self-regulation out of fear that the industry would abuse the power is termed the "jealousy impulse" by commentator Robert Heidt.[260] Heidt postulates that this impulse may arise from the uniquely American experience with vigilantes. According to this theory, the court's fear of the Ku Klux Klan and other similar manifestations of private rule has resulted in an extreme judicial reluctance to allow private groups to exercise substantial power.[261]

The American judicial hostility toward industry self-regulation has been tempered in recent years by an innovative approach that emerged in 1978 to deal with the antitrust aspects of voluntary codes. The approach, formulated by the so-called Chicago School, seeks to maximize economic efficiency. The court's role in this approach is to determine whether the restrictions resulting from self-regulation are justified by increased efficiency. The court attempts to determine whether the restriction will result in lower prices or better products for consumers, or will help to overcome market

---

256. See also *Structural Laminates v. Douglas Fir Plywood Association* 261 F. Supp. 154 (D. Or. 1966).

257. 312 U.S. 457 (1941).

258. 75 F. 2d 733 (8th Cir. 1935).

259. Ibid., p. 737.

260. Heidt (footnote 254), p. 49.

261. Ibid., p. 57.

imperfections such as free riders. The result is that the Chicago School approach tolerates most self-regulation, except when it serves to fix prices or other terms of sale.[262] Although the Chicago School approach has been criticized for failing to consider non-economic factors,[263] it continues to be given significant weight by the American courts and has recently been reaffirmed by the Supreme Court.[264]

In keeping with the more tolerant approach to voluntary codes taken by American courts in recent years, leading American regulatory officials have also endorsed self-regulatory approaches, except when they are used to put new rivals or new forms of competition at a disadvantage.[265] The use of clear and fair procedures has been expressly acknowledged as helping prevent abuses of the self-regulation process.[266] It would appear that properly functioning formal standards bodies, which operate with meaningful participation of all stakeholders, according to a transparent, rules-based process, are in a good position to withstand challenges that their operation contravenes antitrust laws.[267] The Chicago School approach is unique to the United States. The British approach differs substantially. In the first place, the British courts, unlike their American counterparts, have never been as hostile toward industry self-regulation. In fact, British courts have long viewed industry self-regulation as a complement to the formal justice system. An important British case that illustrates the deference shown to self-regulatory bodies by the British courts is *McInnes v. Oslow Fane* (discussed earlier).[268] This case dealt with the British Boxing Board of Control, an organization with no governmental authority. The Board had devised a licensing system to control people who wished to participate in boxing. The plaintiff in the matter was an applicant rejected by the Board.

The court upheld the Board's decision and noted that "there are many bodies that, though not established or operating under the authority of statute, exercise control, often on a national scale, over many activities that are important to many people, both in providing a means of livelihood and for other reasons."[269] In contrast to the American approach, the court indicated that it would give wide discretion to self-regulatory organizations, stating, "There are many reasons why a license might be refused to an applicant of complete integrity, high repute and financial stability. Some may be wholly unconnected with the applicant, as where there are already too many licenses for the good of boxing under existing conditions."[270] This statement would likely shock those

262. Ibid., p. 45. The seminal case in the Chicago School approach was the 1978 decision *National Society of Professional Engineers v. United States* 435 U.S. 679 (1978).

263. Ibid., p. 61.

264. *Northwest Wholesale Stationers v. Pacific Stationery and Printing Co.* 472 U.S. 284 (1985).

265. See R. Pitofsky, Chairman, Federal Trade Commission, "Self Regulation and Antitrust," prepared remarks for presentation at the D.C. Bar Association Symposium, Washington, February 18, 1998, available at <www.ftc.gov/speeches/pitofsky/self4.htm>. Although Chairman Pitofsky's remarks are explicitly stated to be his, not necessarily reflecting those of the Commission or other Commissioners, they have been posted on the FTC Web site since 1998.

266. Ibid.

267. See generally, A. Marasco (footnote 145), and J. Q. Smith, J. P. Bolger and A. Marasco (footnote 145).

268. See footnote 230.

269. Ibid., p. 1527.

270. Ibid., p. 1532.

familiar with the American conception of competition law, since it suggests that a private group acting without governmental authority could legitimately decide to restrict competition in a particular industry. American courts would clearly not accept this.[271]

In *Greig v. Insold*,[272] the traditional governing bodies of cricket, the International Cricket Conference (ICC) and the Test and County Cricket Board (TCCB), banned players who participated in matches sanctioned by the World Series Cricket Party from playing in ICC and TCCB matches. In a challenge of the ban heard by a British court, a group of players who were banned by the ICC and TCCB argued that the ban was a restraint of trade. The court ruled that the actions of the ICC and TCCB were justified, since they were "in a sense custodians of the public interest."[273] The public interest the court was protecting was that cricket be "properly organized and administered."[274] The court tacitly, and without further elaboration, determined that the ICC and TCCB were the custodians of that interest. Heidt has concluded that this approach is far different from that of American courts, which would tend not to concern themselves with protecting a particular organization, even if it were traditionally ingrained.[275]

British courts have not emulated the largely economic approach of the Chicago School, preferring to consider non-economic factors such as the necessity of the sanctions for preserving the self-regulatory body, and the public-oriented role of the body in society. A case that illustrates the British approach is *Re: Association of British Travel Agents, Ltd. Agreement*.[276] This involved around enforcement measures used by the Association of British Travel Agents (ABTA) to stabilize their membership. These measures had the effect of preventing members from dealing with non-members. The restrictions limited competition between members, as well as nearly eliminating foreign travel agents from the British market, since few foreign travel agents were ABTA members. In supporting the Association's sanctions, the British court looked at four factors: how much the restrictions injured third parties, whether the restrictions were necessary to preserve the Association, whether the restrictions threatened the existence of non-members, and whether the restraint is customary in the industry. Ultimately, the court ruled that the restrictions were necessary to preserve the association and were not severe enough to drive non-members out of business.

In addition to the actions of U.K. courts concerning voluntary codes, the U.K. Office of Fair Trading (OFT) has also been called upon to review potentially anti-competitive practices concerning voluntary codes. In 1996, the OFT was called upon to review the activities of the U.K. "95 Plus" Buyers Group, which was organized by the

---

271. See, in contrast, *Hoover v. Ronwin*, 466 U.S. 558 (1984).

272. *Greig v. Insold* [1978] 1 W.L.R. 302.

273. Ibid., p. 347.

274. Ibid., p. 347.

275. Heidt (footnote 254), p. 76.

276. *Re: Association of British Travel Agents, Ltd. Agreement* [1984] I.C.R. 12.

World Wildlife Fund for Nature.[277] Its 84 members, largely U.K. retail wood product traders, distributers and retailers, initially stipulated that they would only receive wood products that were certified by the Forest Stewardship Council's sustainable forestry program. In an apparent response to the OFT review, the buyers group broadened their purchasing stipulation to encompass both "FSC certification or comparable certification schemes."

In Canada, it is a criminal offence to "conspire, combine, agree or arrange to restrain or injure competition unduly."[278] Nonetheless, the *Competition Act* provides a defence for those whose arrangement relates to the exchange of statistics, the definition of product standards, the definition of terminology used in an industry, protection of the environment, or the standardization of containers used by an industry.[279] However, this defence does not apply when the arrangement results in a reduction of competition in respect of prices, quantity or quality of production, markets or customers, or when the alliance prevents or deters anyone from entering or expanding a business.[280] According to the Commissioner of Competition, the defence will fail not only when the agreement is explicitly directed at reducing competition, but also when the indirect effect is to substantially reduce competition.[281]

So far, the courts have not considered a case in which the defences and exceptions contained in ss. 45(3) and 45(4) have been used.[282] However, in a Competition Bureau publication on strategic alliances, an example is provided that illustrates the Bureau's typical treatment of voluntary codes. In the example, the four largest manufacturers in an industry that is under pressure to be more environmentally responsible create an alliance to develop new technology for reducing emissions. In this example, the alliance falls under one of the ss. 45(3) defences, namely protecting the environment.[283] On the basis of the Competition Bureau's discussion, it would appear that the Commissioner will only initiate an inquiry when, for example, the environmental goal of the alliance required a reduction of final product outputs rather than of emissions.[284] The publication also notes that there is less chance of anti-competitive behaviour when all interested parties are involved in the development process.[285] In light of the uncertainty concerning what constitutes acceptable and unacceptable voluntary

---

277. The following information is derived from "Industry Rounds on FSC," *Forestry and British Timber*, 1996, and Department of Foreign Affairs and International Trade (Canada), *Forests: A National Experience*, submitted to the World Trade Organization's Committee on Trade and Environment, and its Committee on Technical Barriers to Trade, March 11, 1998, WT/CTE/W/81 G/TBT/W/61, p. 20.

278. *Competition Act*, R.S.C. 1985 c. C-34. s. 45(1)(d)

279. Ibid, s. 45(3).

280. Ibid, s. 45(4).

281. Director of Investigation and Research (Canada), *Strategic Alliances Under the Competition Act* (Hull, Que.: Ministry of Supply and Services, 1995), p. 8.

282. Ibid.

283. *Competition Act*, s. 45(3)(i).

284. Director of Investigation and Research (footnote 281), p. 18.

285. Ibid.

code activity, from a competition law perspective, the Competition Bureau has invited firms contemplating entering into a voluntary code-type arrangement to take advantage of the Bureau's advisory opinion services.[286]

Although the Bureau's interpretation of the provision does not have the force of law, and is merely an indication by the Commissioner as to whether a proposal is likely to attract liability under the Act, the opinion will provide a basis for assessing the risk of prosecution under the Act, and may provide the foundation for a defence. The Canadian Chemical Producers' Association has twice sought and received approval for their Responsible Care program, as discussed by Moffet, Bregha and Middelkoop in their chapter in this volume.

Canadian courts have in some cases found the actions of industry associations to be anti-competitive, and in others have allowed the activities to continue. In *R. v. Electrical Contractors Association of Ontario*[287] a voluntary association of electricians was found to have unduly lessened competition by restricting membership in the organization.[288] However, successful actions against self-regulatory associations are rare in Canada, an apparent indication that the courts do not view them in the same critical manner evidenced historically in the United States. The case of *R. v. British Columbia Fruit Growers Association et al.*[289] illustrates the amount of leeway Canadian courts will give to self-regulatory bodies. In this case, the growers association, composed of many members of the industry, adopted a rule that prevented storage facilities from offering their services to non-members. This effectively limited independent fruit growers to selling their products fresh. The court acquitted the fruit growers association, noting that non-members could still sell their fruit.

Because any sort of cooperation between competitors is viewed with suspicion, it would appear to be prudent for industry associations attempting to establish voluntary codes to solicit the participation of outside interests from the very outset of code development. Voluntary codes developed through a transparent process and with the meaningful involvement of outside interest groups are less likely to trigger suspicions of collusion because participation of outside groups representing, for example, consumer interests, diminishes the likelihood of anti-competitive and collusive behaviour taking place. Early consultation with the Competition Bureau (including seeking an advisory opinion from the Bureau) would appear to be prudent for any industry association considering developing a voluntary code.

Trade Agreements and Voluntary Codes

Trade agreements, such as those developed and implemented through the World Trade Organization, are systems of rules established by member countries that typically have the objectives of open, fair and undistorted competition across participating

---

286. Ibid., p. 14.

287. *R. v. Electrical Contractors Association of Ontario and Dent* [1961] O.R. 265.

288. Note that this case demonstrates court scrutiny of industry associations, but does not pertain to voluntary codes.

289. *R. v. British Columbia Fruit Growers Association et al.* (1986) 11 C.P.R. (3d) 183.

jurisdictions.[290] To achieve these objectives, the agreements restrict the ability of member countries to adopt measures (including laws, technical regulations and "standards")[291] that impede trade, unless the measures take an approved form and can be justified as compatible with certain identified and legitimate public policy objectives (e.g. protection of health and safety and the environment).[292] Typically, measures are required to be transparent, non-discriminatory and the least trade-restrictive in order to fulfil a legitimate objective[293] and, when possible, governments are to use international standards established by recognized bodies as the basis for technical regulations and national standards.[294] Processes are established to allow member-States to challenge measures that might be considered improperly trade-restrictive, and to compel member-States that are challenged to justify their measures according to a rules-based approach.[295] When findings by a properly constituted trade panel or appellate body show that a measure is unjustifiably trade-restrictive,[296] and once all subsequent procedural requirements are met and avenues of appeal are exhausted, then the member-State that has been found to have engaged in improperly restrictive trade may face significant trade sanctions.

---

290. So described in World Trade Organization, *Trading into the Future* (Geneva: WTO, 1999), p. 7.

291. In the context of the WTO's *Agreement on the Application of Sanitary and Phytosanitary Measures* (the "SPS Agreement"; 1997, available at www.wto.org/english/tratop_e/sps_e/spsagr_e.htm), *measures* is described as including "all relevant laws, decrees, regulations, requirements and procedures ..." (Annex A, para. 1). In the context of the WTO's *Agreement on Technical Barriers to Trade* (the "TBT Agreement"), the possible use of technical regulations and standards is the focus of concern. A *technical regulation* is described as a document "which lays down product characteristics or their related processes and production methods ... *with which compliance is mandatory*" (Annex 1, para. 1; emphasis added) and a *standard* is described as a document "approved by a recognized body, that provides, for common and repeated use, rules, guidelines or characteristics for products or related processes and production methods, *with which compliance is not mandatory*. It may include ... symbols, packaging, marking or labelling requirements as they apply to a product, process or production method." (Annex 1, para. 2; emphasis added) Thus, depending on the meaning of *recognized bodies*, many voluntary codes could be considered standards. This is discussed in detail below.

292. For example, the TBT Agreement recognizes "... that no country should be prevented from taking measures necessary to ensure the quality of its exports, or for the protection of human, animal or plant life or health, of the environment, ... subject to the requirement that they are not applied in a manner which would constitute a means of arbitrary or unjustifiable discrimination between countries where the same conditions prevail or a disguised restriction on international trade, and are otherwise in accordance with the provisions of this Agreement." (Preamble)

293. See articles 2 and 5 of the SPS Agreement and Article 2 of the TBT Agreement.

294. See, e.g., Article 3, para. 1 of the SPS Agreement, which states that, to harmonize SPS measures on as wide a basis as possible, Members shall base their SPS measures on international standards, guidelines or recommendations ... ." See also Article 2.4 of the TBT Agreement. When challenged, a Member whose regulations are inconsistent with existing international standards is required to provide a justification for the variance. If the variance is not in conformity with categories provided in the trade agreement, the measure may be found to be contrary to the agreement. For example, see the decisions of the WTO Dispute Panel and Appellate Body in the U.S.-E.U. dispute concerning hormones in beef, which ruled that there was inadequate scientific evidence to show a serious identifiable health risk that would justify EU regulations prohibiting the use of hormones in beef, in variance from existing CODEX standards. See discussion in P. Holmes, "The WTO Beef Hormones Case: A Risky Decision?" *Consumer Policy Review* 10 (March–April 2000), pp. 61–70.

295. For example, see the process for dispute settlement in Article 11 of the SPS Agreement, which references Articles XXII and XXIII of the General Agreement on Trade and Tariffs, 1994.

296. For example, see the decisions of the WTO Dispute Panel and Appellate Body in the U.S.-E.U. dispute concerning beef hormones (footnote 294).

Trade agreements appear to take a less restrictive approach towards the use of voluntary approaches than they do towards the use of laws and regulations. For example, trade panels have held that provisions in the General Agreement on Tariffs and Trade (GATT)[297] restrict the ability of countries to prohibit imports on the basis of the way products are produced, and have held that GATT also restricts the ability of countries to take trade action for the purpose of attempting to enforce its own domestic laws in another country (extra-territoriality), even when the trade action is designed to protect animal health or exhaustible natural resources.[298] On the other hand, properly constituted voluntary standards — including those that address non-product-related process and production methods (e.g. sustainable forestry practices) and are affiliated with labelling regimes — would appear to be[299] less restricted by trade agreements such as WTO.[300] In effect, by significantly constraining the ability of member countries to use laws and technical regulations to address non-product-related process and production method issues, such as sustainable forestry practices, trade agreements indirectly create an incentive for developing and using voluntary measures as another way of achieving the

---

297. See, especially, GATT Article I (which prohibits discrimination between importing countries), III (which prohibits discrimination between importing and domestic producers) and XI (which constrains imports).

298. See e.g., discussion of the U.S.-Mexico tuna-dolphin dispute, and the 1991 GATT panel decision concerning this dispute, in WTO, *Trading into the Future* (footnote 290), p. 49. Note that, while holding that Member countries could not prohibit imports because of the way the products were produced, nor could the United States engage in extraterritorial application of its own laws in other countries, the panel also ruled that a U.S. law requiring labelling of tuna products as "dolphin-safe" (leaving to consumers the choice of whether or not to buy the product) did not violate GATT rules because it was designed to prevent deceptive advertising of all tuna products, whether imported or domestically produced (Ibid). It should also be noted that the report of this panel, and the report of a subsequent panel on the same issue, was never adopted (Ibid). Moreover, these decisions were made under the pre-WTO, GATT dispute settlement process. Thus, for all these reasons, it is not clear just how "authoritative" this interpretation of the GATT provisions is. A later, 1998, WTO Appellate Body decision concerning U.S. restrictions on the importation of shrimp, while holding that the restriction was contrary to GATT provisions, has been interpreted by some commentators as implicitly suggesting that a production method could serve as a criterion for differentiation if the method contributes to the protection of a migrating species at risk of extinction, if there was a nexus to the jurisdiction imposing the restriction (e.g. the turtles migrated through the U.S.), and if the measure was reasonably related to the ends it was to achieve, and was not disproportionately wide in scope and reach. See, S. Droge, *Ecological Labelling and the World Trade Organization* (Discussion Paper No. 242), (Berlin: Deutsches Institut für Wirtschaftsforschung, February 2001), p. 13, available at <www.diw.de/deutsch/produkte/publikationen/diskussionspapiere/docs/papers/dp242.pdf>; see also I. Cheyne, "Trade and the Environment: The Future of Extraterritorial Unilateral Measures after the Shrimp Appellate Body," *Web Journal of Current Legal Issues* 5 (2000), available at <http://webjcli.ncl.ac.uk/2000/issue5/cheyne5.html>.

299. The expression "would appear to be" is purposely used, to emphasize the fact that no authoritative decision has been made on this point at the time of writing.

300. On this point, Droge (footnote 298), p. 17, concludes as follows:

> The investigation of relevant WTO-rules shows that non-product-related criteria used in governmental eco-labelling programmes are not explicitly regulated under the WTO-legal regime. ... In cases were [sic] labels are voluntary it should be more difficult to proof [sic] a violation of WTO-rules. Labels from private initiatives are even harder to control through WTO mechanisms, because WTO rules are tailored for international official regulation rather than for private programmes.

same or similar public policy objectives.[301] This is one of the likely reasons why governments and non-governmental bodies are turning to market-oriented voluntary standards to stimulate and influence private sector activity at home and elsewhere. Thus, for example, the Canadian federal government is participating (with a variety of other stakeholders) in the development of standards pertaining to the voluntary labelling of foods that are, or are not, products of gene technology,[302] while mandatory regulations on the same issue would appear to be more vulnerable to challenge under a WTO agreement. But even though subject to fewer restrictions, the development and implementation of voluntary standards may still directly or indirectly be subject to constraints through trade agreements. These points are discussed below.

The WTO Technical Barriers to Trade (TBT) Agreement governs technical regulations and voluntary standards relating to product characteristics or their *"related processes and production methods"* (emphasis added) and associated labelling requirements. However, it is considerably less clear whether the TBT's rules apply to *non-product-related* processes and production methods (e.g. rule regimes that pertain to how a product is made but are typically not apparent in the characteristics of the product itself, such as processes concerning sustainable forestry or fisheries, good labour practices, and humane treatment of animals). Commentators have suggested that a review of the history of the negotiation of the TBT Agreement reveals that non-product-related process and production methods were explicitly excluded from discussions during the Uruguay Round.[303] The WTO's Trade and Environment Committee has stated that the subject of how to handle, under the TBT Agreement, labelling used to describe the way a product is produced, as distinct from the product itself, "needs further discussion,"[304] while countries continue to debate whether the TBT rules should apply.[305]

---

301. This is not to suggest that voluntary codes or standards may not have trade distorting effects, but rather that it is harder for trade agreements to constrain these effects. For example, if a code or standard were to be developed or implemented in such a manner that only products from a certain jurisdiction could comply with its criteria, it might be discriminatory and trade distorting. The Association of South East Asian Nations (ASEAN) has stated that, given the absence of an internationally agreed-upon definition of sustainable forest management, efforts to ensure that forestry products only come from sustainably managed forests could impede market access (WTO, *Trade and Environment News Bulletin*, TE/023, May 14, 1998). However, as discussed above and below, it is unclear to what extent the relevant WTO agreements apply to voluntary codes and standards concerning non-product-related process and production methods — particularly those developed and implemented by private non-governmental organizations.

302. For information concerning this standard, see <www.pwgsc.gc.ca/cgsb/032_025/standard-e.html>.

303. See Droge (footnote 298), pp. 10–11, citing S. Chang, "GATTing a Green Trade Barrier: Eco-Labelling and the WTO Agreement on Technical Barriers to Trade," *Journal of World Trade* 31 (1997), pp. 137–159, p. 147.

304. WTO, *Trading into the Future* (footnote 290), p. 47.

305. For example, Canada's position is that the TBT Code of Good Practice should be interpreted "to provide for ecolabelling programs that include the use of certain standards based on non-product-related PPMs provided that these programs are developed according to multilaterally-agreed guidelines in order that the possibility of discrimination and trade distortion is minimized." Department of Foreign Affairs and International Trade (Canada), *Canada's Position on the TBT Code of Good Practice*, submitted to the World Trade Organization's Committee on Trade and Environment, and its Committee on Technical Barriers to Trade, February 21, 1996, WT/CTE/W/21, G/TBT/W/21, paragraph 16). On the other hand, Egypt "and other countries" are on record as saying that the TBT Code of Good Practice should not apply to process-related standards. See WTO, *Trade and Environment News Bulletin* (footnote 301), p. 9.

For the purposes of the TBT Agreement, a standard is defined as a document approved by a "recognized body," that provides, for common and repeated use, rules for products or related processes and production methods, *with which compliance is not mandatory*, and may also include or deal with terminology, symbols or labelling requirements as they apply to a product, process or production method.[306] Leaving aside the issue of "related processes and production methods," a plain language reading of this definition would suggest that many voluntary codes — including the chemical producers' Responsible Care program, the sustainable forestry management program of the Forest Stewardship Council (FSC), and the sustainable fisheries management program of the Marine Stewardship Council (MSC) — could qualify as "standards," since they are non-legislatively required rules designed for common and repeated use. But, is the term *standard* as used in the TBT Agreement limited to documents that emerge from formalized, State-sanctioned (i.e. "recognized") systems (such as those of the Standards Council of Canada, the British Standards Institution, or the American National Standards Institute)? Or are standards that emerge from more informal, less systematized processes (such as those of the FSC and MSC) also subject to the TBT rules? The key to determining which type of standard (or voluntary code) qualifies for coverage under the Agreement seems to be the meaning of the phrase *recognized body*. Unfortunately, the phrase is not defined in the TBT Agreement, so one is compelled to engage in a somewhat frustrating and not entirely fruitful hunt through the Agreement, its Annexes, and beyond, for clues about the defining characteristics of a recognized body.[307]

Annex 3 of the TBT Agreement sets out the *Code of Good Practice for the Preparation, Adoption and Application of Standards*. Among other things, standardizing bodies that have accepted the Code are required to notify the ISO/IEC Information Centre of this fact, to be non-discriminatory in their treatment of products, to not develop standards with a view to creating unnecessary obstacles to trade, to publish a work program at least once every six months, to allow a period of at least 60 days for the submission of comments on draft standards by interested parties, to take into account the comments received, and to promptly publish the standard once accepted.[308]

According to Paragraph B, the Code is "open to acceptance by any standardizing body within the territory of a Member of the WTO, whether a central governmental body, a local government body, or a non-governmental body; to any governmental regional standardizing body one or more members of which are Members of the WTO; and to any non-governmental regional standardizing body one or more members of which are situated within the territory of a Member of the WTO." So a standardizing body can be a governmental or non-governmental body, and also a regional governmental or non-governmental standardizing body.

---

306. TBT Agreement, Annex 1, para. 2.

307. Note that Annex 1 does not stipulate that a standard is a document *developed* by a recognized standardizing body, but rather that it is "approved" by one. The significance of this is unclear. It could mean that the trigger for application of the TBT Agreement, and the focus of attention, is not necessarily the standardizing body that drafted the standard, but rather the body that uses it (and therefore, by its actions, approves it). Alternatively, it could be argued that a standardizing body that drafts standards ultimately approves them, and so the drafting and approving functions belong to one and the same body. Either interpretation is plausible.

308. TBT Agreement, Annex 3, paras. C, D, E, J, L, N and P, respectively.

Central government body is defined as "central government, its ministries and departments or any body subject to the control of the central government in respect of the activity in question." Following this definition, the Standards Council of Canada would appear to qualify, since it is a creature of federal legislation (a Crown corporation) and it reports to Parliament through the Minister of Industry. *Local government body* is defined as "government other than a central government [e.g. states, provinces, etc.], its ministries or departments or any body subject to the control of such a government in respect of the activity in question." Following this definition, it would appear that the Bureau de normalisation du Québec would qualify, since it is a local government body, and is a creature of the Quebec government. *Non-governmental body* is defined as "a body other than a central government body or a local government body, including a non-governmental body which has legal power to enforce a technical regulation."[309] On its face, this would appear to encompass industry bodies, environmental or consumer bodies, or multistakeholder non-governmental bodies that develop documents intended for repeated use (i.e. standards) with which compliance is mandatory, insofar as industry, environmental, consumer, or multistakeholder non-governmental bodies can impose their standards on participants in their programs.

As of November 8, 2001, the Standards Council of Canada is the only Canadian body that has notified the ISO/IEC Information Centre of acceptance of the TBT Code of Good Practice, and is therefore acknowledging that it is under an obligation to meet the requirements of the TBT Code. Because the Standards Council of Canada is the custodian of the standards process in Canada, this would appear to mean that the standards development organizations that the Council has recognized are also now subject to the Code of Good Practice.[310] Similarly, the American National Standards Institute is the only U.S. standards body to have notified the ISO/IEC Information Centre, and the British Standards Institute is the only British standards body to have done the same. A total of 136 standardizing bodies from 94 countries have notified the ISO/IEC Information Centre. The vast majority of the notifying bodies appear to be government-created or -approved bodies.

According to the Code's paragraph B, the Code addresses itself only to national, local and regional standardizing bodies. What about those that are international in scope? In its *Second Triennial Review of the Operation and Implementation of the Agreement on Technical Barriers to Trade* (2000),[311] the WTO TBT Committee noted that international standards, guides and recommendations are important elements of the agreement, forming a basis for national standards, technical regulations and conformity assessment procedures, with the objective of reducing trade barriers. Nevertheless, the Committee also noted that adverse trade effects might arise from standards emanating from international bodies that have no procedures for soliciting input from a wide range of interests. The Committee observed that a diversity of bodies were involved in the

---

309. TBT Agreement, Annex 1, para. 8.

310. For example, the four standards development organizations recognized by the Standards Council of Canada are the Bureau de normalisation du Québec, the Canadian Standards Association, the Canadian General Standards Board, and Underwriters Laboratories of Canada.

311. WTO document G/TBT/9, November 13, 2000, (00-48111), available at www.dfait-maeci.gc.ca/tna-nac/documents/WTO-TBT-13-e.pdf.

preparation of international standards (the report stipulates that this could encompass intergovernmental or non-governmental bodies specialized in standards development or involved in other related activities), and that different approaches and procedures were adopted by them in their standardization activities. For this reason, the Committee agreed that there was a need to develop principles that would clarify and strengthen the concept of international standards under the Agreement and contribute to the advancement of its objectives. In this regard, in Annex 4 of the Review, the Committee articulated a set of principles it considered important for international standards development. Annex 4 stipulates that international standardizing bodies should embody such principles as transparency, openness, impartiality and consensus, relevance and effectiveness, coherence and the need to take into consideration the special circumstances of developing country interests.

While, as discussed, there is a designated official repository for national and regional standards bodies that wish to declare compliance to the Agreement's Code of Good Practice (the ISO/IEC Information Centre), there is no similar repository for international standardizing bodies wishing to declare compliance to the principles set out in Annex 4 of the TBT Committee's Second Triennial Review. As a result, although it would be possible for any international standardizing body to self-declare its intention to abide by WTO-approved principles of operation, third parties (including the author) cannot turn to a centralized documentation centre such as the ISO/IEC Information Centre to ascertain at a glance which bodies have indicated their intention to comply with the principles. Just as national and regional standardizing bodies have done, it would be useful for international standardizing bodies — including ISO, IEC, CODEX and perhaps some of the newer bodies — to declare their observance of WTO principles of good operation. And it would be useful for the WTO or some other body to establish a central repository of names of international standardizing bodies that have declared their compliance with Annex 4 principles.[312]

In 1999, apparently recognizing that their standards development, accreditation and labelling practices may have WTO TBT implications, several of the more recently created non-governmental international voluntary codes/standards bodies — including the Forest Stewardship Council, the Marine Stewardship Council, the International Federation of Organic Agriculture Movements, the International Organic Accreditation System, Social Accountability International, Fairtrade Labelling Organizations International, and the Conservation Agriculture Network — formed the International Social and Environmental Accreditation and Labelling (ISEAL) Alliance.[313] A key objective of ISEAL is positive environmental and social change "through the implementation of international standards-setting and accreditation systems that comply

---

312. Self-declaration — whether by a national, regional or international standardizing body, governmental or non-governmental — should not be accepted as the final word on the subject. Ultimately, some form of authoritative third-party assessment of the veracity of these self-declarations may need to be undertaken. Ross Wraight, Chief Executive of Standards Australia International, and Vice President Technical and Chairman, ISO Technical Management Board, has suggested that ISO should accredit other standardizing organizations to write ISO standards. See R. Wraight, "ISO: What Do We Need to Do Next?" *ISO Bulletin*, May 2001.

313. The following information is derived from documents available from the ISEAL Web site, <www.isealalliance.org>.

with internationally accepted criteria; that do not act as technical barriers to trade ... ."[314] In 2001, following a review of member practices, ISEAL published documents identifying possible weaknesses with its standardizing practices. A three-step process was proposed to bring ISEAL member standard-setting activities into line with a generic standard-setting methodology, as follows:

- production of a standard-setting methodology guidance document for ISEAL standard-setting members' core standards, based upon ISO/IEC directives and the WTO-TBT Code of Practice, Annex 4;
- a standard-setting methodology for the production of certifier core standards and national/regional variations and interpretations of core standards based on need rather than political reasons; and
- a peer review process, administered by the ISEAL Secretariat, to ensure that the standard-setting methodology is being followed by each of the ISEAL standard-setting members. (This peer review is intended to provide checks and balances on the standard-setting activities of all ISEAL members.)[315]

The efforts of ISEAL members are significant in at least three respects: they provide evidence of recognition by them that their current practices might not meet WTO TBT requirements and principles and that they believe these requirements *may apply* to them or have implications on their acceptability in the eyes of other parties; evidence of a desire to bring these practices in line with such requirements and principles; and evidence of a desire to be seen as credible and accepted international standardizing bodies (and, perhaps, therefore, more likely to have their standards accepted and used by both State and non-State parties).

On the basis of a reading of the TBT Agreement and its Annexes, the TBT Committee Second Triennial Review document and its Annexes, the list of national and regional standardizing bodies that have notified the ISO/IEC Information Centre of their intention to comply with the TBT Code of Good Practice, and the activities of ISEAL, it is at best unclear whether the TBT Agreement does, in fact, apply to private voluntary codes and standards activities, such as those engaged in by industry associations, multistakeholder groups of private sector firms, environmental groups, labour groups and aboriginal groups, and individual firms — particularly those that have developed non-product-related process and production method standards. However, even assuming that the TBT Agreement were found to apply to non-product-related processes and production method standards, such as those concerning sustainable forestry practices, and to apply to the activities of non-conventional private standards bodies such as industry associations or the FSC, this would not necessarily present an insurmountable barrier to the development and application of TBT-compatible standards by these bodies. As the activities of ISEAL show, such bodies could respond by developing and implementing their voluntary standards in ways that comply with the requirements and principles set out in the TBT Agreement and Annexes, as well as subsequent requirements and principles stipulated by the TBT Committee, such as Annex 4 of the

---

314. ISEAL Alliance, "Mission Statement," *Membership Requirements: Public Requirements,* Public Draft 2 (July 4, 2001).

315. *ISEAL Member Standard-Setting Review Public Background Document,* Issue 1 (July 2001).

Second Triennial Review (e.g. concerning transparency, openness, impartiality and consensus, relevance and effectiveness, coherence and addressing developing country interests). If they did so, it is difficult to see how their standards could be considered unacceptable for purposes of WTO analysis.

Because it is member-States that are the direct signatories of trade agreements such as GATT, the TBT Agreement and the SPS Agreement — and not individual firms, multistakeholder groups or standards bodies — it seems clear from a reading of the relevant provisions that, at first instance, the obligations associated with WTO-acceptable standards apply to *governments*, and not to conventional or unconventional standards bodies. This is not to suggest that the operations of standards bodies (of any sort) are not controlled or influenced by such trade agreements. But such operations are affected indirectly, through the obligations of member-States. Of particular significance is Article 4.1 of the TBT Agreement, which stipulates that member-States are under an obligation *"to ensure* that their central government standardizing bodies" accept the Code of Good Practice, and that member-States must also *"take such reasonable measures as may be available to them* to ensure that local government and non-governmental standardizing bodies ... accept and comply with ..." the Code of Good Practice.[316] Moreover, Article 4.1 goes on to state that member-States are

> *not* to ... take measures which have the effect of, directly or indirectly, requiring or encouraging such standardizing bodies to act in a manner inconsistent with the Code of Good Practice. The obligations of Members with respect to compliance of standardizing bodies with the provisions of the Code of Good Practice shall apply *irrespective of whether or not a standardizing body has accepted the Code of Good Practice*. (emphasis added)

In light of these provisions, it seems clear that member governments have positive and negative obligations to ensure that non-governmental standardizing bodies comply with the terms of the TBT Agreement, even if these "reasonable measure" obligations are of a lesser nature than those applying to central government standardizing bodies. In carrying out these "reasonable measure" obligations, it would appear that the behaviour of non-governmental standardizing bodies can be influenced or controlled by member governments through at least three techniques:

- *Leading by example.* Governments could draw on the standards that emanate from bodies operating in compliance with TBT criteria, but not draw on standards developed by bodies operating in a manner inconsistent with such criteria. This could manifest itself in direct incorporation by governments of such standards in regulations, use of such standards in procurement and governmental voluntary instruments, or by adhering to such standards in government operations. In this way,

---

316. At this point, the question of what constitutes "reasonable measures" has not been the subject of an authoritative interpretation or adjudication. Pursuant to Article 14, a Member may invoke dispute settlement procedures including a WTO Dispute Settlement Body when a Member considers that another Member has not achieved satisfactory results under Article 4 (and other articles) and its trade interests are "significantly affected." Exactly what would be the consequences of such actions, and the meaning of "significantly affected" have not been the subject of an authoritative interpretation or adjudication.

bodies that develop standards in accordance with WTO-approved criteria would be encouraged, and those that are not TBT-compatible would be discouraged.

• *Providing support for TBT-compatible standards activity.* This could entail developing guides for code development and implementation,[317] interpretive assistance, and tax incentives for firms adopting TBT-compatible standards. If a TBT-compatible standard for voluntary codes were to be promulgated by a body such as ISO, this could assist bodies developing voluntary codes, and could be used by governments as a practical yardstick to distinguish TBT-compatible from non-TBT-compatible voluntary codes activity.[318]

• *Discouraging non-TBT-compliant standards activity.* This could include governments bringing actions against bodies engaging in or supporting standards activities seen to be incompatible with the TBT Agreement.[319]

In these ways, through the activities of member-States, the activities of conventional and non-conventional standards bodies alike can be brought in line with TBT obligations.

To summarize the foregoing, trade agreements constrain the ability of governments to regulate in ways that distort trade, and to a lesser extent, constrain the ability of governments to use voluntary approaches. Members (i.e. governments) are obligated to use international standards as the basis for their regulations and national standards, unless variances from those international standards can be justified under certain exceptions. Trade agreements may restrict governments from using laws and technical regulations to achieve certain objectives when it would appear voluntary approaches may be less constrained. By so doing, trade agreements indirectly create an incentive for development and use of voluntary measures as another way of achieving the same or similar public policy objectives. However, even subject to fewer restrictions, the development and implementation of voluntary standards may still be directly or indirectly subject to constraints through trade agreements.

Members are obligated to ensure that their central government standardizing bodies accept and comply with a Code of Good Practice, and are to take "reasonable

---

317. For example, in 1998, following the lead of counterparts in Australia and New Zealand, the Office of Consumer Affairs, Industry Canada, working in conjunction with the Regulatory Affairs Directorate, Treasury Board (since disbanded), published *Voluntary Codes: A Guide for Their Development and Use* (footnote 180). This guide sets out suggested best practices, including the value of openness and transparency. In its current form, however, it does not specifically refer to or draw on the TBT Code of Good Practice.

318. This would be similar to government use of ISO 14021, which provides guidance concerning what constitutes acceptable environmental claims. Governments use ISO 14021 to help them interpret their deceptive advertising legislation.

319. For example, according to one report, a U.K. Office of Fair Trading review of the activities of a Buyers Group organized by the World Wildlife Fund that was purchasing exclusively from the Forest Stewardship Council (FSC) led to the group reorienting its purchasing activity to "FSC certification or *comparable certification schemes.*" See Department of Foreign Affairs and International Trade (Canada) (footnote 277). For another example, Colombia has claimed that its flower sector had encountered difficulties with market access because private organizations in certain importing countries had promoted a campaign to denigrate Colombian flowers. According to the government of Colombia, these organizations had developed eco-labelling schemes that had conditions that were unacceptable to Colombian exporters, discriminatory and prohibitively costly. See WTO, *Trade and Environment News Bulletin,* footnote 301.) Thus, the government of Colombia, on its own initiative, or in cooperation with other governments, could bring legal actions to challenge the alleged problematic standards.

measures" to ensure that local and regional governmental and non-governmental standardizing bodies accept and comply with the Code of Good Practice. Recently, the TBT Committee articulated principles of good practice for international standardizing bodies similar to those in place for national, local, regional governmental and non-governmental bodies, but there is no central official repository for international standardizing bodies wishing to declare compliance with the principles. As a result, although it would be possible for an international standardizing body to declare its intention to abide by WTO-approved principles, third parties cannot turn to a centralized documentation centre to ascertain which bodies have declared their intention to be in compliance.

The application of WTO agreements to non-conventional voluntary codes and standards activity, such as that of industry associations, NGO-led ventures, or multistakeholder arrangements, is unclear. It is member-States that are signatories to trade agreements, not private sector actors and NGOs. At best, such private standards activity would appear to be indirectly affected by such agreements. When such bodies develop *non-product-related* process and production standards (e.g. sustainable forestry management standards, good labour practices, humane treatment of animals, etc.), there is even greater uncertainty about the application of, for example, the TBT Agreement (which expressly defines standards in terms of *product-related* process and production standards). To fulfil their obligation to take "reasonable measures" to ensure that private standardizing activities comply with the Code of Practice, member-States could lead by example, thus providing support for TBT-compatible standards activity and discouraging non-TBT compliant activity. There do not appear to be significant obstacles preventing non-governmental bodies from developing and implementing private voluntary codes and standards in a manner compatible with TBT criteria, and, moreover, the criteria do not appear to be unduly onerous. Indeed, the efforts of certain non-governmental standards bodies to make their practices TBT-compatible show both a willingness and a capability to make these changes, and recognition that compatibility with WTO agreements such as the TBT Agreement may have implications for them.

Conclusions: the Next Generation of Law-Voluntary Codes Relations

As is evident from the many examples in this volume, industry, NGOs, standards organizations and governments develop, participate in and support voluntary codes for a host of reasons that do not relate in any direct manner to the legal system. For example, some of the non-legal impulses underlying voluntary initiatives include meeting consumer demand, increasing operational efficiency and effectiveness, responding to supplier demand, enhancing public image, addressing worker, shareholder, investor and community concerns, and countering NGO pressure. By the same token, however, we have seen in this chapter that there is a tangled and complex relationship between the legal system and voluntary measures. The law can and does play an important role in shaping and structuring voluntary codes, through implicit or explicit threats of legal action when appropriate and prompt voluntary actions are not taken, through enabling instruments and processes such as contract law, through legislation that explicitly encourages use of voluntary instruments, and through legislation pertaining to competition, misleading practices and trade law that can constrain the development and implementation of certain voluntary measures.

We have also seen that, while laws have a significant effect on voluntary codes, so too do voluntary codes on laws, acting as precursors, refining or elaborating vague legal concepts, extending the ability of the State to address activities outside its legislative jurisdiction, employed by judges and regulators as interoperable parts in legal regimes, substituted in some circumstances for legislation when effective development and application of law are difficult, and used to enhance the performance and the credibility of government bodies and government regulatory programs. Analysis suggests that both regulatory and voluntary code approaches to rule making and implementation have their advantages and disadvantages, so that, in the final analysis, the key challenge is determining how to make both approaches as effective as possible and determining when they can be used to maximum advantage.

Voluntary initiatives that are developed in an open and fair manner with the meaningful participation of all affected stakeholders and effectively implemented — particularly those that subject to independent third-party conformity assessment — can supplement regulatory and private law approaches at the same time as they are reinforced by the legal system. In countries with well-developed regulatory and justice systems, where governments rigorously enforce laws and promptly respond to new problems, a favourable environment for the development of voluntary codes is created. Where the existing regulatory regimes and justice systems are weak (as might be the case in developing countries), voluntary codes may in some cases provide a stronger impetus for private sector action than do legal regimes in those jurisdictions.[320]

While a positive symbiotic relationship between the legal system and voluntary measures might seem to resemble the proverbial and elusive "win-win" situation, it is also apparent that the various rule systems of NGO-supported bodies, industry associations, conventional standards bodies and regulators are competitors, vying for public and market credibility, legitimacy and acceptance.[321] It is clear that all parties concerned need to thoroughly understand the legal implications of such initiatives before becoming involved. As we have seen, there are many ways in which the regulatory, tort, contract, competition and trade law, and other legal aspects of voluntary measures can trip up the unwary. No firm, industry association, standards organization, government, court, NGO or private citizen is immune to the legal effects of poorly planned or implemented voluntary initiatives. The potential for legal liability can discourage governments, the private sector and NGOs from participating in such initiatives.

---

320. See, e.g., S. Pargal and D. Wheeler, "Informal Regulation of Industrial Pollution in Developing Countries: Evidence from Indonesia," *Journal of Political Economy* 104 (1996), pp. 1314–1327; and Kernaghan Webb and David Clarke, "Other Jurisdictions," Chapter 13, below.

321. This is perhaps most evident in the discussion of competing sustainable forestry management rule systems, in Gregory T. Rhone, David Clarke, and Kernaghan Webb, "Sustainable Forestry Practices," Chapter 9, below. See also discussion of recent government efforts to seek certification from the Forest Stewardship Council, the Marine Stewardship Council, and ISO, as referred to in footnote 19. This idea of competing rule systems seems to be a repetition of earlier experiences in medieval times, as discussed in T. Walde in "Non-Conventional Views on Effectiveness: The Holy Grail of Modern International Lawyers," *Austrian Review of International & European Law* 4 (1999), pp. 164–203, p. 201.

In Canada, to date, voluntary initiatives have spread with little government effort to give them formal recognition or to encourage their development (the publication of the *Voluntary Codes: A Guide for Their Development and Use* and the operation of the on-line Voluntary Codes Research Forum notwithstanding). In some ways, this bodes well for the future of voluntary initiatives in Canada. It suggests there is already the proper "climate" for voluntary measures (in the form of demanding and well-informed consumers, innovative firms and industry associations, a diversity of capable, high-profile consumer, environmental, health, human rights and other non-governmental organizations, a competitive marketplace, a basic framework of regulatory laws with adequate enforcement, a comparatively efficient and fair justice system and a modern national standards system), so that government officials, judges, and private sector and NGO representatives tend to turn to voluntary measures instinctively with minimal prompting.

Indeed, one can argue that the self-regulatory "systems" now being developed in Canada and elsewhere may offer a glimpse of the regulatory landscape of the future: against a backdrop of government regulations, industry associations transforming themselves from being simply lobbyists to brokers for the development and implementation of rules on their members, NGOs moving from protest groups "on the outside looking in" to developers and implementors of codes, and respected participants in the codes of others, and governments and courts providing the framework for all these activities to happen, but tending to play more of a reinforcing and facilitating role unless direct regulatory or enforcement action is needed.

Alternatively, governments could more consciously and explicitly encourage and structure the development of voluntary initiatives, and integrate them into statutory regimes. In this regard, probably the most innovative developments are emerging in Europe.[322] An attempt to explicitly "build" a voluntary environmental program on a legislative base is currently being undertaken by the European Union through the Eco-Management and Audit Scheme (EMAS).[323] The legal framework for EMAS, launched in 1993, encourages industry (and other organizations) to adopt explicit and comprehensive environmental management procedures, as verified and audited by independent third parties. In the future, EMAS may become a mandatory system in

---

322. A recent European study on "soft law" (defined as rules other than laws, regulations and contracts, or a set of instruments applied by professionals on their own initiative or in cooperation with others, or on the basis of State authorization, to be applied on a consensual basis, with no legal force) suggests that there is greater development of "soft law" concepts in Anglo-Saxon countries as opposed to those in Europe. It may be that Europeans are more comfortable with government-initiated voluntary initiatives, and less at ease with private sector measures. See <www.europa.eu.int/comm/consumers/index_en.html>. Distinctions in approach are discussed in greater detail in Webb and Clarke, "Other Jurisdictions," Chapter 13, below.

323. As discussed in E. Orts (footnote 168).

Europe, but for now it is not. There are currently no statutory penalties for failing to put in place an EMAS. As of 2003, there were close to 4000 registered EMAS sites in Europe.[324]

The ISO 14001 environmental management system standard, which is available for use by business and other organizations throughout the world, represents a similar initiative to EMAS, except that it was developed without the statutory encouragement along the lines of the European approach.[325] According to the most recent survey available from ISO, there were more than 36 000 ISO 14000 certificates awarded worldwide by the end of 2001, 49 percent in Europe (in 1996, Europe accounted for 63.58 percent of ISO 14000 certificates), 38 percent in the Far East and Australia/ New Zealand, 9 percent in the Americas, and 2.5 percent in Africa/West Asia.[326]

Another example of a legislated approach to voluntary codes comes from the United Kingdom's Office of Fair Trading (OFT). In 2001, the U.K. government announced its intention to introduce new legislation to establish a scheme for giving formal approval to good codes of practice.[327] The approach, which came into effect in 2002, involves promoting sound core principles for codes of practice, publication of which codes have been approved or rejected, communication to consumers of the benefits of the overall scheme and the benefits of dealing with businesses that comply with approved codes, introduction of a seal of approval for approved codes so consumers can see whether a trader is committed to code standards, and removal of the seal from codes that fail to deliver.[328] This builds on existing U.K. OFT legislation that creates a statutory duty on OFT to encourage trade associations to prepare codes of good practice.[329]

Whether the current, largely "hands-off," approach to voluntary initiatives seen outside of Europe, or a more aggressive and systematic approach following the European examples, will ultimately prevail, is difficult to say now.[330] What is clear is that voluntary

---

324. See the EMAS Web site, <www.europa.eu.int/comm/environment/emas/index_en.htm>.

325. In 2001, the EMAS scheme was revised to incorporate ISO 14001 as its environmental management component. EMAS goes beyond ISO 14001 in a number of ways, most notably the requirement to make relevant information available to the public and other parties. See EMAS, *EMAS and ISO/EN ISO 14001: Differences and Complementarities* (April 2001), available at <http://europa.eu.int/comm/environment/emas/pdf/factsheet/fs_iso_en.pdf>.

326. ISO, *The ISO Survey of ISO 9000 and ISO 14000 Certificates, Eleventh Cycle: Up to and Including 31 December 2001*, available at: <www.iso.ch/iso/en/prods-services/otherpubs/pdf/survey11thcycle.pdf>.

327. See U.K. Department of Trade and Industry, *Enterprise Act*, available at <www.dti.gov.uk/ccp/enterpriseact/intro.htm>.

328. These details are outlined in the U.K. Department of Trade and Industry White Paper (1999), *Modern Markets, Confident Consumers* (footnote 78), especially pp. 26–30.

329. Section 124 of the *Fair Trading Act 1973*, as discussed in R. Thomas, "Alternative Dispute Resolution: Consumer Disputes," *Civil Justice Quarterly* (1988), pp. 206–218, p. 208.

330. Commentator Geunther Teubner has suggested that it is more realistic to "replace the over-optimistic model of 'incentives through legal norms' by the more modest 'social order from legal noise'." G. Teubner, "The Invisible Cupola," in G. Teubner, L. Farmer and D. Murphy, eds., *Environmental Law and Ecological Responsibility: The Concept and Practice of Ecological Self-Organization* (Chichester: John Wiley and Sons, 1994), pp. 17–47, p. 33.

measures are playing an increasingly important role in a host of policy contexts, in Canada and elsewhere, and that a clear-headed understanding of the legal implications of such initiatives is essential for all stakeholders.

Analysis suggests that the incentives in Canada to participate seriously in voluntary initiatives are closely but somewhat accidentally linked to a number of legal instruments or stimuli, such as the threat of regulations, as well as prosecutions, and tort and contract liability. These legal instruments are rarely specifically framed or applied so as to promote the development and use of voluntary initiatives. Perhaps an intelligently integrated and well-focussed strategy of credible regulatory threats, exemplary regulatory prosecutions, tort legal suits and contract law actions might provide a powerful boost for voluntary initiatives. This type of "strategic" encouragement of voluntary initiatives might be more effective at stimulating effective voluntary action than either the current "hands-off" approach or the more interventionist European statute-based approach. If successful, this approach could be supplemented through strategic and coordinated use of economic instruments and education campaigns.

PART THREE

Case Studies

Chapter 6
Responsible Care: A Case Study of a Voluntary Environmental Initiative

John Moffet, François Bregha and Mary Jane Middelkoop

Introduction

When Dow Canada measured public opinion as a function of distance from its facilities in the early 1980s, the results were instructive. Within six kilometres of the plants, people held specific opinions about Dow that were different from their opinions about the industry as a whole. But beyond six kilometres, peoples' image of Dow was shaped by their image of the industry. As then Dow President David Buzzelli observed, the exemplary behaviour of Dow's plants was practically irrelevant; Dow was being judged by the behaviour of the industry as a whole.[1] At that time, this behaviour was coming under increasing public criticism as a result of a series of highly publicized accidents in Europe, Asia and North America. Dow and several of its fellow members of the Canadian Chemical Producers' Association (CCPA)[2] therefore realized that they had to take collective action both to prevent the occurrence of such an incident in Canada and to restore and maintain the industry's public image.[3] It was this realization that gave birth to Responsible Care.

On one level, Responsible Care is a collective name that applies to a statement of policy, guiding principles, a national advisory panel, a chemical referral centre (since replaced by a Web site), a verification process, and six codes of practice with 152 individual elements covering i) Community Awareness and Emergency Response (CAER), ii) research and development, iii) manufacturing, iv) transportation, v) distribution and vi) hazardous waste management. (Appendix A summarizes the codes.) As such, Responsible Care is an elaborate environmental management system.

At another level, Responsible Care is a statement of "moral obligations," "an ethic, an attitude, a method of thinking" regarding the responsible management of

---

1. Cited in A. J. Green, *Assessing Organizational Culture: Do the Values and Assumptions of Canadian Chemical Companies Reflect Those Espoused by 'Responsible Care,'* submitted to the Department of Chemical Engineering, Massachusetts Institute of Technology, in partial fulfilment of the requirements of the degree of Master of Science in technology and policy, August 11, 1995, p. 18.

2. The Canadian Chemical Producers' Association (CCPA), established in 1962, represents the Canadian manufacturers of a broad range of petrochemicals, inorganic chemicals, polymers, and other organic and specialty chemicals. In 1994, its 63 member companies accounted for more than 90 percent of the chemical manufacturing capacity in Canada. CCPA members operate more than 200 manufacturing and distribution facilities and employ some 30,000 people. See the CCPA website at <www.ccpa.ca>.

3. As Jean Bélanger, President of the CCPA, observed, "If a paint company or a plating company does something wrong the headlines the next day will scream that chemicals have been wrongly handled and so we will all be tarred by the same brush." See J. Bélanger, *Responsible Care: Developing a Promise*, presentation to the First International Workshop on Responsible Care, European Chemical Industry Council, Rotterdam, 1991.

Kernaghan Webb, Editor, *Voluntary Codes: Private Governance, the Public Interest and Innovation.*
This chapter ©2004 John Moffet, François Bregha and Mary Jane Middelkoop, pages 177–208.
Published by the Carleton Research Unit for Innovation, Science and Environment, Carleton University, Ottawa, Canada.

chemicals and chemical products.[4] Responsible Care is therefore much more than a set of operational procedures to protect the people and the environment; it can be said to represent an attempt at making a fundamental change in corporate culture.

Introduced in the mid-1980s, Responsible Care is now recognized as probably the leading sectoral voluntary environmental program in the world. By 2000, the chemical industries in 45 countries have adopted versions of Responsible Care programs.[5] Other industry sectors have based similar programs on Responsible Care (e.g. electricity, pulp and paper). In 1990 the United Nations Environment Programme granted CCPA President Jean Bélanger a Global 500 award to recognize the significant environmental benefits that have flowed from the program. And, in 1993, the Province of Ontario honoured the CCPA with the Lieutenant Governor's Conservation Award.

This chapter describes the program, explains why it was initiated and evaluates the impacts it has had. The chapter also seeks to extrapolate lessons about the design and use of voluntary measures from an examination of the context within which the program was introduced and operates, the process by which it was developed, and the actual design features of the program.

The Evolution of Responsible Care

"Responsible Care is absolutely essential to the survival of our industry."
Pierre Choquette, President, Plastics Division, NOVA[6]

Until the 1970s, the chemical industry, both in Canada and internationally, lived largely out of the limelight, believing that few members of the public understood or cared about its operations.[7] In 1977, the explosion of a chemical factory in Seveso, Italy, marked the first of several high-profile and extensively reported accidents that rapidly undermined public confidence in the industry and led to demands for stricter government regulation. In the words of the CCPA President, "we went from being an 'invisible industry' to one under a microscope. Our employees found themselves being stigmatized simply because they worked in the chemical industry."[8]

Significantly, opinion polls commissioned by the industry showed that the public did not discriminate among companies, and that the actions of one company could tarnish the industry as a whole. The third largest industry in Canada, the chemical

---

4. CCPA, *Responsible Care 1992: A Total Commitment* (Ottawa: CCPA, 1992), p. 1.

5. See International Council of Chemical Associations (ICCA), *Responsible Care Status Report 2000* (ICCA, 2000), available at <www.cefic.org/activities/hse/rc/icca/report2000/Report2000.pdf>. Not all Responsible Care programs are as rigorous as Canada's. Whereas the programs in Australia and the U.S. are arguably stronger in some respects, Responsible Care is not a condition of membership in many countries' chemical industry associations, and many programs in developing countries do not (yet) have audit/verification elements.

6. P. Choquette, *NOVA Responsible Care Report* (Calgary: NOVA Chemicals Corporation, December 1990).

7. C. Limoges and L. Davignon, *L'initiative gestion responsable de l'association canadienne des fabricants de produits chimiques* (Montréal: Centre interuniversitaire de recherche sur la science et la technologie, UQAM, June 15, 1995).

8. J. Bélanger, *Being Responsible Partners in Canadian Society*, presentation to the Air and Waste Management Association Environmental Government Affairs Seminar, Ottawa, 1990, p. 5.

industry has close to 70 companies, some very large but also a number of medium-sized producers. Large companies such as Dow Canada realized that only a concerted approach would restore public confidence in the industry.[9] Given that the CCPA represented (and continues to represent) almost all chemical manufacturers in Canada, it was the logical body to coordinate the required action. Concerned about its eroded credibility, not just with the public but also with government decision makers, the CCPA therefore developed a *Statement of Policy on Responsible Care* in 1979.

At the time, the Statement of Policy was no more than a one-page statement of good intentions; it was neither binding on CCPA membership nor backed up by operational codes of practice, as it would become later. In 1983, after the extent of the chemical contamination at Love Canal became better appreciated, a dozen members of the CCPA agreed to sign the Statement; this was their first public commitment to the principles underlying it.[10] This commitment encouraged the CCPA to ask the senior executives of all its members to sign the Statement.

Although compliance with the Statement remained voluntary and was not yet a condition of membership in the Association, several CCPA members balked at committing themselves publicly to such a code of ethics, in part because of concerns raised by their lawyers about the potential legal liability of doing so; they were afraid that a judge might use it as a standard in determining due diligence in the event of an accident.[11]

Various concerns were also raised about possible conflicts with the federal *Competition Act*.[12] The CCPA has twice requested opinions from the Competition Bureau, which administers the Act, about Responsible Care. In both cases, the opinion provided was favourable.

In 1984, a public opinion poll revealing wide public distrust of the industry[13] and the Bhopal disaster in India tipped the balance in favour of more forceful action. That year, the CCPA made a commitment to the *Statement of Policy on Responsible Care* a condition of membership in the association. In addition, the CCPA asked its member companies to conduct safety audits of their facilities and the handling of their products.

The CCPA hoped that voluntary action would forestall restrictive government regulation. Canadian chemical company leaders were concerned about the proliferation of regulations in the United States and the renewed interest in Canada in tightening

---

9. Green (footnote 1).

10. Limoges and Davignon (footnote 7).

11. See section on the impacts of Responsible Care in this chapter, below, and in Kernaghan Webb and Andrew Morrison, "The Law and Voluntary Codes: Examining the 'Tangled Web'," Chapter 5, above.

12. Some European jurisdictions have undertaken significant reviews of the potential competition law issues raised by voluntary and negotiated environmental measures. See, e.g., E. M. Basse, "Environmental Contracts: An Example of the Interplay Between Environmental Law and Competition Law," in E. M. Basse, ed., *Environmental Law: From International Law to National Law* (Copenhagen: GadJura, 1997).

13. In mid-1987, a survey of the members of the U.S. Chemical Manufacturers Association revealed that "everyone's number-one or number-two problem [was] the negative public perception of the industry."

regulatory controls,[14] particularly in a climate of public mistrust. As the CCPA President acknowledged in a speech, "Couple mistrust with a growing public belief that environmental laws and regulations are too lax and you can see that an industry like ours could suddenly find itself the target of harsh and perhaps unmanageable restrictions."[15] CCPA members decided that collective action was required to avoid a similar fate in Canada.

Recognizing that the *Statement of Policy on Responsible Care* needed to be backed up to be credible, the CCPA commissioned internal task forces to identify possible courses of action. One of the most important recommendations of this exercise was to adopt a "cradle to grave" approach. The need to control chemical substances from "cradle to grave" had been one of the main recommendations of the "Niagara process," the multistakeholder group established by the federal government to recommend improvements to the *Environmental Contaminants Act*. The CCPA accepted this approach and decided to develop a detailed code of practice for every step in a chemical's life cycle. It established six specialized task forces, comprised of representatives of member companies who were experts in the area, to translate the principles in the Statement of Policy into operational terms. These task forces presented draft codes to a National Advisory Panel (NAP). Run by a professional facilitator, the NAP was comprised of 12 (unpaid) external experts and environmental and labour advocates. After an average of six or seven iterations of each draft code, the NAP and the CCPA Board of Directors agreed to appoint one NAP member to revise each of the codes to ensure consistency. This process resulted in the six codes of practice.

Responsible Care has evolved significantly since its inception. The NAP continues to provide ongoing advice on the program's development and implementation. In 1991, the CCPA added the collection and publication of emissions and waste data to the program, and made it mandatory in 1993. Members began reporting on greenhouse gas emissions in 1992 on a voluntary basis, and by 1999 the chemical companies responsible for 90 percent of the sector's CO_2 emissions had registered with the Voluntary Climate Change Challenge and Registry (VCR).[16] The CCPA now reports this data together with information on transportation and employee health and safety annually. In addition, Responsible Care emphasizes the central importance of community consultations, requiring each member company to engage in ongoing community advisory processes. Finally, in 1993, the program required members to conduct internal audits of compliance with the codes of practice and, in 1994, introduced a system of external verification of performance (discussed below). At present, all CCPA members, except for the newest members, have completed or initiated external evaluations.

---

14. In the early 1980s, the Canadian government had begun its review of the *Environmental Contaminants Act* and launched a high-profile public consultation process to remedy its weaknesses. Public concern about the threat chemical substances posed both to human health and the environment, fuelled by the industry's perceived poor environmental record, would lead the government to strengthen its control over toxic substances in the new *Canadian Environmental Protection Act*.

15. Bélanger (footnote 8), p. 12.

16. For information on the VCR, see <www.vcr-mvr.ca>.

Responsible Care's evolution may not yet be over if its philosophy of "continuous improvement" continues to inspire the CCPA. According to NAP, the CCPA must continue its consideration of:[17]

* Round Two verifications ("re-verification");
* company management succession to prevent interruption in Responsible Care;
* an orientation primer for community advisory panels;
* support for scientific literacy through the education system;
* research on effects on communities of emission mixtures;
* protecting the environment through product stewardship;
* net collective reduction in emissions towards the goal of zero;
* research into safe alternatives to toxics, with displaced worker support;
* work on endocrine modulator research and mitigation; and
* education on industry impact and ethics in engineering schools.

The Impacts of Responsible Care

The main objectives of Responsible Care were to regain public trust and forestall or influence future regulatory developments by improving the environmental performance of the industry as a whole and by improving community relations. In this section we evaluate the degree to which the program has achieved these objectives by reviewing its impacts on environmental performance and workplace health and safety, financial costs and benefits, corporate culture, public policy, and the public image of the chemical industry.

Environmental and Workplace Health and Safety Impacts

CCPA members have steadily improved their environmental and workplace health and safety records over the past decade. Their records indicate a steady decline in workplace injuries and a marked reduction in the frequency and severity of transportation incidents. Members have also reduced their emissions of various pollutants significantly over the past decade. By 1999, CCPA member companies had achieved a 63 percent reduction in their total emissions of substances (excluding CO_2) compared to 1992.[18] This included cuts in emissions of:

* 74 percent in heavy metals (to water);
* close to 100 percent in sulphuric acid to water; 31 percent in sulphuric acid to air;
* 94 percent in chlorfluorocarbons;
* 43 percent in volatile organic compounds;
* 50 percent in stratospheric ozone depleting chemicals; and
* 72 percent in known carcinogens.

---

17. CCPA, *Responsible Care: The Picture is Getting Brighter* (Ottawa: CCPA, 1999).

18. CCPA, "1999 Emissions Inventory and Five-Year Projections," *Reducing Emissions 8: A Responsible Care Initiative* (Ottawa: CCPA, 1999).

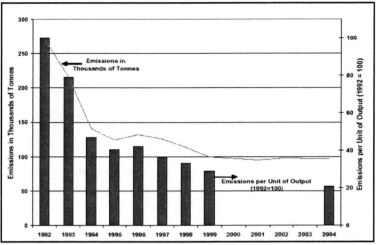

Figure 1: Product Output vs. Emissions from CCPA Member Operations

From: CCPA, "1999 Emissions Inventory and Five-Year Projections," *Reducing Emmissions 8: A Responsible Care Initiative* (Ottawa: CCPA, 1999).

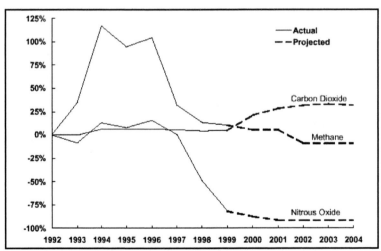

Figure 2: Emissions and Projections of Total Carbon Dioxide, Methane, Nitrous Oxide from CCPA Member Operations

From: CCPA, "1999 Emissions Inventory and Five-Year Projections," *Reducing Emmissions 8: A Responsible Care Initiative* (Ottawa: CCPA, 1999).

These cuts have been made at the same time the industry has grown in output, and thus cannot be attributed to economic slowdowns. These reductions are the result of several factors, including mandated government reporting requirements (embodied in National Pollutant Release Inventory or NPRI), government-sponsored voluntary programs (the Accelerated Reduction/Elimination of Toxics Program, or ARET), and legislated targets (e.g. for CFCs) and cannot therefore be attributed entirely to Responsible Care.[19] Both CCPA members and third parties[20] agree, however, that Responsible Care has played an important role in ensuring that these emissions cuts have been made by all members, rather than by a few industry leaders.

Financial and Economic Impacts

Like most initiatives related to environmental change, Responsible Care requires action with a long-term perspective. As such, participation inevitably conflicts with the myriad pressures facing companies to forego long-term environmental investments in favour of short-term profit. Such pressures come from financial institutions, markets and investors, which typically have focussed on short-term considerations with little understanding or appreciation for the long-term potential for environmental investments. Individual managers too are often evaluated largely on the basis of short-term performance.

The disincentives to participate in the type of collective action contemplated by Responsible Care are particularly acute among small companies.[21] The CCPA currently represents 70 chemical manufacturers. While its membership includes both giants such as Dow and a limited number of small, specialized producers, most members are medium-sized firms, ranging from 150 to 500 employees. The CCPA does not include many of the smaller "specialty chemical manufacturers," most of whom belong to a parallel industry association. Nor does it represent the hundreds of (typically medium and small) companies that blend chemicals in the process of manufacturing items such as carpets.

While the image of the industry as a whole may be a critical factor for large multinational firms, corporate image may not be as significant a concern for smaller firms more concerned about short-term economic performance. In addition, small companies often have less knowledge about new "green" technologies, and typically have fewer resources and less money available to invest in change that has little prospect of short-term payback.

The implementation of Responsible Care represents a considerable investment by the Canadian chemical industry. In addition to the work involved in the development of the detailed codes of practice, the CCPA has held training workshops for its members on each of the codes, published newsletters, prepared user guides, set up a chemical referral centre, developed compliance and reporting protocols, established a national

---

19. For information on NPRI, see <www.ec.gc.ca/pdb/npri/npri_home_e.cfm>. For information on ARET, see <www.ec.gc.ca/nopp/aret/en/index.cfm>.

20. Including, for example, various federal and provincial government officials and environmental advocates interviewed for this chapter.

21. As a recent study observed, for example, costs represent a disincentive to small chemical companies to belong to the CCPA. See Limoges and Davignon (footnote 7).

advisory committee and organized regional "leadership groups" to allow member companies to share information and apply peer pressure on industry laggards. To pay for these collective investments, the CCPA significantly increased its membership dues shortly after introducing Responsible Care. On top of this collective effort, individual companies have had to train staff, collect information, develop "written policies, standards and procedures" for each of the six codes, set up reporting systems, make necessary process changes, engage in community consultations and monitor compliance.[22]

Notwithstanding this investment, according to Brian Wastle, CCPA Vice President for Responsible Care as of 1998, only one company had ever left the CCPA over concerns about the cost of compliance.[23] What financial benefits have offset these costs?

There are two schools of thought dominating the debate over the impact of these sorts of costs. Some argue that the costs of continuous environmental improvement are investments in competitiveness.[24] Others argue that once the low-hanging fruit (e.g. energy retrofit investments with short payback times) have been picked, these types of investments will become increasingly expensive. When evaluated against all other opportunities, such investments may only be justifiable from a social perspective — not from an individual firm's perspective — and may therefore require government intervention to ensure that they are made.[25]

Sorting out the precise financial impact of Responsible Care on the Canadian chemical industry is very difficult. Proponents identify a wide range of possible benefits. Most participants have reduced their workers' compensation, waste management, clean up and disposal costs. During the mid-1980s, for example, pollution prevention research spending was reported to yield returns of 150 percent on investment for Dow Chemical.[26] Some proponents argue that Responsible Care helps companies reduce the costs of product research and development by helping them avoid costly investments in environmentally inappropriate products. Most participants have improved their ability to respond to emergencies, due both to improved systems and improved community relations, which enables them to avoid protracted disputes based on distrust. Some members also credit their Responsible Care certification status with helping ensure faster permitting, and with a renewed ability to obtain financing and insurance at reasonable rates. At least one company has reported that its participation in Responsible Care has led its banks to reduce their lending rates because they were satisfied that the company

---

22. CCPA (footnote 4).

23. According to Wastle, only two members have left the Association over Responsible Care. The CCPA asked one to leave because it was not implementing the public outreach requirements. Another left over a philosophical disagreement about Responsible Care advertising.

24. See, e.g., M. Porter and C. van der Linde, "Green and Competitive: Ending the Stalemate," *Harvard Business Review* 73:5 (September–October 1995), pp. 120–123.

25. See, e.g., C. Stevens, ed., *Environmental Policies and Industrial Competitiveness* (Paris: Organisation for Economic Co-operation and Development, 1993); N. Walley and B. Whitehead, "It's Not Easy Being Green," *Harvard Business Review* 72:3 (May–June 1994), pp. 46–52; A. Jaffe, S. Peterson, P. Portney and R. Stavins, *Environmental Regulation and International Competitiveness: What Does the Evidence Tell Us?* Discussion Paper 94-08 (Washington: Resources for the Future, 1994).

26. K. Loos and S. Stricoff, "Responsible Leadership," *Chemical Week*, July 5–12, 1995, p. 112.

represented a lower risk. Many participants also believe that they have reduced their potential legal liability.

Economists such as Michael Porter argue that many of the elements of Responsible Care are consistent with Total Quality Management. They argue that, particularly for small companies, the information that participants have developed and shared as a result of Responsible Care has helped companies learn, plan and manage in a more systematic manner. The resulting improvements can range from significant savings in inputs and waste disposal costs to more intangible benefits such as strengthened communications between plant and corporate offices.[27] Some speculate that this management system orientation has also helped the sector adapt to the ISO 9000 and 14000 standards more easily than some other sectors.

While implementation of the program inevitably entails costs, some in the industry prefer to characterize Responsible Care's stewardship approach as expanding the nature of the services the industry offers. In the words of one U.S. industry official:

> how much new business did you get because you did a good job at a customer's site? How many lawsuits did you avoid because you kept a customer from misusing a product? Or how much did you save on environmental cleanup because of safer handling or disposal? Those are things that are very difficult to measure, but they are services that a company might not have provided 10 years ago.[28]

The degree to which the chemical industry will continue to realize these benefits in an era of increasing international trade is unclear. Some proponents argue that trade pressures enhance the salience of the program because it helps the Canadian chemical industry differentiate itself from foreign competitors, helping attract investment in new plants in Canada, for example. On the other hand, the competitiveness pressures are sharper today, leading to restructuring, downsizing and potentially less focus on environmental issues. In the mid-1990s, for example, it was reported that environmental managers in the chemical industry were in a less influential position than they had been five years previously.[29] The pressure to demonstrate a short-term return on environmental investments may therefore grow.

International trade dynamics are also generating more generic environmental management certification programs. The European Union, for instance, has established the Eco-Management and Auditing Scheme (EMAS 14001), which applies to firms operating in member countries.[30] Furthermore, many transnationals have focussed on obtaining ISO 14001 certification. Neither of these standards is as comprehensive as

---

27. See J. Nash and J. Ehrenfeld, "Code Green: Business Adopts Voluntary Environmental Standards," *Environment* 38:1 (January–February 1996), pp. 16–45.

28. Cited in S. J. Aynsworth and A. M. Thayer, "Chemical Manufacturers Welcome Challenge of Product Stewardship," *Chemical and Engineering News*, October 17, 1994, p. 10.

29. R. Begley, "Advocacy Conflict With Deregulatory Congress," *Chemical Week*, July 5–12, 1995, p. 40.

30. See discussion of EMAS in Kernaghan Webb and David Clarke, "Voluntary Codes in the United States, the European Union and Developing Countries: A Preliminary Survey," Chapter 13, below.

Responsible Care. If these schemes become the accepted standard for international commerce, will the Canadian chemical industry continue to be willing to enforce their own, more comprehensive standard as well?[31]

Impacts on Corporate Culture

"Responsible Care ... is our culture and, above all, it is not a program. Programs have beginnings and ends — Responsible Care must be our ongoing way of life."
Jean Bélanger[32]

The philosophy embodied even in the earliest versions of Responsible Care amounted to a new attitude towards environmental protection and worker safety. It called on the industry to reject its traditional stance of doing the minimum required by law, maintaining a low profile and downplaying public concerns. Instead, it exhorted the industry to seek out and address public concerns and lead the policy process. Such a transition had to overcome not only immediate concerns about cost and risk but also deep-seated inertia. In short, Responsible Care ideally entails changing corporate culture. To what extent has this occurred?

Some anecdotal evidence suggests that the initiative has helped change organizational culture to a certain extent. On the basis of several interviews with three CCPA member companies, for example, Green argued that Responsible Care has helped promote cultural change in the Canadian chemical industry.[33] He cites numerous examples of changed beliefs and attitudes directly attributable to Responsible Care: investments made in increased safety, recognition of the value of consulting neighbouring communities despite the difficulties in doing so, adjustments in compensation approaches to remove conflicts with Responsible Care objectives, slower, more rigorous decision making, greater emphasis on pollution prevention, acceptance for responsibility over products after they leave the plant, and grudging acceptance of loss of sales to customers who did not meet Responsible Care standards.[34]

Responsible Care may have also helped enhance employee pride and satisfaction. As proponents of Total Quality Management (and its corollary, Total Environmental Quality Management) emphasize, these developments can enhance productivity as well as helping to create a cadre of ambassadors to the community. Green quoted one company executive as saying, "It's morally good. It's righteous. It's great. It

---

31. The U.S. Chemical Manufacturers Association has started to explore the possibility of combining an evaluation of Responsible Care compliance with an ISO 14001 audit. To date, however, the CCPA has been reluctant to link the two initiatives.

32. Bélanger, (footnote 3).

33. Green (footnote 1).

34. In a review of Responsible Care in the U.S., Nash and Howard reach similar conclusions, observing that "Responsible Care, as a coordinated effort by the whole industry, provided a legitimate framework that enabled them to make changes that might not otherwise have been high priority." (J. Nash and J. Howard, *The U.S. Responsible Care Initiative: The Dynamics of Shaping Firm Practices and Values*, presented to the Fourth International Research Conference on the Greening of Industry Network, Massachusetts Institute of Technology, Cambridge, Mass., November 12–14, 1995, p. 26.

was a lot of fun working on it. ... Responsible Care breeds happier people."[35] Finally, the strong emphasis on public outreach in Responsible Care may also have helped foster a more consumer-oriented attitude in what was traditionally a very inward-oriented industry.

Cultural change, however, is a long-term process. A 1995 survey by the U.S. Chemical Manufacturers Association showed that, seven years into its version of the program,[36] fully 35 percent of the industry's employees did not know what Responsible Care was.[37] David Powell, a University of Toronto academic and consultant who has been extensively involved in Responsible Care since its inception similarly observes that although the Canadian industry has changed considerably, many companies still have difficulty understanding the need for ongoing public dialogue — a concept that was antithetical to the pre-Responsible Care industry, and whose implementation remains a challenge for many traditionally trained engineers and business managers.

Impacts on Government Policy

One of the main objectives of Responsible Care was to foster a less adversarial relationship with government and to pre-empt or at least influence the content of additional regulation. In this section, we evaluate the degree to which Responsible Care has achieved this objective. We also review a number of the concerns that critics have raised about the relationship of Responsible Care to the policy process, in terms of its influence on the development of new regulations, on the implementation of existing regulations and on the legal status of existing regulatory obligations.

Relationship With Existing Regulatory Obligations

One of the most significant impacts of Responsible Care is that it may have helped increase the standard of care to which the chemical industry is subject with respect to *existing* regulatory obligations. Most public welfare legislation in Canada — including most environmental regulations — establishes strict liability offences. Once the Crown has proved the *actus reus*, strict liability offences reverse the onus onto the defendant to avoid liability by demonstrating due diligence.[38] Canadian courts have emphasized that due diligence requires a management system, with such elements as regular audits, clear assignment of responsibilities, training, instruction and supervision

---

35. Green (footnote 1), p. 150.

36. Each participating country has its own version of Responsible Care.

37. L. Ember, "Responsible Care: Chemical Makers Still Counting on it to Improve Image," *Chemical and Engineering News*, May 29, 1995, pp. 10–18.

38. See the landmark Supreme Court of Canada case, *R. v. Sault Ste. Marie* (1978), 40 CCC (2d) 353.

of employees, information systems and effective lines of communication.[39] One of the leading factors relied on by the courts in defining what constitutes a reasonable management system is the prevailing industry norm.[40] Thus, it is widely expected that chemical companies will increasingly be held to a Responsible Care-like standard.

That said, it is interesting to note that on January 25, 1996, the Alberta Provincial Court issued an order under the Alberta *Environmental Protection and Enhancement Act* endorsing a settlement agreement that included, in addition to a $100,000 fine, the obligation to become ISO 14001 certified by June 30, 1998.[41] Prospec Chemicals had made an application to join the CCPA at the time of the judgment, but was not yet certified under Responsible Care. The fact that the International Organization for Standardization (ISO) and not Responsible Care certification was chosen raised issues with respect to whether ISO 14001 would supplant Responsible Care as the industry norm in the eyes of regulators and the judiciary. As no similar cases have arisen since the Prospec agreement, it is difficult to determine the significance of the case.

In any event, it is also conceivable that Responsible Care could influence the standard of care owed by a participant to a third party. Civil suits of negligence and nuisance are based on tests of reasonable behaviour. If Responsible Care ratchets up the standard of care reasonably expected of a chemical manufacturer, it may also indirectly influence the standard of care owed by that business to its neighbours.

While Responsible Care may therefore have an indirect positive impact on regulatory and common law standards of care, the program also presents a related challenge with respect to the administration of those laws. To what extent should resource strapped government enforcement officials use membership in Responsible Care as the basis for placing a CCPA company low on their list of inspection priorities? Is it valid to assume that a Responsible Care company will always comply with environmental regulations?

The empirical evidence does not support the assumption that companies certified under Responsible Care will necessarily always be in compliance. The federal and provincial governments have prosecuted various CCPA members for environmental violations over the last five years. Indeed, Tioxide, a (then) CCPA and Responsible Care member, received the largest penalty ever imposed under federal environmental legislation in a widely publicized 1995 case. Moreover, Responsible Care membership is not contingent on 100 percent compliance. Companies can become members of the program upon making a commitment to comply with the program. They then have three years to fulfill the obligations, after which time they are subject to evaluation. Even once

---

39. The courts continue to elaborate the precise elements of due diligence as it relates to environmental management. See, e.g., *R. v. Bata Industries* (1992), 7 CELR (New Series) 245 (Ont. Ct. Prov. Div.); *R. v. Crown Zellerbach Properties Ltd.* (1988), 49 DLR (4th) 161 (S.C.C.); *R. v. Toronto Electric Commissioners* (1991), 6 CELR (New Series) 301 (Ont. Ct. Gen. Div.); *R. v. Courtaulds Fibres Canada* (1992), 9 CELR (New Series) 304 (Ont. Ct. Gen. Div.). More generally, see the discussion of the environmental due diligence jurisprudence in J. Swaigen, "Negligence, Reverse Onuses and Environmental Offences: Some Practical Considerations," *Journal of Environmental Law and Practice* 2 (1992), p. 149; E. Hughes, "The Reasonable Care Defenses," *Journal of Environmental Law and Practice* 2 (1992), p. 214.

40. See *R. v. Consumer's Distributing Co. Ltd.* (1980), 57 CCC (2d) 317 (Ont. C.A); *R. v. Dupont* (unreported, January 23, 1986, Ont. Dist. Ct.); *R. v. Hodgson* (1985), 4 F.P.R. 251 (N.S. Prov. Ct.).

41. *R. v. Prospec Chemicals* (1996), 19 CELR (NS) 178 (Alta. Prov. Ct.).

---

certified, however, a company will not automatically be decertified upon violating a law. The CCPA's policy is that a violation raises a "red flag" and that individual incidents and patterns of behaviour will be dealt with on their own merits.

Responsible Care officials acknowledge that this issue creates a dilemma. Failure to expel a violator could undermine the credibility of the program, one of the main objectives of which is to enhance the industry's credibility. On the other hand, some violations may be minor in nature. Moreover, expulsion from CCPA means that member companies lose their leverage to improve the performance of a fellow chemical company, whose performance will inevitably affect the entire industry's reputation.

Even its strongest proponents do not argue that participation in Responsible Care is a guarantee of compliance. Instead, proponents argue, Responsible Care certification means that companies will more likely *want* to be in compliance. Thus, they say, a Responsible Care company will less likely be systematically non-compliant, and will more likely be willing to take remedial measures without a threat of prosecution if it inadvertently falls out of compliance. In short, it is argued, government enforcement officials should treat Responsible Care companies differently from other companies by emphasizing a compliance-promotion approach versus a stricter enforcement approach.

Most environmental advocates take strong exception to this assertion, arguing that examples such as Tioxide illustrate that officials must continue to exercise enforcement discretion on a case-by-case basis. Critics further warn that reliance on a non-governmental program to establish enforcement priorities may be the start of a slippery slope to deregulation.

Relationship With the Policy Development Process: Cooperation and Influence

One of Responsible Care's explicit objectives was to build up industry credibility with government decision makers so as to pre-empt stricter government control of the industry. The precise degree to which Responsible Care has influenced policy outcomes is hard to discern. Some specific linkages may be possible. The fact that the CCPA developed and implemented its own reporting process in the early 1990s, for example, may have helped influence the form of the federal National Pollutant Release Inventory scheme, which is less intrusive than the U.S. Toxics Reduction Inventory model (both in terms of the total number of substances reported and in terms of intracompany transfers of listed substances, for example). It is also possible that Responsible Care's high profile may have increased the government's comfort with voluntary measures generally, thereby helping foster support for the proliferation of recent government-sponsored initiatives. Finally, CCPA officials credit Responsible Care with the government's increased willingness to consider voluntary commitments in lieu of regulations for specific issues such as benzene emissions from chemical manufacturers.

More generally, most observers and participants agree that the chemical industry now enjoys a much more cooperative and influential role with government policy makers than before it initiated the program. Opinion is divided, however, as to whether these new dynamics are desirable. The CCPA has argued for almost a decade that an important benefit of the initiative has been that the Association now has the "confidence that it can speak externally regarding the responsible nature of its membership."[42] Both industry and government officials agree that the program has helped increase the level of trust between the government and the industry. Some point to the recent Memoranda of Understanding between the chemical industry, the federal government and various provincial governments as evidence of a new partnership.[43] To a certain extent, however, this development simply reflects a recent trend towards a more transparent and inclusive regulatory development process that has applied also to other sectors that do not have the equivalent of a Responsible Care program.

Reflecting on this trend, critics within the environmental and labour community argue that one of the potentially most dangerous aspects of government involvement in voluntary initiatives is the increased potential for capture. They argue that government involvement may amount to tacit approval of certain policies, and may effectively amount to promises not to regulate in other cases. They point to the prominent role CCPA officials and member companies played in lobbying against some of the changes the federal government had proposed for strengthening its authority in the *Canadian Environmental Protection Act* during the process of revising the Act in the late 1980s. The CCPA has long argued that voluntary programs "need to be backed up by a government willing to actually regulate."[44] However, over the past decade, it has increasingly used the Responsible Care program as a rationale for government not to regulate its members. To a number of critics, the extended lobbying exercise concerning the new Act illustrated the tremendous influence the program has developed, when it could be used to lobby not against regulation, but against an enabling statute so as to reduce the likelihood and potential significance of regulations in the future. At a minimum, these concerns point to the need for strong accountability mechanisms and public involvement in voluntary measures.

Impacts on the Industry's Public Image

The CCPA describes the benefits of Responsible Care as follows:[45]

Collectively, [member companies] succeed in their goal of self-regulation and public confidence in the industry. Individually, each member increases its standing in the community in which it operates and with those with whom it does business. It experiences increased employee satisfaction and morale. Member companies and their people can be justly proud of their efforts and commitments. It makes them leaders.

---

42. CCPA (footnote 4).

43. During the last five years, the governments of Canada, Ontario and British Columbia have all signed memoranda of understanding with the CCPA focussing on the mutual promotion of pollution prevention.

44. Gordon Lloyd, Vice President CCPA, cited in A. Duffy, "Industry Told its 'Free Ride' on Pollution About to End," *Ottawa Citizen*, March 20, 1999.

45. CCPA, *How to Communicate and Promote Responsible Care* (Ottawa: CCPA, undated).

The chemical industry was one of the first and remains one of the only major Canadian sectors to have opened itself up to extensive public scrutiny through annual environmental reports, the creation of public advisory committees and third-party verification of its performance. It has invested heavily in improving its public image: it has run national advertising campaigns and encouraged its member companies to place ads in local newspapers; it has developed and cosponsored a course for environmental journalists with the University of Western Ontario; it has developed a week-long course for teachers on environmental and chemical issues (Knowledge of the Environment by Youth); it has developed communications material and tips for its member companies; and, of course, it encourages member companies to reach out to their communities and keep them informed of their activities.

There is widespread agreement that Responsible Care has improved community-level public relations. Green cited company officials saying that community members on their compliance verification teams had been "blown away" by their experience.[46] Scott Munro, General Manager of the Lambton Industrial Society in Sarnia, similarly observed that "we have seen and measured significant improvements to the environment, but the biggest change is the openness in providing information."[47]

Although these efforts have increased the industry's transparence, and arguably have helped improve its environmental performance, they have not yielded the expected dividends in improved public perception. Although Responsible Care may have helped arrest the precipitous decline in trust that marked the early to mid-1980s, CCPA polls continue to reveal low overall levels of public confidence in the industry. A survey completed in 1999 indicates that although the public believes the chemical industry provides valuable products, creates employment, and contributes to positive economic growth, it "does no better than a fair job when it comes to minimizing risks to health and the environment, considering the future effects of chemicals, and assuming responsibility for their activities."[48] Addressing this mistrust remains one of the major challenges facing the program.

One of the reasons for this failure may be found in the attitude of environmental and labour advocates, who appear to be divided in opinion about Responsible Care. Some acknowledge the significant changes carried out by the chemical industry since the inception of Responsible Care, pointing to features of the program such as the emphasis on public involvement and reporting as models for voluntary measures in other sectors. Some critics argue that Responsible Care has not prompted much change, however. A union leader at Dow Canada, for example, argued in 1995 that Responsible Care had brought no great change to the company's operations, just an evolution in the understanding of worker safety and health.[49]

More commonly, however, as noted in the previous section the criticism levelled against Responsible Care is not that the program has been ineffective, but that its very success is now being used inappropriately as a shield against further government

---

46. Green (footnote 1).

47. G. Morris, "Why Canada?" *Chemical Week*, July 5–12, 1995, p. 68.

48. Earnscliffe Research and Communications, *Results of Key Audience Research*, conducted for the Canadian Chemical Producers' Association, 1999.

49. Loos and Stricoff (footnote 26).

regulatory intervention. Paul Muldoon, of the Canadian Environmental Law Association, argues that these problems almost inevitably arise when governments become involved in voluntary measures — as they have with the CCPA pursuant to the federal and provincial memoranda of understanding signed in 1995. Similarly, David Bennett of the Canadian Labour Congress argues that the use of Responsible Care as a lobbying device against further regulation is engendering cynicism among third parties about the program's objectives.

This problem may be exacerbated in the case of Responsible Care by the high-profile role played by the CCPA both in administering the program and in handling the industry's government-relations interests. A number of critics argue that the CCPA has adopted contradictory roles by using the success of Responsible Care as the basis for adopting an increasingly anti-regulatory lobbying stance.[50]

Influence on Other Sectors' Approaches to Environmental Programs

The Responsible Care program has stimulated other sectors to develop their own environmental management programs. In addition to the CCPA, the Mining Association of Canada, the Canadian Petroleum Products Institute, the Canadian Electricity Association, the Steel Association, the Vinyl Council, the Canadian Association of Petroleum Producers and the Forest Products Association of Canada and many other smaller industry associations all have or are developing active environmental management programs. While each of these programs differs in various ways from Responsible Care, each is at least in part based on Responsible Care, which is now a standard reference point for any discussions about new sectoral environmental management initiatives in Canada.

Explaining Responsible Care's Impacts

The CCPA understood early that Responsible Care had to have two significant dimensions in order to succeed: doing the right things, and, equally important, being seen to be doing the right things. From its inception, the designers of Responsible Care understood that achieving these twin goals would require a commitment to collective action and mutual help. How successfully has Responsible Care overcome these challenges? And why? This section suggests that it is important to understand the different roles played by a) the social, economic and political context in which the program was designed, b) the process by which it was developed, and c) the actual design of the program itself.

---

50. This problem is not confined to Canada. In 1993, for example, a senior official of the U.S. Environmental Protection Agency's Office of Pollution Prevention and Toxics noted that "One of the problems I think the Responsible Care program suffers from is its connection with CMA [the Chemical Manufacturers Association], because CMA plays many roles for the industry. And one of the things CMA does on behalf of the industry is attack regulations. ... It appears sometimes that the positions CMA is taking in public policy debates are not consistent with Responsible Care." See R. Begley, "Will the Real Chemical Industry Please Stand Up," *Chemical Week*, July 7–14, 1993, p. 18.

The Role Played by Contextual Factors

The conditions facing the Canadian chemical industry in the 1980s — loss of public trust and growing pressure for stricter government regulation — were no different than those in most other industrial countries. Indeed, the major events that had eroded this trust — Seveso, Love Canal, Bhopal — had all happened outside Canada's borders, although a few lesser incidents (e.g. the Mississauga train derailment, the St. Clair toxic "blob," the PCB fire in St. Basile-le-Grand) and growing scientific concern over the effects of persistent, bio-accumulative toxic chemicals on wildlife and humans, particularly around the Great Lakes, contributed to the changing public mood. Yet, it was in Canada that Responsible Care was born. Why?

And why the chemical industry? No other sector had — or has since — put in place as rigorous an environmental management approach. Yet other sectors (e.g. oil) also pose significant environmental risks, and have been the subject of intense public scrutiny. Although the environmental practices of many industries have improved in the past decade, no sector has set collective standards as rigorous as those established by the CCPA. Common sense suggests that industry is more likely to undertake voluntary action when it sells directly to the consuming public. What explains the development of such a strong initiative from the chemical industry, which does not sell to the public?

The answer lies in an understanding of the development of environmental policies in the 1980s, and of the particular circumstances of the Canadian chemical industry at that time. As Roy observes,[51] the pressure for responsible action facing North American industries had expanded during that period to encompass employees, consumers, and spouses and children of executives, each of whom plays an important role in shaping the "culture" within which businesses make pollution-related decisions. In responding to such wide-ranging demands, industry began to search "both inward and outward for answers of what society expects of them."[52]

These pressures were accentuated for the chemical industry in the early 1980s. Because it is highly capital intensive, the chemical industry places a premium on regulatory certainty and good employee relations in order to ensure adequate investment levels. In the wake of Seveso and Bhopal the industry faced a rapidly growing loss of public confidence. While it was not concerned about direct consumer boycotts, it was very concerned that public mistrust could lead to a decline in interest in working in the industry, and in increased demand for new regulations.

In Canada, these concerns took on particular significance given the federal government's announced intention to reform the *Environmental Contaminants Act* and the renewed interest in environmental reform expressed by many of the provinces in the mid-1980s. At the same time, a number of distinctive features of the Canadian chemical industry allowed it to respond to these pressures in a positive way. The Canadian

---

51. M. Roy, "Pollution Prevention, Organizational Culture and Social Learning," *Environmental Law* 22:1 (1992), pp. 189–252.

52. A. J. Hoffman, *The Environmental Transformation of American Industry: An Institutional Account of Organizational Evolution in the Chemical and Petroleum Industries (1960–1993)*, PhD dissertation, submitted to the Department of Civil and Environmental Engineering, and the Sloan School of Management, Massachusetts Institute of Technology, February 1995.

industry was relatively small compared to that of the U.S., for example. And although it largely consisted of foreign-owned branch plants, it operated relatively autonomously. The industry had also recently enjoyed positive experiences in a couple of high-profile multistakeholder processes, which may have suggested to some of the participants that there existed a possibility of a new, more proactive and participatory approach to the policy process, as opposed to the industry's traditional defensive approach.[53]

The single most important factor, however, appears to have been the role of specific leaders. A number of CEOs of the largest Canadian chemical companies were instrumental in developing the new vision and pushing their peers to accept it. They were supported by the CCPA's President, Jean Bélanger, who had been appointed in 1979. A former civil servant, he was sensitive to the industry's need to re-establish its credibility in order to influence government policy, and he understood the growing importance of working collaboratively with external partners.

Each of these factors helps explain why the Canadian chemical industry took action in the mid-80s. The important fact, however, is that the Canadian industry acted before other countries, and developed a program that has become a model for the chemical industry worldwide, and for other sectors. In the face of continued worries about the competitive disadvantages of unilateral environmental action — particularly in Canada, where the policy debate is dominated by a fear of getting too far ahead of the U.S. — the history of Responsible Care is an important reminder of the potential merits of environmental leadership.

How Has the Process by Which Responsible Care was Developed and Continues to be Delivered Influenced its Impact?

An Incremental Process

The development of Responsible Care typifies the difficult balance that must be achieved by voluntary measures. If standards are set too high initially, industry may be reluctant to participate. Almost all commentators interviewed for this study agreed that peer pressure and culture change require time to evolve. Yet if standards are not rigorous and transparent, the public may criticize the initiative for being ineffective.

Proponents of Responsible Care emphasize that the incremental nature of its development contributed significantly to its effectiveness. Internal buy-in and the effective use of peer pressure to minimize laggards have been enhanced by the gradual development of the program and by the fact that the participants have designed each aspect themselves. In order to continue to be effective, and in order to overcome the continuing distrust described above, however, many commentators recognize that Responsible Care must now confront the challenges associated with going the next step to ensuring the independent evaluation of clear performance. In short, in order to ensure its ongoing effectiveness, it must commit its members to continuous improvement.

---

53. And as compared to the more confrontational U.S. approach or the more corporatist approach relied on in Europe.

Resources

The CCPA has dedicated considerable resources to support Responsible Care. Two people work full time on the program, aided by a part-time consultant, in addition to the support provided by the President and the Vice President for Government Relations. To ensure that it had sufficient resources to implement the program, the CCPA doubled its membership fees. As described above, each member also designates at least one Responsible Care coordinator as well as paying for the costs of the compliance verification at its plants and providing various technical and management resources to support the program.

Peer Pressure and Mutual Assistance

Responsible Care had to overcome resistance to participation both from those worried about the costs and from members reluctant to place all their environmental activities under the Responsible Care umbrella. Some worried that participation in a collective program would undermine the market benefits that they were or could receive by proceeding unilaterally. Finally, even if they were willing to participate themselves, many companies may have been reluctant to participate due to a concern that others might not. In short, the program faced a mutual assurance problem — in order to ensure success, it had to ensure each member that all others would contribute their fair share and not "free ride."[54]

The program makes very effective use of peer pressure and internal accountability to overcome these challenges. The CCPA uses peer pressure effectively to create an atmosphere of mutual accountability and to encourage laggards to improve their performance. Among the main vehicles for the delivery of Responsible Care are the six Regional Leadership Groups, comprised of the chief executive officers from each member company. These groups meet quarterly to "compare notes on their progress, or lack thereof, and their difficulties, and offer each other help in approaches or expertise."[55] Beyond providing a forum for trading advice and reporting on progress, the groups demonstrate the personal commitment of the chief executive officers and prove to be an effective means of applying peer pressure. According to Brian Wastle, "The

---

54. These challenges can be understood in one of two ways. The traditional explanation is that rational, self-interested firms will tend to free ride — to try to obtain the benefit of improved industry reputation without making the individual investments necessary to participate themselves. See, e.g., M. Olson, *The Logic of Collective Action* (Cambridge, Mass.: Harvard University Press, 1965). An alternative explanation is that the basic obstacle to effective self-regulation is an "assurance" problem: "the group member (i.e. the firm) does not withhold its contribution to a public good [e.g. a cleaner environment] based on a rational calculation of costs and benefits involved ... but rather does so because it is unable to obtain necessary assurance that other firms will contribute their fair share." See I. Maitland, "The Limits of Business Self-Regulation," *California Management Review* 27:3 (1985), pp. 132–147, p. 134. From the first perspective, to be effective, Responsible Care must prevent firms from free riding. From the second perspective, collective action could be assured if Responsible Care could provide firms with the necessary assurance that others will contribute their fair share.

55. Bélanger (footnote 3), p. 4.

consequences of a chief executive having to stand up in front of his peers and say, 'We didn't make it' are severe enough that only once has a member withdrawn not meeting even the minimum standards."[56]

One of Responsible Care's most important innovations is that it fostered the transfer of technical know-how among chemical companies in reducing their emissions of certain toxic substances. In particular, large companies helped smaller ones in establishing the necessary control systems to reduce emissions, notwithstanding initial unease about the implications for competition. Through this sharing of information and management approaches, the program achieved both greater gains than if each company had worked on its own and a higher level of participation by companies by overcoming concerns that Responsible Care would be too difficult or would cost too much.

The CCPA has been instrumental in promoting this collective action among its members by i) acting as a catalyst in maintaining the commitment of the industry's chief executive officers, ii) providing a mechanism for mutual assistance, and iii) coordinating joint action (e.g. the evaluation of motor carriers' practices under the transportation code).[57] The CCPA also produces extensive publications and fosters ongoing informal exchanges of technical and management advice among company personnel and Responsible Care coordinators.

What Design Features of Responsible Care Strengthened/Weakened its Impact?

Responsible Care is a Condition of Membership in the CCPA

One of the most important factors behind the program's impact appears to be the fact that Responsible Care certification is a prerequisite for membership in the CCPA. The chief executive officer of each CCPA member company must commit formally, as a condition of membership in the Association, to the *Statement of Responsible Care and Guiding Principles*. Companies that do not perform their activities in accordance with the program are required to cease them or leave the Association.

This requirement is an important source of motivation. Membership provides a variety of important benefits, ranging from the extensive information provided by the Association to the informal networking that occurs among the member companies. And because Responsible Care now effectively defines the standard of care expected of the chemical industry, former members would have a hard time justifying to a court that they had decided to leave the CCPA because they did not want to adopt Responsible Care. In short, membership may send important signals to government officials, to the courts, and to suppliers and customers about the environmental quality of a company's operations.

---

56. G. Morris, "Third Party Verification Keeps Initiative Fresh," *Chemical Week*, July 5–12, 1995, p. 66.

57. See Bélanger (footnote 3).

Reporting

The proponents of Responsible Care have long recognized that effective measurement, monitoring and public reporting of performance are required in order to maintain its credibility. This raises a number of difficult issues. What should such a system measure and report, for example? At a minimum, companies should obviously track toxic emissions. Ideally, however, reports should also address other dimensions of a company's environmental performance. For example, reports should allow third parties (other companies, government officials and the public) to verify that emission reductions have not come about at the expense of the creation of some new risk, or simply because of an economic slowdown. More fundamentally, in the opinion of some, reports should allow readers to compare firms' overall environmental performance, rather than just track changes in specific substances. As the U.S. Chemical Manufacturers Association Vice President, Jon Holtzman, observed, emissions-based reports "are important to get the [Responsible Care] process in place, but they're not a company-by-company comparison."[58] Finally, in order to maximize public trust, any system of reporting ought to be independently verifiable.

While the chemical industries in other countries are also trying to address these challenges,[59] public reporting under Responsible Care is occurring at an increasing number of different levels in Canada. The Transportation Incident Measurement program provides annual measures of transportation-related incidents. The CCPA aggregates workplace health and safety information under the 1982 Safety, Health and Accident Reporting Experience initiative, which collects statistics on accidents that cause employee injuries. CCPA member companies also report to the Association on their implementation of the management systems they have put in place for Responsible Care's six codes. Similarly, emissions reporting is also a condition of membership in the CCPA. In 1999, 69 members with 160 facilities reported on the releases of 599 substances. These included the 254 substances on Environment Canada's National Pollution Release Inventory (NPRI) and the 117 on the Accelerated Reduction/ Elimination of Toxics (ARET) list. The remaining substances tracked by member companies are those that have been identified by the CCPA or individual companies as being emissions of concern from either a human health or an environmental perspective.

The CCPA has published annual *Reducing Emissions* reports since 1992. The reports provide aggregated information on member company emissions of chemical substances to air, water and land. These reports differ significantly from the NPRI data in

---

58. Quoted in N. Gunningham, "Environment, Self-Regulation, and the Chemical Industry: Assessing Responsible Care," *Law & Policy* 17:1 (1995), pp. 57–109, p. 71.

59. The U.S. relies heavily on the Toxics Release Inventory. The French group *Rhône Poulenc* has developed an environmental index that can be applied in every plant, and allows reports to be combined to produce a measure of the environmental performance of each company. The U.K. Chemical Industries Association and France's *Union des Industries Chimiques* have adopted this index as an environmental performance indicator. Similarly, the Australian Chemical Industry Council is developing a set of performance indicators ranging from emissions reductions to local community consultation panels. These indicators are designed to be closely related to the codes in the Australian version of Responsible Care, and to take into account both compliance with the processes set out in the codes and performance in relation to output and quality of operation. (See Gunningham, ibid., p. 72.)

that they also contain projected emissions for a five year period. The 1999 report, for example, predicted that CCPA members will achieve a 79 percent reduction in aggregate emissions in 2004, compared to 1992 levels. Since 1994, the CCPA has also published Responsible Care annual reports. These include the reports of Responsible Care's National Advisory Panel (NAP).

Members also provide information to the public on a company-by-company basis. An increasing number are issuing environmental reports to their communities and shareholders, outlining their environmental emissions and describing planned remedial and preventive activities. Many CCPA members are registered with the Voluntary Climate Change Challenge and Registry, a voluntary initiative that requires companies to prepare annual and progress reports of greenhouse gas emissions from their respective facilities.

Compliance Verification

When a company joins the CCPA, it commits to implementing fully the 152 elements of the codes of practice within three years. In 1994, the CCPA reported that some 98 percent of the code elements had been implemented by companies that have been members for three years or more. The problem with this assertion, of course, is that it was based on self-reported information and is not easily verifiable. This problem led early critics of the program (including some members of the National Advisory Panel) to push for independent evaluations.

In 1994, the CCPA took steps towards addressing this issue by developing the Responsible Care public-peer verification protocol. Under the protocol, each company must verify its compliance with Responsible Care's codes of practice through an exhaustive and comprehensive review and assessment. The review is completed by a verification team consisting of industry experts, an independent representative from the National Advisory Panel, and a member of the community in which the company operates. The verification process includes a review of the plant's management system, based on interviews with plant officials, suppliers, customers and community residents, as well as document reviews, site visits, and extensive community consultations. With the exception of the newest CCPA members, all companies have completed or at least initiated external evaluations.

The CCPA recently introduced a "re-verification" process that is completed three years after the first external evaluation. Re-verification is now mandatory every three years. The purpose of re-verification is to

> re-verify, for credibility with peers and the public and for continuous
> improvement of the implementation of the Responsible Care ethic and
> codes across the membership, that each company's management
> processes, previously verified, are still in place or improved upon, and
> are producing performance improvement, in areas important to itself
> and its various stakeholders, that is acceptable to these stakeholders.[60]

---

60. CCPA, *Responsible Care Re-verification: A Protocol to Help Us Improve* (Ottawa: CCPA, 1999).

The re-verification team produces a report describing significant findings, and any areas in need of follow-up by either the team or by the Leadership Group, Community Advisory Panel, annual re-commitment, or next re-verification process. The report also highlights "opportunities for improvement," "significant improvements," "extra miles" or observed "best practices" that could be used by others in the industry.

While they are among the most advanced evaluation requirements compared to other countries' Responsible Care programs, these measures only partially address the need for independent evaluation. The evaluation focusses on the presence of a management system that is committed to continuous improvement. Instead of measuring actual performance, however, the evaluation assesses whether the company has a sound basis for its practices (e.g. conformity with a standard industry practice or an international norm, comparative research, etc.). Some of the criteria relied on by the evaluators is therefore vague and subjective. Nor are these evaluations completely independent: they are not conducted by independently licensed external auditors as a financial audit would be, for example. Many participants and critics therefore argue that moving from the current system to a more objective and independent evaluation process focussed on actual performance represents one of the most important challenges for Responsible Care to overcome in order to improve its credibility with the public.

Public Involvement

There is considerable variation as to the degree of public involvement in the various voluntary environmental initiatives that have emerged in Canada in recent years. Some justify very little involvement on the grounds that outsiders might be too adversarial and would undermine any opportunities for developing programs that foster cultural change over time. Others argue that the public does not have any legitimate role since the action is by definition voluntary. Many involved in voluntary initiatives appear, however, to be moving in the direction of the CCPA, which has long emphasized the importance of public involvement to the success of Responsible Care.

Although the CCPA developed Responsible Care itself, it has sought the input of outside stakeholders from the outset of the initiative. This input is both formal and informal, and occurs at both the national and local levels. Since its establishment in 1986, for example, the National Advisory Panel (NAP) has emerged as an influential yet controversial aspect of Responsible Care. The introduction of external compliance audits and the strengthening of the "right-to-know" provisions of the *Community Awareness and Emergency Response (CAER) Code of Practice* both resulted from recommendations of the NAP, for example. On the other hand, critics charge that the NAP represents an attempt to control public input. There is no mechanism in place to ensure that Responsible Care members address NAP recommendations. And there are few other formal mechanisms for public consultation at the national level. The question therefore arises as to how much public input is required by an initiative that is nominally voluntary and unilateral, but which has the guise of public policy.

Responsible Care also requires participating companies to support local involvement. The *CAER Code of Practice* encourages member companies to establish community advisory committees and to report and communicate directly to the communities of which they are part through a "community dialogue" process. As explained in Responsible Care's 1995 annual report, "If a CCPA plant is located near you, or ships chemicals through your community, it's your right to be told about all the risks you're exposed to. It's your right to ask tough questions and to expect clear answers."[61] Many companies have established such advisory committees. Many also report to their communities through open letters, open houses, community meetings and articles in the local press.

Future Challenges

The factors described above explain why the CCPA initiated Responsible Care and why members remain supportive of the program. To remain effective from an environmental perspective and, in particular, in order to enhance public trust, however, the program must also promote continuous improvement, both on the part of individual members and on the part of the program itself. As well as continuing to improve the industry's ability to interact with the public, the main continuous improvement challenges facing Responsible Care involve extending the program both upstream and down (product stewardship), and moving beyond cleanup operations and processes to questioning the environmental legitimacy of certain chemical products. In addition, the future of the initiative will increasingly be influenced by international issues.

Stewardship

The easiest part of Responsible Care — improved in-plant controls — has largely been implemented. The more difficult part — applying stewardship principles once the product leaves the direct control of the manufacturer — remains ahead.[62]

Although it has endorsed the need to extend Responsible Care both up and down stream,[63] CCPA members are currently struggling with the concept of stewardship. In theory, product stewardship has significant potential. In practice, however, its impact depends in part on the companies' ability to overcome practical impediments such as how to reward a salesperson for *not* selling to an inappropriate customer. Although some Responsible Care companies have started to address this issue, it remains an ongoing challenge.

The degree to which the CCPA is able to enforce stewardship principles also depends on the degree to which suppliers and users can be convinced to adopt similar programs of their own accord. When the CCPA developed Responsible Care, few related

---

61. CCPA, *Responsible Care Annual Report* (Ottawa: CCPA, 1995).

62. H. Fattah, "Taking Care Outside," *Chemical Weekly*, July 5–12, 1995, p. 53.

63. Responsible Care's *Distribution Code of Practice* requires CCPA member companies to ensure "with due diligence" that their suppliers, distributors and resellers "meet the minimum standards of this code of practice." Although this approach represents a very significant departure from traditional industry codes of practice (see Limoges and Davignon [footnote 7]), the Association justifies it on the premise that any negative news about chemical products will hurt the industry as a whole regardless of whether one of its members is directly involved.

industries were interested in participating or developing parallel initiatives. Over the past five years, however, some — like the specialty chemical manufacturers — have initiated processes to develop similar programs. This interest is partly due to the increased leverage Responsible Care companies can apply to their suppliers and customers as a result of the international recognition and endorsement of the program. Compliance with the basic elements of the program has become the industry norm around the world. This interest is also partly due to a growing realization that the implementation of a credible voluntary measure may be an effective means to strengthen an industry's negotiating hand in the policy development and review process.

From Principles to Targets

The Canadian version of Responsible Care now lags behind its U.S. counterpart in at least one important respect. In January 1999, the U.S. Chemical Manufacturers Association Board approved enhancements to its version of Responsible Care by:

- adopting an association-wide performance commitment to "make continuous progress toward the vision of no accidents, injuries or harm to the environment";
- adding a condition of membership requiring each member (and non-chemical "partner company") to establish its own performance goals and publicly report progress toward those goals; and
- agreeing to determine if individual company performance goals can be harmonized into additional association-wide commitments or goals.

As a result of these decisions, the U.S. program now requires members to:

- establish at least one goal for a performance result;
- make steady performance improvement toward the goal(s);
- publicly communicate the identified performance goal(s) and progress toward meeting the goal(s) at least annually; and
- annually report the established goal(s), progress, and public reporting mechanisms to the Chemical Manufacturers Association.

To date, the CCPA has no equivalent requirement to set and report on beyond compliance targets.

From Processes to Products

To date, Responsible Care has encouraged CCPA members to focus on ensuring that they produce their products in a safe and environmentally appropriate manner. The re-verification process has also focussed on assessing members' progress towards adopting life-cycle stewardship practices. The program has also exercised some influence over the development of new products. It has *not*, however, forced members to ask in a rigorous and systematic manner whether they ought to continue producing existing products. Making this transition from minimizing the environmental impact of ongoing activities to questioning the ongoing use and production of environmentally damaging products and processes represents the next level of environmental management and pollution prevention to which Responsible Care and similar voluntary programs must rise. The willingness of the chemical industry to address emerging debates such as those surrounding endocrine hormones and the use of chlorine as a feedstock by various industries will therefore be an important litmus test of the capacity of Responsible Care to continue to engender positive change within the chemical industry.

Responding to International Dynamics

As noted above, the increasing internationalization of the economy may have important implications for the status and form of Responsible Care as a domestic initiative. The emergence of international certification standards such as ISO 14001, for example, may have two important consequences for the program. First, the Prospec Chemicals case raises questions about whether the less comprehensive[64] ISO 14001 will replace Responsible Care as the norm to which government officials and the judiciary hold the industry. Second, some companies may start to question the cost implications of certifying with two similar programs. To the extent that ISO 14001 becomes a dominant international norm, will the Canadian chemical industry continue to be willing to invest in Responsible Care? Presumably, its willingness to continue to do so depends in part on its perceived need to differentiate itself. To date, the chemical sector appears to have perceived a benefit in retaining its own program.

The status of voluntary domestic initiatives such as Responsible Care under international trade laws such as the Code of Good Practice of the World Trade Organization's Agreement on Technical Barriers to Trade[65] is also unclear. The Code applies certain rules to the development and use of voluntary measures for domestic policy. There is an unsettled question regarding the extent to which these rules could constrain domestic capacity to implement environmental policy through measures such as eco-labelling, voluntary codes of practice or negotiated agreements.

Conclusion

The Responsible Care program is the most far-reaching voluntary environmental initiative launched by an industry sector in Canada. Its main objectives were to improve the chemical industry's environmental performance, to improve its relationship with government and to foster increased public trust. To date, the program appears to have made considerable progress towards the first two objectives. The Canadian chemical industry has achieved substantial reductions in the emissions of many toxic chemicals, helped regain the confidence of some environmental policy makers after a series of well publicized accidents had eroded it, and, arguably, forestalled tighter, more prescriptive

---

64. See CCPA, *A Primer on Responsible Care and ISO 14001* (Ottawa: CCPA, 1995) — a CCPA-sponsored comparison of Responsible Care and ISO 14001, which illustrates the broad range of issues, such as public involvement and reporting, that are not included in the ISO regime.

65. See World Trade Organization, "Code of Good Practice for the Preparation, Adoption and Application of Standards," *Agreement on Technical Barriers to Trade*, Annex 3, Uruguay Round of Trade Agreements (Geneva: World Trade Organization, 1994, available at the WTO Web site: <www.wto.org/english/docs_e/legal_e/17-tbt.pdf>.

regulatory controls. Although not all of these changes have resulted solely because of Responsible Care, most evidence suggests that the program has served as an important catalyst and focus for the industry's environmental and government relations efforts over the past decade.

Evaluating the program's impact on public trust is more complicated. While individual companies report improved community relations and while the industry is much more open than it has ever been, polls indicate that it remains low in the public's esteem. One possible test of its overall success is whether it has become once again the "invisible" industry described by CCPA President Jean Bélanger.[66] On this test, Responsible Care scores well. Because it has improved its environmental and workplace safety performance, the industry has avoided much of the public scrutiny that led to the development of the program in the first place. Continued prosecutions of CCPA and non-CCPA chemical companies have aroused skeptics, however. In addition, particularly as the program's ability to influence the ongoing government policy development process has grown, critics have become increasingly vocal in their demands for additional accountability mechanisms such as clear objectives, more openness to public input and a system of independent verification.

What lessons can be drawn from Responsible Care? We have suggested in this chapter that the program's impacts are in part attributable to the way in which it was designed and implemented, and in part the result of the context in which it was developed. Important lessons about design and process that may be transferable to other initiatives include the following:

- the importance of outside input in all phases, including the initial design, implementation and verification;
- the importance of sustained, senior-level leadership;
- the need to commit sufficient resources;
- the value of relying on an incremental process;
- the benefits of well orchestrated peer pressure;
- the need to support individual action with information sharing, and technological and management know-how;
- the need to back up the program's benefits with negative incentives for collective action (e.g. making membership in the CCPA conditional on Responsible Care certification); and
- the requirement for strong internal and external accountability mechanisms, including mandatory public review, involvement and reporting requirements.

The program also owes its impact to the unique situation facing the Canadian chemical industry in the 1980s. It is not often that another sector will face a similar juxtaposition of crises together with the leadership that helped initiate Responsible Care and ensured that it received high-profile support. The question to ask, then, is to what extent can additional design features or supplementary government action substitute for these contextual features to create the requisite drivers for similar voluntary programs in other sectors?

---

66. See footnote 8.

It is also important to distinguish factors that may have supported the development of a voluntary initiative from those factors that stimulate its ongoing improvement over time. In this regard, one of the most difficult questions with respect to Responsible Care — as with most other voluntary environmental initiatives — is how important is a credible threat of regulatory intervention for the initiative's development and ongoing success? There is no question that the threat of regulation served as a major incentive for the development of the program. The more difficult issue is how important an ongoing threat (or lack thereof) has been to the program's evolution and its ability to ensure continuous improvements. Would Responsible Care have changed to the extent it has without any threat of intervention? Would a more credible threat have prompted more significant change, or averted the use of Responsible Care as a lobbying tool to avoid regulatory reform under the *Canadian Environmental Protection Act*?

To a certain extent, Responsible Care has taken on a life of its own. It has become a more demanding code of practice than it was 10 years ago. Through the accountability mechanisms and reporting requirements, the CCPA has established powerful drivers for further improvement of the program. Proponents of Responsible Care as an alternative to future regulations also point to the continued evolution of the program notwithstanding the decline in public pressure for environmental regulations and notwithstanding the decline in governments' capacity to intervene in recent years. They also point to the growing interest in Responsible Care on the part of other industries.

It is difficult to accept the case that there is no role for government in promoting and monitoring voluntary measures, however. It is in the interest of Responsible Care companies to ensure that the entire chemical industry is subject to strong backstop regulation and monitoring, for example. Although the CCPA represents 90 to 95 percent of the chemicals that are manufactured in Canada, it does not represent some small manufacturers, nor does it represent upstream suppliers or downstream users of chemicals, including the specialty manufacturers, which blend products from CCPA-produced chemicals. The CCPA argues that the best way to address this issue is to convince other companies to adopt Responsible Care-style programs. In the absence of such initiatives, however, effective government control over this full spectrum of users and producers is required to address the risk that free riders will undermine the CCPA's efforts to restore the tarnished public image of the chemical industry as a whole. And unless public advocates are satisfied that the government is at least tracking the program's effectiveness on the basis of highly transparent and accessible information, they will remain dissatisfied with the program and mistrustful of any suggestion that it replace regulations.

In our opinion, there is no question that a credible threat of government intervention will often be required to motivate action. Responsible Care was initiated in response to such a threat. Other sectors are now developing similar programs precisely in order to avoid regulatory intervention.

An equally important point is that governments have many other levers they can pull both to induce and to help sustain environmentally beneficial behaviour, including the following:

- backing up self-enforcement, even if just through the realistic threat of regulatory intervention if voluntary action is not effective;
- ensuring accountability (e.g. through mandatory public-involvement requirements; through reporting initiatives such as Accelerated Reduction/Elimination of Toxics, etc.);
- facilitating information exchange to enable small companies to participate;
- educating consumers (to support demand for green products);
- encouraging financial institutions to fund environmental investments; and
- supportive procurement, research and development, and trade policies.

Finally, regardless of the form of government action to support or monitor voluntary initiatives, the Responsible Care experience suggests that government must coordinate those activities carefully with its ongoing policy administration and development processes. Overt support for a voluntary measure exposes governments to potential defenses of officially induced error and abuse of process.[67] More fundamentally, active participation may expose governments to concerns about capture. Again, then, we return to the overarching importance of developing rigorous and effective accountability mechanisms so that the public can judge the value of the actions undertaken. With its public reporting requirements and its evolving compliance verification mechanism, Responsible Care appears to reflect this lesson more than most similar environmental initiatives. The importance of designing voluntary initiatives to engender public trust is emphasized, however, by the fact that accountability nonetheless remains one of the main issues raised by critics of the program.

---

67. As discussed in Chapter 5.

Appendix A
Key Elements of the Responsible Care Codes of Practice

Community Awareness and Emergency Response (CAER)

The CAER requirements relate to each of the other five codes. This code requires companies to establish a "right to know" program at any site where chemicals are handled. Each company must:

- know and respond sensitively to community concerns;
- advise the community of potential hazards associated with its operations;
- have an emergency plan; and
- integrate the emergency plan with the community emergency response plan.

Research and Development

This code applies to each stage of development (from initial research to marketing and beyond) of all investigative technical work regarding new technical products, processes, equipment and applications, as well as all new uses for existing products. Members may not sponsor or conduct research unless it complies with the code. Members are also precluded from introducing new products not developed in accordance with the code.

Manufacturing

This code applies to all aspects of manufacturing and operations — including siting and decommissioning — of both new and existing sites. Members must develop systems covering plant design, construction and operation to protect employees, the community and the environment from any harmful effects of chemical manufacturing.

Transportation

Members must have an active program to ensure that they transport chemicals and chemical products in a manner that minimizes the risk of accidents and of injury to the persons involved in transportation activities, and to the public and the environment along transportation routes. They must provide to people situated along those routes information concerning any dangers.

Distribution

This code covers all activities related to the sale of chemicals and chemical products and services as well as the movement of goods that come from suppliers to be resold or to be converted into new products. The code establishes standards and procedures and provides training guidance for the storage and handling of chemicals and chemical products. Members may not buy from suppliers or sell to distributors and customers who do not comply with the code.

Hazardous Waste Management

Members are encouraged to assess best practices, to reduce, reuse, recycle or recover hazardous waste, and to cooperate in remediating contaminated sites.

Chapter 7
Gap Inc.'s Code of Conduct for Treatment of Overseas Workers

Gregory T. Rhone, John Stroud and Kernaghan Webb

Introduction

Gap Inc. is a U.S.-based company that operates a chain of more than 4,200 retail clothing stores around the world, under the Gap, Old Navy and Banana Republic names.[1] The company's annual revenues have recently exceeded US$13 billion. It employs approximately 165,000 people. None of its employees make any clothing. Rather, Gap Inc. does business with more than 3,500 manufacturers operating in 50 countries who supply the company with the clothing it sells.[2]

In the early 1990s, following criticisms of the labor conditions prevailing within the apparel industry, Gap Inc. became one of many multinational corporations to develop codes of conduct relating to treatment of those workers.[3] Gap Inc.'s *Sourcing Principles and Guidelines* were originally established in 1993. In 1996, following a negative publicity campaign spearheaded by non-governmental organizations (NGOs) alleging violations of the *Sourcing Principles and Guidelines* at Mandarin International — a Taiwan-owned garment factory in El Salvador that provided clothing on contract to Gap Inc. — the retailer introduced a new, more rigorous *Code of Vendor Conduct*. Several aspects of Gap Inc.'s initiative are noteworthy:

- Unlike codes designed to apply to an entire sector or to all members of an association, Gap Inc.'s code was developed and implemented by a single firm; nevertheless, the code is expressly designed to apply to firms *other than* Gap Inc. — to those that supply products to Gap Inc. In this sense it is a multifirm initiative.
- The code exemplifies the "leveraging" ability that companies can wield through their procurement activities to induce behavioural changes by other private sector actors.
- Gap Inc. is one of the first companies with a labour code to integrate the participation of NGOs into compliance verification of selected suppliers.
- The code is explicitly designed to have multijurisdictional application to supplier companies no matter where they are located. Indeed, given the global nature of the garment manufacturing industry, a code that applied only within a single jurisdiction would have limited effect.

---

1. Statistics are culled from Gap Inc., *Annual Report 2001*, available at the company's corporate Web site at <http://media.corporate-ir.net/media_files/IROL/11/111302/fin_annual_01.pdf>.

2. Gap Inc., *Ethical Sourcing*, formerly available at <www.gapinc.com>.

3. Others include Levi-Strauss, Nike, Reebok, Sears, Wal-Mart and Starbucks. See generally, L. Compa and T. Hinchliffe Darricarrere, "Private Labor Rights Enforcement Through Corporate Codes of Conduct," in L. Compa and S. Diamond, *Human Rights, Labor Rights, and International Trade* (Philadelphia: University of Pennsylvania Press, 1996), pp. 181–197.

Kernaghan Webb, Editor, *Voluntary Codes: Private Governance, the Public Interest and Innovation.*
This chapter ©2004 Gregory T. Rhone, John Stroud and Kernaghan Webb, pages 209–226.
Published by the Carleton Research Unit for Innovation, Science and Environment, Carleton University, Ottawa, Canada.

Although the labour-oriented subject matter of codes of conduct such as Gap Inc.'s is addressed in international and domestic laws — in numerous international human rights and labour conventions, as a condition of favoured treatment in the domestic trade law of countries such as the United States, and in the domestic labour legislation of developed and developing countries — the primary impetus for firms putting such codes in place would not appear to be legal in nature, but rather a desire to be seen as "doing the right thing" in the eyes of customers, and thus attracting or maintaining a client base. In fact, effective government enforcement of such labour-oriented rights has been elusive to date; thus, voluntary approaches may stand a better chance of implementation than a purely statutory approach.

In this chapter, analysis is undertaken of the background conditions that led to Gap Inc. preparing a code, the process of code development, the components of the code, implementation of the code, and the strengths and weaknesses of Gap Inc.'s approach, with a view to determining the broader implications of such initiatives. Throughout the chapter, reference will be made both to the original *Sourcing Principles and Guidelines* and the new *Code of Vendor Conduct*. It is the use of third-party compliance verification as part of the *Code of Vendor Conduct* program that breaks new ground in the area of multijurisdictional codes, and thus the *Code of Vendor Conduct* and its related third-party verification program are the focal points of analysis.

A basic conclusion emerging is that, in a globalized economy, the attention of Western consumers is increasingly focussing on the ethical dimensions of how products are made, and the need for companies to uphold basic labour and environmental standards in all their operations, wherever they are located. Companies such as Gap Inc., which have put global codes in place and are beginning to work with human rights and labour organizations on code implementation, are attempting to respond to these concerns. In so doing, they are providing evidence of what can and cannot be accomplished in this domain through voluntary, market-based approaches, against a variable backdrop of domestic and overseas legal regimes. These and other points are discussed further in the body of the chapter.

Background Conditions

To understand how and why Gap Inc.'s original *Sourcing Principles and Guidelines* and the replacement *Code of Vendor Conduct* were developed, this section examines both the market and the legal environments in which they emerged. Given that Gap Inc. is a U.S. company, and U.S. NGOs and trade laws have been driving forces behind the development of the Gap Inc. codes, the focus of attention is on that country's players and laws.

The Market Environment

A discussion of market conditions can usefully be divided into supply-side and demand-side considerations. Looking first to supply-side factors, many aspects of the garment industry's labour-intensive production and assembly have moved out of high-wage, developed countries in recent years to developing countries in Central and South

America and Asia.[4] These locations are attractive, not as an access point to the local market but as a source of plentiful, low-wage labour, and thus serve as a manufacturing site for the export (Western) market.[5]

The depressed economies, mass unemployment, extreme poverty, corruption, and underdeveloped legal systems of many developing countries provide an environment ripe for human rights (including worker) abuse. By the mid-1990s, reports of child and prison labour, overworked and underpaid employees, and restrictions on labour union activities in developing countries had become commonplace in the Western media[6] and in government hearings.[7] Although the focus of this study is on codes of conduct pertaining to worker treatment *overseas*, it is worth pointing out that garment worker abuse within North America has also been well documented. For example, *The Economist* reported that, in 1995, California state officials freed 72 Thai immigrants from a sweatshop in Los Angeles. They had been held captive and forced to work for up to 17 hours a day, and were being paid between $0.60 and $1.60 an hour.[8] When such worker abuse can take place in developed countries such as the United States — countries with healthy economies, high standards of living, generally well-resourced governments with extensive human rights and health and safety laws, and only occasional incidents of public-servant corruption — it is apparent that the potential for abuse and difficulty in finding effective solutions is arguably far greater in the conditions of developing countries.

A number of factors make it difficult for retailers to effectively monitor the activities of their contractors. It is not uncommon for large garment retailers to enter into contracts with a myriad of supplier factories located in a large number of countries, as evidenced by Gap Inc.'s 3500 suppliers in 50 countries. Factories can range widely in size, and many make clothing for more than one company. For example, in addition to supplying clothing to Gap Inc., Mandarin International has also made clothing for such companies as JC Penney, and Eddie Bauer.[9] Over the course of a week, workers may manufacture different shirts for different retailers. As is discussed below, this can make consistent application of retailer-based labour codes problematic. Retailers often

---

4. See, generally, A. Mody and D. Wheeler, "Towards a Vanishing Middle: Competition in the World Garment Industry," *World Development* 15 (1987), p. 1269. See also C. Green, "At the Junction of the Global and Local: Transnational Industry and Women Workers in the Caribbean," in L. Compa and S. Diamond, eds., ibid., pp. 118–141.

5. As discussed in P. Wilson, *Exports and Local Development: Mexico's New Maquiladoras* (Austin, Tex.: University of Texas Press, 1992), p. 9.

6. See, e.g., A. Borgman, "Garment Workers Show U.S. the 'Child Behind the Label'," *Washington Post*, July 24, 1995; M. Gibb-Clark, "Sweatshops Leave Big Gap in Workers' Rights," *The Globe and Mail*, August 16, 1995; P. Edwards, "'Virtual Slavery' in Sweatshops," *Toronto Star*, August 16, 1995.

7. For example, the Subcommittee on Sustainable Human Development of the House of Commons (Canada) Standing Committee on Foreign Affairs and International Trade, which looked at ending child labour exploitation. See the report of the Subcommittee, *Ending Child Labour Exploitation — A Canadian Agenda for Action on Global Challenges* (February 1997), available at <www.parl.gc.ca/committees352/fore/reports/5_1997-02/fore-05-cov-e.html>.

8. "Dress Code: Stamping out Sweatshops," *The Economist*, April 19, 1997, p. 28.

9. C. Forcese, "Overcoming the Gap: New 'Gap' Code of Conduct Plugs Holes," *Amnesty International Legal Network Newsletter* (Ottawa: Amnesty International, 1996), p. 1.

purchase clothing through buyers who may or may not actually see the factory locations or conditions in which garments are made. As a result, at a practical level, a host of factors — the long-distance retailer-supplier relationship and varied languages and cultures involved, the diversity of contractors who may work with a single retail firm, and the use of intermediary buyers — detract from the ability of retailers in the U.S. and elsewhere not only to make demands concerning worker treatment but also to ensure that those demands are met.

The apparel industry is also noted for the fierce competition between developing countries for apparel contracts. Jobs and capital are highly mobile. When labour is more expensive in one country, there is often another that is cheaper just down the road. Countries such as El Salvador compete with even poorer countries such as Honduras and Nicaragua "where wages are lower and the population even poorer and more eager to work."[10]

Turning to an examination of the demand side of the equation, the increased interest being expressed by some retail firms in how their products are made reflects growing interest by Western consumers in such matters. A Reebok spokesman is reported as saying, "Consumers today hold companies accountable for the way products are made, not just the quality of the product itself."[11] Another factor at play is interjurisdictional — the perceived unfairness of companies meeting rigorous labour, environmental and other standards only in their facilities located in developed countries, and not in their operations located in developing countries. As Warren Allmand, President of the Canadian-based International Centre for Human Rights and Democratic Development put it, "It is no longer enough to say 'When in Rome, do as the Romans do.' The question is rather, Can companies who are responsible at home be irresponsible abroad?"[12] Studies in recent years have suggested that consumers are willing to pay higher prices for apparel that is not manufactured in sweatshops. For example, as part of the U.S. government-spearheaded Apparel Industry Partnership announced in August 1996 (now known as the Fair Labor Association), a survey was reported as suggesting that three quarters of America's shoppers would willingly pay higher prices for clothes and shoes bearing a "No Sweat" label.[13] Whether survey results translate into actual sales remains to be seen.

As is discussed in greater detail later in the chapter, institutional investors and individual shareholders may represent another source of market pressure for action with respect to worker treatment. Unions in developed countries are also beginning to take an increasing interest in the plight of their fellow workers in developing countries. Some commentators have noted that, in recent years, U.S. unions have moved aggressively to

---

10. L. Kaufman and D. Gonzalez, "Labor Standards Clash With Global Reality," *New York Times*, April 24, 2001.

11. Compa and Hinchliffe Darricarrere (footnote 3), p. 183.

12. W. Allmand, "Foreword," in C. Forcese, ed., *Commerce With Conscience? Human Rights and Corporate Codes of Conduct* (Montréal: International Centre for Human Rights and Democratic Development, 1997), p. 8.

13. As reported in *The Economist* (footnote 8). The Apparel Industry Partnership (now the Fair Labor Association) is discussed in Kernaghan Webb and David Clarke, "Voluntary Codes in the United States, the European Union and Developing Countries," Chapter 13, below (referred to as "Other Jurisdictions," below).

develop international solidarity programs with foreign workers and unions.[14] It is perhaps self-evident that improving the working conditions and wages of workers in developing countries is likely to decrease the attractiveness of firms "outsourcing" work overseas, and this might, in the longer term, mean more jobs for union workers in developed countries. As discussed below, one American labour organization (the National Labor Committee)[15] has played a key role in spurring Gap Inc. to use third-party monitors in its supplier factories.

The Legal Environment

The shift to using labour in developing countries has been further encouraged through structural changes to the trade-oriented framework laws of many countries. Particularly since the Reagan administration of the 1980s, there has been increased emphasis in American trade policy away from direct government aid and intervention, toward granting preferential treatment of imports from developing countries that agree to work toward better protection of labour (and other) rights.[16]

Many developing countries have changed their tariff schedules to make investment in their countries more profitable. "Export processing zones" have been established within many developing countries. Perhaps the most well known export processing zones are the *Maquiladoras*, located on the Mexico-U.S. border.[17] By agreement between participating developing countries and developed countries, firms within the export processing zones are allowed to process goods for export without paying duties on imported components.[18] While management decisions, the source of capital, raw materials and technology originate largely outside the developing countries (and that is where much of the profit and finished products are destined), the export processing zones represent an infusion of much-needed jobs and foreign capital into developing countries' economies.[19] There are now export processing zones in some 35 countries.[20]

In 1971, the Generalized System of Preferences (GSP) was authorized under the General Agreement on Tariffs and Trade. The GSP grants tariff preferences to developing countries to foster exports and economic development. Participating developing countries are required to eliminate or reduce significant barriers to trade in goods, services and investment, and to provide adequate and effective means for foreign nationals to secure, exercise and enforce exclusive intellectual property rights. All of

---

14. Compa and Hinchliffe Darricarrere (footnote 3), p. 182.

15. See the National Labor Committee's Web site, <www.nlcnet.org>.

16. D. Ramnarine, "The Philosophy and Developmental Prosects of the CBI," in A. Bakan et al., eds., *Imperial Power and Regional Trade: The Caribbean Basin Initiative* (Waterloo, Ont.: Wilfrid Laurier University Press, 1993), p. 83.

17. As for the Mandarin facility, it is located in a free trade zone in San Marcos, El Salvador. See Forcese (footnote 9), p. 27.

18. Wilson (footnote 5), p. 9.

19. Green (footnote 4), p. 120.

20. Wilson (footnote 5), p. 9.

these factors make it easier for multinationals to do business in participating developing countries.[21] Under the GSP program, specified products imported from more than 140 designated developing countries and territories are granted duty-free treatment.[22]

Under U.S. law, the beneficiary country must undergo an annual review in order to preserve eligibility for GSP status. Among other things, this review involves demonstrating that the country is taking steps to afford internationally recognized worker rights.[23] However, due to language ambiguities and the discretionary nature of the grant of GSP status, some commentators have been critical of the program,[24] although others describe the review process as beneficial.[25]

Regional initiatives of the United States, such as the Caribbean Basin Initiative (CBI), operate in a similar manner to the GSP, and have helped encourage the location of garment factories in these regions.[26] Apparel imported to the U.S. from the Caribbean increased from 5.5 percent of all CBI imports in 1984 to 48 percent in 1998.[27] As with the GSP, the CBI program includes an ambiguous discretionary power authorizing the President to take into account the extent to which workers are afforded "reasonable workplace conditions and enjoy the right to organize and bargain collectively."[28]

In addition, the U.S. government has, for many years, encouraged American businesses to adopt voluntary codes of practice pertaining to labour and other matters for their operations abroad. Examples include the *Sullivan Principles* (a code first drafted in 1977 that sought to promote racial equality in South Africa), the *MacBride Principles* (a 1984 code intended to overcome antipathy between the Protestant majority and Roman Catholic minority of Northern Ireland), and the *Slepak Principles* and *Miller Principles* (which promoted human rights in the former Soviet Union and China, respectively).[29] Most recently, the Apparel Industry Partnership has been spearheaded by the U.S. federal

---

21. For more on the GSP, see *Quantifying the Benefits Obtained by Developing Countries from the Generalized System of Preferences,* note by the Secretariat of the United Nations Commission for Trade and Development, October 7, 1999, available at <www.unctad.org/en/docs/poitcdtsbm52.en.pdf>.

22. Ibid.

23. *Generalized System of Preferences Renewal Act of 1984,* Pub. L. No. 98-573, tit. V, 98 Stat. 3018 (codified at 19 USC § 2461–2465) (Supp. III, 1985). Under § 2462(a)(4), "internationally recognized worker rights" include the right of association, the right to organize and bargain collectively, a prohibition on the use of any form of forced or compulsory labour, a minimum age for the employment of children, and acceptable conditions of work with respect to minimum wages, hours of work and occupational safety and health.

24. P. Alston, "Labor Rights Provisions in US Trade Law," *Human Rights Quarterly* 15 (1993), p. 21.

25. See, e.g., Forcese (footnote 9), p. 5. According to Forcese, in Canada, under the *Customs Tariff,* GSP benefits have been extended to developing countries, but without any legislative requirements necessitating consideration of labour conditions in the exporting nation.

26. See, generally, W. Corbett, "Shortcomings of the Caribbean Basin Initiative," *Law and Policy in International Business* 23 (1992), p. 953; United States International Trade Commission, Office of Economics, *Impact of the Caribbean Basin Economic Recovery Act on U.S. Industries and Consumers* (1992), pp. 8–9.

27. U.S. Trade Representative, *Third Report to the Congress on the Operation of the Caribbean Basin Economic Recovery Act,* October 1, 1999, p. 17, available at <www.ustr.gov/regions/whemisphere/camerica/3rdreport.pdf>.

28. *Caribbean Basin Economic Recovery Act,* Pub. L. No. 9867, tit. II, 97 Stat. 384 (1983) (codified at 19 USC § 2702 (c)(8)) (Supp. IV 1986).

29. See, generally, J. F. Perez-Lopez, "Promoting International Respect for Worker Rights Through Business Codes of Conduct," *Fordham International Law Journal* 17 (1993), pp. 1–23.

government.[30] Other international and intergovernmental bodies have also developed labour-oriented codes of conduct, guidelines, conventions and declarations for use by multinationals:[31]

- In the early 1970s, the United Nations drafted (but did not formally adopt) the *Code of Conduct on Transnational Corporations*, which addressed human rights and fair treatment of workers.
- The Organisation for Economic Co-operation and Development (OECD) established *Guidelines for Multinational Enterprises* in 1976, which included provisions pertaining to workers' rights. The Guidelines have recently been revised and strengthened.[32]
- The International Labor Organization (ILO) has adopted numerous labour-related conventions and standards, with heavy emphasis on worker protection.[33]

Within developing countries, the willpower, resources and infrastructure necessary to ensure governmental protection of worker rights is often lacking. Governments may be falling over themselves to attract new contracts and jobs and thereby pump needed money into the economy, ties to factory owners may be uncomfortably close, labour ministries may be hopelessly understaffed or indifferent, and attempts to expose bad working conditions may be suppressed.[34] While a rigorously enforced regulatory regime is clearly the preferred alternative, in these types of circumstances, a voluntary code such as Gap Inc.'s may be more effective in the immediate term at inducing its suppliers to respect labour standards by these supplier companies than inadequately enforced legislated standards.

Process of Code Development

Gap Inc.'s original *Sourcing Principles and Guidelines* were prepared internally in 1993. Research has revealed no evidence of there being a public consultation process, or outside involvement of NGOs or government officials in the development of the *Sourcing Principles and Guidelines*. In the mid-1990s, labour groups — in particular the U.S.-based National Labor Committee (NLC) — began to examine the implementation of workers' rights-oriented codes, including Gap Inc.'s *Sourcing Principles and Guidelines* initiative. The NLC's attention became focussed on one particular Gap Inc. contractor factory: the Mandarin International facility. One young woman who worked at the Mandarin factory, and who reported numerous breaches of the *Sourcing Principles and Guidelines*, was sponsored by the NLC in a tour of the U.S. and Canada to discuss

---

30. For more on the Apparel Industry Partnership, see Webb and Clarke, "Other Jurisdictions," Chapter 13, below.

31. The following is derived from Compa and Hinchliffe Darricarrere (footnote 3), pp. 183–185.

32. For the text of the OECD Guidelines, see <www.oecd.org/daf/investment/guidelines>.

33. The texts of ILO legal documents are available at <www.ilo.org/public/english>.

34. Kaufman and Gonzalez (footnote 10).

her plight. This resulted in considerable media coverage.[35] Media scrutiny intensified in the fall of 1995. *New York Times* columnist Bob Herbert visited the Mandarin factory in October, reporting on overworked and underpaid women supporting malnourished families.[36] The president of the Mandarin factory was reported as saying that if the wages were any higher American retailers would take their business elsewhere.[37]

Labour, religious, women's, student, consumer and human rights groups petitioned Gap Inc. to acknowledge the problems at the factory. The NLC publicly contemplated bringing a suit in the U.S. for consumer fraud.[38] Gap Inc. responded with a counterthreat of a libel suit should the NLC continue in its accusations.[39] Neither legal action materialized. Instead, in November 1995, Gap Inc. announced that it would no longer place orders from Mandarin. However, Gap Inc. was urged to address the problems instead, and thus avoid punishing the Mandarin workers. Gap Inc. officials eventually met with the NLC and two representatives of the Presbyterian Church to work out a settlement. On December 15, 1995, in a Statement of Resolution, the parties announced agreement on three broad points, as follows:

- The factory owners agreed to meet with non-working union officials and workers to negotiate and resolve their differences, with a view to reinstating seven non-working union leaders and other members.
- Gap Inc. agreed to work with U.S. groups such as the Interfaith Center on Corporate Responsibility (ICCR)[40] and the Business for Social Responsibility (BSR)[41] Education Fund to explore the viability of an independent industry monitoring program in El Salvador (this is the genesis of the American Independent Monitoring Working Group, or IMWG, discussed below); meanwhile, Gap Inc. and the NLC agreed to use the Human Rights Ombudsman's offices in El Salvador and other Central American countries to monitor factory compliance with the *Sourcing Principles and Guidelines*. The involvement of ICCR in independent monitoring is noteworthy because it indicates some awareness and concern among the investment community — and not just the labour, human rights and consumer communities — about the issue. Market pressure from investors and shareholders represents yet another lever to stimulate private sector action in ways that further public policy objectives.

---

35. Alleged breaches of the code included payment of wages below an adequate level, overworking of employees, such as shifts lasting up to 21 hours, the use of child workers, improper payment of overtime, harassment, physical punishment, and the dismissal of employees who attempted to unionize. See such press coverage as Borgman, Gibb-Clark and Edwards (footnote 6).

36. B. Herbert, "Not a Living Wage," *New York Times*, October 9, 1995.

37. Ibid.

38. Forcese (footnote 9), p. 3.

39. National Labor Committee, press release, October 26, 1995, p. 2.

40. ICCR is a coalition of Protestant, Jewish and Roman Catholic institutional investors from the U.S. and Canada that uses its investments to hold corporations accountable for their effect on society and the environment. See the ICCR's Web site at <www.iccr.org>.

41. BSR is a U.S.-based organization that helps companies develop policies and practices that contribute to the sustained and responsible success of their enterprises. See BSR's Web site, <www.bsr.org>.

- Gap Inc. agreed to re-approve the Mandarin factory for production of Gap Inc. garments when it felt confident that Mandarin could meet or exceed its *Sourcing Principles and Guidelines*, and there were other positive signs of progress concerning fair treatment of workers in El Salvador.

Following the Statement of Resolution, Gap Inc. took these steps:

- It worked with the IMWG to explore the feasibility of independent monitoring (January–March 1996). In January 1996, a month after the Statement of Resolution was released, the IMWG began negotiating the terms for an acceptable third-party monitoring arrangement. As part of these efforts, some members of the IMWG travelled to El Salvador to meet with factory managers and workers, and confer with representatives of various local religious, labour, government, and human rights organizations.
- It signed a resolution on worker-management relations with managers, workers and current and former union leaders at Mandarin to strive for the creation of a humane and productive business (March 22, 1996).
- It consented to the formation of a team of local independent monitors in El Salvador to help ensure that Mandarin stays in compliance with its code (March 22, 1996). The monitoring group, called the El Salvador GMIES,[42] consisted of representatives of Tutela Legal (the human rights office of the Catholic Archdiocese of San Salvador), the Institute of Human Rights of Central American University, and a labour studies institute known as CENTRA.
- It hired two Central American "sourcing compliance" officers whose sole responsibility was to ensure that Gap Inc. contractors operate in full compliance with local laws and Gap Inc.'s standards (April 1996).
- It replaced its *Sourcing Principles and Guidelines* with the *Code of Vendor Conduct*.[43]

According to some reports, the move to the use of third-party monitoring by Gap Inc. was resisted by other organizations, such as the U.S. National Retailers Association.[44] The Association's objection related to the fact that factories such as Mandarin actually do garment work for a number of companies simultaneously, so that Gap Inc.'s agreement with Mandarin would affect other retailers as well.

It appears that the next step in the evolution of monitoring programs is to attempt to encourage sustainable worker policies that continue within particular supplier facilities after contracts with leading Western name-brand apparel companies have ended. Over the past three years, Gap Inc. (along with Nike) has piloted this concept through its financial and logistical support of an organization called Global Alliance for

---

42. An acronym for *El Grupe de Monitoreo Independiente de El Salvador*.

43. Information derived from Gap Inc., "To Our Customers," May 1996; Letter from Interfaith Center on Corporate Responsibility, April 19, 1996, Re: Independent Working Group Progress Report.

44. Forcese (footnote 9), p. 1.

Workers and Communities (GA).[45] As is indicated on the Global Alliance Web site, the GA works through a two-step process that begins and ends with the workers themselves. The first step is to give voice to the concerns and aspirations of factory workers, through worker surveys, in-depth interviews and focus groups. Second, is the design and delivery of education, training, personal development and other programs that respond directly to workers' identified needs, both inside and outside the workplace. The GA publishes regular public reports and updates on its work, and posts assessment tools and results, as well as full country reports, on its Web site. The long-term goal of the GA is to develop practical and sustainable multisector partnerships that deliver mutual benefits to workers, factory owners, local NGOs and global companies.[46]

The controversies that swirled around Gap Inc. in the mid- to late 1990s seem to have died down somewhat in recent years. The American IMWG worked in apparent obscurity, releasing a public report in May 2001 (discussed in the section on implementation, below). According to the most recent information from Gap Inc., the company now employs vendor compliance officers throughout the world, representing 25 nationalities (though an exact number of individuals is not provided).[47]

Components of the Code of Vendor Conduct[48]

As mentioned above, one aspect of the fallout from the negative publicity associated with Gap Inc.'s activities in El Salvador in the mid-1990s was the introduction of a new *Code of Vendor Conduct*, to replace the first-generation *Sourcing Principles and Guidelines*. On the surface, there is a good deal of similarity between the two codes. Both articulate objectives calling for an ethical workplace, and stipulate that those contractors who fail to live up to the conditions risk losing Gap Inc. as a purchaser. Both address a nearly identical set of issues — e.g. discrimination, forced labour, child labour, working conditions, wages and hours, environment, freedom of association and compliance.

However, there are significant differences. First, remedying a deficiency of the *Sourcing Principles and Guidelines* revealed by the unfavourable media coverage of 1995, the *Code of Vendor Conduct* includes a section on monitoring and enforcement. The section reads as follows:

---

45. The GA was launched in April 1999 to improve the workplace experience and life opportunities for workers in developing countries, and to promote collaborative multisector efforts in support of these activities. A partnership of foundations, global companies and international institutions, the GA places particular emphasis on reaching young adult workers involved in global productions and service supply chains worldwide. GA partners include the International Youth Foundation, the World Bank, Gap Inc., Nike, St. John's University and Penn State University.

46. For more information, see <www.theglobalalliance.org>.

47. See Gap Inc., *Our People and Partners*, available at <www.gapinc.com>.

48. Citations in this section are from Gap Inc.'s *Code of Vendor Conduct*, available at <www.dol.gov/ILAB/media/reports/iclp/apparel/5c7.htm>.

As a condition of doing business with Gap, each and every factory must comply with this Code of Vendor Conduct. Gap will continue to develop monitoring systems to assess and ensure compliance. If Gap determines that any factory has violated this Code, Gap may either terminate its business relationship or require the factory to implement a corrective action plan. If corrective action is advised but not taken, Gap will suspend placement of future orders and may terminate current production.

This provision is rather open-ended, particularly the statement that Gap Inc. "will continue to develop monitoring systems." However, given that the viability of NGO monitoring was intended to be subject to fairly long-term study, this is perhaps not surprising. According to communications by the authors with Gap Inc. compliance officials, Gap Inc.'s own internal monitoring program has grown since the development of the Code, in the sense that encouraging factories to adopt internal monitoring departments has also become more common as a way to further "develop monitoring systems."

The key difference between *Sourcing Principles and Guidelines* and the *Code of Vendor Conduct* is the amount of detail that each document presents. While the *Sourcing Principles and Guidelines* reads like a public relations pamphlet, the language of the *Code of Vendor Conduct* more closely resembles that of a legal document. For example, the *Sourcing Principles and Guidelines* provision pertaining to working conditions consists of one paragraph, and is very general. It requires that factories be clean, safe, and well-lit. In contrast, section VII of the *Code of Vendor Conduct* — pertaining to working conditions — fills three-and-a-half pages of text, and is very specific. There are prohibitions on "corporal punishment or any other form of physical or psychological coercion," and 16 other mandatory requirements pertaining to all manner of factory conditions, as well as another 16 requirements pertaining to housing (when applicable). Unlike the *Sourcing Principles and Guidelines*, the *Code of Vendor Conduct* is to be translated into the language of the workers in each factory, and posted throughout each facility. For consumers, a plain-language English version of the *Code of Vendor Conduct* is available, and related information can be obtained from Gap Inc.'s corporate affairs Web site.[49]

Nevertheless, the *Code of Vendor Conduct* does have a number of ambiguities and weaknesses. For example, with respect to wages, the requirement in section VI that workers be paid "at least the minimum legal wage or a wage that meets local industry standards, whichever is greater," may prove to be of marginal protection if the local minimum wage or local industry standards are below the poverty line (as is common[50]). There is no provision in the *Code of Vendor Conduct* requiring review and revision of the Code after a set period, no requirement of publication of compliance data, and no whistleblower protection for employees who report incidents of code non-compliance.

---

49. See <www.gapinc.com>.

50. *The Economist* (footnote 8), p. 28.

Gap Inc. set out the following approach for dealing with cases of non-compliance:

> When a compliance issue is identified, corrective action is required. Typically, this results in continuous improvement at a factory over time. But, if serious violations occur or a pattern of non-compliance emerges at an approved factory, we may suspend production or terminate business. For example, we terminated business at 15 factories in China for falsifying payroll records. In 2001, we quit doing business with vendors representing more than 120 factories worldwide for compliance-related reasons.[51]

There remains some degree of ambiguity in this approach (e.g. what constitutes a "serious violation"?) but, as with regulatory enforcement contexts, some discretion is arguably necessary to give parties the flexibility to facilitate creative solutions.[52]

Implementation

The media coverage of the Mandarin factory's non-compliance with Gap Inc.'s *Sourcing Principles and Guidelines* pointed to a major deficiency with an *ad hoc* and purely internal auditing approach. As has been discussed, since then, a more systematic, and widespread internal compliance system has been put in place, with vendor compliance officers working for Gap Inc. throughout the world. But what about the third-party monitoring, a process that was to begin with the Mandarin facility and then extend to other facilities if it proved viable?

In its May 2001 report, the IMWG summarized the progress to date:

> Originally designed to respond to a crisis, independent monitoring has evolved into a method of providing consistent, systematic, on-going compliance with applicable national law and Gap Inc.'s Code of Vendor Conduct.[53]

Over the years, the independent monitoring process has continued to be conducted by the El Salvador local independent monitoring group (GMIES):

> GMIES began visiting the factory shortly after the March 22 [1996] agreement was reached. At first, the visits occurred about three times per week, and focused on worker interviews. Later, the visits became less frequent. GMIES has monitored the range of issues covered in Gap Inc.'s Code of Vendor Conduct and applicable laws. It has

---

51. See <www.gapinc.com>.

52. For discussion of discretion in regulatory enforcement contexts, see, e.g., K. Webb, "Between Rocks and Hard Places: Bureaucrats, Law and Pollution Control," in R. Paehlke and D. Torgerson, eds., *Managing Leviathan: Environmental Politics and the Administrative State* (Kitchener, Ont.: Broadview Press, 1993), pp. 201–227.

53. Independent Monitoring Working Group, *Public Report*, May 14, 2001, p. 2, available at <www.somo.nl/monitoring/reports/IMWG-report.pdf>.

accomplished this through a variety of means including regular on-site visits, worker interviews, meetings with management, formal surveys, monthly meetings attended by the independent monitors, management, union representatives and Gap Inc. representatives.[54]

The El Salvador independent monitors are also available to hear complaints from workers.[55]

Following initial start-up problems related to the devastation caused by Hurricane Mitch in 1998, and difficulties finding local non-governmental partners similar to those carrying out monitoring in El Salvador, the American IMWG established local monitoring of Gap Inc's supplier operations in Honduras in 1999,[56] and Guatemala in June 2000.[57] In April 2001, monitoring was expanded to other El Salvador factories supplying Gap Inc., and the American IMWG began exploring "independent sources of funding to support the work of the monitors in the three countries."[58] The American IMWG resolved to disband at the end of 2001, having agreed that it had succeeded . . .

> ... in exploring the viability of independent monitoring in Central America, as evidenced by the establishment of pilot projects in each of the countries where the IMWG had made an effort to do so. Indeed, the IMWG succeeded in establishing the first independent monitoring project anywhere, which has resulted in a demonstration that a diverse range of civil society organizations can work in a transparent, collaborative manner to promote the observance of fair working conditions that promote a productive and harmonious workplace.[59]

A key potential problem with the use of local third-party monitors revolves around the question of who bears the cost of monitoring. Effective compliance monitoring is an onerous task, requiring both expertise and time to carry out in a proper manner. On the one hand, no funding from Gap Inc. to third-party monitors may be viewed as necessary to ensure the continued credibility of such surveillance activities. On the other, if Gap Inc. does not pay, who does? In El Salvador, the local monitors were originally funded through a charitable foundation, but this proved to be unfeasible over time. Now, the monitors operate under an arrangement whereby Gap Inc. provides the necessary funding to an intermediary, which in turn pays the monitors; this, according to the report, "remove[s] the possibility of direct influence on the monitors by the company."[60]

---

54. Ibid., p. 8.

55. Kaufman and Gonzalez (footnote 10).

56. Independent Monitoring Working Group (footnote 53), p. 13.

57. Ibid., p. 10.

58. Ibid., p. 16.

59. Ibid.

60. Ibid., p. 14.

The independent monitoring activity in El Salvador, Honduras and Guatemala could be taken as evidence that independent monitoring[61] is a workable option. However, these activities can fairly be described as a pilot project operating in a handful of factories in three countries. Outside the pilot project, monitoring for compliance to the *Code of Vendor Conduct* is performed by vendor compliance officers working for Gap Inc. Is it feasible to extend the full independent monitoring and associated management of labour disputes found in El Salvador, Honduras and Guatemala to all of Gap Inc.'s 4,000 suppliers around the world? The costs of doing so have been estimated by some commentators to be around 4.5 percent of Gap Inc.'s annual profit[62] — a significant burden if competitors do not engage in similar activities. As discussed below, industry-wide code programs have now moved to the forefront, in apparent recognition of some of the cost and other limitations of single-firm apparel code initiatives.

Conclusions

In 1995, a worker in Mandarin's factory in San Salvador making apparel for Gap Inc. earned $0.55 an hour, was compelled to spend 18-hour days in an unventilated factory, with no drinkable water, and could be denied bathroom breaks if bosses were displeased.[63] As of 2001, at the same factory, while the wages have only gone up $0.05 an hour, workers now have coffee breaks and lunch on an outside terrace cafeteria, bathrooms are unlocked, the factory is ventilated and clean, and employees can complain to a board of independent monitors. "It's not paradise," reports Carolina Quinteros, co-director of the Independent Monitoring Working Group of El Salvador, "But at least it works better than others down here. They don't have labor or human rights violations."[64]

The Gap Inc.'s *Code of Vendor Conduct* represents a marked improvement over the first-generation *Sourcing Principles and Guidelines* in its detail and assertive language, although it lacks mandatory review and publicity requirements and whistleblower protection. As for the wage protections, as is apparent from the $0.05 an hour wage increase from 1995 to 2001, improvements may be slow and modest. Clearly, the use of third-party monitoring can be considered a breakthrough that, in the event it were effectively carried out and expanded to all Gap Inc. contractors, would increase the likelihood that Gap Inc. officials and Gap Inc.'s contractors would treat the *Code of Vendor Conduct* and its implementation seriously. In turn, this may increase worker confidence in the initiative.

The experience of Gap Inc. in the evolution and development of its code may demonstrate a somewhat perverse phenomenon affecting companies that adopt socially oriented codes, which might be referred to as the "roach motel" syndrome. Roach motels

---

61. The IMWG has defined *independent monitoring* as "…an effective process of direct observation and information-gathering by credible and respected institutions and individuals to ensure compliance with corporate codes of conduct and applicable laws to prevent violations, process grievances, and promote humane, harmonious, and productive workplace conditions." Cited in Forcese (footnote 9), p. 29, and repeated in IMWG, ibid., p. 3.

62. Kaufman and Gonzalez (footnote 10).

63. The following before-and-after description is taken directly from Kaufman and Gonzalez, ibid.

64. Ibid.

are devices used to rid dwellings of unwanted insects. They consist of small boxes with several holes and an attractive scent. The scent lures insects in, and they are subsequently killed by an insecticide. Hence, insects can check in to a roach motel, but they can never leave. It is possible that a similar effect is at work with socially oriented codes. Thus, the initial commitment to abide by a code is likely to be comparatively easy, and compliance with the code may attract minimal attention and have little positive effect on sales. But any evidence of foot-dragging or reneging on commitments can have a negative media and consumer impact and may compel the firm to adopt a more aggressive code and carry out associated implementation activity. Opting out or relaxing the code in many cases is not a real option (i.e. checking out of this "motel" is particularly difficult).[65]

The *Code of Vendor Conduct* can be seen as one of an increasing number of market-based initiatives being developed to address problems of worker abuse in developing countries. Through its purchasing power, Gap Inc. is able to contractually impose conditions concerning workplace treatment on supplier factories located all over the world. While the standards are not perfect, the second-generation *Code of Vendor Conduct* can be viewed as a serious attempt to address many of the major issues associated with maintaining a humane workplace, and a marked improvement over the original guidelines. Efforts by Gap Inc. to integrate NGOs into compliance monitoring represent a potentially significant move away from a purely internal program that lacked credibility and toward an accountable self-regulatory regime. That said, the *ad hoc* nature of the NGO involvement, and the need for NGOs to obtain independent funding assistance to engage in their activities, are issues needing a more long-term solution.

At a fundamental level, it is important to stress that market-driven programs such as Gap Inc.'s *Code of Vendor Conduct* will never represent a complete solution to the problem of abusive treatment of employees in less developed countries. For one thing, Gap Inc.'s code only applies to Gap Inc. contractors: workers who are employed in the making of non-export commodities, or firms who are not participating in the program, will not be directly affected by such initiatives. Moreover, there is no guarantee that, over time, consumers will, through their purchasing decisions, continue to support firms that attempt to safeguard the interests of workers in this way.

Clearly, the most appropriate solution is the full implementation of international conventions on workers' rights, and domestic enforcement of human rights and worker safety legislation, buttressed through trade laws encouraging compliance with such laws. Unlike these public law solutions, market-driven programs represent an attempt to harness an additional lever — that of consumer marketplace demand — to address the same problem. While driven by market demand, Gap Inc.'s code is specifically designed to operate within the conventional legal system, albeit using *private*, not public law

---

65. Gap Inc. has continued to face occasional unfavourable publicity, despite the establishment of its third-party monitoring program and its worldwide system of internal monitors. In 1999, Gap Inc. and numerous other U.S. apparel manufacturers were the object of several lawsuits brought by NGOs over the labour practices of the companies' suppliers on the Western Pacific island of Saipan. Many of the companies agreed to a settlement that is said to include the establishment of third-party monitoring of Saipan factories by a group called Verité. See Global Exchange, *Top U.S. Clothing Retailers Agree to Settle Saipan Garment Worker Lawsuits*, available at <www.globalexchange.org/campaigns/sweatshops/saipan/pr032800.html>.

mechanisms (i.e. contractual instruments enforceable through the ordinary civil courts).[66] These market-driven initiatives are intended to reinforce the legislative regimes in place (as seen in the code requirements that contractors adhere to all local environmental, workplace and labour laws), not replace such regimes. Gap Inc.'s senior vice-president for global affairs confirms this point:

> We are not the all-powerful Oz that rules over what happens in every factory. Do we have leverage? Yes. Is it as great as our critics believe? Not by a long shot. ... We can't be the whole solution. The solution has to be labor laws that are adequate, respected and enforced.[67]

While Gap Inc's precedent-setting agreement to work with civil society organizations from both North and South in monitoring could hardly be described as an unmitigated success, a good argument can be made that it has shown the way for other initiatives, including COVERCO (a Guatemalan-based independent monitoring group),[68] commercial apparel monitoring agencies such as Verité[69] and the Apparel Industry Partnership/American Fair Labor Association (AIP/FLA).[70] The development and implementation of the AIP/FLA initiative — with its use of an industry-wide voluntary standard, an institutionalized multistakeholder monitoring and enforcement group, and a high-profile label — seem to build on and be entirely compatible with Gap Inc.'s program. Although Gap Inc. is not a member of the AIP/FLA, it is reasonable to suggest that the media scrutiny of Gap Inc.'s initiative, and Gap Inc.'s willingness to bring NGOs into compliance verification, has provided impetus for the development of the AIP/FLA. Retailer acceptance of the need for a rigorous approach, and labour, human-rights and consumer group support for such programs, is likely to be enhanced when the leaders in each of these fields are meaningfully involved in their articulation and implementation. The likelihood of consumer acceptance may also be improved when a single, highly publicized label, standard and approach is adopted. The role of the U.S. government in assembling the AIP/FLA, provides an example of how governments can participate in and encourage the development of market-driven voluntary code initiatives.

Against a backdrop of Gap Inc.'s code and independent monitoring, the AIP/FLA initiative and other experiences, public policy commentators are now beginning to suggest innovative ways of combining the power of the marketplace with enhanced legal regimes, to create effective new hybrids.[71] In so doing, they are arguably

---

66. The use of contractual mechanisms to enforce voluntary codes is discussed in Kernaghan Webb and Andrew Morrison, "The Law and Voluntary Codes: Examining the 'Tangled Web'," Chapter 5, above.

67. Kaufman and Gonzalez (footnote 10).

68. For discussion of COVERCO, see H. Fuentes and D. Smith, "Independent Monitoring in Guatemala: What Can Civil Society Contribute?" in R. Thamotheram, ed., *Visions of Ethical Sourcing* (London: Financial Times Prentice Hall, 2001), pp. 36–42.

69. For discussion of Verité's work in China, see H. White, "Monitoring in China," in Thamotheram, ed., ibid., pp. 43–49.

70. See comments to this effect by Sam Brown of the Fair Labor Association in Kaufman and Gonzalez (footnote 10). The AIP/FLA is discussed in Webb and Clarke, "Other Jurisdictions," Chapter 13, below.

71. A. Fung, D. O'Rourke, and S. Sabel, "Realizing Labor Standards: How Transparency, Competition, and Sanctions Could Improve Working Conditions Worldwide," *Boston Review* 26 (2000), available at <http://bostonreview.mit.edu/BR26.1/fung.html>.

acknowledging the value of voluntary measures such as that of Gap Inc.'s, while attempting to build on them to devise more robust, sustainable solutions that work in an increasingly globalized marketplace.

Perhaps this is an appropriate note on which to end this chapter. Gap Inc.'s *Code of Vendor Conduct* and its use of NGOs in monitoring should not be considered as substitutes for effective implementation of law, nor as permanent solutions. To factory owners, workers, governments and NGOs in El Salvador and other developing countries Gap Inc.'s initiative acts as a positive model that perhaps can be emulated with appropriate adjustments by others. To Western retailers, the code and monitoring initiative paved the way for more sophisticated industry-wide labelling initiatives. For public policy makers and commentators, Gap Inc.'s efforts are, it is hoped, a point of departure for imaginative, sustainable solutions that can draw together the legal and market instruments available in effective, sustainable hybrids.

Chapter 8
Privacy Self-Regulation in a Global Economy:
A Race to the Top, the Bottom or Somewhere Else?

Colin J. Bennett

Introduction

In a borderless world, public policies to protect personal privacy are inextricably interdependent. This interdependence could hypothetically produce two possible broad dynamics. In one, countries would progressively fashion their privacy protection policies according to the highest possible standard, a "trading up" or a "race-to-the-top." Conversely, countries might consider that a less regulatory climate would attract global businesses that would want to circumvent the higher standards at work elsewhere. This competitive deregulation would lead to a race to the bottom, as countries progressively weaken their standards to attract global investment in the information technology and services industries.

The race-to-the-bottom argument is based on the underlying premise that there might be competitive advantages for any State to have regulatory policies that are, in some way, distinctive. It is based on a classic "prisoner's dilemma"[1] and the constant temptation to fashion regulatory policies that might improve one's own condition. Assuming that firms will seek the locations with lowest costs, States will need, despite their own preferences, to reduce or weaken their regulations to gain competitive advantage. The prisoner's dilemma metaphor is invoked because the individually rational behaviour is collectively irrational, and constitutes a particular kind of market failure. Under the assumed "pay-off," States would value the higher investment and employment over and above the public good that their regulations purport to achieve, whether that be cleaner air, higher workplace standards or, indeed, greater protection for the personal privacy of their citizens.[2]

The race-to-the-bottom phenomenon may be particularly acute when the factors of production are highly mobile, as is the case with many industries within the new information economy. Hypothetically, vast quantities of information can be transmitted instantaneously for processing in jurisdictions that have lower regulatory (including privacy) standards. The phenomenon may also be observed when there is a genuine diversity of policy choices. There can only be a race-to-the-bottom when there are clear

---

1. Credit for devising this classic game theory problem, which highlights the difficulty of deciding between one's individual benefit and the common good, is usually attributed to scientists working at the RAND Corporation in the 1950s. See W. Poundstone, *Prisoner's Dilemma* (New York: Anchor Books, 1993), pp. 8–9.

2. P. Swire, "The Race to Laxity and the Race to Undesirability: Explaining Failures in Competition Among Jurisdictions in Environmental Law," *Yale Journal on Regulation* 14 (1996), pp. 67–110, p. 89.

Kernaghan Webb, Editor, *Voluntary Codes: Private Governance, the Public Interest and Innovation.*
This chapter ©2004 Colin J. Bennett, pages 227–248.
Published by the Carleton Research Unit for Innovation, Science and Environment, Carleton University, Ottawa, Canada.

and multiple levels of regulatory action. Obviously, if there are only two possible ways to solve a particular policy problem, then the "race" will stop as soon as the second, lower, level is reached.

There is, however, little support either theoretically or empirically for the crude version of the race-to-the-bottom hypothesis. There is a large literature in economics that has debated at length whether the prisoner's dilemma can be at work in these situations. First, there are questions about whether States would use regulation as an instrument to compete for capital. Second, there are questions about the applicability of the model when one moves from a two-player game to the more realistic multiplayer game. Third, there are questionable assumptions about the ability of State actors to measure the consequences of their actions. There are cogent reasons to believe that an "efficiency" model based on cost-benefit calculus cannot, and should not, form the basis of regulatory decision making.

This thesis is also questioned by empirical work conducted on the actual process by which standards are set within a competitive state environment. David Vogel has described the "California effect," which denotes the ratcheting upward of regulatory standards in competing political jurisdictions.[3] He has concluded that this pattern applies to such diverse regulatory activities as animal hormones, genetically engineered crops, meat inspection, pharmaceutical regulation and inspection, fuel economy standards, leg-hold trap bans, eco-labelling, chemical testing standards and ozone depletion: "There does not appear to be a single instance in which either the United States or the European Union (EU) lowered any health, safety or environmental standard to make its domestic producers more competitive."[4]

Much of this debate does rely on analysis of environmental policy, and is probably more relevant to product standards than process standards. The incentive to harmonize production to that higher standard is stronger when the economies of scale dictate that it is more efficient for a firm to meet the higher standard than to tolerate different products in different jurisdictions. Process standards, however, of which privacy protection is a clear example, are perhaps more difficult to enforce outside a State's borders. Both race-to-the-top and race-to-the-bottom theses are based on an underlying premise that States might benefit from having divergent regulations. There is considerable evidence, however, that a more cooperative mode of regulation is in the interests of States. First, compatible regulations facilitate trade and access to different markets. Second, harmonized regulations reduce the cost of production. When a firm is forced to produce multiple versions of the same product, the unit costs are significantly increased.

This model says nothing, of course, about the level at which a coordinated compromise might be struck. Harmonization of standards could conceivably be struck at any point along a hypothetical scale of regulation, from extreme laxity on the one end, to extreme strictness on the other. It should also be noted that coordinative activity need not necessarily lead to the raising of standards. Many instruments of policy coordination may

---

3. D. Vogel, *Trading Up: Consumer and Environmental Regulation in a Global Economy* (Cambridge, Mass.: Harvard University Press, 1995).

4. D. Vogel, *Barriers or Benefits? Regulation in Transatlantic Trade* (Washington: Brookings Institution, 1997), p. 57.

have a symbolic purpose and/or effect. It is commonly assumed that any policy instrument that lacks compulsion must inevitably and ultimately constitute a weakening of privacy standards and contribute to a race to the bottom. Law, on the other hand, based on a model of command and control must reflect a race to the top. Law tries to set a clear line for acceptable behavior. Organizations whose practices fall below that line are susceptible to a variety of penalties, depending on the context and seriousness of the offence. Laws are necessary to frame a system of rights and responsibilities, to provide a degree of certainty for all participants in information processes, and to redress the imbalance between data controllers and data subjects. "Self-regulation," on the other hand, has none of those characteristics. It is inherently "voluntary." If an organization does not want to comply, there is no legal penalty for not doing so. The term *voluntary* is often used in a number of different senses, but it does capture the simple point that self-regulation typically lacks any statutory force or focus.[5]

However, there is no clear distinction between regulation and self-regulation, because instruments of self-regulation do not suggest a freedom from compulsion of any kind. The possible incentives for compliance fall along a continuum, when a complicated and fluctuating range of incentives and sanctions is continuously in play. The more important and interesting task, therefore, is to attempt to understand the conditions under which self-regulation is more likely to change organizational behavior. Effectiveness will depend on a range of non-legal incentives. Evaluating self-regulatory efforts, therefore, involves looking at data protection in wider dimensions — as a social, organizational, political and technological practice, and as an increasingly international and global problem.

Self-regulatory instruments for privacy protection operate almost exclusively in the private sector. However, they now come in a great variety of forms with no correlation between name and function. There has always been a symbolic purpose associated with much of this activity, with the result that organizations are apt to claim more from their self-regulation than is perhaps warranted. So the first aim of this chapter is to develop some greater conceptual clarity, by developing a typology of four interrelated policy instruments: privacy commitments, privacy codes, privacy standards and privacy seals. These instruments are not mutually exclusive, but they do have some distinctive features. I then consider how these instruments have come together within the Safe Harbour Agreement between the United States and the European Commission. The conclusion attempts to outline the conditions under which these various instruments are more likely to be successfully adopted, and analyzes whether this activity represents a trading up of standards or the opposite.[6]

---

5. This is not to deny that voluntary approaches operate within a framework of law, and may have legal implications, as discussed in Kernaghan Webb and Andrew Morrison, "The Law and Voluntary Codes: Examining the 'Tangled Web'," Chapter 5, above.

6. The argument in this chapter also appears in a book entitled *The Governance of Privacy* (London: Ashgate Press, 2003) written with Charles Raab of the University of Edinburgh. Our purpose is to explore the various policy instruments for privacy protection in the context of globalization.

Instruments of Self-Regulation

Privacy Commitments

The very first examples of self-regulatory action from business tended to take the form of brief statements of commitment to a set of privacy principles. The most typical examples emerged in North America in the 1980s as private sector companies and associations were encouraged to "adopt" the 1981 Organisation for Economic Cooperation and Development (OECD) *Guidelines on the Protection of Privacy and Transborder Flows of Personal Data*.[7] But examples are also found in the privacy statements on contemporary Web sites. Often called "codes," "guidelines" or something else that would indicate a self-regulatory function, privacy commitments more often play no other role than to indicate to clients, consumers and regulators that the organization had considered privacy protection at some level, and believed that it would be good public relations to state a set of commitments.

Privacy commitments tend to be relatively brief pledges, often more public relations than substantive. They are often designed more for external consumption than to affect internal organizational functioning. They also have probably not been produced as a result of careful and thorough analysis of an organization's personal information holdings. These commitments tend to be statements of what top management believes is happening (and ought to happen) rather than comprehensive instruments of self-regulation that bind employees and reflect a deep organizational culture that respects privacy. Privacy commitments may inform data subjects about certain rights, to access and correction, to opt-out of disclosures and so on. But they may also tend to finesse crucial questions about how those rights might be exercised. Quite often, privacy commitments are produced as a reaction to bad publicity. There are several recent examples in which public scrutiny of a company's or industry's practices led to a rushed attempt to save face. Jeff Smith demonstrates how "drifting and reacting" is a quite typical response of major American companies to the privacy issue.[8] Unless the organization finds itself the subject of front-page articles or frenzied discussion on privacy newsgroups on the Internet, there is often little incentive to make privacy a priority. It tends to be one of those issues that can always be placed below something else in a corporation's priorities. But privacy commitments need not be symbolic. Frequently, it is quite useful for a company to state its policies in a brief, open and user-friendly manner, provided that is not the only instrument of self-regulation. Privacy commitments can supplement more detailed and thorough codes of practice that are based on a realistic and comprehensive analysis of how an organization collects, uses, stores and processes personal information.

---

7. See Organisation for Economic Cooperation and Development *Guidelines on the Protection of Privacy and Transborder Flows of Personal Data* (Paris: OECD, 1981), available at <www1.oecd.org/publications/e-book/9302011E.pdf>.

8. H. J. Smith, *Managing Privacy: Information Technology and Corporate America* (Chapel Hill, N.C.: University of North Carolina Press, 1994).

Privacy Codes of Practice

Privacy codes may perform crucial functions within the framework of statutory data protection regimes, such as those of the Netherlands, New Zealand, Ireland and the U.K. Article 27 of the European Union's *Data Protection Directive* requires the European Commission and Member States to "encourage the drawing up of codes of conduct intended to contribute to the proper implementation of ... national provisions ... taking account of the specific features of various sectors."[9] Codes of practice may also operate in the absence of a regulatory framework, not only to state commitments but also to specify in more detailed terms how employees should and should not treat personal information in their custody. Terminology is again confusing, but we can make a distinction between five kinds of privacy code, according to the scope of application: the organizational code, the sectoral code, the functional code, the technological code and the professional code.[10]

The simplest instrument is the *organizational code* that applies to one corporation or agency bounded by a clear organizational structure. Typically, these codes have been developed by large, high-profile organizations whose practices have come under scrutiny from the media or privacy advocates, or who may have received a volume of consumer complaints. Some companies, meanwhile, such as Equifax, a major credit reporting service, have developed policies as a result of consumer surveys. Some policies have been pursued to an indeterminate extent to gain a competitive advantage within the respective industries.[11]

A second category — perhaps more important than the first — is that of the *sectoral code* developed by trade associations for adoption by their memberships. Perhaps the country in which these instruments were developed most extensively, in the absence of law, is Canada. The model codes of the Canadian Bankers Association, the Canadian Life and Health Insurance Association, the Insurance Bureau of Canada, Stentor and the Canadian Cable Television Standards Council fall within this category.[12] In each of these sectors, a "model code" has been adapted from the OECD *Guidelines*, or the Canadian Standards Association's *Model Code for the Protection of Personal Information* (see below) and promulgated within the member companies, some of whom then distribute their own publicity and privacy commitments. These examples are national in scope. Sectoral codes have begun to emerge within industries that operate on a global scale, such as those of the International Air Traffic Association and the Federation of European Direct Marketing Association.[13]

---

9. *Directive 95/46/EC of the European Parliament and of the Council of 24 October 1995 on the Protection of Individuals with Regard to the Processing of Personal Data and on the Free Movement of Such Data*, Official Journal L 281, 23/11/1995, pp. 0031–0050.

10. C. J. Bennett, *Implementing Privacy Codes of Practice: A Report to the Canadian Standards Association* (Toronto: Canadian Standards Association, 1995).

11. See <www.privacyexchange.org> for examples of company codes of practice, as well as for evidence of the variety of instruments that fall within this broad classification.

12. See the Insurance Bureau of Canada's *Model Personal Information Code*, and Canadian Bankers Association's *Privacy Model Code*.

13. Neither organization's code was found on its respective Web site.

The major defining feature of the sectoral code is that there is a broad consonance of economic interest and function, and by extension a similarity in the kinds of personal information collected and processed. Sectoral codes permit, therefore, a more refined set of rules tailored to the issues within each industry. Sectors also tend to operate within an already defined set of regulatory institutions and rules, which in turn have established a relatively cohesive policy community that is engaged on an ongoing basis in the negotiation of new rules for the industry and the implementation of existing rules. Trade associations vary in the extent to which they might represent a sector. Some may be relatively inclusive. In other sectors, there are clearly players (perhaps free riders) that operate outside an association's oversight by choice.

Trade or industry associations also differ in their structure and thus in the balance they strike between lobbying and policy development activities. A continual tension exists for trade association officials between representing interests and encouraging new policies and better practices. At one extreme, the leadership can simply reflect the views of members and offer no leadership role. At the other, it can act more authoritatively, trying to communicate to members what is in their best interests and encouraging them to pursue practices they would not otherwise follow. The leadership in successful associations needs to strike the right balance along this continuum. This assessment clearly influences the processes through which privacy codes of practice have been negotiated and developed.

The idea of the sectoral code was taken one step further in Japan when that country's Ministry of Trade and Industry (MITI) published guidelines on the content and substance of industry codes of practice, and on procedures for development and implementation. As a result, various sectors have prepared codes, tailored to the circumstances of individual industries. In 1998, MITI extended its guidelines to electronic commerce.[14] This form of oversight is possible in Japan because of very close ties between industry associations and MITI, and relatively established understandings about the boundaries between industry sectors.

The final three types of code clearly span these more traditional sectoral boundaries. What are called *functional codes* are defined less by economic sector and more by the practice in which the organization is engaged. The most obvious example is direct mail and telemarketing. The direct marketing associations in the United States, Canada and many other countries represent businesses in a wide range and growing number of sectors. Both have responded to longstanding concerns about direct marketing by developing privacy codes of practice that have tried to regulate members and keep up to date with evolving technologies, including the Internet. The Canadian Marketing Association states that its code is compulsory because members are expected to sign a commitment to its provisions and may be expelled from the association if found in violation of its provisions.[15]

A fourth set of codes can be defined not by function, but by *technology*. As new potentially intrusive technologies have entered society, so codes have developed to deal with the specific privacy problems associated with their application and distribution. *Technological codes* typically apply to very new applications. They may be developed

---

14. See <www.ecom.or.jp/ecom_e>.

15. See <www.the-cma.org>.

within societies that already have statutory data protection, as is the case with the code of practice on closed-circuit television cameras in Britain.[16] They may also play an important role in societies that do not. In 1992, for instance, the Canadian banks developed a code for the governance of electronic funds transfers.[17] This code attempts to regulate the issuance of debit cards and personal identification numbers, the content of agreements between the issuer of the card and the cardholder, the nature of transaction records and statements, and security issues. Smart card technology is also amenable to specific regulation through privacy codes of practice. In some countries, specific trade associations have emerged to promote research into, and applications of, smart card technology. Such associations can also play a self-regulatory role, in the same way as more established trade associations.[18]

A final category of privacy codes includes those that have been developed by professional societies. Typically, these codes apply to those directly engaged in information processing activities. *Professional codes* have been developed for information processing professionals, for survey researchers, for market researchers, and for a range of health and welfare-related professionals.[19] They are created by professional rather than trade associations, and can be reinforced by some significant disciplinary measures entailing a loss of professional reputation. They may also be incorporated into larger sets of ethical guidelines and codes of conduct.

In conclusion, privacy codes of practice differ from privacy commitments in the simple fact that they may embody a set of rules for employees, members or member organizations to follow. They state more than a simple claim; they also provide important guidance about correct procedure and behaviour, based on a version of the information privacy principles. But privacy codes of all kinds have been developed for various reasons, have no consistent format, and have been formulated with varying amounts of care and analysis. Procedures for implementation, complaint resolution and communication vary substantially.[20] Their success, therefore, is unpredictable and variable. Privacy codes of practice operate within a complicated and fluctuating set of political, organizational, cultural, technological and economic incentives that vary between and even within business sectors. Absent a regulatory framework, which can impose sanctions for non-compliance, they also suffer from the perception that the individual's privacy rights are in the hands of those who have the most to gain from the processing of personal data.

---

16. The code of practice for closed-circuit television is downloadable from <www.informationcommissioner.gov.uk/ cms/DocumentUploads/cctvcop1.pdf>.

17. See Electronic Funds Transfer Working Group, *Canadian Code of Practice for Consumer Debit Card Services*, available at <http://strategis.ic.gc.ca/ epic/internet/inoca-bc.nsf/en/ca01581e.html>.

18. The Association of Card Technologies in Canada is an example.

19. An example is the Canadian Medical Association's *Health Information Privacy Code*.

20. See Bennett (footnote 10).

Privacy Standards

The phenomenon of a privacy standard extends the self-regulatory code of practice in some important ways. Standards imply not only a common yardstick, but also a process through which organizational claims about adherence to a set of norms can be more objectively tested. Standardization means a common code, but also a conformity assessment procedure that might more effectively determine whether an organization says what it does, and does what it says.

Technical standards have played an important role in computer security for some time. One example is the certification system established under the British Standards Institution's BS7799.[21] This standard comprises a code of practice for computer security, as well as a standard specification for security management systems, including a risk analysis of the categories of information stored by the organization. There is also a certification scheme, called "c:cure," that can operate in conjunction with the ISO 9000 range of generic quality management standards.[22]

The idea of a more general privacy standard that could incorporate the entire range of privacy protection principles is a more recent innovation. The first comprehensive privacy standard was negotiated in Canada. In 1992, representatives of the major trade associations joined with key government officials and consumer representatives ostensibly to harmonize the codes of practice that had already been developed and also in recognition that the process of code development under the OECD *Guidelines* had not been successful. Later that year, it was decided to formalize the process by using the more institutionalized process of standard development under the Canadian Standards Association (CSA), which then acted as facilitator and secretariat. The major participants contributed financial support to the process. The negotiation proceeded through the CSA Technical Committee, which finally comprised about 40 representatives from government, industry and consumer groups. The *Model Code for the Protection of Personal Information* was finally passed by the Technical Committee without dissent on September 20, 1995, and was subsequently approved as a National Standard of Canada by the Standards Council of Canada, and was published in March 1996.[23]

The CSA Model Code standard is organized around 10 principles, each of which is accompanied by an interpretive commentary. Organizations have been advised that all principles must be adopted in their entirety; in other words, organizations may not cherry-pick. They are also expected to reproduce the CSA principles in their codes, although they may adapt the commentary to their own personal information practices. The standard may be adopted by any organization (public or private) that processes personal data. An accompanying workbook, giving more practical advice about the development and implementation of a privacy policy, has also been released.

Although the standard uses prescriptive language ("shall" and "must"), it is clearly a *voluntary* instrument. Various participants have, however, different

---

21. British Standards Institution, *Information Security Management System*, BS7799 (London: British Standards Institution, 1995).

22. See <www.c-cure.org/bs7799.htm>.

23. CSA, *Model Code for the Protection of Personal Information*, CAN/CSA-Q830-96 (Toronto: CSA, 1996).

interpretations of what this means. For most private sector participants, it serves as no more than a *template*. The major trade associations began to tailor their codes of practice to the CSA model with the intention that any further oversight would take place mainly within the industry concerned. For many others, it was envisaged that the code should operate as a *standard*. Within CSA, the Quality Management Institute (QMI) registers companies to the series of quality assurance standards, principally those within the increasingly popular ISO 9000 series. There are some interesting parallels between the goals of total quality management and the implementation of fair information principles.

In September 1996, QMI announced a three-tier recognition program. Even though few businesses have so far demonstrated an interest in this program, there might in fact be several incentives to adopt a privacy standard. Moral suasion, the desire to avoid adverse publicity and the possible use of privacy protection for competitive advantage are the kinds of incentives that operate at the moment. But more coercive inducements might also operate. A standard can be referenced in contract either between private enterprises or between government and a private contractor. For instance, if a private contractor processed personal data under government contract, a simple way for the government agency to ensure adherence to the same data protection standards as apply in government would be to require the contractor to register to the standard. The same would apply to international contracts and the transborder flow of data. It is possible that European data protection agencies could also enforce Article 25 of the new European Union *Data Protection Directive*,[24] by requiring any recipient of European data in Canada to be registered to the CSA Model Code.[25]

In Canada, the CSA standard was also used to broker a *de facto* agreement between the federal government and the provinces on some basic legislative principles, something that would have been exceedingly difficult within a formal federal-provincial lawmaking exercise. There are some similar patterns in other countries. General standards, similar to those of the CSA, have more recently been negotiated in Australia and Japan. In 1999 the Japanese Standards Association released JIS Q 15001, which adapts the environmental management standard ISO 14001 to personal data protection.[26] In Australia, the Privacy Commissioner issued National Privacy Principles, similar to those of the CSA, in February 1998. Although there was no explicit certification scheme

---

24. Article 25 forbids entities in the European Union from transferring personal data to non-European Union countries whose data protection measures are not deemed to be "adequate." See Article 25, EU *Data Protection Directive* (footnote 9).

25. However, adoption of the code would still be incremental and piecemeal, even though governments, international data protection authorities and market forces can exert pressures. For this reason, the Canadian government decided that legislation should be introduced to make the principles within the CSA standard mandatory. The *Personal Information Protection and Electronic Documents Act* (S.C. 2000, c. 5,) came into effect in 2001 for many private sector companies operating in Canada, with a phased introduction thereafter. As a result of this legislation, there has never been a pure test of whether the standard could be adopted in the absence of legislation. Companies in most sectors decided that they would wait to see what the law said before committing resources to implementation.

26. See J. Dumortier and C. Goemans, *Data Privacy and Standardization*, discussion paper prepared for the CEN/ISSS Open Seminar on Data Protection, Brussels, March 23–24, 2000.

offered, the overall aim was to get Australian business to formally adopt the National Principles. As in Canada, this initiative has been overtaken by the general desire for a legislative approach.[27]

A further attempted extension of the standard occurred at the international level. In September 1996, as a result of initial pressure from the Consumer Policy Committee of the International Organization for Standardization (ISO), the ISO Council recommended that work begin on developing an international standard for the protection of privacy. The 12-member Technical Management Board of ISO met in January 1997 and decided to refer the issue to an Ad Hoc Advisory Group, which was to pave the way for a positive Technical Management Board resolution in 1998.[28] The expected resolution, however, did not materialize, mainly because of some very intensive lobbying by certain U.S. multinational interests. The Ad Hoc Advisory Group was maintained for another year in order to study the issue further, but was disbanded in June 1999.

Since then, the initiative has moved to Europe. The *Comité européen de normalisation* (CEN), responsible for the negotiation of standards within Europe, has begun to study the feasibility of an international privacy standard, supported by the Article 29 Data Protection Working Party, the group of national privacy officials responsible for overseeing the implementation of the European Union *Data Protection Directive*. At a seminar in Brussels in March 2000, it was proposed to begin standardization activities along three paths: a general data protection standard that would set out practical operational steps to be taken by an organization to comply with relevant data protection legislation, principally the European Union directive, a series of sector-specific initiatives in key areas such as health information and human resources management; and task-specific initiatives mainly related to the on-line environment.[29]

Proponents contend that an international standard would have a number of advantages over national models. It would carry far greater weight and credibility in both Europe and the United States. It would attract attention and international certification efforts from various national standards bodies. It would give North American businesses a more reliable and consistent method by which to demonstrate their conformity to international data protection standards. It would also provide a more reliable mechanism for the implementation of Article 25 of the *Directive*. The scrutiny of laws and contracts provides no assurances to European data protection agencies that data protection rules are complied with in the receiving jurisdiction. Required registration to a standard, which would oblige independent and regular auditing, would provide greater certainty that "adequate" data protection is being practised by the receiving organization, wherever it is located. This does, of course, require concomitant efforts to harmonize systems of

27. See the Australian Privacy Commissioner's Web site, <www.privacy.gov.au/business/index.html>.

28. The arguments for such a standard were provided in C. J. Bennett, *Prospects for an International Standard for the Protection of Personal Information: A Report to the Standards Council of Canada* (1997), available at <http://web.uvic.ca/~polisci/bennett/research/iso.htm>.

29. Dumortier and Goemans (footnote 26).

conformity assessment and auditor certification. At the end of the day, bilateral and multilateral mutual recognition agreements need also to be negotiated to ensure that domestic conformity assessment programs are commonly respected.[30]

Privacy Seals

One logical corollary of any standard is a commonly understood mark, symbol or cachet that can be awarded to any organization that is successfully certified or registered. The Canadian Standards Association's mark is generally regarded as a symbol of quality within the Canadian marketplace, and its use is jealously guarded and restricted to those companies that have followed an appropriate registration or certification process. The claim that an organization might make about its compliance is also carefully monitored.

The development of a specific mark or seal for privacy protection has, however, proliferated on the Internet. Several schemes can be mentioned. The most notable have been developed by the TRUSTe organization, by the Better Business Bureau's BBBOnLine, and by the Japanese Information Processing Development Centre.[31] TRUSTe was founded in 1996 as a non-profit organization dedicated to building global confidence in the on-line environment, and developed a program built upon the *Fair Information Practices and the Privacy Guidelines* established by the Online Privacy Alliance, a consortium of corporations and associations devoted to promoting privacy-friendly practices on-line.[32] This approach allows Web publishers to develop privacy statements that reflect the specific information-gathering and usage practices of their site(s). As a result, TRUSTe's trustmark rapidly became the most widely deployed privacy protection brand on Web sites, although most licensees are U.S.-based companies.

The program was built on the premise that consumers should be able to have consistent disclosure of privacy practices from all sites with which they interact. To build this consistency, TRUSTe's licensing program requires participating Web sites to post a privacy policy disclosing their on-line information-gathering and dissemination practices. A cornerstone of the program is the TRUSTe trustmark, an branded seal displayed by member Web sites that is awarded only to sites that adhere to established privacy principles and agree to comply with ongoing TRUSTe oversight and dispute resolution procedures. All TRUSTe licensees display the resulting trustmark either on their Web site with a link to their site's privacy policy or directly on the privacy statement.

---

30. See C. J. Bennett, *An International Standard for Privacy Protection: Objections to the Objections*, paper presented at CFP 2000, Toronto, April 2000, available at <www.cfp2000.org/papers/bennett.pdf>.

31. See, respectively, <www.truste.org>, <www.bbbonline.org> and <www.privacymark.jp>. TRUSTe and BBBOnline are also discussed in Kernaghan Webb and David Clarke, "Voluntary Codes in the United States, the European Union and Developing Countries," Chapter 13, below.

32. See the Online Privacy Alliance Web site, <www.privacyalliance.org>.

TRUSTe claims that:

When you see our TRUSTe seal, you can be assured that the Web site will disclose:

- What personal information is being gathered about you
- How the information will be used
- Who the information will be shared with, if anyone
- Choices available to you regarding how collected information is used
- Safeguards in place to protect your information from loss, misuse, or alteration
- How you can update or correct inaccuracies in your information.[33]

The full list of licensees is published on the Internet.[34]

TRUSTe monitors its licensees' sites and performs periodic reviews, including database "seeding" of unique identifiers to ensure licensees comply with their posted privacy policy. Currently, there is no provision in the TRUSTe program for an on-site examination of a site's privacy practices as a pre-condition for receiving a TRUSTe trustmark. In the case of a privacy violation, licensee sites are contractually liable to undergo a comprehensive examination of its privacy practices. For now, a TRUSTe-designated public accounting firm investigates the alleged violations committed by the organization holding the TRUSTe seal. However, this comprehensive examination is only performed "for cause" at TRUSTe's request, in response to formally stated concerns about a licensed site's compliance with TRUSTe's requirements. The accounting firm Ernst and Young has proposed an enhanced certification system through a third-party front-end audit, especially for those businesses that process sensitive personal data. The third-party assurance would focus on the site's data protection practices to ensure the organization "does what it says." This language is obviously reminiscent of the arguments for standardization presented above.[35]

In March 1999, the Council of Better Business Bureaus (CBBB) — an organization representing North America's 135 Better Business Bureaus — released a privacy seal program called BBBOnLine.[36] Within the BBBOnline program there are three types of seals available to participating companies: Reliability, Privacy and Kids' Privacy, each seal indicating the company's agreement to abide by a set of principles outlined by the CBBB. BBBOnLine claims that participants can take advantage of the longstanding expertise of the Better Business Bureau network in self-regulation and dispute resolution. As with the TRUSTe licensees, Web sites displaying the BBBOnLine Privacy seal have established a privacy policy to protect consumer information that meets

33. See <www.truste.org/consumers/users_how.html>.

34. Available at <www.truste.org/users/users_lookup.html>.

35. The credibility of TRUSTe certification was brought into question in 1999 as a result of a complaint against Microsoft, specifically the registration process for Windows '98. TRUSTe investigated the complaint but concluded that the breach of privacy protection was outside the initial licence agreement, and that it could not, then, initiate an audit. That credibility was also questioned when it was reported that the TRUSTe Web site itself collected cookies from unsuspecting visitors to the site.

36. See BBBOnLine Web site, <www.bbbonline.org>.

all the program's standards. As part of the privacy policy, businesses must include notification to consumers of how information is collected, used and shared, provide adequate data security, provide opt-outs for third-party information transfers, provide reasonable access to information, and use encryption for the receipt and transfer of sensitive information.

Web sites or online services displaying a BBBOnLine Privacy seal have also committed to using the BBBOnLine dispute resolution process, and are subject to an independent and random audit of their information practices. In this respect, the conformity assessment program is more extensive than that of TRUSTe. Web sites displaying the BBBOnLine Kids' Privacy seal must meet all the requirements of the BBBOnLine Privacy program *and* comply with requirements that address the special privacy concerns that can arise when very young children go on-line.

The final example of a seal program is the Privacy Protection Mark system devised in Japan in 1998.[37] This system was conceived to apply to any organization, not just those operating on the Internet. The Japan Information Processing Development Center serves as the granting organization, and is responsible for examining private enterprises' applications for the privacy mark, certifying them and operating the system. The Privacy Mark System Committee — consisting of experts, representatives of business groups, representatives of consumers, lawyers and so on — oversees the regime.

The system also allows for a designated organization, such as a trade association, to oversee the application of the Privacy Protection Mark within its own sphere of competence. The scope of a designated organization's responsibility is based on an application by the business group and deliberation by the Privacy Mark System Committee. A designated organization is responsible for establishing guidelines for the industry to which the business group belongs. Besides the above requirement, an enterprise must have a compliance program complying with MITI's *Guidelines for Protection of Personal Information Related to Computer Processing in the Private Sector* (or, alternatively, the industry guidelines established based on the Guidelines by the business group to which the enterprise belongs).[38] It must also demonstrate that personal information is appropriately managed (based on the compliance program), or that a feasible structure has been established. The certification is then in effect for two years. Front-end audits are not a precondition of certification, but they may be required during the application process or as a result of consumer complaints.

Privacy protection marks or seals certainly represent an extension of the code of practice and the standard. In countries such as the United States and Japan, which have yet to pass comprehensive privacy protection laws for the private sector, they should provide an empirical test of the hypothesis that privacy protection is in the interests of any business that processes personal information. Ideally, privacy seals should operate to distinguish the compliant from the non-compliant and present consumers with clear statements by which to make informed choices in the marketplace, particularly the on line marketplace. None of these systems, however, has yet achieved general recognition and credibility. Ironically, the more privacy seal programs there are, the more

---

37. Formerly at <www.jipdec.or.jp/security/privacy/pamph-e.html>.

38. *Guidelines for Protection of Personal Information Related to Computer Processing in the Private Sector*, MITI Notification No. 98, March 4, 1997.

consumers will be confused, and the more difficult it will be for any one system to achieve a reputation as the methodology by which privacy protection practices can be claimed and assured.

An Instrument of Co-Regulation: The Safe Harbour Agreement

Elements of each of the above instruments have come together on an international scale in the negotiation of the Safe Harbour Agreement between the European Commission and the United States Department of Commerce. As the United States has no comprehensive laws protecting personal information in the hands of the private sector, the Safe Harbour Agreement is designed to give U.S. companies that import data from Europe a more predictable and "adequate" framework of privacy protection to meet the requirements of Article 25 of the European Union's *Data Protection Directive.*

The Agreement includes seven privacy principles: notice, choice, onward transfer, security, data integrity, access and enforcement. The benefits of the "safe harbour" are assured from the date on which an organization self-certifies to the Department of Commerce (or a designated organization) its adherence to these principles. Self-certification consists of a letter (to be updated annually), signed by a responsible corporate officer, that contains all contact details, a description of the activities of the organization in the area of personal information received from the EU, and a description of the organization's privacy policy for such information, including its date of implementation, the contact person, the specific statutory body that has jurisdiction over the organization, the method of verification (whether in-house or third-party) and the independent recourse mechanism for investigating unresolved complaints. The Department maintains and publishes a list of all organizations filing such letters.[39]

The central enforcement mechanism is embodied in the requirement that any public misrepresentation concerning adherence to the safe harbour principles may be actionable by the Federal Trade Commission, which has statutory responsibility to monitor "unfair and deceptive trade practices."[40] Thus the act of self-declaration to the safe harbour principles, while voluntary, also binds the organization to a set of legal requirements. It should be noted, however, that the safe harbour only applies to data transmitted from Europe to the U.S.; data on American citizens is therefore not covered, an irony that has not been lost on U.S. privacy advocates.

Earlier drafts of the Safe Harbour Agreement were criticized by the TransAtlantic Consumer Dialogue, a coalition of EU and U.S. consumer groups and by the Article 29 Data Protection Working Group.[41] The latest draft of the Agreement, it

---

39. The list is available at <http://web.ita.doc.gov/safeharbor/shlist.nsf/webPages/safe+harbor+list>.

40. See s. 5(a) of the *FTC Act*, 15 U.S.C. § 45(a). There is a parallel requirement in Canada. Those companies that make representations about their personal information protections that then turn out to be false are vulnerable to prosecutions under the deceptive advertising provisions of the Canadian *Competition Act*, R.S.C., 1985, C-34, s. 52.

41. See <www.epic.org/privacy/intl/art29wp_report_1299.pdf>

should be noted, was also passed over the objections of the European Parliament. It is an innovation, the effectiveness of which is still very unclear. With respect to the involvement of the Federal Trade Commission, however, the Agreement does embody an element of compulsion for those businesses that will make the public commitment. It does not, however, stipulate the method of self-regulation, and certainly does not require an external certification process. The Safe Harbour Agreement is perhaps best described as a co-regulatory instrument.

The Conditions for Effective Self-Regulation

We can reach two broad conclusions as a result of the analysis of self-regulatory instruments sketched above. First, the *scope* of self-regulatory activity has expanded. Privacy commitments and the early privacy codes were largely based on the individual organization. Codes of practice then spread to sectors, to functions, to professions and to specific technologies. The process of standardization then pushed these instruments to the national level (in the case of the CSA, and the American and Japanese privacy marks), and even to the international levels in the case of the Safe Harbour Agreement. Perhaps the final step in this process is represented by the drafting of the *Global Code of Conduct* by the International Commerce Exchange, directed primarily to organizations engaged in international data flows.[42]

It would be tempting to conclude that there is a progressive logic behind this pattern of adoption, and that each form of self-regulation is a prerequisite for the next. The reality is obviously less tidy. A second conclusion, therefore, is that the development of privacy commitments, privacy codes, privacy standards and privacy seals is not a cumulative or linear one. A pre-condition for adoption of a standard is a commitment (say what you do) and a code (do what you say). The privacy seal is then awarded. Privacy seal programs often require a privacy commitment, but they tend not to mandate the development of a proper code of practice, nor to require external certification through an audit program. So, in the abstract, there appears to have been a steady expansion of the understanding of what it means for an organization to "adopt" a privacy protection policy. But this is often not reflected in organizational practices, which have become very confused, largely as a result of the frenzy to self-regulate on the Internet. There is most certainly not a serial evolution from vague principles through codes to seals and standards and then laws. Instead we see a complex dialectic, with one approach to some extent being a response to the other. This applies both within and across jurisdictions.

Critics remain sceptical that codes and other self-regulatory rules will be applied forcefully. Self-regulation will always suffer from the perception that it is more symbolic than real, because those who are responsible for implementation are those that may have the most to gain from the processing of personal data. Those who argue from more critical positions have contended that the appetite for the collection and processing of greater quantities and increasingly more refined types of personal information is inherent in the logic of the capitalist enterprise.[43] The incentive to breach privacy rules, in

---

42. See International Commerce Exchange Web site, <www.icx.org>.

43. See, for example, O. Gandy, *The Panoptic Sort* (Boulder, Colo.: Westview Press, 1993).

particular to collect, process and disclose personal information without consent, will tend to overwhelm the desire to be privacy-friendly. Other commentators have argued exactly the opposite: the protection of privacy fosters a greater trust among consumers and is therefore a relatively inexpensive way to promote the image of corporate social responsibility.[44] There is indeed evidence that privacy protection is linked to higher levels of consumer trust, and that this is a powerful motive for serious self-regulation.[45]

The truth is more complicated and contingent. What we are seeing is recognition that voluntary approaches are not something to be ignored or scorned, but rather an integral part of protecting our privacy, on-line and off. Sometimes the conditions for effective self-regulation are present; sometimes they are not. But, to grapple with this larger question, we do need to specify in a more systematic manner the various conditions that might promote an organization to self-regulate to a contemporary privacy protection standard. These conditions relate to the international, technological and business environments.

On an *international* dimension, we might first hypothesize that in those enterprises in which there is a greater need for the free international flow of personal data the exposure to international privacy standards will be greater and the motivation to self-regulation will be higher.[46] The global impact of the EU Directive, in particular, has been a significant force behind the development of privacy standards and seal programs in North America and Japan, as well as the Safe Harbour Agreement. If one scans the list of licensees to TRUSTe, for example, it is immediately obvious that those companies with an actual, or intended, global reach are those that have tended to sign on.

A second set of factors, *technological factors,* can be mentioned. New technologies tend to raise privacy fears more so than old ones. To the extent that new information technologies with privacy implications are continually introduced, the motive to self-regulate will be higher. As electronic commerce has penetrated the activities of every sector, there has been a corresponding need to anticipate privacy problems before they arise, and to assure consumers that their privacy is not at risk. Quite often, the same practices as are conducted in the offline world raise far greater fears when they are conducted on-line. The provision of credit card information, for example, is generally less secure when a card is physically handed over the counter in a traditional retail store, than when it is transmitted via a secure server with strong encryption over the Internet. Nevertheless, the subjective perception of risk associated with a new technology is a powerful motive to anticipate concerns and produce higher levels of self-regulation.

A final set of factors stems from the *business environment.* An initial concern would be the level of publicity. A strong motivation for self-regulation is the extent to

---

44. A. Cavoukian and D. Tapscott, *Who Knows: Safeguarding Your Privacy in a Networked World* (Toronto: Random House, 1995).

45. M. Culnan and D. Bies, "Managing Privacy Concerns Strategically: The Implications of Fair Information Practices for Marketing in the 21st Century," in C. J. Bennett and R. Grant, eds., *Visions of Privacy: Policy Choices for the Digital Age* (Toronto: University of Toronto Press, 1999), pp. 149–164.

46. For some empirical analysis of international flows of personal data, see C. D. Raab, C. J. Bennett, R. M. Gellman and N. Waters, *Application of a Methodology Designed to Assess the Adequacy of the Level of Protection of Individuals With Regard to Processing Personal Data: Test of the Method of Several Categories of Transfer,* (Luxembourg: Office for Official Publications of the European Communities, 1999), available at <http://europa.eu.int/comm/internal_market/privacy/studies/adequa_en.htm>.

which the enterprise (or sector) is the subject of negative publicity in both the traditional media and on the Internet.[47] A second variable is the existence or proximity of regulation. As the threat of law increases, so does the more responsible organization try to ward off, or at least anticipate, the regulator by self-regulating. A third political factor is the level of concern about privacy. The motivation to self-regulate will be higher when there is a demonstrated consumer concern about the privacy practices of the sector concerned. Public opinion surveys tend to suggest that privacy concerns remain high in most countries, and, if anything, they have increased as a result of the Internet. The incentive to self-regulate will be higher the more the sector is controlled by a broadly representative trade (peak) association that can self-regulate to minimize the influence of free riders. The more that actors within a sector abide by any standard, the more likely it is that the non-compliant will be exposed.[48]

However, the world is not neatly divided into sectors in which laws and codes of practice can be devised.[49] In practice, there is a rather incoherent categorization of sectors or industries in which privacy protection codes are established. A particularly clear exposition of the confusion that may arise in sectoral approaches is given by Robert Gellman in this hypothetical example:[50]

> [A]ssume that there are privacy codes for the banking, direct marketing, and insurance industries. Assume further that a bank is a member of all three industry associations that promulgated the codes. Which code applies when the bank sells insurance through direct mail? Which code applies to corporate activities of the bank holding company that operates banking, insurance, and marketing subsidiaries, each of which has promised to comply with the applicable industry codes? If all codes are general or identical, then there may be no problem. But if the codes have different standards or procedures, then jurisdictional conflicts will occur.

---

47. The very first company to register to the CSA standard, for instance, was IMS Health Canada, whose practices of collecting data on drug prescribers had come under significant media scrutiny.

48. A graphic example relates to the Canadian Marketing Association, which claims to represent about 75 percent of the direct-marketing activity in Canada. It is no accident that the CMA was one of the first associations to develop a privacy code, and the very first to call for legislation based on the CSA standard. The free riders who ignore basic consent requirements for the collection and disclosure of personal information were tainting the reputations of the more responsible players. The rational solution for the CMA was to attempt to raise the barrier for entry into the sector.

49. C. D. Raab, "Governing Privacy: Systems, Participants and Policy Instruments," in *Proceedings of Ethicomp99: Fifth International Conference*, Rome, 1999.

50. R. Gellman, *Conflict and Overlap in Privacy Regulation: National, International, and Private*, paper presented to the Symposium on Information, National Policies, and International Infrastructure, The Global Information Infrastructure Commission, Harvard University, January 28–30, 1996, available at <www.ksg.harvard.edu/iip/GIIconf/gellman.html>.

Information industries, entertainment industries, broadcasting industries and communication industries are in the midst of a dramatic restructuring that poses serious questions for privacy regulators and self-regulators. As the boundaries between sectors break down, the potential for the reputation of any business to be negatively affected by the actions of others increases. In an electronic commerce environment, old roles and functions are being radically redefined, with the result that bad actors might have a more widespread effect, far beyond the traditional sector in which they operate.

Conclusion: A Race to the Top, the Bottom or Somewhere Else?

Despite the continuing differences between U.S. privacy protection policy and that of most of the rest of the advanced industrial world, it is fair to say that privacy protection has never assumed a higher importance on national political agendas.[51] Certainly the arrival of the Internet and its use for on-line commercial activity is a major force behind this increased concern for personal privacy. But the impact of the international agreements (from the OECD, the Council of Europe and most notably the European Union[52]) has been very significant. The EU Directive has established the rules of the road for the increasingly global character of data processing operations.

There continues to be a high level of policy convergence in the area of data protection. Over time, these international harmonization efforts and an increasing cross-fertilization of policy ideas have motivated a considerable consensus (at least among the industrialized countries) about what it means for an organization to pursue privacy-friendly practices.[53] These fair information principles now appear in about 30 national laws, in international agreements, in voluntary codes of conduct, in the CSA's Model Code and with some variations in the Safe Harbour Agreement. The EU Directive, with its insistence that a "supervisory authority" should oversee data protection laws, is beginning a process of convergence, not only around the statutory principles but also around the policy instruments through which those principles should be enforced.[54] The United States currently resists the establishment of a privacy protection agency or commissioner. Most other countries (including New Zealand, Hong Kong, Australia and Canada) have accepted the need for an independent privacy watchdog.

51. See for example, the cover story "The End of Privacy," *The Economist*, May 1–7, 1999.

52. The OECD and EU initiatives have been referred to above. The *Council of Europe Convention for the Protection of Individuals with Regard to Automatic Processing of Personal Data*, which dates from 1981, can be found at <www.coe.int/T/e/legal_affairs/Legal_co-operation/Data_protection>.

53. C. J. Bennett, *Regulating Privacy: Data Protection and Public Policy in Europe and the United States* (Ithaca, N.Y.: Cornell University Press, 1992).

54. C. J. Bennett, "Convergence Revisited: Toward a Global Policy for the Protection of Personal Data?" in P. E. Agre and M. Rotenberg, *Technology and Privacy: The New Landscape* (Cambridge, Mass.: MIT Press, 1997), pp. 99–124.

Does all this policy activity constitute, however, a race to the top? So far, the convergence dynamic seems to have operated to harmonize data protection rules to the highest, rather than the lowest, common denominator. This process seems to approximate what David Vogel has described as "trading up."[55] I suggest, however, that the reasons are somewhat different from those offered by Vogel.

Vogel's first explanation is that stricter regulations represent a source of competitive advantage for domestic firms, which then support them in the international arena. When the burdens of compliance fall disproportionately on international competitors, this may make domestic firms more willing to support stricter regulations than would have been the case in the absence of foreign competition. The liberalization of trade (in data or anything else) may actually provide nations with an economic incentive to strengthen regulations, says Vogel. One problem with this argument as it relates to data protection is that many European industries (particularly direct marketing and consumer credit) lobbied hard *against* the EU Directive. Some even made common cause with American multinationals.

Vogel's second explanation concerns market access. Political jurisdictions that have developed stricter product standards force foreign producers in nations with weaker domestic standards either to design products to meet those standards or sacrifice export markets. Having made these initial investments, they now have a stake in encouraging their home markets to strengthen its standards as well, since their exports are already meeting those standards. This is obviously an important argument, with some validity. But the costs of making different automobiles to different emission standards are generally a lot higher than the costs of complying with different privacy standards. Fundamentally, this debate comes down to one of consent: should one have to get the data subject's consent before using personal data for secondary purposes? The value of this personal information for a major direct-marketing firm is probably a greater incentive to seek the lowest possible standard. If it has to design its systems to allow an "opt-in" in Germany, and an "opt-out" in Canada, so be it. The economies of scale are perhaps not strong enough to dictate an across-the-board trading-up dynamic.

Vogel's third explanation, however, is more plausible. This has to do with the politics of integration. To the extent that treaties or trade agreements provide formal mechanisms for establishing harmonized or equivalent standards, they provide an opportunity for richer, more powerful countries to play a greater role in setting those standards. "The more authority nations concede over the making of national regulatory standards," says Vogel, "the more likely these standards will be strengthened."[56] Politics makes the difference: "Trade agreements and treaties are likely to maintain or raise regulatory standards when a powerful and wealthy nation insists that they do so."[57] In the case of data protection, the EU Directive was driven by the efforts of the Germans and the French. We therefore see a considerable effort to pressure those without comprehensive privacy protection laws to adopt them. This pressure has stemmed from officials within the European Commission, as well as from certain influential data protection commissioners, who, after all, now have the power to disrupt the international

---

55. See Vogel (footnote 3).

56. Ibid., p. 264.

57. Ibid.

trade in personal information. In this regard, I would add another important factor relating to culture and history. Privacy is a deeply felt value in Western Europe. Experiences of totalitarianism raise questions about what Hitler could have done if he only had computers and other surveillance tools.

A more satisfactory explanation for the trading up of standards in this particular case is provided by Shaffer,[58] who offers five reasons for the raising of privacy standards in the United States. First, he argues that business demand for trade liberalization leads to a need to compete in Europe, and a concomitant need to conform their data processing standards to the EU's. The important implication of trade liberalization is the spillover effect permitting U.S. advocates to highlight the lower level of privacy protection in the United States. Secondly, the authority of EU law is bolstered by the power of the European market, producing an ability to negotiate rules that govern firm behaviour. A third argument relates to the relative importance of privacy in the public consciousness, and the belief that privacy becomes a good that is increasingly demanded as individuals become richer. A fourth reason relates to the externalities of data privacy policies, and the need within Europe to ensure that laws are not undermined by the processing of personal data in offshore "data havens." This factor is strengthened by the final reason, which relates to the application of international trade rules to data privacy. World Trade Organization rules, which otherwise constrain a country's ability to restrict imports and exports, include exemptions for data protection. As a result, "trade liberalization rules do not abate the pressure on the United States to raise effectively its data privacy standards. On the contrary, they constrain the ability of the United States to retaliate, again further facilitating a trading up of standards."[59]

Shaffer's analysis links the interests of European governments, private industry and privacy advocates. He is correct in saying that the EU Directive can be, and has been, used by privacy advocates as "leverage to force domestic regulators and businesses to raise privacy standards at home."[60] In general terms, the trading-up argument, as applied by Shaffer, is correct. But his analysis just applies to the United States. Moreover, it is by no means clear that the trading-up dynamic operates with equal force in different sectors. Privacy protection policy cuts across traditional sectoral categories, with the result that the market incentives of a bank will not be the same as those of an airline or a retailer. Cross-sectoral comparisons are necessary, as well as cross-national ones.

Within this context, the proliferation and the broadening scope of self-regulatory instruments mean that the overall trajectory and dynamic constitutes, if not a race to the top, than at least a steady walk. Many self-regulatory tools are admittedly designed to stem this process and avoid regulatory intervention. Many have no effect on organizational behaviour. But, overall, the bar has been raised. Symbolic statements of good intention are being distinguished from serious efforts at self-regulation. For the

---

58. G. Shaffer, "Globalization and Social Protection: The Impact of EU and International Rules in the Ratcheting Up of U.S. Privacy Standards," *Yale Journal of International Law* 25:1 (Winter 2000).

59. Ibid., p. 86.

60. Ibid., p. 88.

reasons that apply to other areas of consumer protection policy, there has been a trading up of privacy protection policy. Self-regulatory, along with legislative and technological instruments contribute to that general process.

Three final reservations are in order. First, we can measure and observe a ratcheting up of standards, but not necessarily of results or compliance. We still need to come to grips with how one measures "success" or "effectiveness" in the achievement of data protection goals.[61] Second, privacy protection policy is not only made by the laws of nation-states. Our ability to protect our personal information depends as much perhaps on decisions made in the labs of Microsoft and Intel, as in international negotiations and in national regulatory bodies. Lawrence Lessig has recently argued the persuasive case that computer "code" can have as significant an impact on the processing of personal information as does legal code.[62] Third, these judgments apply to the countries of the advanced industrial world. And with information policy, it is increasingly difficult to draw neat lines between regions of the globe. For very few countries outside of the OECD has privacy protection been a salient issue. The test of the international data protection regime, administered through the EU Directive, may not be the extent to which a trade war with the U.S. can be avoided, but whether or not this regime can prevent the processing of personal data in the lower-wage economies of the developing world. A truly global solution to this problem will require, therefore, more than legislation and regulatory oversight. Only a range of approaches, including privacy-enhancing technologies, market inducements and certifiable privacy standards, will promote a ratcheting up of organizational practices, as well as a trading up of national policies.

---

61. C. D. Raab and C. J. Bennett, "Taking the Measure of Privacy: Can Data Protection Be Evaluated?" *International Review of Administrative Sciences* 62:4 (December 1996), pp. 535–556.

62. L. Lessig, *Code and Other Laws of Cyberspace* (New York: Basic Books, 1999).

Chapter 9
Two Voluntary Approaches to Sustainable Forestry Practices

Gregory T. Rhone, David Clarke and Kernaghan Webb

Introduction

This is an account of two voluntary initiatives pertaining to sustainable forestry, that of the Forest Stewardship Council (FSC) and of the Canadian Standards Association (CSA). Although they claim similar objectives, these initiatives differ in approach, operation and key players. The FSC is a stand-alone international program spearheaded by environmental non-governmental organizations (ENGOs) that, from its inception, has very actively promoted the value of its on-product eco-label. The CSA initiative, on the other hand, originated with the forestry industry and was developed within the framework of Canada's National Standards System, with the objective of improving forest management.[1] Initially, the proponents of the CSA Sustainable Forest Management (SFM) System refrained from entering into the area of on-product labelling. Only recently has a chain of custody labelling component been added to SFM. The differences between the two initiatives do not take away from the fact that they have fundamentally the same goals, seeking to serve as a vehicle through which a company may send credible messages to the public about its forestry practices.[2]

A comparison of the two initiatives is undertaken in this chapter to provide readers with some insights as to how industry-supported and ENGO-supported voluntary codes interact in the marketplace. It consists of a discussion of the origins of the two standards,[3] the development of their rules, their respective auditing and certification

---

1. The National Standards System is coordinated by the Standards Council of Canada (SCC), a federal Crown corporation. SCC accredits organizations involved in standards development (of which there are four in Canada, CSA being the best known) and conformity assessment or auditing (of which there are about 250). The SCC also determines policies and procedures for developing National Standards of Canada. For an overview of the National Standards System, see Industry Canada, *Standards Systems: A Guide for Canadian Regulators* (Ottawa: Industry Canada, 1998), available at <http://strategis.ic.gc.ca/sc_mrksv/regaff/stdguide/engdoc/english.pdf>. See also Andrew Morrison and Kernaghan Webb, "Bicycle Helmet Standards and Hockey Helmet Regulations: Two Approaches to Safety Protection," Chapter 11, below.

2. These are two of the most prominent sustainable forestry initiatives in Canada; there are others, both within Canada and abroad, such as the American Forest and Paper Association's Sustainable Forestry Initiative Program (see <www.afandpa.org>) and the Pan European Forestry Certification Council (see <www.pefc.org>). For further discussion, see Kernaghan Webb and David Clarke, "Voluntary Codes in the United States, the European Union and Developing Countries," Chapter 13, below.) The American program has, in fact, made some inroads into Canada. An example of another ENGO-led initiative is the Silva Forest Foundation, based in British Columbia (see <www.silvafor.org>).

3. The term *standard* is used throughout this case study to refer to the rules developed by both initiatives, though only one was developed within the framework of the National Standards System. The term fits equally well to describe the documents produced by both initiatives, according to the general definition provided by the Standards Council of Canada: "Standards are publications that establish accepted practices, technical requirements and terminologies for diverse fields of human endeavour." See <www.scc.ca>.

Kernaghan Webb, Editor, *Voluntary Codes: Private Governance, the Public Interest and Innovation.*
This chapter ©2004 Gregory T. Rhone, David Clarke and Kernaghan Webb, pages 249–272.
Published by the Carleton Research Unit for Innovation, Science and Environment, Carleton University, Ottawa, Canada.

processes and the extent of their acceptance and implementation, one in the light of the other. The relationship of the standards to the regulatory process is also discussed.

Origins of the Standards

FSC Principles and Criteria

Many participants involved in the genesis of the FSC — which currently claims that almost 24 million hectares[4] of forest area worldwide have been certified by FSC-accredited organizations — admit that the program's success and high visibility were entirely unexpected in the beginning. Indeed, they thought they were creating, according to one participant, a niche market.[5] The idea of certification had been bandied about independently by a variety of environmental groups in the late 1980s as a positive alternative to boycotting tropical timber. Notable among the groups were the Canadian and U.S.-based Woodworkers' Alliance for Rainforest Protection and the U.K. chapter of the World Wide Fund for Nature (WWF).[6] Meanwhile, in 1989, the Rainforest Alliance, an international nonprofit organization dedicated to preserving tropical forests, became involved in forest certification through its Smart Wood certification program.[7] From about 1990, these and other environmental groups started discussing the issue of certification and proposing drafts for standards.[8] These discussions were usually conducted informally and did not include contributions from significant commercial interests. A meeting in Washington in 1992 was a significant turning point. It was there that the various drafts for standards formulated by the attending groups started coalescing

---

4. See FSC, *Forests Certified by FSC-Accredited Certification Bodies*, available at <www.fsc.org/keepout/content_areas/77/55/files/ABU_REP_70_2004_06_01_FSC_Certified_Forest.pdf>.

5. This cursory history is constructed from interviews in December 1998 and January 1999 with Jamison Ervin, the then-coordinator of the FSC's United States Initiative, Andrew Poynter, an Ontario woodworker, Paul Griss, an Alberta-based environmental consultant and key catalyst of the New Directions Group virtual dialogue between environmental and industry interests, and James Sullivan, FSC's Operations Director at the time of the interview. Mr. Sullivan had also served on the CSA SFM Technical Committee before joining FSC.

6. Founded in 1961 as the World Wildlife Fund (the full name that is still used by its national chapters in Canada and the U.S., though elsewhere it calls itself the World Wide Fund for Nature), WWF is frequently described as the world's largest environmental group. WWF International's Secretariat is based in Switzerland, although there are 26 national and territorial WWF organizations throughout the world, and offices in 20 other countries. WWF International and its national organizations reported an income of 575 million Swiss francs (CAN$585 million) in 1999–2000, with the principal income sources being individuals' contributions (45 percent) and governments and aid agencies (20 percent). See The Fridtjof Nansen Institute, *Yearbook of International Co-operation on Environment and Development*, available at <www.ext.grida.no/ggynet/ngo/wwf.htm>. WWF's approach to environmental activism includes partnerships with other ENGOs, industry and government. A notable example of the last is The Endangered Species Recovery Fund, a partnership between WWF Canada and Environment Canada.

7. See Rainforest Alliance Web site, <www.rainforestalliance.com>. Today, the Rainforest Alliance is one of FSC's accredited certifiers.

8. An intergovernmental organization, the International Tropical Timber Organization, had also become interested in certification at this time, but some of its member countries dismissed the concept as a boycotting effort or as unworkable. See E. Meidinger, "'Private' Environmental Regulation, Human Rights and Community," *Buffalo Environmental Law Journal* 7 (2000), pp. 123–237, p. 131, available at <www.law.buffalo.edu/homepage/eemeid/scholarship/hrec.pdf>.

into something of a coherent document. Representation by this time had widened: the large U.K. building supply retail chain B & Q[9] was represented, along with Greenpeace, Friends of the Earth and WWF International. At this meeting, the groups agreed that more work on the drafts was needed. An interim board was elected to carry out consultations and develop the set of Principles and Criteria that would serve as a basis for certification.

The drafts were distributed to various national contact people, who then circulated them within their own countries. Canada's contact person sent out about 50 copies of the drafts, to every deputy minister of forestry, most industry associations, some senior officials of large companies, some academics and environmental groups. He received about a dozen responses and synthesized them into a report that was sent to the international coordinating body. Most replies came from industry.

While the documents were circulating, funding was solicited. At first, minor charitable organizations gave small contributions. A significant boost came when a grant of $100,000 was received from the MacArthur Foundation, with more money following soon thereafter from WWF-UK, and the Austrian and Dutch governments. The Ford Foundation also made a contribution, as did the WWF chapters in Austria and the Netherlands. When FSC established its international secretariat in Oaxaca, Mexico, the Mexican government contributed funds to offset startup costs for the office.

FSC's Founding Assembly in Toronto in September 1993 was attended by 130 participants from 25 countries. It was at this meeting that FSC was established as a membership organization. Founding members included Greenpeace International and various national organizations of the WWF.[10] FSC's Principles and Criteria, adopted at the Assembly, were later approved by mail-in ballot. The membership roll did not include any large-scale forestry *producers*. However, some very large wood-product *retailers* were founding members, including Home Depot and B & Q.[11] A major step forward for FSC came in early 1997, when the Swedish company AssiDoman, described as the largest private forest owner in the world, became the first major forest products company to join FSC.[12] From 1998 to 2000, AssiDoman's Chief Ecologist was chair of FSC's board of directors.

FSC's members constitute the General Assembly, which was originally divided into two voting "chambers": "economic interests" (includes timber traders, forest industry representatives, certifiers and retailers); and "social and environmental

---

9. With almost 300 stores in the United Kingdom, B & Q claims to hold 19 percent of that country's retail building supply market.

10. FSC's current membership list includes 13 WWF national chapters, such as those of Canada, the U.K. and the U.S. The current membership list is available at the FSC Web site, <www.fsc.org/fsc>.

11. By this time, too, the 1992 Earth Summit in Rio de Janeiro was already history. The failure there to reach a State-sanctioned agreement on forestry conservation was said to have sparked an increased interest among ENGOs in finding market-based conservation instruments, such as certification. See S. Bernstein and B. Cashore, "Globalization, Four Paths of Internationalization and Domestic Policy Change: The Case of Eco-forestry Policy Change in British Columbia," *Canadian Journal of Political Science* 33 (2000), pp. 67–99.

12. "It's Official: AssiDoman Makes History With FSC Membership," *Timber Trade Journal*, January 4, 1997, p. 4.

organizations."[13] Originally, the former group wielded 25 percent of the voting power and the latter, 75 percent. These proportions were officially modified in 1996 to create three chambers: 33 percent social, 33 percent ENGO and 33 percent commercial.[14] This change was designed to ensure a greater voice for the last group. The voting power within each chamber is divided evenly between North and South[15] to ensure equal representation. The board of directors comprises two representatives of economic interests, and seven of social, indigenous and environmental interests.[16] The board's voting power is divided according to the same categories and proportions as the General Assembly.[17] In 2003, the office of chair of the board of directors was held by a representative of the Algonquins of Barriere Lake, Canada.[18] There were five representatives from the South and four from the North.[19] FSC by-laws are designed to ensure that these proportions are reversed every three years.[20]

FSC Regional and National Standards

Perhaps as important as the original development of the Principles and Criteria is the development of standards that are specific to a country or region. It is against these standards that a company seeking certification is assessed. These local standards are developed not by FSC's Mexico-based international body, but by national or regional working groups, though FSC International ultimately must approve the final document. FSC's stated objectives in developing this structure are "to decentralize the work of FSC and encourage local participation."[21] Canada has a national office,[22] based in Toronto, but because of the country's size and the variety of its forest types, there is no attempt to create national standards, as there are in smaller countries. Rather, a number of working groups are at various stages of developing regional standards. These groups represent British Columbia, the Great-Lakes-St. Lawrence region of Ontario, the "Boreal Pilot

---

13. C. Elliott and A. Hackman, *Current Issues in Forest Certification in Canada: A WWF Canada Discussion Paper* (Toronto: WWF Canada, 1996), p. 5. There was said to have been vigorous debate at the Founding Assembly over the extent to which commercial interests should be allowed to participate in the development of standards; this according to an anonymously written document, "Acting in the Public Interest: Policy Considerations which shape governments [sic] role and responsibility in standards development and administration, natural resource regulation and development policy and the maintenance of free and open markets," supplied by the Canadian Pulp and Paper Association to the authors, April 1998.

14. FSC, *Forest Stewardship Council A.C. By-laws*, s. 12, available at the FSC Web site, <www.fsc.org/keepout/content_areas/77/84/files/FSC_By_laws___revised_November_2002.PDF>.

15. FSC's terms for high-income countries, and low-, middle- and upper-middle-income countries, as determined by "United Nations Criteria": ibid., ss. 13–14.

16. Ibid., s. 51.

17. Chris Elliott, *WWF Guide to Forest Certification* (Surrey, U.K.: World Wildlife Fund, 1996), p. 8.

18. FSC, *Address List for FSC Directors and Secretariat*, available at FSC Web site, <www.fsc.org/fsc>.

19. Ibid.

20. See FSC, *By-laws* (footnote 14), ss. 51–52.

21. Ibid., s. 71.

22. See FSC Canada Web site, <www.fsccanada.org>.

Project" in Ontario, and the Maritimes.[23] While FSC International calls for national and regional working groups to have three chambers, one of each representing social, economic and environmental interests, Canadian working groups actually have a fourth chamber, representing Aboriginal interests.[24]

The Canadian working group with the highest profile has been the one in British Columbia. The early standards development work of the group was described by one observer as being conducted by "a close-knit group of environmentalists," with little outside participation.[25] According to the B.C. group's original coordinator, throughout the early years of the group's work the provincial government consistently sent observers to meetings and offered technical expertise.[26] She said that some representatives of industry (both large and small producers) attended meetings, describing their involvement as "cautious."[27] Until fall 1998, the development process had been carried out on a very tight budget, with participants generally paying their own way to meetings. Then, faced with increasing interest from the media and from industry, the working group realized that it was time to accelerate the process of writing the draft. To do this, the group had by 1999 raised operating funds from some large environmental groups as well as from FSC International's secretariat.[28] A five-member team was contracted to write the first draft standard.[29] According to the B.C. initiative's Web site, the final standard was in place in July 2002.[30] The B.C. initiative has apparently become much more successful in fundraising now than it had been in earlier years; its Web site lists a wide variety of contributors (of "financial gifts or in-kind resources"), ranging from environmental groups such as Greenpeace Canada and WWF Canada, as well as industry associations and the provincial government of British Columbia.[31]

---

23. Ibid.

24. See <www.fsccanada.org/about/chamber_rep.shtml.

25. G. Hoberg, "The Coming Revolution in Regulating our Forests," *Policy Options* (December 20, 1999), pp. 53–56, p. 54, available at <www.irpp.org/po/archive/dec99/hoberg.pdf>.

26. Interview with Lara Beckett, then-regional coordinator of the B.C. FSC initiative, 1998.

27. Beckett, ibid.

28. This according to Marty Horswill, who in 1999 was regional coordinator of the B.C. initiative, in interview with the authors. Mr. Horswill did not go into detail about the names of environmental groups involved and the specific amounts received.

29. The five members were a forest consultant to industry, an agronomist who was a consultant to both government and industry, an environmental lawyer, a representative knowledgeable of issues relating to First Nations, and a writer. (Ibid.)

30. See <www.fsc-bc.org>.

31. See <www.fsc-bc.org>.

The CSA Sustainable Forest Management System Standards

The depletion of the world's tropical forests became the subject of international attention in the late 1980s and early 1990s.[32] However, the interests of international media and ENGOs gradually expanded to encompass more northerly forests, including those of Canada, in particular, British Columbia.[33] Among the principal stakes in the debate that arose was the European share of British Columbia's exports of lumber, pulp, paper and other wood products.[34] As one B.C. forest industry spokesman was quoted as saying at the time, Europeans were "getting a very bad impression about B.C."[35] Canadian and international media focussed in particular on Clayoquot Sound, an area on the west coast of Vancouver Island that attracted hundreds of protesters over the spring and summer of 1993 who called for a halt to forestry company MacMillan Bloedel Ltd.'s logging operations there. The protesters' logging road blockades, subsequent arrests and mass trials became a *cause célèbre* among environmental activists throughout the world.

Faced with the pressure of negative public opinion abroad and in Canada, representatives of major Canadian forestry industry associations, led by the Canadian Pulp and Paper Association, saw that to remain competitive in international markets, it would be useful to develop a system of certification for sustainable forestry that would be independent and reliable, and perceived as such by the public. In the spring of 1994 the Association contracted with CSA to direct the standards development process. CSA received funding for this endeavour from the forestry industry, though the standards were to be developed in conjunction with a government-funded pilot project that would test the draft CSA standard, on a working scale, in six test areas across Canada.[36]

The forest industry had concluded that CSA, as a well-established and independent standards development organization with an affiliated (but independent)

---

32. Concerns were expressed not just by ENGOs but among intergovernmental organizations as well. For instance, the intergovernmental International Tropical Timber Organization (ITTO) developed the *ITTO Guidelines for the Sustainable Management of Natural Tropical Forests*, released in May 1990. Then, in 1991, ITTO committed to the Year 2000 Objective, which was the "goal of having all tropical timber entering international trade come from sustainably managed sources by 2000." See *ITTO Objective 2000*, available at the ITTO Web site, <www.itto.or.jp/live/PageDisplayHandler?pageId=5>.

33. See F. Gale and C. Burda, "The Pitfalls and Potential of Eco-Certification as a Market Incentive for Sustainable Forest Management," in C. Tollefson, ed., *The Wealth of Forests: Markets, Regulation and Sustainable Forestry* (Vancouver: UBC Press, 1998), pp. 278–296, p. 281.

34. See W. Stanbury, I. Vertinsky and B. Wilson, *The Challenge to Canadian Forest Products in Europe: Managing a Complex Environmental Issue* (Victoria, B.C.: Natural Resources Canada, 1995).

35. Patrick Watson of the B.C. Forest Alliance, quoted in R. Matas, "Foreign Eyes on Canadian Forests," *The Globe and Mail*, February 6, 1993, p. A7.

36. Interview with Ahmad Husseini, Program Manager, CSA Standards Development, 1996. See also *Canada's Model Forest Program*, available at <www.nrcan.gc.ca/cfs-scf/national/what-quoi/modelforest_e.html>.

certification/registration[37] body, was best suited to develop the standard.[38] The CSA struck the multistakeholder Technical Committee, which included 32 voting members, and sought to ensure what it calls a "balanced matrix" of representation. By the time the standards were ultimately published (in October 1996), the four categories of representation were as follows: academia (22.5 percent), government/regulatory (22.5 percent), environmental/general interest (32.5 percent) and product/industry interests (22.5 percent).[39] Because the inclusion of government representatives from each of the provinces would have made the Technical Committee unwieldy, only provincial government officials from British Columbia, Alberta, Ontario, Quebec and Nova Scotia participated on the Committee.[40]

The development of the standards was thus said to be a broad-based multistakeholder process. Drafts of the standards were brought to public attention by various means.[41] Anxious to show that it was ensuring significant environmentalist input in the development process, the CSA hosted a Canadian Environmental Network[42] information session in Ottawa, which brought the process to the attention of ENGOs.[43]

In additional, consultations were held across the country toward the end of October 1995 in Vancouver, Toronto and Montréal. Of the environmental organizations invited to attend these consultations, approximately 135 were present at the three

---

37. A note on the term *certification*. CSA documents employ the term *registration* to denote the process of confirming that a company conforms to the standard. Certification usually implies a mark or label, whereas registration usually refers to a recording of a successful system audit. Given that there was no initial intention by the industry proponents of the CSA initiative to create a label, the word *registration* was used to denote system auditing, not labelling. However, the Canadian Sustainable Forestry Certification (CSFC) Coalition prefers the term *certification*, because that is the more common term for the process and is more readily understood by overseas customers. For the purposes of this case study, the words are synonymous. See CSFC Coalition, *Communicating Your Certification to the Sustainable Forest Management System Standards, CAN/CSA Z809* (Montréal: CSFC Coalition, 1997), p. 1.

38. As we will see, there were in fact two standards published. One document (CSA, *A Sustainable Forest Management System*, CAN/CSA-Z808-96 [Toronto: CSA, 1996], hereafter "*Z808 Guidance Document*") is a guide for companies, outlining in some detail the steps they need to take to obtain certification. The shorter document (CSA, *Specifications Document, A Sustainable Forest Management System*, CAN/CSA-Z809-96 [Toronto: CSA, 1996], hereafter "*Z809 Specifications Document*") is a checklist for certification bodies to determine whether the necessary elements of a management system are present. Thus, it is to the Z809 standard that a management system is certified.

39. According to Mr. Husseini, who was chair of the Technical Committee, the voting membership of the Committee changed little over the course of the development process. Voting environmental representatives were constant throughout the entire process. (Interview with Mr. Husseini, May 1999.)

40. However, Alberta's representative spoke for Saskatchewan and Manitoba. Nova Scotia represented the Atlantic provinces. The federal government was also represented on the Technical Committee.

41. The task of writing the drafts as well as the final standards was contracted out to professional writers. This was supervised by an editing team comprising representatives of the four categories of the matrix. (Husseini [footnote 36].)

42. The Canadian Environment Network provides a forum for ENGOs of all sizes and mandates, ensuring that they have coordinated input into national environmental policy discussions (see <www.cen-rce.org>).

43. See CSA, *Background and Proceedings of the Non-Governmental Organization (NGO) Consultation Sessions for the Canadian Standards Association's Sustainable Forest Management (SFM) Project*, summary report (Toronto: CSA, November 29, 1995), pp. 3–6.

sessions.[44] The consultations led to redrafts that incorporated many of the suggestions of attending parties, as well as the comments sent in by those who did not attend.[45] The redrafted documents were again sent to any interested party for comment. Further public consultations were conducted in February and March 1996, in a widely advertised process. The ENGO conferences and consultations were organized and funded by CSA (and therefore ultimately by the Canadian Pulp and Paper Association), and interested ENGOs could attend without incurring any costs.[46] Hence, the problem of lack of funds for interested parties was largely negated as an issue in the consultation process. The final documents were published as National Standards of Canada in October 1996.[47]

Although at first glance this would seem to represent an example of the thorough multistakeholder development process required by the Standards Council of Canada, critics raised a number of concerns, as follows:[48]

- ENGOs were not invited to participate on the Technical Committee "until decisions about the process, membership, time frames and other key aspects of the SFM Technical Committee had been made, the terms of reference of the CSA's contract negotiated, and the background document prepared."[49] Strictly speaking, this is correct. However, it is worth pointing out that frequent requests to ENGOs to become part of the CSA process and attempts to include members of the Canadian Environmental Network were rejected. In specific regard to time frames, the Technical Committee's consumer representative points out that industry representatives on the Committee were particularly amenable to setting back the development process for several months to allow for country-wide NGO consultations.[50]

---

44. Ibid.

45. Ibid.

46. Husseini (footnote 36).

47. See footnote 38.

48. Some of these concerns were related to efforts to bring the CSA SFM System immediately to the international level. As Rachel Crossley describes it, the original intent of the Technical Committee was to bring the Canadian standards, once developed, to the International Organization for Standardization (ISO) for approval as international standards. In April 1995, the ISO national bodies of Australia and Canada proposed to formally request that ISO develop international standards based upon the Canadian model. It was at this point that groups opposed to the Canadian standards started becoming more vocal in their opposition, saying that there was an attempt to avoid national debate on the standards by shifting their development to the international level. See R. Crossley, *A Review of Global Forest Management Certification Initiatives: Political and Institutional Aspects*, draft paper for the Conference on Economic, Social and Political Issues in Certification of Forest Management, Malaysia, May 1996, available at <www.forestry.ubc.ca/concert/ crossley.html>.) ISO did not ultimately publish a sustainable forest management standard; rather, it published a technical report, a guide for companies wishing to apply the ISO 14001 or ISO 14004 environmental management standard to the forestry context. See *ISO 14061, Information to Assist Forestry Organizations in the Use of Environmental Management System Standards ISO 14001 and ISO 14004* (Geneva: ISO, 1998).

49. Paul Griss, letter to Jean-Claude Mercier, Chair, Sustainable Forest Management Technical Committee, March 10, 1995. Mr. Griss, an Alberta-based environmental consultant, was an associate (non-voting) member of the Technical Committee at the time he wrote the letter. As we have seen, he also participated in the development of the Forest Stewardship Council's Principles and Criteria. A similar criticism is made by Gale and Burda (footnote 33), p. 285.

50. Interview with Jennifer Hillard, Vice-President, Policy, Consumers' Association of Canada, July 1999.

- ENGOs were critical of the management basis of the standards, preferring what they called performance-based standards (a distinction discussed in further detail below), which the FSC purported to be producing during the same period.[51]
- There were allegations that CSA misrepresented the role of environmentalists in the process. This was said to be manifest in several ways. First, it was said that one prominent environmentalist was listed as a consistently absent member of the Technical Committee for a year, when in fact she had informed CSA that she would be unable to participate.[52] Second, the calibre and kind of ENGOs that did participate were criticized as not representing the views of larger, more well-known ENGOs that did not participate. Third, and more generally, CSA boasted of a wide representation from ENGOs on the Technical Committee. However, according to critics, these were not the "groups most experienced and independent regarding forest ecology and protection work."[53]

Content of the Standards

FSC Principles and Criteria, Standards, and Certificates

The FSC's base rules are 10 very general principles, each of which is fleshed out with a number of criteria.[54] Many of the Principles and Criteria are arguably quite vague, but perhaps necessarily so, since they are meant to apply to forest types throughout the world — tropical, temperate and boreal forests, as well as plantations. They form the basis for national or regional standards that, as noted earlier, are developed by the national or regional working groups.

---

51. Forest Caucus of the Canadian Environmental Network, *An Environmentalist and First Nations Response to the Canadian Standards Association Proposed Certification System for Sustainable Forest Management*, paper presented to the Canadian Standards Association, October 20, 1995. The paper was endorsed by 25 organizations, most notably Friends of the Earth and Sierra Club of Canada. A similar document, spearheaded by Greenpeace and signed by more than 40 groups, had been released in June 1995.

52. The misrepresentation was apparently caused by the fact that the list of participants also included individuals wishing to receive documents related to Technical Committee meetings. Some industry representatives were overly enthusiastic about a prominent environmental activist's presence on the list. CSA offered a full apology to Elizabeth May. (Authors' correspondence with Elizabeth May, January 1999.)

53. Forest Caucus of the Canadian Environmental Network (footnote 51), p. 5. One commentator has written of the groups who were included: "None of these groups are what one would call forest activist groups — Wildlife Habitat Canada is primarily involved in collaborative initiatives with government and the private sector, while the other two groups [the B.C. Federation of Mountain Clubs and the Ontario Federation of Anglers and Hunters] have mandates that limit them to specialized interests." (M. von Mirbach, *Reward the Best or Improve the Rest? Questions About Forest Certification in Canada and Internationally*, paper prepared for February 23–27, 1998, meeting of ENGOs in Ottawa, cited in T. Burrell, *CSA Environmental Standards Writing: Barriers to Environmental Non-Governmental Organization Involvement*, Canadian Institute for Environmental Law and Policy, May 1997.) The response from CSA to this has consistently been to point out that environmental activist groups had always been encouraged to participate. Indeed, a WWF representative was present for some of the earliest Technical Committee meetings.

54. See *FSC Principles and Criteria*, available at <www.fsc.org/fsc/whats_new/documents/Docs_cent/2,16>.

Some critics have nevertheless expressed concerns that the Principles and Criteria will be applied inconsistently, because of their imprecision.[55] For instance, the Principles and Criteria do not explicitly forbid clearcutting, though some supporters and critics have interpreted them thus. Rather, they only forbid conversion of a primary or well-developed secondary forest to other uses.[56]

At the same time, FSC documents are very similar in some of their procedural requirements to those of the CSA SFM System. First, management must respect local laws (Principle 1), as well as Aboriginal interests. Second, the Principles and Criteria require the production of a management plan that, though far from identical in format to the plan called for in the CSA SFM System standard, nevertheless appears similar: management objectives must be clearly stated, along with detailed analyses of the means of achieving them. Furthermore, the plan must be updated to reflect the results of ongoing monitoring. Also, there are public input requirements built in to the process: "Consultations shall be maintained with people and groups directly affected by management operations."[57]

An apparent difference lies in the fact that FSC's public input requirements, though less detailed, appear to place more weight on objections from interested parties. According to Criterion 2.3, disputes "of substantial magnitude involving a significant number of interests will normally disqualify an operation from being certified."[58]

Turning to substantive aspects of the Principles and Criteria, FSC is frequently described by its proponents as emphasizing on-the-ground performance over management.[59] Despite this characterization, however, the Principles and Criteria contain few specific performance requirements. Rather, on the whole they emphasize general social goods — respect for laws and the rights of Aboriginals, workers and communities — as well as outlining performance guidelines that are frequently articulated in imprecise language. Only two of the principles lay down substantive rules about a company's actions within forests. Of these, Principle 5 — Benefits from the Forest — and its related criteria are surprisingly vague. The related criteria tend to use the word *should* rather than *shall*, suggesting either that they are optional or that they will be applied with less rigour than will the other requirements. In contrast, it must be said that Principle 6 — Environmental Impact — lays down firmer and more specific rules for minimizing the impact of the use of pesticides and other chemicals. But it is less specific on what

---

55. See, e.g., M. von Mirbach, "Demanding Good Wood." *Alternatives Journal* 23 (Summer 1997), p. 12.

56. Len Aipedale, a representative of FSC-accredited SGS International Certification Services Ltd., outlined some of the confusion in this way:

> A lot of people have their own ideas about what certification means, about what FSC certification means and about what the FSC Principles and Criteria mean. ... Some people interpret it on one end of the scale as no logging in natural forests. That's certainly not the common interpretation or the intent of the FSC Principles and Criteria, but some people believe very strongly that this is what it means.

Quoted in D. Jordan, "Forest Certification Behind Schedule," *Business in Vancouver*, January 19–25, 1999, p. 1.

57. Criterion 4.4 (footnote 54).

58. Criterion 2.3, ibid.

59. See, for instance, Elliott and Hackman (footnote 13), pp. 24ff.

appropriate measures should be taken to protect animal and plant species. Thus, there is a great deal of flexibility built in to the Principles and Criteria.

As well as developing and occasionally amending the Principles and Criteria and other documents, an important role of FSC's international secretariat is to accredit organizations to carry out the certification process. Eleven organizations have been accredited as of this writing, one of them Canadian.[60] The accredited certifier will, ideally, assess (or "audit") an area (a "management unit") according to region-specific standards that are in keeping with the globally applicable Principles and Criteria. The qualifier "ideally" is used because in many cases forests are not actually being certified to regional or national standards. During the period that the standards are being developed, a management unit can be certified to the auditor's own, generic set of standards employed in combination with consultations among local interested parties. This explains how, for instance, there can be forest areas commonly described as "FSC-certified" in British Columbia,[61] even though, as we have noted above, no standards for the province were finalized until July 2002.[62]

Discussion has thus far focussed on FSC's forest management certificate. From a consumer perspective, however, the most visible aspect of the FSC process is the on-product logo, a stylized checkmark melding into the outline of a tree. Before a product or its packaging may bear the logo, the product's manufacturer is required to establish and document a chain of custody, the link between the certified management unit and the product. Unless the link can be positively traced, the product may not carry the logo. So there are, in effect, two certificates involved in the FSC process, the forest management certificate and the chain of custody certificate. The holder of a forest management certificate alone cannot put the logo on a product or packaging, though it may, with permission, use the logo on promotional materials. While it has been pointed out that the chain of custody requirement makes FSC a rather difficult system to implement for some large operations that obtain wood from various sources,[63] such criticisms may become more muted with time, given that those promoting the CSA SFM System have now found some value in the use of on-product logos.

---

60. See *FSC-Accredited Certification Bodies*, available at <www.fsc.org/keepout/content_areas/77/78/files/FSC_Accreditated_CBs__June_1__2004_.pdf>.

61. See "Progress in Implementation," below.

62. As for costs incurred by a company seeking certification, they have been described as "shrouded in mystery" and varying anywhere from "$500 to $130,000 US." See Meidinger (footnote 8), p. 150.

63. See T. Rotherham, *Chain of Custody*, a paper presented to the International Conference on Certification Criteria and Indicators: Global Approaches to Sustainable Forest Management, Prince George, B.C., September 1997, available at <www.mcgregor.bc.ca/publications/GlobalApproaches/GAPanel2.pdf>. Products bearing the FSC logo must contain a specified percentage of wood from an FSC source. The amount originally specified was 70 percent, but was subsequently lowered to 30 percent, and is to rise to 50 percent by 2005. This percentage and its variability have been the subject of criticisms by consumer groups such as the Consumers' Association of Canada, the U.S. Consumers Union and Consumers International. These groups have also pointed out that the FSC label is not life-cycle based. These points are discussed in *Forest Certification Watch*, Issue 23 (April 30, 2002), pp. 8–9 (see http://certificationwatch.org), and Consumers International, *Green Claims: Environmental Claims on Products and Packaging in the Shops: An International Study* (London: Consumers International, March 2000).

The CSA Sustainable Forest Management System Standards

The CSA SFM system standards have been described as "ISO 14000 plus."[64] They contain a management component based on the ISO 14001 and 14004 environmental management system standards, which principally call for a commitment to comply with applicable environmental laws and to continuous improvement, as well as the adoption of a management system designed to ensure conformity with that commitment.[65] One "plus" element is the requirement for public consultation throughout the process as the system is proposed, drawn up and implemented. Another "plus" element is the performance side of the standards; an organization's management plan must identify "values, goals, indicators and objectives" for a given Defined Forest Area and declare how it will implement them on the ground. Third-party audits must examine not only the management system, but also on-the-ground performance, including whether the organization is living up to its commitment to continually improve.

The CSA standards organize this process into four components, which merit closer examination in light of a principal criticism, that in the absence of minimal on-the-ground performance requirements, a company can receive certification without changing its *status quo*.[66] To judge strictly by the text of the standards, this outcome is possible, since specific performance indicators are not predefined. However, the very public nature of the planning and certification process makes this unlikely, given the ample opportunity for interested parties to air their views on the process.

The first component of the standard requires a company to commit to the process — to make "readily available to internal and external parties" a policy statement that includes a commitment at the highest levels of the company not only to manage the forest in a sustainable manner, but also to provide for public participation, with particular attention to the needs of Aboriginal peoples, in the setting of "objectives, goals and indicators"[67] and "values."[68] These key terms are defined mainly by their relationship to one another,[69] though they all ultimately find their basis in the Canadian Council of

---

64. The CSFC Coalition, for its part, says that the CSA SFM System "builds on the ISO 14001 system framework." See Coalition Web site, <www.sfms.com/iso.htm>.

65. The ISO 14001 and 14004 international standards for environmental management systems were published by the International Organization for Standardization in September 1996. They are the first of a group of standards collectively called ISO 14000. While supporters of ISO 14001 and 14004 contend that they provide a competitive advantage to companies along with ensuring good environmental stewardship, critics feel that they were developed with little ENGO input, are essentially procedural standards with no substantive requirements, and entail a certification process that is of little value. For a discussion of these and other issues, see P. S. Evers, "ISO 14000 and Environmental Protection," *Mississippi Law Journal* 67 (1996), pp. 463–526.

66. Elizabeth May of the Sierra Club of Canada, for instance, said the following about the CSA SFM system standard: "[The companies] are audited by independent auditors against the plan they have chosen for themselves. They are not audited to see if the outcome was enhanced biodiversity; they are audited to see if they did what they said they would do." (*Proceedings of the Subcommittee on the Boreal Forest*, Standing Senate Committee on Agriculture and Forestry, April 24, 1997.)

67. *Z809 Specifications Document*, p. 7.

68. Ibid., p. 8.

69. *Z808 Guidance Document*, p. 8.

Forest Ministers' Criteria and Indicators for Sustainable Forestry.[70] At the top of the order is a "value" — that is, "a principle, standard or quality considered worthwhile or desirable."[71] A "goal" is a "broad, general statement that describes a desired state or condition related to one or more forest values."[72] One or more goals must be set for each value. An "indicator" is a "measurable variable used to report progress toward the achievement of a goal."[73] An "objective," which is set for each indicator, "is a clear, specific statement of expected quantifiable results, related to one or more goals."[74] Next in order is the "practice" — the "on-the-ground forest management activity designed to achieve an objective."[75]

All but the last of these elements are determined by the public participation process. The public participation process is the second component of the CSA SFM approach. In this component, the company determines which participants to invite (and is audited to ensure that this is done fairly) by making efforts to identify "local people and others who are affected by or who have an interest in the Defined Forest Area and ask them to participate."[76] The rules of the process — time lines, decision making and dispute settlement, for example — must be developed and agreed to by the participants, and then must be clearly described. The company is obliged to provide participants with access to relevant information about the Defined Forest Area, consider all input from participants, and provide responses to it. It is from this public process that values, goals, indicators and objectives are to be set. Actual practices, as we have noted, are not determined by the public participation process.

The third component is the establishment of the Sustainable Forest Management System. This component entails rather extensive documentation requirements, including an account of the public participation process (including its outcomes), and the drawing up of an SFM plan and manual. Apart from documenting its intentions in this way, the applicant must show that the system is implemented on the ground.[77]

---

70. In 1993, the Canadian Council of Forest Ministers (CCFM) produced a national framework of criteria and indicators to help track progress toward achieving sustainable forest management. See CCFM, *Criteria and Indicators of Sustainable Forestry Management in Canada, Technical Report 1997* (Ottawa: Canadian Council of Forest Ministers, 1997), p. i. For details on the Criteria and Indicators, see the Canadian Forest Service Web site, <www.nrcan.gc.ca/cfs/proj/ppiab/ci/indica_e.html>.

71. *Z808 Guidance Document*, p. 4.

72. Ibid., p. 3.

73. Ibid.

74. Ibid.

75. Ibid., p. 12.

76. Ibid., p. 15.

77. Ibid., pp. 17–21.

The final component — "continual improvement" — is closely linked to the ongoing process of review, measurement and assessment. Ongoing performance is measured against objectives, and new information that results from past practices, audits and performance reviews must be incorporated into the CSA SFM System.[78]

For the first five years of its existence, the CSA SFM System did not provide for a CSA logo to appear on a product, allowing time for the management system to be put in place and begin working, and apparently reflecting the fact that it was not initially intended to be used as an on-product marketing tool. While this arguably limited the potential visibility of the certification process, the Canadian Sustainable Forestry Coalition[79] sought to overcome any such weakness by encouraging companies to widely publicize their certification and provide background information about it.[80] Recommended techniques ranged from putting information on the company letterhead, to contacting the media.[81] Logos on products or packaging, however, did not form a part of the system. Such logos are intimately tied to the concept of "chain of custody," which is the tracking of forest products originating from the certified forest of origin, "through all phases of ownership, transportation and transformation" to the end consumer.[82] Coalition representatives occasionally offered reasons why such a system was neither feasible nor ecologically sound.[83]

This attitude had apparently changed by the summer of 2001, when CSA released a document providing for the optional use of an on-product and/or on-package logo by companies establishing a chain of custody from the forest to the product.[84] Three logo options are available, the most stringent indicating to the consumer that 100 percent of the "product has been tracked and monitored from its point of origin (a Z809-certified forest) to the end consumer."[85] The precise motivations for developing a product-centred logo after years of resistance are a matter of speculation. It is safe to assume, however, that the success of FSC in promoting its own logo (as discussed below) provided at least some of the inspiration. Even without FSC's influence, however, it is obvious that companies that make the effort to implement the CSA SFM System, and companies manufacturing products derived from certified forests, would all be anxious to see those efforts communicated effectively to the consuming public at the retail level.

---

78. Ibid., p. 21. The CSA certification process is said to cost a company more than $200,000. See D. Brown and D. Greer, *Implementing Forest Certification in British Columbia: Issues and Options*, prepared for the Trade and Sustainable Development Group, Policy and Economics Division, B.C. Ministry of Forests, March 2001, p. 113, available at <www.for.gov.bc.ca/HET/certification/ResearchStudyReport0301.pdf>.

79. The Canadian Sustainable Forestry Coalition is dedicated to the promotion of certification standards by Canadian industry (footnote 37).

80. CSFC Coalition (footnote 37), p. ii.

81. Ibid.

82. See CSA, *Chain of Custody for Forest Products Originating from a Defined Forest Area Registered to CSA Standard CAN-CSA-Z809*, CSA Special Publication PLUS 1163 (Toronto: CSA, June 2001), p. iv.

83. Chain of custody was said not to be feasible because of the difficulty of distinguishing wood that originated in a certified area from wood that was not. See, e.g., T. Rotherham (footnote 63). For a contrary view, see R. P. Vlosky and L. K. Ozanne, "Chain of Custody Vital to Certification Process," *Wood Technology*, March 13, 1995, p. 35.

84. CSFC Coalition (footnote 37).

85. See Coalition Web site, <www.sfms.com/csa.htm#chain>.

Progress in Implementation

Forest Stewardship Council

In Canada, as of early 2003, 10 forest areas were subject of FSC Certification, in locations ranging from Nova Scotia to B.C. The largest of these forest areas is about 19,180 ha; the total of all areas is a modest 35,553 ha.[86] Five of the areas are under 1,000 ha each. Though modest, FSC's progress in implementation has frequently been fraught with controversy. An 11th area, managed by J. D. Irving Ltd. at Black Duck Brook in New Brunswick, is no longer certified; in early 2000, Irving renounced its certification when it felt that the standards finally endorsed in the region were too strict because they forbid the use of biocides.[87] The Sierra Club of Canada, for its part, had been calling for the Irving certification to be withdrawn.[88] The certification of the privately owned Haliburton Forest and Wildlife Reserve in Ontario also drew some public criticism — in this case from a member of the CSA SFM System Technical Committee.[89]

In spite of international success measured in total hectares of forests certified around the world,[90] FSC has also experienced a number of administrative missteps at the international level. In its early years, FSC received some unfavourable media attention in the Netherlands when its name became associated with a controversial Costa Rican teakwood plantation.[91] More recently, FSC had to suspend the authority of one of its accredited certifiers to issue certificates because of non-compliance with FSC procedures.[92] In combination with some of the highly criticized Canadian certifications, these experiences seem to indicate an organization that has occasionally struggled with the difficult task of developing a good reputation (by associating it with valid, well-performed certification processes), while also ensuring that the name has a high profile in the marketplace.

The challenge of balancing success and credibility may have been one motivation for FSC joining with other environmental and social labelling programs in the

---

86. *Forests Certified by FSC-Accredited Certification Bodies* (footnote 3).

87. See discussion of the controversy in M. Lansky, "If Certification was the Answer, What was the Question? A Close Look at J. D. Irving and the Certification of Industrial Forestry," *Understory* 9 (Summer 1999); responses to this story are published in "Touching a Nerve," *Understory* 10 (Winter/Spring 2000). For a discussion of the Maritimes standard development process, see E. Meidinger (footnote 8), pp. 156–162.

88. Sierra Club of Canada, *Evidence Confirms Sierra Club of Canada Concerns Over Black Brook Certification Process*, press release, January 21, 2000, available at <www.sierraclub.ca/national/media/fsc-cert-concerns-00-01-21.html>.

89. See K. Armson, letter to the editor, *The Forestry Chronicle* 74 (May/June 1998), p. 284. Among the criticisms: the certification took place over only four days, in December 1997, when the forest was covered with snow; there was no completed forestry management plan; and there was no documentation to "clearly demonstrate that the rate of harvest of forest product does not exceed levels that can be sustained."

90. As of early 2003, the certified forests approached 24 million hectares in total area worldwide. See *Forests Certified by FSC-Accredited Certification Bodies* (footnote 3).

91. For more information on this controversy, see an unofficial archive of the United Nations Environment Program's Infoterra mailing list, available at <www.ee/lists/infoterra/>.

92. See World Wide Fund for Nature, *Skal's Authority Suspended to Issue FSC Certificates, Forests For Life Certification Updates*" May 2001, and *Skal's Chain-of-Custody Accreditation Reinstated*, June 2001.

International Social and Environmental Accreditation and Labelling (ISEAL) Alliance.[93] Just as FSC purports to lend credibility to individual sustainable forestry efforts, so does ISEAL offer its members the opportunity to maintain and enhance their own credibility. ISEAL has indicated that it intends to enable its members to gain credibility in the eyes of government and international trade bodies, in part by establishing transparent and professional mechanisms for peer review of member operations (see more detailed discussion in Chapter 5).

CSA SFM System

As of early 2003, 14.5 million hectares of Canadian forest had become registered to the CAN/CSA Z809 standard.[94] While this represents significantly more area than that certified by FSC, the management of the CSA forest areas is much more concentrated: the certified forest areas are managed by three major companies.

Approaches to Regulation and Their Effect upon Certification

Both standards require that forestry practices conform to domestic laws. Even if the standards contained no such obligation, forestry companies would need to comply with the law. A certification scheme's practical impact on a company's operations will heavily depend upon the extent to which the scheme's requirements are already covered by (and are compatible with) local laws. Two examples from Canadian jurisdictions (British Columbia and Ontario) serve to highlight this fact. One commentator noted that a company operating in British Columbia may have an easier task of implementing an FSC standard than would a company operating in Ontario; the reverse would be true for the CSA SFM system standards. This is because the commentator concluded that forestry regulation in B.C. to be generally more performance-based, while Ontario relies more upon a management approach.[95] Other observers point out that the tenure rights granted to companies operating in B.C. may hamper those companies' ability to make the long-term commitments necessary for certification to any of the currently available programs.[96] In either case, one point prevails: government regulation always looms in the background, and frequently in the foreground, of the certification process.

---

93. See ISEAL Alliance Web site, <www.isealalliance.org>. See also E. Meidinger, *Emerging Trans-Sectoral Regulatory Structures in Global Civil Society: The Case of ISEAL*, paper prepared for the Tools for Regulation Panel at the Joint Annual Meetings of the Law and Society Association and the Research Committee for the Sociology of Law, July 4–7, 2001, Budapest, available at <http://law.buffalo.edu/homepage/eemeid/scholarship/ISEAL.pdf>.

94. CSFC Coalition, *Certification Status and Intentions in Canada*, available at the Coalition Web site, <www.sfms.com/status.htm>.

95. P. Griss (footnote 5).

96. Brown and Greer (footnote 78), p. 113.

Attitudes of Regulators Toward Certification

The attitude of forestry regulators to voluntary certification is worthy of discussion, because regulators regularly balance the interests of industry, environmentalists, other government sectors, those people who directly depend upon the forest for their living, and those who do not. British Columbia provides an interesting focal point for discussion, because forestry is not only that province's most important industry, but is also the scene for some of the most intense conflicts among the varying interests.[97]

It would seem that any *voluntary* process would not have entered into an overly welcome legal environment in British Columbia in the early to mid-1990s. According to the provincial government's own history, the B.C. *Forest Practices Code* (the principal law governing the forest industry in the province, which was brought into force in 1995) was "a reaction to the old framework, which relied much more heavily on contractual obligations and voluntary incorporation of forest practices guidelines into operational plans and permits."[98] The Code was, in part, the product of the government's commitment to toughen its regulation of forest practices in response to growing pressure from environmental groups. The intense negative international publicity resulting from the 1993 Clayoquot Sound demonstrations seems to have been one spur to more stringent regulation.

This detailed, complex body of law has required extensive inspection measures.[99] The apparent hope was that this sort of detailed inspection and oversight regime would improve the image of B.C.'s forest industry. By many accounts, it has not achieved that objective. The Code has been criticized by industry and environmental groups. Industry complained about the paperwork, which was adding $8 to $20 to the cost of a cubic metre of wood: a company was required to file six different plans before it could proceed to log an area.[100] On the other side, environmental groups perceived the Code as ineffectual.[101]

---

97. For its part, Canada's federal government, or at least the Department of Natural Resources, has explicitly stated that it "supports" the efforts of both initiatives, even though it was actively involved in the development of only the CSA SFM System standards. See Natural Resources Canada, *Sustainable Development Strategy: Safeguarding our Assets, Securing our Future* (Ottawa: Natural Resources Canada, 1998), p. 67.

98. Kristine Weese, Research Officer, Integrated Resources Policy Branch, British Columbia Ministry of Forests, in *Introduction to the Forest Practices Code*, September 1996.

99. According to the Compliance and Enforcement Branch, the Ministry of Forests provides reports of its extensive inspection and enforcement activities. See <www.for.gov.bc.ca/hen>.

100. "B.C. Not Backsliding with Forest Practices," *Financial Post*, April 4, 1998, p. 18.

101. See, e.g., Greenpeace, *What is Happening in B.C.'s Forests* (undated, 1997?), available at <www.greenpeace.org/~comms/97/forest/logging.html>. It should be noted that the government announced an overhaul of the Code that was geared in part to reducing companies' paperwork. See P. Lush, "B.C. Forest Firms to Reap Savings. Changes to Code Will Cut Logging Costs," *The Globe and Mail*, April 3, 1998.

To judge from published reports, the Forestry Minister was frustrated by Greenpeace's efforts to convince European companies to cancel contracts unless they sought FSC certification.[102] But once MacMillan Bloedel[103] announced its intention to halt clearcutting and seek certification, the Minister became more upbeat about the FSC: "This is a positive move on the part of MacMillan Bloedel, and we're interested in working with other forest companies in this regard. ... Other recent announcements about companies seeking Forest Stewardship Council certification reflect important changes in the forest industry, which we have been encouraging and promoting through the *Forest Practices Code* and other major forestry initiatives."[104]

In September 1998, the Ministry announced a decidedly qualified position on voluntary forestry certification:

> In British Columbia, government has stated it supports voluntary certification in the marketplace if certification will support real progress in sustainable forest management. Government wants to ensure that certification is based on standards that are equally challenging and meaningful for all jurisdictions, and that certification systems are compatible with definitions, standards, and processes developed domestically and in the international arena.[105]

The position remains unchanged at the time of writing, based on a review of Ministry materials.[106]

For more detail on what it seeks from a certification system, the Ministry reverts to a set of guiding principles, agreed upon by federal, provincial and territorial governments in 1996.[107] The principles are hardly revealing, and the extent to which the CSA SFM system or the FSC conforms to some of these principles is open to debate. For instance, some of the criteria reflect the government's desire that any given certification system be fully welcomed by all major consumer markets. Obviously, this is a delicate goal that has not yet been fully achieved by either the CSA or the FSC initiative. But it is

---

102. See "British Columbia Forest Expert Calls for Certification," *Vancouver Sun*, April 3, 1998: "Forests Minister David Zirnhelt said FSC standards have no more scientific support than the standards B.C. is moving towards under the CSA process. However, he acknowledged the process of setting standards is moving too slowly."

103. MacMillan Bloedel was British Columbia's largest forest products company at the time. It was purchased by U.S.-based Weyerhaeuser Company in 1999. See Weyerhaeuser's Web site, <www.weyerhaeuser.com>.

104. Ministry of Forests (British Columbia), *Forests Minister Welcomes MacMillan Bloedel's Plan to Phase Out Clear Cutting Old Growth*, press release, June 10, 1998, available at <www.news.gov.bc.ca/hnr/content/1998/1998nr/1998045.asp>.

105. From Ministry Web site, ibid.

106. The Ministry commissioned a major comparative study of the various certification processes available, without stating any particular preference for which fit best into its regulatory framework. See P. Wood, *A Comparative Analysis of Selected International Forestry Certification Schemes* (Victoria, B.C.: Ministry of Forests, 2000), available at <www.for.gov.bc.ca/het/certification/WoodReportOct00.PDF>.

107. See *Framework of Guiding Principles For Voluntary Certification System for Sustainable Forest Management Prepared by the Federal/Provincial/Territorial Ministers Responsible for Forestry* (1992), as discussed in Brown and Green (footnote 78).

just as true that many parties have been unhappy with the *Forest Practices Code*, and it is unlikely that this situation will change as long as there are differing views on the proper use of forest resources as a source of economic wealth. To require the same of a voluntary initiative seems a lot to ask.

Conclusions

In this chapter, an attempt has been made to describe the origins of two approaches to voluntary verification of sustainable forestry management practices used in Canada, the processes of rule development, the content of the rules, implementation to date, and relations to the Canadian regulatory forestry management system. While the terms and operation of the programs differ in some respects, both seem to offer a real prospect of substantive achievement of sustainable forestry practices to those companies that adhere to their requirements. Both now offer product labelling based on chain-of-custody attribution programs.

From a Canadian perspective, the FSC initiative can be seen as a program driven originally by European consumers, created by international environmental organizations (ENGOs) working in partnership with large European (and, later, North American) retail interests, which is now in the process of regional elaboration for Canadian forestry conditions. To achieve "traction" in Canada (and in other regions where it operates), the challenge for FSC has been to attract forestry companies and not simply appeal to retailers, who to date have been its most receptive commercial constituency in North America. If measured in terms of hectares of forests that are certified as in compliance with FSC standards, success in Canada has been limited, particularly when compared with the CSA SFM program. Nevertheless, initial outright resistance by the Canadian forest industry to FSC seems to be giving way to some degree of industry acceptance. While Canadian forestry industry certification to FSC has been limited to date, several large North American and European retailers have committed themselves to purchasing FSC or similarly labelled products.

In contrast to the FSC initiative and its reception in Canada, the CSA SFM program is "home-grown," yet it too is attempting to appeal to the same largely non-Canadian (i.e. European) consumer audience. The primary sponsors of the CSA initiative have been Canadian forestry companies, using the services of the Canadian Standards Association. As a recognized standards development body, the CSA is under an obligation to develop standards in an open way through a balanced matrix. A key challenge has been to find ways of attracting ENGO support, particularly from the high-profile international ENGOs that are backing the FSC. (Indeed, the refusal of many ENGOs to participate in the CSA process, or the withdrawal of participation of some of these ENGOs, would most appear to resemble a boycott of the process.) These ENGOs have shown themselves to be wary of what they perceive as an industry-driven process. Some have also suggested that part of the discomfort may stem from the fact that the development of many environmental norms has a higher public policy content than most technical standards, which traditionally have been the bread-and-butter of conventional standards developers. In a report prepared for CSA, Terry Burrell observes that the development of environmental standards involves:

> ... broad policy issues in a way that technical standard setting does not.
> ... Public policy making has demands and constraints appropriate to a
> different form and style of consultation. It requires the commitment to
> a distinct brand of stakeholder consultation, including a commitment to
> transparency and a willingness to do what is necessary to ensure that
> the appropriate interests are represented in decision making. It can also
> involve a willingness to entertain questions about scope and purpose
> and be open to alternative ways of looking at issues.[108]

While participation in and support of the CSA SFM initiative from high profile international ENGOs has been slow in coming, the program has been more successful in terms of total hectares of forests committed to compliance with its provisions. Subsequent environmental standards development activity of CSA seems to have received a more positive reception from ENGOs, suggesting that the CSA has learned from the SFM experience and adjusted its processes in a manner more conducive to ENGO participation.[109] The ultimate acceptance, credibility and sustainability of either SFM initiative in the marketplace is unclear at this time.

As Ben Cashore of the Yale School of Forestry and Environmental Studies has discussed in several recent publications,[110] the two programs have from the outset struggled for legitimacy in the eyes of several constituencies.[111] Cashore describes similar struggles for legitimacy taking place in other jurisdictions. He suggests that, in the early days of FSC operation, with few exceptions, forestry companies and landowners gave pragmatic[112] and moral[113] legitimacy to industry-driven (e.g. CSA SFM, or the American

---

108. Burrell, (footnote 53), p. 29.

109. Environmental groups were said to have been hesitant to participate in the development of Z770, an environmental assessment standard that was spearheaded by the federal government (rather than by industry). The Environmental Assessment Caucus of the Canadian Environmental Network was convinced to participate, with a promise that it could choose six of the eight Technical Committee representatives in the environmental/general interest category. This is according to Nathalie Séguin of the Canadian Environmental Assessment Agency, in communication with the authors. Note, however, that this standard is essentially domestic in scope with no evident international market implications.

110. For example, B. Cashore, "Legitimacy and the Privatization of Environmental Governance: How Non State Market-Driven (NSMD) Governance Systems (Certification Eco-labelling Programs) Gain Rule Making Authority," *Governance: An International Journal of Policy, Administration and Institutions* 15:4 (October 2002), pp. 503–529; Bernstein and Cashore (footnote 11).

111. Cashore, in "Legitimacy and the Privatization of Environmental Governance," ibid., defines legitimacy as "... a generalized perception or assumption that the actions of an entity are desirable, proper, or appropriate within some socially constructed system of norms, values, beliefs and definitions." In so doing, he is quoting Mark Suchman, "Managing Legitimacy: Strategic and Institutional Approaches," *Academy of Management Review* 20 (1995) pp. 571–610, p. 574.

112. Cashore, ibid., defines *pragmatic legitimacy* as resting on "self-interested calculations of an organization's most immediate audiences."

113. *Moral legitimacy* reflects a "positive normative evaluation of the organization and its activities. It rests not on judgments about whether a given activity promotes the goals of the evaluator, but rather on judgements about whether the activity is 'the right thing to do'." Cashore, ibid., drawing on Suchman (footnote 111).

Forestry and Paper Sustainable Forestry Initiative), as opposed to ENGO-driven SFM programs such as FSC, but that since 1998 the supply-side audience in B.C. and the United Kingdom has started to give the FSC pragmatic legitimacy. Cashore concludes that forestry companies are more likely to support the FSC program if:

- there is a high reliance on foreign markets, since these international buyers can make demands for FSC wood without risking political backlash that domestic companies might experience; and
- forest management practices in a region have reached the status of "problem" on the policy agenda, so that FSC is seen as a way to gain "social licence" and thus resolve the problem.[114]

On the other hand, a high level of forest industry sector group cohesion was identified by Cashore as being closely related to the ability of such supply-side interests to resist the pressure for FSC certification. This appears to have been the historical situation in both Canada and the United States, although this resistance seems to be lessening over time.

Arguably, the single most significant observation emerging from the foregoing examination of the FSC and CSA SFM experience in Canada is that international ENGOs have flexed their muscles and moved from being, at best, invited (and, often, token or tolerated) participants in government- or industry-led policy initiatives, to powerful rule makers and implementors in their own right,[115] or sought-after participants in government- and industry-led initiatives. This transformation from bit-player to kingpin seems to have occurred as a result of several factors:

- ENGO frustration with, in their eyes, the inadequate development and implementation of conventional public law instruments at both the international[116] and domestic[117] level;
- a decrease in public confidence in government — particularly its regulatory efforts — aided no doubt by mounting evidence of its fallibility;[118]

---

114. Cashore, ibid.

115. See discussion of allegations of anti-competitive behaviour of an FSC "buyers group" in the United Kingdom, in Kernaghan Webb and Andrew Morrison, "The Law and Voluntary Codes: Examining the 'Tangled Web'," Chapter 5, above.

116. As noted earlier, one reason for ENGO movement on market-driven SFM initiatives was frustration with the lack of progress at the 1992 Earth Summit toward development of an international agreement on forestry conservation (see footnote 11).

117. See earlier discussion of ENGO criticisms of the B.C. regulatory regime.

118. For example, the tainted blood scandals in several jurisdictions, the U.K. mad cow and foot-and-mouth disease containment problems, the Nova Scotia Westray mining disaster, and the Walkerton, Ontario, water tragedy are recent examples of incidents in which regulatory failure was identified as at least a contributing factor to the problem.

- increased public confidence in NGOs as credible sources of information, and public interest watchdogs;[119]
- recognition by ENGOs of an opportunity to exploit a market niche.[120]

These points are perhaps no more clearly demonstrated than with recent announcements by Canadian provincial and American state governments that they themselves are obtaining or have obtained certification from FSC and its related entity, the Marine Stewardship Council, for their private forestry and fishery resource management regulatory regimes.[121] In effect, such actions seem to represent government acknowledgment that, as currently operated, their regulatory regimes are lacking in some element of public credibility, and that ENGO-led certification schemes might assist them in providing that needed credibility.

Not only do these actions demonstrate a commodification of environmental values (an old story[122]), but also a commodification of ENGOs themselves (who have, through the creation of their spin-off private regulatory bodies such as FSC and the Marine Stewardship Council, attempted to transform their credibility as critics of public policy into a marketable rule-and-label commodity) and even a commodification of regulatory regimes. In keeping with this notion of commodification and markets, there is

---

119. "Public surveys reveal that NGOs often enjoy a high degree of public trust, which can make them a useful — but not always sufficient — proxy for the concerns of society and stakeholders." International Institute for Sustainable Development, *Business and Sustainable Development: A Global Guide*, at <www.bsdglobal.com/ngo/roles.asp>.

120. In "The NGO-Industrial Complex," *Foreign Policy* July–August 2001, authors Gary Gereffi, Ronie Garcie-Johnson, and Erika Sasser of Duke University state:

> NGOs have become highly sophisticated in using market-campaigning techniques to gain leverage over recalcitrant firms. Market campaigning, which focuses protests against highly visible branded retailers, is only about 10 years old, but in the words of one Greenpeace activist, "it was like discovering gunpowder for environmentalists."

121. In March 2001, "The Honourable John Snobelen, Minister of Natural Resources for the province of Ontario, and Dr. Maharaj Muthoo, Executive Director of the Forest Stewardship Council (FSC), initiated a bilanteral process that will result in FSC certification of all Crown-owned forests managed in compliance with Ontario law and the products derived from those forests." Per Ontario Ministry of Natural Resources, *Ontario First in World to Receive Environmental Forest Certification*, press release, March 23, 2001. E. Meidinger, in "Environmental Certification Programs and U.S. Environmental Law: Closer Than You May Think," *Environmental Law Reporter* 31 (2001), pp. 10162–10179, p. 10169, reports sources indicating that the agencies responsible for managing State-owned lands in Minnesota, New York and Pennsylvania have either achieved Forest Stewardship Council certification or announced they intended to do so. The State of Alaska's commercial salmon fisheries management program has been certified as sustainable by the non-governmental Marine Stewardship Council, pursuant to its sustainable fishery standards. See Office of the Governor of Alaska, *Alaska's Salmon Fishery Certified as Sustainable*, press release, (September 5, 2000). Note that the Marine Stewardship Council differs in significant respects from the FSC.

122. See discussion of the history of environmental product labels in K. Harrison, "Promoting Environmental Protection Through Eco-Labelling: An Evaluation of Canada's Environmental Choice Program," Chapter 10, below.

now a high degree of domestic and international competition among public and private rule-making bodies — be they ENGO-led regimes, or those of conventional standards bodies, industry associations or governments — concerning who is the most credible and why.[123]

These activities represent a blurring of public and private spheres, or a "hybridization of law and market, state and non-state,"[124] which has led some commentators to suggest that a new conception of "government" is needed, capable of encompassing "the entire complex of ideals, goals, rationales, techniques, procedures and programs by which a diversity of state and non-state authorities seek to shape human conduct to desired ends."[125] In this broader sense, it is possible for non-State actors such as ENGOs to use "governmental technologies"[126] to achieve their aims. Arguably, the FSC represents a good example of a "governmental technology" employed by ENGOs: through trial and error, the FSC has developed into a fairly conventional bureaucratic rule-making and implementation structure, and indeed there are indications that, in an effort to be seen as acceptable for trade purposes, it will become even more conventional in its operations.[127] Thus, an ENGO-spearheaded body is submitting to the "discipline" of an intergovernmental rule regime (World Trade Organization) in an effort to be seen as acceptable by governments and others.

As ENGOs develop rule-making and development bodies, some familiar questions arise. Just how accountable and transparent are these bodies in their decision-making processes? Are there meaningful opportunities for all affected parties to participate in their decision making? And what is the basis for their decisions?[128] These, of course, are the very questions ENGOs have asked for years of governments. Looked at from this broader perspective, it is not clear whether bodies such as FSC will eventually represent the triumph of ENGOs over governments and the private sector, or the reverse, since in the final analysis it is not apparent that an ENGO-led body subject to the same

123. A similar point is made by T. Walde in "Non-Conventional Views on Effectiveness: The Holy Grail of Modern International Lawyers," *Austrian Review of International & European Law* 4 (1999), pp. 164–203, p. 201.

124. S. Wood, "Green Revolution or Greenwash? Voluntary Environmental Standards, Public Law and Private Authority in Canada," in *New Perspectives on the Public-Private Divide* (Vancouver: UBC Press, 2004)..

125. Wood, ibid, drawing on, among others, M. Foucault, "Governmentality," in G. Burchell, C. Gordon and P. Miller, eds., *The Foucault Effect* (Chicago: Chicago University Press, 1991), pp. 87–104, and N. Rose and P. Miller, "Political Power Beyond the State: Problematics of Government," *British Journal of Sociology* 43 (1992), p. 173.

126. Wood, ibid.

127. The FSC and the Marine Stewardship Council are both members of the ISEAL (International Social and Environmental Accreditation and Labelling) Alliance, which has the express purpose of positive environmental and social change "through the implementation of international standards-setting and accreditation systems that comply with internationally accepted criteria; that do not act as technical barriers to trade. ..." See ISEAL Alliance, "Mission Statement," *Membership Requirements: Public Requirements*, Public Draft 2 (July 4, 2001), available from the ISEAL Web site, <www.isealalliance.org>. ISEAL, and the implications of the trade agreements such as those of the World Trade Organization, are discussed in greater detail in Webb and Morrison, "The Law and Voluntary Codes," Chapter 5, above.

128. See, e.g., A. Warleigh, "NGOs: More Influence Means More Responsibility," *Consumer Policy Review* 11:3 (2001), pp. 101–104. See also A. Adair, *A Code of Conduct for NGOs: A Necessary Reform* (London: Institute for Economic Affairs, 1999).

fairness, accountability, accessibility and transparency constraints as governments and conventional standards bodies will operate in a manner markedly different from how governments and conventional standards bodies operate.

Now that ENGOs are acting as rule makers and rule implementors, it is reasonable to predict that they will experience many of the same problems that have plagued more conventional rule-making and implementation bodies, such as regulatory agencies and state-supported standards bodies — that is, they too will be subject to the usual array of allegations of unfairness, conflicts of interest, corruption and incompetence, some well founded, some not. When these problems arise, then the credibility of these ENGO-supported organizations will inevitably be tested, and will likely diminish. Like a film critic who becomes a director, the barbs will now be pointed in the other direction. Just how sustainable such initiatives will be in the long-term, once some of these problems do arise, remains to be seen.

In the final analysis, as is common with other market goods, the public has more choice as to rule makers now that ENGOs have entered the field (and governments and conventional standards bodies have new competition). It is probably a choice the public would prefer not to have, but as confidence in governments has diminished, an opening has been created for others to fill the gap. Whether ENGO spin-off bodies such as FSC can maintain the aura of legitimacy, and adjust to the constraints they are subject to as rule makers is an open question. Undoubtedly, governments and conventional standards bodies will respond to the competition as well.[129] While it is too early to predict exactly what will happen, a likely scenario is that ENGO-supported bodies such as FSC will become established and accepted standards developers, conventional standards organizations will adjust their processes and perspectives to become more amenable to the more policy-oriented work of environmental, labour and human rights standards, and governments as well as other stakeholders will draw on the services of both as they feel is appropriate in the circumstances.

---

129. For example, the Technical Committee of ISO that is responsible for development of environmental management standards (ISO 14000) is currently sponsoring research led by ENGOs concerning how to improve the functioning of the committee.

Chapter 10
Promoting Environmental Protection Through Eco-Labelling: An Evaluation of Canada's Environmental Choice Program

Kathryn Harrison[1]

Introduction

When Canada's Environmental Choice Program was established in 1988, it was at the leading edge of an international eco-labelling movement. The Environmental Choice Program seeks to harness market forces to achieve environmental protection by helping environmentally aware consumers identify products that are less harmful to the environment. The Program does so by licensing manufacturers of preferred products to display the "EcoLogo" as a symbol of their products' reduced burden on the environment. The logo depicts three doves intertwined to form a maple leaf, the doves representing the three Program partners: government, industry and consumers.

Eco-labelling programs are distinguished by a number of characteristics.[2] First, in contrast to government-mandated warnings on cigarette packages and nutritional labels on food packaging, participation in an eco-labelling program is completely voluntary. Indeed, manufacturers must pay for the right to display the logo and demonstrate continued adherence to relevant product guidelines to maintain their licences. The approach thus has been hailed as an innovative voluntary alternative to more coercive policy instruments, including mandatory product labelling and regulation of process discharges and product quality. Second, eco-labels convey only positive information about a product or service. No effort is made to flag products that are especially hazardous to the environment; negative labelling of that sort would clearly be infeasible in a voluntary program. Third, eco-labels are, ideally, awarded by independent third parties (governmental or private). This distinguishes them from environmental labels that firms may include on their own products.[3]

Contemporary eco-labelling programs represent an evolution of environmentally oriented product claims popular in the 1970s, including claims of energy efficiency and organic farming methods. A critical distinction is that while earlier labelling efforts were largely directed at consumers' immediate self-interest, the second generation of labelling programs rely more heavily on consumers' altruism, that is, their willingness to consider

1. I would like to thank the many people who granted interviews and/or provided comments on earlier drafts, David Cohen and Allan McChesney for sharing documents, and Aaron Delaney and Barb Everdene for research assistance.

2. Environmental Protection Agency (EPA; U.S.), *Environmental Labelling: Issues, Policies, and Practices Worldwide* (Washington: EPA, 1998).

3. Ibid. Arguably, eco-labelling programs are also distinguished by their focus on multiple product categories and multiple attributes of products within each product category, which distinguishes them from programs that focus on a single attribute (such as recycled content) or a single product category (such as lumber).

Kernaghan Webb, Editor, *Voluntary Codes: Private Governance, the Public Interest and Innovation.*
This chapter ©2004 Kathryn Harrison, pages 273–298.
Published by the Carleton Research Unit for Innovation, Science and Environment, Carleton University, Ottawa, Canada.

environmental impacts felt by all members of society, even though the direct benefits to themselves may be outweighed by higher product costs.[4] This reliance on consumer altruism is both a strength of the new programs and, as discussed below, a potential limit to their effectiveness.

This chapter seeks to evaluate the effectiveness of this new approach. However, it is first necessary to review the concept of eco-labelling, the history of the Environmental Choice Program, and brief case studies of several product guidelines.

The Concept of Eco-Labelling

Why Eco-Labels?

West Germany was the first country to launch an environmental labelling program when it introduced the "Blue Angel" in 1978. By 1999, the German program included roughly 4000 labelled products in 86 product categories.[5] Ten years later, Canada's Environmental Choice Program was the second national eco-labelling program. It was followed closely by two dozen other eco-labelling initiatives in both industrialized and developing countries.[6]

Eco-labelling programs emerged in response to two factors. First, a rise in environmental consciousness among consumers in the late 1980s and early 1990s prompted a deluge of self-proclaimed "green" products. In 1990, 81 percent of Canadians reported a willingness to pay a 10 percent premium for more environmentally friendly products.[7] Manufacturers responded to this consumer demand enthusiastically. Although "green" products constituted only 0.5 percent of new products in 1985, that figure had increased to 9.2 percent by early 1990.[8] Indeed, one study found that 26 percent of new household products in 1990 made environment-related claims.[9]

The second factor was the subsequent emergence of widespread consumer skepticism regarding manufacturers' claims of environmental friendliness. At the limit, some claims involved outright deception; other product claims were merely vague, selective, or misunderstood. An Australian study reported that two thirds of environmental claims on dishwashing liquids were meaningless or incomplete,[10] while

---

4. Organisation for Economic Co-operation and Development (OECD), *Environmental Labelling in OECD Countries* (Paris: OECD, 1991).

5. Information gleaned from the Blue Angel Web site, <www.blauer-engel.de/englisch/navigation/body_blauer_engel.htm>.

6. See Environmental Protection Agency (footnote 2) and the Global Ecolabelling Network Web site, <www.gen.gr.jp/germany.html>.

7. "Synopsis: The Environmental Monitor," prepared for the Environmental Choice Program, November 1993.

8. J. Salzman, "Green Labels for Consumers," *The OECD Observer* 169, pp. 29–30, p. 29.

9. J. Fierman, "The Big Muddle in Green Marketing," *Fortune*, June 3, 1991, pp. 91–101.

10. M. J. Polonsk and J. Bailey, et al., "Communicating Environmental Information: Are Marketing Claims on Packaging Misleading?" *Journal of Business Ethics* 17 (1998), pp. 281–294.

U.S. national surveys found that only half of respondents demonstrated basic comprehension of the widely used terms "recycled" and "recyclable."[11]

The result was that consumers became increasingly mistrustful of manufacturers' environmental claims. Various studies reported that between 42 percent and 56 percent of consumers "dismiss environmental claims as 'mere gimmickry' or believe that brands advertised as environmentally benign are no better for the environment."[12] Policy makers became concerned that consumer distrust would undermine the potential benefits of the green marketing movement. As David Cohen observed, "A distrustful public with no way of verifying environmental benefit claims may be prone to ignore even those that are legitimately made and to continue to use those products that give them the best immediate results, irrespective of their environmental value, in their quest to get clothes whiter, dishes cleaner, and infants diapered more conveniently."[13]

The extent of consumer deception and confusion is consistent with two types of market failure. The first is information asymmetry. Many environmental impacts of consumer goods can be considered "credence" qualities. In other words, consumers can neither assess the environmental impact of the product through inspection in advance of purchase, nor increase their knowledge through frequent purchase. The second market failure is that information about the environment, like the environment itself, is in many respects a public good. While the societal benefits of collecting information about a product's environmental impacts may well exceed the costs, the benefits to a single consumer do not exceed the costs to that individual of conducting a detailed life-cycle assessment of each product he or she buys. Consumers thus rationally decline to conduct extensive research to verify manufacturers' environmental claims.

The problems of consumer confusion and deception spawned two simultaneous policy responses. The first was increased regulation of green advertising. Efforts were made in many jurisdictions to crack down on deceptive claims as well as to promote greater standardization of the use of common terms such as "recycled" and "biodegradable." Consumer and Corporate Affairs Canada published its Guiding Principles for Environmental Labelling and Advertising in 1991 to clarify for advertisers what the government considers to be false and misleading representations or labels under the *Competition Act* and the *Consumer Packaging and Labelling Act*.[14] The Canadian Standards Association also developed a private standard, Guidelines on Environmental Labelling, in 1993 to help advertisers voluntarily seeking to go beyond minimum

---

11. L. Morris, M. Hastak and M. B. Mazis, "Consumer Comprehension of Environmental Advertising and Labelling Claims," *Journal of Consumer Affairs* 29:2 (Winter 1995), pp. 328–350.

12. J. M. Church, "A Market Solution to Green Marketing: Some Lessons from the Economics of Information," *Minnesota Law Review* 79 (1994), pp. 245–324, p. 285.

13. D. Cohen, "The Regulation of Green Advertising: The State, the Market, and the Environmental Good," *UBC. Law Review* 25 (1991), pp. 225–276, pp. 240–241.

14. Consumer and Corporate Affairs Canada (CCAC), *Principles and Guidelines for Environmental Labelling and Advertising* (Ottawa: CCAC, 1991), available at <http://strategis.ic.gc.ca/pics/cp/envguide.pdf>. Most of the functions of the former CCAC were incorporated into the newly created Industry Canada in 1995.

compliance with the law.[15] In 2001, the federal Competition Bureau proposed to replace these Guidelines as its reference point for compliance with a new National Standard for self-declared environmental claims.[16]

The second policy response was the creation of eco-labelling programs. The intent of eco-labels is to go beyond merely ensuring that advertisers' claims are not misleading. Rather, the objective is to interpret a vast array of information on environmental impacts and present the conclusions to consumers in the form of a simple and credible label.

How Eco-Labels Work

Eco-labelling programs seek to achieve their primary goal of reducing environmental impacts via two market-based mechanisms. The first is to encourage consumers to purchase less harmful products and thus to increase the market share of those products relative to more environmentally harmful alternatives. The second is to encourage manufacturers to redesign their products to reduce their environmental impact. As the market share of "green" products is enhanced by the eco-label, there is an incentive for competitors who did not qualify to reformulate their products to compete. Consistent with this second mechanism, an essential feature of most eco-labelling programs is a commitment to regularly review and, as appropriate, strengthen product criteria to ensure continuing incentives for improvement for licensees and their competitors alike.

Most eco-labelling programs follow a similar approach. First, categories of products or services are selected for development of guidelines. Issues for consideration in selecting product categories include potential interest in the logo among consumers and producers of the product and potential for environmental improvements. The second step is development of product or process criteria for chosen product categories. Criteria are usually based on a simplified model of life-cycle assessment, which in its ideal form attempts to evaluate all environmental impacts of a product (e.g. on soil, air, water and resources) at all stages of the life cycle, from resource extraction, through manufacture, to product use and disposal. Although many early eco-labelling guidelines were based on a small number of factors, indeed often just one,[17] in recent years most eco-labelling programs have moved toward multi-criteria guidelines that approximate life-cycle assessment. The third step is licensing of products after evaluation of individual manufacturers' applications relative to the relevant product guidelines. Finally, eco-labelling programs to varying degrees monitor compliance with licensing agreements and apply contractual sanctions in response to non-compliance.

---

15. Canadian Standards Association, *Guideline on Environmental Labelling Z761-93* (Toronto: Canadian Standards Association, 1993).

16. For details of this proposal, see Competition Bureau (Canada), *Proposed Adoption of New Environmental Labelling and Advertising Guidelines*, July 10, 2001. See also Canadian Standards Association, *14021-00 Environmental Labels and Declarations: Self-Declared Environmental Claims,* CAN/CSA-ISO14021-00 (Toronto: Canadian Standards Association, 2000).

17. OECD (footnote 4), p. 19.

A critical issue in program design is the form of the eco-label. A number of options have been considered, ranging from a simple seal, like Canada's EcoLogo, to graded seals (e.g. offering one, two or three "stars"), to report card-type labels offering more plentiful information. The obvious advantage of a single symbol of certification is its simplicity. Once consumers are familiar with the logo, it can serve as an effective prompt to alert environmentally conscious consumers to opportunities to choose products that are less environmentally harmful. Simplicity has its drawbacks, however. A single level of certification does not allow a consumer to distinguish among products bearing the logo, thus limiting their ability to promote environmental improvements. Indeed, if there is sufficient variability among the products that qualify for the logo, an eco-label could actually have a *negative* impact on the environment if it prompts an increase in the market share of "browner" firms relative to "greener" ones.[18] This problem could be mitigated, though not eliminated, by a system of graded logos. Another drawback is that while a simple seal facilitates consumers' desire to "do good," it does not enhance their understanding of what doing good involves.[19] A coalition of U.S. businesses opposed to eco-labelling thus has argued that affixing a simple logo is "akin to a food label that simply says 'good for you,' rather than providing objective information about calories, fat and sodium content."[20]

An alternative to a simple logo is a more complex labelling system, like the U.S. Scientific Certification Systems' "Eco-Profile."[21] The most obvious benefit of a report card approach is that more information is provided, which can help to educate consumers about the environmental implications of their purchases. It may also encounter less political resistance, since trade associations tend to be more receptive to a report card approach that can apply to the products of all their members, rather than just those deemed to be environmental leaders. A report card also allows consumers to assign their own weights to different types of environmental impacts, rather than relying on the value judgments of a certification board. However, even complex reporting systems still involve extensive judgment calls (e.g. concerning which impacts to report and how), so claims of total objectivity are unjustified.[22] The greatest problem with providing additional information, however, is the reduced likelihood that consumers will actually read and act on it.[23] Consumers confronted with detailed information may simply ignore

---

18. A. Nadai and B. Morel, *Product Ecolabelling, Competition, and the Environment*, Working Paper 82.2000 (Milan: Fondazione Eni Enrico Mattei, 2000).

19. R. D. Wynne, "Defining 'Green': Toward Regulation of Environmental Marketing Claims," *University of Michigan Journal of Law Reform* 24 (Spring and Summer 1991), pp. 785–820, p. 820.

20. B. Wildavsky, "Sticker Shock," *National Journal*, March 9, 1996, pp. 532–535.

21. A description of the program is available in Environmental Protection Agency (footnote 2), pp. B-173–B-178.

22. See Wynne (footnote 19).

23. Wynne, ibid., pp. 98 and 119. Various studies showing that parsimonious labels generally are more effective are summarized in S. Hadden, *Read the Label: Reducing Risk by Providing Information* (Boulder, Colo.: Westview Press, 1986), Chapter 9. Although Hadden reports that detailed labels enhance understanding when the information provided has high salience for consumers, given the collective goods nature of environmental impacts, one would expect eco-labels to have relatively low salience for most consumers.

it or, alternatively, mistakenly assume that the mere presence of the label is indicative of environmental benefits.[24]

After weighing the pros and cons of these alternative approaches, the vast majority of eco-labelling programs have opted for a single symbol to indicate certification. However, report cards have had some impact further up the supply chain, where firms typically contract for frequent and large-scale purchases and thus may be more willing to invest in analysis of more detailed information.[25]

Evaluating the Effectiveness of Eco-Labels

The primary goal of eco-labelling programs is to reduce the environmental impacts of consumer goods and services by increasing the market share of environmentally preferred products without increasing consumption overall. However, it is important to recognize that eco-labels tend to have an impact at the margin. If consumers demand less environmentally harmful products, manufacturers will have incentives to produce such products and to advertise their products' environmental assets, with or without eco-labels. An eco-label will enhance the market share of a labelled product only to the extent that consumers mistrust comparable information provided by the manufacturer, competitors or other information sources, such as interest groups and the media. It is noteworthy that just as the environmental attributes of a product are "credence" goods, so too is the eco-label itself.[26] Shoppers confronting an eco-label are in no better position to assess the validity of the label than the producer's own claims. The impact of an eco-label thus rests squarely on its credibility with consumers *relative to* other sources of comparable information.

Rigorous measurement of the environmental benefits of an eco-label would require data on the environmental burden posed by different products throughout their life cycle, as well as analysis of the impact of the eco-label on the market share of both labelled and unlabelled products, controlling for other factors, such as manufacturers' own marketing strategies, that might also cause concurrent changes in consumption patterns. Such an analysis is impracticable since data concerning the market impact of eco-labels are difficult to obtain, and when data do exist, are typically confidential among participating firms.[27] In the absence of direct evidence, one can consider several secondary criteria for evaluation of eco-labelling programs. Environmental effectiveness requires that certification standards meaningfully distinguish between labelled and unlabelled products based on their environmental impacts, that environmentally aware

24. The Good Housekeeping Seal of Approval serves as an example. Although the seal means only that the product manufacturer is willing to grant a refund to dissatisfied consumers, many consumers mistakenly perceive that the seal is based on rigorous product testing and evaluation. (See further discussion in Kernaghan Webb and David Clarke, "Voluntary Codes in the United States, the European Union and Developing Countries," Chapter 13, below.)

25. Environmental Protection Agency (footnote 2).

26. A. Nadai, "Conditions for the Development of a Product Ecolabel," *European Environment* 9 (1999), pp. 201–211.

27. Organisation for Economic Co-operation and Development, *Eco-Labelling: Actual Effects of Selected Programmes*, document ECDE/GD(97)105 (Paris: OECD, 1997).

consumers recognize and trust the logo, and that they be willing to purchase products bearing the eco-label. In addition to environmental effectiveness, one can also evaluate eco-labelling programs based on their transparency and openness to various interests, both of which also support soundness and credibility of standards.[28] The following discussion considers the issues of standard setting and credibility in greater detail.

Standard Setting

Setting Sound Standards

The greener the product, the greater the opportunity to lessen the burden on the environment by shifting consumers to that product. However, the task of developing product criteria is not as simple as choosing the most strict standards technically achievable.[29] Assuming, all else being equal, that reducing the environmental burden of a product increases its cost, one can expect that beyond some point the demand for a product will decrease the "greener" and thus more expensive that product becomes.[30] Eco-labellers thus face an optimization problem. If a standard is too strict, few products will be labelled and few consumers will be willing to pay the necessary premium for them, thus resulting in minimal environmental impact. If a standard is too lax, almost all products will qualify without reformulation. Consumers may well buy products bearing the logo, but in most cases they will be the same products that they bought before, and there will thus be negligible environmental benefit.

In order to address this optimization problem, those establishing product guidelines ideally need extensive information on the implications of different criteria for environmental impacts, product costs and consumer demand. Since such information is seldom available in practice, most programs instead choose a target level of market eligibility for compliance. For instance, the Environmental Choice Program has tried to set guidelines so that roughly 20 percent of products in a category are initially eligible.[31] However, while market share provides a convenient rule of thumb in seeking optimal stringency of standards, it should be noted that there is in fact no reason to assume that the same market share would be optimal for all product categories in light of different control cost functions and consumer sensitivity to price changes. Adoption of a target market share thus should not replace efforts to obtain reliable information on elasticity of demand and the environmental impacts and costs of alternative product or process designs.

---

28. Although cost-effectiveness of operations may also be relevant, particularly when the public purse is involved, it is noteworthy that it is not the task of eco-labelling programs to pursue economic efficiency by balancing environmental improvements and economic costs. With a voluntary eco-labelling program, that task is left to individual consumers, who assess their own willingness to pay for environmental improvements.

29. D. Cohen, "Procedural Fairness and Incentive Programs: Reflections on the Environmental Choice Program," *Alberta Law Review* 31 (1993), pp. 544–574.

30. This is a reasonable assumption, since if environmental protection were free, manufacturers would by now all have responded to consumer demand with environmentally benign products.

31. The Hickling Corporation, *Evaluation of the Environmental Choice Program: Final Report*, prepared for Environment Canada, November 29, 1993.

An important challenge for eco-labelling programs is that this essential expertise rests largely within the industry. Eco-labelling programs thus rely heavily on industry cooperation in developing guidelines. However, they typically invite participation of other interests as well, including representatives of environmental and consumer groups, who can offer additional expertise concerning environmental impacts and consumer demand. The independence of decision making from any of these interests is critical. Undue influence of environmentalists or industry could yield standards that are either too strict or too lax. Industry influence presents a greater concern for most eco-labelling programs, however, since industry participants in the process typically substantially outnumber consumer and environmental group representatives.

The challenge lies in the fact that different manufacturers within a product category face different incentives concerning the eco-label. The "greenest" manufacturers can be expected to seek standards reflecting the characteristics of their current products and production processes, though no stricter. Less environmentally progressive manufacturers may still perceive potential for a boost in sales, or may fear a loss in sales to competitors who qualify for the eco-label, but will resist investing in product or process redesign to qualify for it. They can thus be expected to lobby for weaker product criteria.[32] Moreover, given the complexity of life-cycle analysis, manufacturers with processes or products with different characteristics can be expected to disagree about the weighting of criteria associated with different environmental impacts. For instance, paper manufacturers who have invested in recycling capacity will emphasize recycled content, while those who have invested in new bleaching processes will place greater emphasis on dioxin discharges.

How such differences are resolved will depend on who is involved in decision making and what decision rules are adopted. A decision rule of consensus will tend to yield standards at the lowest common denominator (or no standards at all), since the least environmentally progressive firm can block consensus and thus effectively veto any standards it considers too strict.[33] Even with a majority decision rule, "green" industries and environmental and consumer advocates could be overruled if "brown" industry representatives are greater in number, a not unrealistic scenario if one recalls that many programs seek to establish standards at a level that 80 percent of products do not meet.

Credibility and Program Design

A contentious issue in program design is the degree to which the State should be involved in establishing and operating eco-labelling programs. Church has argued that government sponsorship of eco-labelling programs is unnecessary because producers have sufficient incentives to provide information that consumers want, and, if necessary,

---

32. Nadai and Morel (footnote 18) note an important exception. Although deadlock on standards can be expected between "green" and "brown" firms in a heterogeneous industry in which each firm produces a single product in a given product category, in a homogenous industry in which each firm produces multiple products with a range of environmental characteristics, an eco-label has the potential to increase each firm's profits. Compromise on effective standards thus can be more readily achieved.

33. Although "green" participants, such as environmentalists and consumer representatives, would also have a veto, it would be less useful to them, since exercising their veto would result in an undesirable outcome, from their perspective, of no standards at all.

to turn to credible non-governmental third parties to reassure skeptical consumers.[34] Private eco-labelling initiatives have emerged in the United States. Why then has government involvement been the norm in most eco-labelling programs established to date?

The most obvious advantage of public sector eco-labelling programs is that government involvement can bring the credibility that is critical to success. Both independence and the perception of independence from industry may be more readily achieved by government programs, in large part because they do not face the same temptation as private certifiers to relax product standards in order to attract licensees and thus increase revenues.[35] Concerns have also been raised about the secretive operations of some private eco-labelling firms, and there is apparently greater confidence that government standard-setting processes will be more transparent and open to diverse interests.[36] On closer examination, however, these claims are not so straightforward. A government-run program may still be tempted to relax standards to attract licensees if there is an expectation that it will be self-financing.[37] Perhaps a greater threat to independence is the potential for political interference, particularly in response to lobbying by industries that do not qualify for the label and thus fear a loss of market share.[38] Another potential drawback of government programs is that public-sector rules may yield cumbersome processes with lengthy consultations and layers of approvals.[39]

In theory, private-sector programs offer greater flexibility of operations, as well as the potential for competition to stimulate efficiencies and innovation.[40] However, these strengths are also easily overstated. The protracted deliberations of government-run programs may simply be the price of greater transparency and openness. Indeed, the non-governmental U.S. Green Seal program,[41] which has adopted a very open and consultative process to promote the credibility of its standards, appears to be no quicker at developing guidelines than its public-sector counterparts in other countries. Competition may also have its downsides, since competition among labels may confuse consumers and undermine their collective impact. While a lack of credibility may be problematic for for-profit private programs, independent non-profit programs may offer comparable or greater credibility than government certification, particularly if the government in question has a weak reputation for environmental protection. Efforts by a

---

34. Church (footnote 12).

35. J. Grodsky, "Certified Green: The Law and Future of Environmental Labelling," *The Yale Journal on Regulation* 10 (1993), pp. 147–227, p. 209.

36. R. D. Wynne, "The Emperor's New Eco-Logos? A Critical Review of the Scientific Certification Systems Environmental Report Card and the Green Seal Certification Mark Programs," *Virginia Environmental Law Journal* 14 (1994), pp. 51–149.

37. It should be acknowledged, however, that both private and public certifiers face cross-pressure to maintain high standards in order to ensure the credibility of the logo, and thus its long-term economic viability.

38. The Hickling Corporation (footnote 31).

39. The Hickling Corporation, ibid., pp. 4–7, notes that, operating within Environment Canada, the Environmental Choice Program was constrained in its marketing efforts by government requirements for approval of advertising campaigns.

40. Grodsky (footnote 35).

41. See Green Seal program Web site, <www.greenseal.org>.

leading Swedish environmental group to certify "dioxin-free" disposable diapers and other sanitary paper products were quite influential in expanding the European market for such products, before the government-run Nordic Swan program was even established. However, although such programs can take steps to insulate their decision making from industry influence — for instance, the Green Seal program does not permit representatives of manufacturing companies to sit on the Board lest they bias the process toward weaker standards[42] — the potential financial influence of licensees remains problematic.

The foregoing discussion identifies two alternatives: government and private programs, with for-profit and non-profit variants of the latter. However, as the following case study of the Environmental Choice Program reveals, hybrid models are also conceivable, depending on the mix of private-sector and government involvement with respect to funding, standard setting and administration.

Evolution of the Environmental Choice Program

The Program's Inception

Prime Minister Brian Mulroney announced the creation of the Canadian government's Environmental Choice Program at an international conference on climate change in Toronto in 1988.[43] The first products bearing the EcoLogo appeared on store shelves in March 1990. By January 2001, guidelines for 122 categories of products and services had been developed and over 2000 products and services had been certified.

Although the goals of the Environmental Choice Program have been constant, the structure and decision-making process of the Program have evolved over time. When the Program was launched in 1988, the federal Environment Minister appointed a voluntary 16-member Advisory Board, comprising representatives from the environmental, consumer, business, health-care and academic sectors. The Board was responsible for selecting product categories and approving guidelines prior to Ministerial approval as well as managing day-to-day Program operations. The original process of developing guidelines was quite cumbersome. At the first stage, the Board chose product categories for guidelines development. The Program secretariat within Environment Canada then contracted a private consultant to prepare a briefing paper, which included a preliminary life-cycle review of the product and a profile of the industry and the consumer market. After the Board approved the briefing note, the Canadian Standards Association (CSA), a private standard-setting body whose services had been contracted by the Program, was directed to develop the guidelines. CSA would convene a task force with expertise in the relevant product category. The task forces tended to be heavily weighted toward industry, but normally did include consumer and environmental

---

42. Wynne (footnote 36), p. 124.

43. The Program was initially named the Environmentally Friendly Products Program, but the name was soon changed to Environmental Choice in recognition of the fact that no consumer product is truly environmentally friendly.

representatives.[44] The draft guidelines were reviewed by a volunteer 18-member Coordinating Technical Committee (CTC) established by CSA before they were forwarded to the Board. Then, after approval by the Board, the draft guidelines were published in the *Canada Gazette* for public comment. Thereafter, the CSA and CTC might amend the guidelines in response to public comments before resubmitting them to the Board. With final approval of the Board, the guidelines were forwarded to the Minister for approval and publication in the *Canada Gazette*.[45]

Once guidelines were established, CSA was responsible for licensing individual products and monitoring compliance with licence provisions. The Environmental Choice Program licensing contract authorizes sampling of products and inspections of manufacturing facilities to monitor compliance, and requires that licensees inform the Program of any instances of non-compliance. Sanctions for non-compliance include termination of licence, recall of products, and damages. Despite these provisions, it does not appear that any formal monitoring program existed in the early years of the Program. The 1994–95 Annual Report noted that surveillance of companies licensed before 1992 had only just begun. A 1998 review noted that "monitoring is not a major part of the program" and that labels are not automatically revoked as long as a firm is forthcoming and commits to correct the problem.[46]

Increasing Governmental Control and Industry Orientation

Program operations were transformed over the next few years, in some cases at the initiative of the Board and in others over its objections. By 1991, the Board and Program staff were frustrated by the 18-month length of the guidelines development process, and undertook reforms to streamline the process. The secretariat within Environment Canada assumed responsibility for guidelines development from CSA, and the CTC, which had often been in tension with the Board, was disbanded.[47] A firm called Calian Technical Services was granted a three-year contract to perform the remaining licensing functions.[48]

One of the most serious problems encountered in the early years of the Program was industry opposition, discussed further below, to guidelines for sanitary paper products, such as toilet paper and facial tissue. Members of the pulp and paper industry concerned about the potential negative economic impact of a proposed guideline on

---

44. As noted in C. Chociolko, *The Environmental Choice Program: A Better "Choice" for the Environment?* (unpublished manuscript, November 30, 1990), the ratio of industry representatives to environmentalists on the sanitary paper products task force was 8:1. Program staff explained that the imbalance resulted from two factors: most of the relevant expertise lay with the industry, and few environmentalists or consumer representatives were available to participate in the highly technical and often time-consuming committees.

45. For other discussions of the CSA standards-development process in this volume, in different contexts, see Gregory T. Rhone, David Clarke and Kernaghan Webb, "Two Voluntary Approaches to Sustainable Forestry Practices," Chapter 9, above, and Andrew Morrison and Kernaghan Webb, "Bicycle Helmet Standards and Hockey Helmet Regulations: Two Approaches to Safety Protection," Chapter 11, below.

46. A. Gesser, "Canada's Environmental Choice Program: A Model for a 'Trade-Friendly' Eco-Labelling Scheme," *Harvard International Law Journal* 39 (1998), pp. 501–544, p. 502.

47. The Hickling Corporation (footnote 31), pp. 4–6.

48. Ibid., pp. 4–15.

non-licensed firms found a sympathetic audience within the Department of Industry, Science and Technology (known as Industry, Science and Technology Canada or ISTC), which resulted in interdepartmental tensions between ISTC and Environment Canada. In response to the industry's concerns, the government undertook a series of reforms to rein in the Advisory Board and increase governmental control of the Program. In February 1992, the Minister issued a directive to the Board to ensure that both environmental and economic considerations were integral in product category selection and guidelines development.[49] The Minister also restricted the role of the Board to its advisory function in guidelines development, shifting responsibility for Program management to Environment Canada and increasing interdepartmental consultation via a new Interdepartmental Advisory Committee. These changes were not welcomed by Board members, who had been reviewing options involving greater, rather than less, Program autonomy.

These reforms failed to resolve tensions with stakeholders and by 1993, "the expected relationship of harmony between the three doves [consumers, government, and industry] had not only not developed, but had, ironically, deteriorated into acrimonious debate."[50] Industry spokespersons complained that the Board was acting as an "environmental lobby group," despite a larger number of industry Board members than environmental or consumer members.[51] While such opposition came from firms that felt the guidelines criteria were too strict, there was also discontent among firms that had qualified to display the EcoLogo. Consumer awareness of the Program was low, leading licensees to question the value of the logo. The first efforts by the Environmental Choice Program to market the logo had been undertaken in 1992, and both Program staff and industry licensees agreed that the $2 million campaign had been ineffective.[52] A 1993 survey found only 30 percent "aided awareness" of the logo, and only 11 percent unaided recognition.[53]

Despite industry complaints that the Board was acting as an "environmental lobby," environmentalists were also increasingly disillusioned with the Program in light of the federal government's unwillingness to approve the sanitary paper guidelines.[54] There was also low morale among Board members and Program staff, who were frustrated by the unresolved conflicts between the Program and both the government and the pulp and paper industry.[55]

An independent Program evaluation conducted in late 1993 was critical of the lack of strategic direction of the Program, inadequate rigour in product category

49. D. Cohen, "Subtle Effects: Requiring Economic Assessments in the Environmental Choice Program," *Alternatives* 20 (1994), pp. 22–27.

50. J. Polak and E. Bozowsky, "Restructuring the Environmental Choice Program," paper prepared for the Conference on Restructuring Strategies for the Public Sector, Institute for International Research, Ottawa, March 1995.

51. Hickling (footnote 31), pp. 4–6.

52. Ibid., pp. 4–26.

53. Ibid., pp. 4–28.

54. Ann Hillyer, West Coast Environmental Law Association, personal communication, March 25, 1996.

55. Graham Hardman, former Director, Environmental Choice Program, personal communication, February 28, 1996.

selection, and inattention to marketing.[56] The consultants also reported that, although the Program originally was intended to be self-financing within five years, when that time came in 1993 it was recovering only 10 percent of its annual budget from licensees. Two of 27 product guidelines accounted for 70 percent of external revenues. Most importantly in terms of the Program's objectives, the reviewers concluded that the Program had little success in changing consumer attitudes and increasing the market share of certified products.

The changes that were instituted in response had the effect of increasing the Program's responsiveness to both the federal government and industry, and further undermining original members of the Board. A new Program Director was appointed by the Minister in mid-1993 without consulting Board members. The number of Board members from industry was increased,[57] and a new Board Chair, a retired oil industry executive, was also appointed, again without consultation with the Board. An "industry challenge" program was adopted to elicit proposed criteria from industry. The approach was welcomed by industry, but generated criticism from some Board members, who were concerned that input was being elicited only from industry. The combination of the more "business-like" orientation of the Program,[58] the new approach to guidelines development, and the new staff and Board appointments did much to restore support among disgruntled industry spokespersons. One industry representative who had been critical of the Program prior to 1993 described the new Director and Board Chair as "a breath of fresh air."[59] However, consumer and environmental Program participants' concerns were, if anything, exacerbated. Completing in-house control of the Program, the Environmental Choice Advisory Board was disbanded in 1994. One effect of the abolition of the Advisory Board was to greatly reduce the influence of non-industry voices, since the remaining guidelines review committees, like the original task forces, tended to be weighted heavily toward industry participants.

Privatization of Operations

The pendulum between Program independence and government control swung back in 1995, when Program operations were privatized. Although the federal government retained ownership of the EcoLogo, management and delivery of the Program was transferred to TerraChoice, a private for-profit enterprise headed by the former Environmental Choice Program Director and employing many of the former government staff. A five-year agreement (since renewed) was signed granting TerraChoice authority to sublicence use of the EcoLogo to individual firms. A second agreement guaranteed continuing financial support for the Program for a period of five years.

---

56. Hickling (footnote 31).

57. Cohen (footnote 49), p. 26.

58. Polak and Bozowsky, (footnote 50).

59. John Philip, former Vice-President, Business Development, Scott Paper, personal communication, March 25, 1996.

Although licensing revenues constituted only 15 percent of the Program budget in 1995,[60] the financial support agreement required that the Program be self-financing by 1997. In response, TerraChoice restructured licensing fees, streamlined operations and reduced spending on activities such as marketing. The fact that the Environmental Choice Program is now self-financing makes it unique among government-sponsored eco-labelling programs worldwide.[61] Although additional revenues have been obtained through an increase in licensing fees,[62] financial self-sufficiency has been achieved largely by reducing the scale of Program operations, from a full-time staff of 22 at the peak of operations within Environment Canada to six part-time or roughly three full-time staff dedicated to the Program today.

A reduction in the scale of operations by a factor of seven inevitably entails more than just streamlining. A firm that must finance its own activities may be reluctant to devote scarce resources to program evaluations or consumer polling; neither have been conducted since 1993. The Environmental Choice Program today is also focussed less on individual consumers than on institutional, including governmental, procurement, where it can obtain more "bang for its buck" on marketing activities. Perhaps most significant, however, is a shift in focus from development of guidelines to an *ad hoc* "panel review certification" process. Although the Environmental Choice Program materials state a commitment to reviewing each guideline every three years, and the Program has eliminated or updated several guidelines accordingly, no record of when each guideline was last updated is available, either on the Web site or from Program staff.[63] Only two new guidelines have been developed in recent years, and in both cases external funds were provided by Environment Canada to support guidelines development.

The panel review process instituted by TerraChoice represents a quicker, less expensive way to develop standards for innovative products. In recognition of the fact that the EcoLogo will have no impact if firms are not willing to apply for it, the panel review process invites applications for licensing of innovative *individual* products, rather than attempting *ex ante* to identify product *categories* offering the greatest potential for environmental improvements. The onus is on the applicant to convince a four-person panel, comprising representatives from a consumer group, an environmental group, industry, and Environment Canada, that its product or service offers significant environmental benefits without sacrificing performance. After a product is approved by the panel, the Environmental Choice Program staff develop and post criteria for that product category so that other producers can apply for licensing as well. The panel review criteria thus serve as informal guidelines. Indeed, the Environmental Choice Program's Web site does not distinguish between panel review criteria and guidelines. However, in contrast to formal guidelines, panel review criteria are not approved by the

---

60. Evan Bozowsky, Manager of Business Operations, TerraChoice, personal communication, February 27, 1996.

61. Environmental Protection Agency (footnote 2).

62. Since privatization, licensing fees have been increased from a range of $400 to $5,000 per licence to $500 to $10,000 per licence.

63. See <www.environmentalchoice.com>. As of 1997 (when guidelines were still dated in Program publications), only about one third of guidelines more than three years old that had licensees had been revised or reviewed.

federal government nor published for public comment prior to being finalized, though products certified under them are still eligible to bear the EcoLogo.

An important advantage of the panel review process is the opportunity to licence niche products and services that might not otherwise warrant development of full-fledged guidelines,[64] a process that can cost from $60,000 to $100,000. It does seem unlikely that development of guidelines for a "source reduced plastic petri dish," a product licensed through the panel process, could be justified. However, the panel process is also being used to develop criteria for more common products, such as dishwashers, washing machines and desktop printers, which would traditionally have been pursued using the more elaborate guidelines process. Only if a significant number of licences have been granted within a product category does TerraChoice proceed to develop more formal guidelines. This approach offers clear efficiencies, since the Program needn't waste resources developing guidelines that will attract few if any licensees, as has been the case for many guidelines in the past. However, much of the cost of guidelines development is associated with contracting for life-cycle and market assessments of the relevant product category. It seems doubtful that an equally rigorous assessment is performed by a single applicant for a panel review. It is noteworthy, however, that Program staff and panel members believe that the standards they set through the panel review process are, if anything, more stringent than those that emerge from a full-fledged guidelines process, since they are keenly aware of the need to protect the credibility of the Program.

The Environmental Choice Program staff contrast the "demand-side" panel review process with the more traditional "supply side" approach of developing guidelines where there is a perceived opportunity for environmental benefits. In many respects, this is a response to reviewers' criticism of the Program in its early years for paying too little attention to industry demand, with the result that most guidelines attracted no licensees.[65] To be fair, it should be noted that this has been the case for many eco-labelling programs,[66] reflecting not merely poor choice of product categories but also sustained resistance to eco-labelling from trade associations.[67] The demand-side approach is also understandably attractive to a program that must finance its own operations, and thus cannot shift the costs of unsuccessful guidelines to taxpayers. The disadvantage is that it is *ad hoc*: criteria are being developed where there is guaranteed demand, but there are no guarantees that resources are being devoted to where they will yield the greatest environmental benefit.

---

64. Global Ecolabelling Network (GEN), *The Ecolabelling Guide* (Tokyo: GEN, October 1999).

65. See Hickling (footnote 31). A market survey conducted for the Environmental Choice Program in 1993–94 drew similar conclusions.

66. Organisation for Economic Co-operation and Development (footnote 4).

67. See H. U. de Haes, "Slow Progress in Ecolabelling: Technical or Institutional Impediments?" *Journal of Industrial Ecology* 1 (1997), pp. 4–6; J. Salzman, "Informing the Green Consumer: The Debate Over the Use and Abuse of Environmental Labels," *Journal of Industrial Ecology* 1 (1997), pp. 11–21; and K. Harrison, "Racing to the Top or Bottom? Industry Resistance to Eco-Labelling of Paper Products in Three Jurisdictions," *Environmental Politics* 8 (1999), pp. 110–137.

The International Context

In recent years, the Environmental Choice Program has operated within an increasingly international context. Eco-labelling has been criticized as a potential barrier to international trade for two main reasons.[68] First, there is concern that national eco-labelling programs will adopt criteria that favour domestic producers. Foreign producers' concerns are amplified by the fact that they often have been afforded few if any opportunities to participate in the development of domestic eco-labelling standards. It can also be significantly more costly for foreign producers to obtain licences from national eco-labelling programs, particularly to the extent that eco-labelling criteria require certification of environmental impacts at the point of production. This emphasis on criteria concerning process and production methods — "PPMs" in international trade parlance — is a second source of some controversy in light of World Trade Organization decisions overturning environmental regulations based on PPMs. Some argue that even though eco-labels must be based on the full range of impacts across a product's life cycle, including those associated with production, because they are entirely voluntary they do not limit foreign producers' access to domestic markets. Others are critical that PPM-oriented eco-labels merely represent a back-door effort to constrain the sovereignty of developing countries. It is noteworthy that after reviewing Program operations and emerging case law concerning international trade, Gesser dubbed the Environmental Choice Program a "model for a 'trade-friendly' eco-labelling scheme."[69]

Apart from the trade issues, there is also international concern that a proliferation of private and government eco-labels will confuse consumers and undermine the impact of all such labels. Such concerns have spurred development of multinational eco-labelling programs, including the Nordic Swan and the European Union's Eco-label, as well as efforts to promote harmonization and mutual recognition among eco-labelling programs through the Global Ecolabelling Network, an association of 24 governmental and private-sector programs. The Environmental Choice Program has played an instrumental role in the Global Ecolabelling Network since its inception.

Environmental Choice has also been active in the International Organization for Standardization's (ISO) efforts to develop international standards for environmental labelling.[70] Input from international eco-labelling program representatives was critical in revising language in early drafts of the ISO eco-labelling standard (ISO 14024), calling

---

68. See B. Driessen, "New Opportunities or Trade Barrier in Disguise? The EC Eco-labelling Scheme," *European Environmental Law Review* 8 (1999), pp. 5–15; and GEN (footnote 64).

69. Gesser (footnote 46).

70. ISO standards 14020 and 14024 offer principles for "type 1" (i.e. third party) eco-labelling programs. ISO has also developed standard 14021 concerning "type 2" (self-declared) claims (see footnote 16), and is working on a 14025 standard for "type 3" (report card-type) labels.

for eco-labelling guidelines to be developed by consensus among relevant stakeholders.[71] However, the fact that the final standard still calls for "reasonable efforts … to achieve a consensus throughout the [standard-setting] process" remains troubling in light of the potential for obstruction by laggard firms noted above. Like other ISO 14000 series standards, ISO's eco-labelling standards concern principles and procedures for operating an eco-labelling program, rather than promoting international harmonization of the content of eco-labelling guidelines. Substantive harmonization and mutual recognition among national programs remain a significant challenge — though it is noteworthy that the Environmental Choice Program has negotiated mutual recognition agreements with the U.S. Green Seal and Taiwanese programs — since different countries tend to weigh environmental impacts differently and thus emphasize different product criteria.

Evaluation of the Environmental Choice Program

Case Studies

The Hickling Program review conducted in 1993 contained four case studies, which are briefly summarized below.[72] In addition, this section summarizes the history of the sanitary paper and "Green Power" guidelines.

The guideline for re-refined motor oil was the first product guideline issued by the Environmental Choice Program. Hickling concluded that although the EcoLogo encouraged an increase in the number of products that met the criteria, there was no evidence that the market share of those products had increased. Consumers apparently had not accepted the products because of a perception of inferior quality. In the absence of consumer demand, Hickling concluded that the logo offered no financial reward for licensees; some reported that with hindsight they would not have entered the Program in the first place.

The impact of the logo on a second product category, building insulation products, also was found to have been negligible. Producers reported that consumers simply were more concerned about price and ease of application than environmental factors. Hickling's case study revealed a tension between cellulose and glass fibre insulation manufacturers, with the cellulose industry resentful that the criteria had been "watered down" in response to the demands of the glass fibre industry.

Two of the original guidelines that attracted the largest number of licensees were oil- and water- based paints. Hickling reported that the logo spurred widespread product reformulation within the industry to reduce the volatile organic compound

---

71. This point was made by the Global Ecolabelling Network, which stated that "it is important to distinguish between the consultation process used for ecolabelling of leadership products and the consensus process used for developing standards of uniformity and acceptability. All stakeholders should be involved at appropriate points in ecolabelling, but ultimately the ecolabelling organization alone must determine the criteria. Consensus about criteria is often not possible because of the different interests represented by stakeholders, particularly in industry, where the majority of manufacturers may not qualify under the leadership criteria." See Global Ecolabelling Network, *Comments and Suggestions of Global Ecolabelling Network on ISO TC 207 SC 3 Type I Labelling Standards* (Tokyo: GEN, November 9, 1995).

72. Hickling (footnote 31).

(VOC) content of paints. By the mid-1990s, paints bearing the EcoLogo had become the industry norm. The oil-based guideline was subsequently deleted and the water-based guideline was tightened in the late 1990s. The paint sector thus appears to be an ideal model for the Environmental Choice Program. However, one puzzling aspect of the Hickling 1993 case study is the widespread view expressed by paint manufacturers that the logo had no impact on consumer demand.[73] Why were producers competing for certification if not to attract customers? The answer may lie in their references to the VOC control program being developed at the time by the Canadian Council of Ministers of the Environment. The impact of the logo in the paint categories thus may owe more to a perception that it was either a harbinger of or alternative to stricter product regulations, than to perceived consumer demand for green products.

The fourth Hickling case study concerned major household appliances. Although the guideline was issued in 1990, there were no licensees as of 1993. The guideline has since been revoked. Manufacturers apparently did not bother to seek the logo because they were already participating in Natural Resource Canada's EnerGuide program, which involved roughly similar product standards.

Although development of a guideline for sanitary paper products (toilet paper, facial tissues, paper towels, and paper napkins) began in 1988, the guideline was not finalized until 1995 after years of conflict both between the industry and the Environmental Choice Program and between the Program and the federal government. The first version of the sanitary paper products guideline was published for public comment in late 1989. The proposal focussed exclusively on the recycled content of sanitary paper products, on the grounds that this would reduce demand for virgin fibre, result in energy savings, and reduce the impact on landfills of the disposable products in question. After the public comment period, the guideline was revised to reduce the recycled content requirements and released for a second public review. Although environmentalists on the task force and several small firms, including Atlantic Packaging Products, supported the proposed criterion,[74] it was strongly opposed by the Canadian Pulp and Paper Association (CPPA) and especially one of its members, Scott Paper, which alone accounts for 50 percent of the national production of sanitary paper products. Opponents of the proposed guideline marshalled an aggressive lobbying campaign, including letters to various Cabinet Ministers and threats of legal action against the Environmental Choice Program.[75]

Scott and CPPA's substantive arguments exemplify two common controversies that can arise in standard setting for eco-labels, those concerning economic impacts and life-cycle analysis. With respect to the former, to the extent that an eco-labelling program is successful in encouraging market shifts, there will inevitably be winners and losers. It

---

73. As one producer put it, "VOCs are a non-issue with the public ... Really, their biggest concern is cost." (Ibid., pp. C3–3.)

74. A letter to CSA from Atlantic Packaging Products noted that "of the 8 paper companies representing 100 % of the Sanitary Paper Industry, 50% of the companies recommended a standard of 100% [recycled content] for bathroom tissue and towels." (Letter from R. E. Adrian, Atlantic Packaging Products Ltd., to Jack Poon, CSA, November 9, 1989.)

75. Environmental Choice Program, *Sanitary Paper Guideline: Involvement of Scott Paper and the CPPA* (Ottawa: Environmental Choice, May 1991.)

should thus come as no surprise that proposed guidelines will be resisted at every opportunity by those who stand to lose market share. In the sanitary paper case, Scott argued that the Environmental Choice guideline would place Canadian mills at a competitive disadvantage relative to mills in the United States, which have greater access to ~~waste paper~~ by virtue of their proximity to major urban centres. Industry criticisms of the environmental basis for the proposed guideline also reveal the vulnerability of truncated life-cycle analysis. Critics of the guideline argued that because the guideline was based on a single criterion, recycled fibre content, there was no guarantee that products certified to bear the eco-label would actually be less harmful to the environment. The benefits of higher recycled fibre content could be outweighed by other environmental factors, such as forestry practices or mill discharges.

After the second public comment period, the Board approved the guidelines for toilet paper and facial tissue in June 1990 over the objections of Scott, the Canadian Pulp and Paper Association (CPPA), and a majority of industry members on the sanitary paper products task force.[76] In response to lobbying by the industry, DIST pressed the Program to conduct an economic impact study, and even offered to share the cost. Although the Environment Minister had already approved the proposed guideline and agreed to forward it to the relevant Cabinet committee, it was subsequently removed from the Cabinet agenda in response to DIST's concerns.[77] The increasingly frustrated Board members agreed to conduct the proposed economic impact analysis in hopes of overcoming interdepartmental opposition. Upon receipt of the economic assessment, they voted again in February 1993 to recommend the guideline to the Minister. However, the Minister declined to take action pending receipt of the recommendations of a panel advising the Environmental Choice Program on a number of paper guidelines under development.[78]

Although that panel did not end up addressing the sanitary paper products controversy, the new Director and Board Chair abandoned the original proposal and called on the industry to offer counter-proposals. CPPA established a task force that developed a consensus-based industry proposal, which was circulated in October 1993. The counter-proposal differed from the original in two respects. First, it included multiple criteria, such as fibre consumption, energy consumption, and process effluent characteristics. Second, it did not establish inflexible hurdles, but instead assigned points for each criterion, thus allowing some tradeoffs among criteria. It is quite understandable that such an approach would emerge from negotiations among firms with facilities with different environmental strengths and weaknesses. A revised version of the CPPA proposal was eventually issued in 1995 in the form of several new guidelines for sanitary paper products. Despite industry consensus behind the new guidelines, as of January 2001, there was only one licensee for toilet tissues and napkins, and two for paper towels. It is striking that the experiences of the European Union and Nordic Swan eco-labelling programs in developing standards for these same products were remarkably

---

76. Chociolko (footnote 44).

77. Environmental Choice Program, *Project Status Report, ECP-09-89, Sanitary Paper from Recycled Paper* (Ottawa: Environmental Choice, August 10, 1992).

78. Environmental Choice Program, *Project Status Report, ECP-09-89, Sanitary Paper from Recycled Paper* (Ottawa: Environmental Choice, February 17, 1993).

similar, including comparable debates between "green" and "brown" firms, and subsequent reluctance to apply for the label even among firms that had supported the guideline.[79]

The experience of developing the sanitary paper products guidelines also resonates in many respects with the Environmental Choice Program's more recent efforts to develop a "Green Power" guideline. Development of such a guideline was undertaken with $60,000 funding from Environment Canada in 1999 in response to the popularity of the "alternative source electricity" panel review criterion. An advisory committee of roughly 25 representatives from consumer and environmental groups and different energy sectors met three times and held several conference calls to advise the Environmental Choice Program. Their input on various drafts was supplemented by that from several dozen other participants in an on-line bulletin board. As with the sanitary paper products guidelines, fault lines quickly emerged between those who would and who would not qualify according to different proposals. For instance, there was debate about whether less environmentally harmful non-renewable sources, such as natural gas, should qualify in addition to renewable sources, and whether existing hydro-electric producers should qualify in addition to those deriving power from innovative, new facilities. Despite opposition from the Canadian Hydro Association, the Canadian Gas Association and the Canadian Electrical Association, Program staff decided in both cases to restrict eligibility. However, it would appear that the aggrieved parties have taken their arguments to Environment Canada. Although a draft guideline was published in the *Canada Gazette* in 2001, a final version has not yet been published in the *Canada Gazette*.

Direct Evidence of Environmental Impacts

As noted previously, eco-labelling programs seek to achieve their primary goal of environmental protection in two ways: by increasing the market share of products that pose a reduced burden on the environment, and by encouraging innovation among manufacturers to design "greener" products and processes. In order to assess the impact of the eco-label, one would thus need extensive information on the fraction of a certified product's success that is attributable to the logo, the extent to which any observed product and process changes can be attributed to the availability of the logo, and the environmental impacts of products that do and do not qualify for the label. Such information, if available at all, tends to be confidential.

With respect to market impact, there are mixed signals. The fact that manufacturers continue to propose new product categories and that 185 firms have invested in licences with the Environmental Choice Program[80] indicates that they believe eco-labelling will have a positive impact on their market share. Various international studies have also offered anecdotal evidence of the impact of eco-labels. For instance, one manufacturer claimed that its sales in some markets tripled after its products

---

79. Harrison (footnote 67).

80. TerraChoice, *The EcoBuyer Catalogue* (Ottawa: TerraChoice Environmental Services Inc., 2000).

qualified for the European eco-label for washing machines.[81] An international study by the OECD[82] found the strongest impacts of eco-labelling in a few product categories, such as paper products and detergents, that have been emphasized in environmental groups' campaigns and that have thus attained symbolic importance for environmentally motivated consumers. The substantial resources that many firms in Canada and elsewhere have committed to opposing particular product guidelines also suggests that they anticipate a positive impact of the logo on sales of their competitors' products.

On the other hand, a 1993 survey of Environmental Choice Program licensees indicated that 62 percent of licensees did not attribute any change in sales to the EcoLogo, compared to 33 percent who perceived a positive impact.[83] No impact on market share was found in any of the case studies discussed above. Although firms must anticipate a market benefit to invest in licensing, current licensing fees are set at only 0.6 percent of the value of product sales, thus offering little evidence of significant market shifts. Moreover, applications for licensing have never been overwhelming. Even though several unsuccessful guidelines have been deleted in recent years, roughly half of the Environmental Choice Program's 48 final guidelines still have no licensees. Perhaps more surprisingly in light of the demand-side emphasis of the panel review program, about a third of the 74 panel review criteria also have no licensees.[84] Since those criteria are developed with a particular applicant in mind, this may indicate that licensees are declining to renew their licences. The majority of product categories, whether guidelines or panel criteria, have only one licensee. In light of the limited interest by both producers and consumers in the majority of eco-label product categories in Canada and elsewhere, an OECD study concluded overall that "eco-labelled products have not had a significant impact on the market."[85] Similar conclusions have been drawn by reviews of international programs by Salzman[86] and the US EPA.[87]

In the absence of conclusive evidence of shifts in market share and associated environmental benefits, one can turn to an evaluation of program operations using the secondary criteria identified above: validity of standards, program recognition and credibility, and consumer willingness to pay for environmentally preferred products.

Validity of Standards

Industry buy-in is essential to a voluntary program, since voluntary eco-labels clearly can have no impact if manufacturers are unwilling to display them. Moreover, manufacturers' cooperation is needed because they have essential information about product characteristics, processing technologies and consumer demand. However, if an

---

81. "Re-evaluating Eco-labels," *Business Europe*, May 15, 1995, pp. 4–5.

82. Organisation for Economic Co-operation and Development (footnote 27).

83. Hickling (footnote 31).

84. These figures are drawn from a September 2000 list of final guidelines and panel review criteria and from TerraChoice (footnote 80).

85. Organisation for Economic Cooperation and Development (footnote 27), p. 67.

86. Salzman (footnote 67).

87. EPA (footnote 2), p. 59.

eco-labelling program is effective in promoting changes in consumer behaviour, it will inevitably result in industry dislocations. While the winners can be expected to support the program and advocate stringent product standards, the influence of the losers in urging relaxation of standards or obstructing the program altogether is a potentially serious problem. Much depends on the relative influence of industry laggards and industry leaders in program decision making. As discussed above, the influence of laggards will be more pernicious since decisions are made by consensus. While consensus is not required of technical committees involved in developing Environmental Choice Program guidelines, the sanitary paper products and green power case studies suggest that a more important obstacle to program effectiveness may lie in the practical requirement of political consensus within the federal government.

The eco-labelling model is predicated on an assumption that markets are competitive: if consumers demand less environmentally harmful products, producers will compete to cater to that demand. Yet there is evidence from eco-labelling program experience in many countries that industry associations resist internal competition with respect to environmental criteria and may even encourage their members to boycott eco-labels.[88] It is noteworthy that in the case of the sanitary paper products guideline, the Canadian Pulp and Paper Association represented the interests of Scott paper, rather than those of small firms supportive of the original proposal. Similarly, the Canadian Electrical Association and Canadian Hydro Association spoke on behalf of the majority of their members in debates over the draft Green Power guidelines, rather than representing members who would qualify. European pulp and paper producers also appear to have boycotted the Nordic Swan eco-label for sanitary paper products and the European Community eco-label for paper products more generally.[89] Finally, a coalition of several major US industry associations has formed to oppose all eco-labelling programs.[90] These examples demonstrate the obstacles faced by eco-labelling programs even in pursuing a voluntary, market-based approach.

Program Recognition and Credibility

Government sponsorship of eco-labelling is often cited as a basis for credibility. However, it is noteworthy that while maintaining a government role, the Environmental Choice Program has experimented with three quite different operational models. The original Program, although created and financed by the federal government, was designed to have a considerable degree of independence with respect to standard setting and administration. It was, in a sense, a hybrid between the government-run and non-profit private-sector models discussed previously. In practice, to the extent that consumers were aware of the Program, it benefited from the government's reputation. Decision making was relatively transparent and open to diverse interests, though more as a result of the diverse Board membership than individual task forces. However, a problem with this hybrid approach was the uneasy fit between independent operations

---

88. See de Haes (footnote 67) and Salzman (footnote 67).

89. See "Eco-labels Stuck on Search for Common Standards," *Pulp and Paper International* 36 (1994), pp. 39–43; "Re-evaluating Eco-labels" (footnote 81); Harrison (footnote 67).

90. Wildavsky (footnote 20).

and government sponsorship. In the end, guidelines still required the approval of Cabinet and thus independence with respect to decision making was in many respects an illusion, a painful lesson for Board members during the sanitary paper products debacle.

The second model was an in-house government operation. A critical reform was the creation of an interdepartmental committee to vet proposed guidelines prior to Ministerial approval. This change to the decision-making process acknowledged the inevitability of Cabinet's role in a way that the original model did not. Although in theory this increased the risk of political interference, it is difficult to assess the significance of the interdepartmental committee, as there were no controversies comparable to that concerning the sanitary paper guidelines during this period. Moreover, the greater industry orientation of the Program after 1993 may have precluded such conflicts. One disadvantage of the move to greater governmental control was the reduction of input from non-industry sources via the Board, which was disbanded in 1994.

Finally, the current model merges government ownership of the EcoLogo with self-financing operation by a private firm. This delivery arrangement is unique among eco-labelling programs, most of which are delivered by either the State or an affiliated non-profit body such as a national standards association with financial support from the state. The Canadian approach seeks to combine the credibility and openness of a governmental enterprise with the efficiency of a commercial one. The advantages of a self-financing program are clear, especially to taxpayers. However, the mandate that the Program be self-financing has had a significant impact on operations. Fewer guidelines have been reviewed and developed as attention has shifted to the less resource-intensive, *ad hoc* panel review process. This has been accompanied by a subtle shift in business philosophy; Program staff stress that unlike other eco-labelling programs, Environmental Choice is a "marketing program" rather than an "awards program." The focus is on helping the Program's paying clients market their environmentally preferred products, which may not always entail the same activities as a program that seeks to maximize environmental benefits based on analysis of industry demand, consumer demand and products' environmental characteristics. Moreover, as the recent Green Power guidelines experience reveals, as long as the federal government reserves final approval of guidelines, there is still potential for political interference.

The Role of Consumers

An effective eco-labelling program can help environmentally conscientious consumers make better product choices. However, ultimately consumer "awareness and concern are necessary prerequisites to successful eco-logo programs, not products of them."[91] The impact of eco-labels is only as great as underlying consumer demand.

Surveys revealed strong demand for greener products in the late 1980s and early 1990s. However, opinion polls undoubtedly overestimated the depth of consumers' commitment. A "halo effect" is observed even in anonymous surveys, with respondents tending to give what they perceive to be the "right" answer. There is evidence that some consumers leave their halos behind when they approach the cash register, however. A

---

91. Wynne (footnote 36), p. 105.

1991 survey found that although 58 percent of adult men said aerosols should not be used, 87 percent had in fact purchased aerosols in the previous six months.[92] Relatively early in the green marketing revolution, producers began to be wary of consumers' reported willingness to pay more for environmentally benign products.[93] Environmental impacts are only one of many characteristics consumers take into account in making product choices, and they are unlikely to be at the top of the list for most consumers.

Moreover, there is evidence that consumer demand for less environmentally harmful products waned with the salience of environmental issues more generally.[94] A Canadian poll found that the fraction of respondents willing to pay a 10 percent premium for environmentally preferred products fell from 81 percent in 1990 to 57 percent in 1993.[95] Trade publications confirm that the green marketing boom cooled by 1993.[96] Finally, in 1995 Scott paper cancelled production of its line of unbleached sanitary paper products, introduced in 1990, in response to declining consumer demand.[97]

Although the decline in consumers' willingness to pay may yet rebound, eco-labelling programs nonetheless must confront the fact that not all consumers were green even at the height of the green consumer movement in 1990. And, there is reason to doubt that even environmentally oriented consumers will fully internalize their share of social costs. If industry shareholders have not been willing to forgo personal wealth to internalize the social costs of pollution, why should we be so sanguine that consumers will exhibit greater altruism?

Conclusions

Eco-labelling programs offer considerable promise. If green consumerism can be fostered and sustained, labelling programs provide a powerful opportunity to harness market forces for environmental protection. In any case, since participation is entirely voluntary on the part of both consumers and business, a credible eco-labelling program probably cannot do much harm (though there may be significant dislocations within an industry sector.) Moreover, eco-labelling offers a unique opportunity to encourage changes to products across the life cycle in a single stroke, in contrast to regulating each ingredient or step in the manufacturing process. As an OECD report observed, "In the absence of labelling programmes, the state will not simply decree that environmentally friendly products be manufactured."[98]

---

92. Cited in Church (footnote 12), p. 254.

93. S. Hume, "Consumer Doubletalk Makes Companies Wary," *Advertising Age*, October 28, 1992, p. GR4.

94. Harrison (footnote 67).

95. Environmental Choice Program, "Synopsis: The Environmental Monitor," (footnote 7). Similarly, a U.S. survey found that the fraction of respondents who indicated that they were willing to pay 15 percent more for environmentally safe packaging decreased from 47 percent in 1990 to 37 percent in 1991. (See J. Dagnoli,"Consciously Green: Consumers Question Marketers' Commitment," *Advertising Age*, September 18, 1991, p. 14.)

96. J. Lawrence, "Green Marketing Jobs Wilt at Big Companies," *Advertising Age*, September 1993, p. 4.

97. N. V. Palmer, letter to the editor, *The Georgia Straight*, February 8–15, 1996, p. 4. (Neil V. Palmer wrote in his capacity as Corporate Vice-President, Scott Paper Ltd.)

98. Organisation for Economic Co-operation and Development (footnote 4), p. 338.

However, eco-labelling also has important limitations. At most, it seeks to shift consumer patterns within a given product category. No effort is made to reduce consumption or encourage responsible use and disposal of products. Depending on program decision rules and the competitiveness of a given industrial sector, industry influence may result in standards that are weaker than desirable. Overly lax standards not only forego potential environmental benefits but could actually increase environmental harm. Finally, at the core, environmental quality remains a public good. Although certification of environmentally preferred products can help to overcome problems of information asymmetry and the public goods nature of information, labels alone will not ensure that individuals voluntarily assume their share of social costs. While the emergence of green consumerism is tremendously encouraging, the current state of the environment suggests that it would be foolhardy to rely exclusively on consumer altruism for environmental protection.

Eco-labelling programs are thus best viewed as a complement, rather than an alternative, to a broad range of governing instruments, including educational programs to encourage reduced consumption and sustain consumer commitment to green purchasing, strategic use of government procurement, mandatory disclosure of environmental impacts, product and process regulations, and regulation of advertising claims. As a German Minister of the Environment remarked, "The environmental label is just one instrument of environmental policy. It ought not and must not be used as an excuse for the state to do nothing if the market is incapable of making the necessary changes on its own."[99]

Epilogue: Eco-Labelling as a Voluntary Code of Practice

Eco-labels share many characteristics of voluntary codes of conduct. Guidelines for individual product categories are, in effect, codes of conduct administered by third parties to which manufacturers of individual products voluntarily agree to adhere. The licensing contract is an explicit statement of that agreement, though as a binding legal document it probably has greater weight than obligations under most voluntary codes.

One difference between eco-labels and other codes of conduct is that consumer demand for less environmentally harmful products creates a direct, positive incentive for producers to sign on. In contrast, development of many voluntary codes may be motivated more by a negative incentive, to avoid more coercive and less flexible government regulation, with public or customer perceptions being at most a secondary factor. However, one insight that emerges from the eco-labelling case study for voluntary codes more generally is the need to acknowledge and address the potential challenge of sustaining an effective voluntary program after the original impetus that led to the Program's creation has faded, whether that impetus was consumer demand or the threat of government regulation.

A second difference lies in the selective nature of eco-labelling programs. The objective is to raise the ceiling rather than the floor. Rather than encouraging participation by all members of an industry, eco-labelling programs quite intentionally

---

99. Ibid., p. 31.

restrict participation to a subset of leaders. Free riding is not an issue, but eco-labelling programs must confront the potential for intra-industry competition. As such, third-party leadership is essential and an objective of consensus in standard setting is quite inappropriate. However, the resistance to eco-labelling by firms who fear a loss of market share may offer a cautionary lesson concerning other voluntary codes. Differences in the ability and willingness of individual firms to pursue social goals is an issue that must be confronted by other types of voluntary codes as well. The evidence from this case study that firms within an industry will resist standards that they cannot meet provides cause for concern more generally about the leadership potential of voluntary codes based on industry-wide consensus.

A final lesson from this case study concerns the lack of data to evaluate program effectiveness. The lack of such data may well be endemic in voluntary programs, since there are few incentives for firms to report their non-compliance and weaker tools for managers of voluntary programs to elicit such information.[100] If this problem is indeed widespread, one must resist the temptation to draw an unfair comparison between regulation, the flaws of which are very public, and an untested theoretical ideal of voluntary alternatives.

---

100. Harrison (footnote 67).

Chapter 11
Bicycle Helmet Standards and Hockey Helmet Regulations: Two Approaches to Safety Protection

Andrew Morrison and Kernaghan Webb

Introduction

Both hockey players and bicyclists engage in activities that can be dangerous and even life-threatening. For self-evident reasons, the heads of hockey players and cyclists are particularly vulnerable to injury. Governments, standards organizations and sports associations have put in place a combination of approaches which are intended to ensure that hockey and bicycle helmets meet certain standards, and that hockey players and cyclists wear these helmets. Yet the approaches adopted vary significantly from one context to the other. Hockey helmets in Canada are required by federal law[1] to meet certain design/performance standards, whereas there is no similar legislated performance requirement for bicycle helmets. At the same time, there is no federal and only one provincial law (in Quebec)[2] requiring the use of hockey helmets, whereas there are several provincial and municipal laws requiring bicycle helmet use.[3]

The purpose of this chapter is to explore and describe the rule-making and implementation regimes in place for hockey and bicycle helmets, with a view to understanding why different approaches have been adopted for seemingly similar situations. Particular attention is paid to the role played by standards associations, in order to illustrate how these bodies operate in practice. Analysis suggests that a range of factors help explain why different approaches have been adopted. These include:

- *The time period when the issue first arose.* From the 1960s to the present, the receptivity of governments towards using conventional command-penalty regulations has decreased, shaped by fiscal constraints and a better understanding of the strengths and weaknesses of regulation and its alternatives. The issue of the need for hockey helmets first arose in the 1960s and 1970s when governments arguably were more willing to use regulations to address many societal problems. In contrast, bicycle helmet safety became an issue in the 1980s and 1990s, when a more restrained approach to the use of regulations predominated.
- *Varying marketplace conditions.* These include the existence in the marketplace of products of substandard quality, the number and size of manufacturers, the mix of domestic and imported products, the existence of competing standards

---

1. *Hazardous Products Act,* R.S.C. 1985, c. H-3, s. 43.

2. *An Act Respecting Safety in Sports,* R.S.Q., c. S-3.1.

3. Provinces with bicycle helmet laws include British Columbia (see *Motor Vehicle Act,* R.S.B.C. 1996, c. 318, s. 184); Nova Scotia (see *Motor Vehicle Act,* R.S.N.S. 1989, c. 293, s. 170A). Municipalities with bicycle helmet by-laws include St. John's and Mount Pearl, Newfoundland and Labrador.

Kernaghan Webb, Editor, *Voluntary Codes: Private Governance, the Public Interest and Innovation.*
This chapter ©2004 Andrew Morrison and Kernaghan Webb, pages 299–314.
Published by the Carleton Research Unit for Innovation, Science and Environment, Carleton University, Ottawa, Canada.

already in the marketplace, and the perceived seriousness of problems and the need for immediate responses.

- *The role and ability of "user" associations to compel conduct on behalf of members.* The Canadian Hockey Association (CHA),[4] which represents a substantial number of amateur hockey players in Canada, was in a position to require the use of helmets for its members, to support use of a legislated standard, and to be held liable should the helmets not adequately protect their members. For a variety of reasons there is no cyclists' association capable of imposing similar requirements on individual bicyclists.

- *External regulatory conditions.* The existence of regulations and standards in other jurisdictions can assist Canada in adopting standards, and developing approaches to problems. The existence of free trade agreements, with their restrictions on trade barriers, can also play a role.

- *Evolving role of standards associations.* Over time, the profile and credibility of standards produced by standards organizations has increased. Such standards now often receive the respect of industry, consumers and government, thus making it increasingly acceptable to use standards produced by standards organizations as instruments of public policy.

While empirical data demonstrating costs and benefits are hard to come by, available evidence suggests that the voluntary approach in place for bicycle helmets has been no less successful than hockey helmet regulations in preventing or reducing head injuries. As a result, a good argument can be made that, if the issue of the need for hockey helmet performance regulations had arisen not in the 1960s and 1970s, but rather at the same time as the need for bicycle helmet performance regulations (in the 1980s, when fiscal constraints on government were more apparent), it is quite possible that design/performance standards for the manufacture of *both* hockey helmets and cycling helmets would have been addressed through non-legislative means.

Before beginning the comparative analysis of the hockey and bicycle helmet standards approaches, it is perhaps worth emphasizing the distinction between design/performance standards and rules respecting use. The best standard for helmets in the world, whether enshrined in law or purely voluntary, is no guarantee of reduced injuries if no one uses the helmets that meet those standards. It is clear, then, that a comprehensive approach to sport safety necessitates both product standards and rules respecting use. The focus of analysis in this chapter is an examination of the standards applying to the design and performance of helmets. There is supplementary discussion of the approaches used to encourage helmet use, which range from legislation (provincial and municipal), to membership requirements set by associations (e.g. the CHA), to civil liability and to education. It is interesting to note that while regulations have been promulgated concerning the safety of hockey helmets, the use of these helmets is stimulated through non-legislated CHA rules, except in Quebec where use requirements are set out in law. In contrast, there are no laws in Canada requiring manufacturers of bicycle helmets to meet certain standards (although there are provincial and municipal

---

4. The Canadian Amateur Hockey Association changed its name in 1994 to the Canadian Hockey Association (CHA). To avoid confusion, the organization is referred to as the CHA throughout this paper.

laws requiring that cyclists wear helmets which meet those standards). This is explained in greater detail in the body of the chapter.

Hockey Helmets

Background

The Canadian Hockey Association requested that the Canadian Standards Association (CSA) develop a standard for hockey helmets in 1969. The CHA was concerned about the number of head injuries, some resulting in death, experienced by young amateur hockey players. The CHA thought that the preparation of a nationally recognized consensus standard on hockey helmets, backed up by a program of testing and certification, would give the players better protection and reduce injuries. The CHA had previously made it mandatory that all players in CHA league games wear helmets, but there was a need to specify the quality of the helmets.[5]

In 1974, following the development of a hockey helmet standard by the CSA, the Product Safety Branch of the federal Department of Consumer and Corporate Affairs amended the *Hazardous Products Act* to require that all hockey helmets sold in Canada conform to certain provisions of the CSA's ice hockey helmet standard.[6] There was no previous regulation of helmets, and accident statistics, particularly relating to young players, were sufficient to persuade the government that action was necessary to ban helmets that did not meet the CSA standard (and might therefore give a false sense of security).[7] After the standard was published the CHA required all amateur hockey players and referees to wear CSA-certified ice hockey helmets. Since the CHA governs the majority of formal hockey leagues in the country, this requirement went a long way toward achieving the objective of all players wearing helmets at all times.[8]

There have been four revisions to the standard since 1973, and three of these have resulted in corresponding amendments to the regulations. Changes made to the *Hazardous Products Act* regulations in June 1987 now allow the referential incorporation of a standard "as amended from time to time" so that it is no longer necessary to amend

---

5. The CHA rules with regard to helmets were introduced in stages. In 1965 helmets were required for all players in the juvenile and lower age groups. In 1966 this rule was expanded to make helmet use mandatory for all players in age groups other than Junior A. Helmet use was made mandatory for Junior A players in 1971. Correspondence with Dave Baker, CHA Manager of Officiating, June 1997.

6. Canadian Standards Association, *Ice Hockey Helmet Standard,* CAN/CSA Z262.1-M1975 (Toronto: CSA, 1975). Note that the Product Safety Branch was later transferred to Health Canada.

7. An example of one type of problem facing consumers of hockey equipment occured when a Canadian supermarket chain advertised a helmet in the *Toronto Star* on November 18, 1972, as having "approved safety design." In fact, no organization had approved the hockey helmet. The supermarket chain was subsequently fined for misleading advertising. E. Amirault and M. Archer, *Canadian Business Law* (Toronto: Methuen Publications, 1988), p. 512.

8. It is important to note that while most organized hockey is governed by the CHA, there are many unorganized hockey games played in Canada. These range from "shinny" games on ponds and outdoor rinks to industrial leagues which operate outside the CHA. Although some industrial leagues and some arenas require that a CSA-approved helmet be worn, enforcement is often lax. The bottom line is that every year thousands of hockey games are played without the required use of a helmet.

the regulations each time the standard is updated, an important advantage of the "incorporated standard" approach.[9]

It appears that there were (and are) only a few Canadian companies making hockey helmets, and that even prior to the incorporation of the CSA standard in 1973 the majority of their products met the standard. The problem had more to do with imported products, which were of variable quality — variances that were not always obvious to consumers. Nowadays, Canadian consumers can be reasonably confident that all hockey helmets on sale are sufficiently robust to meet the rigours of the game. According to government, standards organization and hockey association officials interviewed in the preparation of this chapter, the structure of the Canadian industry did not change as a result of introducing the regulation, but the number of non-compliant imported products was significantly reduced.[10]

Process

The federal government's Product Safety Branch had the choice of writing its own standard, or using the standard that was being developed by CSA. Up to that time, all the *Hazardous Products Regulations* had been written by government after consultation with industry and consumer groups. Previous regulations had sometimes incorporated parts of existing standards; however, it was something of an innovation for government to approach CSA with a view to referencing a complete standard.

CSA derives its income from several sources, primarily through the testing of products, as well as the sale of CSA standards materials and logos; however, standards are occasionally financed by a one-time grant from an interested party. The standards development process begins when CSA receives a request for a new standard.[11] This request is evaluated based on various criteria, including the level of support for the proposed standard.[12] If CSA accepts the request to develop a new standard, it informs the public of this decision and proceeds to develop the standard through a Technical Committee. The Technical Committee is composed of a "matrix" of constituents with diverse viewpoints. Typically, a matrix includes representatives from academia, the manufacturing sector, the regulatory sector and consumers.[13] The Technical Committee, taking into account relevant national and international standards, prepares a draft standard. This standard is debated by the members of the Technical Committee. Once a consensus is reached in regard to the content of the draft standard, it is put to a vote for

---

9. *Hazardous Products (Ice Hockey Helmets) Regulations*, SOR/89-257, s. 3. It is important to note that the referential incorporation of a standard set by a non-governmental body might be viewed as undesirable by some, since it constitutes a delegation of "law-making" powers from an elected body to a non-elected body. Indeed, some might suggest that a delegation of this sort may be illegal, since Parliament may not have the constitutional power to delegate "law-making" ability to non-elected bodies.

10. We have been unable to find statistics regarding foreign/domestic market share to support this observation.

11. Canadian Standards Association, *CSA Directives and Guidelines Governing Standardization, Part 2: Development Process*, CSA-SDP-2.2-98 (Toronto: CSA, 1998), Clauses 4.1.2 and 4.1.3.

12. Ibid., Clause 4.3.

13. Canadian Standards Association, *CSA Directives and Guidelines Governing Standardization, Part 1: Participants and Organizational Structure*, CSA-SDP-2.1-99 (Toronto: CSA, 1999), Clause 3.3.

approval by the Technical Committee. Generally, the affirmative votes must constitute at least 50 percent of the total voting membership and at least two thirds of the votes actually cast.[14] CSA standards have a built-in sunset clause requiring that the standards be reviewed by the Technical Committee every five years.[15] CSA standards that are to be considered for acceptance as national standards are then reviewed and approved by the Standards Council of Canada.[16]

The 1983 revision of the hockey helmet standard followed the criteria established by the Standards Council of Canada for National Standards of Canada and it was then approved as National Standard CAN3-Z262.1-M83. The Technical Committee participants were selected[17] and the process financed by CSA according to its usual procedures; as well, the development of the consensus standard was in accordance with Standards Council of Canada guidelines. Earlier versions of the standard had not been submitted for approval as National Standards, but were developed in accordance with CSA policies, which differ only marginally from the Standards Council of Canada criteria. The average time for the development of a CSA standard is approximately 18 months, but revisions usually take less time than that.

Standard Components

The CSA hockey helmet standard is based on three types of tests: impact, penetration and roll-off. The impact test requires that a helmet be attached to a head form, which is then dropped onto a flat steel slab.[18] The penetration test ensures that ventilation holes in the helmet are not too large and the roll-off test determines whether the helmet will come loose in a collision.[19] Because the CSA standard for hockey helmets has been incorporated into legislation, it has the force of law. The penalties for non-compliance as set out in the *Hazardous Products Act* include a fine of up to $1 million and/or imprisonment for two years.[20]

Implementation

The hockey helmet regulations, aided by the CHA rules, are among the most widely known requirements under the *Hazardous Products Act*. Perhaps because of this there have been no public awareness campaigns for many years, and even the periodic

14. Canadian Standards Association (footnote 11), Clause 9.

15. Ibid., Clause 12.

16. The Standard Council of Canada is a federal Crown corporation that oversees and encourages the development and use of national standards in Canada. See Web site, <www.scc.ca>.

17. The 1983 amendments to Z262.1 were developed and approved by the CSA Technical Committee on Protective Equipment for Ice Hockey and Box Lacrosse Players. Membership of the Committee included representatives from the CHA, the Canadian Lacrosse Association, the Canadian Ball Hockey Association Inc., the American Society for Testing and Materials, the Canadian Dental Association, the Canadian Medical Association, the federal Department of Consumer and Corporate Affairs and all levels of industry.

18. CAN/CSA Z262.1 1-M90, *Ice Hockey Helmets*, section 6.2.

19. Ibid., ss. 6.3 and 6.4.

20. *Hazardous Products Act*, op. cit., section 28(1)(b).

reminders from the CHA to its members have now ceased. Although Health Canada (through its Product Safety Bureau) has inspectors across the country to administer the law, enforcement actions are very rare, and relate primarily to uncertified imported products — usually initiated as the result of complaints by consumers or competitors. Official sampling and testing of products may follow, with actions taken on non-complying products ranging from negotiation for a voluntary product withdrawal from the market to prosecution. According to discussions with Health Canada officials, there has never been a prosecution of a helmet manufacturer and there have been very few instances of non-compliance. Even in these few cases, prosecution was unnecessary, as the manufacturer was persuaded to withdraw or modify the helmet.[21]

Head injuries to hockey players have markedly decreased and nowadays injuries sustained by players hitting the boards head first are frequently to the neck rather than the skull.[22] Those involved in hockey suggest that the wearing of helmets leads to players taking greater risks.[23] Overall, however, the benefits of allowing for sale only helmets that meet the standard are manifest.[24]

The fact that the CHA requires the use of CSA-certified helmets is an important factor in the success of the regulations. By compelling its players to wear the CSA-approved helmets, the CHA created an enormous market of captive buyers. The CHA rule was buttressed in Quebec by provincial legislation that requires the use of helmets in every game of hockey played in an arena in the province, whether sanctioned by the CHA or not.[25]

Foreign hockey players who are under the jurisdiction of other hockey federations, such as USA Hockey or the International Ice Hockey Federation, must comply with the rules of their own governing body.[26] In the case of American teams this means that their players must wear helmets approved by the Hockey Equipment Certification Council, which uses the American Society for Testing and Materials (ASTM) hockey helmet standard.[27]

---

21. Interview with Georges Desbarats, Health Canada, Senior Project Officer, Product Safety Bureau, Mechanical and Electric Hazards Division, June 1996.

22. Interview with Glen McCurdy, CHA, Manager Health Benefit Program, July 1996. These sentiments are echoed by Dr. Tom Pashby, an ophthalmologist who is recognized as one of the major advocates for broader helmet use. (Interview, July 1996.)

23. This according to Glen McCurdy, ibid. This phenomenon, known as the "offsetting behaviour hypothesis," has been observed in other fields. For example, researchers have determined that drivers of cars equipped with airbags drive more aggressively than drivers of non-airbag-equipped cars. See S. Peterson and G. Hoffer, "Are Drivers of Air-Bag Equipped Cars More Aggressive? A Test of the Offsetting Behavior Hypothesis," *Journal of Law and Economics* 38:2 (1995), pp. 251–264.

24. Dr. Pashby (footnote 22) suggests that the primary reason players are taking greater risks is coaching style combined with a feeling of invincibility.

25. *An Act Respecting Safety in Sports*, op. cit. The law also requires the use of a CSA-approved face protector and a neck protector approved by the *Bureau de normalisation du Québec*, a Quebec-based standards organization. The law exempts professional and major-junior hockey.

26. Dave Baker (footnote 5).

27. The current version of the standard is published as ASTM, *Standard F1045-95: Ice Hockey Helmets* (West Conshohocken, Pa.: ASTM, 2001).

Measuring the true costs and benefits of codes and regulations is not simple. In the case of hockey helmets, for instance, the costs of medical treatments that have been avoided could be included as a benefit. The costs for the development of, and revisions to, the regulation are long hidden in government accounts. One estimate for the cost of development of the original standard is $17,275.[28] It is difficult to isolate the costs of implementing the hockey helmets regulation from the general administration costs of the *Hazardous Products Act*. In addition to the costs incurred by the government, the requirement that all helmets comply with the CSA standard increases the costs to manufacturers — a cost that is ultimately passed on to the consumer. Although the consumer benefits from the higher quality of the helmets, the consumer is unable to purchase a helmet of lesser quality for a lower price.

Interpretive Analysis

The objective of the regulation — namely, to ensure that all hockey helmets are adequately safe and thereby to reduce the number and seriousness of head injuries suffered by hockey players — would appear to have been substantially achieved. The CHA requirement that hockey players wear helmets during play complements the regulation since the regulation controls only the sale of the product, not its use. The increasing prevalence of legal action over the past few decades has likely also contributed to increasing the safety of the helmets that were being used by hockey players.[29] Health Canada has since regulated the manufacture of face protectors under the *Hazardous Products Act*.[30]

Bicycle Helmets

Background

As bicycles became an increasingly popular mode of transportation in the 1960s and 1970s, manufacturers began to address the risk of head injury by developing bicycle helmets. Although the first bicycle helmets were relatively primitive, helmet use gradually increased. Soon American standards organizations began to test and certify helmets.[31] Canada lagged behind the U.S. in this respect until the mid-1980s, when CSA began to develop a bicycle helmet standard, which was finally published in 1989.[32]

---

28. Donald J. Lecraw, *Voluntary Standards as a Regulatory Device* (Ottawa: Economic Council of Canada, 1981).

29. Helmet manufacturers generally, including hockey helmet manufacturers, were reported as being subject to an increasing number of product liability suits in the 1980s. See, e.g., J. Davidson, "Helmet Makers Drowning in Sea of Litigation," *The Globe and Mail*, March 31, 1986, p. C1.

30. *Hazardous Products Act*, s. 20, incorporating CSA, *Face Protectors and Visors for Ice Hockey Players Standard CAN3-Z262.2-M78* (Toronto: CSA, 1990).

31. Organizations include Snell, in 1973 (see information on current Snell standards at <www.smf.org/stds.html>), and the American National Standards Institute (ANSI), in 1984 (see <www.ansi.org>).

32. CSA, *Cycling Helmets Standard*, CAN/CSA-D113.2 M89 (Toronto: CSA, 1989), available in a 2001 revision.

In the early 1990s the federal Department of Consumer and Corporate Affairs considered regulating the sale of bicycle helmets through the *Hazardous Products Act*. If carried out, this proposal, announced in both 1990 and 1991, would have referentially incorporated the CSA standards into the *Hazardous Products Act*,[33] in the same manner as hockey helmets. However, in 1992, the Department of Consumer and Corporate Affairs published a withdrawal of its regulatory proposal in the *Canada Gazette*.[34] This action was taken for the stated reason that marketplace compliance with one of the major standards was nearly universal.[35] The Department of Consumer and Corporate Affairs committed itself to monitoring the industry's compliance with these standards and to introducing regulations at a later time if necessary.[36]

The decision to withdraw the proposal to regulate bicycle helmets deserves closer scrutiny. If the regulation of hockey helmets was acceptable in the 1970s, what changes occurred to make the regulation of bicycle helmets unacceptable in the 1990s? While governments of the 1970s often saw regulation as a favoured tool to protect society from hazardous products, governments of the 1990s tended to resort to the use of regulations only when all other means were impractical. The movement to regulate the sale of hockey helmets occurred during an era in which government was inclined to use regulation as a policy instrument.[37] This was particularly true in the context of consumer protection.[38] By the 1990s attitudes toward regulation had shifted, and the limitations and costs of regulation were felt to be increasingly apparent, so that alternatives were favoured unless proven to be impractical.[39] However, the federal government did not reject the concept of regulation outright. Indeed, it was recognized that regulation could play a key role if "public protection requires it."[40]

Government's desire to prevent the proliferation of unnecessary regulation resulted in the creation of the Office of Privatization and Regulatory Affairs (OPRA) in the 1980s. OPRA's influence came from its relationship to the Special Committee of Cabinet. The Special Committee, which approved all regulations, was advised by both the Privy Council Office and OPRA. Recommendations from the Privy Council Office or OPRA to approve or oppose a regulation were apparently given considerable weight by the Special Committee.[41]

---

33. Office of Privatization and Regulatory Affairs, 122-CCAC, *Federal Regulatory Plan* (Ottawa: 1990); Office of Privatization and Regulatory Affairs, 138-CCAC, *Federal Regulatory Plan* (Ottawa: 1991).

34. *Canada Gazette*, Part I, March 9, 1991, p. 756.

35. Ibid.

36. Ibid.

37. R. J. Schultz, "Regulating Conservatively: The Mulroney Record, 1984–1988," in A. B. Gollner and D. Salee, eds., *Canada Under Mulroney: An End-of-Term Report* (Montreal: Véhicule, 1988), p. 192.

38. Ibid.

39. Ibid., p. 201.

40. Office of Privatization and Regulatory Affairs, *Regulatory Reform Strategy* (Ottawa: 1986), p. 4.

41. Interview with Georges Desbarats, (footnote 21).

In the case of bicycle helmets, the Department of Consumer and Corporate Affairs, with the full cooperation of industry and CSA, had initiated bicycle helmet regulations.[42] However, our interviews suggest that, because of concerns raised in particular by OPRA, it was decided that regulation was not appropriate, and the proposal was withdrawn.

The decision to withdraw the regulation stemmed from several factors. The vast majority of helmets on the market met one of the major standards. It was felt that if manufacturers were compelled to meet the CSA standard in addition to whichever American standard they complied with, they would pass on the costs of adherence to the consumer through higher helmet prices. Concerns were also raised that the potential increase in price would result in lower helmet usage among cyclists. In the final analysis, it was concluded that the potential reduction in head injuries achieved through the improvement of the helmets would not be offset by the potential increase in head injuries due to lower helmet usage.

It is interesting to note that in the case of bicycle helmets there is no powerful user association akin to the CHA which can compel the wearing of bicycle helmets in the same way that the CHA can compel the use of CSA-approved hockey helmets by its members. Although there are bicycle racing associations, they have far less influence on bicyclists than the CHA has on hockey players. Whereas hockey is a sport most often played in an organized forum, bicycling is primarily a leisure activity or a means of transportation and is not generally organized. However, as will be discussed later, the increasing number of provincial, state and municipal bicycle helmet-use laws are compelling cyclists to wear approved helmets in particular jurisdictions.

Process

The CSA bicycle helmet standard was published in 1989 following a development process similar to the one described above with respect to hockey helmets. Like the CSA hockey helmet standard, the bicycle helmet standard is a technical document requiring that the helmets pass a particular impact test. At present, bicycle helmet manufacturers are under no Canadian legislated obligation to meet any safety standard. In contrast, as of 1999, all helmets sold in the U.S. had to meet a separate, legislated standard that was developed by the Consumer Product Safety Commission.[43]

Companies complying with the CSA standard are entitled to place the CSA logo on their helmets, thus offering a signal of assurance to safety-conscious consumers. Helmets that comply with more than one standard will often bear several logos. However, an advantage of CSA certification is that the CSA logo is more familiar to

---

42. *Federal Regulatory Plan 1990* (footnote 33), p. 51. *Federal Regulatory Plan 1991* (footnote 33), p. 49.

43. This stands in contrast to the situation in the U.S., where federal legislation known as the *Children's Bicycle Helmet Safety Act of 1994*, § 201-207, Pub. L. 103-267, 108 Stat. 726-729; 15 U.S.C. 6001-6006, requires that all helmets meet any one of a prescribed set of standards. Although the title of the Act specifically refers to children's helmets, it actually covers all types of helmets. The Act contains two initiatives, the first is to promote the use of bicycle helmets by children (hence the name), the second is to develop a national safety standard for bicycle helmets.

Canadian consumers than most other logos.[44] This may provide a company with a competitive advantage if it plans to service the Canadian market.

Implementation

CSA enforces its standard by first testing samples of a prototype batch from the applicant. If the prototypes pass the CSA tests, then CSA authorizes the use of its logo for that particular helmet. Twice a year CSA inspects the manufacturing site — to ensure that quality control measures are in place — and randomly tests helmets from the site. If any of the samples fails to meet the standard, CSA launches a confidential investigation. CSA does not provide an estimate of how much the cost of certification adds to each helmet. However, the manufacturer pays $450 for each of the two inspections CSA conducts each year.[45] Re-testing fees are $700, and there is a licensing fee of between $800 and $1000 per year. Each label costs $0.04.[46]

Effectiveness of Voluntary Bicycle Helmet Standards

Overall, the CSA standard, like its U.S. counterparts, appears to have successfully ensured that bicycle helmets are safe. Virtually every manufacturer of bicycle helmets adheres to at least one of the major safety standards. As the Department of Consumer and Corporate Affairs noted when withdrawing its regulatory proposal, a market survey had shown that retail outlets did not carry helmets which did not meet at least one of the predominant standards.[47] *Consumer Reports* magazine surveys of the U.S. market in the past (i.e. before the mandatory standard came into effect) have confirmed this conclusion. In 1990 the magazine tested a wide variety of helmets available in the U.S. and found only one that did not meet the impact test.[48] There is no

---

44. A 1984 survey found that more Canadian consumers recognized the CSA logo than recognized the logo of any other certification body. T. A. Watts, *Consumer Awareness and Perception of Canadian Marks of Conformity* (Ottawa: Standards Council of Canada, 1984), p. 23. The information is admittedly dated, but casual observation shows that the CSA label is, if anything, even better known today.

45. Interview with Charlie Caruara of CSA, June 1996.

46. Ibid. In contrast, Snell regulates usage of its logo in a unique manner. Operating on the theory that the best test subjects are products actually available to the public, Snell buys its test-sample helmets directly from retailers. If a helmet purchased by Snell fails to meet the Snell standard, another three are purchased. If any of these is not up to standard, Snell will require the manufacturer to correct the defect. If no action is taken Snell will recall its certification and in some cases publish a retraction of their certification.

47. *Canada Gazette* (footnote 34), p. 756. In the U.S., incidents of non-compliance with standards, resulting in Consumer Product Safety Commission (CPSC) recalls, do occur from time to time. (The Bicycle Helmet Safety Institute gathers information in this regard at <http://www.helmets.org/recalls.htm>.) In one U.S. case, the manufacturer of a toy helmet (clearly marketed as such) claimed that it had no obligation to comply with the regulations since its product was not intended for use as a real helmet. (Described by Scott Heh, Division of Engineering, CPSC, in interview, June 1996.) Since the the CPSC came into full effect, such non-compliance can carry with it serious legal penalties.

48. "Bike Helmets: Unused Lifesavers," *Consumer Reports,* May 1990, p. 348.

indication that this helmet was ever sold in Canada. A follow-up survey in 1994 found that every helmet tested met acceptable standards.[49]

The apparent high rate of compliance among bicycle helmet manufacturers appears to be related to the fact that consumer awareness of safety issues has grown in recent years. In Canada, consumers are so accustomed to seeing the CSA logo on virtually every piece of protective equipment that they are hesitant to purchase helmets that are not CSA-approved. Since consumers desire safe helmets and associate the logos with safety, manufacturers have an incentive to ensure that their helmets meet these standards.

Interpretive Analysis

Canada's voluntary bicycle helmet performance standards are effective primarily because industry compliance is almost total. It is possible to identify four main reasons for the overwhelming industry compliance with bicycle helmet standards: the maturation of standards organizations, high consumer awareness of safety issues, legal liability risks, and helmet-use laws requiring that cyclists wear certified helmets. These are discussed in greater detail below.

The Maturation of Respected Standards Organizations. Most of today's prominent standards-writing organizations were created in the early part of the last century.[50] The early years of these organizations were spent developing a reputation with both industry and consumers. As standards organizations have become better established, it has become easier to convince industry, government and consumers that they offer valuable services. By the early 1980s, it was clear that a majority of consumers recognized the logos of the major standards organizations.[51] Thus, by the early 1990s bicycle helmet manufacturers were aware of the benefits of complying with one of the major standards as a signal of assurance to consumers.

Increased Consumer Awareness of Safety-related Issues. The consumer movement of the 1960s and 70s demonstrated a growing public awareness of marketplace safety issues. In the 1990s consumers seem to use several factors when determining which products to purchase. Although price is often important, safety appears to be a critical factor as well.[52] In the current marketplace consumers tend not to accept products that have not undergone testing to ensure their safety. This is particularly true of protective equipment such as helmets. If consumers will not buy unsafe products, even less expensive ones, there is little reason for the manufacturer to make them or the vendor to stock them.

---

49. "Bicycle Helmets," *Consumer Reports*, August 1994, p. 518.

50. CSA was established in 1919, ANSI in 1918 and ASTM in 1898. Snell, on the other hand, was formed in 1956.

51. Watts (footnote 44), p. 21.

52. The above-mentioned survey found that 94 percent of respondents always or sometimes looked for the CSA logo when purchasing products. Ibid., p. 73.

The Legal Liability of the Helmet Manufacturer and Vendor. Since the 1970s there has been an increasing awareness on the part of manufacturers and vendors of their potential tort liability for unsafe products. In the case of bicycle helmets, most manufacturers will not make products which do not pass the tests of a major standards organization, since this is the best way to show insurers, vendors, consumers and the courts that the product is safe. While the fact that a bicycle helmet is certified by a major standards organization will not necessarily relieve the manufacturer and vendor of liability, selling a helmet that could *not* be certified will increase the likelihood of being found liable in negligence when injuries occur.[53]

The Emergence of Mandatory Bicycle Helmet Use Laws. In the late 1980s various jurisdictions began to make wearing bicycle helmets mandatory for some or all cyclists. The helmets must meet approved standards. The first North American jurisdiction to adopt such legislation was California, which required bicycle helmets to be worn by all passengers under five in 1987, and other U.S. jurisdictions have followed this example.[54] The bicycle helmet industry understood that there would be more such legislation in the future. Since, inevitably, this legislation would specify that the helmet must be approved by a particular standards organization, manufacturers realized that they must conform their helmets to these standards if they wished to sell them. The move toward mandatory helmet-use legislation has also taken place in Canada. An Ontario law, making helmet-use mandatory for all cyclists under the age of 18, came into effect October 1, 1995. The law states that helmets must conform to at least one of nine different standards, including Snell, CSA, ANSI and ASTM.[55] Then, British Columbia in 1996 became the first North American province or state to make the wearing of certified helmets mandatory for *all* riders.[56] Because of the trend towards legislating helmet use, the industry has had a strong incentive to ensure that helmets are capable of passing the various standards. Failure to do so would make the helmets virtually unmarketable in areas that have mandated their use.

---

53. See, e.g., *Hohlenkamp v. Rheem Mfg. Co.* (1982) 655 P2d 32, discussed in 47 ALR 4th, 621), a U.S. products liability case involving an allegedly defective water heater. In this case, the defendant manufacturer's evidence that it had complied with applicable ANSI standards was deemed admissible. According to ALR, "the court expressed the belief that industry standards promulgated by organizations like the ANSI, through their use of committees of experts in the particular industry, were more representative of the consensus of the industry than any single learned treatise or expert's opinion." Such admissibility is a selling point used by standards organizations in touting their services. For instance, in promotional literature, the U.K's British Standards Institution tells businesses that the use of its logo "provides you with evidence to help show due diligence in product liability cases. It shows you have sought the approval of the world's most respected standards body." See BSI-Global, *The Kitemark: Business Benefits*, London: 2000, available at <www.bsi-global.com/Kitemark/Overview/Business_Benefits.xalter>. For further discussion of the legal aspects of voluntary codes see Kernaghan Webb and Andrew Morrison, "The Law and Vountary Codes: Examining the 'Tangled Web'," Chapter 5, above.

54. The Bicycle Helmet Safety Institute provides an inventory of such laws; see *Helmet Laws for Bicycle Riders*, available at <www.helmets.org/mandator.htm>.

55. *Highway Traffic Act*, s. 104; Ont. Reg. 411/95, 610.4(1).

56. See footnote 3. The effectiveness of British Columbia's law has been the subject of a study (*British Columbia Bicycle Helmet Study*) by the University of North Carolina's Highway Safety Research Center, available at <www.hsrc.unc.edu/pubinfo/bike_bchelmets.htm>.

The high rate of industry compliance with bicycle helmet standards has helped to mask two other possible reasons why bicycle helmet standards are not regulated under the *Hazardous Products Act*: the belief that the problem was insufficient to merit regulation; and concerns surrounding the free trade implications. These two points merit a closer look.

Insufficient justification to merit regulation. Since the proposed regulation was not designed to increase the number of bicycle helmet wearers, but only guarantee the integrity of the helmets worn by cyclists, the regulation, by itself, would have had only a minimal effect in reducing injuries. Without some means of increasing the use of bicycle helmets among bicyclists, it was felt that any increase in the quality of bicycle helmets would not result in a significant decrease in head injuries sustained in bicycle accidents. The problem was not so much that the helmets on the market were unsafe, but that helmets were not widely used. This stands in contrast to hockey, in which players have been injured while wearing an unsafe helmet.

Canada-U.S. Free Trade Agreement (FTA). In Chapter Six of the FTA (which came into effect on January 1, 1989), Canada and the U.S. pledged not to introduce product standards that would create unnecessary barriers to trade between the two countries.[57] As a result, Canada can only introduce standards-related regulations if it can demonstrate that the purpose of doing so is to achieve health and safety objectives. When the proposal for regulation was reviewed, concerns surfaced that referential incorporation of the CSA standard into the *Hazardous Products Act* might constitute a trade barrier contrary to Article 603. Although it was suggested that the regulation could be justified under the health and safety exception, there was no concrete evidence that the CSA standard was superior to the major American standards. The possibility of a trade dispute over a regulation that was ultimately considered to be unnecessary to achieve its safety objective, was yet another reason for withdrawing the proposal to regulate.[58]

In short, there have been a number of factors that help to explain the particular approach to adoption of bicycle helmet standards and bicycle helmet use laws in Canada.

Distinctive Nature of Hockey and Bicycling Activities

A final possible explanation for the different approaches might be the distinctive nature of hockey and bicycling. People usually play hockey in groups — teams — against others. Although the team formation does not have to be formally undertaken, it is clear that a user organization which establishes leagues, and allows for graduation from one tier to another, can be extremely important in the sport's development and popularity among young people. In Canada, user organizations (notably, the Canadian Hockey Association) perform an important intermediary role in ensuring that many

---

57. International Trade Communications Group, *The Canada-U.S. Free Trade Agreement* (Ottawa: 1987), Article 603. The FTA was incorporated into the subsequent North American Free Trade Agreement, Chapter 9, available at the Web site of the Organization of American States, <www.sice.oas.org/trade/nafta/naftatce.asp>.

58. This information was provided by Georges Desbarats (footnote 21).

Canadians play hockey. Organized hockey also usually requires a rink, a costly item that few individuals would ever be in a position to build and maintain. Therefore, user organizations encourage governments to create and maintain the much-needed rinks. Thus, such organizations act both as gatekeepers (giving associations such as the CHA a certain latitude to impose conditions upon its members) and as facilitators (ensuring the availability of appropriate fora for play). Both roles make them potentially liable when things go awry. Given the powerful position of the CHA with respect to its members, combined with its potential vulnerability, it is not surprising that a predominantly non-legislative approach has been largely successful in persuading hockey players to use standardized helmets.[59]

This situation is in contrast to cycling. For many, cycling is a solitary activity. It can be a mode of transportation or a leisure activity. It is not necessary for a cyclist to join a bicycling association in order to ride his or her bicycle. Cycling need not involve teams and, therefore, many cyclists — even avid ones — see no need for organized bicycling activities. Cycling does not require the use of specialized facilities: any road or path will suffice (although specialized facilities do exist, and may attract clubs). As a result, with the exception of racing organizations that tend to rigorously enforce helmet requirements, cycling associations do not play a central role in the pursuit of cycling. In turn, cycling associations are not in as powerful a position as hockey associations in terms of their ability to perform gate-keeping functions and impose rules on users. Nor would they, in normal circumstances, be as likely to attract liability as a result of a cyclist's activities. Thus, for the average cyclist, a rule requiring the wearing of a helmet prescribed by a bicycling association would hold no sway. Yet cyclists' head injuries can impose costs on many public services and bodies (particularly health-related costs). It is not surprising, then, that laws regarding the use of bicycle helmets have been considered necessary in an increasing number of Canadian jurisdictions. Looked at this way, the nature of the activity in question would appear to have played an important role in determining the approach to policy-instrument selection.[60]

Conclusion

The divergent approaches adopted to implement performance and use requirements for hockey and bicycle helmets provide a number of interesting insights concerning why and how regulatory and non-regulatory instruments and institutions are used in consumer safety contexts. At its most basic level, this chapter suggests that it is wrong to view the selection of regulatory and non-regulatory approaches as an either/or proposition. In practice, the two may work in tandem. Thus, for example, there are

59. Another factor may be the relatively high level of consumer knowledge regarding hockey equipment, which ensures that sub-standard helmets will not find a market in Canada. See M. E. Porter, *Canada at the Crossroads* (Ottawa: Ministry of Supply and Services, 1991), pp. 227–228.

60. Another example of the way the nature of the activity can play a role in policy development is equestrian helmets. Equestrian helmets are certified by ASTM. There are no laws or regulations requiring that they meet the ASTM standard, but major equestrian bodies such as the United States Pony Club and the American Horse Shows Association require the use of certified helmets in the events they sponsor. See J. Woodward, "The New Regulations: Prepare for Impact," *Tack 'n Togs Merchandising*, December 1989, p. 30.

federal regulatory product standards for hockey helmets, yet use requirements are (with the exception of Quebec) implemented through non-regulatory means. In the case of bicycle helmets, performance standards are not set out in law, but several jurisdictions have use requirements enshrined in law.

Moreover, it is worth emphasizing that in both the hockey and bicycling contexts, the mix of regulatory and voluntary techniques in place operates against a backdrop of tort liability. That is, should an injury take place, there is a potential for the harmed party to bring an action in negligence against manufacturers, vendors, member associations, standards organizations, facility owners and even governments, if it can be established that a duty of care was owed, and that a reasonable care standard has been violated. This potential for private civil law actions provides an important stimulus for many parties to put in place both regulatory and voluntary measures.

As to why one particular set of regulatory and voluntary measures is in use in the case of hockey helmets, and another for bicycle helmets, we have seen how a combination of factors seems to be at play, including the distinctive nature of the activity itself, different governmental attitudes over time toward the use of regulation and its alternatives, divergent market conditions, the ability of user associations to compel use on members, the existence of regulations in other jurisdictions, and the increasing credibility of standards bodies in the eyes of government, the private sector, the courts and consumers.

PART FOUR

The Codes Experience Outside Canada

Chapter 12
Codes of Practice: The Australian Experience

Neil Gunningham

   This chapter seeks to encapsulate the considerable Australian experience of codes of practice[1] rather than to rehearse the various potential benefits and pitfalls of codes in the abstract. It does so in three parts. First, it describes a variety of Australian government initiatives intended to nurture this approach, including the development of a Guide to Codes of Conduct and principles about their use. Second, it focusses on one code which contains many of the best features of this approach, and in relation to which there is considerable empirical evidence: the *Australian Code of Practice for Computerised Checkout Systems in Supermarkets*.[2] Third, it draws broader lessons about the factors necessary for codes of practice to function effectively and in the public interest, and about their potential role as an alternative or complement to government regulation.

When are Codes of Practice Appropriate?

The Australian Government Experience

   A 1988 Trades Practices Commission (TPC) report on self-regulation provided the impetus for a reassessment of the role of codes of conduct in Australian industry. Australia first considered developing a manual on the appropriate uses, design and implementation of codes of conduct in 1989. From this original concept, the *Guide to Codes of Conduct* gradually evolved in the early 1990s. Draft guidelines were developed and distributed to industry informally. The Commission then consulted business and consumer representative bodies for comment and input. At this stage, further reflection went into the design of the Guide, which was then formally released in October 1996.[3]

---

1. In keeping with this book's definition of voluntary codes, in this chapter codes of practice will be taken to encompass non-legislatively required commitments by industry designed to change or influence firm behaviour, and which ensure that industry practices comply with basic principles of consumer protection. Later in the chapter I will explore why it is important not to describe them as necessarily "pure" self-regulation. Nevertheless, the term *self-regulation* is often used by government and others to describe codes of practice; see, e.g., the work of the Australian Taskforce on Industry Self-Regulation, *Industry Self-Regulation in Consumer Markets* (Canberra: Department of the Treasury, August 2000), available at <www.selfregulation.gov.au/publications/TaskForceOnIndustrySelf-Regulation/FinalReport/download/final_report.pdf>.

2. Australian Retailers Association (ARA), *Australian Code of Practice for Computerised Checkout Systems in Supermarkets* (Sydney: ARA, 2001), available at <www.ara.com.au/asi/SCANNING_CODE.PDF>.

3. Australian Consumer and Competition Commission (ACCC), *Fair Trading Codes of Conduct: Why Have Them, How to Prepare Them* ["*The Guide*"] (Canberra: ACCC, 1996), p. 1.

Kernaghan Webb, Editor, *Voluntary Codes: Private Governance, the Public Interest and Innovation.*
This chapter ©2004 Neil Gunningham, pages 317–334.
Published by the Carleton Research Unit for Innovation, Science and Environment, Carleton University, Ottawa, Canada.

In subsequent years, the Commonwealth government has continued to study the value of codes of conduct and self-regulation generally. In March 1998, the Minister of Customs and Consumer Affairs released *Codes of Conduct Policy Framework.*[4] This document shares common themes with the Guide, but places codes of conduct in the context of the government's policy objectives, describing "the Government's likely response to problems that arise in the marketplace and, in particular, when a code of conduct might be the appropriate response to answer that problem."[5] More recently, there have been other significant developments. In 1999, the Minister for Financial Services and Regulation established a Task Force on Industry Self-Regulation, which produced its final report in August 2000.[6] Also, the Commonwealth Treasury commissioned a consultancy group to produce a report on the efficacy of self-regulation. Released in 2000, this report identifies "the characteristics of markets where various forms of self-regulation are likely to operate effectively and the circumstances where self-regulation is likely to be inappropriate."[7] Finally, the Australian Government announced its intention to develop another guide to self-regulation for industry.[8]

The stated purpose of the current Guide is to serve as a "useful reference tool," promoting codes as a "means of improving the economic and social well-being of Australia."[9] The other documents produced over the past few years expand upon this purpose. The Task Force, for its part, associates the use of self-regulatory schemes with cost-efficiency. According to the Task Force, "Self-regulatory schemes tend to promote good practice and target specific problems within industries, impose lower compliance costs on business, and offer quick, low cost dispute resolution procedures. Effective self-regulation can also avoid the often overly prescriptive nature of regulation."[10] The consultancy group similarly recognized the argument that self-regulation tends to lead to efficiencies, but notes that the extent to which market failures can be redressed by self-regulation depends entirely on a set of contextual circumstances.[11] For instance, among its key findings, the group notes that self-regulation is more likely to reach its stated

---

4. Minister of Customs and Consumer Affairs, *Codes of Conduct Policy Framework* (Canberra: MCCA, 1998), available at <www.selfregulation.gov.au/publications/CodesOfConduct-PolicyFramework/index.asp>.

5. Ibid., p. 7.

6. Task Force on Industry Self-regulation (footnote 1).

7. J. Wallace, D. Ironfield and J. Orr, *Analysis of Market Circumstances Where Industry Self-Regulation is Likely to be Most and Least Effective* (Canberra: Tasman Asia Pacific Pty Ltd., May 2000), available at <www.selfregulation.gov.au/publications/TaskForceOnIndustrySelf-Regulation/ConsultantReport/ch1.pdf>.

8. On December 13, 2000, the Minister for Financial Services and Regulation announced that the government would publish a guideline for businesses, consumers and government advisers. This guideline is intended to provide practical advice on self-regulation and to be a gateway to other resources on self-regulation. This initiative responded to a suggestion made by the Minister's Task Force on Industry Self-Regulation. The guideline is currently being drafted and the government promises that it will appear at <www.selfregulation.gov.au/ind_self_reg.asp>.

9. *The Guide* (footnote 3), p. 3.

10. Task Force on Industry Self-regulation (footnote 1), p.21.

11. See "Key Findings," Wallace, Ironfield and Orr (footnote 7), p. iv.

goals in a market that is competitive and when the products in question are homogeneous; it is less likely to do so in an uncompetitive market and when the products are "complex and heterogeneous in the eyes of consumers."[12]

The overall problem to which the Guide, and the codes themselves, are addressed, is that of protecting consumers from the abuses sometimes generated by completely unregulated competition. For example, in a deregulated marketplace, consumers commonly confront problems relating to the supply of inferior-quality or unsafe goods, costs of access to redress when there are problems with a product, inadequate service standards, and lack of information about product use and after-sales service.

As the consultancy group indicated,[13] there are a number of ways in which market failures can be addressed, of which codes of conduct are only one,[14] and one which is not appropriate to every market imperfection. It is important, therefore to first ask whether intervention is really required. It might be, for example, appropriate (if the problem is trivial) to take no action at all, or if action is justified, codes may not be the most effective and cost-efficient option. While the consultancy group drew up its own elaborate list,[15] the Task Force highlighted a checklist developed by the Commonwealth Office of Regulation Review. The checklist calls for self-regulation when:

- there is no strong public interest concern, in particular, no major public health and safety concern;
- the problem is a low risk event, of low impact/significance, in other words, the consequences of self-regulation failing to resolve a specific problem are small; and
- the problem can be fixed by the market itself, in other words there is an incentive for individuals and groups to develop and comply with self-regulatory arrangements (e.g. for industry survival or to gain a market advantage).[16]

Even in circumstances when a code *does* seem a viable approach, the creation of such a code does not necessarily imply that government should completely vacate the field. On the contrary, it may still have a continuing role in enforcing the general consumer protection legislation when code participants breach that legislation, and it must be prepared to escalate up a regulatory pyramid by introducing legislation if the code proves to be ineffective. By keeping such sticks in the closet, an industry has more incentive to regulate itself effectively. Consistent with the above, the *Codes of Conduct*

---

12. Ibid.

13. Noting that different contexts create very different circumstances, the group states that "the development of effective regulation involves a careful analysis and comparison of the relative merits of alternative forms of self-regulation, government regulation, and legislation, and mixes of those regulations." (Wallace, Ironfield and Orr [footnote 7], p. ix.)

14. Alternatives to the use of codes of practice include no action, fostering improved market responses such as improved information, guidance by the regulator, establishing a complaint handling mechanism, either at the firm or industry association level, co-regulation, direct regulation, and taxes and charges to ensure that the costs of externalities are borne by producers and users. See Trade Practices Commission (Australia), *Final Report by the Trades Practices Commission on the Self-Regulation of Promotion and Advertising of Therapeutic Goods*, Canberra: Trade Practices Commission, July 1992, p. 8.

15. See footnote 11.

16. Task Force on Industry Self-Regulation (footnote 1), p. 43.

Policy Framework, released by the Minister of Customs and Consumer Affairs in 1998, suggests implementing the following four principles:

- The general presumption is that competitive market forces deliver greater choice and benefits to consumers.
- The government will consider intervention when there is market failure or demonstrated need to achieve a particular social objective.
- Effective voluntary codes of conduct are the preferred method of intervention.
- When a code of conduct is not effective, the government may assist industry to regulate effectively.[17]

Necessary Elements of a Code

Assuming that, in the circumstances, a code is an appropriate response to market failure — because it will potentially produce a more efficient market outcome than other solutions —the crucial question then becomes how to design and structure codes so as to best achieve their public interest goals. It is here that the Guide makes its most important contribution in identifying some basic criteria and suggesting some options for use within those criteria. That is, drawing upon the experience of existing codes that agencies believe have been successful in delivering fair trading outcomes, the Guide provides a reference for any party interested in developing a new code.

The Guide only very briefly addresses the process of code development, emphasizing the importance of participation by industry members, consumer affairs agencies and consumer public interest groups.[18] It deals far more extensively with substantive matters, proposing seven sections that a "code should contain," while recognizing that "there will be variations between industries in the content and extent of detail in each of these sections."[19] The sections are:

- scope (who it applies to and who is bound by the code);
- objectives (the expected outcomes);
- core rules (technical standards and performance benchmarks to be delivered by members of the industry);
- complaints, dispute procedures and sanctions;
- administration of the codes;
- publicity and reporting; and
- monitoring, review and amendments.[20]

---

17. Minister of Customs and Consumer Affairs (footnote 4), p. 3.

18. *The Guide* (footnote 3), pp. 4–5.

19. Ibid., p. 5.

20. Ibid.

The Guide itself is somewhat terse in its requirements. It is, therefore, worth noting a more detailed list of requirements, proposed by the TPC in 1992:

- a clear statement of the objects of the code principles that address common complaints about industry practices and/or that set performance standards for industry;
- a mechanism to provide for administration of the code that contains some form of outside representation (such a body would have direct responsibility to supervise the ongoing administration of the code, ensuring that it was adequately resourced, publicized and modified to meet prevailing market conditions);
- membership covering a substantial proportion of the relevant industry;
- provision for an independent complaints-handling body that can deal with complaints from the public and industry members when there are breaches of the codes principles (such a body to be easily accessible and to provide quick and inexpensive remedies for complainants);
- provision for commercially significant sanctions for breaches of the code of practice;
- ensuring knowledge of the existence of the code and its complaints handling provisions amongst relevant groups through widespread publicity and other methods;
- training, so that association members and their employees are conversant with the provisions of the code;
- data collection, so that the association members or the association itself have a good profile of what practices or which members are giving cause for concern, and to give some indication of how practices may have changed over time;
- ongoing monitoring for compliance with standards of practice;
- transparency provisions, such as the production of annual reports on the operation of the code to allow for a period assessment of the scheme's effectiveness by industry members, its customers and the public at large; and
- regular review to ensure that the standard is meeting current community expectations.[21]

However, the gap between theory and practice may be considerable, and further insights can be gained as to the value of the principles articulated above, by examining the application of a particular industry code in concrete circumstances.

Testing by Results: the *Australian Code of Practice for Computerised Checkout Systems in Supermarkets*

Origins and Administration

During the late 1980s, major supermarket chains in Australia began to implement new bar code scanning technology for the sale of goods to consumers. Under this new system, prices are no longer visible on the product. Instead, a price appears on the shelf, and a bar code is present on the product itself, which in turn correlates to a

---

21. TPC (footnote 14), pp. 8–9.

centralized price register kept on the store's computer database. As each individual product passes through a checkout scanner, a price appears on the checkout's display unit. This system provides a number of efficiencies for supermarkets, particularly for those with a larger turnover of stock.

At the time of its introduction, however, concerns were raised about the accuracy of prices and potential scope for abuse. Such concerns arose because of a potential gap in information between the consumer and the retailer. In particular, consumers have to remember the shelf price if they want to be sure they are charged the correct price when they reach the checkout. Since this may not be easy, particularly when a person is buying large numbers of items, discrepancies between the shelf price and the price charged at the checkout may go unnoticed by the consumer. There is a risk that supermarkets could exploit this possibility to systematically overcharge shoppers.

In order to address such fears, a supermarket industry association[22] introduced the *Australian Code of Practice for Computerised Checkout Systems in Supermarkets* (the "Scanning Code" or "Code") in 1989, with the support of the then Trade Practices Commission (TPC).[23] The aims of the Scanning Code are to minimize discrepancies between the shelf price and the price charged, ensure shelf labels and receipts are informative and readable, provide a remedy for customers when overcharges or other problems arise, and inform customers and store staff about these safeguards and remedies.[24] The TPC gave permission for its name and logo to appear on signs and leaflets promoting the Code, and the ACCC's name and logo continue to appear on the current (2001) version of the Code. According to a 1992 review of the Code, at least 83 percent of scanning supermarkets in Australia subscribed to the Code.[25] A number of incentives are built into the Code to discourage abuse. With regard to overcharging for a single item, for example, the customer receives the item free of charge. In the case of multiple items with the same bar code being charged at more than the shelf price, then the first item is free of charge, with the remainder being charged at the lower price.

However, these provisions are only effective to the extent that consumers are able to bring price discrepancies to the attention of supermarket staff and obtain redress. To this end, the Code sets out the course of action consumers must follow in terms of complaint handling and dispute resolution procedures. First, consumers must speak to the store manager or supervisor. In turn, retailers are required to ensure that all such complaints are taken seriously and treated courteously. Second, and failing a successful resolution in the first instance, the store manager or supervisor is required to inform the customer of the formal complaints procedures available: completion of a complaints form

---

22. The original supermarket association was replaced by the Australian Supermarket Institute, which is now a division of the Australian Retailers Association (ARA). ARA administers the Scanning Code for its member supermarkets. See *Scanning Code* (footnote 2), s. 1.

23. Since then, the TPC was replaced by the current Australian Competition and Consumer Commission (ACCC). See *Scanning Code*, ibid.

24. While not explicitly stated in the text of the Scanning Code itself, these aims are noted in Wallace, Ironfield and Orr (footnote 7), pp. 95–96.

25. This information is taken from TPC, *Checkout the Price: Review of Supermarket Scanning Code Report* (Canberra: TPC, July 1992). Exact percentages for today are not available, though the consultancy report indicates that supermarkets subject to the Code now number approximately 5000. (Wallace, Ironfield and Orr, footnote 7, p. 96.)

made available by the supermarket (along with a reply-paid envelope) or by a telephone call to the relevant industry association. Complaints are then heard by a state-based administrative committee made up of industry, government and consumer representatives, and a decision is made within 28 days. Third, if a decision cannot be reached by the committee, or if a decision is unacceptable to either party, then an independent arbitrator is appointed.

The overall administration of the Code is conducted by a National Administrative Committee (NAC) chaired by the ASI Executive Director and made up of executive directors from each of the state/territory industry associations. In addition, a consumers' representative must be present, and a representative of the Commonwealth government may attend as an observer. The NAC is responsible for continually reviewing the Code, and, when it is deemed appropriate, initiating modifications (following a call for submissions from interested parties). While the Code itself does not have force of law, all supermarkets (whether or they use scanners or not) are subject to an enforceable regulatory background, in particular the provisions of both state and Commonwealth legislation which make it illegal to mislead a customer about the selling price or description of any item.

Evaluating the Code

Has the Code been effective in minimizing discrepancies between the shelf price and the price charged; ensuring shelf labels and receipts are informative and readable; providing a remedy for customers when overcharges or other problems arise; and informing customers and store staff about these safeguards and remedies?

Based on a series of reviews, the then TPC concluded that price discrepancies had been within reasonable limits and shelf labels and receipts were, on the whole, informative and readable.[26] However, whether this was due to the Code was hard to gauge, "but it seemed likely that the current code and its predecessors, which date back to 1989, played a role in achieving this."[27] The following were particularly significant: in both scanning and non-scanning supermarkets, undercharges usually outweigh overcharges, so that customers have a good chance of coming out ahead over time in monetary terms; customers fare no worse on average in scanning stores than in non-scanning stores, in terms of overcharging; and this was the situation as early as 1987–1988, pre-dating the formal launching of the Code in 1989.[28]

Another important performance indicator is the number of formal complaints, which has been trending downwards. While by 1999 some 299 phone calls and 52 letters had been received by the ASI, the majority of these were not actually complaints.[29] Rather, they were a range of suggestions for store improvements or other non-Code-related matters. When consumers did have a complaint about pricing, all of these were resolved without further customer complaint.

---

26. TPC, ibid., p. 8.

27. Ibid.

28. Ibid., p. 9.

29. Wallace, Ironfield and Orr (footnote 7), p. 99.

From the evidence it had gathered, the TPC (and its successor, the ACCC) concluded that there was no justification for making the Code mandatory. Not only had the Code performed acceptably well, but it covered more than 83 percent of the supermarket scanning industry, and was already underpinned by the general legislative provisions concerning misleading selling. However, the TPC did identify several areas of possible improvement of the Code. In particular, it noted that past monitoring had been deficient in a number of areas, that complaints data had not been uniformly recorded, that some data that might have been useful had not been recorded at all, and that no analysis of national performance had been attempted by the industry body. This led the TPC to suggest a number of modifications to the Code. Prominent among these were the following:

- making the complaints system more accessible to consumers;
- reducing the size of in-store signs, but making them more eye-catching and informative;
- enhancing consumer representation on the Code committees;
- providing the public with annual reports of the Code's operation; and
- setting out the scope of the item-free policy in the Code.[30]

The TPC concluded that it would be impractical to extend the Code to cover non-supermarket retail scanning in all retail sectors, given the variety of store circumstances and the possibility of very expensive consumer items being obtained free of charge. Instead, it was determined that the TPC would write to the industry associations of each of the major retail sectors recommending that the Code be used as a guide for developing their own codes.

The question, however, of how much of the supermarkets' performance (in terms of the rate of overcharging) can be attributed directly to the Code, remains difficult to answer. For example, the extent to which customers have received free items when overcharged is only an estimate because the Code does not require stores to actually record this. Numbers of consumer complaints may be more an indicator of the public awareness of the complaints system than a measure of overall consumer satisfaction. On the issue of customer awareness of the Code, for example, the TPC review suggested there was room for improvement, and further, that checkout staff's awareness of the item-free policy and ability to provide consumers with a copy of the explanatory leaflet on the Code was patchy.[31]

To provide a more definitive answer to the question of Code performance, the ASI has commissioned a series of surveys to determine consumer awareness. These have revealed a relatively high consumer recognition rate, in the order of 70 percent. Additional ASI-commissioned surveys have confirmed the TPC review's conclusion that there has been no widespread overcharging of consumers. Overall, it is hard to disagree with their view that the Code, "while far from perfect, has probably played a role, along

---

30. TPC (footnote 25), p. 9.

31. Ibid., p. 8.

with improvements over time in scanning management systems and technology, together with competition, in helping stores make a relatively smooth transition to scanning and in helping allay consumer concerns about scanning."[32]

Accepting that the Code has been successful in achieving its stated objectives (that is, allaying consumer concerns) in improving the ability of consumers to verify the accuracy of displayed prices, providing cost efficient dispute resolution procedures, and providing compensation via the "item free policy," then what are the reasons for its success? Crucially, there is evidence to suggest that there is a substantial coincidence of interest between that of consumers in not paying misleading prices and that of large supermarket chains in protecting their reputation.[33] We explore in more detail below how to harness this coincidence of interest and, more important, how best to face the challenges to regulatory design in circumstances when public and private interest substantially diverge.

Ensuring that Codes of Practice Function Effectively

Co-Regulation: the Role of Government and Third Parties

Drawing from the experience of the Australian Scanning Code, from impressionistic evidence of a broader range of codes gathered during the course of our research, and from the experience of other self-regulatory initiatives, such as Responsible Care, this section identifies the wider lessons that can be learned about the prerequisites for successful codes and for the design of such codes. In particular, it examines the extent to which an underpinning of State control is necessary for the successful functioning in the public interest of the large majority of codes of practice.

In considering this last question, it is important to recognize that there is no clear dichotomy between self-regulation on the one hand and government regulation on the other. Rather, there is a continuum, with pure forms of self-regulation and government regulation at opposite ends. However, those pure forms are rarely found in the real world, in which distinctions between self-regulation and government regulation are incremental rather than dichotomous.

While codes of practice are conventionally viewed very much as a form of self-regulation, there is no reason in principle why they should be located at the voluntary self-regulation extreme of the continuum. Indeed, there are considerable reasons in practice why they should not. For reasons we explore below, in the majority of circumstances, codes of practice are likely to more effective when they function in combination with some form of outside (usually government) regulation or control.

Such models are often referred to as "co-regulation," this being defined variously as "the formulation and adoption of rules and regulations done in consultation

---

32. Ibid., p. 17.

33. Consistent with this, the consultancy report draws three general conclusions: First, the regularity and familiarity of consumer supermarket shopping habits mean that they are likely to be more price conscious than in other retail circumstances. Second, in a competitive environment, supermarkets place a premium on their reputation. And third, there is a shared interest between supermarkets and their consumers in ensuring true pricing. See Wallace, Ironfield and Orr (footnote 7).

with stakeholders, negotiated within prescribed boundaries"[34] and as industry-wide voluntary standards that are ratified by government and enforced by industry associations and public interest groups.[35] Since there are numerous possible forms of co-regulation, no single definition adequately encapsulates them all. To illustrate why a variety of different forms of self- and co-regulation may be desirable, the following categorization of codes of practice and of the settings in which they may be used, is helpful:[36]

(i) those that advance the private interests of industry members but have no detrimental effect on consumer or public interests;

(ii) those having the primary purpose of pursuing the industry's private interests at the expense of consumer and public interests (e.g., through collusive, anti-competitive arrangements);

(iii) those intended to reduce the costs of market failure by imposing restrictions on the competitive process to achieve an overall net public benefit; and

(iv) those intended to overcome a market failure without imposing significant public detriments including restrictions on the competitive process.

As one commentator has pointed out:

> Category (i) is of no direct interest to competition or public policy, while category (ii) arrangements are likely to be in breach of the *Trade Practices Act* and will be vigorously pursued by the Commission. Category (iii) represents the most difficult case and a mechanism is needed to ensure that net public benefits are achieved and delivered over time and to ensure that the arrangement is not "captured" by the private interests of the industry. Category (iv) cases are less

---

34. Australian Manufacturing Council, *The Environmental Challenge: Best Practice Environmental Regulation* (Canberra: Australian Manufacturing Council, 1993).

35. See for example, I. Ayres and J. Braithwaite, *Responsive Regulation: Transcending the Deregulation Debate* (London: Oxford University Press, 1992).

36. TPC (footnote 14), p. 7. The former Trade Practices Commission provided another useful typology as follows:

- a code designed primarily to *improve the image* of an industry by setting minimum standards in the area of product/service quality and information disclosure, and to provide a complaint mechanism when there is a breach of code principles;
- a code which sets down minimum quality standards as a *competitive tool* for members of the association within a particular industry when such an association does not have full coverage of industry members;
- a code which operates *in addition to* existing law, in which the government regulators "move back" and allow the industry to regulate its own members and only intervene if they consider that the code of conduct breaks down;
- a code which operates *instead* of government regulation following repeal of such regulation; and
- a code that comes into operation *as an alternative to* enacting government regulation.

In the last three circumstances above, government may choose to confer a large degree of industry ownership of regulation even when there is a significant market failure or "mischief" to be addressed, as an alternative to public enforcement. Note that if the public benefits of a code outweigh its anti-competitive effects then the Commission may authorize the Code, with the consequence that those who are bound by the Code will be immune from court action brought under the competition provisions of the federal *Trade Practices Act 1974* (Cth).

controversial ...[most] codes on which the TPC has provided advice fall into this category.[37]

An example of category (iv) is the *Electronic Funds Transfer Code of Conduct*, which is intended, *inter alia*, to provide an efficient mechanism for disseminating information about the service to customers. It is there to reduce information asymmetries between providers and users and to resolve consumer disputes.[38]

Why "Pure" Self-Regulation is Usually Inadequate

In the following paragraphs some general reservations are expressed about the likely utility of codes of practice, at least if they are used as a stand-alone mechanism of social control, and as a form of pure self-regulation. Pure self-regulation in this context means total or voluntary self-regulation, whereby an enterprise, industry or profession establishes codes of practice or enforcement techniques that are entirely independent of government. Some important prerequisites to the success of codes of practice, over and beyond those identified in the Guide, will also be identified.

There are only a very limited range of circumstances where total or voluntary self-regulation, without any form of oversight or external intervention, can work in the public interest. The best documented such example is Rees' study of self-regulation in the nuclear power industry, which works well precisely because there are compelling reasons of self-interest why the industry as a whole must avoid a nuclear incident (let alone an accident) and where there is a sufficiently small number of players (all of them large) to make such self-regulation viable.[39]

Similarly, studies of occupational health and safety have found that the greatest motivation to comply with voluntary codes is in circumstances when an industry has a public image to protect, when improved safety can contribute significantly to profits (or, as in the chemical industry, when poor safety can lead to catastrophic explosions) and when, in short, companies have a self-interest in improved health and safety performance. When this is not the case, then the track record of self-regulation is a poor one.[40] Since only in a minority of circumstances will the self-interest of the target group and the public interest coincide, voluntary self-regulation, and voluntary codes of practice, are only capable of operating successfully under very narrow conditions.

In the very large majority of circumstances, the gap between private and public interest is so large that in the absence of external controls or oversight, the former overwhelms the latter. As Martin puts it, "this approach [purely voluntary] can be

---

37. J. Tamblyn, *Industry Codes of Conduct: Their Role in the Competitive Marketplace*, a paper presented to TPC Consultative Committee, Canberra, March 17, 1990, p. 2.

38. For information on the Electronic Funds Transfer Code, see the Web site of the Australian Securities and Investments Commission, <www.asic.gov.au/asic/asic.nsf/lkuppdf/ASIC+PDFW?opendocument &key=eft_code.pdf>.

39. J. Rees, *Hostages of Each Other: The Transformation of Nuclear Safety Since Three Mile Island* (Chicago: University of Chicago Press, 1994).

40. See H. Genn, "Business Responses to the Regulation of Health and Safety in England," *Law & Policy* 15:3 (1993), pp. 219–233; N. Gunningham, "Environment, Self-Regulation and the Chemical Industry: Assessing Responsible Care," *Law & Policy* 17:1 (1995), pp. 57–109.

effective where compliance efforts will largely coincide with best business practices, or where there are strong and effective non-government pressures to comply (which could be just peer group pressure)."[41] In general, however, it is unlikely that "an industry regulating itself can deliver any credible outcomes either to its members or its users."[42]

There are also a further range of other circumstances, beyond the public-private interest divide, which will also limit the potential for pure self-regulation. Some of these, acknowledged in a draft of the Australian Guide, include economic circumstances that force a focus on short-term profit, particularly when firms are economically marginal, the size, mobility and public profile of participating firms, whether the industry or industry sub-sector has had a positive record on the issue in the past, and whether a breach of the code would be readily transparent.[43] A particularly useful checklist of such factors has been suggested by the Netherlands' former Minister for Environment, Pieter Winsemius, as including a small number of firms in each sector, domination of each sector by large firms, and sectoral associations that are able to negotiate on behalf of their members.[44] Also important is the prevailing business culture.

Finally, even assuming that, in a particular instance, the gap between public and private interest is modest, and that the relevant industry association wants the code to work, there may still be serious weaknesses with it — weaknesses that only a broader mix of policy instruments, including direct government intervention, would be likely to compensate for. For example, even a broader range of sanctions under the code may not work against recalcitrants. Shaming cannot work against firms with no reputation to protect. Expulsion cannot work when firms can still operate effectively outside the industry association. This is a particular example of the free-rider problem examined below, a problem likely to require government intervention to overcome it.

To the extent that there is a significant gap between public and private interests, or when other circumstances identified above suggest there are limits to effective self-regulation, then from the standpoint of public policy (accepting, for reasons considered earlier, the desirability of industry involvement when this is practicable), the issue becomes how best to design co-regulatory mechanisms. The latter should be designed to take advantage of the strengths and virtues of codes of practice and industry self-regulation, while compensating for their weaknesses as stand-alone mechanisms by underpinning them with sufficient state intervention to ensure that they do operate in the public interest — that is, that they are effective in achieving their purported social and economic goals and have credibility in the eyes of the public or their intended audience. Precisely what form of state intervention will provide the most appropriate underpinning is likely to vary with the particular circumstances of the case. Unfortunately, there are no

---

41. J. Martin, *Performance-Oriented Regulatory Programs*, a paper presented to New South Wales Regulatory Review Conference, Sydney, Australia, June 20, 1995, p. 6.

42. B. Dee, *Can Codes of Conduct be an Effective Alternative to Government Regulation?* a paper presented to the Ethics and Codes of Conduct Conference, Sydney, Australia, November 1993. See examples cited in Gunningham, 1995 (footnote 40).

43. Australian Consumer and Competition Commission, *Guide to Fair Trading Codes of Conduct* (Canberra: ACCC, 1995).

44. R. Gerits and J. Hissen, "Environmental Covenants for the Oil and Gas Producing Industry," *Environmental Law and Policy* 24:6 (1994), p. 323.

magic bullets or universally appropriate prescriptions. However, it is at least possible to identify some of the most commonly important variables, and to illustrate by example how co-regulation might operate to optimal effect in particular circumstances.

The Role of the General Law

First, it is usually crucial that the self-regulatory code operates in the shadow of rules and sanctions provided by the general law, for it is these that are the most obvious and visible (but not the only) means of giving regulatees the incentive to comply with the code. For example, the Scanning Code operates against the backdrop of the general law, which makes misleading pricing an offence. As one astute commentator has put it:

> Society cannot expect miracles from self-regulation when the
> substantive law is weak. Traders will be part of a self-regulatory code
> when it offers an alternative to legislation and/or litigation. In many
> ways the best thing government can do for self-regulation is to provide
> for effective general laws. No trader will submit her/himself to
> stringent standards if she or he has little liability at general law. ... All
> codes have to work against the background that the law itself will
> provide a less palatable sanction to industry than will self-regulatory
> codes. This is the incentive to make self-regulatory codes operate
> effectively.[45]

Certainly, there is considerable evidence from a variety of jurisdictions that it is largely fear of government regulation that drives the large majority of self-regulatory initiatives.[46] Since those initiatives are more concerned with keeping government at bay that with genuinely self-regulating their industry, it seems unlikely that they will perform the latter task well, in the absence of continuing government oversight and the threat of direct intervention.

A related and important role for government is in preventing free riding. If 80 percent of the industry agrees to comply with a code, but 20 percent refuses to sign on, a failure to address the misconduct of the latter (which since they are outside of the code, is beyond the scope of the self-regulatory scheme) will almost certainly result in the failure of the code. This is because those who sign the code cannot afford to be put at a competitive disadvantage as against those who do not. For example, if traders are competing on price and quality but only those covered by the code agree to provide the quality while the others (unknown to the consumer) do not, it is unlikely that the code will be successful.[47] That is, there is a considerable threat to support for code

---

45. W. Pengilley, "Competition Law and Voluntary Codes of Self-regulation: An Individual Assessment of What Has Happened to Date," *University of NSW Law Journal* 13:2 (1990), pp. 212–301. See also Kernaghan Webb and Andrew Morrison, "The Law and Voluntary Codes: Examining the 'Tangled Web'," Chapter 5, above.

46. See a Dutch study in M. Aalders, "Regulation and In-Company Environmental Management in the Netherlands," *Law & Policy* 15:2 (1993), pp. 75–94.

47. W. Richardson and D. Morris, "Towards More Effective Consumer Marketplace Interventions," *Journal of Consumer Policy* 11 (1988), pp. 315–334 at p. 321.

implementation created by outsiders who adopt lower standards while competing strongly on price, and by free-riding traders who provide lower standards while taking advantage of the higher industrial image created by codes.[48] Here, government must intervene directly to curb the activities of non-code members.

Significantly, the *Codes of Conduct Policy Framework* does recognize that legislative backing is sometimes necessary to make a code effective. Such legislative backing may include, *inter alia*, enforcement of undertakings to comply with a code, prescribing a code as a regulation (though the code would only apply to those subscribing to it), and setting out standards that can be overridden by a more stringent industry code, should the industry choose to implement one.[49] Again, the degree of legislative backing will necessarily vary from industry to industry [50]and will depend on the broader economic circumstances.

In this context, the authorization process used by the Australian Competition and Consumer Commission is of particular significance. This specifies that if industry members agree to a code of conduct which substantially lessens competition in a particular market for goods and services, they may leave themselves open to court action under the competition provisions of the *Trade Practices Act*. However, it is open to the Commission to authorize a code of conduct (though never one that involves price fixing) if the code's proponents can prove to the Commission's satisfaction that the benefits to the public flowing from the agreement outweigh the detrimental effects the code would have on competition. Authorization in this context means that the code subscriber will have immunity from court action brought under the competition provisions of the *Trade Practices Act* in relation to the code.[51]

Other Co-Regulatory Strategies

While a legislative underpinning to codes of practice is perhaps the most obvious way of giving them "bite" and credibility, it is not necessarily the only way. In some circumstances, the mere threat of imposing legislation may provide sufficient incentive to the target group to make its actual imposition unnecessary. In others, less direct forms of State oversight or control will be sufficient. For example, it may be appropriate for a State agency to endorse a particular code by permitting it to use the agency's logo or other official seal of approval, thereby giving the public greater confidence in the code's credibility.[52] This in turn may help the industry sell its product or provide other commercial benefits. In these circumstances, the capacity of the agency

---

48. Ibid.

49. Minister of Customs and Consumer Affairs (footnote 4), pp. 21–24.

50. In Australia, most of the state/territory trade practices statutes provide for statutory recognition of industry codes of practice and machinery for their enforcement, making possible, through regulation, their application to entire industries.

51. D. Rickard, *Codes of Conduct: Their Place in the Regulatory Framework and Making Them Work in the Interest of Consumers*, a paper presented to the Working Together for Change Consumer Affairs Forum for the Commonwealth Trade Practices Commission, Adelaide (undated), p. 11.

52. There is no provision under the *Trade Practices Act* (Cth.) that gives the ACCC the authority to endorse a code, although the Scanning Code is one case in which this has happened.

to withdraw its endorsement may provide a significant inducement to the target group to self-regulate effectively. For example, under the Scanning Code, the regulator has allowed its logo to be used to give legitimacy to the scheme, and by doing so has leverage over the industry to maintain its standards. It remains an open question whether there is a serious danger of an agency — by promoting and becoming closely identified with a particular code — being thus captured by the regulated industry.

Another means of incorporating codes into a broader co-regulatory strategy is to harness third parties to act as surrogate regulators, policing the code as a complement or alternative to government involvement. The most obvious third parties with an interest in playing this role are consumers themselves. This contribution may be through their direct involvement in administration of the code itself (in which case it has greater credibility as a genuinely self-regulatory scheme) or in their capacity as potential victims of code malpractice, in taking direct action against firms that breach the code. For example, under the Scanning Code, consumers who are overcharged have a right to receive the item free.[53] Assuming (heroically) that consumers know of this provision, then their capacity to enforce it directly, in their own self-interest, may make this aspect of the Code largely self-enforcing.

Moreover, consumers are not the only ones whose self-interest in policing a code is sufficient to make it effective. Rival traders provide another important group whose self-interest in ensuring a level playing field, and that their competitors do not abuse the code and thereby gain a competitive advantage, can be used to good effect. In Australia, the best illustration of this is the *Code of Practice and Administrative Rules for the Fruit Juice Industry*.[54] There is a considerable temptation for fruit juice manufacturers to make claims as to the fruit juice contents of their products, but to then dilute the product contrary to those claims. This practice is difficult to detect once the product is in the store. However, by providing for inspection at the production stage by rival manufacturers, the code is largely self-policing.

One major consequence of codes that can be made self-enforcing — whether through harnessing the self-interest of consumers, rival traders or others — is that there is consequently far less need for direct involvement of government regulators, who may take a back seat, intervening only to the extent that the self-enforcing mechanisms break down in practice, or need external support in order to make them effective. Finally, the importance of utilizing a broader regulatory mix cannot be over-emphasized. In the past, policy makers have often assumed that various instruments should be treated as alternatives rather than as complementary mechanisms, and have tended to embrace one or more of these instruments without regard to the virtues of the others. This single-instrument approach is misguided in that all instruments have strengths and weaknesses and none are sufficiently flexible and resilient as to be able successfully to address all problems in all circumstances. Accordingly, in the large majority of circumstances a mix of instruments will achieve far more than single-instrument approaches, though the nature of the mix will necessarily vary with the nature of the problem and its particular context.

---

53. *Scanning Code* (footnote 2), s. 3.

54. Available for download from the Australian Business Limited Web site, <www.australianbusiness.com.au>.

For example, in the case of the chemical industry's Responsible Care program,[55] even though the industry as a whole has a self-interest in improving its environmental performance, collective action problems and the temptation to free ride mean that self-regulation and its related codes of practice alone will be insufficient to achieve that goal. However, a tripartite approach, involving co-regulation and a range of third-party oversight mechanisms, may be a viable option. This might involve creating greater transparency (through ensuring a community's right to know about chemical emissions), which in turn enables the community to act as a more effective countervailing force; greater accountability (through the introduction of independent third-party audits which identify whether code participants are living up to their commitments under the code); and an underpinning of government regulation which, in the case of companies that are part of the scheme, needs to kick in only to the extent that the code itself is failing or when individual companies seek to defect from their obligations under it and free ride.

One convenient means of encapsulating the potential dynamic between government, business and third parties in achieving effective co-regulation is a three-dimensional instrument pyramid (see next page),[56] conceived of as having three faces or sides, one side each representing respectively: first parties (government), second parties (business), and third parties (commercial and non-commercial).

In this model, escalation (i.e. increasing coercion) would be possible up any face of the pyramid, and not merely in terms of government action. That is, it would also be possible up the second face (through self-regulation), or up the third face (through a variety of actions by commercial or non-commercial third parties or both).[57]

In this model, one might regulate (in the broadest sense) using a number of different instruments across a number of dimensions (or faces of the pyramid). Escalation

---

55. See John Moffet, François Bregha and Mary Jane Middelkoop, "Responsible Care: A Case Study of A Voluntary Environmental Initiative," Chapter 6, above.

56. The original enforcement pyramid, on which we build, is John Braithwaite's (see Ayres and Braithwaite, footnote 35). Our own conception of the pyramid is broader in two main respects. First, Braithwaite's pyramid is concerned with the behaviour of, and interaction between, only two parties: (state) regulator and (business) regulatee, whereas we are concerned with the potential regulatory role not just of the state but also of second and third parties. Second, Braithwaite's pyramid is concerned with how best to tailor enforcement responses within a single instrument category, specifically, state regulation, rather than with how best to utilize a range of instruments. In contrast, our pyramid conceives of the possibility of regulation using a number of different instruments across a number of dimensions (or faces of the pyramid). Our conception of the three-dimensional pyramid was first mooted in Gunningham, *Codes of Practice: The Australasian Experience*, a paper presented to the Voluntary Codes Symposium, Office of Consumer Affairs, Industry Canada, and Regulatory Affairs Division, Treasury Board Secretariat (Canada), Ottawa, September 1996, and is further developed in N. Gunningham and D. Sinclair, "Integrative Regulation: A Principle-Based Approach to Environmental Policy," *Law & Social Inquiry* 24:4 (Fall 1999), pp. 853–896.

57. To give a concrete example of the latter, the Forest Stewardship Council (FSC) is a global environmental standards-setting system for forest products. The FSC both approves standards that can be used to certify forestry products as sustainably managed and certifies the certifiers. It relies for its "clout" on changing consumer demand and upon creating strong "buyers groups" and other mechanisms for institutionalizing green consumer demand. That is, its success will depend largely on influencing consumer demand. While government involvement — for example, through formal endorsement or government procurement policies that supported the FSC — would be valuable, the scheme is essentially a freestanding one: from base to peak (consumer sanctions and boycotts), the scheme is entirely third-party based. (See Gregory T. Rhone, David Clarke and Kernaghan Webb, "Two Voluntary Approaches to Sustainable Forestry Practices," Chapter 9, above.)

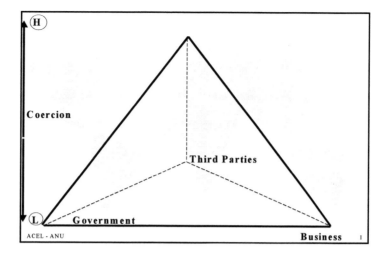

to higher levels of coercion would also be possible not only within an instrument but also across instruments and across different faces of the pyramid That is, our model of three-dimensional regulation holds out the possibility of escalating degrees of coercion through interaction between different but complementary instruments and parties. Thus one might begin with one less intrusive instrument such as business-initiated self-regulation (i.e. using second parties), but then recruit another instrument when the first exhausts its responsive potential (e.g. third-party audit or government-mandated community right to know) and end up (when all else fails) with highly coercive instruments such as government enforcement of command and control or third-party foreclosure of a loan. Ideally, one would use a combination of instruments in sequence to achieve a seamless, coordinated and gradual escalation up one or more faces of the pyramid from base to peak.[58]

Conclusions

Judging by the Australian experience, there is no doubt that codes of practice, properly designed and administered, in appropriate circumstances, and in combination with an underpinning of government oversight or regulation, can provide important benefits to consumers, industries and governments. As the Australian Competition and Consumer Commission has put it, summarizing its experience over the last few years:

> There is considerable scope for using voluntary codes of practice to
> improve the operation of the marketplace by overcoming elements of
> market failure without imposing significant restrictions on competition
> .... in such circumstances effective codes of conduct can provide
> benefits for business, customers and the community at large, compared

---

58. In practice, such seamless escalation is not always possible. See further Gunnningham and Sinclair (footnote 56).

with the alternatives of open competition and direct government regulation.[59]

Based on the experience of the Australian codes, the Guide and the various other government-commissioned studies of recent years, one may conclude that certain features are required of codes if they are to achieve public credibility and therefore public acceptance.[60] Notwithstanding the considerable potential of codes of practice that have the above-mentioned features, great care should be taken not to adopt codes in inappropriate circumstances, when they are likely to do far more harm than good, and may seriously devalue the concept of industry self-regulation in general.

Equally important, codes are likely to make their greatest contribution in combination with, rather than in the absence of, government regulation. It is in this context that they make their greatest contribution to "sustainable governance." (For a more detailed discussion of sustainable governance, see Chapter 14.) In the enthusiasm to embrace voluntary mechanisms in general, and codes in particular, this crucial qualifying factor is all to often forgotten.

59. J. Tamblyn (footnote 37), p. 2.

60. See "Necessary Elements of a Code," above.

Chapter 13
Voluntary Codes in the United States, the European Union and Developing Countries: A Preliminary Survey

Kernaghan Webb and David Clarke

Introduction

Any attempt to review worldwide use of a particular policy instrument is almost invariably destined to be cursory and incomplete, and this review of market-oriented voluntary codes in use in the United States, the European Union and developing countries is no exception. While admittedly far from comprehensive, our preliminary research of voluntary initiatives in these jurisdictions suggests some intriguing themes deserving further exploration. These themes revolve around the relationship between how receptive the legal system and government agencies are to voluntary codes (what could be called "the regulatory culture" of voluntary codes) and what voluntary instruments emerge (the number, shape and content of those codes).

In the United States, the federal government has explicitly encouraged the use of self-regulatory instruments in the areas of environmental, human rights, worker and consumer protection. It is not surprising, therefore, that there has been significant voluntary code activity in all of these sectors. In some cases, U.S. governments have played direct and primary roles in the development and implementation of these voluntary instruments, while in others a more "hands-off" approach has been adopted, leaving the leadership role to businesses or others.

In Europe, at the European Union level, the direct involvement of government is apparently preferred for developing and operating voluntary instruments. In the case of both environmental and consumer protection instruments, European governments have played central roles in ensuring that key voluntary instruments are of a certain quality. In developing countries, given their wide diversity, it is harder to make useful generalizations concerning the experience with voluntary instruments, although there is evidence from India and Indonesia suggesting that a strong government role can help facilitate development of effective voluntary approaches.

In an effort to provide the reader with a sense of the breadth of voluntary initiatives activity currently being undertaken, this chapter reviews voluntary initiatives in four major sectors: environmental protection, human rights and worker safety, consumer protection in the conventional (non-Internet) marketplace, and consumer protection in the context of e-commerce. Analysis of each of these sectors is then subdivided by examining initiatives in terms of who is the lead proponent — that is, we review voluntary initiatives spearheaded by government, the private sector and non-governmental organizations.

Kernaghan Webb, Editor, *Voluntary Codes: Private Governance, the Public Interest and Innovation.*
This chapter ©2004 Kernaghan Webb and David Clarke, pages 335–376.
Published by the Carleton Research Unit for Innovation, Science and Environment, Carleton University, Ottawa, Canada.

Environmental Voluntary Initiatives

Our research suggests that governments, the private sector and non-governmental organizations (NGOs) in the United States, the European Union and developing countries are demonstrating growing openness to the use of voluntary approaches as one way of responding to environmental challenges, although the degree of interest and the approaches taken vary significantly from jurisdiction to jurisdiction and from player to player. Increasingly, governments in each of these jurisdictions seem to be promoting voluntary initiatives in tandem with regulatory incentives (e.g. firms that go "beyond compliance" with the law are potentially subject to reduced inspections or greater regulatory flexibility) and public recognition schemes. Meanwhile, the voluntary initiatives spearheaded by businesses and NGOs often seem to be directed as much at gaining marketplace advantage (e.g. with consumers, investors, suppliers and insurers) as at relieving government pressure, and in many cases business and NGO codes seem to be in competition, with both sides trying to prove to the public (or their particular stakeholders) that their respective rules, development and enforcement processes provide the most credible path to environmental protection. While similar patterns are seen in developing countries, these countries have their own distinctive operational environments that, in part, shape their voluntary initiatives, including particularly weak regulatory infrastructures, and fixations with concerns that the voluntary initiatives do not interfere with economic development.

The United States: Government-led Voluntary Environmental Initiatives

U.S. government interest and involvement in voluntary initiatives seem to stem primarily from recognition of the need to find ways of avoiding some of the limitations of traditional command-and-control environmental regulation.[1] Framed more positively, one commentator has stated that government-led voluntary environmental initiatives:

> ...can motivate beyond compliance environmental performance that otherwise would not occur...may also enable regulators to create detours around existing regulatory obstacles.....[and] respond to a long-standing industry position that the current system unnecessarily

---

1. For example, see M. Stoughton, K. Shapiro and D. Reda, in *Do Voluntary Mechanisms Work? An Evaluation of Current and Future Program Performance* (Boston: Tellus Institute, 2000, an executive summary of which is available at <www.tellus.org/b&s/publications/r8-031.pdf>), who note that government-led voluntary environmental programs in the U.S. "have emerged in response to the belief that traditional regulatory approaches have significant limitations in driving pollution prevention and in addressing the next generation of environmental problems." (p. 1). See also E. Orts, "Reflexive Environmental Regulation," *Northwestern University Law Review* 89 (1995), pp. 1227–1340, especially pp. 1235–1241. Orts outlines a range of criticisms of traditional regulatory approaches, ranging from concerns about their inefficiencies, dependence on regulator capacity and competence, the potential for capture or bureaucratic empire-building, limited ability to adapt to changing circumstances and the sheer burden of regulatory prescriptions. See also J. Nash and J. Ehrenfeld, "Codes of Environmental Management Practice: Assessing Their Potential as a Tool for Change," *Annual Review of Energy and the Environment* 22 (1997), pp. 487–535.

burdens business and that equal or superior environmental outcomes can be achieved less expensively.[2]

Perhaps reflecting this view, the federal government has actively promoted voluntary approaches in which corporations agree to meet certain goals in exchange for regulatory flexibility and, occasionally, public recognition as a good corporate citizen. Nash and Ehrenfeld describe two generations of government-led voluntary environmental initiatives that have emerged from this regulatory reform effort. According to their research, the first generation was dedicated to recognizing companies that were taking voluntary pollution prevention steps, and to providing direct technical assistance to firms.[3] An example of this first generation was the U.S. Industrial Toxics Project, also known as the "33/50 Program," because it called for 33 percent reductions of 17 toxic chemicals by 1992 and 50 percent by 1995. The program met its ultimate goal of a 50 percent reduction one year ahead of schedule, in 1994.[4] Over the life of the program, 7,500 companies were invited to participate, of which nearly 1,300 responded (13 percent) with commitments, and their facilities reported more than 60 percent of the 1988 releases and transfers of 33/50 chemicals.[5] The Environmental Protection Agency concentrated much of its outreach on those 500 or so companies responsible for the largest releases and transfers; of those, 64 percent participated in the program.[6] While the rates of participation were not outstanding, the 33/50 Program provided evidence of industry interest in such programs, and showed considerable success in meeting targeted objectives.

The second generation of voluntary environmental initiatives focussed on what Nash and Ehrenfeld describe as "reinventing" environmental regulation. This has included the Common Sense Initiative, described generally as an attempt to move away from a regulatory focus on a single environmental medium (air or water, for example) to addressing the full impact of individual industrial sectors. Common Sense Initiative proposals included offering regulatory flexibility in exchange for superior environmental performance.[7] A recent study concludes that voluntary environmental programs have now become an established activity of environmental regulatory agencies at all levels of government, with an increasing focus on pollution prevention.[8] In 1999, the Environmental Protection Agency proposed a two-track regulatory system, with a new performance track that invites facilities to meet certain voluntary stipulations in return for

---

2. M. Crow, "Beyond Experiments," *The Environmental Forum* 17:3 (May–June 2000), pp. 19–29, p. 19.

3. Nash and Ehrenfeld, (footnote 1). For a discussion of a different typology of voluntary environmental programs involving agreements between government and industry, see J. Dowd and G. Boyd, *A Typology of Voluntary Agreements Used in Energy and Environmental Policy*, draft working paper (Washington: Department of Energy, January 1998).

4. Environmental Protection Agency (U.S.), Office of Pollution Prevention and Toxics, *33/50 Program: The Final Record* (Washington: EPA, 1999), p. 2, available at <www.epa.gov/opptintr/3350/3350-fnl.pdf>.

5. Ibid., p. 4.

6. Ibid.

7. Nash and Ehrenfeld (footnote 1).

8. Stoughton, Shapiro and Reda (footnote 1).

a mix of regulatory, financial and other benefits, while the remaining facilities stay on the existing compliance-oriented system.[9]

Increasingly, legislation is being amended to explicitly acknowledge and encourage companies to adopt environmental management systems such as ISO 14001.[10] Examples have included Wisconsin's Cooperative Environmental Agreements Program and Oregon's Green Permits Program,[11] both described by one researcher as offering several regulatory tiers "to distinguish the good or better actors from the poor ones and to treat the categories differently [by providing] incentives for performance at the higher tier levels."[12] Similarly, Connecticut has taken the step of explicitly incorporating voluntary initiatives into a regulatory scheme. Under *An Act Concerning Exemplary Environmental Management Systems*,[13] the Connecticut Commissioner of Environmental Protection may provide regulatory flexibility (in the form of expedited review of permit applications, for example) to companies registered as adhering to environmental systems such as ISO 14001.[14]

At the federal level, another incentive for firms to establish environmental management systems and pollution prevention systems is the *Federal Sentencing Guidelines for Organizations*, developed by the United States Sentencing Commission.[15] The Guidelines set out a series of aggravating and mitigating circumstances to be

---

9. Crow (footnote 2), p. 19.

10. Published in 1996 by the International Organization for Standardization (ISO), ISO 14001 is an environmental management system standard. The standard specifies requirements for an environmental management system, to enable an organization to formulate a policy and objectives taking into account legislative requirements and information about significant environmental impacts. It applies to those environmental aspects which the organization can control and over which it can be expected to have an influence. It does not itself state specific environmental performance criteria. For a more complete discussion of ISO, particularly in the U.S. context, see P. S. Evers, "ISO 14000 and Environmental Protection," *Mississippi Law Journal* 67 (1996), pp. 463–526.

11. See discussion of the Oregon and Wisconsin performance track programs in National Academy of Public Administration (NAPA), *Environment.Gov: Transforming Environmental Protection for the 21st Century*, (Washington: NAPA, 2000), pp. 49–53.

12. Professor Jerry Speir, Director, Tulane Institute for Environmental Law and Policy, whose discussion is summarized in *ISO 14001 Environmental Management Systems and Public Policy: Proceedings of a Workshop Held on July 29, 1999, Oakland, California*, p. 8, available at <www.pacinst.org/reports/iso_14001/isoproceedings.pdf>.

13. *Connecticut Public Act No. 99-226*; the Act is available at <www.cga.state.ct.us/ps99/Act/pa/1999PA-00226-R00HB-06830-PA.htm>.

14. Ibid., ss. (b).

15. See United States Sentencing Commission, *Chapter Eight: 2000 Federal Sentencing Guideline Manual*, available at <www.ussc.gov/2000guid/tabconchapt8.htm>. In 2000, 23 percent of sentences for organizations under the guidelines were related to environmental pollution. (See U. S. Sentencing Commission, *1998 Annual Report*, p. 42, available at <www.ussc.gov/annrpt/1998/ar98toc.htm>.) Draft sentencing guidelines specifically pertaining to environmental misconduct have also been developed, which stipulate that adherence to the terms of environmental compliance programs can considerably reduce the penalties imposed. See *Report from Advisory Group on Environmental Sanctions* (1993), available at <www.ussc.gov/publicat/environ.pdf>, and discussion in Orts (footnote 1), pp. 1281–1283.

weighed in considering appropriate penalties for corporate criminals.[16] Among the most novel of the mitigating considerations is whether a corporation exercised due diligence by establishing "compliance standards and procedures to be followed by [the organization's] employees and other agents that are reasonably capable of reducing the prospect of criminal conduct."[17] Essentially, a corporation that establishes a coherent and comprehensive management system, and ensures effective communication and compliance to it, is better protected from exposure to onerous penalties (and indeed is less likely to contravene the law) than one that has no such management system. The Guidelines thus provide an additional government incentive for companies to adopt proactive, preventative practices.

The United States: Business-led Voluntary Environmental Initiatives

Among the most significant business-led voluntary environmental initiatives in operation in the United States is ISO 14001, an environmental management system that has been the focus of serious public policy debate.[18] As mentioned above, ISO 14001 has recently started to be directly recognized in U.S. environmental legislation. In addition to this direct form of governmental approval, there are indications that ISO 14001 is gaining momentum for non-governmental, market reasons.[19] For example, large U.S. firms are increasingly requiring that their suppliers put in place ISO environmental management system approaches, thus creating market-driven supply-chain pressure on

---

16. For background on this part of the Guidelines, see D. Thorne LeClair et al., "Federal Sentencing Guidelines for Organizations: Legal, Ethical and Public Policy Issues for International Marketing," *Journal of Public Policy and Marketing* 16:1 (Spring 1997), pp. 26–37. See also D. E. Murphy, "The Federal Sentencing Guidelines for Organizations: A Decade of Promoting Compliance and Ethics," *Iowa Law Review* 87 (2002), pp. 697–719, available at <www.ussc.gov/corp/Murphy1.pdf>. Judge Murphy is Chair of the United States Sentencing Commission.

17. United States Sentencing Commission, *Chapter Eight: 2000 Federal Sentencing Guideline Manual* (footnote 15).

18. See, for example, NAPA (footnote 11). According to NAPA, "the emergence of ISO 14001 and other voluntary, private efforts by firms to identify and manage their environmental responsibilities is likely to raise the level of compliance and create some opportunities for pollution prevention. ... Although third-party registration is not a guarantee of a firm's compliance, state and federal regulators are justified in presuming that certified firms are less likely to pose compliance problems than uncertified firms, and thus less desirable as targets for inspection. That conclusion could change if the integrity of the third-party registration process were to be compromised." (p. 61). See also Pacific Institute for Studies in Development and Security, *ISO 14001: Environmental Management Systems and Public Policy* (footnote 12); K. Kao-Cushing, "Why Environmental Management System Standards Matter," *Pacific Institute Report* (Fall 2000), pp. 6–10; K. Kollman and A. Prakash, "Green by Choice?: Cross-National Variations in Firms' Responses to EMS-based Environmental Regimes," *World Politics* 53:3 (2001), pp. 399–430; C. Coglianese and J. Nash, eds., *Regulating from the Inside: Can Environmental Management Systems Achieve Policy Goals?* (Washington: Resources for the Future, 2001).

19. See R Florida and D. Davison, "Why Do Firms Adopt Advanced Environmental Practices (And Do They Make a Difference)?" in Coglianese and Nash, eds., ibid. On the basis of survey evidence, the authors conclude that business benefits, such as cost savings, improved business performance and improved stakeholder relations, are important motivations for adopting environmental management systems, along with regulatory compliance.

companies to adopt environmental management systems.[20] While ISO 14001 may be gaining in popularity, this is not to suggest that it is without weaknesses: criticisms to date have focussed on its lack of substantive performance requirements and inadequate public reporting obligations.[21]

Aside from the growing U.S. acceptance of ISO 14001, there have also been some ambitious attempts by particular American industry sectors to establish their own environmental programs. The chemical and forestry industries offer two particularly interesting and occasionally controversial examples.[22] The programs demonstrate the significance of non-governmental factors as incentives for development and operation of voluntary environmental initiatives — in particular, the need to address negative public perceptions of the industries.

Chemical manufacturers had a serious public relations problem on their hands in the 1980s, following the release of toxic chemicals from a plant owned by a U.S.-based company in Bhopal, India, in 1984. Following Bhopal, the Chairman of the U.S. Chemical Manufacturers Association's (CMA) Public Perception Committee championed the adoption of the Canadian Chemical Manufacturers Association's Responsible Care program, because it was clear to him that the "industry had a performance problem that it could not advertise [its] way out of."[23] The CMA's board unanimously adopted Responsible Care in September 1988. It is a condition of membership in the CMA that companies comply with the 10 principles of Responsible Care and six codes of management practice.[24] In the past, commentators have questioned Responsible Care's effectiveness in achieving actual improvement in the industry, noting among other things that the Program focusses on inputs, not outputs (e.g. reduced what levels of pollutants will be achieved), lacks coercive sanctions, and does not involve independent expert third-party compliance verification.[25] On the positive side, however, the same commentators have also noted that the CMA is working to create mechanisms for measuring performance on some aspects of its codes, and is moving toward a third-party verification system.[26] Commentators have also lauded the Responsible Care

---

20. For instance, Kao-Kushing, (footnote 18), p. 7, notes that "Major multi-national corporations, such as Ford and GM, are already requiring or strongly recommending that their suppliers conform to the ISO 14001 standard."

21. Ibid.

22. For insightful recent comparative analysis of the American chemical, forestry and ISO 14001 environmental management systems, see Coglianese and Nash (footnote 18).

23. Paul Oreffice (then Chairman of Dow Chemical), cited in Nash and Ehrenfeld (footnote 1), p. 499. For a more comprehensive treatment of the Canadian Responsible Care Program, see John Moffet, François Bregha and Mary Jane Middelkoop, "Responsible Care: A Case Study of a Voluntary Environmental Initiative," Chapter 6, above.

24. A. King and M. Lenox, ""Industry Self-Regulation Without Sanctions: The Chemical Industry's Responsible Care Program" *Academy of Management Journal* 43:4 (2000), p. 7, available at <www.aom.pace.edu/amj/August2000/king.pdf>.

25. Ibid., pp. 33–36.

26. Ibid., p. 35.

Program's call on firms to adopt a "no accidents, injuries, or harm to the environment" approach to operation.[27] Responsible Care members are to...

> establish a policy of openness with surrounding communities but decide for themselves which information to disclose about their operations. About half of the American Chemistry Council's members have had their Responsible Care programs externally verified, but results of these assessments generally are not available to the public. Firms participating in the Canadian Responsible Care program, however, must provide a copy of their verification report to anyone who requests it.[28]

In short, the program has problematic aspects, but is still evolving. The evolution seems to be toward increased openness and independent compliance auditing, but there are many steps to go before reaching that objective.

As with the American chemical industry, the American Forest and Paper Association (AF&PA)[29] was also concerned with the public image associated with its logging activities, and so instituted the Sustainable Forestry Initiative (SFI) in 1994.[30] An independent expert review panel, with representatives from government, academic, conservation and other sectors, reviews the program and advises AF&PA on its progress. The program provides a system of "principles, objectives and performance measures" to ensure the perpetual growth and harvesting of trees and the protection of wildlife, plants, soil and water.[31] Participation in the program has been mandatory for AF&PA members since 1996.[32] In its 2000 annual report for SFI, AF&PA reported that 90 percent of industrial forest land in America is controlled by its membership, who are required to comply with the SFI program.[33] AF&PA has stated that it has expelled 17 companies to date for failure to comply, and another 23 have been suspended,[34] but it does not disclose on its Web site the names of these companies.

Although the AF&PA SFI initiative does not subject members to independent third-party field audits, the Association has made a number of adjustments to the

---

27. Coglianese and Nash (footnote 18). In this regard, the American Responsible Care initiative is now superior to the Canadian originator, as discussed in Moffet, Bregha and Middelkoop, "Responsible Care," Chapter 6, above.

28. Coglianese and Nash. Ibid.

29. See the AF&PA Web site, <www.afandpa.org>.

30. The AF&PA industry initiative was and is in direct competition with the environmental NGO-supported Forest Stewardship Council. See discussion in B. Cashore, "Legitimacy and the Privatization of Environmental Governance: How Non State Market-Driven (NSMD) Governance Systems (Certification Eco-labelling Programs) Gain Rule Making Authority," *Governance: An International Journal of Policy, Administration and Institutions* 15:4 (October 2002), pp. 503–529.

31. American Forest and Paper Association, *SFI Program*, brochure (Washington: AF&PA, 1998).

32. Ibid.

33. "Statement of AF&PA President and CEO, W. Henson Moore," *The SFI^SM Program Fifth Annual Progress Report* (Washington: AF&PA, 2000), available at <www.internationalpaper.com/our_world/ SFI_2000_1to6.pdf>.

34. See the AF&PA Web site, <www.afandpa.org>.

program which seem to have prompted such third-party evaluations to be undertaken.[35] In 1999, it developed a verification system (facilitating compliance audits) and introduced a Forest Monitoring Project. The Izaak Walton League of America manages the project, which involves random visits to companies with significant holdings in selected sites, as well as field inspections at a combination of company-selected and randomly chosen sites. These initiatives have apparently stimulated many AF&PA members to engage in third-party audits; in 2001, AF&PA reported that 100 million acres are enrolled in the SFI program in North American and 85 million will be third-party certified by June 2002. More than a third of its members' forest lands "[had] been either committed to or [had] already undergone an independent third-party audit for certification under the SFI Standard."[36] Thus, as with the U.S. Responsible Care initiative, the SFI program seems to be evolving toward a more publicly accountable program, with performance measurements and third-party verification of results.

Similar to Responsible Care, however, the AF&PA SFI is not without its critics, including representatives of such environmental NGOs as the World Wildlife Fund and the Natural Resources Defense Council,[37] who have put their support behind the U.S. version of the Forest Stewardship Council (FSC). Until 2001, a key distinction between the two programs was that the FSC initiative involved "chain of custody" labelling of forest products while the AF&PA SFI program did not. However, in 2001, the AF&PA SFI announced that "an on-product labeling system for organizations that have successfully completed 3rd party certification and meet comprehensive label use requirements on fiber sources" would be available as of the fall of 2001.[38] As in other countries, there has been a competition for credibility between industry-driven forestry industry certification initiatives and environmental NGO-driven programs — particularly FSC, which has certified forests in more than 30 countries.[39] It is a competition for credibility, not only among the public but also among important commercial players. It was widely seen as a victory for FSC when the building-supply chain Home Depot, having been the target of numerous protests from environmental groups over the years, opted to publicly endorse the efforts of FSC and promised to carry FSC-certified wood products.[40]

---

35. "Statement of Independent Expert Review Panel," *5th Annual Progress Report* (Washington: AF&PA, 2000).

36. *2001 Sustainable Forestry Initiative (SFI) Program Overview*, at <www.aboutsfi.org>.

37. See, e.g., Kate Heaton (Natural Resources Defense Council), Nicholas Brown (World Wildlife Fund), et al., "Forest Stewardship's Rigorous Standards," *Wall Street Journal*, December 16, 1999, p. A23. Both the Natural Resources Defense Council and World Wildlife Fund have long been active supporters of FSC.

38. See footnote 36.

39. See, e.g., the Canadian experience on this issue in Gregory T. Rhone, David Clarke and Kernaghan Webb, "Two Voluntary Approaches to Sustainable Forestry Practices," Chapter 9, above.

40. J. Hunter, "Home Depot Gives Green Light to Forest Products Certification," *Vancouver Sun*, March 10, 1999.

The United States: NGO-promoted Voluntary Environmental Initiatives

Non-governmental organizations can be a significant source of pressure for change on U.S. corporations, as demonstrated by the above-noted example of a building supply company endorsing use of a particular forestry labelling scheme for wood products sold in its stores following targeted protests by environmental groups. One method of applying such pressure is for an NGO to lead the development of a set of standards, and then exhort corporations to adhere to them. This kind of NGO-led rule making can be viewed as problematic, of course, for the targeted companies, which are expected to submit to rules that they may have had no hand in developing. Conscious that voluntary codes are of little value when they are simply ignored, activists have, in some cases, engaged some of the targeted companies in the rule-making process, in the hope that this would increase the likelihood of their initiative being adopted and influencing market behaviour.

The CERES Principles, though hardly alone in this regard, provide a useful example of this evolution from antagonism to engagement. Motivated by the massive environmental damage resulting from the oil spill from the tanker *Exxon Valdez* off the Alaska coast in 1989, a coalition of investors, environmental activists, labour unions and religious groups formed the Coalition for Environmentally Responsible Economics (CERES).[41] The group envisioned an ambitious system of corporate disclosure of "consistent and comparable" environmental information, in much the same way that corporations are required to disclose financial data in accordance with generally accepted accounting principles. Unfortunately, from the group's perspective, fewer than 20 relatively small corporations originally endorsed the principles. However, through an intensive and somewhat lengthy process of negotiation and compromise (which, among other things, resulted in such concessions as a name change from the antagonistic original "Valdez" program name, and substantial changes to the obligations and operation of the program), the initiative has now attracted some much more prominent endorsers, including American Airlines, Bank of America Corporation, Bethlehem Steel Corporation, Body Shop International PLC, Coca Cola USA, Ford Motor Company, General Motors, Polaroid Corporation, Sunoco Inc. and Vancouver City Savings Credit Union. This willingness to work with industry has permitted the CERES Principles to flourish to a much greater extent than would have been possible under CERES's original regime: it now boasts nine Fortune 500 endorsers and more than 50 corporate endorsers in total.[42]

CERES started a related program in 1997, in collaboration with the United Nations Environment Programme, called the Global Reporting Initiative (GRI). As the name suggests, its focus is global. In essence, GRI seeks to establish uniformity in sustainable development reporting by companies of their performance and progress toward the environmental, social, and economic aspects of sustainable development.[43]

---

41. CERES Web site, <www.ceres.org>.

42. See <www.ceres.org/about/endorsing_companies.htm>.

43. See the GRI Web site, <www.globalreporting.org>.

The GRI's *Sustainability Reporting Guidelines* were released in draft form in March, 1999, and were released in revised form in June 2000. In 2002, the GRI established a permanent, independent, international body with a multistakeholder governance structure. Its core mission is the maintenance, enhancement and dissemination of the Guidelines through ongoing consultation and stakeholder engagement. CERES and GRI may be said to blur the lines between those programs that are led by business and those led by NGOs. Now that GRI is collaborating with the United Nations Environment Programme, there is an element of international government organization (IGO) support as well. Clearly, activists were the primary players at the program's inception; however, the program's growing credibility is the result of industry-NGO-IGO partnerships contributing to its ongoing evolution.

The European Union: Government-led Voluntary Environmental Initiatives

The Eco-Label and Eco-Management and Auditing Scheme

The European Eco-label (as well as some of the corresponding national labelling schemes) and the Eco-Management and Auditing Scheme represent two examples of market-oriented voluntary environmental initiatives spearheaded by the European Union (EU). While both attempts have met with, at best, mixed success so far, both programs' administrators have been seeking ways to improve them, focussing on keys to increasing legitimacy in the eyes of stakeholders.

The European Commission established the European Eco-label in 1992,[44] with the stated goals of promoting "products which have a reduced environmental impact during their entire life cycle," and providing "consumers with better information on the environmental impact of products,"[45] without compromising worker or product safety or significantly affecting the product's fitness for use.[46] Clearly, the success of the program depends upon its acceptance by those participating interest groups and by the market itself. Since its creation, an estimated 250 products have been awarded the European Eco-label, in 17 products groups, ranging from footwear to textiles to light bulbs.[47]

In 1994, the European Commission started working on a proposal to revise the scheme. In the memorandum accompanying the proposal, the Commission acknowledged the tepid response from industry and consumers.[48] It admitted that industry had taken "a very reserved position" toward the scheme and only supported it to the extent that it

---

44. European Parliament, *Council Regulation (EEC) No. 880/92 of 23 March 1992 on a Community Eco-label Award Scheme*, O.J. L 99, p. 1.

45. Ibid., article 4.

46. For a more comprehensive treatment of the issues associated with eco-labels, see Kathryn Harrison, "Promoting Environmental Protection through Eco-labelling: An Evaluation of Canada's Environmental Choice Program," Chapter 10, above.

47. The complete list of product groups is available at the European Union Web site, <http://europa.eu.int/comm/environment/ecolabel/producers/productgroups.htm>.

48. The memorandum was formerly available at <www.europa.int/comm/dg11/ecolabel/proprev.htm>, but seems to have been removed from the EU Web site.

might replace national eco-labelling schemes. Industry's principal difficulty appeared to be that eco-labels are awarded selectively — that is, as the Commission itself put it, "only a number of products on the market can qualify for the label."[49] This, however, has not been the only barrier to the program's success. Studying the Eco-label's past (and potential future) fortunes in Benelux and Italy, researchers found a number of barriers, including a lack of information about the scheme among companies, and the perception that the label was a weak marketing tool.[50] Others, outside the EU, have called the scheme a barrier to trade.[51] A key challenge for the Eco-label's administrators has been to redesign the program to address these problems.[52] In 2000, the Eco-label program was substantially revised.[53] Among other things, the revisions widened the program's scope to cover services as well as products, reinforced stakeholder participation in developing the environmental criteria, reduced fees for small and medium-sized enterprises, introduced a ceiling on the annual fee, renewed emphasis on promotion of the scheme and reinforced coordination with national eco-label schemes.[54] It is too early to assess whether these revisions will increase the market take-up of the scheme. Notable, however, is the central role that the European Commission played in developing this scheme, which is similar to the strong role played by the Canadian federal government in the original development of its Eco-Logo scheme, but markedly more interventionist than the American approach, in which there is no direct government involvement or leadership in eco-labelling initiatives.

This pattern of an interventionist leadership role for the European Commission in the development of voluntary eco-labelling initiatives, and a lack of similar leadership in the United States, repeats itself in the area of voluntary environmental management systems (most notably, ISO 14001), with this role largely being left to the business sector. This is in stark contrast to the European model: the European Eco-Management and Auditing Scheme (EMAS) is without question a product of the EU.

Originally envisaged as a regulatory initiative that would apply in a compulsory manner to all relevant businesses,[55] EMAS was introduced in June 1993 by the EU with a

---

49. Ibid.

50. M. Frey and M. de Clercq, et al., *Project for the Promotion and the Diffusion of the EU Eco-label in Italy and the Benelux: Final Report*, submitted to the European Commission, DG XI, February 1, 1998 (Gent and Milan: University of Gent and Bocconi University, 1998), pp. 61–65.

51. See, e.g., "EU's New 'Eco-label' Called Trade Barrier," *Pulp and Paper*, October, 1996, p. 19.

52. The problems faced by the EU Eco-label are occasionally contrasted with the relative success of the Nordic White Swan and the German Blue Angel programs. See Germany's Blue Angel Web site, <www.blauer-engel.de> and Organisation for Economic Co-operation and Development, *Eco-labelling: Actual Effects of Selected Programmes,* document OCDE/GD(97)105 (Paris: OECD, 1997), for discussion of a number of national eco-label progams. For a discussion of the contrast between the national labels and the EU Eco-label, see S. Zadek, S. Lingayah and M. Forstater, *Social Labels: Tools for Ethical Trade*, report prepared for the European Commission, DG V (London: New Economics Foundation, 1998), p. 59.

53. As set out in European Parliament, *Regulation (EC) No. 1980/2000 of the European Parliament and of the Council of 17 July 2000 on a Revised Community Eco-label Award Scheme*, O.J.L. 237, 21.9.2000, p. 1.

54. Ibid.

55. See Orts (footnote 1) especially from pp. 1289 ff.

framework established by regulation, but operating as a voluntary program.[56] All EU member states were then required to operationalize EMAS in their respective jurisdictions (e.g. to designate the competent body to verify environmental statements made by companies as part of their EMAS public disclosures).[57] EMAS is open to any company operating an industrial site (that is, manufacturing or energy production) in the EU.[58] EMAS has also been applied on an experimental basis to the public service and sites involved in distribution. The objective of EMAS is to "promote continuous improvements in the environmental performance of industrial activities."[59]

EMAS has been forced to compete for credibility with other programs having similar objectives, most notably ISO 14001, with which it has much in common. However, in two respects, EMAS is more stringent: it incorporates performance elements and public disclosure requirements, which ISO 14001 lacks.[60] Responsibility for these differences is almost universally attributed to U.S. business participation in the ISO process and its absence from EMAS.[61] Given the success of ISO 14001 in comparison to EMAS, the EU has had to consider what place there will be for EMAS in the future. After all, given the growing visibility of ISO 14001, it is not on the face of things very obvious what incentive a company would have for implementing EMAS. The European Commission appears confident in the possibilities of EMAS, despite the competition. In 2001, the EMAS scheme was revised to incorporate ISO 14001 as its environmental management component.[62]

It seems apparent that the direct, central role played by the EU in developing EMAS, and the failure of the American and Canadian governments to play a similar role in the development of ISO 14001 (a business-led initiative), has contributed to one program being more rigorous (EMAS) but the other more popular (ISO 14001). The rationalization of the two systems that occurred in Europe in 2001 demonstrates the influence of ISO 14001 in Europe. In terms of reception by companies, in early 2002, there were more than 3,700 registered EMAS sites in Europe.[63] In 2002 (the last year for which statistics are available), there were more than 23,000 companies with ISO 14001 certification in Europe.[64] Commentators have explored the cross-national differences in reception of environmental management systems, and have concluded that the

---

56. European Parliament, *Council Regulation (EEC) No 1836/93 of 29 June 1993 Allowing Voluntary Participation by Companies in the Industrial Sector in a Community Eco-management and Audit Scheme*, O.J. L 168, 10.7.93, p. 1. For a most cogent description of EMAS in its original state, see Orts (footnote 1).

57. Orts, ibid., p. 1291.

58. European Parliament, Council Regulation (EEC) No 1836/93 (footnote 56), article 5.

59. Ibid., article 1.

60. See, e.g., S. Parto, "Aiming Low," in R. Gibson, ed., *Voluntary Initiatives: The New Politics of Corporate Greening* (Peterborough, Ont.: Broadview Press, 1999), p. 186.

61. See, e.g, Parto, ibid., p. 187.

62. See EMAS, *EMAS and ISO/EN ISO 14001: Differences and Complementarities* (April 2001), available at <http://europa.eu.int/comm/environment/emas/pdf/factsheet/fs_iso_en.pdf>.

63. See the EMAS Web site, <http://europa.eu.int/comm/environment/emas/index_en.htm>.

64. International Organization for Standardization, *The ISO Survey of ISO 9000 and ISO 14000 Certificates, Twelfth Cycle: Up to and Including 31 December 2002*, available at <www.iso.ch/iso/en/iso9000-14000/pdf/survey12thcycle.pdf>.

differences may in part reflect the regulatory climate within the countries.[65] These commentators have suggested that the United States is more adversarial and legalistic, while European countries such as Germany are more proscriptive and interventionist.

Individual European Government-led Voluntary Environmental Agreements

Another important European government-led form of voluntary initiative in the environmental area is the voluntary environmental agreement — sometimes also called the voluntary covenant — which has been defined as a collective agreement between a "public authority and an industrial sector focussing on one particular industrial pollution concern and including a collective quantified pollution target to be met by the firms of the industry."[66] Such agreements have been struck at the national level in all EU countries. In 1996, they numbered 300, with many more at the subnational level. Their innovative distinguishing features have been described as twofold: "the *jointness* of policy formulation and implementation and *voluntariness* of the mode of governance that stress the importance of co-operation and partnership between private and public actors."[67] Writers have noted that these two qualities actually appear on a continuum, which explains the variety of approaches; for instance, while many agreements within EU countries exert only a moral obligation on companies, most (90 percent) in the Netherlands are binding contractual obligations.[68] In such cases, of course, the agreements cease to be voluntary once they are negotiated, but retain their element of voluntariness throughout the development stage.

The willingness of European governments and businesses to work together to develop joint, quasi-contractual and individuated agreements that exceed regulatory requirements represents yet another example of the distinctive regulatory environment in Europe as compared to that in North America. The American governmental approach appears to support voluntary pollution-prevention initiatives, and often involves government in a leadership role, but tends to rely more on regulatory incentives (e.g. reduced inspections, easier permit processes) and public recognition than individuated agreements.[69] It is apparent that, whenever individuated agreements are negotiated between government and industry, care must be taken to develop them in an open and transparent manner that will not be seen by competitors as unfair favouritism and by the public as a "closed-door" relaxation of legal standards.[70]

---

65. Kollman and Prakash (footnote 18).

66. M. Glachant, "The Cost Efficiency of Voluntary Agreements for Regulating Industrial Pollution: A Coasean Approach," in C. Carraro and F. Lévêque, eds., *Voluntary Approaches to Environmental Policy* (London: Kluwer, 1999), pp. 75–89, p. 75.

67. Ibid. Emphasis in original.

68. See V. Ingram, "From Sparring Partners to Bedfellows: Joint Approaches to Environmental Policy-Making," *European Environment* 9 (1999), pp. 41–48.

69. For discussion of the situation in Canada, and the legal implications of using such agreements, see Kernaghan Webb and Andrew Morrison, "The Law and Voluntary Codes: Examining the 'Tangled Web'," Chapter 5, above.

70. Ibid.

European Business-led and NGO-led
Voluntary Environmental Initiatives

One of the most prominent voluntary sustainable forestry initiatives in Europe is the Forest Stewardship Council (FSC).[71] An international non-governmental organization, FSC calls for the certification of forest areas harvested in an environmentally and socially sound way and the labelling of products derived from those forests.[72] From the outset, FSC has been led by timber users, traders and representatives of environmental and human rights organizations,[73] not the forest resource extraction industry. This industry has in turn developed its own certification schemes, as has been the case in Canada and the United States.[74] Until recently, such efforts were focussed at the national levels.[75] In 1999, however, national forestry organizations in Europe banded together to form the Pan European Forestry Certification Council, which offers its own option for certification.[76] The program operates in a manner similar to that of FSC, with a logo available for wood products, and specific rules regarding chain of custody.[77]

This seems to represent another example of competition between business-led and NGO-led voluntary processes, similar to that in the United States and Canada.[78] While it is too early to predict which (if either) initiative will ultimately emerge as the dominant player in the marketplace, it is clear that consumers, non-governmental organizations, the media and public perception will play a central role in determining the success or failure of the processes. What is also clear is that governments in Canada, Europe and the United States have all tended to play a comparatively minor role in developing and promoting these sorts of initiatives, leaving it instead to the businesses and environmental organizations to assume leadership roles. This likely reflects recognition that the issue (of what constitutes acceptable sustainable forestry practices, and how this is measured) has an important market element to it, and that governments

---

71. Almost 10 million ha of forests have been certified in Sweden, 1 million in the United Kingdom, and an additional 600,000 in other European Union countries. Former Eastern Bloc countries such as Croatia, the Czech Republic, Estonia and Poland have more than 3 million hectares of FSC-certified forests. (See *Forests Certified by FSC-Accredited Certification Bodies*, available at <www.fsc.org/keepout/content_areas/77/55/files/ABU_REP_70_2004_06_01_FSC_Certified_Forest.pdf.) In Europe, funding for FSC has been received from the European Commission, the Austrian and Dutch governments, WWF-Netherlands, IUCN-Netherlands and the Swedish Society for Nature Conservation. (See "Frequently Asked Questions," available at <www.fsc.org/fsc/about/about_fsc/faqs>.) FSC has "received endorsement and activity commitment from a wide range of NGOs, including WWF, Friends of the Earth and Greenpeace." (See "Frequently Asked Questions," ibid.)

72. See, generally, the FSC International Web site, <www.fsc.org/fsc>.

73. "Frequently Asked Questions" (footnote 71).

74. See Rhone, Clarke and Webb, "Sustainable Forestry Practices," Chapter 9, above, and the discussion of the United States FSC initiative in this chapter, above.

75. However, there had been at least one at the supranational level, the Nordic Forest Certification project, launched by Sweden, Norway and Finland in 1996.

76. See generally the Pan European Forestry Certification Council Web site, <www.pefc.org>.

77. Ibid.

78. See Rhone, Clarke and Webb, "Sustainable Forestry Practices", Chapter 9, above, and the discussion of the United States FSC initiative in this chapter, above.

are not well placed to lead, although they maintain important roles in terms of setting out and enforcing the ground rules about what constitutes accurate and inaccurate representations of sustainable forestry practices, and regulating the forest extraction industry in their jurisdictions.

Developing Countries: The Environmental Protection Challenge

Voluntary environmental initiatives — whether in the form of a consumer product eco-labelling program, or some form of environmental management system or other voluntary code — are mechanisms that are inherently intended to maintain a certain level of behaviour according to an environmental standard. One of the difficulties in establishing such initiatives in developing countries is that firms there may claim that they are not able to meet such standards. This problem was exemplified in a case study presented to the World Trade Organization (WTO) by the government of Colombia, regarding a Colombian flower growers' association that complained of effectively being barred from the German market because of a (voluntary) environmental standard developed by German importers.[79] This represented a situation in which the rule-makers were Europeans (developing environmental standards found acceptable for German consumers), while the Columbians were rule-takers (feeling compelled to adhere to the standard, in order to gain access to the market, in spite of the cost implications).

One of the immediate questions raised by the Colombian flower situation is, if the demands of German consumers for higher environmental standards concerning flowers were to necessitate increased costs for the product or service in question, would these consumers pay for it, or would they abandon their principles in favour of less costly flowers from elsewhere? If German consumers were willing to pay for their principles, this should not be problematic for Colombian flower growers, as long as the costs of meeting with these standards were passed on to the consumers. From the standpoint of producers in developing countries who are faced with high environmental standards being demanded by consumers in developed countries, a key concern is that they have an opportunity to participate in the rule-making process that will affect them. The WTO has established a code of good practice concerning the development of standards, which, among other things, calls for openness, transparency and access to rule making.[80] However, it is not clear that WTO rules apply to voluntary, non-governmental schemes, particularly when these are developed by bodies other than recognized standards organizations.[81]

A second distinctive issue for many developing countries is the adequacy (or more accurately, the inadequacy) of the domestic regulatory framework for environmental protection, and these countries' capacity to effectively implement such a framework. As commentators have noted, environmental regulatory institutions in

---

79. *Environmental Labels and Market Access: Case Study in the Colombian Flower Industry.* Document from Colombia, Committee on Trade and Environment and the Committee on Technical Barriers to Trade, World Trade Organization, document WT/CTE/W/76-G/TBT/W/60, March 9, 1998. Available for download from WTO Web site, <www.wto.org>.

80. See discussion in Webb and Morrision, "The Law and Voluntary Codes," Chapter 5, above.

81. Ibid.

developing countries "are chronically short of funding, expertise and political support."[82] In the absence of a well-functioning regulatory framework, some of the pressure for industry to adopt voluntary environmental approaches may decrease (at least insofar as that pressure comes from government). Looked at another way, this might signal the need for a different and more central role for voluntary environmental approaches in developing countries, to compensate for a weaker regulatory framework. In the absence of a strong regulatory presence, one of the many challenges for governments in developing countries is to devise mechanisms that harness non-regulatory forces to stimulate the private sector to meet environmental standards.

Government-led Voluntary Environmental Initiatives in Developing Countries

The government of Indonesia has shown leadership in devising voluntary environmental schemes as adjuncts to a regulatory regime. In 1995, Indonesia's environmental regulatory agency established PROPER (Program for Pollution Control Evaluation and Rating), with the objective of creating "incentives for compliance through honor and shame."[83] Under the PROPER program, government regulators, using data from inspections and other sources, rate individual emitters who participate in the program.[84] The results and process are vetted by an advisory panel that includes environmental organizations. The results are selectively made public through both a press conference and an Internet site. Two of the five "colour" ratings are for companies that exceed the standards required by law (a "gold" and a "green" rating). The other three ratings are for companies that do not comply with the standards required by law (black, blue and red).

A recent study[85] that examined PROPER over time provides evidence that community pressure, negative media attention and other non-regulatory (market) factors, are major stimuli for improved environmental performance, but that increased environmental information to plant managers (i.e. managers learn more about problems through an environmental audit program) is also a significant factor.[86] Thus, both external (community, media and market) and internal factors (valuable information gleaned from the audit) help explain why abatement activity takes place. The research seems to support the view that, for a variety of reasons, voluntary reporting programs can be a useful incentive for environmental improvements, even when the regulatory regimes are weak. The PROPER program has led to the establishment of a similar program in the

---

82. S. Afsah, A. Blackman and D. Ratunanda, *How Do Public Disclosure Pollution Control Programs Work? Evidence from Indonesia* (Washington: Resources for the Future, 2000), p. 1, available at <www.rff.org/Documents/RFF-DP-00-44.pdf>.

83. See S. Afsah and D. Ratunanda, "Environmental Performance Management and Reporting in Developing Countries: The Case of Indonesia's Program for Pollution Control Evaluation and Rating," in M. Bennett and P. James, eds., *Sustainable Measures: Evaluation and Reporting of Environmental and Social Performance* (Sheffield: Greenleaf Publishing, 1999), pp. 185–201.

84. The following description of PROPER is a paraphrase from Afsah, Blackman and Ratunanda (footnote 82).

85. Ibid.

86. Ibid., pp. 12–14.

Philippines,[87] and the development of PROPER-like programs in China, Mexico, India, Colombia, Bangladesh and Thailand.[88]

Industry-led Voluntary Environmental Initiatives in Developing Countries

A recent study comparing use of regulatory and private-sector-led environmental protection measures in Mexico suggests that in the "informal sector" (i.e. small firms with few pre-existing ties to the State, operating in pollution-intensive activities such as leather tanning, brick and tile making and metal working), peer monitoring can be a useful supplement to regulatory approaches, and that industry-led initiatives show considerable promise in addressing pollution problems.[89] Author Allen Blackman's research into the environmental impact of Mexico's traditional brick-making kilns indicated that brick making is highly polluting, and yet for a variety of technical and political reasons, difficult to regulate. In these circumstances, industry-led monitoring initiatives may work well to buttress regulatory command-and-control process standards. In particular, Blackman says the following about private-sector-led initiatives:

> Private sector-led initiatives would seem to enjoy a number of advantages over state-run programs. First, the willingness of the majority of the brickmakers ... to cooperate with the project suggests that private sector-led projects may be best suited to engage firms that by their nature are bound to be wary of sustained contact with regulatory authorities. Second, the enthusiasm that the ... Project generated among founders, participants and the public at large suggests that private sector-led projects may be able to draw more freely on public sympathy for environmentalism than top-down bureaucratic initiatives. And finally, the Projects' success at consensus building among a diverse set of stakeholders suggests that private sector-led-initiatives may be better able to sidestep the politics and bureaucracy that often plague public sector-led initiatives.[90]

Blackman goes on to note, however, that the brick-making initiative would not have had as much success without governmental support.

For larger firms operating in developing countries, particularly those exporting to developed countries or attempting to attract investment from developed countries, participation in business-led voluntary initiatives that emanate from developed countries may be considered "the price of doing business." For example, there is evidence to

---

87. Called Eco-watch, the program was established in 1997. More information on the program is available at the World Bank Web site, <www.worldbank.org/nipr/ecowatch/ecowatch2.htm>.

88. See Afsah, Blackman, and Ratunanda (footnote 82), p. 8.

89. A. Blackman, *Informal Sector Pollution Control: What Policy Options Do We Have?* (Washington: Resources for the Future, 1999, revised 2000), available at <www.rff.org/Documents/ RFF-DP-00-02-REV.pdf>.

90. Ibid., p. 16.

suggest that the ISO 14001 Environmental Management·Standard is increasing popular in Indonesia. A recent study suggests that industry representatives wish to comply with the standard to gain access to new markets and investment because compliance is demanded of them.[91]

NGO-led Voluntary Environmental Initiatives in Developing Countries

Commentators have suggested that, in the absence of effective regulatory environmental protection mechanisms, local citizens will seek other forms of "informal regulation" to address the problem. Local community associations, for example, may create contractual pacts directly with industries concerning such matters as emission controls or compensation.[92] The incentive for firms to negotiate such pacts may come from a number of sources, including "social ostracism of the firm's employees, the threat of physical violence, boycotting the firm's products, and monitoring and publicizing the firm's emissions."[93]

In addition to this local, community-oriented approach to stimulating voluntary environmental protection from industry, the private sector in developing countries may also comply with voluntary environmental protection codes that are spearheaded and supported by environmental non-governmental organizations. Perhaps the most well known of these is the Forest Stewardship Council and its initiative for sustainable forestry practices, which is discussed earlier in this chapter and elsewhere in this volume. The FSC head office is in Mexico. Its organizational structure specifically includes members from developing countries (referred to as "the South"), in both economic and social positions.[94] There are now more than 2 million hectares of FSC-certified forests in developing countries, including 884,000 in Bolivia, 600,000 in Brazil, 72,000 in Indonesia, 55,000 in Malaysia, 400,000 in Mexico, 14,000 in the Philippines, 41,000 in the Solomon Islands and 91,000 in Zimbabwe.[95] While such programs operate in and apply to forestry activity in Canada, the United States and Europe, it is clear that they operate as adjuncts to regulatory structures pertaining to forestry management. The same is not necessarily true in developing countries, where FSC obligations and monitoring

---

91. Afsah, Blackman, and Ratunanda (footnote 82), p. 1.

92. See examples discussed in S. Pargal and D. Wheeler, "Informal Regulation of Industrial Pollution in Developing Countries: Evidence from Indonesia," *Journal of Political Economy* 104 (1996), pp. 1314–1327, p. 1314.

93. See S. Pargal, H. Hettige, M. Singh and D. Wheeler, *Formal and Informal Regulation of Industrial Pollution: Comparative Evidence from Indonesia and the United States* (Washington: World Bank, 2000), p. 1.

94. For discussion of FSC's organizational structure, particularly its General Assembly (which includes a social and indigenous chamber, an environmental chamber and an economic interest chamber, each with 33.3 percent of voting power in the General Assembly, and each subdivided into Northern and Southern sub-chambers), see *Forest Stewardship Council A.C. By-laws*, available at <www.fsc.org/keepout/content_areas/77/84/files/ FSC_By_laws___revised_November_2002.PDF>.

95. *Forests Certified by FSC-Accredited Certification Bodies* (footnote 71). It should be noted that the independent non-profit Malaysian Timber Certification Council (MTCC), which has a board with government, non-governmental, industry and academic representatives, operates in a manner similar to FSC, and that the two organizations have entered into a collaboration. See "Good Fellers," *The Economist*, January 27, 2001.

may be the primary force for environmental protection, and regulatory action assumes a more secondary role.

Thus, while government, the private sector and NGOs have all set up voluntary environmental initiatives in developing countries, their role and importance may be quite different from what is common in developed countries. The challenge is finding the right set of incentives to stimulate good environmental behaviour in the absence of a strong regulatory presence. Evidence suggests that the incentives may come as much from community and media pressure, as from consumer and investor pressure (largely originating in developed countries). Proponents of "Western" voluntary initiatives operating in developing countries, which could be seen to have significant direct benefits to developed as opposed to developing countries, need to be sensitive to allegations that the programs are "imposing" (albeit via non-governmental, non-coercive instruments) Western interests and values on developing countries. The best response to this appears to be to fully and meaningfully involve developing country participants in establishing and operating the program, so that it is not perceived as an externally imposed initiative.

Human Rights and Worker Safety-Oriented Initiatives

For financial reasons, over the course of the 1980s and 1990s, much of the labour-intensive production of industries such as the clothing and shoe sectors migrated out of high-wage developed countries and into the low-wage developing economies of Central and South America and Asia.[96] During that time and since, consumers in developed countries have been showing increased interest in the conditions under which the products they purchase are made, not just the quality of the products themselves. For example, a 1996 American survey reported that three quarters of U.S. shoppers would be willing to pay higher prices for apparel that had not been made by workers in oppressive working conditions.[97]

In this context, "fair trading" or "ethical trading" voluntary initiatives have been developed to assure consumers that workers have not suffered in the making of particular products. More specifically, the initiatives stipulate standards for factory or agricultural workers in developing countries who produce goods for the developed world, stating that the workers should be fairly compensated for their labour and products, and have the opportunity to work under humane conditions. Typically, an item produced in conformity with the criteria established by a given initiative bears a label to communicate this fact to consumers in developed countries. Ultimately, the success of these initiatives depends almost entirely on the consumers, whose purchasing decisions drive the process.[98]

---

96. For further discussion, see Gregory T. Rhone, John Stroud and Kernaghan Webb, "Gap Inc.'s Code of Conduct for Treatment of Overseas Workers," Chapter 7, above.

97. As reported in "Dress Code: Stamping out Sweatshops," *The Economist*, April 19, 1997, p. 28. Of course, surveys may not translate into purchases at the cash register.

98. A recent Environics International poll found that one in five respondents had "punished" a company in the previous year for failing to behave in a socially responsible manner, as reported in "Consumers Punishing Abusive Companies," *USA Today*, April 1, 2001, p. 16.

The great variety of "fair trade" initiatives in the marketplace — some developed with the strong encouragement of government, some emanating from the private sector, others from non-governmental organizations — is indicative of the belief of these various parties that large numbers of consumers are concerned with the issues, and are looking for labels that indicate ethical behaviour. In some situations, the initiatives (and the groups that support them) are in direct competition. Ideally, the competition can breed a culture of constant evolution and improvement, as each player attempts to outperform the others. However, some argue that it can also cause problems for consumers, who face a barrage of somewhat confusing, all apparently legitimate programs. Of course, there is no guarantee that good programs (i.e. the most effective or most protective) will necessarily emerge victorious over the others.

Another important question is whether the programs actually do for workers in developing countries what they purport to do — that is, improve the quality of the lives of workers. It is possible to argue that to raise standards in any given developing country is to deprive that country of its competitive advantage (as was discussed above in regard to environmental issues). A counterargument could be made that the presence of a well-run factory that is subject to strict standards and monitoring will not only improve the lives of the workers concerned, but will also provide a model of good practice to the rest of that country. Others simply see the phenomenon of Western standards and monitoring as ineffective — a means of alleviating Western consumers' guilty feelings. One writer expressed the issue this way:

> Many in the South and in the trade unions in general suspect that "Codes of Conduct" and "independent monitoring" constitute but the most recent of all public relations gimmicks and privatization of enforcement of labor rights.[99]

On the other hand, when representatives of non-governmental organizations in developing countries participate in compliance monitoring exercises, and come away from the experience supportive of the initiatives in question, it certainly suggests that the programs have some merit.[100] Research also suggests that when compliance verification is looked at more as a learning and empowering experience for workers, and not simply a commercial exercise carried out by outsiders, it is more rewarding in the long run.[101]

In contrast to the voluntary environmental initiatives examined above, which entail a wide variety of initiatives that apply to activities in both developed and developing countries, it is apparent that the phenomenon of fair trade initiatives pertaining to labour seems to have a distinct developing-country focus. In effect, there is

---

99. A. Bendana, of the Centro de Estudios Internacionales, Managua, Nicaragua, *Which Way for NGOs: A Perspective From the South*, e-mail article posted on the Voluntary Codes Research Forum, 2000. For information concerning the Forum, see the Office of Consumer Affairs, Industry Canada, Web site, <www.strategis.ic.gc.ca/epic/internet/inoca-bc.nsf/en/ca00973e.html>.

100. This was the experience of Magaly Pineda, of the Research Center for Feminist Action of the Dominican Republic, as related at a September 21, 1998, North-South Institute social labelling workshop in Toronto. The program review, *An Independent Evaluation of Levi Strauss & Co.'s Code of Conduct Process: A Pilot Program in the Dominican Republic* (August 1998), is available from the authors of this chapter.

101. See J. Bendell, *Towards Participatory Workplace Appraisal: Report from a Focus Group of Women Banana Workers* (London: New Academy of Business, September 2001).

little apparent consumer concern about the safety and human rights of workers in developed countries. While the perception may be wrong,[102] it is assumed that government (and perhaps unions) are adequately protecting workers in developed countries, and that there is no need for companies to comply with voluntary codes of conduct for their developed-country workers and no need for non-governmental third parties to attest to that. On the other hand, there is considerable concern that there is no effective governmental presence to protect workers' rights in developing countries, so that compliance with a code of conduct, particularly when attested to by a qualified independent third party, can become a proxy for effective regulatory protection in those jurisdictions.

The United States: Government-led Voluntary Ethical Trading Initiatives

In August 1996, U.S. President Clinton convened a task force of labour, human rights and consumer groups, and several major apparel makers to create the Apparel Industry Partnership (AIP). AIP sought to protect the rights of workers around the world, while providing consumers with the means to make informed choices about their clothing purchases. After eight months of negotiations, AIP presented its *Workplace Code of Conduct* and *Principles of Monitoring* to President Clinton on April 14, 1997.[103] Companies participating in the AIP must implement a code of conduct that meets or exceeds the standards, and must also undergo internal and external monitoring.[104] They also commit to remedying any problems revealed through the monitoring process and to releasing a public report of their performance. Despite hopes that the program would put an end to the companies' significant image problems, the AIP and its corresponding monitoring body, the Fair Labor Association (FLA), have continued to be dogged by criticism — some of the most vocal emanating from U.S. college student associations — that the programs do not effectively protect overseas clothing workers.[105]

Regardless, the program is now operating, and seems to have retained major private sector support and participation, as well as the support of labour, consumer and student organizations.[106] In 2002, FLA revised its monitoring program so that FLA rather

---

102. See discussion of use of "Compliance Monitoring Agreements" as part of U.S. labour law enforcement, in A. Fung, D. O'Rourke, and S. Sabel, "Realizing Labor Standards: How Transparency, Competition, and Sanctions Could Improve Working Conditions Worldwide," *Boston Review* 26 (2000), available at <http://bostonreview.mit.edu/BR26.1/fung.html>

103. For more information on the history and development of the program, see generally <www.fairlabor.org>.

104. This information is derived from the Fair Labor Association press release, *FLA Makes Major Strides*, October 24, 2001, available at <www.fairlabor.org/html/press.html#Press102401>.

105. See, e.g., "17 Colleges Join Against Sweatshops," *New York Times*, March 16, 1999, p. A22; "Student Critics Push Attacks on an Association Meant to Prevent Sweatshops," *New York Times*, April 25, 1999, p. A18.

106. Supporters include the International Labor Rights Fund, the Lawyers Committee for Human Rights, the National Consumers League, the National Council of Churches, and 172 colleges and universities. See <www.fairlabor.org>.

than member companies select the compliance verifiers and the factories to be audited.[107] The FLA also committed to greater transparency so that consumers and the public will have access to the results of factory audits, including the name of the FLA member company whose facility was audited, the country and region where the facility is located, the size of the facility and the type of product manufactured, areas of non-compliance and status of remediation. As of September 2002, 176 U.S. and Canadian universities had joined the FLA, and more than 1,100 university suppliers were affiliated with the FLA, as a result of university code of conduct requirements that companies manufacturing university-licensed products must participate in the FLA. The FLA has also accredited independent external monitoring organizations, including multinational and local commercial auditing firms, non-profit companies and several southern NGOs, such as COVERCO, an independent, Guatemala-based group that has conducted monitoring of a Liz Claiborne supplier.[108] The U.S. government continues to provide major financial assistance for the program, most recently a $750,000 grant from the Department of State in support of Fair Labor's external monitoring program.[109]

United States: Industry Versus NGO-led Fair Trade Initiatives

While AIP's multistakeholder approach has been developing, several other programs have also been taking shape. A U.S-based industry group, the American Apparel and Footwear Association first developed its standards in 1999, called the Worldwide Responsible Apparel Production (WRAP) Certification program.[110] WRAP places responsibility for seeking and paying for certification in the hands of the factory owners.[111] The WRAP Board includes major corporate members such as Sara Lee (Hanes, Leggs, Playtex, etc.), Vanity Fair Corporate (Lee, Wrangler and Chic Jeans), Kellwood (which produces private label goods for Wal-Mart), as well as former U.S. labour and government leaders, and one NGO representative. WRAP is also endorsed by maquiladora and manufacturers' associations in a dozen developing countries. As of December 2002, WRAP had certified more than 330 factories in 32 countries as being in compliance with the WRAP Principles. According to the WRAP Web site, a total of 1,025 factories in 68 countries have registered to be certified. One report has concluded that "WRAP is generally considered to have the lowest code standards and the least thorough or transparent monitoring program."[112]

---

107. The following information is derived from Maquila Solidarity Network, *Memo: Codes Update*, Number 13 (December 2002–January 2003), available at <www.maquilasolidarity.org/resources/codes/memo13.htm>.

108. See COVERCO report (August 2001) on the Web site of the Maquila Solidarity Network, at <www.maquilasolidarity.org/resources/codes/coverco3.htm>

109. FLA Press release, *Fair Labor Association Awarded $750,000 Grant as Part of the Department of State Anti-Sweatshop Initiative*, January 16, 2001, available at <www.fairlabor.org/html/press.html#Press011601>.

110. See WRAP Web site, <www.wrapapparel.org>.

111. The following information derived from the WRAP Web site (see footnote 110) and the Maquila Solidarity Network (footnote 107).

112. Maquila Solidarity Network, *Memo: Codes Update*, Number 9, November, 2001, available at <www.maquilasolidarity.org/resources/codes/memo9.htm>

A number of student groups have placed their support behind the Workers' Rights Consortium (WRC), officially launched in April 2000.[113] Unlike FLA or WRAP, the WRC does not certify factories or brands. It carries out investigations (both proactive and in response to worker and third-party complaints) of factories producing for member universities. Investigations are carried out by joint investigative teams made up of WRC members and local NGO and labour organizations. As of November 22, 2002, 110 U.S. and Canadian universities were members of the WRC.[114]

One of the most established labor code initiatives is Social Accountability 8000 (SA8000), developed by the New York-based charity Social Accountability International (SAI).[115] SA8000 is a factory certification system based on the ISO management system model. SAI accredits compliance verification organizations to carry out factory audits. Accredited auditors are selected and paid for by the companies rather than by SAI. SAI was founded in 1997 as the Council on Economic Priorities Accreditation Agency to address the growing consumer concern with labour conditions. SAI's affiliate, the Council on Economic Priorities, carried out studies on codes of conduct, finding them to be inconsistent and difficult to monitor. In response to these inadequacies, SA8000 was developed, using an international advisory board that includes experts from trade unions, businesses and NGOs. While not immune to criticism, the SA8000 approach has been generally recognized as one of the more rigorous labour-oriented code initiatives. As of December 31, 2002, there were 190 SA8000-certified facilities in 31 industries and 31 countries, employing 123,810 workers.

What is apparent is that despite government support and a comparatively transparent and inclusive process, the AIP/FLA initiative is still not universally accepted by manufacturers or student consumers as the most appropriate program for the promotion of their interests. Thus, the "honest broker" image that is sometimes bestowed on government-supported programs has not, at least to date, prevented others from launching parallel programs.

European Government-led Ethical Trading Voluntary Initiatives

Although no EU-led ethical trade voluntary programs have emerged to parallel the European Eco-label or the Eco-Management and Audit Scheme (discussed earlier in the chapter), the European Parliament has expressed support for a new European code of conduct for ethical business.[116] The proposal, made by a British Labour European MP, called for voluntary codes of conduct to be adopted by companies doing business in developing countries. The proposal also called for independent monitoring and verification, a new legal base for a statutory European framework governing companies'

---

113. Information from the WRC Web site, <www.workersrights.org>, and the Maquila Solidarity Network (footnote 107).

114. Information from the Maquila Solidarity Network (footnote 107).

115. The following information comes from the SAI Web site, <www.cepaa.org>, and the Maquila Solidarity Network (footnote 107).

116. See R. Howitt, *European Breakthrough in Combatting Multinational Abuses*, press release, January 15, 1999, reported on the on-line Voluntary Codes Research Forum, January 25, 1999, available at <http://strategis.ic.gc.ca/epic/internet/inoca-bc.nsf/en/ca00973e.html>.

operations worldwide, the setting up of an independent European monitoring and verification body with public hearings in the European Parliament, and a mechanism to cut off European funding when companies breach fundamental rights.[117] To date, the proposed initiative has not materialized.

In a manner similar to the U.S. government's support of the Apparel Industry Partnership/Fair Labor Initiative (discussed above), the government of the United Kingdom has supported the Ethical Trading Initiative (ETI), particularly at the financial level. Supporters of ETI have noted that "governments have become aware that globalization can create losers both in the developing and developed worlds — possibly jeopardising fresh steps to liberalise world trade."[118] ETI grew from this context. ETI was established in the United Kingdom in January 1998 and describes itself as an alliance of companies, NGOs and trade union organizations. Substantial operations funding has come from a £530,000 grant from the U.K. Department of International Development, as well as contributions from its membership,[119] which includes a significant number of large, U.K.-based retail chains, food and clothing manufacturers and importers, NGOs and trade union coalitions.[120] Government, too, has involved itself by guaranteeing at least one bank loan in support of an ETI project.[121] ETI has taken a relaxed, incremental approach to gaining acceptance, encouraging company input into the development of ethical trade benchmarks and their implementation. Had they followed a more prescriptive approach, the argument goes, ETI risked having commercial buy-in from companies holding a marginal part of the market. As it stands, ETI claims to have buy-in from companies with a total annual turnover of £50 billion. ETI is apparently recognizing the value of gradual change on a large scale, over immediate change on a small scale.[122]

European Business-Led Ethical Trading Initiatives

Perhaps the best known private sector ethical trading initiative to emerge from Europe is that of The Body Shop, a beauty products retail chain. The Body Shop has committed itself to developing and maintaining trading relationships (with customers, franchisees and suppliers) that are commercially viable, mutually beneficial and based on trust and respect.[123] This includes commitments to safe and healthy working environments, fair wages and non-discrimination, use of environmentally sustainable resources whenever possible, and no use of animals in testing of Body Shop products.[124]

---

117. Ibid.

118. Ethical Trading Initiative, *Learning from Doing* (London: Ethical Trading Initiative, 1999), available at the ETI Web site, <www.ethicaltrade.org/Z/lib/1999/04/lfdr/eti-lfd-review.pdf>.

119. Ibid., p. 9.

120. Membership list is available at <www.ethicaltrade.org>.

121. "Divine Moment for Fair-trade Crusader," *The Express* (U.K.), October 8, 1999.

122. This discussion admittedly does not do justice to the other fair trading programs in Europe. See, e.g., the Clean Clothes Campaign, at <www.cleanclothes.org>.

123. The Body Shop, *Trading Charter*, available at <www.thebodyshop.com/web/tbsgl/images/values97.pdf>, p. 209.

124. Ibid.

Community Trade is a special purchasing program to support long-term sustainable trading relationships with communities in need.[125] The goal is to "help create livelihoods, and to explore a trade-based approach to supporting sustainable development by sourcing ingredients and accessories directly from socially and economically marginalised producer communities."[126]

The Body Shop releases Values Reports and conducts independent third-party social, environmental and animal protection auditing.[127] In 1997, the *Body Shop Values Report* scored the highest rating for the second year running, evaluated by SustainAbility for the United Nations Environmental Programme. As mentioned earlier, The Body Shop is also a member of CERES, the global sustainability reporting program.

European NGO-led Ethical Trading Initiatives

The pioneering Max Havelaar Foundation, a non-profit NGO based in the Netherlands, was established in 1988 to promote a seal of approval for ethically traded coffee. The Foundation bases its program on some fundamental marketplace practicalities: to be successful, a label must be visible and accessible to consumers, and the program should operate so that farmers' interests "coincide with the long-term interests of the consumer, trade and industry" rather than on charitable principles.[128] Under the program, a minimum price is set, one that is well above what the open commodities markets are tolerating at any given time. Of course, consumers, the final participants in this private rule-making structure, ultimately assume the cost. The consumer market's acceptance of the label, meanwhile, can perhaps fairly be described as moderate. Recent indications are that acceptance is steadily rising, with 3.3 million kg of Max Havelaar-labelled coffee having been sold in 1998, a seven percent increase over 1997; still, this constitutes only three percent of the Dutch coffee market.[129]

While the Netherlands branch of Max Havelaar was the first major fair trading scheme in Europe, it is certainly no longer alone. Similar labelling organizations now exist in 14 European countries, as well as in Canada, the United States and Japan. They are grouped under an umbrella body called Fairtrade Labelling Organizations International, headquartered in Bonn, Germany.[130] The group focusses efforts on promoting fair trade, in particular to the EU and national governments, to demonstrate to politicians the viability of labelling as a consumer-oriented market option.

---

125. The Body Shop, *What is Community Trade?* available at <www.thebodyshop.com/web/tbsgl/values_sct_what.jsp>.

126. Ibid.

127. The Body Shop, *Values Report*, available at <www.thebodyshop.com/web/tbsgl/images/values97.pdf>.

128. Max Havelaar Foundation, *The Basic Principles of Max Havelaar*, formerly available at the Max Havelaar Web site <www.maxhavelaar.org>. (Although the particular document cited appears to be no longer available, the philosophy of the company does not seem to have changed.)

129. Figures cited culled from "Max Havelaar Gains Ground on Coffee Market (Max Havelaar wint terrein op koffiemarkt)," *Het Financieele Dagblad*, June 3, 1999, p. 5.

130. See <www.fairtrade.net>.

Developing Countries: Ethical Trading Initiatives

Most human rights and labour-oriented initiatives originate in developed countries. Rugmark, however, is an example of one that originated in the very country whose people it was designed to help. Rugmark was started in India by the South Asia Coalition on Child Servitude in 1989.[131] A producing-marketing partnership was established with German non-governmental organizations in 1994. The Rugmark Foundation provides for the monitoring of child labour in the carpet weaving industries of that country.[132] The initiative has since expanded to Nepal and Pakistan. Rugmark's national branches in these exporting countries are responsible for establishing locally applicable criteria, and carrying out monitoring and inspection of registered looms against those criteria. Meanwhile, Rugmark Foundation offices have been set up in the United States and Germany, the two largest importers of handwoven carpets.

A carpet bearing the Rugmark label purports to ensure, among other things, that no child younger than 14 was involved in manufacturing it.[133] In addition, import and export levies are employed to finance schools for former labourers. Rugmark labels carry individual serial numbers to ensure a clear chain of custody from the loom to the consumer. Clearly, programs such as Rugmark are not a panacea for unfortunate conditions in developing countries. Indeed, no social labelling scheme can be, because the presence of large numbers of workers who are willing to do labour-intensive tasks for low wages is the primary competitive advantage of these countries. The key would appear to be to design rules that permit them to capitalize upon this competitive advantage, while at the same time eliminating the worst forms of abuse.

It is clear that market-driven ethical trading initiatives such as those discussed above will never represent a comprehensive solution to problems associated with poor worker treatment in developing countries. Their weaknesses are self-evident: only workers in participating factories benefit,[134] factories not engaged in the manufacture of export-oriented products will be outside of the reach of the programs, and the programs themselves depend on consumers making the purchases. It is also self-evident that, first and foremost, there must be adequate laws and enforcement of those laws. Until such legal regimes are effectively in place, voluntary ethical trading initiatives with third-party monitoring represent a prototype for the legal regimes that, it is hoped, will eventually materialize. The proliferation of such programs around the world, and the support of

---

131. From Rugmark Canada, *Rugmark Labels Carpets to End Exploitative Child Labour* (undated).

132. For more information, see <www.rugmark.org>.

133. The Kaleen label, administered by a government/industry organization called the Carpet Export Promotion Council, purports to take similar steps towards improving the lot of children in the Indian carpet weaving industry. Promoted as the "Hallmark of Commitment to Child Welfare," the label assures the consumer that a given carpet has been made by a company committed to eliminating child labour, but is generally considered as taking a much more moderate approach than Rugmark to dealing with the problem. (A Rugmark U.S.A. spokesperson stated in conversation with the authors that Kaleen performs no monitoring at all.) It is, of course, a product of a government that has vigorously complained of outsiders' standards and other measures creating barriers to trade.

134. This having been said, all other things being equal, a progressive factory owner who treats workers well may not only increase his or her ability to attract good workers, but may also put pressure on other factory owners to provide similar improved conditions, in an effort to maintain the supply of good workers.

governments for them in several jurisdictions, suggests recognition of the value of these programs, as one small step toward a more comprehensive and effective solution.

Perhaps the most significant development in the area of social labelling has been increased recognition of the importance of, and actual participation by, developing country workers, NGOs, academics and others in the monitoring of compliance with labour-oriented code programs.[135] The potential for learning and empowerment that can take place through such participation is significant, and suggests the need to move away from a single-focussed conventional commercial auditing approach to a more hybrid model involving local actors.

Approaches to Consumer Protection in the Conventional Marketplace [136]

As the following discussion makes clear, market-oriented voluntary approaches to consumer protection have been used for many years. Their development seems to stem largely from private sector recognition that consumers are often looking for more than the basic protections provided through the law, and that it is good business to provide protections to consumers that go beyond those required by law. In addition, businesses develop voluntary consumer protection approaches to stave off new laws. Finally, there is an evident relationship between the existence of adequate consumer protection laws and the development of voluntary consumer protections — that is, businesses are more likely to put effective voluntary approaches in place when there is a strong legal framework.

The United States: Two Examples of Private Consumer Protection

In the United States, governments engage in considerable consumer protection activity through well-established regulatory regimes at both the federal and state levels — activity that has spurred private sector consumer protection initiatives. However, it appears that governments have not directly developed voluntary consumer protection approaches. The late 19th and early 20th centuries saw increased public and governmental concern with misleading advertising and deceptive marketing claims.[137] This led to the introduction of more aggressive misleading advertising legislation, and the response by some businesses to organize into "vigilance committees" to self-regulate and encourage good advertising practices. As the movement grew and shifted from a focus on misleading advertising to more general concern with ethical business practices, its name changed, and in 1912 the Better Business Bureau was born.

The entity commonly known to consumers as the Better Business Bureau actually consists of hundreds of local BBB chapters, groups of local businesses that have

---

135. See, in particular, discussions in Bendell (footnote 101), and Maquila Solidarity Network (footnote 112).

136. *Conventional* refers to the non-on-line marketplace. Electronic commerce presents its own set of issues, as we note below, and is thus dealt with separately.

137. This historical material is culled from *History and Traditions* (1996), available at <www.bosbbb.org/about/history.asp>.

licensed the use of the name and the familiar torch logo from the umbrella group, the Council of Better Business Bureaus, Inc. (CBBB), based in Arlington, Virginia.[138] CBBB and the BBB chapters are supported by more than 250,000 businesses in the United States. Virtually any kind of business that deals with consumers in any way may join the organization.[139] The local BBBs provide several services, including information about individual companies, consumer complaint handling and dispute resolution. Companies that agree to adhere to the BBB standards of ethical behaviour, submit to its dispute resolution process, and pay BBB membership dues are entitled to display the BBB insignia on their premises and in their promotional material. As well, at the national level, the CBBB runs a program to ensure integrity in advertising.

The BBBs garner considerable respect from government and business groups, and millions of consumers continue to call upon the BBBs as the first line of protection, whether to prevent an unsatisfying transaction from occurring (by checking on a company before doing business with it) or to complain when one does. It is true that the rules established by the BBBs in the marketplace may be viewed by some as weak — in the sense that they may not be consistently applied and enforced, and that businesses are not required to become members. Nevertheless, the program is so well branded as a leader in ethical market conduct that a tremendous number of businesses continue to see value in membership. This is a kind of regulation through mutual reinforcement of reputations: the BBBs help member businesses demonstrate that they abide by rules of ethical market conduct; meanwhile, good member businesses help reinforce the public view of BBBs. While the BBBs have been the subject of some criticism, focussing in particular on the variable quality of service from one chapter to another,[140] it is clear that BBBs perform a useful front-line function, ensuring ethical standards in business and providing information on reliable merchants to consumers.[141]

Another century-old veteran in the marketing of integrity arose in the publishing world: *Good Housekeeping* magazine and its Good Housekeeping Seal of Approval, which first appeared in the magazine in 1909.[142] Under the program, a manufacturer wishing to advertise in the magazine requests approval for its products. If the product is approved, then it may carry the seal, and the magazine promises refunds to unsatisfied

---

138. See the Council of Better Business Bureau's Web site, <www.bbb.org>.

139. This is in contrast to industry-specific attempts to ensure integrity and quality of service. Notable examples in the United States include the Direct Marketing Association's codes of ethics (see <www.the-dma.org/channels/businessethics.shtml>) and the American Automobile Association's (AAA) Approved Auto Repair Program. Under the AAA program, 4,600 garages have been approved as meeting the Association's standards for quality work. The garage guarantees that it will not only meet the standard, but will also abide by AAA decisions in disputes between certified shops and AAA members who complain. (This information gleaned from <www.aaa.com> and affiliated regional AAA Web sites.)

140. See, e.g., L. Marable, "Better Business Bureaus are a Bust," *Money*, October 1995, p. 106.

141. Supportive testimonials from presidents Clinton and Reagan, and others, were formerly at <www.bbb.org/bnd/bbbpraise.asp>.

142. For historical information on the Good Housekeeping Seal, see *The 100th Anniversary of the Good Housekeeping Institute*, available at <http://magazines.ivillage.com/goodhousekeeping/consumer/institute/articles/0,,284511_290558,00.html>.

customers.[143] In exchange, the manufacturer commits to purchasing a set amount of advertising in the magazine. Like the BBB system, the Seal represents a double commitment from both the company and from *Good Housekeeping*. As long as the promise of the warranty is kept, then the scheme appears to be a model combination of ethical marketing and good business sense.

There is a symbiotic relation between government and business-driven initiatives such as the BBB and the Good Housekeeping Seal of Approval, in the sense that these sorts of private sector initiatives provide up-front information to consumers about product or merchant reliability, set and apply standards of ethical business behaviour, and provide a form of redress when problems arise, thus decreasing the need for government intervention. But when an organization such as the BBB is confronted with a problem deserving of legal action (for example, when an advertiser refuses to abide by a BBB National Advertising Division decision), the matter is often passed on to the Federal Trade Commission (FTC).[144] The then Chairman of the FTC stated publicly that self-regulation can serve as an important complement to FTC consumer protection enforcement efforts, and in that regard referred to the BBB's advertising self-regulatory program as "an effective model."[145]

The European Union: EU-led Voluntary Consumer Protection Initiatives

As can readily be understood, in the European internal market, there is tremendous potential for cross-border consumer problems to arise. In 1998, the European Commission adopted a "Communication" on the out-of-court settlement of consumer disputes, with the goal of encouraging and facilitating the settling of consumer disputes before going to court.[146] The Communication recognizes the benefit that would accrue to Europe's cross-border consumers if the tremendous variety of out-of-court systems for consumers already in operation across Europe were brought together in a network.

The Communication thus established the principles to which out-of-court settlement bodies would have to adhere in order to participate in the network: independence, transparency, respect of the adversarial principle, effectiveness, legality, liberty and representation.[147] Member states soon began to identify those bodies that met

---

143. The Good Housekeeping Seal of Approval itself does not appear to denote that the Good Housekeeping Institute has tested the product, simply that the purchase price will be refunded if the product proves defective within two years. The Institute does test products, but the indicator of such testing is a different logo: the GH Report Stamp. See *The GH Institute Reports*, available at <http://magazines.ivillage.com/goodhousekeeping/consumer/institute/articles/ 0,,284511_290570-2,00.html>.

144. As discussed in R. Pitofsky, Chairman, Federal Trade Commission, "Self Regulation and Antitrust," prepared remarks for a presentation to the D.C. Bar Association Symposium, Washington, February 18, 1998, available at <www.ftc.gov/speeches/pitofsky/self4.htm>.

145. Ibid.

146. European Commission, *Communication from the Commission on the Out-of-court Settlement of Consumer Disputes*, COM-198 (1998), and *Commission Recommendation on the Principles Applicable to the Bodies Responsible for Out-of-court Settlement of Consumer Disputes*, 98/257/CE, available at <http://europa.eu.int/scadplus/leg/en/lvb/l32031.htm>.

147. Ibid.

these basic guarantees. In 2001, the European Extra-Judicial Network (EEJ-NET) entered a pilot phase, having brought together the acceptable out-of-court settlement bodies, coupled with a linked centralized system for communication and assistance (a clearing house) in each participating jurisdiction.[148] Reflecting the widely diverging approaches in place in each jurisdiction (and the degree of involvement of centralized government consumer agencies), 20 out-of-court bodies were identified (some public, some private) in the United Kingdom, while in Germany there are 203, only 1 in Denmark (the government-funded Consumer Complaints Board) and 2 in France.[149]

A complement to this process is FIN-NET, which came into effect on February 1, 2001.[150] FIN-NET is an out-of-court complaints network for financial services to help businesses and consumers resolve disputes in the internal market in a fast and efficient manner. In the United Kingdom, the Financial Ombudsman Service (FOS) is identified.[151] FOS is funded by levies on the participating companies and free to the consumer; it was created by statute.

EEJ-NET and FIN-NET can be seen as ambitious schemes to link and rationalize public and private non-judicial bodies providing recourse for consumers, a process that has particular relevance in an internal market consisting of many jurisdictions with widely divergent regulatory, market and social cultures and tremendous variation in consumer redress approaches. The private and voluntary consumer redress schemes that are part of the process are all vetted to ensure that they meet minimum standards, and undoubtedly those that do not meet the threshold will be under strong pressure to make the appropriate adjustments. In a way, the resulting integration and rationalization of public and private systems can be seen as a possible model, and logical evolution, for private voluntary systems (i.e. their acceptance by and conformity to governmental authorities and standards). A key challenge is determining when to "let all flowers bloom" (i.e. encourage the development of voluntary approaches with little externally imposed structure) and when to begin culling, trimming and insisting on minimum standards.

European Union: National Government-led Voluntary Consumer Protection Model

The United Kingdom is witnessing a process of revising a regulatory process that was quite innovative when first proposed in the 1970s. The Office of Fair Trading (OFT) is the United Kingdom's consumer protection agency and competition regulator.

---

148. See European Commission, Health and Consumer Protection Directorate-General, *New European Network to Help Consumers Settle Cross-border Disputes Out-of-court,*" press release, October 16, 2001, available at <http://europa.eu.int/comm/dgs/health_consumer/library/press/press197_en.pdf>. The current status of the pilot project is not clear.

149. See European Commission, Health and Consumer Protection Directorate-General, *Out-of-court Bodies Responsible for the Settlement of Consumer Disputes*, available at <http://europa.eu.int/comm/consumers/redress/out_of_court/ commu/acce_just04_en.html>.

150. See "EEJ-Net Gears Up to Take on Cross-Border Consumer Disputes," *Consumer Voice* 3 (October 2001), available at <http://europa.eu.int/comm/dgs/health_consumer/newsletter/200110/02_en.htm>.

151. Ibid.

One of the duties of its director general has been to encourage trade and professional associations to establish codes of practices to promote the interests of consumers, and many such codes have been put in place. However, in the past few years the OFT has concluded that systemic problems with the codes have made many of them ineffective: many of them remain little known among the firms they are supposed to be regulating, some have tended to adopt lowest common denominator standards, and their disciplinary procedures have caused difficulties for the associations (in the sense that expulsion of non-compliant members would sometimes result in weakening those associations).[152]

In an attempt to resolve these problems, in 1999, the U.K. Department of Trade and Industry (to which OFT is responsible) proposed a new approach to consumer protection,[153] under which the OFT would bestow a Seal of Approval on codes that would adhere to a set of "core principles," including truthful advertising, clear and adequate pre-contractual information, and the availability of low-cost third-party redress.[154] Before receipt of the Seal of Approval, a code's sponsors must establish a supervisory body with wide-ranging representation, ensure compliance with the code, and publish reports on the code's successes and failures.[155] A program for approval and promotion of codes of conduct is now in place as part of the *UK Enterprise Act, 2002.*[156] It is interesting to note the parallels between the development at the EU level of the EEJ-NET, whereby qualifying public and private consumer redress schemes must meet certain basic standards, and the initiatives of the Department of Trade and Industry to require domestic voluntary codes schemes to meet certain basic standards.

EU-level Private Sector-led Voluntary Consumer Protection Scheme

In 1992, the European Advertising Standards Alliance was created, in response to a direct challenge from the then EU Competition Commissioner, to show how the issues affecting advertising in the Single Market could be successfully dealt with through cooperation rather than detailed legislation.[157] The national self-regulatory bodies, with the support of the respective parts of the European advertising industry (i.e. the advertisers, the agencies and the media), then established the Alliance. The aims of the Alliance are to promote and support the development of effective self-regulation and to coordinate the handling of cross-border complaints and to provide information on

---

152. The issues are addressed in a series of OFT reports. See Office of Fair Trading, *Raising Standards of Consumer Care: Progressing Beyond Codes of Practice* (London: Office of Fair Trading, February 1998), available at <www.oft.gov.uk/NR/rdonlyres/D7BC7340-436F-4E13- A77D-B22F04337D1E/0/oft206.pdf>, and *Raising Standards of Consumer Care: Report on a Conference Held at Newhall College, Cambridge, 22 September 1998* (London: Office of Fair Trading, February 1999), available at the OFT Web site, <www.oft.gov.uk/NR/rdonlyres/9E2832FF-BB50-49E0-90F5-FC08C139ED77/0/OFT259.PDF>.

153. U.K. Department of Trade and Industry, *Modern Markets, Confident Consumers* (London: Secretary of State for Trade and Industry, July 1999), available at <www.dti.gov.uk/consumer/whitepaper>.

154. Ibid., p. 37.

155. Ibid.

156. See <www.oft.gov.uk/Business/Codes/default.htm>.

157. The following description is based on *About EASA*, available at the Alliance Web site, <www.easa-alliance.org/about_easa/en/about.html>.

advertising self-regulation in Europe. Cross-border consumer complaints are adjudicated according to the rules of the competent Alliance member in the country of origin of the medium concerned, but the process is coordinated through the Alliance. The results of cross-border complaints are published in a publicly available quarterly report. For example, a U.K. consumer complained to the U.K. Advertising Standards Authority (ASA) about a direct mailing from a Dutch advertiser. ASA referred the complaint to the Dutch equivalent of the ASA (the SRC NL). SRC contacted the advertiser, who indicated that the advertisement had been stopped and that in the future the SRC would contact the ASA in advance of publication to discuss mailing content.[158]

The Alliance would appear to be an example of "regulation by raised eyebrow," where the threat of legislative action prompts industry self-regulatory action. Notably, there appears to be little interest in developing a pan-European advertising code, on the grounds that each jurisdiction has its own unique cultural, economic, legal and social context.[159]

European Union: National Level Private Sector-led Consumer Protection Schemes

Although the U.K. Office of Fair Trading is playing an increasingly supportive role in promoting voluntary codes, it is worth noting that a number of very successful voluntary codes have operated with little support or attention from the OFT. The U.K. Press Complaints Commission and the U.K. Advertising Standards Authority are decades-old examples of self-regulatory initiatives offering an adjudicatory forum for members of the public who are unhappy with the conduct of a member of the respective industry.[160] Both organizations emphasize the importance of transparency and public understanding of their operation. Both have been aided in this task by the advent of the Internet: their respective Web sites abound in such information as complete details regarding previous adjudications, guides to the adjudicative process, and reports providing statistics on the nature of complaints and how they have been handled.

Developing Countries: Voluntary Consumer Protection Initiatives

Strongly enforced consumer protection laws are an uncommon phenomenon in developing countries. Misleading advertising may be prevalent and product safety standards lax, but rectifying the situation may not be a high priority for authorities there. In such a situation, there may therefore be a role for non-governmental entities (business or consumer) in establishing at least some baseline standards for business. This may come about in a number of ways. It may be a natural byproduct of globalization; international companies entering developing countries may sometimes bring their own

---

158. Case No. 233, discussed in *Alliance Update* 16 (February 2000), p. 15.

159. See "FAQ" under *About Self-Regulation* at <www.easa-alliance.org/about_sr/en/sr_faq.html>.

160. See <www.pcc.org.uk> and <www.asa.org.uk>. It should be noted that, as a result of regulations introduced in 1998, the ASA can now refer complaints to the Office of Fair Trading for possible injunctive relief. See discussion in Webb and Morrison, "The Law and Voluntary Codes," Chapter 5, above.

standards, which can raise the bar for local companies, who will have to compete to survive.[161] Alternatively, the pressure may come from within, from local groups seeking to improve the ethical conduct of businesses.[162] For example, within six months of the first consumer organization being established in India (in 1966), the Fair Trade Practices Association was established by the private sector.[163] Or, it may come from outside groups. At least one group, Consumers International, has established an international code of business ethics, which is intended to be as applicable in the developing world as in the developed world.[164] In any of these cases, given the reluctance or inability of governmental authorities to act, there is definitely a place for others to fill the void.

Studies also suggest that the introduction of effective consumer protection legislation in developing countries can be an important stimulus for self-regulatory activity by the private sector. A study of business self-regulation and consumer protection in India concludes that there was an increased amount of self-regulation by the public as well as by the private corporate sector as a result of the enactment and implementation of the *Consumer Protection Act, 1986*.[165] The author of that study suggests that mounting pressure by consumer organizations and the growing number of cases filed by consumers before the publicly financed quasijudicial Consumer Disputes Redressal Agencies (established pursuant to the 1986 legislation) have stimulated the private sector to become more socially accountable. For example, the enactment of the legislation

> ...had a visible effect on the CFBP [the Council for Fair Business Practices] and its member businessmen. In the same month when the Act came into being, the CFBP and the Rotary Club jointly organized a workshop on the Consumer Protection Bill and the consensus was that "the business community should think of ways and means to prevent further doses of government legislation."[166]

---

161. *New York Times* columnist Thomas L. Friedman recently discussed at length the popularity of U.S. franchise restaurants in some non-Western countries. The attraction of such establishments, he noted, included "a clean bathroom, international sanitation standards, smiling service and quality controls — all at a cheap price they could afford." See T. Friedman, *The Lexus and the Olive Tree* (New York: Anchor Books, 2000), p. 293. The phenomenon of Western companies offering their services to developing countries is not an undiluted good, however; witness U.S. cigarette companies increasing their marketing in developing countries in order to compensate for declining sales at home.

162. See, e.g., E. C. Limbs and T. L. Fort, "Nigerian Business Practices and Their Interface With Virtue Ethics," *Journal of Business Ethics* (July 2000), pp. 169–179.

163. As discussed in G. Singh, "Business Self-regulation and Consumer Protection in India: A Critique," *Journal of Consumer Policy* 16 (1993), pp. 1–33, p. 17.

164. See the Consumers International Web site, <www.consumersinternational.org>. It must be admitted that the code does not seem to have experienced any significant take-up among international businesses.

165. Singh (footnote 163).

166. Ibid., p. 19. In the context of the author's discussion, this reaction "to prevent further doses of government legislation" seems to be intended to indicate a desire by the private sector to constructively resolve consumer disputes before they go to the public redress institutions, not simply to engage in rearguard actions against new legislation.

Thus, it would appear that voluntary consumer protection approaches may be developed and be particularly important in developing countries where the regulatory system is weak, but that the introduction and implementation of consumer protection legislation in those countries may also stimulate voluntary private sector consumer protection activity.

On-line Consumer Protection, Including Protection of Consumer Privacy

Electronic commerce is an area in which innovative voluntary approaches to consumer protection may be particularly well suited. The increased ability to use the Internet to search for and purchase goods and services from merchants located both locally and around the world represents a tantalizing prospect full of potential advantages for consumers.[167] There is the potential for enhanced consumer convenience, increased access to information about products and services, improved choice, and cheaper prices. This potential, if realized, will also benefit merchants. In particular, small and medium-sized businesses may be able to expand their markets substantially through e-commerce applications, unencumbered by conventional expenses associated with building and operating new facilities.

However, the on-line purchasing experience is considerably different from the conventional "off-line" experience of a consumer buying an item at a "bricks and mortar" establishment. Instead of a consumer directly seeing, touching and feeling products and services he or she wishes to buy, and thereby judging the appropriateness of the product or service at the time of sale (and similar judgments concerning the reliability of the merchant), the on-line consumer is more dependent on information-technology-based substitutes for appraising products and the reliability of merchants.[168] When dealing with an on-line merchant, there also needs to be increased attention paid to issues of delivery and return, what consumer information is gathered, how it is used, held and when it is disclosed to third parties, and techniques for dealing with consumer concerns should problems arise. For all of these reasons, consumers have consistently expressed reservations concerning on-line purchases,[169] and to date the amount of business activity undertaken over the Internet has been relatively low, compared to on-line business-to-business activity.

---

167. It should be acknowledged that consumer access to computers and the Internet, varies widely from jurisdiction to jurisdiction. Consumers in developing countries are at a particular disadvantage in this regard.

168. It is true that on-line *merchants* are also at a disadvantage in terms of assessing the reliability and honesty of their customers. E-commerce consumer security standards can also be of assistance to merchants.

169. See, e.g., a 1999 Consumers International survey revealing that sites were hard to find, product choice was limited, researchers had to call to find out whether the retailer delivered in their own country, poor information was provided, researchers were sometimes re-routed to other sites, the price of an item was sometimes difficult to evaluate, delivery was frequently unreliable, receipts were provided less than 50 percent of the time, seldom was there mention of applicable law, and crucial contract terms were frequently missing. Privacy was another serious concern. See Consumers International, *Consumers@Shopping: An International Comparative Study of Internet Shopping* (London: Consumers International, September 1999). See also a 2001 update of the study, showing similar results. See also a report of the National Consumer Council (U.K.), *E-commerce and Consumer Protection*, (London: National Consumer Council, August 2000), available at <www.ncc.org.uk/pubs/pdf/ecommerce.pdf>.

In apparent recognition of both the differences between the off-line and on-line consumer experiences, as well as the significant potential benefit of e-commerce to consumers and merchants alike, intergovernmental organizations, governments, the private sector, non-governmental organizations and standards organizations have each variously attempted to develop solutions to problems associated with on-line purchasing activity. The result has been a proliferation of voluntary approaches, all variously attempting to protect consumers, including principles and guidelines,[170] merchant reliability codes, seal and trustmark programs,[171] complaints-handling and money-back guarantee services,[172] third-party mediation and dispute resolution initiatives,[173] escrow/insurance[174] and credit card charge-back programs,[175] and information initiatives.[176]

The focus of attention here is on a selection of key merchant reliability and privacy voluntary code, seal and trustmark initiatives being developed in the United States and Europe, as well as in developing countries.

---

170. See, e.g., OECD, *Guidelines for Consumer Protection in the Context of Electronic Commerce* (Paris: OECD, 1999), available at <www1.oecd.org/publications/e-book/9300023E.PDF>; Working Group on Electronic Commerce and Consumers, *Canadian Principles of Consumer Protection for Electronic Commerce*, available at <http://strategis.ic.gc.ca/epic/internet/inoca-bc.nsf/en/ca01180e.html>; and the European Commission, *E-confidence Consumer Forum Principles for E-commerce Codes of Conduct*, available at <http://econfidence.jrc.it>.

171. For example, the former U.K. Web Trader initiative, <www.which.net/webtrader/index.html>, as well as its partner programs in other countries, such as the Netherlands, <www.consumentenbond.nl/>, the Singapore CASETRUST initiative, <www.case.org.sg/casetrust1.htm>, the U.S. BBBOnline initiative, <www.bbbonline.org>, the U.K. TrustUK initiative, <www.trustuk.org.uk/>, the WebTrust initiative, <www.webtrust.org/>, the Global Business Dialogue initiative, <www.gbde.org>, and the Danish Electronic WebSeal Scheme <www.e-fokus.dk>.

172. For example, the U.K. Web Trader initiative offered to reimburse consumers for the first £50 of loss due to credit card fraud in the course of purchases from any of its merchant members (credit card companies pay the rest, by law). America Online offers a money-back guarantee on all purchases from its "certified merchants": see <www.ftc.gov/bcp/icpw/comments/aol.htm>.

173. See, e.g., <www.squaretrade.com> and <www.cybersettle.com>. For a recent review of these schemes, which, among other things, calls for the development of international standards pertaining to on-line dispute resolution, see Consumers International, *Disputes in Cyberspace: Online Dispute Resolution for Consumers in Cross-Border Disputes — An International Evaluation* (London: Consumers International, December 2000), an executive summary of which is available at <www.consumersinternational.org/Publications/ ViewADocument_search.asp?langid=1&regid=135&ID=29>.

174. Escrow services offered by trusted intermediaries operate to protect each party against loss in the event that the other party does not follow through according to the agreement of sale. Insurance services, like escrow services, offer the consumer recovery of losses due to non-delivery of goods. Such services may already be available to the consumer through the consumer's credit card, when that payment method is used.

175. Such programs can be an effective method of achieving redress when a credit card has been used to make the purchase. As the intermediary, the credit card company serves as the preliminary verifier of the reliability of the merchant and the dispute resolver when things go wrong.

176. See, e.g., the U.S. Consumers' Union Ratings scheme, as used in its magazine *Consumer Reports*. See <www.consumerreports.org>.

The United States: Government-led Voluntary On-line Consumer Initiatives

For the most part, American governments have allowed the private sector to take the lead in developing voluntary approaches to on-line consumer protection,[177] but this has not meant that government agencies have not been active in identifying key issues and concerns, monitoring the progress of private sector initiatives, and in certain cases, threatening legislative action when private regulation has not proven sufficient. In September 2000, following a conference held jointly by the Federal Trade Commission and the Department of Commerce on consumer protection in the global e-commerce marketplace, the FTC released a report that, among other things, encouraged continued development of industry programs that better inform consumers and prevent disputes. Industry initiatives that address consumer concerns, such as certification programs, rating systems, codes of conduct and escrow and insurance programs, were described as key to the continued growth of e-commerce.[178]

On the other hand, with regard to on-line consumer privacy, in May 2000, the FTC recommended congressional action to protect on-line consumers' personal information.[179] An FTC Web survey revealed that only 20 percent of the busiest commercial sites had implemented all four of the basic fair information practices that underlie personal information protection (notice, choice, access and security). Although the FTC praised industry self-regulatory practices, only 8 percent of sites in the random sample, and 45 percent of sites in the most popular group, displayed a privacy seal. As a result, the FTC concluded that self-regulatory efforts alone cannot ensure that the on-line marketplace as a whole will emulate standards adopted by industry. The FTC noted that industry initiatives should continue to play an important role within any statutory structure and widely adopted seal programs could be an important component of that effort. "While the Commission applauds the efforts by the private sector to address the issue of online privacy," said then Chairman Robert Pitofsky, "the survey results show that such efforts have not been enough."[180] As a result, the FTC recommended that Congress enact legislation to ensure a minimum level of privacy protection for on-line consumers, establishing "basic standards of practice for the collection of information

---

177. American governments continue to work on a legal framework for jurisdiction and applicable law in cross-border consumer transactions. See Federal Trade Commission, *Consumer Protection in the Global E-commerce Marketplace: Looking Ahead* (Washington: FTC, 2000), available at <www.ftc.gov/bcp/icpw/lookingahead/global.htm>. The FTC has also now recommended legislation to protect online personal information, as discussed below.

178. Information gleaned from Federal Trade Commission, *Consumer Protection in the Global Electronic Marketplace: Looking Ahead,* ibid.

179. The following is derived from Federal Trade Commission, *Privacy Online: Fair Information Practices in the Electronic Marketplace,* (Washington: FTC, May 22, 2000), available at <www.ftc.gov/reports/privacy2000/privacy2000.pdf>.

180. Robert Pitofsky, cited in Federal Trade Commission, *FTC Recommends Congressional Action to Protect Consumer Privacy Online,* press release (May 22, 2000), available at <www.ftc.gov/opa/2000/05/privacy2k.htm>.

online."[181] In the meantime, a "safe habour" approach has been adopted by the FTC, as discussed in Chapter 8.

U.S. Private Sector-led Voluntary On-line Consumer Initiatives

As mentioned in the introduction to this section, there has been a veritable explosion of voluntary on-line consumer protection initiatives introduced by the private sector in the United States and elsewhere. In this section, we focus on only a handful of the better known ones.

BBBOnLine Inc., a wholly owned subsidiary of the Council of Better Business Bureaus, Inc., has adapted old rules to a new medium and adopted new rules when that medium has created new problems.[182] Through its Reliability Program, BBBOnLine applies BBB's traditional roles — advertising regulation, information provision, merchant certification and dispute resolution — to the field of electronic commerce. At the same time, BBBOnLine has also attempted to address consumers' new concerns regarding the fair handling of their personal information through its Privacy Program and its Kid's Privacy Program — the latter essentially providing assurances that personal information will not be solicited (without parents' permission) from minors surfing on-line.[183] Businesses wishing to participate in these programs agree to adhere to a given set of rules (and, in the case of the two privacy programs, undergo an audit of their Web sites). In return, they are permitted to display a logo or seal that informs the consumer of their adherence to the program. When the consumer clicks on the logo, he or she is brought to the BBBOnLine site, where a profile of the company is available. BBBOnLine has marketed the virtues of these programs to the public and the business community, and now claims that nearly 15,000 Web sites have qualified to display one or both of the BBBonLine trustmarks.[184]

Perhaps spurred on by this success, BBBOnLine has added a *Code of Online Business Practices* to its set of voluntary mechanisms.[185] The Code was introduced in November 2000, after a year-long drafting and consultation process during which more than 1000 comments were received from consumer, business, BBB and government representatives. The five principles that underlie the Code are truthful and accurate communications, adequate and upfront disclosure about the business and its goods and services, safe and secure personal information practices, appropriate consumer redress should things go wrong, and special protections for children.[186] At the time of the principles' introduction, an FTC Commissioner stated, "The Commission is active in providing baseline standards to protect consumers through law enforcement efforts and

---

181. Ibid.

182. See the BBBOnLine Web site, <www.bbbonline.org>.

183. See <www.bbbonline.org/privacy/kid.asp>.

184. Figures from Better Business Bureau, *Better Business Bureau Joins With Internet Leaders in GetNetWise Campaign*, press release (July 23, 2003), available <www.bbb.org/alerts/article.asp?ID=176>.

185. The Code is available at <www.bbbonline.org/code/code.asp>.

186. Better Business Bureau, *BBBOnLine to Develop Code of Online Business Practices*, press release (June 8, 1999), available at <www.bbb.org/alerts/article.asp?ID=23>.

other activities. Accordingly, I welcome the BBB's initiative to give businesses the tools to provide confidence to consumers shopping online."[187]

In the field of privacy protection, there are many other codes and trustmarks in addition to BBBOnline's initiative. Another prominent program is Truste, and it too is entirely privately funded. Still other programs have been developed to compete in the on-line consumer protection arena. Webtrust is a product of the American Institute of Certified Public Accountants in collaboration with the Canadian Institute of Chartered Accountants. It distinguishes itself from BBBOnline by undertaking very thorough and costly audits with client companies.[188] Clicknsettle offers an automated program designed to help parties reach monetary settlements, particularly in insurance-related disputes.[189] Squaretrade provides on-line mediation services to consumers.[190] These initiatives all take different approaches, but all are efforts by American business to self-regulate and thereby assure consumers that their concerns about electronic commerce can be met — with a minimum of government intervention.

As discussed earlier, the FTC continues to closely monitor issues associated with consumer protection in the on-line context, holding workshops, issuing discussion papers, outlining basic acceptable practices, and recommending to Congress that legislation be introduced when they feel that self-regulatory approaches have not been sufficient. In effect, continuing dialogue is taking place between the FTC, the business community and consumers about what constitutes adequate consumer protection in the on-line context. The FTC, while apparently predisposed towards market-based private regulatory solutions, is not shy about recommending legislation when it feels that business has not met the challenge. The fact that the FTC has done so with regard to personal information protection could very well have a salutary effect on self-regulatory on-line business practices in general.

European Union: Voluntary Online Consumer Initiatives

Government-led or Supported Initiatives

EU-Level

With the exception of personal information protection (in the case of which all member states have been required by an EU directive to put legislation in place[191]), the EU has so far resisted the temptation to regulate consumer protection in e-commerce. As with the American federal government, the European Commission has actively encouraged the development of effective voluntary approaches. In this regard, the Commission has established the eConfidence Forum, which includes as its main

---

187. Ibid.

188. See <http://webtrust.org>.

189. See <www.clicknsettle.com>.

190. See <www.squaretrade.com>.

191. See Colin J. Bennett, "Privacy Self-Regulation in a Global Economy: A Race to the Top, the Bottom or Somewhere Else?" Chapter 8, above.

components the promotion of high standards of good business practices (e.g. codes of conduct, trust marks, complaint settlement procedures), as well as easy and affordable access to third-party alternative dispute resolution systems, especially for cross-border disputes.[192] The Forum has also been used to support the work of the Commission's eConfidence group of stakeholders, which is working with the Commission to develop general principles that, if necessary, could be applied to codes of conduct and trust mark schemes by accreditation bodies in EU member states. In late 2001, a joint European Consumers' Organisation (BEUC) and industry program was announced, and the European Commission indicated its intention to promulgate a resolution concerning it. Essentially, it is similar to the TrustUK model (see below) — that is, it is a "seal of seals" initiative to endorse codes of conduct and trustmark schemes covering on-line shopping.[193]

EU Member State Government-Supported Voluntary On-line Consumer Initiatives

While government-supported voluntary on-line consumer protection schemes are operating in several EU jurisdictions, discussion here focusses on the experience in the United Kingdom. The U.K. government, and in particular the Department of Trade and Industry, has indicated that it believes that codes and conduct and alternative dispute resolution have an important contribution to make to consumer confidence in e-commerce.[194] The U.K. government has strongly supported the establishment of TrustUK, a private sector body that involves the participation of business, consumer and regulatory organizations in approving e-commerce codes. The U.K. government has also indicated that it is a priority to develop a way of linking such national initiatives at the EU level.

Industry-initiated Voluntary On-line Consumer Initiatives

As mentioned, the TrustUK scheme is a private sector initiative supported by government.[195] Under the program, promoters of codes of practices and seal programs (such as the former Web Trader program, for example) may submit their own consumer protection programs to TrustUK. Those that meet the criteria will be able to carry the TrustUK logo. This sort of "seal of seals" program is designed to provide consumers with an extra level of assurance of the quality of a given voluntary program. TrustUK approved the on-line codes of the former *"Which? Web Trader"* (a voluntary approach initiated by the U.K. Consumers Association, which is discussed below), the U.K. Direct Marketing Association, and the Association of British Travel Agents.[196]

---

192. Information in this section has been derived from the eConfidence Web site, <http://econfidence.jrc.it>.

193. A second draft is available from the eConfidence Web site, ibid.

194. See European Commission, *David Byrne Welcomes Breakthrough in Helping Consumers Shop Online With Confidence*, press release, December 10, 2001. The full text of the project document can be downloaded at <www.beuc.org>.

195. TrustUK Web site, <www.trustuk.org.uk>.

196. See <www.trustuk.org.uk/default.asp?option=5>.

NGO-initiated Voluntary Online Consumer Initiatives

Launched in July 1999 and closed at the end of 2002, the "*Which?* Web Trader" on-line seal program of the U.K. Consumers' Association was a good example of a voluntary e-commerce consumer protection initiative run by a non-governmental organization. The program operated in conjunction with *Which?*, the Association's publication for consumers. The "*Which?* Web Trader" scheme was a program designed to ensure that consumers get a fair deal and to protect them when things go wrong. Merchants in the United Kingdom who agreed to meet and abide by the Web Trader Code of Practice could display the Web Trader logo. The program was free for participating merchants. When the Consumers' Association received complaints from consumers about the service from a merchant displaying the Web Trader logo, it investigated and could withdraw permission to use the logo (following a procedure that allowed merchants to explain their side). More than 2600 commercial organizations were accepted into the Web Trader scheme. In its function as an up-front verifier of merchant reliability, and a follow-through resolver of disputes, the program was similar to those operated by the BBB discussed earlier in this chapter, the key exception being that this program was run not by and for business (and in turn, consumers) but by a consumer organization for consumers (although participating businesses, in turn, benefit).

The Consumers' Association formed Web Trader links with consumer groups in other European and non-European countries. Through these links, businesses in those countries have the opportunity of belonging to a program similar to Web Trader, and under which the businesses may display a logo virtually identical to the Web Trader logo.[197] A system of mutual recognition was established as well, whereby an unsatisfied consumer may complain to the national consumer organization of his or her own country when the complaint arises from dealings with a business bearing the foreign "equivalent" to the Web Trader.

Developing Countries: Voluntary On-line Consumer Initiatives

Much of what is true of the off-line world in developing countries applies equally in the realm of electronic commerce: the lack of effective government standards for consumer protection can be problematic. While in many ways the Internet represents a new venue for exploitation of vulnerable consumers, it does have the virtue of providing a low-cost means of disseminating consumer information. In China, for example, a Web site with the somewhat cryptic domain name, <www.e315.com>, offers a platform for consumers wishing to complain publicly about goods or services with which they are unsatisfied. Before the Internet, such information would likely have been available only in hard copy to consumers. A more organized approach to offering on-line consumer information is that of the Consumers' Association of Singapore (CASE), with its CASE Trust seal of approval program, operating in a fashion similar to the U.S. and

---

197. European Commission, Enterprise Director General, *WEBTRADER Trust Scheme for B@C E-commerce, Supported by the Enterprise DG — Main Results of the Pilot Operation*, at <http://europa.eu.int/comm/ enterprise/ict/policy/webtrader.htm>.

European on-line programs already discussed.[198] While Singapore may no longer qualify as a developing country, it is clearly a non-Western one, and the example of the CASE Trust program demonstrates the adaptability of the seal of approval model to any number of cultures. This adaptability, combined with the Internet's affordability as a medium of information dissemination, shows the potential of the Internet as a vehicle for increasing consumer information (and thus improving consumer protection) in developing countries. Of course, numerous obstacles remain — on-line access to this information is hardly a priority to those whose basic needs are barely met or not met at all. However, the fact is that at least in some countries, in the absence of effective government regulation the Internet may be the most cost-effective and efficient method there is of making information available to the people to help them protect themselves.

Conclusions

Even from this admittedly inadequate preliminary review, it is apparent that voluntary initiatives to protect the environment, workers and consumers are flourishing in the United States, Europe and developing countries. Different styles and approaches are apparent from jurisdiction to jurisdiction, and from context to context. In the United States, there is an apparent predisposition to let the private sector lead in developing voluntary approaches, with government encouraging and supporting but generally not intervening, except when it is apparent that the self-regulatory techniques are proving insufficient. The support comes in many forms, including positive public statements and endorsements from high-ranking officials, government-run workshops and discussion papers that monitor progress and set out baseline standards, and the facilitation of multistakeholder processes. American federal and state governments have shown a proclivity to lead in the development of voluntary pollution prevention approaches rather than in other sectors, particularly with respect to those with no immediate and apparent market "drivers" (e.g. consumer, supplier or investor demand). Nevertheless, private sector- and NGO-led market-driven voluntary environmental approaches are also flourishing in the United States.

In Europe, the European Commission appears to show more willingness to play a lead role in the development and operation of voluntary approaches. This is particularly evident in the environmental area, where the Eco-Management and Auditing System, while voluntarily applied, is based on a European-wide regulatory framework. The roughly comparable system in operation in America (and elsewhere), ISO 14001, was developed largely by and for industry, with the participation of others. Perhaps not surprisingly, EMAS seems, on the whole, to be a more rigorous approach to environmental management than ISO 14001, although efforts are under way to make the two more compatible. Operating alongside EMAS are voluntary industry and NGO-driven environmental initiatives, such as the Pan European Forest Certification system and the Forest Stewardship Council.

---

198. See Web site: <www.case.org.sg>.

With regard to consumer protection, the European Commission has demonstrated leadership in developing an ambitious cross-jurisdictional alternative redress system that incorporates both public and private redress systems that meet certain basic standards. In a sense, the European approach seems to be one of coordination and integration of public and private voluntary approaches that have previously been allowed to operate without significant governmental oversight. As such, it represents an interesting model of evolution for voluntary approaches (i.e. their eventual integration into government regimes) that, if successful, may be emulated in other contexts and jurisdictions. The e-commerce context may be one candidate for such an integrated EU-level approach, although it is too early to predict.

In developing countries, several insights of importance seem to emerge from the preceding review. First, governments, the private sector and non-governmental organizations all seem to be increasingly recognizing the important role that voluntary approaches can play, regardless of and sometimes specifically in recognition of, the often weak regulatory infrastructures. On the other hand, empirical evidence from at least one jurisdiction seems to suggest that industry may be stimulated to develop or make more effective its voluntary approaches upon the introduction and implementation of effective legal techniques. Thus, in various ways, whether the regulatory system is weak or is quite effective, there is an apparent role for voluntary initiatives. A promising and distinctive development is an apparent increased recognition of the importance and use of developing country NGOs, workers, academics and others in the monitoring of labour-oriented codes. Such involvement has potential to be both empowering and educational for the parties involved, and could operate alongside commercial audits.

Looking at the experiences *in toto*, Europe seems to be providing the most innovative examples of use of voluntary approaches in direct support of public policy objectives. Whether it be the development of EMAS, or the new European alternative redress system, there is an apparent willingness on the part of governments to overtly draw on and rationalize voluntary approaches into a systematic public policy framework. It is difficult at this stage to say whether other jurisdictions will follow the European lead or develop their own unique approach.[199]

---

199. See discussion on this topic in Webb and Morrison, "Law and Voluntary Codes," Chapter 5, above.

PART FIVE

Conclusions

Chapter 14

Ind vo dust

Voluntary Codes: Where To From Here?

Kernaghan Webb

It is perhaps fitting that, as governments, the private sector and civil society organizations variously find their feet in a new century, this volume should attempt to bring together descriptions and analysis of a different approach to governing from that which dominated in the 20th century. Taken together, the chapters depict a changing, increasingly borderless world, in which old assumptions about the appropriate roles and instruments of governments, the private sector and non-governmental organizations are being challenged, and new approaches are being put to the test. It is a world in which State and non-State actors alike are displaying a growing willingness to engage in new and innovative approaches to public interest-oriented rule-making and implementation. This willingness seems to stem from conscious or subconscious recognition that conventional approaches have limitations, and that the full potential of alternative approaches has yet to be fully exploited.

The chapters show a rich diversity of voluntary initiatives currently in use to address environmental, worker and consumer protection problems. Characteristic of Clayton Christensen's concept of *breakthrough innovation* described in Chapter 1, public interest-oriented governing, drawing significantly on the use of voluntary codes, is increasingly being taken up by individual firms and industry associations, as well as non-governmental civil society organizations. In other cases, it is government that is initiating and supporting voluntary codes to support public policy objectives. In all cases, the effect is a move to embrace "bottom up" consent-based voluntary codes and related governing measures, as a complement or alternative to exclusive reliance on the more familiar centralized, top-down, command-and-control approaches.

Looking at the evolution in use of voluntary instruments in Canada and elsewhere, a number of general patterns emerge. Increasingly, voluntary approaches are being used to address problems associated with new technologies (e.g. voluntary codes concerning personal information protection, electronic commerce, toxic pollutants, the accuracy of price scanners, and ongoing work to develop a voluntary code in Canada concerning foods that are the product of genetic engineering). This perhaps reflects the potential for voluntary codes to be developed and implemented more quickly than conventional approaches. A second observable trend is the increasing use of voluntary codes to address the way products are produced, and not simply to address the quality of a corporation's products or services. This phenomenon, which is perhaps most clearly evidenced through the increasing interest in "corporate social responsibility," is discussed later in the chapter. A third trend is the creation of new institutions and processes to work in conjunction with voluntary codes. Thus, for example, a new international governing body, the Forest Stewardship Council, with its own distinctive processes for rule development and implementation, has developed alongside the Forest Stewardship Council principles, the Cable Television Standards Foundation now operates in Canada to oversee operation of the Canadian cable television customer service standards, the United States Fair Labor Association has developed a compliance

Kernaghan Webb, Editor, *Voluntary Codes: Private Governance, the Public Interest and Innovation.*
This chapter ©2004 Kernaghan Webb, pages 379–402.
Published by the Carleton Research Unit for Innovation, Science and Environment, Carleton University, Ottawa, Canada.

verification process to ensure conformity with its standards, and the Canadian Chemical Producers' Association has developed a peer and community/NGO process for reviewing member firms' progress in implementing its Responsible Care program codes. The development of such new institutions and processes seems to suggest a recognition that voluntary codes may need some degree of "support bureaucracy" to ensure their continued long-term operation. More is said about the administrative aspects of voluntary codes below.

In resorting to using voluntary codes, it is apparent that all parties are taking risks. Businesses that initiate code initiatives may find their efforts criticized as failing to accurately and fully reflect the interests of those affected, as not being rigorous or transparent enough, and as being nothing more than thinly disguised public relations exercises designed to win new customers or discourage the introduction of new laws. Non-governmental organizations that initiate voluntary codes may be attacked for their bias and unrepresentativeness (and hence the illegitimacy and non-credibility of their initiatives), as engaging in get-rich-quick schemes to fill depleted coffers, and as lacking the experience and business acumen to run the programs. Governments run the risk of criticism that they are abdicating their regulatory responsibilities, are engaging in favouritism when program formulation and implementation are not scrupulously open, accessible and fair, and (when initiatives fail) of backing the wrong horse.

If the risks are self-evident, then why do all three sets of players continue to develop the codes? The most obvious explanation is that they all variously *feel compelled* to initiate the programs.[1] Individual firms and industry associations may develop the programs to "answer their critics" (be they governments, non-governmental organizations, the media, community members, or others) or to "get ahead of the curve" (by anticipating and addressing problems before solutions are imposed on them) and thereby maintain or increase profitability. Non-governmental organizations may initiate voluntary programs to "get things done directly" (out of frustration with perceived inaction or inadequate action from government or industry) or to exploit an opportunity to influence action through the market and thereby gain revenue and influence. Governments may resort to voluntary programs to reinforce regulatory programs, because regulatory approaches are ineffective, cumbersome, slow, expensive, inefficient or inappropriate, because resistance to new regulatory programs is too great, or to stimulate action that goes "beyond compliance." In all cases, the proponents have apparently concluded that the command-and-control regulatory model is not enough, and that it is necessary to develop non-command-and-control initiatives.

On reading the analysis and case study descriptions in this volume, some might conclude that this impulse of businesses, non-governmental organizations and

---

1. While, as noted in Chapter 1, voluntary codes are defined in this volume as *non-legislatively required* commitments, it should be apparent from the examples discussed that a wide variety of market, peer, governmental and community pressures can stimulate private sector action that, in the eyes of the actors involved, may have a distinctly involuntary feel to it. Thus, defining voluntariness purely in terms of legislative requirements is clearly unsatisfactory on many levels. However, it does have the value of re-directing attention away from conventional tools of public policy, such as command-and-control regulation, and instead focussing attention on those instruments and societal forces that draw their power from sources other than directly imposed or threatened State coercion. More subtle investigations of the concept of voluntariness outside of the context of legislative compulsion would be a very fruitful area for further research.

governments to resort to use of voluntary codes bespeaks of a State receding when it should be expanding or at least holding course, of a breakdown on the part of government to fully, responsibly and imaginatively exercise its proper command-and-control regulatory responsibilities. If governments were to fully and rigorously fulfil their regulatory responsibilities, some contend, there would be no need for voluntary measures. Some might also characterize the resort to market-based mechanisms to protect the environment, workers, consumers and the greater community as the commodification of heretofore non-market values of respect and dignity for each other as human beings and for our broader environment. Or, alternatively, they might argue that the current initiatives are simply ineffective and inadequate, a distraction to anyone seriously interested in the proper protection of important human interests, since the market and altruism are not strong enough impulses to protect basic human interests.

There are important truths in each of these observations. Unquestionably, the State should not simply recede in the face of new problems. Undoubtedly, governments are capable of more fully, responsibly and imaginatively exercising their responsibilities and more rigorously enforcing existing legislation and regulations. As for the commodification of non-market values, surely it is true that the "purchase" by consumers of proper environmental and worker behaviour by corporations has a thoroughly repulsive and non-equitable ring to it — particularly when reliance is placed exclusively on the market to deliver these "goods." And certainly it is as difficult to directly attribute beneficial results to use of specific voluntary instruments as it is to attribute results to particular laws.

But while these truths are important to keep in mind, the position taken here is that they are not sufficient reasons to reject or downplay voluntary approaches. It is not so much a question of the State receding in the face of new problems as it is other societal players assuming greater responsibility for governing, drawing on attributes and capacities that make them uniquely qualified to take on these responsibilities. Full and rigorous enforcement of existing legislation and regulations and the use of voluntary approaches should not be seen as an either/or proposition: indeed, as we have seen, evidence suggests that voluntary initiatives may be stimulated by diligent regulatory action, and experience suggests that the two instruments often work in a mutually supportive and positive manner. It is true that the use of market-based voluntary codes in the area of environmental, worker and consumer protection can be characterized as the commodification of basic human values. But it can equally be viewed as the expansion or injection of basic human values into the market — and, in that regard, surely "commerce with a conscience"[2] is an encouraging development. While evidence of the effectiveness of voluntary initiatives is anecdotal and thus inadequate, this should be seen as an area in which improvement in evaluations is needed, not as a justification for rejecting such programs. Finally, it should be clear from the case studies that voluntary initiatives are rarely a substitute for regulatory action, and are much more likely to be a supplement to a regulatory regime that builds on, and indeed depends on, the legal system for its proper implementation, or are transitional instruments that precede regulatory action.

---

2. This is the title of a monograph by Craig Forcese, *Commerce with a Conscience? Human Rights and Corporate Codes of Conduct* (Montréal: International Centre for Human Rights and Development, 1996).

Voluntary Codes: Private Governance, the Public Interest and Innovation

The available evidence, while far from definitive, suggests that voluntary codes have been successful on two levels (although unquestionably, there is much room for improvement). First, with regard to discerning modifications of private sector behaviour, the examples discussed in this volume have provided preliminary if not conclusive evidence of real change. There are now industries developing and implementing environmental programs that, in conjunction with regulatory initiatives, are reducing certain harmful substances and increasing public reporting and community accountability. There is also considerable evidence of retail firms requiring their contract supplier factories to provide protection to their apparel workers in developing countries (whose governments do not have the capacity to enforce whatever worker protection laws they have in place), of forests being harvested in a sustainable fashion under the terms of market-based certification programs, of personal information being protected in accordance with privacy seal programs (and voluntary privacy standards becoming the basis for laws), of products being reformulated to be less environmentally harmful under "ecologo" certification programs, of other products such as helmets being designed to meet voluntary safety standards, and of on-line merchants abiding by e-commerce consumer protections in accordance with the terms of voluntary merchant reliability programs.

But perhaps the more important success has been at the macro level: through voluntary codes, industries, non-governmental organizations and governments are articulating and implementing rule systems, working together and engaging in public policy discourse in ways they have not done before. Non-governmental organizations are aggregating demand-side voices, channelling them into voluntary code initiatives and working directly with businesses and others to make their codes practical and effective. Firms and industry associations are making commitments about their behaviour to communities, environmental organizations and the public at large, not just to government, and in the process are opening up their internal decision-making and implementation processes to others in ways previously unheard of. Governments are working directly with business and other stakeholders to develop and implement consent-based voluntary initiatives that expand and supplement their command-and-control regulatory programs.

In this volume, Bruce Doern describes non-State actors that develop and implement voluntary codes as "surrogate States." There is much to be said for this description, since in many ways the rule-articulation and implementation processes of successful voluntary codes tend to involve the creation of rule-making organs, the hiring of bureaucrats responsible for rule implementation, and the development of accountability and reporting mechanisms that, when taken together, seem to replicate the State in miniature. But as noted by Bryne Purchase in this volume, one key difference is the pressing need for consent, which underlies voluntary codes and is only indirectly at play with State command-and-control measures. To put it more bluntly, voluntary codes cannot be imposed; parties must agree to comply. This puts considerable pressure on proponents to work with those who are to be governed by the code, and all other affected interests, or risk serious challenges to the legitimacy and credibility of the initiative (and, indeed, of the proponent). This pressure to work with others in a meaningful way is arguably the dynamic that makes the discourse surrounding development and implementation of voluntary codes so powerful and interesting as a social phenomenon.

But the position taken here is that both the initial impulse of code proponents to develop voluntary initiatives and the subsequent feeling of compulsion that drives them to work in a meaningful manner with others in order for the initiative to be credible are currently largely spontaneous, ad hoc and subconscious responses, not systematically stimulated nor structured. In some ways, that is part of the appeal and power of the current generation of voluntary codes: no government agency can claim credit for the members of the chemical industry taking it upon themselves to develop the Responsible Care program, the World Wildlife Fund's decision to spearhead the development of the Forest Stewardship Council, or the U.K. Consumers' Association's decision to create its on-line Web Trader program, to name but three initiatives. However, it is also arguably one of the deficiencies of current voluntary code usage: there is no overall accepted understanding of how voluntary codes "fit" in society, in the market, in public policy discourse and in the pantheon of "instrument choice" literature. And there is no effective structure for such initiatives that will not only stimulate parties to develop voluntary codes, but will also ensure that they continue to be effective, accountable and sustainable. In effect, to move from the current, and non-systematic, "let all flowers bloom" phase to one in which the initiatives are both more likely to occur when needed and to be successful would necessitate conscious articulation of an approach, and development of a framework to guide and shape the creation and use of voluntary codes.

What follows is an attempt to sketch a more systematic approach to the use of voluntary codes, to explore its underlying tenets and describe two possible scenarios for operationalization.

Sustainable Governance: A New Approach to Governing in the 21st Century

Sustainable governance[3] begins with the understanding that even though conventional approaches to public interest governing such as command-and-control regulation are powerful in many circumstances they are not without limitations. As Bryne Purchase indicates in his chapter in this volume, command-and-control regulation can be slow, cumbersome and expensive to develop and implement, may stifle innovation, can impose unnecessary costs, and may not be particularly well suited to an environment of rapid technological, social or economic change. Command-and-control regulation can also be a rather blunt instrument to address a varied set of regulated actors, ranging from those who consistently make efforts to fully comply and even attempt to exceed regulatory requirements, to those who comply only when prodded, to those who are in chronic non-compliance.

---

3. *Sustainable governance* is a concept developed by the author that draws on the notion of *sustainable development*, as championed by the Commission on Environment and Development in its report *Our Common Future* (Oxford: Oxford University Press, 1988), and *governance*, as defined by the Commission on Global Governance, in *Our Global Neighbourhood* (Oxford: Oxford University Press, 1995), p. 2. The following section draws substantially on K. Webb, "Sustainable Governance in the 21st Century: Moving Beyond Instrument Choice," in P. Eliadis, M. Hill and M. Howlett, eds., *Designing Government: From Instruments to Governance* (Montréal: McGill-Queen's Press University Press, 2004).

Moreover, full enforcement of command-and-control regulation is a condition that is rarely attained or maintained (due to, for example, budgetary cutbacks, staffing reductions and changing political and management priorities). Full enforcement of command-and-control regulation may be particularly difficult to attain in developing countries, where the legal structure may be weak and financial and human resources limited. For all of these reasons, it is important and indeed prudent to draw on a diversity of both State and non-State actors, structures, processes, instruments and approaches to advance public policy objectives, and to not rely too extensively on any one technique.

Sustainable governance also starts from the premise that the State does not necessarily have a monopoly on governance approaches or activities — the instruments, institutions or resources. As has been discussed in this volume, an increasing number of imaginative approaches to private voluntary governance with public interest-oriented dimensions are springing up in many jurisdictions, but they are not necessarily being developed or promoted in a systematic way. Nor has their development necessarily been motivated by any apparent recognition of the problematic nature of over-reliance on the conventional command-and-control regulatory approaches enforced by government. As a result, there may be situations in which the quality of the private governance approaches could be improved, and in which State encouragement, support or coordination of private governance approaches could be undertaken to good effect.

In the sense that sustainable governance is premised on the understanding that others than simply the State are capable of and willing to take on governing responsibilities, the concept of sustainable governance resonates in important respects, at the level of theory, with some of the work of Michel Foucault (in particular, his broad conception of government and governmentality) and Jürgen Habermas (in particular, his notion of *juridification*).[4] For Foucault and those who have elaborated on his ideas, the concepts of government and governmentality are not limited to activities of the State, and instead refer more generally to ways in which entities (individuals and others) place themselves under the management, guidance or control of others, or seek to place others under their own sway. Looked at in this way, law is simply one of many forms of governance, and non-State bodies — including the individual, and entities between the individual and the State such as the family, the community, individual firms, industry associations and non-governmental organizations — are all capable of creating or being subject to non-State governance techniques. According to some writers who have explored Foucault's ideas, the notion of governmentality, when considered in light of modern liberal fixations with the proper limits of the State, generates an inclination to locate responsibility on actors other than the State. This phenomenon — referred to as *responsibilization* — takes place when actors accept and internalize obligations.[5]

---

4. The following description of the relevant thinking of Foucault and Habermas draws substantially on A. Hunt, "Legal Governance and Social Relations: Empowering Agents and the Limits of Law" in M. MacNeil, N. Sargent, and P. Swan, eds., *Law, Regulation and Governance*, (Don Mills, Ont.: Oxford University Press, 2002), Chapter 3, pp. 54–77. See also Stepan Wood, "Green Revolution or Greenwash? Voluntary Environmental Standards, Public Law and Private Authority in Canada," *in New Perspectives on the Public-Private Divide* (Vancouver: UBC Press, 2004).

5. See e.g., D. Garland, "The Limits of the Sovereign State: Strategies of Crime Control in Contemporary Society," *British Journal of Criminology* 36 (1996), p. 445.

The writings of Habermas are centrally concerned with the tendencies of law to engage in processes of "colonization of the life-world" (what he calls *juridification*), whereby informal means of structuring relations and activity are increasingly replaced by more formal, law-like approaches. While juridification can be positive, such as when notions of justice are imported into the resolution of disputes, it can also lead to increasing bureaucratization and complexity, in which the individual is ultimately rendered less capable of protecting his or her own interests.

There appears to be implicit recognition in these interpretations of Foucault and Habermas that there are limits in terms of the capability of the State and of the law, and, in view of these limits, that there is a space for co-existing and sometimes competing forms of governance, including alternatives to law (this co-existence or competition has been referred to as *legal pluralism*). In light of these potential limitations, there also appears to be some acknowledgement that restraint in the use of law may be useful in some circumstances, as would development of legal approaches that increase the self-regulatory capacity of non-State actors (this has been referred to as *reflexive law*). Building on the work of Habermas, Gunther Teubner describes the emerging strategy as follows: "The task of the law then is still to control power abuses, but the central problem becomes rather to design institutional mechanisms that mutually increase the power of members and leadership in private institutions."[6]

It is perhaps self-evident that there are potential dangers associated with devising systems and approaches that acknowledge or encourage non-State actors to take on governance responsibilities, and to internalize obligations that have important public interest dimensions. For example, there is the potential for the State to abdicate its legitimate responsibilities in favour of private bodies that are less accountable, transparent and democratic. However, the notion of sustainable governance should in no way be considered as a call for or support of the idea of the State withdrawing from its legitimate governing responsibilities, or as support for developing sub-par governance approaches by non-State parties. Rather, sustainable governance is based on recognition that bodies other than the State can take on certain governance responsibilities, in a coordinated, accountable way that supplements those governance activities of the State. Sustainable governance is also based on recognition of the limitations of the State and its conventional governance mechanisms. Sustainable governance is a structured and systematic approach to State and non-State actor governing activities working in tandem, in the public interest, in an accountable, transparent manner.

As part of the implementation of sustainable governance approaches, many innovative instruments, institutions and processes are or could be used by the State to support conventional regulatory enforcement activities, some of these taking the form of voluntary codes, others not.[7] Sustainable governance recognizes that evolution in the mix

---

6. G. Teubner, "After Legal Instrumentalism? Strategic Models of Post-Regulatory Law," *International Journal of the Sociology of Law* 12 (1984), pp. 375– 400, p. 394.

7. Examples of non-voluntary code State-based techniques that could support sustainable governance approaches include specialized independent government investigative bodies that have the authority, upon receipt of citizen petitions, to initiate reviews of enforcement effectiveness and, when necessary, to recommend corrective action; government-operated information disclosure programs that form the basis for direct individual, community, non-governmental organization or industry action; financial incentives to stimulate changes in behaviour that would otherwise not be forthcoming, or at least not as quickly; use of procurement

and use of governance approaches is natural and to be expected. Put another way, public policy is dynamic, not static. This is an important element of sustainable governance, because sustainable governance is governance over the long term, and is an ongoing learning process. For example, in the short term, governments, industry and/or non-governmental actors may put in place voluntary market-based code instruments that in the longer term can become the basis for a command-and-control regulatory approach when the understanding and support for such a transformation has developed. This has occurred in Canada with the transformation of the voluntary Canadian Standards Association's model privacy code into federal legislation, as discussed elsewhere in this volume.

The concept of sustainable governance is also sensitive to the fact that, at any given moment, for any particular policy problem, it may be necessary to offer a range of governance responses to address a range of behaviours. For example, as has been noted earlier, it is well known that not all regulated actors are the same. Some are more than willing to exceed legal requirements. Some will meet legal requirements when pushed. Others will do everything possible to avoid compliance. Voluntary codes and standards can be helpful in addressing this sort of range of behaviours. Consider how the ISO 14001 environmental management systems standard (a standard developed by a non-governmental international organization) has been employed by regulators. As discussed in Chapter 5, in some jurisdictions governments have offered firms the possibility of expedited permit processes when those firms choose to put in place an environmental management system in compliance with ISO 14001 standard. Here, the ISO 14001 standard is being employed by government as a reward or inducement, in a manner that may be particularly attractive to "over-achieving" firms who are willing to exceed regulatory requirements. In other cases, legislation provides that courts, when determining liability, may take into account use of environmental management systems that meet international standards. Here, governments seem to use these systems to reinforce the command-and-control regime — to address those firms who are generally law-abiding, and simply need a nudge or "another good reason" to engage in law-abiding behaviour. Finally, courts have imposed ISO 14001 registration on firms found to be not in compliance with law, as part of sentencing. Here, ISO 14001 is being used to address laggards, and although the ISO 14000 series was designed by non-State actors to operate as a voluntary regime, in these instances it has become decidedly non-voluntary. These three examples show how a private voluntary standard can be used by governments and courts in various ways to address three types of regulated actor, as a supplement to a command-and-control regulatory scheme.

A key theme underlying the concept of sustainable governance is the value of harnessing the energies and expertise of multiple actors, instruments, institutions and processes. Diversity of viewpoints, and even some degree of conflict, rivalry and overlap among actors and instruments, helps to create a thriving (if somewhat chaotic and confusing), multivariate "ecosystem" of approaches addressing a particular policy issue

---

powers or government foreign aid programs in which funding is conditional on compliance with certain public policy conditions; government-industry covenants or agreements that structure and encourage behaviour beyond that required by regulations; and structured access to the court system that allows for actions by private individuals and others on public policy issues (e.g. through private prosecutions, private civil actions and class actions). These are all discussed in greater depth in K. Webb (footnote 3).

or problem, with the effect that the failure of any one technique does not necessarily mean an overall implementation failure, but rather that another actor, instrument, institution or process is in a position to "pick up the slack" or otherwise act as a check and balance concerning a particular behaviour. There is a form of "mutually assured implementation" that can occur when multiple actors, instruments, institutions and processes are all brought to bear on the same activity. Sustainable governance should not be looked upon as a zero-sum game: that is, energy and resources spent on developing and implementing one initiative take away from attention devoted to another initiative. A key value of sustainable governance is its ability to bring to bear currently underutilized governance capacity latent in existing actors and institutions, and thereby increase the total attention spent on addressing a particular problem.

Use of the sustainable governance approach is intended to assist policymakers in determining whether any particular policy context is as "robust" as it could be. It leads to questions such as these:

- Is the full range of actors, instruments, policies and processes in use? If not, why not?
- Where can adjustments and additions be made?
- What sort of interactions between instruments and actors are taking place?
- Could the system be better coordinated?
- Where are the gaps?

By mapping the range of instruments and actors employed in a particular context using the sustainable governance model, it may be possible to identify under- or overutilized approaches or actors, as well as opportunities for better coordination.

The concept of sustainable governance should in no way be considered a call for the abandonment or even necessarily a reduction in command-and-control regulation. Rather, a key message underlying sustainable governance is acknowledgement of the limitations of the command-and-control model and the value of drawing on approaches that may not be so limited. Undoubtedly, these other approaches have limitations of their own. For example, limitations of voluntary approaches discussed in this volume include difficulties addressing free riders, lower visibility and often lower credibility than conventional regulatory approaches, the possibility of less rigorous standards being developed and applied than those associated with regulatory regimes, variable public accountability, and the potential for conflicts with regulatory approaches. As discussed in Chapter 5, some of these limitations of voluntary approaches may be rectified or minimized through imaginative use of legal approaches (e.g. court recognition of voluntary codes as representative of "reasonable care" standards for purposes of tort or regulatory liability can effectively widen the application of such voluntary codes to cover free riders).

While the concept and realization of sustainable governance involves much more than simply welcoming voluntary approaches into the pantheon of available governing instruments, it is the role of voluntary approaches in sustainable governance that is the focus of attention here. What follows is an attempt to depict the role of voluntary codes as part of a sustainable governance model in three policy contexts: consumer protection in Canada, environmental protection in Canada and environmental

Sustainable Governance:

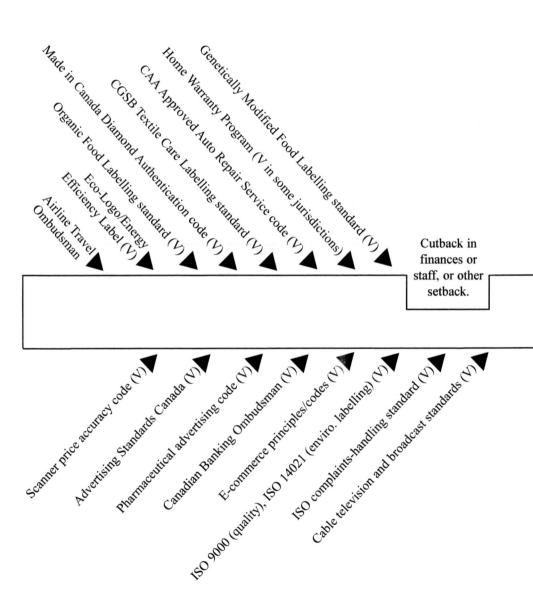

Cutback in finances or staff, or other setback.

Made in Canada Diamond Authentication code (V)
Organic Food Labelling standard (V)
CGSB Textile Care Labelling standard (V)
CAA Approved Auto Repair Service code (V)
Home Warranty Program (V in some jurisdictions)
Genetically Modified Food Labelling standard (V)
Eco-Logo/Energy Efficiency Label (V)
Airline Travel Ombudsman

Scanner price accuracy code (V)
Advertising Standards Canada (V)
Pharmaceutical advertising code (V)
Canadian Banking Ombudsman (V)
E-commerce principles/codes (V)
ISO 9000 (quality), ISO 14021 (enviro. labelling) (V)
ISO complaints-handling standard (V)
Cable television and broadcast standards (V)

Consumer Protection in Canada

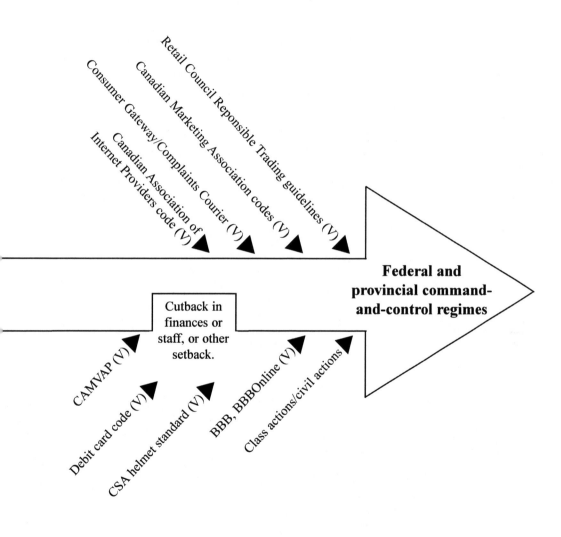

Consumer Gateway/Complaints Courier (V)

Canadian Association of
Internet Providers code (V)

Canadian Marketing Association codes (V)

Retail Council Reponsible Trading guidelines (V)

Federal and
provincial command-
and-control regimes

Cutback in
finances or
staff, or other
setback.

CAMVAP (V)

Debit card code (V)

CSA helmet standard (V)

BBB, BBBOnline (V)

Class actions/civil actions

V=Voluntary code or initiative

protection in Indonesia. In each policy context, a diagram is provided to illustrate how the various voluntary code and other initiatives interact.[8]

Looking first at *Sustainable Governance: Consumer Protection in Canada*, there are a host of federal and provincial (and other levels of government) command-and-control regulatory instruments and other laws that together form the backbone of consumer protection efforts. Included here are federal laws such as the *Competition Act*, the *Consumer Packaging and Labelling Act* and the *Hazardous Products Act*, and provincial laws such as the Ontario *Consumer Protection Act* and the Alberta *Fair Trading Act, 1998*. In recognition of their pivotal role, these command-and-control instruments comprise the large arrow in the centre of the diagram. On both sides of these regulatory instruments are a range of other support instruments, including the Internet-based Consumer Gateway (a portal to government, industry and non-governmental organization consumer information) and Complaints Courier (facilitating the ability of consumers to effectively resolve problems with merchants directly on-line), private law civil and class actions, and the Airline Ombudsman. All of these approaches are administered by federal, provincial or other levels of government.

The remaining 22 small arrows identify voluntary codes or approaches pertaining to product safety, use of products, claims about foods, products and drugs, the reliability of on-line and conventional merchants, characteristics of the foods, accuracy of check-out scanner technologies, protections associated with certain services, quality assurances, and private redress mechanisms.[9] Some of these voluntary codes and

---

8. In all three diagrams, the large arrow represents the dominant instrument used in the particular context (typically a conventional command-and-control regulatory instrument), with the smaller arrows representing programs and instruments that support the main arrow in impact, even if not in intention. The indentations on either side of the large arrows in all three diagrams are intended to represent an occasional budget cutback or other setback occurring to regulatory programs. The indentations do not relate to any particular cutback or setback — their specific location on the side of the arrows is not significant. In all three diagrams, the smaller arrows are not placed in any particular order on either side of the main arrows. In other words, no attempt should be made to interpret the placement of any of the small arrows as particularly significant in relation to the main arrow or to the other small arrows. Simply put, the smaller arrows represent supplementary or secondary instruments. In all three diagrams, many more secondary instruments could be included: the instruments identified should be considered a more or less representative sampling of what is currently in operation.

9. The Canadian Motor Vehicle Arbitration Program, Canadian Banking Ombudsman, Better Business Bureau, Canadian Automobile Association Approved Auto Repair Service, Advertising Standards Canada, Canadian Marketing Association, Cable Television Standards Council and Alberta New Home Warranty Program are all discussed in David Clarke and Kernaghan Webb, *Market-Driven Consumer Redress Case Studies and Legal Issues* (Ottawa: Office of Consumer Affairs, Industry Canada, 2002), available at <http://strategis.ic.gc.ca/epic/internet/inoca-bc.nsf/en/ca01643e.html>. The *Voluntary Code of Conduct for Authenticating Canadian Diamond Claims* is available at <www.canadiandiamondcodeofconduct.ca/html/EN_code.htm>. The *Scanner Price Accuracy Voluntary Code* is available at <http://cb-bc.gc.ca/epic/internet/incb-bc.nsf/vwapj/ct02381e.pdf/$FILE/ct02381e.pdf>. The Canadian Standards Association's Helmet Standard and Eco-Logo programs are the subject of case studies in this volume. Summary discussions of the Textile Care Labelling Standard and Debit Card Code (Electronic Funds Transfer) are available at <http://strategis.ic.gc.ca/epic/internet/inoca-bc.nsf/en/ca00880e.html>. The *Principles of Consumer Protection for Electronic Commerce* are available at <http://strategis.ic.gc.ca/epic/internet/inoca-bc.nsf/en/ca01185e.html>. The ISO complaints-handling standard and genetically modified food labelling standard are in final draft stages. Information about the National Standard for Organic Agriculture is available at <www.pwgsc.gc.ca/cgsb/032_310/intro-e.html>. The Canadian Association of Internet Providers *Code of Conduct* is available at <www.caip.ca/issues/selfreg/code-of-conduct/code.htm>. The Pharmaceutical Advertising Advisory Board code of advertising and guidelines are available at <www.paab.ca/index_en.html>.

initiatives involve the State in some capacity (e.g. governments have approved, sponsored, funded or participated in the development of the codes), and some do not. A voluntary initiative "small arrow" can eventually be transformed into a regulatory initiative "big arrow," as in the case of the transformation of the Canadian Standards Association privacy code into federal law. Overall, the diagram seems to suggest a thriving ecosystem of instruments, institutions, and processes — an ecosystem in which a blow to any one instrument (such as a sudden cutback of regulatory enforcement resources or staff) does not necessarily lead to a crippling of all protection efforts, and one that can potentially respond to a new problem through a variety actors and techniques more quickly than is possible when reliance is placed primarily on command-and-control approaches.

Clearly, the diagram cannot do justice to the full and complex interaction between instruments and actors taking place in a sustainable governance model. For example, it does not portray the dynamic relationship between the Better Business Bureau as a front-line consumer complaints response, redress and market intelligence mechanism and government regulators, who regularly share information and work out coordinated responses to emerging problems. In viewing consumer protection in Canada through a sustainable governance perspective, the suggestion is not that it works as fairly, efficiently and effectively as possible, or indeed that all available information concerning its current operation is known. Unanswered questions at this stage include the following: whether the range of voluntary codes and initiatives are as effective as they could be; whether there are practical mechanisms available for some form of "quality control" of the voluntary instruments; whether there is adequate information disclosure and sharing among players and instruments; whether there is adequate coordination between the instruments; whether consumers are confused by or unsatisfied with the range of instruments; and whether there are gaps that need to be addressed.

Looking next at *Sustainable Governance: Environmental Protection in Canada*, again it is federal and provincial command-and-control regulation that is the dominant policy instrument, so command-and-control regulation occupies the "main arrow" position in the centre of the diagram. Included here are such federal statutes as the *Canadian Environmental Protection Act, 1999*, and the *Fisheries Act* pollution control provisions, as well as provincial legislation such as the Ontario *Environmental Protection Act* and the British Columbia *Waste Management Act*. Supporting the command-and-control regulatory approach are intergovernmental, federal and provincial process instruments facilitating citizen petitions concerning instances of alleged problematic enforcement, private prosecutions and private civil actions (including class actions on environmental matters), information disclosure initiatives, financial incentives and a range of voluntary codes and agreements pertaining to the environmental and energy characteristics of products, the reduction of toxic substances, the reduction of harmful climate change activity, as well as sector-specific and generic environmental management initiatives.[10] As discussed above with respect to the use of the ISO 14001 environmental management standard, there are a wide range of ways in which voluntary approaches can interact with and supplement regulatory command-and-control approaches. Useful interaction between other instruments is also possible. For example,

---

10. See Webb (footnote 3).

Sustainable Governance:

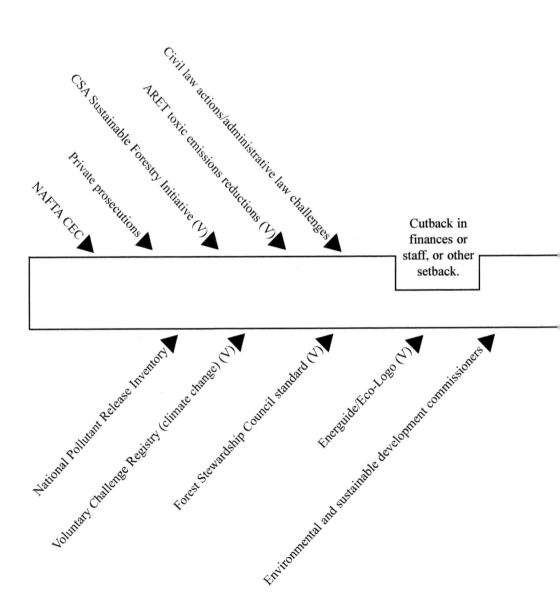

Environmental Protection in Canada

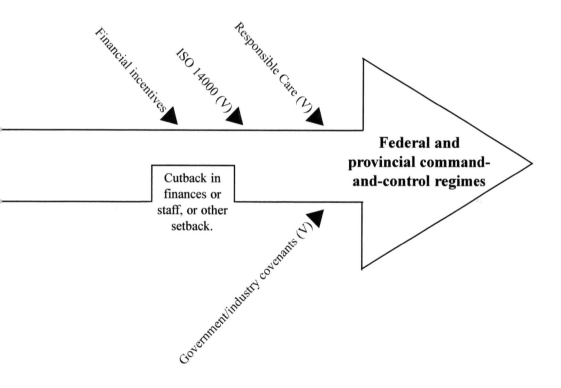

V=Voluntary code or initiative

Sustainable Governance:

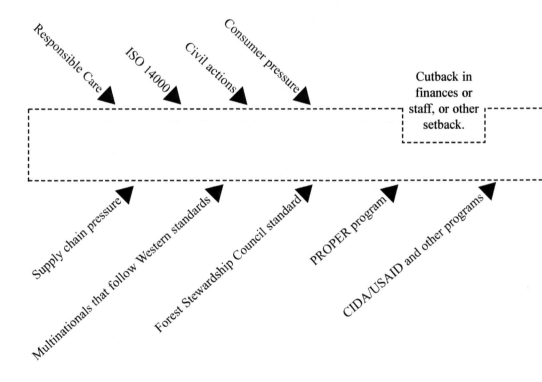

Responsible Care

ISO 14000

Civil actions

Consumer pressure

Cutback in
finances or
staff, or other
setback.

Supply chain pressure

Multinationals that follow Western standards

Forest Stewardship Council standard

PROPER program

CIDA/USAID and other programs

Environmental Protection in Indonesia

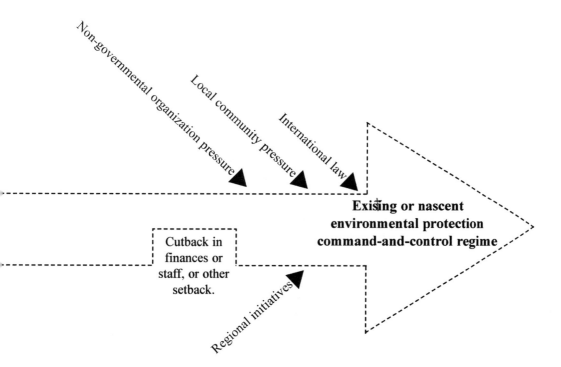

Non-governmental organization pressure

Local community pressure

International law

Exising or nascent environmental protection command-and-control regime

Cutback in finances or staff, or other setback.

Regional initiatives

use of the National Pollutants Release Inventory, an information instrument in which firms are required to publicly report their use of certain toxic substances, can help communities, citizens and other interested parties verify progress or lack of progress with voluntary toxic reduction programs. As with the questions articulated above concerning coordination of instruments and processes, effectiveness and quality control in the context of Canadian consumer protection, similar questions can be posed concerning the range of instruments and actors involved in the Canadian environmental protection sustainable governance model.

The final diagram, *Sustainable Governance: Environmental Protection in Indonesia*, is provided to illustrate the somewhat different dynamic typically at work among command-and-control regulatory instruments and other approaches in developing countries. Again, the command-and-control regulatory approach occupies the "main arrow" position, but here it is more of a work-in-progress than fully actualized. In light of the comparatively weak nature of the command-and-control instrument, the support approaches are particularly important in developing countries. Thus, community information programs such as PROPER (discussed in Chapter 13), as well as foreign aid programs, international conventions, pressure at the local community, supplier, non-governmental organization, consumer and regional levels, and international voluntary programs such as ISO 14001 and the Forest Stewardship Council sustainable forestry standards, can all play important roles in stimulating environmentally sensitive behaviour. While a modern, fully funded, properly administered command-and-control regulatory instrument might be the preferred option, in its absence, the other approaches can at least provide some degree of market and community pressure for private sector companies to meet basic environmental protection norms.

The sustainable governance model was developed by the author in an attempt to convey more clearly the value of diverse, multivariate and multi-actor approaches to governing, and to illustrate the important role that voluntary codes can play in contributing to more robust, flexible and effective public policy. Sustainable governance is essentially a lens for better understanding how instruments and actors can and do interact, but it is also intended to assist in critical analysis of the effectiveness of current governance approaches in particular policy contexts. Making the shift from conventional thinking about governing to sustainable governance may be difficult for some, who have ideological predispositions in favour of or against certain approaches, who are uneasy about the varying degrees of control offered by different approaches, and who are troubled by a complex non-linear approach to achieving public policy objectives. The immediate issue here, however, is more modest: if the potential value of voluntary approaches is accepted, then how can the State more systematically stimulate and integrate the use of voluntary approaches into public policy design and implementation thinking and activities, and thereby improve the quality of life and the economic well-being of its citizens and businesses, and those of the broader global community?

Sustainable Governance and Voluntary Codes: Next Steps

Operationalization of the concept of sustainable governance, particularly as it pertains to the use of voluntary codes, can be pursued in at least two different ways. The first approach could be called *aggressive stimulation*, because many of the incentives for voluntary action and much of the structure for the operation of voluntary codes are explicitly predetermined in an effort to ensure that certain results are achieved. The second could be described as *conscious minimalism*, in that it involves minor, incremental adjustments to the current system designed to encourage but not directly control the development and operation of effective voluntary codes. There are advantages and disadvantages associated with each. The two approaches are briefly described below.

One of the best examples of an aggressive stimulation approach to using voluntary codes is the European Union's Eco-Management and Audit Scheme (EMAS), described earlier in this volume. EMAS is an attempt to explicitly "build" a voluntary environmental program on a legislative base. The legal framework encourages industry to adopt explicit and comprehensive environmental management procedures, as verified and audited by approved independent third parties. In the future, EMAS may become a mandatory system for Europe, but for now it is not. There are currently no statutory penalties for failing to implement EMAS.

What is apparent in the EMAS example is that government is very much in control of every aspect of EMAS, save actual use by industry (and even in this regard, a requirement is being considered that companies would need to have EMAS in place if they wish a contract with an EU government). One clear advantage of this approach is the opportunity for a very high degree of quality control by government over the substantive terms and procedural aspects of the program.

Conscious minimalism, as the name suggests, is a more modest approach to encouraging voluntary codes. It involves rigorous enforcement of existing legislation, and a well-recognized willingness to initiate new legislative and regulatory solutions when circumstances warrant,[11] since evidence suggests that this sets a strong incentive for industry to take the initiative in developing new voluntary codes (or risk being the subject of a new regulation). Governments may also engage in wide-ranging information initiatives, such as pollution release inventories, the development of guides on how to develop and implement voluntary codes, evaluative frameworks to assist in identifying areas for improvement with existing codes, and monitoring and reporting on compliance levels with existing voluntary codes.

The conscious minimalist approach to sustainable governance as it pertains to voluntary codes may consist of, among other things, government leadership and support of particular market-based and regulatory-oriented voluntary approaches, as circumstances warrant, but not necessarily under a specialized legislative framework for voluntary action, as with EMAS. Development by governments of national and international principles, benchmarks and guidelines, and support of the formal

---

11. It is recognized that the regulatory infrastructure may be lacking or inadequate in developing countries, in which case conscious minimalism may involve encouragement of certain voluntary initiatives in spite of or because of a lack of a regulatory regime.

State-supported standards system, are other elements of the conscious minimalist approach. The principles, benchmarks and guidelines can be drawn on by all parties in the development of specific voluntary codes, as can the standards system.

The development of an international standard for customer satisfaction codes of conduct could act as a particularly useful benchmark that could help separate the useful codes from those that are misleading or ineffective.[12] This standard could entail procedural elements, such as stipulations regarding meaningful participation of all stakeholders in code development and implementation, and requirements concerning the content of codes, such as the need for provisions requiring clear performance obligations, monitoring, reporting, internal and external audits and effective incentives and penalties. While not overtly creating a legislative framework within which voluntary codes are to operate, such a standard could, if widely accepted and promoted, stimulate code proponents to meet or exceed its terms, and thereby increase the likelihood that existing voluntary codes are effective and credible.

The advantage of the conscious minimalist approach is that it does not attempt to decide in advance exactly how any particular voluntary approaches should operate. As a result, experimentation is encouraged. On the other hand, this feature of the conscious minimalist approach is also a disadvantage in the sense that it provides less guidance and control over what voluntary codes are developed and how.

In many ways, the aggressive stimulation and conscious minimalist approaches represent fairly divergent positions that a particular society might adopt as part of operationalization of a voluntary codes strategy within a sustainable governance approach. In reality, within the general concept of sustainable governance, there is more of a continuum of options. There would be no barrier to developing an explicit legislative framework for voluntary codes in one context, and a more relaxed approach in another. In short, the foregoing should be considered as no more than a "broad strokes outline" of how a strategy for use of voluntary instruments may be operationalized within a sustainable governance framework.

The Next Wave: Corporate Social Responsibility

Corporate social responsibility (CSR) has been described as "...business decision-making linked to ethical values, compliance with legal instruments, and respect for people, communities and the environment."[13] While this indicates its breadth, it leaves the actual content undefined. What constitutes "ethical values"? When does a corporation cross the line between acceptable conduct with respect for people or communities or the environment, and unacceptable conduct? What is apparent is that, increasingly, corporations are recognizing that, while obtaining a legal licence from government is an obvious first step before beginning activity in any area, failure to negotiate an additional "social licence" with the broader range of affected stakeholders can leave them vulnerable to frictions and problems that can undermine their ability to proceed with their operations in a constructive and profitable manner. In short,

---

12. Such a standard is now being developed through the International Organization for Standardization (ISO).

13. Quote from the Business for Social Responsibility Web site, <www.bsr.org>.

corporations are learning to "get the permission" not only of government, but also of affected stakeholders, and to be accountable and transparent in their actions to more than just shareholders and governments. In so doing, voluntary codes can play a key role. The topic of CSR — why it has arisen, its implications, the reactions and next steps of various actors — is both intriguing and clearly beyond the scope of this volume. In a way, CSR starts just where this volume ends. For current purposes, it is only necessary here to sketch how it could emerge as a prime example of a phenomenon in which both the concept of sustainable governance and the use of voluntary instruments could play central roles.

The rise to prominence of corporate social responsibility is in many ways the not unpredictable outcome of government, private sector and non-governmental organization activity that has taken place over the past several decades. Since World War II, Western governments have been taking on a mounting number of economic, social and environmental responsibilities on behalf of society. Since the 1990s, many Western governments have also been asked to reduce their tax burden. This has raised questions concerning the capacity of Western governments to deliver on their regulatory promises while simultaneously meeting their fiscal responsibilities. (In developing countries, weak governmental capacity has been a longstanding problem.) As discussed in Chapter 1, there is growing recognition that the State cannot achieve all of its objectives exclusively through conventional approaches. At the international level, the limitations of international law regimes are also very apparent, as is the power and influence of multinational corporations. As the weaknesses of the State and the strength of large corporations have become apparent, some non-governmental organizations have assumed watchdog roles over both government and corporate activity. But this role is problematic in the sense that non-governmental organizations do not necessarily have the capacity or the legitimacy to effectively carry out the watchdog function.

The long-term solution might be widespread adoption by governments of the sustainable governance approach, in which the "load" of governing is shared among a variety of actors. In addition, development of an effective international legal regime with powerful democratic organs of rule-making and enforcement might also be considered to be desirable. But, clearly, the full realization of these solutions — even if they were agreed to by all — is many years away. In the meantime, what can be done? The suggestion made here is that, in the short term, a combination of domestic legislation in Western countries devoted to improving corporate transparency and accountability, coupled with market pressure from consumers, shareholders, investors, insurers and other demand-side interests using voluntary codes, could supply corporations with the impetus and guidance they need to address in an open and transparent way their economic, social and environmental impacts. A host of stakeholders in developing countries could also assist firms in devising and meeting their CSR commitments. If firms developed and implemented CSR approaches in this manner, they may be able to obtain the "social licence" they need for the immediate future, and these short-term solutions could demonstrate the feasibility of more comprehensive and systematic solutions for the longer term.

In designing regimes in which the State stimulates greater corporate accountability, transparency and responsibility through legal mechanisms, which are then developed and "made real" through non-State activity, the resultant sustainable governance model for corporate social responsibility resembles in important respects the trend toward *proceduralization*, which is discussed in the works of Habermas. This proceduralization is described as "providing a framework within which an expanding diversity of conflicts can be regularized through procedures that open up the possibility of 'dialogue' between participants."[14] One commentator observes:

> In an increasingly stratified and pluralist world — an agnostic society
> in which agreement on substantive issues is less and less possible —
> identifying procedures that require participants to take some steps
> towards the recognition of the other is the best that we can aspire to.[15]

A structured approach leading to corporations engaging in meaningful dialogues with the full range of stakeholders who are impacted by their activities — an approach to obtaining a "social licence" involving a combination of State and non-State actors and governance techniques — is an achievable if modest objective of corporate social responsibility, using the concepts underlying sustainable governance discussed in this chapter.

Is this sufficient? Is this ideal? Few would say that it is. But the model for constructive interrelations between State and non-State actors and conventional and voluntary approaches is one that has worked in the past. As in the case of the development of a federal law in Canada for the protection of personal information, which started life as a voluntary code, the momentum created by combined government-business-NGO action can build the trust for and show the practicality of a particular approach, thereby overcoming seemingly intractable obstacles to progress in a given area of public policy. Of course, there is no guarantee that this will occur — in the context of corporate social responsibility, or any other issue of concern. But it may lead to the critical mass, or tipping point of State and non-State action taking place in the form of a systematically employed range of actors, institutions, instruments and processes that together are an example of the sustainable governance model in action.

As is apparent from the research in this volume, to do a voluntary code right (and to thereby receive the positive rewards that flow from doing it right) is not easy. It is expensive, time-consuming, and fraught with traps for the unwary. Moreover, there are no guarantees that a favourable response from the full range of stakeholders will be forthcoming. The irony is that the short-term "favourable case" scenario of individuated voluntary CSR arrangements may be sufficiently intimidating in terms of the energy it takes to make such arrangements work, that it will drive all parties back to the State capacity-building table, and perhaps even the international law table, where real institutional reforms are needed.

At some point, there may be realization that, in light of the transaction costs associated with each firm developing and implementing its own voluntary approach, the most cost-effective solution may be one in which State and non-State actors work together in a systematic way using a combination of international law, domestic law and voluntary approaches. And if it does lead to greater corporate support for the development of effective international law and domestic legal regimes, then it provides a

---

14. Hunt (footnote 4).

15. Ibid.

good illustration of the significance of evolution in sustainable governance, as discussed earlier — that is, one approach may give way to another over time as the players and capacities evolve. This sort of recognition of an evolving approach seems to be reflected in a recent statement by the Taizo Nishimuro, Toshiba Board Chairman, that, while Toshiba requires its operations around the world to adhere to strict environmental standards (stricter, he notes, than are currently in place in many jurisdictions), Toshiba will at the same time help governments to establish global standards.[16] To this statement could usefully be added the following: parallel to establishment of global standards, there also needs to be development of effective means of implementing global standards, and effective capacity for norm development and implementation at the domestic level in countries around the world.

Conclusion

Sustainable governance is intended to describe a more nuanced understanding of how communities order themselves, an understanding that recognizes the important and different roles that voluntary codes can play, alongside more conventional governing approaches that fall almost exclusively within the control of the State. The world of sustainable governance is one in which normative rule development involves a complex interplay of domestic and international legal instruments, voluntary codes, and State and non-State actors. It is an interplay that harnesses the energies of markets and communities, as well as citizens, communities, businesses, non-governmental organizations, legislatures, governments, intergovernmental organizations and the courts. Operationalization of a strategic approach to voluntary codes within the sustainable governance model could involve overt stimulation within a tightly circumscribed legislative framework, a more minimalist and laissez-faire approach, or something in between.

The analysis and case descriptions of the voluntary codes discussed in this volume suggest that businesses, non-governmental organizations and governments have all felt compelled to resort to the use of voluntary codes, although it is clear that their reasons for doing so differ widely. The exact implications of using voluntary codes are difficult to predict at this early stage in their evolution. Nonetheless, it is clear that a growing number of businesses are making public commitments about their activities, increasing numbers of non-governmental organizations are now attempting to change business behaviour directly rather than relying solely on governments to compel behaviour modifications, communities are being invited to participate in rule processes and decisions that have never been open to them before, and governments are increasingly resorting to consensual approaches to governing, alongside use of more conventional coercive techniques. The instrument for carrying out much of this activity

---

16. "Toshiba, he noted, requires its manufacturing operations around the world to adhere to the strictest environmental standards in effect anywhere — even though regulations in most countries are far less burdensome. 'We are moving towards global standards and we have to be responsible as we help governments establish those standards.'" World Economic Forum, *Corporate Leaders Discuss Social Role*, press release, (February 4, 2002).

has been the voluntary code. In effect, voluntary codes act as information-rich methods of discourse among various parts of society — methods of discourse that seem to reflect a restructuring in the way the public and private sectors operate, and deep changes in the relative power, roles and responsibilities among the participants.

The exploration of voluntary codes provided in this volume suggests that there is much that can be learned from the codes phenomenon as we collectively search for what is possible and what is desirable with respect to governance in the public interest at the domestic and global level in the 21st century.

Bibliography

Aalders, M., "Regulation and In-Company Environmental Management in the Netherlands," *Law & Policy* 15:2 (1993), pp. 75–94.

Adair, A., *A Code of Conduct for NGOs: A Necessary Reform* (London: Institute of Economic Affairs, 1999).

Advertising Standards Authority (U.K.), *ASA Welcomes High Court Victory* (January 17, 2001), at <www.asa.org.uk/news/show_news.asp?news_id=57&news_section=General>.

———, *Misleading Advertisements: The Law,* at <www.asa.org.uk/issues/background_briefings>.

Afsah, S., and D. Ratunanda, "Environmental Performance Management and Reporting in Developing Countries: The Case of Indonesia's Program for Pollution Control Evaluation and Rating," in M. Bennett and P. James, eds., *Sustainable Measures: Evaluation and Reporting of Environmental and Social Performance* (Sheffield: Greenleaf Publishing, 1999).

Afsah, S., A. Blackman and D. Ratunanda, *How Do Public Disclosure Pollution Control Programs Work? Evidence from Indonesia* (Washington: Resources for the Future, 2000), at <www.rff.org/Documents/RFF-DP-00-44.pdf>.

Allmand, W., "Foreword," in C. Forcese, ed., *Commerce With Conscience? Human Rights and Corporate Codes of Conduct* (Montréal: International Centre for Human Rights and Democratic Development, 1997).

Alston, P., "Labor Rights Provisions in US Trade Law," *Human Rights Quarterly* 15 (1993), p. 21.

American Forest and Paper Association, *SFI Program* (brochure), (Washington: American Forest and Paper Association, 1998).

———, "Statement of AF&PA President and CEO, W. Henson Moore," *The SFI^{SM} Program Fifth Annual Progress Report* (Washington: American Forest and Paper Association, 2000), at <www.internationalpaper.com/our_world/SFI_2000_1to6.pdf>.

———, "Statement of Independent Expert Review Panel," *5th Annual Progress Report* (Washington: American Forest and Paper Association, 2000).

American Society for Testing and Materials, *Standard F1045-95: Ice Hockey Helmets* (West Conshohocken, Pa.: American Society for Testing and Materials, 2001).

Amirault, E., and M. Archer, *Canadian Business Law* (Toronto: Methuen Publications, 1988).

Aristotle, *Nicomachean Ethics*, T. Irwin, trans. (New York: Hackett Publishing Company, 1985).

Armson, K. (letter to the editor), *The Forestry Chronicle* 74 (May/June 1998), p. 284.

Association of British Insurers, *Investing in Social Responsibility: Risks and Opportunities* (2001), at <www.abi.org.uk/Display/File/364/csr_Report.pdf>.

Atkinson, M., *Governing Canada: Institutions and Public Policy* (Toronto: Harcourt Brace Jovanovich, 1993).

Aucoin, P., *The New Public Management: Canada in Comparative Perspective* (Montréal: McGill-Queen's University Press, 1997).

Australian Consumer and Competition Commission, *Guide to Fair Trading Codes of Conduct* (Canberra: Australian Consumer and Competition Commission, 1995).

———, *Fair Trading Codes of Conduct: Why Have Them, How to Prepare Them* (Canberra: Australian Consumer and Competition Commission, 1996).

Australian Manufacturing Council, *The Environmental Challenge: Best Practice Environmental Regulation* (Canberra: Australian Manufacturing Council, 1993).

Australian Retailers Association, *Australian Code of Practice for Computerised Checkout Systems in Supermarkets* (Sydney: Australian Retailers Association, 2001), at <www.ara.com.au/asi/SCANNING_CODE.PDF>.

Australian Securities and Investments Commission, Electronic Funds Transfer Code of Conduct, at <www.asic.gov.au/asic/asic.nsf/lkuppdf/ASIC+PDFW?opendocument&key=eft_code.pdf>.

Axelrod, R., *The Evolution of Cooperation* (New York: Basic Books, 1984).

Aynsworth, S. J., and A. M. Thayer, "Chemical Manufacturers Welcome Challenge of Product Stewardship," *Chemical and Engineering News* (October 17, 1994), p. 10.

Ayres, I., and J. Braithwaite, *Responsive Regulation: Transcending the Deregulation Debate* (New York: Oxford University Press, 1992).

Bardach, E., and R. A. Kagan, *Going by the Book: The Problem of Regulatory Unreasonableness* (Philadelphia: Temple University Press, 1982).

Basse, E. M., "Environmental Contracts: An Example of the Interplay Between Environmental Law and Competition Law," in E. M. Basse, ed., *Environmental Law: From International Law to National Law* (Copenhagen: GadJura, 1997).

Becker, G. S., "A Theory of Competition Among Pressure Groups for Political Influence," *Quarterly Journal of Economics* 98 (August 1983), pp. 371–400.

Begley, R., "Advocacy Conflict With Deregulatory Congress," *Chemical Week* (July 5–12, 1995), p. 40.

Begley, R., "Will the Real Chemical Industry Please Stand Up," *Chemical Week* (July 7–14, 1993), p. 18.

Bélanger, J., *Being Responsible Partners in Canadian Society* (presentation to the Air and Waste Management Association Environmental Government Affairs Seminar, Ottawa, 1990).

————, *Responsible Care: Developing a Promise* (presentation to the First International Workshop on Responsible Care, European Chemical Industry Council, Rotterdam, 1991).

Bendana, A., *Which Way for NGOs: A Perspective from the South* (e-mail article posted on the Voluntary Codes Research Forum, 2000), at <www.strategis.ic.gc.ca/epic/internet/inoca-bc.nsf/en/ca00973e.html>.

Bendell, J., ed., *Terms for Endearment: Business, NGOs and Sustainable Development* (London: New Academy of Business, 2000).

————, *Towards Participatory Workplace Appraisal: Report from a Focus Group of Women Banana Workers* (London: New Academy of Business, September 2001).

Bennett, C. J., *Regulating Privacy: Data Protection and Public Policy in Europe and the United States* (Ithaca, N.Y.: Cornell University Press, 1992).

————, *Implementing Privacy Codes of Practice: A Report to the Canadian Standards Association* (Toronto: Canadian Standards Association, 1995).

————, "Convergence Revisited: Toward a Global Policy for the Protection of Personal Data?" in P. E. Agre and M. Rotenberg, *Technology and Privacy: The New Landscape* (Cambridge, Mass.: MIT Press, 1997).

————, *Prospects for an International Standard for the Protection of Personal Information: A Report to the Standards Council of Canada* (1997), at <http://web.uvic.ca/~polisci/bennett/research/iso.htm>.

————, *An International Standard for Privacy Protection: Objections to the Objections* (paper presented at CFP 2000, Toronto, April 2000), at <www.cfp2000.org/papers/bennett.pdf>.

Bernstein, M., *Regulating Business By Independent Commission* (Princeton, N.J.: Princeton University Press, 1955).

Bernstein, S., and B. Cashore, "Globalization, Four Paths of Internationalization and Domestic Policy Change: The Case of Eco-forestry Policy Change in British Columbia," *Canadian Journal of Political Science* 33 (2000), pp. 67–99.

Better Business Bureau, *History and Traditions* (1996), at <www.bosbbb.org/about/history.asp>.

————, *Nuclear Energy Advertising Compliance Referred to Government* (press release), (May 13, 1999).

————, *BBBOnLine to Develop Code of Online Business Practices* (press release), (June 8, 1999), available at <www.bbb.org/alerts/article.asp?ID=23>.

————, *Better Business Bureau Joins With Internet Leaders in GetNetWise Campaign* (press release), (July 23, 2003), at <www.bbb.org/alerts/article.asp?ID=176>.

————, *Code of Online Business Practices*, at <www.bbbonline.org/code/code.asp>.

Bicycle Helmet Safety Institute, *Helmet Laws for Bicycle Riders*, at <www.helmets.org/mandator.htm>.

Biodiversity Stewardship in Resource Industries Initiative, *About CBIN*, at <www.cbin.ec.gc.ca/ about/default_e.cfm>.

Blackman, A., *Informal Sector Pollution Control: What Policy Options Do We Have?* (Washington: Resources for the Future, 1999, revised 2000), at <www.rff.org/ Documents/RFF-DP-00-02-REV.pdf>.

Blair, R. D., and S. Rubin, *Regulating the Professions* (London: DC Heath, 1980).

Body Shop, The, *What is Community Trade*? at <www.thebodyshop.com/web/tbsgl/ values_sct_what.jsp>.

———, *Trading Charter*, at <www.thebodyshop.com/web/tbsgl/images/values97.pdf>, p. 209.

———, *Values Report*, at <www.thebodyshop.com/web/tbsgl/images/values97.pdf>.

Borgman, A., "Garment Workers Show U.S. the 'Child Behind the Label'," *Washington Post* (July 24, 1995).

Braithwaite, J., and P. Drahos, *Global Business Regulation* (Cambridge: Cambridge University Press, 2000).

Braithwaite, J., J. Walker and P. N. Grabosky, "An Enforcement Taxonomy of Regulatory Agencies," *Law and Policy* 9 (1987), pp. 323–350.

Bregha, F., and J. Moffet, *From Challenge to Agreement? Background Paper on the Future of ARET* (Ottawa: Resource Futures International, December 8, 1997).

British Standards Institution, *Information Security Management Systems*, BS7799 (London: British Standards Institution, 1995).

Brown, D., and D. Greer, *Implementing Forest Certification in British Columbia: Issues and Options* (prepared for the Trade and Sustainable Development Group, Policy and Economics Division, B.C. Ministry of Forests, March 2001), at <www.for.gov.bc.ca/ HET/certification/ResearchStudyReport0301.pdf>.

Browning, D., and F. Fiorenza, eds., *Habermas, Modernity and Public Theology* (New York: Crossroads, 1992).

BSI-Global, *The Kitemark: Business Benefits* (London: BSI-Global, 2000), at <www.bsi-global.com/ Kitemark/Overview/Business_Benefits.xalter>.

Buchanan, J. M., "An Economic Theory of Clubs," *Economica 32* (February 1965), pp. 1–14.

Buchanan, J. M., and G. Tullock, *The Calculus of Consent* (Ann Arbor, Mich.: University of Michigan Press, 1962).

Burrell, T., *CSA Environmental Standards Writing: Barriers to Environmental Non-Governmental Organizations Involvement* (Toronto: CIELAP, 1997).

Burton, P., and S. Duncan, "Democracy and Accountability in Public Bodies: New Agendas in British Government," *Policy and Politics* 24:1 (January 1996), pp. 5–16.

Canadian Chemical Producers' Association, *Responsible Care 1992: A Total Commitment* (Ottawa: Canadian Chemical Producers' Association, 1992).

———, *A Primer on Responsible Care and ISO 14001* (Ottawa: Canadian Chemical Producers' Association, 1995).

———, *Responsible Care Annual Report* (Ottawa: Canadian Chemical Producers' Association, 1995).

———, *Does Responsible Care Pay? A Primer on the Unexpected Benefits of the Initiative* (Ottawa: Canadian Chemical Producers' Association, 1996).

———, "1999 Emissions Inventory and Five-Year Projections," *Reducing Emissions 8: A Responsible Care Initiative* (Ottawa: Canadian Chemical Producers' Association, 1999).

———, *Responsible Care: The Picture is Getting Brighter* (Ottawa: Canadian Chemical Producers' Association, 1999).

———, *Responsible Care Re-verification: A Protocol to Help Us Improve* (Ottawa: Canadian Chemical Producers' Association, 1999).

———, *How to Communicate and Promote Responsible Care* (Ottawa: CCPA, Canadian Chemical Producers' Association, undated).

Canadian Council of Forest Ministers, Criteria and Indicators of Sustainable Forestry Management in Canada, Technical Report 1997 (Ottawa: Canadian Council of Forest Ministers, 1997).

Canadian Marketing Association, *Direct Marketing Industry Welcomes Federal Privacy Bill* (October 1, 1998).

Canadian Standards Association, *Ice Hockey Helmet Standard,* CAN/CSA Z262.1-M1975 (Toronto: Canadian Standards Association, 1975).

———, *Cycling Helmets Standard,* CAN/CSA-D113.2 M89 (Toronto: Canadian Standards Association, 1989) (available in a 2001 revision).

———, *Face Protectors and Visors for Ice Hockey Players Standard*, CAN3-Z262.2-M78 (Toronto: Canadian Standards Association, 1990).

———, *Guideline on Environmental Labelling Z761-93* (Toronto: Canadian Standards Association, 1993).

———, *Background and Proceedings of the Non-Governmental Organization (NGO) Consultation Sessions for the Canadian Standards Association's Sustainable Forest Management (SFM) Project* (summary report), (Toronto: Canadian Standards Association, November 29, 1995).

———, *Model Code for the Protection of Personal Information,* CAN/CSA-Q830-96 (Toronto: Canadian Standards Association, 1996).

————, *A Sustainable Forest Management System,* CAN/CSA-Z808-96 (Toronto: Canadian Standards Association, 1996).

————, *Specifications Document, A Sustainable Forest Management System,* CAN/CSA-Z809-96 (Toronto: Canadian Standards Association, 1996).

————, *CSA Directives and Guidelines Governing Standardization, Part 2: Development Process,* CSA-SDP-2.2-98 (Toronto: Canadian Standards Association, 1998).

————, *CSA Directives and Guidelines Governing Standardization, Part 1: Participants and Organizational Structure,* CSA-SDP-2.1-99 (Toronto: Canadian Standards Association, 1999).

————, *Environmental Labels and Declarations: Self-Declared Environmental Claims,* CAN/CSA-ISO 14021-00 (Toronto: Canadian Standards Association, 2000).

————, *Chain of Custody for Forest Products Originating from a Defined Forest Area Registered to CSA Standard CAN/CSA-Z809,* CSA Special Publication PLUS 1163 (Toronto: Canadian Standards Association, June 2001).

Canadian Sustainable Forestry Certification Coalition, *Communicating Your Certification to the Sustainable Forest Management System Standards, CAN/CSA Z809* (Montréal: Canadian Sustainable Forestry Certification Coalition, 1997).

————, *Certification Status and Intentions in Canada,* at <www.sfms.com/status.htm>.

Carraro, C., and F. Lévêque, eds., *Voluntary Approaches in Environmental Policy* (Dordrecht: Kluwer, 1999).

Carrette, J., ed., *Religion and Culture by Michel Foucault* (Manchester: Manchester University Press, 1999).

Cascio, J., *Implications of ISO 14001 for Regulatory Compliance* (paper presented to the Fourth International Conference on Environmental Compliance and Enforcement, Thailand, 1996), at <www.inece.org/4thvol1/cascio.pdf>.

Cashore, B., "Legitimacy and the Privatization of Environmental Governance: How Non State Market-Driven (NSMD) Governance Systems (Certification Eco-labelling Programs) Gain Rule Making Authority," *Governance: An International Journal of Policy, Administration and Institutions* 15:4 (October 2002), pp. 503–529.

Cavoukian, A., and D. Tapscott, *Who Knows: Safeguarding Your Privacy in a Networked World* (Toronto: Random House, 1995).

Chang, S., "GATTing a Green Trade Barrier: Eco-Labelling and the WTO Agreement on Technical Barriers to Trade," *Journal of World Trade* 31 (1997), pp. 137–159.

Chayes, A., and A. Handler Chayes, *The New Sovereignty: Compliance with International Regulatory Agreements* (Cambridge, Mass.: Harvard University Press, 1995).

Cheyne, I., "Trade and the Environment: The Future of Extraterritorial Unilateral Measures after the Shrimp Appellate Body," *Web Journal of Current Legal Issues* 5 (2000), at <http://webjcli.ncl.ac.uk/2000/issue5/cheyne5.html>.

Chociolko, C., *The Environmental Choice Program: A Better "Choice" for the Environment?* (unpublished manuscript, November 30, 1990).

Choquette, P., *NOVA Responsible Care Report* (Calgary: NOVA Chemicals Corporation, December 1990).

Christensen, C., *The Innovator's Dilemma: When New Technologies Cause Great Firms to Fail* (Boston: Harvard Business School Press, 1997).

Christensen, C., and T. Petzinger, "Innovation in the Connected Economy: A Conversation with Clayton Christensen," *Perspectives on Business Innovation*, Issue 5: The Connected Economy (September 2000).

Church, J. M., "A Market Solution to Green Marketing: Some Lessons from the Economics of Information," *Minnesota Law Review* 79 (1994), pp. 245–324.

Clarke, D., and K. Webb, *Market-Driven Consumer Redress Case Studies and Legal Issues* (Ottawa: Office of Consumer Affairs, Industry Canada, 2002), at <http://strategis.ic.gc.ca/epic/internet/inoca-bc.nsf/en/ca01643e.html>.

Clifford, J., and K. Webb, *Policy Implementation, Compliance and Administrative Law* (Ottawa: Law Reform Commission of Canada, 1986).

Cochrane, M., *Class Actions in Ontario: A Guide to the Class Proceedings Act 1992* (Toronto: Canada Law Book, 1992).

Coglianese, C., and J. Nash, eds., *Regulating from the Inside: Can Environmental Management Systems Achieve Policy Goals?* (Washington: Resources for the Future, 2001).

Cohen, D., "The Regulation of Green Advertising: The State, the Market, and the Environmental Good," *UBC Law Review* 25 (1991), pp. 225–276.

————, "Procedural Fairness and Incentive Programs: Reflections on the Environmental Choice Program," *Alberta Law Review* 31 (1993), pp. 544–574.

————, "Subtle Effects: Requiring Economic Assessments in the Environmental Choice Program," *Alternatives* 20 (1994), pp. 22–27.

Collier, R., and J. Strasburg, "Clothiers Fold on Sweatshop Lawsuit," *San Francisco Chronicle* (September 27, 2002).

Commission on Environment and Development, *Our Common Future* (Oxford: Oxford University Press, 1988).

Commission on Global Governance, *Our Global Neighbourhood* (Oxford: Oxford University Press, 1995).

Commissioner of the Environment and Sustainable Development, *Responding to Climate Change: Time to Rethink Canada's Implementation Strategy* (Ottawa: Office of the Auditor General, 1998), at <www.oag-bvg.gc.ca/domino/reports.nsf/html/c8menu_e.html>.

————, *Managing the Risks of Toxic Substances* (Ottawa: Office of the Auditor General, 1999).

————, *Working With the Private Sector* (Ottawa: Office of the Auditor General, 2000), at <www.oag-bvg.gc.ca/domino/reports.nsf/html/c0menu_e.html>.

Compa, L., and T. Hinchliffe Darricarrere, "Private Labor Rights Enforcement Through Corporate Codes of Conduct," in L. Compa and S. Diamond, *Human Rights, Labor Rights, and International Trade* (Philadelphia: University of Pennsylvania Press, 1996), pp. 181–197.

Competition Bureau (Canada), *Proposed Adoption of New Environmental Labelling and Advertising Guidelines* (July 10, 2001).

Connor, T., *Still Waiting for Nike to Do It* (San Francisco: Global Exchange, 2001), at <http://store.globalexchange.org/nike/html>.

Consumer and Corporate Affairs Canada, *Principles and Guidelines for Environmental Labelling and Advertising* (Ottawa: Consumer and Corporate Affairs Canada, 1991), at <http://strategis.ic.gc.ca/pics/cp/envguide.pdf>.

Consumers International, *Consumers@Shopping: An International Comparative Study of Internet Shopping* (London: Consumers International, September 1999).

————, *Green Claims: Environmental Claims on Products and Packaging in the Shops: An International Study* (London: Consumers International, March 2000).

————, *Disputes in Cyberspace: Online Dispute Resolution for Consumers in Cross-Border Disputes — An International Evaluation* (London: Consumers International, December 2000), at <www.consumersinternational.org/Publications/ViewADocument_search.asp?langid=1&regid=135&ID=29> (executive summary).

Corbett, W., "Shortcomings of the Caribbean Basin Initiative," *Law and Policy in International Business* 23 (1992).

Council of Europe, *Council of Europe Convention for the Protection of Individuals with Regard to Automatic Processing of Personal Data* (1981), at <www.coe.int/T/e/legal_affairs/Legal_co-operation/Data_protection>

Cragg, W., *Business Ethics and Stakeholder Theory* (unpublished manuscript available from the author), (November 2001).

Crossley, R., *A Review of Global Forest Management Certification Initiatives: Political and Institutional Aspects* (draft paper for the Conference on Economic, Social and Political Issues in Certification of Forest Management, Malaysia, May 1996), at <www.forestry.ubc.ca/concert/crossley.html>.

Crow, M., "Beyond Experiments," *The Environmental Forum* 17:3 (May–June 2000), pp. 19–29.

Crowe, R., and S. Williams, *Who are the Ethical Consumers?* (London: The Cooperative Bank, 1999).

Culnan, M., and D. Bies, "Managing Privacy Concerns Strategically: The Implications of Fair Information Practices for Marketing in the 21st Century," in C. J. Bennett and R. Grant, eds., *Visions of Privacy: Policy Choices for the Digital Age* (Toronto: University of Toronto Press, 1999).

Customs and Excise Department (Hong Kong), *Toys and Children's Products Safety Ordinance* (1992), at <www.info.gov.hk.customs/eng/major/consumer/toys_e.html>.

Dagnoli, J., "Consciously Green: Consumers Question Marketers' Commitment," *Advertising Age* (September 18, 1991), p. 14.

Davidson, J., "Helmet Makers Drowning in Sea of Litigation," *The Globe and Mail* (March 31, 1986), p. C1.

Day, P., and R. Klein, *Accountabilities* (London: Tavistock Publications, 1987).

de Haes, H. U., "Slow Progress in Ecolabelling: Technical or Institutional Impediments?" *Journal of Industrial Ecology* 1 (1997), pp. 4–6.

Dee, B., *Can Codes of Conduct be an Effective Alternative to Government Regulation?* (paper presented to the Ethics and Codes of Conduct Conference, Sydney, Australia, November 1993).

DeMesquita, B. B., D. Newman and A. Rabushka, *Forecasting Political Events: The Future of Hong Kong* (New Haven: Yale University Press, 1985).

Department of Foreign Affairs and International Trade (Canada), *Canada's Position on the TBT Code of Good Practice* (submitted to the World Trade Organization's Committee on Trade and Environment, and its Committee on Technical Barriers to Trade, February 21, 1996), WT/CTE/W/21, G/TBT/W/21.

———, *Forests: A National Experience* (submitted to the World Trade Organization's Committee on Trade and Environment, and its Committee on Technical Barriers to Trade, March 11, 1998), WT/CTE/W/81 G/TBT/W/61.

Department of Trade and Industry (United Kingdom), *Modern Markets, Confident Consumers* (London: Secretary of State for Trade and Industry, July 1999), at <www.dti.gov.uk/consumer/whitepaper>.

———, *Enterprise Act*, at <www.dti.gov.uk/ccp/enterpriseact/intro.htm>.

———, Information Commissioner, *CCTV Code of Practice*, at <www.informationcommissioner.gov.uk/cms/DocumentUploads/cctvcop1.pdf>.

Dewees, D., ed., *The Regulation of Quality* (Toronto: Butterworths, 1983).

Dingwall, R., *A Respectable Profession? Sociological and Economic Perspectives on the Regulation of Professional Services* (paper presented to the Conference on Regulating the Professions, University of Strathclyde, Glasgow, April 20–21, 1995).

Director of Investigation and Research (Canada), *Strategic Alliances Under the Competition Act* (Hull, Que.: Ministry of Supply and Services, 1985).

Doern, G. B., *Political Accountability and Efficiency,* Government and Competitiveness Discussion Paper Series (Kingston, Ont.: School of Policy Studies, Queen's University, 1993).

———, *The Road To Better Public Services: Progress and Constraints in Five Federal Agencies* (Montréal: C. D. Howe Institute, 1994).

———, *Fairer Play: Canadian Competition Policy Institutions in a Global Market* (Toronto: C. D. Howe Institute, 1995).

———, "A Political-Institutional Framework for the Analysis of Competition Policy Institutions," *Governance: An International Journal of Policy, Administration and Institutions* 8:2 (April 1995), pp. 195–217.

Doern, G. B. and T. Conway, *The Greening of Canada: Federal Institutions and Decisions* (Toronto: University of Toronto Press, 1992).

Doern, G. B., M. Hill, M. Prince and R. Schultz, *Changing The Rules: Canada's Changing Regulatory Regimes* (Toronto: University of Toronto Press, 1999).

Doern, G. B., and R. W. Phidd, *Canadian Public Policy: Ideas, Structure, Process*, 2nd ed. (Toronto: Nelson Canada, 1992).

Doern, G. B., and S. Sutherland, *Bureaucracy in Canada: Control and Reform 1985* (Toronto: University of Toronto Press, 1985).

Doern, G. B., and S. Wilks, eds., *Changing Regulatory Institutions in Britain and North America* (Toronto: University of Toronto Press, 1998).

Dowd, J., and G. Boyd, *A Typology of Voluntary Agreements Used in Energy and Environmental Policy* (draft working paper), (Washington: U.S. Department of Energy, January 1998).

Driessen, B., "New Opportunities or Trade Barrier in Disguise? The EC Eco-labelling Scheme," *European Environmental Law Review* 8 (1999), pp. 5–15.

Droge, S., *Ecological Labelling and the World Trade Organization* (Discussion Paper No. 242), (Berlin: Deutsches Institut für Wirtschaftsforschung, February 2001), at <www.diw.de>.

Duffy, A., "Industry Told its 'Free Ride' on Pollution About to End," *Ottawa Citizen* (March 20, 1999).

Dumortier, J., and C. Goemans, *Data Privacy and Standardization* (discussion paper prepared for the CEN/ISSS Open Seminar on Data Protection, Brussels, March 23–24, 2000).

Dunleavy, P., *Democracy, Bureaucracy and Public Choice: Economic Explanations in Political Science* (London: Harvester Wheatsheaf, 1991).

Earnscliffe Research and Communications, *Results of Key Audience Research* (conducted for the Canadian Chemical Producers' Association, 1999).

Economic Council of Canada, *Responsible Regulation* (Ottawa: Economic Council of Canada, 1979).

————, *Reforming Regulation* (Ottawa: Economic Council of Canada, 1981).

Edwards, P., "'Virtual Slavery' in Sweatshops," *Toronto Star* (August 16, 1995).

Electronic Funds Transfer Working Group, *Canadian Code of Practice for Consumer Debit Card Services*, at <http://strategis.ic.gc.ca/epic/internet/inoca-bc.nsf/en/ca01581e.html>.

Elliott, C., *WWF Guide to Forest Certification* (Surrey, U.K.: World Wildlife Fund, 1996).

Elliott, C., and A. Hackman, *Current Issues in Forest Certification in Canada: A WWF Canada Discussion Paper* (Toronto: World Wildlife Fund Canada, 1996).

Ember, L., "Responsible Care: Chemical Makers Still Counting on it to Improve Image," *Chemical and Engineering News* (May 29, 1995), pp. 10–18.

Environics International, *Consumers Worldwide Expect Business to Achieve Social as Well as Economic Goals* (press release), (September 30, 1999).

Environment Canada, *Court Orders Unique Environmental Penalties* (press release), (August 20, 1998), at <www.ec.gc.ca/press/pen0898_n_e.htm>.

————, *Enforcement and Compliance Policy for the Canadian Environmental Protection Act, 1999* (March 2001), at <www.ec.gc.ca/CEPARegistry/documents/policies/candepolicy/CandEpolicy.pdf>.

Environmental Choice Program, *Sanitary Paper Guideline: Involvement of Scott Paper and the CPPA* (Ottawa: Environmental Choice, May 1991).

————, *Project Status Report, ECP-09-89, Sanitary Paper from Recycled Paper* (Ottawa: Environmental Choice, August 10, 1992).

————, *Project Status Report, ECP-09-89, Sanitary Paper from Recycled Paper* (Ottawa: Environmental Choice, February 17, 1993).

————, *Synopsis: The Environmental Monitor* (Ottawa: Environmental Choice, November 1993).

Environmental Protection Agency (United States), *Environmental Labelling: Issues, Policies, and Practices Worldwide* (Washington: Environmental Protection Agency, 1998).

————, Office of Pollution Prevention and Toxics, *33/50 Program: The Final Record* (Washington: Environmental Protection Agency, 1999), at <www.epa.gov/opptintr/ 3350/3350-fnl.pdf>.

Ethical Trading Initiative, *Learning from Doing* (London: Ethical Trading Initiative, 1999), at <www.ethicaltrade.org/Z/lib/1999/04/lfdr/eti-lfd-review.pdf>.

European Advertising Standards Alliance, *EASA Guide to Self-Regulation* (Amsterdam: European Advertising Standards Alliance, 1999).

————, "Case No. 233," *Alliance Update* 16 (February 2000), p. 15.

————, *About EASA*, at <www.easa-alliance.org/about_easa/en/about.html>.

————, "FAQ," *About Self-Regulation*, at <www.easa-alliance.org/about_sr/ en/sr_faq.html>.

European Commission, *Communication from the Commission on the Out-of-court Settlement of Consumer Disputes*, COM-198 (1998), at <http://europa.eu.int/scadplus/ leg/en/lvb/132031.htm>.

————, *Commission Recommendation on the Principles Applicable to the Bodies Responsible for Out-of-court Settlement of Consumer Disputes*, 98/257/CE, at <http://europa.eu.int/scadplus/leg/en/lvb/132031.htm>.

————, *David Byrne Welcomes Breakthrough in Helping Consumers Shop Online With Confidence* (press release), (December 10, 2001).

————, *E-confidence Consumer Forum Principles for E-commerce Codes of Conduct*, at <http://econfidence.jrc.it>.

————, *New European Network to Help Consumers Settle Cross-border Disputes Out-of-court* (news release), (October 16, 2001), at <http://europa.eu.int/ comm/dgs/health_consumer/library/press/press197_en.pdf>.

————, Enterprise Director General, *WEBTRADER Trust Scheme for B@C E-commerce, Supported by the Enterprise DG — Main Results of the Pilot Operation*, at <http://europa.eu.int/comm/enterprise/ict/policy/webtrader.htm>.

————, Health and Consumer Protection Directorate-General, "EEJ-Net Gears Up to Take on Cross-border Consumer Disputes," *Consumer Voice* 3 (October 2001), at <http://europa.eu.int/comm/dgs/health_consumer/newsletter/200110/02_en.htm>.

————, Health and Consumer Protection Directorate-General, *Out-of-court Bodies Responsible for the Settlement of Consumer Disputes*, at <http://europa.eu.int/comm/ consumers/redress/out_of_court/commu/acce_just04_en.html>.

————, Health and Consumer Protection Directorate-General, *New European Network to Help Consumers Settle Cross-border Disputes Out-of-court* (press release), (October 16, 2001), at <http://europa.eu.int/comm/dgs/health_consumer/library/press/ press197_en.pdf>.

European Eco-Management and Audit System, *EMAS and ISO/EN ISO 14001: Differences and Complementarities* (April 2001), at <http://europa.eu.int/comm/ environment/emas/pdf/factsheet/fs_iso_en.pdf>.

European Parliament, *Council Regulation (EEC) No. 1836/93 of 29 June 1993 Allowing Voluntary Participation by Companies in the Industrial Sector in a Community Eco-management and Audit Scheme*, O.J.L. 168, 10.7.93 (superseded by *Regulation (EC) No. 761/2001 of the European Parliament and of the Council of 19 March 2001*).

————, *Directive 95/46/EC of the European Parliament and of the Council of 24 October 1995 on the Protection of Individuals with Regard to the Processing of Personal Data and on the Free Movement of Such Data*, Official Journal L 281, 23/11/1995.

————, *Council Regulation (EEC) No. 880/92 of 23 March 1992 on a Community Eco-label Award Scheme*, O.J.L. 99.

————, *Regulation (EC) No. 1980/2000 of the European Parliament and of the Council of 17 July 2000 on a Revised Community Eco-label Award Scheme*, O.J.L. 237, 21.9.2000.

Evans, J., H. Janish, D. Mullan and R. Risk, *Administrative Law: Cases, Text and Materials*, 4th ed. (Toronto: Emond Montgomery, 1995).

Evers, P. S., "ISO 14000 and Environmental Protection," *Mississippi Law Journal* 67 (1996), pp. 463–526.

Fair Labor Association, *Fair Labor Association Awarded $750,000 Grant as Part of the Department of State Anti-Sweatshop Initiative* (press release), (January 16, 2001), at <www.fairlabor.org/html/press.html#Press011601>.

————, *FLA Makes Major Strides* (press release), (October 24, 2001), at <www.fairlabor.org/html/press.html#Press102401>.

Fallon, G., and R. Berman Brown, "Does Britain Need Public Law Status Chambers of Commerce?" *European Business Review* 12 (2000), pp. 19–27.

Fattah, H., "Taking Care Outside," *Chemical Week* (July 5–12, 1995), p. 53.

Federal Trade Commission, *Consumer Protection in the Global E-commerce Marketplace: Looking Ahead* (Washington: Federal Trade Commission, 2000), at <www.ftc.gov/bcp/icpw/lookingahead/global.htm>.

————, *Privacy Online: Fair Information Practices in the Electronic Marketplace* (Washington: Federal Trade Commission, May 22, 2000), at <www.ftc.gov/reports/ privacy2000/privacy2000.pdf>.

————, *FTC Recommends Congressional Action to Protect Consumer Privacy Online* (press release), (May 22, 2000), at <www.ftc.gov/opa/2000/05/privacy2k.htm>.

Ferguson, C., *Voluntary Industry Self-Management in Ontario* (draft case study prepared for the Voluntary Codes Symposium, Office of Consumer Affairs, Industry Canada, and Regulatory Affairs Division, Treasury Board Secretariat [Canada], Ottawa, September 1996), at <http://strategis.ic.gc.ca/epic/ internet/inoca-bc.nsf/en/ ca00880e.html> (summary).

Fierman, J., "The Big Muddle in Green Marketing," *Fortune* (June 3, 1991), pp. 91–101.

Fisher, R., and W. Ury, *Getting to YES: Negotiating Agreement Without Giving In* (Markham, Ont.: Penguin Books, 1981).

Florida, R., and D. Davison, "Why Do Firms Adopt Advanced Environmental Practices (And Do They Make a Difference)?" in C. Coglianese and J. Nash, eds., *Regulating From the Inside: Can Environmental Management Systems Achieve Policy Goals?* (Washington: Resources for the Future, 2001).

Florini, A., ed., *The Third Force: The Rise of International Civil Society* (Washington: Japan Center for International Exchange and Carnegie Endowment for International Peace, 2000).

Foote, S. B., "Corporate Responsibility in a Changing Legal Environment," *California Management Review* 26 (1984), pp. 217–228.

Forcese, C., *Commerce with Conscience? Human Rights and Corporate Codes of Conduct* (Montréal: International Centre for Human Rights and Development, 1997).

———, "Overcoming the Gap: New 'Gap' Code of Conduct Plugs Holes," *Amnesty International Legal Network Newsletter* (Ottawa: Amnesty International, 1996), p. 1.

Forest Caucus of the Canadian Environmental Network, *An Environmentalist and First Nations Response to the Canadian Standards Association Proposed Certification System for Sustainable Forest Management* (paper presented to the Canadian Standards Association, October 20, 1995).

Forest Stewardship Council, *Forest Stewardship Council A.C. By-laws*, at <www.fsc.org/ keepout/content_areas/77/84/files/FSC_By_laws___revised_November_2002.PDF>.

———, *FSC Principles and Criteria*, at <www.fsc.org/fsc/whats_new/documents/ Docs_cent/2,16>.

———, *Address List for FSC Directors and Secretariat*, at <www.fsc.org/fsc>.

———, *FSC-Accredited Certification Bodies*, at <www.fsc.org/keepout/content_areas/ 77/78/ files/FSC_Accreditated_CBs__June_1__2004_.pdf>.

———, *Forests Certified by FSC-Accredited Certification Bodies*, <www.fsc.org/keepout/content_areas/77/55/files/ABU_REP_70_2004_06_01_FSC_ Certified_Forest.pdf>.

———, *Forest Stewardship Council Suspends Activities of Europe-Based Certification Body* (press release), (March 30, 2001).

———, *Frequently Asked Questions*, at <www.fsc.org/fsc/about/about_fsc/faqs>.

Foucault, M., "Governmentality," in G. Burchell, C. Gordon and P. Miller, eds., *The Foucault Effect* (Chicago: Chicago University Press, 1991).

Francis, J., *The Politics of Regulation: A Comparative Perspective* (Oxford: Blackwell, 1993).

Frey, M., M. de Clercq, et al., *Project for the Promotion and the Diffusion of the EU Eco-label in Italy and the Benelux: Final Report* (submitted to the European Commission, DG XI, February 1, 1998), (Gent and Milan: University of Gent and Bocconi University, 1998).

Fridman, G., *The Law of Contract in Canada* (Scarborough, Ont.: Thomson, 1994).

Fridtjof Nansen Institute, *Yearbook of International Co-operation on Environment and Development*, at <www.ext.grida.no/ggynet/ngo/wwf.htm>.

Friedman, T., *The Lexus and the Olive Tree* (New York: Anchor Books, 2000).

Fuentes, H., and D. Smith, "Independent Monitoring in Guatemala: What Can Civil Society Contribute?" in R. Thamotheram, ed., *Visions of Ethical Sourcing* (London: Financial Times Prentice Hall, 2001).

Fukuyama, F., *Trust: The Social Virtues and the Creation of Prosperity* (London: Penguin, 1995).

Fung, A., D. O'Rourke and S. Sabel, "Realizing Labor Standards: How Transparency, Competition, and Sanctions Could Improve Working Conditions Worldwide," *Boston Review* 26 (2000), at <http://bostonreview.mit.edu/BR26.1/fung.html>.

Gale, F., and C. Burda, "The Pitfalls and Potential of Eco-Certification as a Market Incentive for Sustainable Forest Management" in C. Tollefson, ed., *The Wealth of Forests: Markets, Regulation and Sustainable Forestry* (Vancouver: UBC Press, 1998).

Galt, V., "Child's Play a Challenge for Engineers," *The Globe and Mail* (December 4, 2001).

Gandy, O., *The Panoptic Sort* (Boulder, Colo.: Westview Press, 1993).

Gap Inc., *Annual Report 2001*, at <http://media.corporate-ir.net/media_files/IROL/11/111302/fin_annual_01.pdf>.

———, *Our People and Partners,* at <www.gapinc.com>.

———, *Ethical Sourcing,* formerly at <www.gapinc.com>.

———, *Code of Vendor Conduct,* at <www.dol.gov/ILAB/media/reports/iclp/apparel/5c7.htm>.

Garland, D., "The Limits of the Sovereign State: Strategies of Crime Control in Contemporary Society," *British Journal of Criminology* 36 (1996), p. 445.

417

Gellman, R., *Conflict and Overlap in Privacy Regulation: National, International, and Private* (paper presented to the Symposium on Information, National Policies, and International Infrastructure, The Global Information Infrastructure Commission, Harvard University, January 28–30, 1996), at <www.ksg.harvard.edu/iip/GIIconf/gellman.html>.

Genn, H., "Business Responses to the Regulation of Health and Safety in England," *Law & Policy* 15:3 (1993), pp. 219–233.

Gereffi, G., R. Garcia-Johnson and E. Sasser, "The NGO-Industrial Complex," *Foreign Policy* (July–August 2001).

Gerits, R., and J. Hissen, "Environmental Covenants for the Oil and Gas Producing Industry," *Environmental Law and Policy* 24:6 (1994), p. 323.

Gesser, A., "Canada's Environmental Choice Program: A Model for a 'Trade-Friendly' Eco-Labelling Scheme," *Harvard International Law Journal* 39 (1998), pp. 501–544.

Gibb-Clark, M., "Sweatshops Leave Big Gap in Workers' Rights," *The Globe and Mail* (August 16, 1995).

Gibson, R., ed., *Voluntary Initiatives: The New Politics of Corporate Greening* (Peterborough, Ont.: Broadview Press, 1999).

Giroux, Y., and D. Waite, *Electronic Funds Transfer Code* (draft case study prepared for the Voluntary Codes Symposium, Office of Consumer Affairs, Industry Canada, and Regulatory Affairs Division, Treasury Board Secretariat [Canada], Ottawa, September 1996), at <http://strategis.ic.gc.ca/epic/ internet/inoca-bc.nsf/en/ ca00880e.html> (summary).

Glachant, M., "The Cost Efficiency of Voluntary Agreements for Regulating Industrial Pollution: A Coasean Approach," in C. Carraro and F. Lévêque, eds., *Voluntary Approaches to Environmental Policy* (London: Kluwer, 1999).

Global Exchange, *Top U.S. Clothing Retailers Agree to Settle Saipan Garment Worker Lawsuits*, available at <www.globalexchange.org/campaigns/sweatshops/saipan/ pr032800.html>.

Global Ecolabelling Network, *The Ecolabelling Guide* (Tokyo: Global Ecolabelling Network, October 1999).

———, *Comments and Suggestions of Global Ecolabelling Network on ISO TC 207 SC 3 Type I Labelling Standards* (Tokyo: Global Ecolabelling Network, November 1995).

Good Housekeeping Institute, *The 100th Anniversary of the Good Housekeeping Institute*, at <http://magazines.ivillage.com/goodhousekeeping/consumer/institute/ articles/0,,284511_290558,00.html>.

———, *The GH Institute Reports*, at <http://magazines.ivillage.com/goodhousekeeping/ consumer/institute/articles/0,,284511_290570-2,00.html>.

Government of Canada, "Metal Mining Liquid Effluent Regulations" (regulations and Regulatory Impact Assessment Statement), *Canada Gazette*, Part II, June 19, 2992, pp. 1412–1462, at <http://canadagazette.gc.ca/partII/2002/20020619/html/sor222-e.html>.

Grabosky, P. N., "Using Non-Governmental Resources to Foster Compliance," *Governance: An International Journal of Policy, Administration and Institutions* 8:4 (1995), pp. 527–550.

Gray, T. S., *UK Environmental Policy in the 1990s* (London: MacMillan, 1995).

Green, A. J., *Assessing Organizational Culture: Do the Values and Assumptions of Canadian Chemical Companies Reflect Those Espoused by 'Responsible Care'* (submitted to the Department of Chemical Engineering, Massachusetts Institute of Technology, in partial fulfilment of the requirements of the degree of Master of Science in technology and policy, August 11, 1995).

Green, C., "At the Junction of the Global and Local: Transnational Industry and Women Workers in the Caribbean," in L. Compa and S. Diamond, eds., *Human Rights, Labor Rights, and International Trade* (Philadelphia: University of Pennsylvania Press, 1996).

Greenpeace, *What is Happening in B.C.'s Forests* (undated, 1997?), at <www.greenpeace.org/~comms/97/forest/logging.html>.

Griffith, P., "Innovation in Not for Profits and Government," *The Innovation Journal* 4:2 (May–August 1999), at <www.innovation.cc/discussion-papers/not-for-profits.htm>.

Grodsky, J., "Certified Green: The Law and Future of Environmental Labelling," *The Yale Journal on Regulation* 10 (1993), pp. 147–227.

Gunningham, N., "Environment, Self-Regulation and the Chemical Industry: Assessing Responsible Care," *Law & Policy* 17:1 (1995), pp. 57–109.

———, *Codes of Practice: The Australasian Experience* (paper presented to the Voluntary Codes Symposium, Office of Consumer Affairs, Industry Canada, and Regulatory Affairs Division, Treasury Board Secretariat [Canada], Ottawa, September 1996).

Gunningham, N., and D. Sinclair, "Integrative Regulation: A Principle-Based Approach to Environmental Policy," *Law & Society* 24:4 (Fall 1999), pp. 853–896.

Gunningham, N., P. Grabosky and D. Sinclair, *Smart Regulation: Designing Environmental Policy* (Oxford: Clarendon Press, 1998).

Hadden, S., *Read the Label: Reducing Risk by Providing Information* (Boulder, Colo.: Westview, 1986).

Hamilton, R., "The Role of Non-governmental Standards in the Development of Mandatory Federal Standards Affecting Safety or Health" *Texas Law Review* 56 (1978), p. 1329.

Harris, S., *The Political Economy of the Liberalization of Entry and Ownership in the Canadian Investment Dealer Industry* (unpublished doctoral dissertation, Department of Political Science, Carleton University, Ottawa, 1995).

Harrison, K., "Racing to the Top or Bottom? Industry Resistance to Eco-Labelling of Paper Products in Three Jurisdictions," *Environmental Politics* 8 (1999), pp. 110–137.

―――, "Voluntarism and Environmental Governance," in E. Parson, ed., *Governing the Environment: Challenges and Trends* (Toronto: University of Toronto Press, 2001).

Haufler, V., *A Public Role for the Private Sector: Industry Self-Regulation in a Global Economy* (Washington: Carnegie Endowment for International Peace, 2001).

Heaton, Kate, Nicholas Brown, et al., "Forest Stewardship's Rigorous Standards," *Wall Street Journal* (December 16, 1999), p. A23.

Heidt, R., "Populist and Economic v. Feudal: Approaches to Industry Self-Regulation in the United States and England," *McGill Law Journal* 34:1 (1989), p. 41.

Heilbroner, R., *The Making of Economic Society*, 4th ed. (Englewood Cliffs, N.J.: Prentice Hall, 1972).

Henry, S., *Private Justice: Towards Integrated Theorising in the Sociology of Law* (London: Routledge & Kegan Paul, 1983).

Herbert, B., "Not a Living Wage," *New York Times*, October 9, 1995.

Hickling Corporation, The, *Evaluation of the Environmental Choice Program: Final Report* (prepared for Environment Canada, November 29, 1993).

Hill, M., *The Choice of Mode For Regulation: A Case Study of the Canadian Pesticide Registration Review 1988–1992* (unpublished doctoral thesis, Department of Political Science, Carleton University, Ottawa, 1994).

Hirschman, A. O., *Exit, Voice, and Loyalty* (Cambridge, Mass.: Harvard University Press, 1970).

Hirst, P., *Associative Democracy: New Forms of Economic and Social Governance* (Cambridge: Polity Press, 1994).

Hobbes, T., *Leviathan* (1651), R. Tuck, ed., (Cambridge: Cambridge University Press, 1996).

Hoberg, G., *Pluralism By Design: Environmental Policy and the American Regulatory State* (New York: Praeger, 1993).

―――, "The Coming Revolution in Regulating our Forests," *Policy Options* (December 20, 1999), pp. 53–56, at <www.irpp.org/po/archive/dec99/hoberg.pdf>.

Hoffman, A .J., *The Environmental Transformation of American Industry: An Institutional Account of Organizational Evolution in the Chemical and Petroleum Industries (1960–1993)* (PhD dissertation, submitted to the Department of Civil and Environmental Engineering, and the Sloan School of Management, Massachusetts Institute of Technology, February 1995).

Holm, H., and G. Sorensen, eds., *Whose World Order? Uneven Globalization and the End of the Cold War* (Boulder, Colo.: Westview Press, 1995).

Holmes, P., "The WTO Beef Hormones Case: A Risky Decision?" *Consumer Policy Review* 10 (March–April 2000), pp. 61–70.

Hood, C., *Administrative Analysis* (London: Harvester Wheatsheaf, 1986).

Hornung, R., "The VCR Doesn't Work," in R. Gibson, ed., *Voluntary Initiatives: The New Politics of Corporate Greening* (Peterborough, Ont.: Broadview Press, 1999).

Howitt, R., *European Breakthrough in Combatting Multinational Abuses* (press release, January 15, 1999, reported on the on-line Voluntary Codes Research Forum, January 25, 1999), at <http://strategis.ic.gc/ca/epic/internet/inoca-bc.nsf/en/ca00973e.html>.

Hughes, E., "The Reasonable Care Defenses," *Journal of Environmental Law and Practice* 2 (1992), p. 214.

Hume, S., "Consumer Doubletalk Makes Companies Wary," *Advertising Age* (October 28, 1992), p. GR4.

Hunt, A., "Legal Governance and Social Relations: Empowering Agents and the Limits of Law" in M. MacNeil, N. Sargent, and P. Swan, eds., *Law, Regulation, and Governance* (Don Mills, Ont.: Oxford University Press, 2002).

Hunter, J., "Home Depot Gives Green Light to Forest Products Certification," *Vancouver Sun* (March 10, 1999).

Independent Monitoring Working Group, *Public Report* (May 14, 2001), at <www.somo.nl/monitoring/reports/IMWG-report.pdf>.

Industry Canada, *Standards Systems: A Guide for Canadian Regulators* (Ottawa: Industry Canada, 1998), at <http://strategis.ic.gc.ca/sc_mrksv/regaff/stdguide/engdoc/english.pdf>.

Ingram, V., "From Sparring Partners to Bedfellows: Joint Approaches to Environmental Policy-Making," *European Environment* 9 (1999), pp. 41–48.

Innovation Journal, The (Editorial Board of *The Innovation Journal*), "Some Thoughts on Definitions of Innovation," *The Innovation Journal* 4:3 (September–December 1999), at <www.innovation.cc/discussion-papers/thoughts-innovation.htm>.

International Council of Chemical Associations, *Responsible Care Status Report 2000* (International Council of Chemical Associations, 2000), at <www.cefic.org/activities/hse/rc/icca/report2000/Report2000.pdf>.

International Institute for Sustainable Development, *Business and Sustainable Development: A Global Guide*, at <www.bsdglobal.com/ngo/roles.asp>.

International Organization for Standardization, *ISO 14061, Information to Assist Forestry Organizations in the Use of Environmental Management System Standards ISO 14001 and ISO 14004* (Geneva: International Organization for Standardization, 1998).

————, *The ISO Survey of ISO 9000 and ISO 14000 Certificates, Eleventh Cycle: Up to and Including 31 December 2001*, at <www.iso.ch/iso/en/prods-services/otherpubs/pdf/survey11thcycle.pdf>.

————, *The ISO Survey of ISO 9000 and ISO 14000 Certificates, Twelfth Cycle: Up to and Including 31 December 2002*, at <www.iso.ch/iso/en/iso9000-14000/pdf/survey12thcycle.pdf>.

International Trade Communications Group, *The Canada–U.S. Free Trade Agreement* (Ottawa: 1987).

International Tropical Timber Organization, *ITTO Guidelines for the Sustainable Management of Natural Tropical Forests* (May 1990).

————, *ITTO Objective 2000*, at <www.itto.or.jp/live/PageDisplayHandler?pageId=5>.

ISEAL Alliance, *ISEAL Member Standard-Setting Review Public Background Document*, Issue 1 (July 2001).

————, "Mission Statement," *Membership Requirements: Public Requirements* (Public Draft 2), (July 4, 2001).

Jaffe, A., S. Peterson, P. Portney and R. Stavins, *Environmental Regulation and International Competitiveness: What Does the Evidence Tell Us?* Discussion Paper 94-08 (Washington: Resources for the Future, 1994).

Jordan, D., "Forest Certification Behind Schedule," *Business in Vancouver* (January 19–25, 1999), p. 1.

Kao-Cushing, K., "Why Environmental Management System Standards Matter," *Pacific Institute Report* (Fall 2000), pp. 6–10.

Kaplan, J., "The Sentencing Guidelines: The First Ten Years," *Ethikos* (November–December 2001).

Kaufman, L., and D. Gonzalez, "Labor Standards Clash With Global Reality," *New York Times* (April 24, 2001).

Kelly, P., and M. Kranzburg, eds., *Technological Innovation: A Critical Review of Current Knowledge* (San Francisco: San Francisco Press, 1979).

Kernaghan, K., "Reshaping Government: The Post-Bureaucratic Paradigm," *Canadian Public Administration* 36:4 (Winter 1993), pp. 636–645.

Kernaghan, K., and D. Siegel, *Public Administration in Canada*, 2nd ed. (Toronto: Nelson Canada, 1991).

King, A., and M. Lenox, "Industry Self-Regulation Without Sanctions: The Chemical Industry's Responsible Care Program," *Academy of Management Journal* 43:4 (2000), p. 7, at <www.aom.pace.edu/amj/August2000/king.pdf>.

Kollman, K., and A. Prakash, "Green by Choice? Cross-National Variations in Firms' Responses to EMS-Based Environmental Regimes," *World Politics* 53:3 (2001), pp. 399–430.

Lansky, M., "If Certification was the Answer, What was the Question? A Close Look at J. D. Irving and the Certification of Industrial Forestry," *Understory* 9 (Summer 1999).

Lawrence, J., "Green Marketing Jobs Wilt at Big Companies," *Advertising Age* (September 1993), p. 4.

LeClair, D. Thorne, et al., "Federal Sentencing Guidelines for Organizations: Legal, Ethical and Public Policy Issues for International Marketing," *Journal of Public Policy and Marketing* 16:1 (Spring 1997), pp. 26–37.

Lecraw, D. J., *Voluntary Standards as a Regulatory Device* (Ottawa: Economic Council of Canada, 1981).

Leiss, W., and C. Chociolko, *Risk and Responsibility* (Montréal: McGill-Queen's University Press, 1994).

Lessig, L., *Code and Other Laws of Cyberspace* (New York: Basic Books, 1999).

Limbs, E. C., and T. L. Fort, "Nigerian Business Practices and Their Interface with Virtue Ethics," *Journal of Business Ethics* (July 2000), pp. 169–179.

Limoges, C., and L. Davignon, *L'initiative gestion responsable de l'association canadienne des fabricants de produits chimiques* (Montréal: Centre interuniversitaire de recherche sur la science et la technologie, UQAM, June 15, 1995).

Linden, A.,*Canadian Tort Law* (Toronto: Butterworths, 1988).

Linder, S., and G. Peters, "Instruments of Government: Perceptions and Contexts," *Journal of Public Policy* 9:1 (1989), pp. 35–58.

Loos, K., and S. Stricoff, "Responsible Leadership," *Chemical Week* (July 5–12, 1995), p. 112.

Lonti, Z., and A. Verma, *Industry Self-Management as a Strategy for Restructuring Government: The Case of the Ministry of Consumer and Commercial Relations (MCCR) and the Technical Standards and Safety Authority (TSSA) in Ontario* (Ottawa: Canadian Policy Research Networks, December 1999), at <www.cprn.org>.

Lukasik, L., "The Dofasco Deal" in R. Gibson, ed., *Voluntary Initiatives: The New Politics of Corporate Greening* (Peterborough, Ont.: Broadview Press, 1999).

Lush, P., "B.C. Forest Firms to Reap Savings. Changes to Code Will Cut Logging Costs," *The Globe and Mail* (April 3, 1998).

Maitland, I., "The Limits of Business Self-Regulation," *California Management Review* 27:3 (1985), pp. 132–147.

Makkai, T., and J. Braithwaite, "In and Out of the Revolving Door: Making Sense of Regulatory Capture," *Journal of Public Policy* 12:1 (January–March 1992), pp. 61–78.

Manheim, J., *Corporate Conduct Unbecoming: Codes of Conduct and Anti-Corporate Strategy* (St. Michaels, Md.: Tred Avon Institute Press, 1999).

Maquila Solidarity Network, *COVERCO Report* (August 2001), at <www.maquilasolidarity.org/resources/codes/coverco3.htm>.

———, *Memo: Codes Update*, Number 9 (November 2001), at <www.maquilasolidarity.org/resources/codes/memo9.htm>.

———, *Memo: Codes Update*, Number 13 (December 2002–January 2003), at <www.maquilasolidarity.org/resources/codes/memo13.htm>.

Marable, L., "Better Business Bureaus are a Bust," *Money* (October 1995), p. 106.

Marasco, A., *Standards Development: Are You At Risk?* (1999), at <www.ansi.org/news_publications/other_documents/risk.aspx?menuid=77>.

Martin, J., *Performance-Oriented Regulatory Programs* (paper presented to the New South Wales Regulatory Review Conference, Sydney, Australia), (June 20, 1995).

———, *Regulating the Regulators: The Canadian Approach to Implementing Government-wide Regulatory Reform Strategies*, (paper presented to the New South Wales Regulatory Review Conference, Sydney, Australia), (June 20, 1995).

Martin, J., and C. Iwankow, *The Canadian Government Perspective on Cost-Effective Regulation* (Fredericton, N.B.: Joint Meeting of the Canadian Nuclear Association and the Canadian Nuclear Safety Society, June 1996).

Matas, R., "Foreign Eyes on Canadian Forests," *The Globe and Mail* (February 6, 1993), p. A7.

Max Havelaar Foundation, *The Basic Principles of Max Havelaar*, formerly at <www.maxhavelaar.org>.

———, "Max Havelaar Gains Ground on Coffee Market (Max Havelaar wint terrein op koffiemarkt)," in *Het Financieele Dagblad* (June 3, 1999).

McGarity, T. O., *Reinventing Rationality: The Role of Regulatory Analysis in the Federal Bureaucracy* (New York: Cambridge University Press, 1991).

Meeran, R., "Victims of Multinational Corporations: What Avenues are Available?" *Mealey's Litigation Report: Asbestos* (March 23, 2001).

Meidinger, E., *Emerging Trans-Sectoral Regulatory Structures in Global Civil Society: The Case of ISEAL* (paper prepared for the Tools for Regulation Panel, Joint Annual Meetings of the Law and Society Association and the Research Committee for the Sociology of Law, Budapest, July 4–7, 2001), at <http://law.buffalo.edu/homepage/eemeid/scholarship/ISEAL.pdf>.

———, "'Private' Environmental Regulation, Human Rights and Community," *Buffalo Environmental Law Journal* 7 (2000), pp. 123–237, at <www.law.buffalo.edu/homepage/eemeid/scholarship/hrec.pdf>.

———, "Environmental Certification Programs and U.S. Environmental Law: Closer Than You May Think," *Environmental Law Reporter* 31 (2001), pp. 10162–10179.

Melnitzer, J., "Fix Environmental Snags Before Seeking ISO 14000 Certification," *Law Times* (June 16–22, 1997), pp. 14–15.

Milgrom, P., D. North and B. Weingast, "The Role of Institutions in the Revival of Trade: The Medieval Law Merchant," *Economics and Politics* 2 (March 1990), pp. 1–23.

Miller, D. T., *Psychological Factors Influencing Compliance: Final Report,* Study for the Federal Statutes Compliance Project, Department of Justice Canada (Vancouver: Vancouver Psychology and Law Institute, Simon Fraser University, 1985).

Minister of Customs and Consumer Affairs (Australia), *Codes of Conduct Policy Framework* (Canberra: Minister of Customs and Consumer Affairs, 1998), at <www.selfregulation.gov.au/publications/CodesOfConduct-PolicyFramework/index.asp>.

Ministry of Forests (British Columbia), *Forests Minister Welcomes Macmillan Bloedel's Plan to Phase Out Clear Cutting Old Growth* (press release), (June 10, 1998), at <www.news.gov.bc.ca/hnr/content/1998/1998nr/1998045.asp>.

Ministry of Natural Resources (Ontario), *Ontario First in World to Receive Environmental Forest Certification* (press release), (March 23, 2001).

Ministry of Trade and Industry (Japan), *Guidelines for Protection of Personal Information Related to Computer Processing in the Private Sector*, MITI Notification No. 98 (March 4, 1997).

Mnookin, R. H., and L. Kornhauser, "Bargaining in the Shadow of the Law: The Case of Divorce," *Yale Law Review* 88 (1979), pp. 950–997.

Mody, A., and D. Wheeler, "Towards a Vanishing Middle: Competition in the World Garment Industry," *World Development* 15 (1987), p. 1269.

Moffet, J., and F. Bregha, "Non-Regulatory Environmental Measures," in R. Gibson, ed., *Voluntary Initiatives: The New Politics of Corporate Greening* (Peterborough, Ont.: Broadview Press, 1999).

Morris, G., "Third Party Verification Keeps Initiative Fresh," *Chemical Week* (July 5–12, 1995), p. 66.

———, "Why Canada?" *Chemical Week* (July 5–12, 1995), p. 68.

Morris, L., M. Hastak and M. B. Mazis, "Consumer Comprehension of Environmental Advertising and Labelling Claims," *Journal of Consumer Affairs* 29:2 (Winter 1995), pp. 328–350.

Mueller, D. C., *Public Choice II, A Revised Edition of Public Choice* (Cambridge: Cambridge University Press, 1989).

Murphy, D. E., "The Federal Sentencing Guidelines for Organizations: A Decade of Promoting Compliance and Ethics," *Iowa Law Review* 87 (2002), pp. 697–719, at <www.ussc.gov/corp/Murphy.pdf>.

Nadai, A., "Conditions for the Development of a Product Ecolabel," *European Environment* 9 (1999), pp. 201–211.

Nadai, A., and B. Morel, *Product Ecolabelling, Competition, and the Environment*, Working Paper 82.2000 (Milan: Fondazione Eni Enrico Mattei, 2000).

Nash, J., and J. Ehrenfeld, "Code Green: Business Adopts Voluntary Environmental Standards," *Environment* 38:1 (January–February 1996), pp. 16–45.

———, "Codes of Environmental Management Practice: Assessing Their Potential as a Tool for Change," *Annual Review of Energy and the Environment* 22 (1997), pp. 487–535.

Nash, J., and J. Howard, *The U.S. Responsible Care Initiative: The Dynamics of Shaping Firm Practices and Values* (presented to the Fourth International Research Conference on the Greening of Industry Network, Massachusetts Institute of Technology, Cambridge, Mass., November 12–14, 1995).

National Academy of Public Administration, *Environment.Gov: Transforming Environmental Protection for the 21st Century* (Washington: National Academy of Public Administration, 2000).

National Consumer Council (United Kingdom), *E-commerce and Consumer Protection* (London: National Consumer Council, August 2000), at <www.ncc.org.uk/pubs/pdf/ecommerce.pdf>.

Natural Resources Canada, *Canada's Model Forest Program*, at <www.nrcan.gc.ca/cfs-scf/national/what-quoi/modelforest_e.html>.

———, *Sustainable Development Strategy: Safeguarding our Assets, Securing our Future* (Ottawa: Natural Resources Canada, 1998).

Nolan, J. R., and J. M. Nolan Haley, eds., *Black's Law Dictionary* (St. Paul, Minn.: West, 1990).

North American Commission for Environmental Cooperation, *North American Environmental Law and Policy* (Cowansville, Que.: Les éditions Yvon Blais Inc., 1998).

Office of Consumer Affairs and Regulatory Affairs Division, Treasury Board Secretariat (Canada), *Voluntary Codes: A Guide for Their Development and Use* (Ottawa: Industry Canada and Treasury Board Secretariat, 1998), at <http://strategis.ic.gc.ca/epic/internet/inoca-bc/nsf/en/ca00880e.html>.

———, *Voluntary Codes Symposium*, Office of Consumer Affairs, Industry Canada, and Regulatory Affairs Division, Treasury Board Secretariat (Canada), held in Ottawa, September 1996, at <http://strategis.ic.gc.ca/epic/internet/inoca-bc.nsf/en/ca00819e.html> (summary).

Office of Fair Trading (United Kingdom), *Raising Standards of Consumer Care: Progressing Beyond Codes of Practice* (London: Office of Fair Trading, February 1998), at <www.oft.gov.uk/NR/rdonlyres/D7BC7340-436F-4E13-A77D-B22F04337D1E/0/oft206.pdf>.

———, *Raising Standards of Consumer Care: Report on a Conference Held at Newhall College, Cambridge, 22 September 1998* (London: Office of Fair Trading, February 1999), at <www.oft.gov.uk/NR/rdonlyres/9E2832FF-BB50-49E0-90F5-FC08C139ED77/0/OFT259.PDF>.

Office of Management and Budget, *Federal Participation in the Development and Use of Voluntary Consensus Standards and in Conformity Assessment Activities* (February 19, 1998), at <www.whitehouse.gov/omb/circulars/a119/a119.html>.

Office of Privatization and Regulatory Affairs, *Regulatory Reform Strategy* (Ottawa: Office of Privatization and Regulatory Affairs, 1986).

———, *122-CCAC, Federal Regulatory Plan* (Ottawa: Office of Privatization and Regulatory Affairs, 1990).

———, *138-CCAC, Federal Regulatory Plan* (Ottawa: Office of Privatization and Regulatory Affairs, 1991).

Office of the Governor of Alaska, *Alaska's Salmon Fishery Certified as Sustainable* (press release), (September 5, 2000).

Ogus, A., *Regulation: Legal Form and Economic Theory* (Oxford: Clarendon Press, 1994).

———, "Rethinking Self-Regulation," *Oxford Journal of Legal Studies* 15 (1995), pp. 97–108.

Olson, M., *The Logic of Collective Action* (Cambridge, Mass.: Harvard University Press, 1965).

———, *The Rise and Decline of Nations: Economic Growth, Stagflation, and Social Rigidities* (New Haven: Yale University Press, 1982).

Organisation for Economic Co-operation and Development, *Guidelines on the Protection of Privacy and Transborder Flows of Personal Data* (Paris: Organisation for Economic Cooperation and Development, 1981), available at <www1.oecd.org/publications/e-book/9302011E.pdf>.

———, *Environmental Labelling in OECD Countries* (Paris: Organisation for Economic Cooperation and Development, 1991).

———, *Eco-Labelling: Actual Effects of Selected Programmes*, document ECDE/GC(97)105 (Paris: Organisation for Economic Cooperation and Development, 1997).

———, *Guidelines for Consumer Protection in the Context of Electronic Commerce*, (Paris: Organisation for Economic Cooperation and Development, 1999), at <www1.oecd.org/publications/e-book/9300023E.PDF>.

Organization of American States, *North American Free Trade Agreement*, at <www.sice.oas.org/trade/nafta/naftatce.asp>.

Orts, E., "Reflexive Environmental Regulation," *Northwestern University Law Review* 89 (1995), pp. 1227–1340.

Osbaldeston, G., *Keeping Deputy Ministers Accountable* (London: National Centre for Management Research and Development, 1988).

Osborne, D., and T. Gaebler, *Reinventing Government* (Don Mills, Ont.: Addison-Wesley, 1992).

Pacific Institute for Studies in Development and Security, *ISO 14001: Environmental Management Systems and Public Policy* (Oakland, Cal.: Pacific Institute for Studies in Development and Security, 1999), at <www.pacinst.org>.

Palmer, N. V. (letter to the editor), *The Georgia Straight* (February 8–15, 1996).

Pargal, S., H. Hettige, M. Singh and D. Wheeler, *Formal and Informal Regulation of Industrial Pollution: Comparative Evidence from Indonesia and the United States* (Washington: World Bank, 2000).

Pargal, S., and D. Wheeler, "Informal Regulation of Industrial Pollution in Developing Countries: Evidence from Indonesia," *Journal of Political Economy* 104 (1996), pp. 1314–1327.

Parloff, R., "Can We Talk?" *Fortune* (September 2, 2002).

Parto, S., "Aiming Low" in R. Gibson, ed., *Voluntary Initiatives: The New Politics of Corporate Greening* (Peterborough, Ont.: Broadview Press, 1999).

Peltzman, S., "Towards a More General Theory of Regulation?" *Journal of Law and Economics* 19 (August 1976), pp. 211–240.

Pengilley, W., "Competition Law and Voluntary Codes of Self-regulation: An Individual Assessment of What Has Happened to Date," *University of NSW Law Journal* 13:2 (1990), pp. 212–301.

Perez-Lopez, J. F., "Promoting International Respect for Worker Rights Through Business Codes of Conduct," *Fordham International Law Journal* 17 (1993), pp. 1–23.

Peterson, S., and G. Hoffer, "Are Drivers of Air-Bag Equipped Cars More Aggressive? A Test of the Offsetting Behavior Hypothesis," *Journal of Law and Economics* 38:2 (1995).

Phillips, S., "How Ottawa Blends: Shifting Government Relationships With Interest Groups" in F. Abele, ed., *How Ottawa Spends 1991–92* (Ottawa: Carleton University Press, 1991), pp. 183–227.

Pildes, R., and C. Sunstein, "Reinventing the Regulatory State," *The University of Chicago Law Journal* 62:1 (1995), pp. 1–129.

Pitofsky, R., "Self Regulation and Antitrust" (prepared remarks for a presentation to the D.C. Bar Association Symposium, Washington, February 18, 1998), at <www.ftc.gov/speeches/pitofsky/self4.htm>.

Polak, J., and E. Bozowsky, "Restructuring the Environmental Choice Program" (paper prepared for the Conference on Restructuring Strategies for the Public Sector, Institute for International Research, Ottawa, March 1995).

Polonsk, M. J., and J. Bailey, et al., "Communicating Environmental Information: Are Marketing Claims on Packaging Misleading?" *Journal of Business Ethics* 17 (1998), pp. 281–294.

Porter, M. E., *Canada at the Crossroads* (Ottawa: Ministry of Supply and Services, 1991).

Porter, M., and C. van der Linde, "Green and Competitive: Ending the Stalemate," *Harvard Business Review* 73:5 (September–October 1995), pp. 120–123.

Poundstone, W., *Prisoner's Dilemma* (New York: Anchor Books, 1993).

Prakash, A., *Greening the Firm: The Politics of Corporate Environmentalism* (Cambridge: Cambridge University Press, 2000).

Prakash, A., and J. Hart, eds., *Globalization and Governance* (London: Routledge, 1999).

Priest, M., "The Privatization of Regulation: Five Models of Self-Regulation," *Ottawa Law Review* 29 (1998), pp. 233–302.

Pross, P., *Group Politics and Public Policy* (Toronto: University of Toronto Press, 1986).

———, *Group Politics and Public Policy*, 2nd ed. (Toronto: Oxford Press, 1992).

Public Policy Forum, "Innovation in the Federal Government: The Risk Not Taken," *The Innovation Journal* 4:2 (May–August 1999) at <www.innovation.cc/discussion-papers/risk2.htm>.

Raab, C. D., "Governing Privacy: Systems, Participants and Policy Instruments," in *Proceedings of Ethicomp99: Fifth International Conference,* Rome (1999).

———, *The Governance of Privacy* (London: Ashgate Press, 2003).

Raab, C. D., and C. J. Bennett, "Taking the Measure of Privacy: Can Data Protection Be Evaluated?" *International Review of Administrative Sciences* 62:4 (December 1996), pp. 535–556.

Raab, C. D., C. J. Bennett, R. M. Gellman and N. Waters, *Application of a Methodology Designed to Assess the Adequacy of the Level of Protection of Individuals With Regard to Processing Personal Data: Test of the Method on Several Categories of Transfer* (Luxembourg: Office for Official Publication of the European Communities, 1999), at <http://europa.eu.int/comm/internal_market/privacy/studies/adequa_en.htm>.

Ramnarine, D., "The Philosophy and Developmental Prosects of the CBI," in A. Bakan et al., eds., *Imperial Power and Regional Trade: The Caribbean Basin Initiative* (Waterloo, Ont.: Wilfrid Laurier University Press, 1993).

Ratushny, E., "What are Administrative Tribunals? The Pursuit of Uniformity in Diversity," *Canadian Public Administration* 30:1 (1987), pp. 1–13.

Raz, J., *The Concept of a Legal System: An Introduction to the Theory*, 2nd ed. (Oxford: Oxford University Press, 1980).

Rees, J., *Hostages of Each Other: The Transformation of Nuclear Safety Since Three Mile Island* (Chicago: University of Chicago Press, 1994).

Rhone, Gregory T., *Canadian Tobacco Manufacturers' Council Tobacco Industry Voluntary Packaging and Advertising Code* (draft case study prepared for the Voluntary Codes Symposium, Office of Consumer Affairs, Industry Canada, and Regulatory Affairs Division, Treasury Board Secretariat [Canada], Ottawa, September 1996), at <http://strategis.ic.gc.ca/epic/internet/inoca-bc.nsf/en/ca00880e.html> (summary).

———, *The Canadian Care Labelling Program* (draft case study prepared for the Voluntary Codes Symposium, Office of Consumer Affairs, Industry Canada, and Regulatory Affairs Division, Treasury Board Secretariat [Canada], Ottawa, September 1996), at <http://strategis.ic.gc.ca/epic/internet/ inoca-bc.nsf/en/ ca00880e.html> (summary).

———, *Investment Funds Institute of Canada Draft Code of Sales Practices for the Mutual Fund Industry* (draft case study prepared for the Voluntary Codes Symposium, Office of Consumer Affairs, Industry Canada, and Regulatory Affairs Division, Treasury Board Secretariat [Canada], Ottawa, September 1996), at <http://strategis.ic.gc.ca/ epic/internet/inoca-bc.nsf/en/ca00880e.html> (summary).

Richard, K. Peter, *The Westray Story: A Predictable Path to Disaster* (Report of the Westray Mine Public Inquiry), (1997).

Richardson, W., and D. Morris, "Towards More Effective Consumer Marketplace Interventions," *Journal of Consumer Policy* 11 (1988), pp. 315–334.

Rickard, D., *Codes of Conduct: Their Place in the Regulatory Framework and Making Them Work in the Interest of Consumers* (paper presented to the Working Together for Change Consumer Affairs Forum for the Commonwealth Trade Practices Commission, Adelaide, undated).

Rose, N., and P. Miller, "Political Power Beyond the State: Problematics of Government," *British Journal of Sociology* 43 (1992), p. 173.

Rosenbaum, S. W., *ISO 14001 and the Law* (California: AQA Press, 1998).

Rosenberg, N., and L. E. Birdzell, *How The West Grew Rich* (New York: Basic Books, 1986).

Rotherham, T., *Chain of Custody* (paper presented to the International Conference on Certification Criteria and Indicators: Global Approaches to Sustainable Forest Management, Prince George, B.C., September 1997), at <www.mcgregor.bc.ca/ publications/GlobalApproaches/GAPanel2.pdf>.

Roundtables on the Environment and Economy in Canada, *Building Consensus for a Sustainable Future: Guiding Principles, An Initiative Undertaken by Canadian Roundtables* (Roundtables on the Environment and Economy in Canada, August 1993).

Rourke, D., *Monitoring The Monitors: A Critique of Pricewaterhousecoopers (PWC) Labor Monitoring* (Boston: Massachusetts Institute of Technology, 2000), at <http://web.mit.edu/dorourke/www/PDF/pwc.pdf>.

Rowley, C. K., R. D. Tollinson and G. Tullock (eds.), *The Political Economy of Rent-seeking* (Boston: Kluwer Academic Publishers, 1988).

Roy, M., "Pollution Prevention, Organizational Culture and Social Learning," *Environmental Law* 22:1 (1992), pp. 189–252.

Rugmark Canada, *Rugmark Labels Carpets to End Exploitive Child Labour* (undated).

Salzman, J., "Informing the Green Consumer: The Debate Over the Use and Abuse of Environmental Labels," *Journal of Industrial Ecology* 1 (1997), pp. 11–21.

———, "Green Labels for Consumers," *The OECD Observer* 169, pp. 29–30.

Schuck, P., "Tort Liability to Those Injured by Negligent Accreditation Decisions," in C. Havighurst, ed., "Private Accreditation in the Regulatory State," *Law and Contemporary Problems* 57:4 (Autumn 1994), p. 192.

Schultz, R. J., "Regulating Conservatively: The Mulroney Record, 1984–1988," in A. B. Gollner and D. Salee, eds., *Canada Under Mulroney: An End-of-Term Report* (Montréal: Véhicule, 1988).

Scott, Sir Walter, *Marmion* (Edinburgh: Constable, 1808).

Shaffer, G., "Globalization and Social Protection: The Impact of EU and International Rules in the Ratcheting Up of U.S. Privacy Standards," *Yale Journal of International Law* 25:1 (Winter 2000).

Shaked, A., and J. Sutton, "The Self-Regulating Profession," *Review of Economic Studies* 48 (1981), pp. 217–234.

Shapland, J., *Self-Regulation of the Professions: Coercion or Free Choice* (paper presented to the Conference on Regulating the Professions, University of Strathclyde, Glasgow, April 20–21, 1995).

Sierra Club of Canada, *Evidence Confirms Sierra Club of Canada Concerns Over Black Brook Certification Process* (press release), (January 21, 2000), at <www.sierraclub.ca/national/media/fsc-cert-concerns-00-01-21.html>.

Singh, G., "Business Self-regulation and Consumer Protection in India: A Critique," *Journal of Consumer Policy* 16 (1993), pp. 1–33.

Skyrms, B., *The Stag Hunt*, at <http://hypatia.ss.uci.edu/lps/home/fac-staff/faculty/skyrms/Hunt.PDF>.

Smith, A., *An Inquiry into the Nature and Causes of the Wealth of Nations* (1776) (London: Oxford University Press, 1997).

Smith, H. J., *Managing Privacy: Information Technology and Corporate America* (Chapel Hill, N.C.: University of North Carolina Press, 1994).

Smith III, J. A., "The CERES Principles: A Voluntary Code for Corporate Environmental Responsibility," *Yale Journal of International Law* 18 (1993), pp. 307–317.

Smith, J. Q. , J. P. Bolger and A. Marasco, *Products Liability Claims Against Voluntary Standards Developers: An Update on Recent Developments* (1996).

Smith, N. C., *Morality and the Market: Consumer Pressure for Corporate Accountability* (London: Routledge, 1990).

Sparrow, M. K., *Imposing Duties: Government's Changing Approach To Compliance* (London: Praeger, 1994).

Speir, Jerry, *ISO 14001 Environmental Management Systems and Public Policy: Proceedings of a Workshop Held on July 29, 1999, Oakland, California*, at <www.pacinst.org/reports/iso_14001/ isoproceedings.pdf>.

Stanbury, W., I. Vertinsky and B. Wilson, *The Challenge to Canadian Forest Products in Europe: Managing a Complex Environmental Issue* (Victoria, B.C.: Natural Resources Canada, 1995).

Steinhardt, R., *Litigating Corporate Responsibility* (2001) at <www.lse.ac.uk/collections/ globalDimensions/seminars/humanRightsAndCorporateResponsibility/steinhardt Transcript.htm>.

Stenzel, P., "Can the ISO 14000 Series Environmental Standards Provide a Viable Alternative to Government Regulation?" *American Business Law Journal* 37 (2000), pp. 237–279.

Stevens, C., ed., *Environmental Policies and Industrial Competitiveness* (Paris: Organisation for Economic Co-operation and Development, 1993).

Stevenson, T., "Regulation, Deregulation, Self-Regulation: The Case of Engineers in Ontario," *Journal of Business Ethics* 4 (August 1985), pp. 253–267.

Stigler, G. J., "The Theory of Economic Regulation," *Bell Journal of Economics and Management Science* 2 (Spring 1971), pp.137–146.

Stone, C., *Where the Law Ends* (New York: Harper, 1975).

Stoughton, M., K. Shapiro and D. Reda, *Do Voluntary Mechanisms Work? An Evaluation of Current and Future Program Performance* (Boston: Tellus Institute, 2000), at <www.tellus.org/b&s/publications/r8-031.pdf> (executive summary).

Subcommittee on Sustainable Human Development of the House of Commons (Canada), Standing Committee on Foreign Affairs and International Trade, *Ending Child Labour Exploitation: A Canadian Agenda for Action on Global Challenges* (February 1997), at <www.parl.gc.ca/committees352/fore/reports/05_1997-02/fore-05-cov0-e.html>.

Suchman, Mark, "Managing Legitimacy: Strategic and Institutional Approaches," *Academy of Management Review* 20 (1995), pp. 571–610.

Sustainable Forestry Initiative, *2001 Sustainable Forestry Initiative (SFI) Program Overview*, at <www.aboutsfi.org>.

Susskind, L. E., and J. Cruikshank, *Breaking The Impasse: Consensual Approaches to Solving Public Disputes* (New York: Basic Books, 1987).

Susskind, L., and G. McMahon, "The Theory and Practice of Negotiated Rulemaking," *Yale Journal of Regulation* 3 (1985), pp. 133–165.

Sutherland, S. L., "Responsible Government and Ministerial Responsibility: Every Reform Has Its Own Problem," *Canadian Journal of Political Science* 24 (1991), pp. 91–120.

Swaigen, J., "Negligence, Reverse Onuses and Environmental Offences: Some Practical Considerations," *Journal of Environmental Law and Practice* 2 (1992), p. 149.

Swire, P., "The Race to Laxity and the Race to Undesirability: Explaining Failures in Competition Among Jurisdictions in Environmental Law," *Yale Journal on Regulation* 14 (1996), pp. 67–110.

Tamblyn, J., *Industry Codes of Conduct: Their Role in the Competitive Marketplace* (paper presented to Trade Practice Commission Consultative Committee, Canberra, March 17, 1990).

Taskforce on Industry Self-Regulation (Australia), *Industry Self-Regulation in Consumer Markets* (Canberra: Department of the Treasury, August 2000), at <www.selfregulation.gov.au/publications/TaskForceOnIndustrySelf-Regulation/FinalReport/download/final_report.pdf>.

Taylor, E., "E-tailers Seek Seal of Approval To Reassure Cautious Customers," *Wall Street Journal Europe* (March 1, 2001).

Taylor, M., "Between Public and Private: Accountability in Voluntary Organizations," *Policy and Politics* 24:1 (January 1996), pp. 57–72.

Technical Safety Standards Association (Ontario), *Consolidated TSSA 2005 Strategy and 2001/2002 Plan* (Ontario: Technical Safety Standards Association, 2001), at <www.tssa.org/about_tssa/pdf/tssa_plan.pdf>.

TerraChoice, *The EcoBuyer Catalogue* (Ottawa: TerraChoice Environmental Services Inc., 2000).

Teubner, G., "After Legal Instrumentalism? Strategic Models of Post-Regulatory Law," *International Journal of the Sociology of Law* 12 (1984), pp. 375–400.

——, "The Invisible Cupola," in G. Teubner, L. Farmer and D. Murphy, eds., *Environmental Law and Ecological Responsibility: The Concept and Practice of Ecological Self-Organization* (Chichester: John Wiley and Sons, 1994).

Teubner, G., L. Farmer and D. Murphy, eds., *Environmental Law and Ecological Responsibility: The Concept and Practice of Ecological Self-Organization* (Chichester: John Wiley and Sons, 1994).

Thomas, R., "Alternative Dispute Resolution: Consumer Disputes," *Civil Justice Quarterly* (1988), pp. 206–218.

Trade Practices Commission (Australia), *Checkout the Price: Review of Supermarket Scanning Code Report* (Canberra: Trade Practices Commission, July 1992).

———, *Final Report by the Trades Practices Commission on the Self-Regulation of Promotion and Advertising of Therapeutic Goods* (Canberra: Trade Practices Commission, July 1992).

———, *Federal Regulatory Process Management Standards Compliance Guide*, at <www.pco-bcp.gc.ca/raoics-srdc/docs/publications/rpms_e.pdf>.

Trebilcock, M., "Regulating Service Quality in Professional Markets," in D. Dewees, ed., *The Regulation of Quality* (Toronto: Butterworths, 1983).

———, "Requiem for Regulators: The Passing of a Counter-Culture?" *Yale Journal of Regulation* 8:2 (Summer 1991), pp. 497–510.

Tuohy, C., and A. Wolfson, "Self-Regulation: Who Qualifies?" in P. Slayton and M. Trebilcock, eds., *The Professions and Public Policy* (Toronto: University of Toronto Press, 1978).

Unattributed, "17 Colleges Join Against Sweatshops," *New York Times* (March 16, 1999), p. A22.

Unattributed, "Industry Rounds on FSC," *Forestry and British Timber* (1996).

Unattributed, "B.C. Not Backsliding With Forest Practices," *Financial Post* (April 4, 1998), p. 18.

Unattributed, "Bicycle Helmets," *Consumer Reports* (August 1994), p. 518.

Unattributed, "Bike Helmets: Unused Lifesavers," *Consumer Reports* (May 1990), p. 348.

Unattributed, "British Columbia Forest Expert Calls for Certification," *Vancouver Sun* (April 3, 1998).

Unattributed, "Consumers Punishing Abusive Companies," *USA Today* (April 1, 2001), p. 16.

Unattributed, "Divine Moment for Fair-trade Crusader," *The Express* (October 8, 1999).

Unattributed, "Dress Code: Stamping out Sweatshops," *The Economist* (April 19, 1997), p. 28.

Unattributed, "Eco-labels Stuck on Search for Common Standards," *Pulp and Paper International* 36 (1994), pp. 39–43.

Unattributed, "The End of Privacy," *The Economist* (May 1–7, 1999).

Unattributed, "EU's New Eco-label Called Trade Barrier," *Pulp and Paper* (October 1996), p. 19.

Unattributed, "Good Fellers," *The Economist* (January 27, 2001).

Unattributed, "It's Official: AssiDoman Makes History With FSC Membership," *Timber Trade Journal* (January 4, 1997), p. 4.

Unattributed, "Reducing Legal Liability With an ISO 14001 EMS," *Standards New Zealand Environmental Newsletter* (February 1996).

Unattributed, "Re-evaluating Eco-labels," *Business Europe* (May 15, 1995), pp. 4–5.

Unattributed, "Student Critics Push Attacks on an Association Meant to Prevent Sweatshops," *New York Times* (April 25, 1999), p. A18.

Unattributed, "Touching a Nerve," *Understory* 10 (Winter/Spring 2000).

United Nations Commission for Trade and Development, Secretariat, *Quantifying the Benefits Obtained by Development Countries from the Generalized System of Preferences* (October 7, 1999), at <www.unctad.org/en/docs/poitcdtsbm52.en.pdf>.

United Nations Environment Program, unofficial archive of the Infoterra mailing list, at <www.ee/lists/infoterra/>.

United States Department of Labor, Bureau of International Labor Affairs, *By the Sweat and Toil of Children: Consumer Labels and Child Labor* (Vol. IV) (Washington: U.S. Department of Labor, 1997).

United States International Trade Commission, Office of Economics, *Impact of the Caribbean Basin Economic Recovery Act on U.S. Industries and Consumers*, (1992).

United States Sentencing Commission, *Chapter Eight: 2000 Federal Sentencing Guideline Manual*, at <www.ussc.gov/2000guid/tabconchapt8.htm>.

———, *Report from Advisory Group on Environmental Sanctions* (1993), at <www.ussc.gov/publicat/environ.pdf>.

———, *1998 Annual Report*, at <www.ussc.gov/annrpt/1998/ar98toc.htm>.

United States Trade Representative, *Third Report to the Congress on the Operation of the Caribbean Basin Economic Recovery Act*, October 1, 1999, at <www.ustr.gov/regions/whemisphere/camerica/3rdreport.pdf>.

University of North Carolina, Highway Safety Research Center, *British Columbia Bicycle Helmet Study*, at <www.hsrc.unc.edu/pubinfo/bike_bchelmets.htm>.

Van Nijnatten, D., "The ARET Challenge," and "The Day the NGOs Walked Out," in R. Gibson, ed., *Voluntary Initiatives: The New Politics of Corporate Greening* (Peterborough, Ont.: Broadview Press, 1999).

Vass, P., "The Accountability of Regulators" in *Regulatory Review 1994* (London: Centre for the Study of Regulated Industries, 1994).

Vlosky, R. P., and L. K. Ozanne, "Chain of Custody Vital to Certification Process," *Wood Technology* (March 13, 1995), p. 35.

Vogel, D., *Trading Up: Consumer and Environmental Regulation in a Global Economy* (Cambridge, Mass.: Harvard University Press, 1995).

————, *Barriers or Benefits? Regulation in Transatlantic Trade* (Washington: Brookings Institution, 1997).

Vogel, E., *Japan as Number 1* (New York: Harper Colophon, 1979).

von Mirbach, M., *Reward the Best or Improve the Rest? Questions About Forest Certification in Canada and Internationally* (paper prepared for February 23–27, 1998, meeting of ENGOs in Ottawa), cited in T. Burrell, *CSA Environmental Standards Writing: Barriers to Environmental Non-Governmental Organization Involvement* (Canadian Institute for Environmental Law and Policy, May 1997).

————, "Demanding Good Wood," *Alternatives Journal* 23 (Summer 1997), p. 12.

Vosburgh, R., "Produce Safety Audits are Consumer Driven," *Supermarket News* (March 6, 2001), at <www.primuslabs.com/ap/SN_0300.htm>.

Walde, T., "Non-Conventional Views on Effectiveness: The Holy Grail of Modern International Lawyers," *Austrian Review of International & European Law* 4 (1999), pp. 164–203.

Wallace, J., D. Ironfield and J. Orr, *Analysis of Market Circumstances Where Industry Self-Regulation is Likely to be Most and Least Effective* (Canberra: Tasman Asia Pacific Pty Ltd., May 2000), at <www.selfregulation.gov.au/publications/ TaskForceOnIndustrySelf-Regulation/ConsultantReport/ch1.pdf>.

Walley, N., and B. Whitehead, "It's Not Easy Being Green," *Harvard Business Review* 72:3 (May–June 1994), pp. 46–52.

Warleigh, A., "NGOs: More Influence Means More Responsibility," *Consumer Policy Review* 11:3 (2001), pp. 101–104.

Wastle, B., *Are We There Yet? The Responsible Care Ethic as an Evolving Secular Religion* (speech given at the University of Ottawa, March 1996).

Watts, T. A., *Consumer Awareness and Perception of Canadian Marks of Conformity* (Ottawa: Standards Council of Canada, 1984).

Weale, A., *The New Politics of Pollution* (Manchester: Manchester University Press, 1992).

Webb, K., *Pollution Control in Canada: The Regulatory Approach in the 1980s* (Ottawa: Law Reform Commission of Canada, 1988).

————, "Regulatory Offences, the Mental Element, and the Charter: Rough Road Ahead," *Ottawa Law Review* (1989).

————, "Between Rocks and Hard Places: Bureaucrats, Law and Pollution Control," in R. Paehlke and D. Torgerson, eds., *Managing Leviathan: Environmental Politics and the Administrative State* (Kitchener, Ont.: Broadview Press, 1993).

————, "Thumbs, Fingers and Pushing on String: Legal Accountability in the Use of Federal Financial Incentives," *Alberta Law Review* 21 (1993), pp. 501–535.

————, *Regulatory Offences: The Quest for a Non-Criminal Approach to Penal Liability* (Doctor of Laws thesis, University of Ottawa, 1999).

————, "Voluntary Initiatives and the Law," in R. Gibson, ed., *Voluntary Initiatives: The New Politics of Corporate Greening* (Peterborough, Ont.: Broadview Press, 1999), pp. 32–50.

————, "Government, Private Regulation, and the Role of the Market," in M. MacNeil, N. Sargent and P. Swan, eds., *Law, Regulation and Governance* (Don Mills, Ont.: Oxford University Press, 2002).

————, "Sustainable Governance in the 21st Century: Moving Beyond Instrument Choice," in P. Eliadis, M. Hill and M. Howlett, eds., *Designing Government: From Instruments to Governance* (Montréal: McGill-Queen's University Press, 2004).

Webb, K., and A. Morrison, "Voluntary Approaches, the Environment and the Law: A Canadian Perspective," in C. Carraro and F. Lévêque, eds., *Voluntary Approaches in Environmental Policy* (London, U.K.: Kluwer Academic Publishers, 1999), pp. 229–259.

Weese, K., *Introduction to the Forest Practices Code* (British Columbia Ministry of Forests, September 1996).

White, H., "Monitoring in China" in R. Thamotheram, ed., *Visions of Ethical Sourcing* (London: Financial Times Prentice Hall, 2001),

Wildavsky, B., "Sticker Shock," *National Journal* (March 9, 1996), pp. 532–535.

Williams, C., "The Securities and Exchange Commission and Corporate Social Transparency," *Harvard Law Review* 112 (1998), pp. 1197–1311.

Wilson, J. Q., *Political Organizations* (New York: Basic Books, 1973).

Wilson, P., *Exports and Local Development: Mexico's New Maquiladoras* (Austin, Tex.: University of Texas Press, 1992).

Wood, P., *A Comparative Analysis of Selected International Forestry Certification Schemes* (Victoria, B.C.: Ministry of Forests, 2000), at <www.for.gov.bc.ca/het/certification/WoodReportOct00.PDF>.

Wood, S., "Green Revolution or Greenwash? Voluntary Environmental Standards, Public Law and Private Authority in Canada," in *New Perspectives on the Public-Private Divide* (Vancouver: UBC Press, 2004).

Woodward, J., "The New Regulations: Prepare for Impact," *Tack 'n Togs Merchandising* (December 1989), p. 30.

Working Group on Electronic Commerce and Consumers, *Canadian Principles of Consumer Protection for Electronic Commerce*, at <http://strategis.ic.gc.ca/epic/internet/inoca-bc.nsf/en/ca01180e.html>.

World Economic Forum, *Corporate Leaders Discuss Social Role* (press release), (February 4, 2002).

World Trade Organization, *Agreement on Technical Barriers to Trade*, (Geneva: World Trade Organization, 1994), at <www.wto.org/english/docs_e/legal_e/17-tbt.pdf>.

————, "Code of Good Practice for the Preparation, Adoption and Application of Standards," *Agreement on Technical Barriers to Trade,* Annex 3, Uruguay Round of Trade Agreements (Geneva: World Trade Organization, 1994), at <www.wto.org/english/docs_e/legal_e/17-tbt.pdf>.

————, *General Agreement on Tariffs and Trade 1994* (Geneva: World Trade Organization, 1994), at <www.wto.org/english/docs_e/legal_e/06-gatt.pdf>.

————, Environmental Labels and Market Access: Case Study in the Colombian Flower Industry, document WT/CTE/W/76-G/TBT/W/60 (March 9, 1998).

————, *Trade and Environment News Bulletin*, TE/023 (May 14, 1998).

————, *Trading into the Future* (Geneva: World Trade Organization, 1999).

————, WTO document G/TBT/9 (November 13, 2000), (00-48111).

————, Agreement on the Application of Sanitary and Phytosanitary Measures, (Geneva: World Trade Organization).

————, TBT Committee, *Second Triennial Review of the Operation and Implementation of the Agreement on Technical Barriers to Trade* (2000), G/TBT/9 (November 13, 2000), (00-48111), at <www.dfait-maeci.gc.ca/tna-nac/ documents/WTO-TBT-13-e.pdf>.

World Wide Fund for Nature, *Skal's Authority Suspended to Issue FSC Certificates, Forests For Life Certification Updates* (May 2001).

————, *Skal's Chain-of-Custody Accreditation Reinstated* (June 2001).

Wraight, R., "ISO: What Do We Need to Do Next?" *ISO Bulletin* (May, 2001).

Wright, R., *Nonzero: The Logic of Human Destiny* (New York: Pantheon, 2000).

Wynne, R. D., "Defining 'Green': Toward Regulation of Environmental Marketing Claims," *University of Michigan Journal of Law Reform* 24 (Spring and Summer 1991), pp. 785–820.

————, "The Emperor's New Eco-Logos? A Critical Review of the Scientific Certification Systems Environmental Report Card and the Green Seal Certification Mark Programs," *Virginia Environmental Law Journal* 14 (1994), pp. 51–149.

Young, O., *Compliance and Public Authority: A Theory with International Implications* (Baltimore: John Hopkins University Press, 1979).

Zadek, S., S. Lingayah and M. Forstater, *Social Labels: Tools for Ethical Trade* (report prepared for the European Commission, DG V), (London: New Economics Foundation, 1998).

Court Cases

340909 Ontario Ltd. v. Huron Steel Products Ltd. [1992] 9 O.R. (3d) 305 (Ont. C.A.).

A.A.A. Khan Transport Inc. v. Bureau d'éthique commerciale de Montréal Inc. [1998] Q.J. No. 226, Quebec Superior Court (General Division) (Q.L.).

Benton v. Tea Tree Plaza (1995) No. SCGRG 94/417, Judgment No. 5144 (SC of South Aus.).

Bolger v. Youngs Drug Products Corp. (1983) 463 U.S. 60.

Carlill v. Carbolic Smoke Ball Co. [1893] 1 Q.B. 256 (C.A.).

Clark v. MacLennan [1983] 1 All E.R. 416 (Q.B.).

Commack Self-Service Kosher Meats, Inc. v. Rubin 106 F. Supp. 2d 445 (U.S. Eastern District Court of New York, 2000).

Currie v. Misa (1875) L.R. 10 Exch. 153.

Department of Labour v. Waste Management N.Z. Limited [1995] CRN No. 40040511262 (Dist. Ct. — Auckland).

Doe v. Unocal (2000) 248 F.3d 915.

Fashion Originators Guild of America v. Federal Trade Commission 312 U.S. 457 (1941).

Federal Trade Commission v. Wallace 75 F. 2d 733 (8th Cir. 1935).

Greig v. Insold [1978] 1 W.L.R. 302.

Hanberry v. Hearst Corp., 81 Cal. Rptr. 519 (Cal. Ct. App. 1969).

Hohlenkamp v. Rheem Mfg. Co. (1982) 655 P2d 32 (discussed in 47 ALR 4th, 621).

Hoover v. Ronwin 466 U.S. 558 (1984).

Hydrolevel Corp. v. American Society of Mechanical Engineers 635 F. 2d 118 (2d Cir. 1980).

Johnson v. Bingley and Others, The Times (London), February 28, 1995 (QB).

Just v. British Columbia [1990] 1 W.W.R. 385 (S.C.C.).

Kasky v. Nike Inc. (2002) 27 Cal. 4th 939 (California Supreme Court).

King v. National Spa and Pool Institute Inc. 570 So. (2d) 612 (Ala. 1990).

Levitts Kosher Foods Inc. v. Levin [1999] 45 OR (3d) 147 (Ont. Superior Ct.).

Martineau and Butters v. Matsqui Institution Disciplinary Board [1978] 1 S.C.R. 118.

McInnes v. Onslow Fane [1978] 1 W.L.R. 1520.

Meisel v. Tolko Industries Ltd. [1991] B.C.J. No. 105 (SC).

Meneely v. S. R. Smith Inc. [2000] WA-QL 1055 No. 18036-1-III (August 3, 2000), Court of Appeals, State of Washington.

Murphy et al. v. Atlantic Speedy Propane Ltd. (1979) 103 D.L.R. (3d) 545 (NSSC).

Murray v. Sperry Rand Corporation (1979) 23 O.R. 456 (H.C.).

National Society of Professional Engineers v. United States 435 U.S. 679 (1978).

Northwest Wholesale Stationers v. Pacific Stationery and Printing Co. 472 U.S. 284 (1985).

R. v. Advertising Standards Authority, ex parte The Insurance Service plc, Queen's Bench Division, 9 Tr L 169, July 6, 1989.

R. v. Bata Industries (1992), 7 CELR (New Series) 245 (Ont. Ct. Prov. Div.).

R. v. British Columbia Fruit Growers Association et al. (1986) 11 C.P.R. (3d) 183.

R. v. Calgary (City) (2000) 272 AR 161, 35 CELR (NS) 253 (Alta. Prov. Ct).

R. v. Cancoil Thermal Corp. (1986) 52 CR (3d) 188.

R. v. Consumer's Distributing Co. Ltd. (1980), 57 CCC (2d) 317 (Ont. C.A).

R. v. Crown Zellerbach Properties Ltd. (1988), 49 DLR (4th) 161 (S.C.C.).

R. v. Corotec (formerly PCI Inc.) and Zadeh (1998) (Ont. Prov. Ct.).

R. v. Courtaulds Fibres Canada (1992), 9 CELR (New Series) 304 (Ont. Ct. Gen. Div.).

R. v. Domtar [1993] O.J. No. 3415 (Ont. C.J. — Gen. Div.).

R. v. Dupont (unreported, January 23, 1986, Ont. Dist. Ct.).

R. v. Electrical Contractors Association of Ontario and Dent [1961] O.R. 265.

R. v. Hodgson (1985), 4 F.P.R. 251 (N.S. Prov. Ct.).

R. v. Panel on Take-overs and Mergers [1987] 1 All E.R. 564.

R. v. Prospec Chemicals (1996) 19 CELR (NS) 178 (Alta. Prov. Ct).

R. v. Sault Ste. Marie (1978), 40 CCC (2d) 353.

R. v. Toronto Electric Commissioners (1991), 6 CELR (New Series) 301 (Ont. Ct. Gen. Div.).

R. v. Van Waters & Rogers Ltd. (1998) 220 AR (315) (Alta. Prov. Ct).

Re: Association of British Travel Agents, Ltd. Agreement [1984] I.C.R. 12.

Re: Evaline Jill Hamlyn and Moppet Grange Pty. Ltd. (1984) Nos. G375-477 of 1983 (Fed. Ct. of Aus.).

Re. Malcolm David Lennox and Megray Pty. Ltd, (1985) Nos. VG23 to VG28 of 1985 (Fed. Ct. of Aus.).

Re: ss. 193 and 195.1 of the Criminal Code (Prostitution Reference) [1990] 1 S.C.R. 1123.

Re: Robert George Quinn and Brian Alexander Given, (1980) 41 F.L.R. 416.

Reed v. McDermid St. Lawrence Ltd. (1991) 52 B.C.L.R. (2d) 265 (CA).

Ripley v. Investment Dealers Association (Business Conduct Committee) [1991] 108 N.S.R. (2d) 38 (N.S.C.A.).

R.J.R. Macdonald v. Attorney General of Canada [1995] 3 S.C.R. 1999.

SmithKline Beecham plc v. Advertising Standards Authority [2001] EWJ No. 49 Queen's Bench Division, Administrative Court, 17 January 2001.

Strasser v. Roberge (1979) 103 DLR (3d) 193.

Structural Laminates v. Douglas Fir Plywood Association 261 F. Supp. 154 (D. Or. 1966)

Swanson and Peever v. Canada (1991) 124 N.R. 218.

Visp Construction v. Scepter Manufacturing Co. (1991) 45 Const. L. Rep. 170 (Ont. Court Gen. Div.).

Wiwa v. Royal Dutch Petroleum Company (2000) 226 F.3d 88.

Index